Lecture Notes in Artificial Intelligence   8922

Subseries of Lecture Notes in Computer Science

LNAI Series Editors

Randy Goebel
University of Alberta, Edmonton, Canada
Yuzuru Tanaka
Hokkaido University, Sapporo, Japan
Wolfgang Wahlster
DFKI and Saarland University, Saarbrücken, Germany

LNAI Founding Series Editor

Joerg Siekmann
DFKI and Saarland University, Saarbrücken, Germany

More information about this series at http://www.springer.com/series/1244

Xinchun Su · Tingting He (Eds.)

Chinese Lexical Semantics

15th Workshop, CLSW 2014
Macao, China, June 9–12, 2014
Revised Selected Papers

 Springer

Editors
Xinchun Su
Xiamen University
Xiamen, Fujian
China

Tingting He
Central China Normal University
Wuhan, Hubei
China

ISSN 0302-9743
Lecture Notes in Artificial Intelligence
ISBN 978-3-319-14330-9
DOI 10.1007/978-3-319-14331-6

ISSN 1611-3349   (electronic)

ISBN 978-3-319-14331-6   (eBook)

Library of Congress Control Number: 2014958983

LNCS Sublibrary: SL7 – Artificial Intelligence

Springer Cham Heidelberg New York Dordrecht London

Printed on acid-free paper

Springer International Publishing AG Switzerland is part of Springer Science+Business Media
(www.springer.com)

Preface

The 15th Chinese Lexical Semantics Workshop (CLSW 2014) was held during June 9–12, 2014 at the University of Macau, Macao, one of two SARs in China. The previous conferences were held in different Asia Pacific cities, including Hong Kong, Beijing, Taipai, Singapore, Xiamen, Hsinchu, Yantai, Suzhou, Wuhan, and Zhengzhou. CLSW is an important conference for scholars of Chinese in Asia to report and discuss the latest progress in Lexical Semantics and related fields, including Theoretical Linguistics, Applied Linguistics, Computational Linguistics, Information Processing, and Computational Lexicography. For 14 years, it has had a broad impact and has greatly promoted the academic research and application development of the related fields.

This conference is jointly organized by Department of Chinese, Faculty of Arts and Humanities, University of Macau and Research Centre for Humanities in South China. A total of 139 papers were submitted to CLSW 2014 for peer review. All submissions went through a double-blind review process. A selection of 44 papers (31.65%) presented in the workshop were published in Springer's LNAI series. Of these, 41 submissions were accepted as regular papers (29.5%) and 3 as short papers (2.16%). Some excellent Chinese papers will be recommended to the Journal of Chinese Information Processing.

As the editors of this volume, we would like to thank all Program Committee members, as well as all attendees for their contribution and participation.

November 2014

Xinchun Su
Tingting He

Organization

The 15th Chinese Lexical Semantics Workshop (CLSW 2014) was held during June 9–12, 2014 at the University of Macau, Macao, China.

Conference Chairs

Xinchun Su   Xiamen University, China

Advisory Committee

Honorary Members

Shiwen Yu   Peking University, China
Chin-Chuan Cheng   University of Illinois, USA

Members

Chu-Ren Huang   Hong Kong Polytechnic University, Hong Kong
Donghong Ji   Wuhan University, China
Kim Teng Lua   COLIPS, Singapore
Mei-chun Liu   National Chiao Tung University, Taiwan
Qin Lu   Hong Kong Polytechnic University, China
Xinchun Su   Xiamen University, China
Shu-Kai Hsieh   National Taiwan University, Taiwan
Jie Xu   University of Macau, China
Hongying Zan   Zhengzhou University, China
Benjamin Tsou   Hong Kong Institute of Education, Hong Kong

Program Committee

Chairs

Tingting He   Central China Normal University, China
Shu-Kai Hsieh   National Taiwan University, Taiwan

Members

Xiaojing Bai   Tsinghua University, China
Xiaohe Chen   Nanjing Normal University, China
Gong Cheng   PLA University of Foreign Languages, China

Yanbin Diao	Beijing Normal University, China
Minghui Dong	Institute for Infocomm Research, Singapore
Guohong Fu	Heilongjiang University, China
Jiafei Hong	National Taiwan Normal University, Taiwan
Minghu Jiang	Tsinghua University, China
Guangjin Jin	Ministry of Education, Institute of Applied Linguistics, China
Jing-Schmidt Zhuo	University of Oregon, USA
Kathleen Ahrens	Hong Kong Baptist University, Hong Kong
Shiyong Kang	Ludong University, China
Olivia Kwong	City University of Hong Kong, Hong Kong
Hui-ling Lai	National Chengchi University, Taiwan
Baoli Li	Henan University of Technology, China
Ting Liu	Harbin Institute of Technology, China
Yao Liu	Institute of Scientific and Technical Information of China, China
Qin Lu	Hong Kong Polytechnic University, Hong Kong
Yao Meng	Fujitsu Research Center, China
Haihua Pan	City University of Hong Kong, Hong Kong
Chong Qi	Paris Diderot University, France
Xiaodong Shi	Xiamen University, China
Le Sun	Chinese Academy of Sciences, China
Chong Teng	Wuhan University, China
Yunfang Wu	Peking University, China
Nianwen Xue	Brandeis University, USA
Erhong Yang	Beijing Language and Culture University, China
Tianfang Yao	Shanghai Jiaotong University, China
Yulin Yuan	Peking University, China
Hongying Zan	Zhengzhou University, China
Yangsen Zhang	Beijing Information Science and Technology University, China
Zezhi Zheng	Xiamen University, China
Qiang Zhou	Tsinghua University, China
Guodong Zhou	Soochow University, China
Chengqing Zong	Chinese Academy of Sciences, China

Organizing Committee

Chair

Jie Xu	University of Macau, China

Vice Chair and Secretary

Mingyu Wang	University of Macau, China

Members

Jianguo Shi	University of Macau, China
Daming Xu	University of Macau, China
Chaoyang Shao	University of Macau, China
Lifeng Zhang	University of Macau, China
Yang Gao	University of Macau, China

Publication Committee

Chair

Pengyuan Liu	Beijing Language and Culture University, China

Vice Chair

Xuri Tang	Huazhong University of Science and Technology, China
Qi Su	Peking University, China

Contents

Lexical Semantics

Embedded Compounding Monosyllabic Morphemes: A Perspective from
the Lexical Study and TCFL 3
    Ling Cen and Jianfei Luo

Word Ordering in Chinese Opposite Compounds 12
    Jing Ding and Chu-Ren Huang

Study on Prosodic Morphology of Chinese Verbal
Monosyllabic-Disyllabic Synonyms. 21
    Jianfei Luo

Semantic Derivation of the " 吃 *[chi] (eat)* + Object" Idiom in Mandarin,
Taiwanese and Hakka 31
    Xiangyun Qiu

On the Lexical Meaning of Conditional Connectives in Chinese 43
    Yan Jiang

Combination of Mandarin Chinese Verb "xiě" and Nouns from the
Perspective of Generative Lexicon Theory. 55
    Qiang Li

The Mechanism Behind Idioms' Meaning Extension. 66
    Hongyan Liu, Peicui Zhang, and Baopeng Ma

A Cognitive Grammar Approach to Relative Antonyms 75
    Fengmei Ren

Instantiations of the Generation Mechanism of A-not-A Question
in Chinese and Some Relevant Syntactic Issues 85
    Yuan Tian and Jie Xu

A Reanalysis of Chinese Passive with a Retained Object. 99
    Juan Wang Villaflor and Ying Li

Quantitative Research on the Origins of Contemporary Chinese Vocabulary
Based on *The Great Chinese Dictionary* 112
    Xueyang Liu, Bin Li, Yingjie Zhang, and Liu Liu

The Ergativization of the Verb "死"[si](Die) in Chinese Language History. . . 124
    Yichen Zhang

Grammaticalization and Subjectivization of "*Po*"   134
  Haifeng Yang

On *chi:* Its Gestalt and Collocations   143
  *Huibin Zhuang, Yichen Zhang, Xiangling Li, Shaoshuai Shen,
  and Zhenqian Liu*

The Nature of *men* and Its Co-occurrence with Numeral Expressions
in Mandarin Chinese   153
  Ying Zhang

A Study on the Causative Alternation from a Non-derivational Perspective . . .   161
  Daran Yang

The Processing of Dummy Verbs in Semantic Role Labeling   170
  Mengxiang Wang, Yang Liu, and Houfeng Wang

Categorization and Intensity of Chinese Emotion Words   181
  Jingxia Lin and Yao Yao

Lexical Semantic Restrictions on the Syntactic Representation of the
Semantic Roles of Pinjie Class   191
  Zhen Tian and Shiyong Kang

Syntactic Distribution of Motion Agents' Concept from the Redundancy
of Leg Nouns   198
  Li Meng and Xiangnong Li

Investigate into the Cognitive Motivation of the Derivative Meaning
of Words: The Case of *Luojuan*   211
  Qingshan Qiu

Applications on Natural Language Processing

A Rule-Based Method for Identifying Patterns in Old Chinese Sentences . . .   221
  Youran Liu and Dan Long

Semi-supervised Sentiment Classification with Self-training on Feature
Subspaces   231
  Wei Gao, Shoushan Li, Yunxia Xue, Meng Wang, and Guodong Zhou

The Effect of Modifiers for Sentiment Analysis   240
  Xin Kou

Word Relevance Computation for Noun-Noun Metaphor Recognition   251
  Yuxiang Jia, Hongying Zan, Ming Fan, Shiwen Yu, and Zhimin Wang

Learning Semantic Similarity for Multi-label Text Categorization 260
Li Li, Mengxiang Wang, Longkai Zhang, and Houfeng Wang

Latent Semantic Distance Between Chinese Basic Words and Non-basic
Words 270
Shanon Yi-Hsin Lin and Shu-Kai Hsieh

Manual Investigation on Context for Word Sense Disambiguation 278
Dan Liu, Min Hua, Maohua Qian, and Xuri Tang

Conventionalizing Common Sense for Chinese Textual Entailment
Recognition 286
Shengjian Ni, Yichen Chen, and Donghong Ji

Scale-Free Distribution in Chinese Semantic Field Network: A Main Cause
of Using the Shortest Path Length for Representing Semantic
Distance Between Terms 296
Hua Yang, Mingyao Zhang, Donghong Ji, and Guozheng Xiao

Recognition and Extraction of Honorifics in Chinese Diachronic Corpora . . . 305
Dan Xiong, Jian Xu, Qin Lu, and Fengju Lo

A Hypothesis on Word Similarity and Its Application 317
Peng Jin, Likun Qiu, Xuefeng Zhu, and Pengyuan Liu

Lexical Resources and Corpus Linguistics

Chinese Near-Synonym Study Based on the Chinese Gigaword Corpus
and the Chinese Learner Corpus 329
Jia-Fei Hong

Semantic Labeling of Chinese Verb-Complement Structure Based
on Feature Structure 341
Bo Chen, Chen Lyu, Xiaomei Wei, and Donghong Ji

Structurally and Functionally Comparative Analysis of Lexlical Bundles
in the English Abstracts of Chinese and International Journals 349
Gui-ling Niu

Corpus Building for the Outcome-Based Education of the Ancient
Chinese Courses 358
Bing Qiu and Qingzhi Zhu

Building Chinese Semantic Treebank for Patent Text on the Basis
of 3 Dimensional Dynamic Concept Model 369
Yateng Wang, Dongfeng Cai, Haoguo Feng, Qiaoli Zhou, and Mingru Wei

Statistics and Analysis of Coordination Structures in Patent Text 380
  Mingru Wei, Guiping Zhang, Qiaoli Zhou, Yateng Wang,
  and Haihong Huang

Syntactic Distribution, Semantic Framework, and Pragmatic Function
of the Modal Adverb *Meizhun* (Maybe). 390
  Hong Xiao

Preliminary Study on the Construction of Bilingual Phrase Structure
Treebank 403
  Kunli Zhang, Hongying Zan, Yingjie Han, and Lingling Mu

Quantitative Analysis of "ADV+N" via Cognitive Property Knowledgebase . . . 414
  Bin Li, Yan Ma, Xueyang Liu, and Xuri Tang

Annotating Principal Event Chain in Chinese Texts 425
  Yu Chen, Han Ren, Jing Wan, Donghong Ji, and Guozheng Xiao

A Study on Metaphors in Idioms Based on Chinese Idiom Knowledge Base . . . 434
  Lei Wang, Shiwen Yu, Zhimin Wang, Weiguang Qu, and Houfeng Wang

Generalized Case Theory and the Argument-Omission Structure
in Mandarin Chinese 441
  Yong Yang

Author Index 449

Lexical Semantics

Embedded Compounding Monosyllabic Morphemes: A Perspective from the Lexical Study and TCFL

Ling Cen[1] and Jianfei Luo[2(✉)]

[1] Central China Normal University, Wuhan, China
`0602windy@163.com`
[2] Beijing Language and Culture University, Beijing, China
`nch1980s@163.com`

Abstract. Many modern Chinese words inherited from the classical Chinese. Therefore, vocabularies used in written Chinese are different from those used in modern Chinese. In written Chinese, an embedded compounding monosyllabic morpheme (hereafter abbreviated as ECMM) has its own prosodic structure and stylistic constraints, the details of which can be further explored. The article discusses the function of EMCC in the lexical system and proposes the corresponding teaching methods based on the characteristic of EMCC and the teaching experience.

Keywords: Embedded compounding monosyllabic morpheme · Prosody · Style · Chinese writing · Chinese teaching

1   Introduction

In Chinese written words, most monosyllabic elements can be used individually, but some cannot, for example,

(1a)*这　一切　具　吸引力。
　　 zhe　yiqie　ju　xiyinli
　　 these　all　have　attraction.
　　 All these are attractive.

(1b)*他　觉　头昏眼花。
　　 ta　jue　touhunyanhua
　　 he　feel　dizzy
　　 He feels dizzy. （Dong, 2006: 51）

具[*ju*](*have*) and 觉[*jue*](*feel*) in these two examples cannot work capable for separate uses, so they are not "word". However, they become grammatical if the relative modifier is added:

(2a) 这　一切　极　具　吸引力。
　　 zhe　yiqie　ji　ju　xiyinli
　　 these　all extremely　have　attraction
　　 All these are extremely attractive.

© Springer International Publishing Switzerland 2014
X. Su and T. He (Eds.): CLSW 2014, LNAI 8922, pp. 3–11, 2014.
DOI: 10.1007/978-3-319-14331-6_1

(2b) 他 顿　　　觉　头昏眼花。
　　ta dun　　　jue touhunyanhua
　　he suddenly feel dizzy
　　He feels dizzy suddenly.

This kind of monosyllabic elements is not a pure "bound morpheme". It sometimes acquires the features of "bound morpheme" and other times acquires the feature of "free morpheme" in Chinese writing vocabulary. Some monosyllabic elements are different from words, and in the meantime simultaneously, they are not exactly the same as bound morphemes. These components have different properties. Thus it is necessary for us to investigate their features and come up with some teaching methods in the aspect of foreign students' language acquisition.

2   The Definition of ECMM and Relative Research

Feng(2006) defined the features of ECMM as "syntactically free and prosodically bound". Huang (2012) summarized the features of these words as follows:

These words come from classical Chinese;
Their register is constrained as formal and elegant;
They have prosodic constraints;
They can form words, phrases, and temporary disyllabic units.

Huang (2012) pointed out that ECMM is a newly discovered language phenomenon in modern Chinese, and it is constrained by syntax and prosody. On one hand, it is syntactically free; on the other hand, it should form a disyllabic unit when used in real language.

3   The Analysis of the Errors Made by the Foreign Students

The writing materials of foreign students (with Chinese 4 and Chinese 5 levels, from Harvard University, Yale University, Chicago University and Massachusetts Institute of Technology) are used to analysis their relative errors in writing.

3.1   The Errors Made when Using ECMM

This kind of ECMM should be used in a disyllabic template with another monosyllabic element, but foreign students use indiscriminately as disyllabic element, for example,

(3)*哈佛大学、　耶鲁大学　这　类　名　　　学校。
　　Hafo daxue , Yelu daxue zhe lei ming xuexiao
　　Harvard　　　Yale　　　these CL well-known universities
　　These well-known universities such as Harvard and Yale

(4)*本　　　　国家　　　一流　　　　　的　　　大学
ben　　　*guojia*　　*yiliu*　　　　*de*　　*daxue*
our　　　country　first class　　DE　　university
The first-class universities in our country

(5)*养老院　　　　　　的　　　社工人。
yanglaoyuan　　　*de*　　*shegongren*
the nursing home　DE　　social　workers
Social workers of the nursing home

(6)*两 个　　人　　互相　　爱　的　　时候，婚姻　　一定　　是　　完美　　的
liang ge　*ren*　*huxiang*　*ai*　*de*　*shihou , hunyin*　*yiding*　*shi*　*wanmei*　*de*
two CL　person　each other　love　DE　time marriage　must　be　perfect　DE
If two people love each other, their marriage must be perfect.

The monosyllabic words used in a disyllabic template in these examples are 校 [*xiao*](*school*), 国 [*guo*](*country*), 工 [*gong*](*worker*), 互 [*hu*](*each other*). Their usages are differently used in templates:

(7a) 校[*xiao*](*school*): 本校[*ben xiao*]/*本学校[*ben xuexiao*](*our school*), 我校[*wo xiao*]/*我学校[*wo xuexiao*](*my school*).

(7b) 国[*guo*](*country*): 本国[*ben guo*]/*本国家[*ben guojia*](*our country*), 我国[*wo guo*]/*我国家[*wo guojia*](*my country*).

(7c) 工[*gong*](*worker*): 童工[*tong gong*] /*童工人[*tong gongren*](*child labor*), 社工[*she gong*]/*社工人[*she gongren*](*social worker*).

(7d) 相[*xiang*](*each other*): 相爱[*xiang ai*]/*互相爱[*huxiang ai*](*love each other*), 相助[*xiang zhu*]/*互相助[*huxiang zhu*](*help each other*).

Foreign students, considering the corresponding disyllable synonymy as a way of expression, add relative monosyllabic elements. Though the meanings are the same, they are invalid for the restriction of prosody.

3.2 Errors Made from the Collocations of the ECMM

Most foreign students don't make any errors in ECMM, but they misuse disyllable and multisyllable constituent as collocations. There are some examples as follows,

(8)*他们　　大　　赞美　　中国　　　的　　经济　　成就。
tamen　*da*　*zanmei*　*zhongguo*　*de*　*jingji*　*chengjiu*
they　highly　praise　China　　DE　economic　achievements
They highly praised the economic achievements of China.

(9)*经济　　对　　大　　选举　　有　　影响。
jingji　*dui*　*da*　*xuanju*　*you*　*yingxiang*
ecnomy　to　big　election　have　influence
The economy has impact on the general election.

(10)*值得　　大家　　传　　阅读。
zhide　*dajia*　*chuan*　*yuedu*
worth　everyone　pass　reading
It's worth everyone passing round for perusal.

(11)*价格   猛   下降。
　　jiage   meng   xiajiang
　　price   sharply   decline
　　The price declines sharply.

(12)*主   角色   表演   得   很   好。
　　zhu   juese   biaoyan   de   hen   hao
　　main   role   play   DE   very   good
　　The leading role played very well.

(13)*各   坚持   己   见。
　　ge   jianchi   ji   jian
　　everyone   nsist   oneself   viewpoint
　　Everyone insists his own viewpoints.

　　大 [da](highly), 传 [chuan](transmit), 猛 [meng](fiercely), 主 [zhu](main),
各[ge](each) are the ECMMs in the above examples. Their usages also differ from
disyllabic words.

　　(14a) 大[da](highly): 大批[da pi]/*大批评[da piping](heavily criticize), 大赞[da
zan]/*大赞美[da zanmei](highly praise).

　　(14b) 传[chuan](transmit): 传阅[chuan yue]/*传阅读[chuan yuedu](pass round
for perusal), 传看[chuan kan]/*传观看[chuan guankan](passed around).

　　(14c) 猛[meng](fiercely): 猛攻[meng gong]/*猛进攻[meng gongji](fierce attack),
猛击[meng ji]/*猛攻击[meng gongji](slap).

　　(14d) 主[zhu](main): 主角[zhu jue]/*主角色[zhu juese](leading actor), 主裁[zhu
cai]/*主裁判[zhu caipan](chief umpire).

　　(14e) 各[ge](each): 各持[ge chi]/*各坚持[ge jianchi](each insist on).

3.3   Element Chosen Errors from the ECMM

There are two examples as follows,

(15)*见到   很多   人   在   碧波   中   畅   泳
　　jiandao   henduo   ren   zai   bibo   zhong   chang   yong
　　see   a lot of people   in the blue waves LOC   delighted swim
　　It has been seen that a lot of people delighted swimming in the ocean.

(16) *求   业   竞争   非常   激烈。
　　 qiu   ye   jingzheng   feichang   jilie
　　 hunt   job   competition   very   fierce
　　 The competition of job hunting is quite fierce.

　　畅[chang](joyful) and 职[zhi](job) are ECMMs in the above examples. Their
major usages are as follows,

　　(17a) 畅[chang](joyful): 畅谈[chang tan]/*畅交谈[chang jiaotan](talk freely),
畅饮[chang yin]/*畅饮酒[chang yinjiu](drink one's fill).

　　(17b) 职[zhi](job): 辞职[ci zhi]/*辞职业[ci zhiye](quit one's job), 求职[qiu
zhi]/*求职业[qiu zhiye](apply for a job).

Though foreign students construct the disyllabic mode correctly, they still make mistakes when choosing the collocations, for example, in the word of 游泳[*you yong*](*swim*) and 职业[*zhi ye*](*job*), foreign students have certain understanding of selecting the monosyllabic element, but they have difficulties in selecting the proper one, like 畅游[*chang you*]/*畅泳[*chang yong*](*swim delightly*), 求职[*qiu zhi*]/*求业 [*qiu ye*](*apply for a job*).

3.4   Reasons of the Errors

3.4.1   The Regulation of ECMM

The meaning of these ECMMs is similar to their corresponding disyllable counterparts and they share analogical functions, such as 校[*xiao*]/学校[*xuexiao*](*school*), 国[*guo*]/国家[*guojia*](*country*). The corresponding disyllables are free words. The main difference lies in prosody, namely the ECMM has the feature of syntactically free and prosodically bound (Feng, 2006: 5). It has its specialties in expression, which is a way to show Chinese elegance expression.

3.4.2   Errors from Practice

When teaching senior foreign students, teachers emphasize the vocabularies and the comparison of synonyms while paying less attention to the difference between mon-osyllable and disyllable. For example, teachers explain the new word案[*an*](*law case*) as "law case" and show the example of 盗窃案[*daoqie an*](*theft case*) to support it. However, 案[*an*](*law case*) cannot be used alone. We cannot say:

(18a) *案   很   重要。
      an   hen   zhongyao
      law case   very   important
      The case is very important.

(18b) *他   无   权   处理   案。
       ta   wu   quan   chuli   an
       he   no   right   settle   case
       He has no right to deal with this case.

(18c) *案   的   审理   已经   结束。
       an   de   shenli   yijing   jieshu
       law case DE   trial   already   over
       The trial of the law case has already finished.
       We can only say:

(19a) 本   案   很   重要。
      ben   an   hen   zhongyao
      this case   very   important
      This case is very important.

(19b) 他   无   权   处理   本   案。
      ta   wu   quan   chuli   ben   an
      he   no   right   settle   this   case
      He has no right to deal with this case.

(19c) 本   案   的   审理   已经   结束。
　　　Ben   an   de   shenli   yijing   jieshu.
　　　this   law case   DE   trial   already over

The trial of the law case has already finished.

So in the case of案[*an*](*law case*), we cannot only use translation methods but also consider more about its prosodic features.

4   Method of Teaching ECMM

We cannot use traditional way to teach these words, nor can we teach them as common monosyllabic morphemes. We should make sure of the meaning of ECMM and emphasize on the collocation words. More specifically, there are four steps.

4.1   Recognition

We should help foreign students to improve the awareness of the ECMM. They should know that not only syntax, semantic and pragmatic, but also "prosody" and "register" are vital important in Chinese writing. Specifically speaking, there are two teaching methods as follows.

4.1.1   Input of Relative Materials

We should supply large amount of material with ECMM, students will aware of the prosody. Take 贤[*xian*](*virtuous*) in the newspaper and magazine as example:

(20a) 追忆   先   贤。
　　　zhuiyi   xian xian
　　　recall   earlier sage

Recall our ancestors.

(20b) 敬   老   尊   贤。
　　　jing   lao   zun   xian
　　　respect olds   respect ancestors

Respect the olds and ancestors.

(20c) 求   贤   若   渴。
　　　Qiu xian   ruo   ke
　　　Seek wise man   seems   thirsty

Seek for the virtuous like a thirsty person for water.

We have先贤[*xian xian*](*ancestor*), 尊贤[*zun xian*](*respect the ancestors*) and求贤若渴[*qiu xian ruo ke*](*seek for the virtuous like a thirsty person for water*). If our students read more about these words, their language intuition will improve a lot.

4.1.2   More Practice

We can show the meaning of its collocation without the concept of ECMM and then let students guess the meaning of other collocations. Such as,

Show the meaning of当选[dang xuan](be elected), and guess the meaning of 参选[can xuan](participate in evaluation and election) and 落选[luo xuan](fail to be elected).

Show the meaning of要员[yao yuan](important official), and guess the meaning of 要事[yao shi](important thing) and要闻[yao wen](important news).

In this way, students can improve the sense of ECMM and master the regulation better.

4.2   Teaching and Practice

Feng(2006,2007)made a deep research on teaching ECMM. He classified the teaching method into three steps. Learn monosyllabic element from disyllabic words, divide disyllabic words into monosyllabic elements and systematically practice. More specifically speaking, we should make sure which element can be used as ECMM in a disyllabic word. Take 朋友[pengyou](friend) for example, 友[you](friend) can get into a new word easily while 朋[peng](friend) cannot. Thus we should teach students which elements can be used as ECMM. After that, we should combine these single elements. For example, we separate友[you](friend) from 朋友(friend), so we can make new words, such as 好友[hao you](good friend), 室友[shi you](roommate), 校友 [xiao you](alumnus), 贵友[gui you](invaluable friend), etc. At last, it comes to the systematical practice. We divide the original words and make the new words.

This kind of practice shows the relative knowledge clearly to foreign students and helps a lot in teaching. So we prefer this method to enlarge the vocabularies of ECMM for foreign students.

4.3   Steps of Consolidation

We should help foreign students to consolidate what we have taught in class. The specific methods are like follows. First of all, diction practice. The teacher asks students to make sentences according to the given mode, such as暗[an](secretly) + [X]v, 大[da](highly) + [X]v, 孤[gu](alone) + [X]n, 返[fan](return) + [X]pw, [X]adv + 感 [gan](feel). When we do the practice, the teacher can show some clues to the students. For example, the teacher tells students the location of the single word (show as[X]) and what kind of words the students should use. Thus, students will pay attention to the prosody according to the clues on syntax.

What's more, we can use the method of "register transmission" to practice. We can tell students how to use the ECMM and ask students to orally explain them or vice verse. When we teach the character of共[gong](together), we can supply them with the following sentences.

(21a) 让   我们   共   创   美好   未来。

rang women gong chuang meihao weilai

let   us   together create bright future

Let's cooperate toward a bright future.

(21b) 跟   同学   共   居   一   室。

gen   tongxue   gong   ju   yi   shi

with classmate together live one room

Share one room with my classmate.

(22a)
让	我们	共同	创造	美好	的	未来。
rang	*women*	*gongtong*	*chuangzao*	*meihao*	*de*	*weilai*
let	us	together	create	bright	DE	future

Let's cooperate toward a bright future.

(22b)
跟	同学	共同	居住	在	一	间	卧室。
gen	*tongxue*	*gongtong*	*juzhu*	*zai*	*yi*	*jian*	*woshi*
with	classmate	togegher	live	in	one	CL	room

Share one room with my classmate.

4.4   Flexible Application

When we finish the above steps, we can encourage students to use these expressions freely in the compositions based on the syntactic and prosodic regulations. For example, the teacher can ask students to use the ECMM as often as possible in their compositions.

5   Conclusion

Based on the previous research and errors of foreign students', the position of ECMM in Chinese vocabulary system and the methods of teaching ECMM are analyzed , this article is a great help for vocabulary research and supplies a good way for foreign students to master the standard Chinese.

Acknowledgments. The study is supported by the Beijing Language and Culture University scientific research project (The central university basic scientific research business special fund project) (Grant No. 13YBT05), and the Youth Elite Project of Beijing Language and Culture University.

References

1. Dong, X.: Chinese Lexicon and Grammar. Peking University Press, Beijing (2006). (in Chinese)
2. Feng, S., Yan, L.: Chinese Grammar and Textbook compilation. Journal of the Chinese Language Teachers Association **49**, 1 (2013). (in Chinese)
3. Feng, S.: Expressions of Written Chinese, vol. 1. Beijing Language and Culture University Press, Beijing (2006). (in Chinese)
4. Feng, S.: On Modern Written Chinese. Journal of Chinese Linguistics **37**(1) (2009). (in Chinese)
5. Feng, S.: On the Properties and Pedagogy of Written Chinese. Journal of Chinese Teaching in the World **78**(04), 98–106 (2006). (in Chinese)
6. Feng, S.: Prosodic Structure and its Implications for Teaching Chinese as a Second Language. Journal of the Chinese Language Teachers Association **39** (2004). (in Chinese)

7. Feng, S.: Written Chinese the Present and the Past. Peking University Press, Beijing (2013). (in Chinese)
8. Feng, S: An Independent Grammar for Written Chinese in Second Language Teaching. Journal of Language Teaching and Linguistic Studies (3), 53–63 (2003). (in Chinese)
9. Grabe, W., Kaplan, R.B.: Theory and practice of writing. Longman, New York (1996)
10. Huang, M.: Prosodic Syntax of Modern Chinese Disyllabic Words Used as a Couplet. Beijing Language and Culture University Press, Beijing (2012). (in Chinese)
11. Lu, J.: Attention Should Be Given To the Written Chinese Teaching in Teaching Chinese as Foreign Language, Research on Chinese as a Second Language (2007). (in Chinese)
12. Lü, S.: On Modern Chinese Monosyllabic and Disyllabic Word. Studies of the Chinese Language (1) (1963). (in Chinese)
13. Skehan, P.: A Cognitive Approach to Language Learning. CUP, Cambridge (1998)

Word Ordering in Chinese Opposite Compounds

Jing Ding[(⊠)] and Chu-Ren Huang

Department of Chinese and Bilingual Studies,
The Hong Kong Polytechnic University, Hung Hom, Hong Kong
amanda.ding@connect.polyu.hk, Churen.huang@polyu.edu.hk

Abstract. The smantic factor is considered to play an important role in deciding the word order of compounds. Previous studies on Chinese opposites generally agree with the Pollyanna Principle, but do not offer detailed statistical analysis, especially for opposite compounds. In this paper, we go through 315 opposite pairs in Sinica Corpus and the result shows that, for Chinese opposite compounds, prosodic factor and cultural hierachy are also crucial for ordering.

Keywords: Chinese opposite compound · Pollyanna Principle · Corpus

1 Introduction

According to the **Pollyanna Principle** (Matlin & Stang, 1978), the positive or evaluatively (more) positive members are more favored than the negative ones and therefore preferred to be placed in the front of the negative ones.

Such a hypothesis is supported by some early dated observations. Tang (1979) mentioned that the word order of "antonymous coordinate construction" (:18) features having the positive meaning one in the front position and the negative, in the latter position. That was, he interpreted, because the positive one also carried the neutral, or unmarked, meaning.

For the exception of 轻重 [*qing1zhong4*] (*weight*), for example, 问题的轻重 [*wen4ti2 de0 qing1zhong4*], Tang thought it was equal to "the importance (of the issue)" and referred to a state, rather than a physical measurement. And therefore it did not follow the general order. Similar cases like *qing1zhong4* are （态度的）冷热 [(*tai4du4 de0*) *leng3re4*] (*attribute*), and （人间的）冷暖 [(*ren2jian1 de0*) *leng3 nuan3*] (*social snobbery*) (:18-20). However, such an interpretation is not convincing enough. As we have mentioned above, *qing1zhong4* is also commonly used as 'weight' in both ancient and modern Chinese. The meaning of 'importance' is actually derived from the initial meaning of 'weight'. So do the cases of *leng3re4* and *leng3nuan4*. But as to the other compounds, which are combined by opposite pairs and refer to the hypernym, it is more often to have the positive ones in prior position: 长短 [*chang2duan3*] (*length*), 高低/高矮 [*gao1di1*]/[*gao1ai3*] (*height*), 多少 [*duo1shao3*] (*quantity*). And it is also seen as to provide a move from the higher point of the scale to the lower point.

X. Su and T. He (Eds.): CLSW 2014, LNAI 8922, pp. 12–20, 2014.
DOI: 10.1007/978-3-319-14331-6_2

In his book, Tang listed out fifteen special word orders in Chinese (:20-26):

(1) '天'>'人' (the concept of *tian1* 'sky' prior to that of *ren2* 'human being')
(2) '人'>'兽'或'物' (the concept of *ren2* 'human being' prior to that of *shou4* 'animal' or *wu4* 'things')
(3) '公'>'私' (the concept of *gong1* 'public' prior to that of *si1* 'private')
(4) '家'>'人' (the concept of *jia1* 'family' prior to that of *ren2* 'human being')
(5) '长'>'幼' (the concept of *zhang3* 'senior' prior to that of *you4* 'junior')
(6) '尊'>'卑' (the concept of *zun1* 'respected' prior to that of *bei1* 'humble')
(7) '亲'>'疏' (the concept of *qin1* 'close' prior to that of *shu1* 'distant')
(8) '男'>'女' (the concept of *nan2* 'male' prior to that of *nv3* 'female')
(9) '优'>'劣' (the concept of *you1* 'good(_quantity)' prior to that of *lie4* 'bad(_quantity)')
(10) '盈'>'亏' (the concept of *ying2* 'surplus' prior to that of *kui1* 'deficit')
(11) '主'>'副' (the concept of *zhu3* 'host' prior to that of *ke4* 'guest')
(12) '鸟'>'（鱼）兽' (the concept of *niao3* 'avifauna' prior to that of *yu2* 'ichthyfauna' or *shou4* 'quadruped')
(13) '上'>'下' (the concept of *shang4* 'up' prior to that of *xia4* 'down')
(14) '软'>'硬'>（或者，'流体'>'固体'） (the concept of *ruan3* 'soft' prior to that of *ying4* 'hard', or, *liu2ti3* 'liquid' prior to that of *gu4ti3* 'solid')
(15) '里'（'进'）>'外'（'出'） (the concept of *li3* 'inside' prior to that of *wai4* 'outside', or, *jin4* 'come in' prior to that of *chu1* 'go out')

Tang's list was not for bi-syllabic compounds only, but served as general rules for the word ordering of related Chinese concepts, be they for compounds, phrases or others.

Besides, Xu also generally mentioned that, in the opposite compounds, it is usual to have the words which bear the positive meaning in front, and the negative one behind. So he demonstrated that the word order of opposite compounds does have relation with their meanings. (2000: 450-1) In that sense, his finding also agreed with that of the Pollyanna Principle.

2   Research Question

Tang's analysis offers a general rule for Chinese opposite compounds. However, his rules do not fully explain the existence of compounds such as 轻重 [*qing1zhong4*] (*weight*). Therefore, corpus-based statistical data is necessary for testing whether the fact agrees with Pollyanna Principle or Tang's list. For this paper, we want to answer following questions: is Pollyanna Principle sufficient to explain all the compound orderings; if not, then, what would be the other deciding factors?

3   Corpus and Method

There are two main steps in our experiment: first, the opposite pairs are selected from modern Chinese dictionaries; then, all the compounds that contain opposite pairs are extracted from the corpus for later analysis.

Notice, in the experiment, we settle a window size of extraction from 2 characters to 4 characters, to avoid the noises which are not considered as compounds. And, all the data are extracted automatically but then manually checked for higher accuracy.

《新华反义词词典》(*Dictionary of Opposites*) (2003) is selected as the base of our candidate list. It is the most authorized dictionary for Chinese opposites and its definition of what an opposite pair is, is based on the lexical meanings. That is to say, for the two members of an opposite pair: the assertion of one member implies the negation of the other,, and vice versa, like 生: 死, [*sheng1: si3*] (*alive: dead*); or, the meanings of two members are contrasts to each, and the negation of one does not necessarily imply the assertion of the other, like 大: 小, [*da3: xiao3*] (*big: small*); or, converse pairs like 买: 卖, [*mai3: mai4*] (*buy: sell*), 敌: 友, [*di2: you3*] (*enemy: friend*). This rule convers most of the Chinese opposite compounds. However, the book does not include the pairs like 夫: 妻, [*fu1: qi1*] (*husband: wife*), or 父: 子, [*fu4: zi3*] (*father: son*), neither the Chinese cultural contrast pairings (对举词 [*dui4ju3 ci2*]), like 水: 火, [*shui3: huo3*] (*water: fire*), which are also very frequent-ly used as opposites in Chinese. In that case, we manually add extra 39 pairs to the initial list hence the final seed list contains 315 pairs, which are supposed to cover most of the opposite pairings in Chinese.

We chose Sinica Corpus because: it is one of the largest balanced corpora for Modern Chinese and it is fully segmented. By using it, we mean to reflect the nature of Modern Chinese, and, for practical aspect, to avoid the problems of word segmentation as well as the argument of what the word is, in Chinese.

4   Data Result

There are four basic kinds of patterns in our data. The first kind of pattern contains only one opposite pairing, which is generalized as [A][-A], such as 美丑[*mei3: chou3*] (*beauty: ugliness*), 胜负[*sheng4: fu4*] (*victory: failure*), 爱恨 [*ai4: hen4*] (*love: hate*) and 男女 [*nan2: nv3*] (*man: woman*). This basic pattern [A][-A] some-times derives into patterns of [A][-A][A][-A] (彼此彼此 [*bi3ci3bi3ci3*] (*there and here*)), [A] [A][-A][-A](来来往往 [*lai2lai2wang3wang3*] (*come and go*)) and [A][-A][A](里外里 [*li3wai4li3*] (*in all*)).

The second pattern is that of one opposite pair explicitly representing a relation be-tween the opposite pairing members within the phrase. The relation may appear in front/behind the pairing, like [A][-A][X] (松紧度 [*song1jin3du4*] (*degree of tight-ness*), 生死与共 [*sheng1si3yu3gong4*] (*share the same destiny*)) or [X][A][-A](见高低 [*jian4gao1di1*] (*show the result*), 不相上下 [*bu4xiang1shang4xia4*] (*be equally good*)), and also in the middle position of the pattern like [A][X][-A](老来少

[*lao3lai2shao4*] (*have a young heart at an old age*)), or, in some of the cases, be separated into two parts interjecting the two opposite members like [X-][A][+X][-A] (反客为主 [*fan3k4wei2zhu3*] (*guest acts like host*)) and [A][X-][-A][+X](今非昔比 [*jin1fei1xi1bi3*] (*things change with time*)).

The third is to have two pairs of opposites combined together. For example, [A1][A2][-A1][-A2], such as古往今来 [*gu3wang3jin1lai2*] (*of all ages*), and, 优胜劣汰 [*you1sheng4lie4tai4*] (*select the fittest*).

The forth one is combined by one opposite pair and one synonymous pair, like 东躲西藏 [*dong1duo3xi1can2*] (*hide hard*) and 阴错阳差 [*yin1cuo4yang2cha1*] (*a mistake caused by fate*) are both marked as [A][S][-A][S']. In some of the examples, the added word repeats in the same patterns, such as 时冷时热 [*shi2leng3shi2re4*] (*sometimes cold sometimes hot*) ([S][A][S][-A]) or 明里暗里 [*ming2li3an4li3*] (*in all places*)

([A][S][-A][S]). Such examples of patterns [A][S][-A][S] and [S][A][S][-A] are also considered as one of the patterns in the second category.

Theoretically peaking, there are more patterns which may, for example, bear three of the above pairs at the same time, but the number of them is not very large in daily language. So they are not considered as the most **basic** patterns, although we will still keep them for discussion in this study.

Table 1. Hits of patterns for four basic categories

category	pattern	hits	total
one opposite pairing	[A][-A]	218	
	[A] [A][-A][-A]	38	
	[A][-A][A][-A]	3	
	[A][-A][A]	1	
			260
One opposite pairing with one relationship	[A][-A][X]	459	
	[X][A][-A]	120	
	[X-][A][+X][-A]	63	
	[A][X][-A]	62	
	[A][X-][-A][+X]	6	
			710
Two opposite pairings	[A1][A2][-A1][-A2]	136	
			136
One opposite pairing with one synonymous pairing	[S][A][S][-A]	216	
	[A][S][-A][S']	129	
	[S][A][S'][-A]	118	
	[A][S][-A][S]	17	
			480
			1586

5   Discussion

As we have mentioned above, previous studies agree with the Pollyanna Principle in general. Our research however, shows that the Pollyanna Principle has its limitation when applied to Chinese opposites as a whole, and the real situation is more complicated than Pollyanna Principle or Tang's list can cover.

Adopting the general rule and list, we went through the 218 bi-syllabic opposite compounds, which are restricted to the [A][-A] pattern. Only 113 out of them agree with the rules. The rest of the examples, including 往来 [wang3lai2] (come and go), 问答 [wen4 da2] (questions and answers), 经纬 [jing1wei3] (horizontal and latitudinal), are not applicable, since it is hard to define the positive or negative in the components.

In the 113 valid instances, 87 (77.0%) agreed with the above rules and only 26 were against it. Both lists contained some highly frequent words, such as 亲疏 [qin1shu1] (close or distant (of social connection)), 利害 [li4hai4] (benefit and harm), 美丑 [mei3chou3] (beautiful and ugly), as positive-in-front order, and, 死活 [si3huo2] (death and living), 悲喜 [bei1xi3] (sad and happy), 贫富 [pin2fu4] (poor and rich), as negative-in-front order.

These exceptions are also found in the experiment. The saying of 雌雄 [ci2 xiong2] (male and female) appears 158 times, is much better accepted than xiong2ci2, which does not appear once in the whole corpus. But as we will see in later this section, for the same concept of gender, nan2: nv3 and gong1:mu3 strongly follows the rules.

Moreover, when the reversed order can also be used, and the two word orders are both acceptable for speakers, it is usually the positive-in-front order more preferred in speaking.

We use the hits of each word in Chinese GigaWord (Simplified) to see which one is better accepted.

The word 真假 [zhen1jia3] (real and fake), it has 331 hits, while the reversed word 假真 [jia3zhen1] does not have any hit. 真真假假[zhen1zhen1jia3jia3] has 16 hits, which is three times higher than that of 假假真真[jia3jia3zhen1zhen1] (4 hits). 生死 [sheng1si3] (living and death) has 1916 hits, but 死生 [si3sheng1] has 0 hit and even for 死活 [si3huo2] (death and living) the hit number reaches is only 156. The gap between 男女 [nan2 nv3] (male and female) and 女男 [nv3nan2] is more obvious. 12576 instances contain the saying nan2nv3 but none for nv3nan2. Similarly, 公母 [gong1: mu3] (male: female) is accepted but mu3gong1 is not.

The variation of the [A][-A] pattern, that is, that the rest patterns is category One, and, the second category, as well as the forth category, follow the order of their according [A][-A] compounds.

The results show that the Pollyanna Principle does have an overwhelming effect on the applicable words but does not cover all the opposite compounds of the [A][-A] pattern. In fact, the word order related to their semantic meanings in different ways, within different kinds of opposites.

For the third category, that is, the one of the compounds having two pairs of opposites within one compound or idiom, the ordering rules are generalized as following:
1. The positive one(s) is/are preferred to take the prior place(s).

There are only three possible orderings in our corpus, and within them: [P(ostive)1][N(egative)1][P(ositive)2][N(egative)2] > [P1][N1][N2][P2](安危祸福 [an1wei1huo4fu2] (fate), 是非曲直 [shi4fei1qu3zhi2] (right and wrong), 是非黑白 [shi4fei1hei1bai2] (right and wrong))>[N1][P1][N2][P2](悲欢离合 [bei1huan1li2he2] (happiness and sadness), 轻重缓急 [qin1zhong4huan3ji2] (various situations).

That is to say, [P1][N1][P2][N2] is the most common pattern.

2. For the ones which share the same natural domain, they are preferred to appear in close positions. Hence, in 男女老少 [nan2nv3lao3shao4] (all the population), nan2 (male) and nv3 (female) are both for gender, while lao3 (old) and shao4 (young) are both for age, is preferred to 男老少女 [nan2lao3shao4nv3] or 男老女少 [nan2lao3nv3shao4] (this compound may be possible when it means 'the male one is elder and the female one is younger', which differs from the meaning of nan2nv3lao3shao4). And, in 亲疏远近 [qin1shu1yuan3jin4], qin1 (close) and shu1 (remote) are both for relationship, while yuan3 (distant) and jin4 (close) are both for distance, 'close and distant', rather than 亲远近疏 [qin1yuan3jin4shu1]; in 利弊得失 [li4bi4de2shi1], li4 (advantage) and bi4 (disadvantage) mean 'cons and pros', and, de2 (win) and shi1(lose) mean two possible results), 'all the aspects', rather than 利失得弊 [li4shi2de2bi4].

3. If the same domain has more than one way to be divided, then the ones which share the same manner of division should be placed together. For example, 前后左右 [qian2hou3zuo3you4] (in four directions), qian2 (front) with hou3(behind), and zuo3 (left) with you4 (right). And, 加减乘除 [jia1jian3cheng2chu2] (four arithmetic operations), jia1 (addition) with jian3 (subtraction), and cheng2 (multiplication) with chu2(division), according to the rules of arithmetic operation.

From the aspect of opposite sub-categories, different kinds of opposite perform differently with the rules. For antonym and complementary compounds, it is the truth that most of the instances prefer to have the positive ones in front: 亲疏 [qin1shu1] (close and distant), 优劣 [you1lie4] (good(_quantity) and bad(_quantity)), 利害 [li4hai4] (benefit and harm), 善恶 [shan4e4] (kindhearted and evil), 多寡 [duo1gua3] (many and few), 尊卑 [zun1bei1] (respected and humble).

For taxonomy words, there are so many compounds like文武 [wen2wu3] (civil and military), 经纬 [jing1wei3] (horizontal and latitudinal), 水火 [shui3huo3] (water and fire), 南北 [nan2bei3] (south and north) that it is hard to evaluate the polarity.

In other words, the hypothesis is not applicable to these examples. Some taxonomy compounds, such as 甘苦 [gan1ku3] (sweet and bitter), 爱恨 [ai4hen4] (love and hate), have the ones which are considered as culturally positive words in front. But, it also has compounds like 悲喜 [bei1xi3] (sad and happy) or 阴阳 [yin1yang2] (Yin and Yang), which have the culturally negative ones in front.

For the converse, the order of the two members is exactly the same as they are in the real event. That is to say, the event order decides the word order of the according converse compound. Let's take 买卖 [mai3mai4] (buy and sell) for example. In the trade activity, to sell something is always after the action of buying or possessing something. Hence the word order keeps the same as their temporal order.

When there is no temporal difference between the two components, the compounds prefer to agree on the positive-in-front order. 婚 [hun1] (man marries woman) and 嫁 [jia4] (woman marries man) describe a marriage from the groom's and bride's aspects, respectively. In the compound of this pairing, hun1 is put in front of jia4, that is, hun1jia4, as the same order of rule (8) "male prior to that one of female". In our data, we did not find any instance which follows the temporal order but are against the Pollyanna hypothesis. From the examples of taxonomy group, we added some rules to Tang's list:

(16) '古'>'今' (the concept of gu3 'ancient' prior to that of jin1 'nowadays')

(17) '东'>'西' (the concept of dong1 'east' prior to that of xi1 'west')

(18) '南'>'北' (the concept of nan2 'south' prior to that of bei3 'north')

(19) '经'>'纬' (the concept of jing1 'horizontal' prior to that of wei3 'latitudinal')

(20) '昼'>'夜' (the concept of zhou4 'day' prior to that of ye4 'night').

(21) '头'>'尾' (the concept of tou2 'head' prior to that of wei3 'end')

(22) '左'>'右' (the concept of zuo3 'left' prior to that of you4 'right')

(23) '前'>'后' (the concept of qian2 'front' prior to that of hou4 'behind')

(24) '天'>'地' (the concept of tian1 'sky' prior to that of di4 'earth').

5.1   A Prosodic Explanation[1]

Apart from the above, the prosodic factor[2] is also possible for the explanation of word ordering in compounds. We compute the tone order of the 218 [A][-A] compounds. 113 examples have first or second tones in the front position and the third or fourth tone in the back position; 62 examples have the reverse situation. That is, with the third or fourth tones in the front position, and the first or second tone in back position; the rest of the 43 compounds have the same tone in both positions. That is to say,

---

[1] Thanks to Yu Shiwen, Chen Keh-Jiann, Su Xinchun and Yuan Yulin, for pointing out this factor and offering a discussion for us, in CLSW 2014, at University of Macau.

[2] Because of the limitations of time and knowledge, this paper only considers the initial tone of each word. The tonal modification, which means the influence and change in actual speaking, is not considered. From the aspect of historical linguistics, it is also possible for the word tone to change since some compounds were created. That kind of change, however, is not discussed in this paper either.

first or second tone (113>62) has an obvious leading position in compounds, than third or fourth tone.

Do the Pollyanna Principle and prosodic factors agree with each other? In our data, there are 84 compounds which are both available to the Pollyanna Principle and show a difference of tone in two positions:

Table 2. The distribution of 84 examples

Pollyanna Principle	Prosodic factor	Example number
+	+	40
+	-	18
-	+	19
-	-	7
		Total: 84

As we can see here, the examples in which the Pollyanna Principle agrees with the prosodic factor overwhelms the other three situations. When the two factors clash with each, the chances for any one of them to win out are almost equal. That is to say, from this table, it is hard to tell which factor is stronger than the other in deciding the order within opposite compounds.

However, there are 7 examples violating both of the two rules. They are: 死生 [*si3sheng1*] (*being dead or alive*), 死活 [*si3huo2*] (*being dead or alive*), 短长 [*duan3chang2*] (*shortness*), 祸福 [*huo4fu2*] (*unfortunate and fortunate*), 冷热 [*leng3re4*] (*cold and hot*), 苦乐 [*ku3le4*] (*unhappy and happy*), 浊清 [*zhuo2qing1*] (*muddy and clear*).

6   Conclusion

In this paper, we use 315 Chinese opposite pairs as the seed list to go through Sinica Corpus, in order to see their ordering rules in compounds from bi-syllabic to quad-syllabic. Based on the data result, we modified the initial observation by previous studies as follows: The Pollyanna Principle is available to around half of the Chinese opposite compounds. In these examples, most agree with the principle. Additionally, when two-word orders are both available, the positive-in-front ones are preferred. Temporal order is an influencial factor for the ones which are not available to the Pollyanna Principle. It is mostly proved in the opposite category of converse.

In general, the result shows that, in Chinese, cultural hierarchy and the Pollyanna Principle together determine the order of opposites in compounds. Moreover, detailed conceptual orders of such cultural hierarchy are also added to previous studies.

We must admit, due to the limit of time and space, this paper only focuses on the semantic factor for Chinese opposite compounds. Other possible factors, such as prosodic, would be considered in our future work.

References

Cruse, D.A.: Lexical Semantics. Cambridge University Press, Cambridge (1986)

Murphy, M.L.: Semantic Relations and the Lexicon: Antonyms, Synonyms and other Semantic Paradigms. Cambridge University Press, Cambridge (2003)

Paradis, C.: Ontologies and construals in lexical semantics. Axiomathes **15**, 541–573 (2005)

Matlin, M.W., Stang, D.J.: The Pollyanna Principle: Selectivity in Language, Memory, and Thought. Schenkman Publishing, Cambridge (1978)

Tang, T.-C.: Studies on Chinese Morphology and Syntax. Taiwan Student Book Press, Taipei (1979). (in Chinese)

Xu, W.: Chinese lexical. Chinese Lexicology in 20th Century. Book Sea Publisher, Taiyuan (2000). (in Chinese)

Chinese Knowledge Information Processing Group (CKIP): CKIP Technical Report No. 95-02/98-04. Academia Sinica, Taipei (1993)

Study on Prosodic Morphology of Chinese Verbal Monosyllabic-Disyllabic Synonyms

Jianfei Luo[✉]

Beijing Language and Culture University, Beijing, China
nch1980s@163.com

Abstract. Chinese verbal synonyms, mainly verbal monosyllabic and disyllabic synonyms (hereafter, verbal monosyllabic-disyllabic synonyms), vary in their semantic and pragmatic performances. However, a systematic research on grammatical and prosodic rules of these verbal synonyms does not exist. Therefore, this paper is to calculate and analyze paired verbal monosyllabic-disyllabic synonyms included in *The Contemporary Chinese Dictionary (6th Edition)* on their corresponding rules and prosodic morphology. It is revealed that 81% non-interchangeable verb pairs are relevant with morphological functions of prosody. More specifically, they are relevant with verb-object collocations, embedded monosyllables, verbal disyllables featuring in weakening concrete space and time, and different register characters of monosyllables and disyllables. All of these above factors lead to non-interchangeability of some paired verbal monosyllabic-disyllabic synonyms in language using.

Keywords: Verbal monosyllabic-disyllabic synonyms · Morphological function of prosody · Register character · Feature of weakening concrete space-time

1   Introduction

Chinese verbal synonyms, mainly verbal monosyllabic and disyllabic synonyms (hereafter, verbal monosyllabic-disyllabic synonyms), vary in their semantic and pragmatic performances. Previous studies mainly zeroed in on three aspects.

The first one is studies on comparisons of monosyllabic and disyllabic verbs. Zhang (1989, 1990) focused on syntactic components and collocation functions of monosyllabic and disyllabic verbs. He pointed out that monosyllabic verbs are the basic words people tend to use in their daily life while disyllabic verbs, mostly emerging after May Fourth Movement, are newly born. Their functions are also quite different. Liu (2005) has extensively researched verbal monosyllabic-disyllabic synonyms including the same morphemes and found out they differed in phonology, grammar, lexicon, rhetoric, etc.

The second is studies on nominalization of disyllabic verbs. According to Chen (1987), disyllabic word is a necessary condition for Chinese verbs to be changed into nouns. A large number of disyllabic verbs enlarges categories of Chinese nouns, which means that verb-oriented language drifts into a noun-oriented one. Analyzing nominalization out of verbs, Zhang & Fang (1996) voiced that nouns, non-predictive ad-

© Springer International Publishing Switzerland 2014
X. Su and T. He (Eds.): CLSW 2014, LNAI 8922, pp. 21–30, 2014.
DOI: 10.1007/978-3-319-14331-6_3

jectives, adjectives, intransitive verbs and transitive verbs form a continuum, where the nominal features weaken while the verbal features strengthen.

The last is studies on application. Zhang (2011) has analyzed semantics of verbal monosyllabic-disyllabic synonyms which possess the same morpheme and the same meaning. According to Zhang, the substitute area of monosyllabic-disyllabic verbs sharing the same morpheme and the same meaning have a positive correlation with their semantic equivalence. It can be inferred from their semantic equivalence calculation and analysis that there are three kinds of semantic equivalences: equivalence, compounding and crossing. Cheng & Xu (2004) carried out a study on verbal monosyllabic-disyllabic synonyms via Chinese Efficiency Test. Enlightened from the major synonym-teaching problems in teaching Chinese as a second language, they have selected 181 verb synonyms from *the Syllabus of Graded Words and Characters for Chinese Proficiency* and discussed the classifications and major differences of those verbal synonyms.

In all, though we have made progress gradually, we still have some theoretical and practical problems. For example, we are lacking in diachronic analysis, comprehensive explanation, corpus, systematical research, etc. Therefore, the author makes a systematical research on verbal monosyllabic-disyllabic synonyms included in *The Contemporary Chinese Dictionary (6th Edition)*. This paper quantitatively and qualitatively describes the interchangeability of verbal monosyllabic-disyllabic synonyms and explains when they are non-interchangeable from the perspective of prosodic morphology, morphology and register.

2   Interchangeability of Verbal Monosyllabic-Disyllabic Synonyms

2.1   Distribution and Number of Verbal Synonyms

100 monosyllabic verbs which have corresponding disyllabic synonyms (taking the annotation from the dictionary as standard) were selected from the Contemporary Chinese Dictionary (6th Edition), such as碍[ai]/妨碍[fang'ai](to hinder), 拜[bai]/拜访[baifang] (to visit), 毙[bi]/枪毙[qiangbi] (to kill), 测[ce]/测量[celiang] (to measure), 编[bian]/创作[chuangzuo] (to create), 怵[chu]/害怕[haipa] (to fear). Some of such paired words share the same morpheme while others do not. In addition, some monosyllabic verbs have several corresponding disyllabic synonyms, such as吃[chi]——吸收[xishou] (to absorb)/消灭[xiaomie] (to wipe out)/承受[chengshou] (to bear). Hence, disyllabic verbs outnumber monosyllabic ones. In order to conduct a research on the usage and substitution of verbal monosyllabic-disyllabic synonyms, the author has collected all the examples in that dictionary. For instance, 充[chong] (to forge)——充行家[chong hangjia] (to pretend to be an expert)/以次充好[yi ci chong hao] (to forge inferior products at high quality prices)/打肿脸充胖子[da zhong lian chong pangzi] (try to satisfy one's vanity when one cannot really afford to do so). Table 1 shows the number and usage of disyllabic verbs corresponding to 100 monosyllabic verbs.

Table 1. Statistic table of 100 pairs verbal monosyllabic-disyllabic synonyms

item	number
Monosyllabic verbs	100
Disyllabic verbs	213
Examples of monosyllabic verbs	369
Examples of disyllabic verbs	464
Total examples	833

2.2   Statistics of Interchangeable Verbal Monosyllabic-Disyllabic Synonyms

In this research, 833 verbal monosyllabic-disyllabic synonyms mentioned in Table 1 were substituted, acceptance by the native Mandarin speakers out of their sense to Mandarin were investigated, and validity of these substituted language materials was tested under the help of Contemporary Chinese Corpus from Peking University. Results revealed that 242 examples (29.1% of the whole) can be substituted, such as:

(1) 爱/爱护　　公物
    ai/aihu　 *gongwu*
    care   public property
    caring for public property

(2) 办/办理　　　　入学手续
    ban/banli　 *ruxueshouxu*
    handle   school enrolment formalities
    go through the formalities

Another 12 examples (1.4% of the whole) is valid as long as combined with function words. Such as,

(3) 这　　几　　天　　他　　好像　　有意　　躲避　　我。
    zhe　*ji*　*tian*　*ta*　*haoxiang*　*youyi*　*duobi*　*wo*
    these　several　day　he　seem　intentionally　avoid　me
    He seems to be avoiding me intentionally these days.

(4) 这　　几　　天　　他　　好像　　有意　　躲　着　我。
    zhe　*ji*　*tian*　*ta*　*haoxiang*　*youyi*　*duo*　*zhe*　*wo*
    these　several　day　he　seem　intentionally　avoid-ZHE　me
    He seems to be avoiding me intentionally these days.

To put these two categories together, 254(30.5%) of these words can be substituted. The specific data can be seen from Table 2.

Table 2. Statistics of interchangeable verbal monosyllabic-disyllabic synonyms

item	number	percentage
Interchangeable words	242	29.1%
Interchangeable (+function word)	12	1.4%
Total number of interchangeable words	254	30.5%
Non-interchangeable words	579	69.5%

2.3   Distribution and Proportion of Non-interchangeable Monosyllabic and Disyllabic Verbs

2.3.1   Monosyllabic and Disyllabic Collocations

Though two verbs share the same meaning, one can be invalid as a result of monosyllabic and disyllabic collocations. In Chinese, a VO combination is unacceptable if the verb contains two syllables while the object consists of only one syllable. Take 编 [*bian*]/编辑[*bianji*] (*to edit*) as an example, when we talk about 编[*bian*] (*to edit*), we have 编报[*bian bao*] (*to edit the newspaper*) and 编杂志[*bian zazhi*] (*to edit the magazine*) in the dictionary. By contrast, we cannot say *编辑报[*bianji bao*] (to edit the newspaper) although they have the same meaning, while we can say 编杂志[*bian zazhi*] (*to edit the magazine*) and 编辑杂志[*bianji zazhi*] (*to edit the magazine*). It is collocation that makes the difference.

2.3.2   Embedded Compounding Monosyllabic Morphemes

In Chinese, some embedded compounding monosyllabic morphemes have to be used in a disyllabic template (Feng, 2006: 5-6). Take 筹[*chou*]/筹措[*choucuo*] (*to raise*) for instance, we can say 自筹资金[*zi chou zijin*] (*to raise money by oneself*), but we cannot say *自筹措资金[*zi choucuo zijin*] (*to raise money by oneself*), because 自[*zi*] (*by oneself*)is an embedded compounding monosyllabic morpheme, but *自筹措[*zi shoujian*] (to raise by oneself) is a trisyllabic word. Therefore, 筹[*chou*] (*to raise*) and 筹措[*choucuo*] (*to raise*) are not interchangeable.

2.3.3   Differences in Collocation Objects

Monosyllabic verbs are clearly and obviously manifested by time and space, while disyllabic verbs always tend to weaken concrete time and space. Take 挖[*wa*]/挖掘 [*wajue*] (*to dig*) as an example, Chinese people can expand 挖[*wa*] (*to dig*) into 挖槽 [*wa cao*] (*to dig a trench*), 挖坑[*wa keng*] (*to dig a hole*), 挖土[*wa tu*] (*earth cutting*), 挖钱[*wa qian*] (*to dig for the money*), among which 槽[*cao*] (*trench*), 土[*tu*] (*earth*), 坑[*keng*] (*hole*), 钱[*qian*] (*money*) are the specific objects. However, 挖掘[*wajue*] (*to dig*) cannot be used in *挖掘土坑[*wajue tukeng*] (*to dig a hole*), *挖掘土壤[*wajue turang*] (*earth cutting*), etc. When it comes to 挖掘[*wajue*] (*to dig*), it is common to use 挖掘财富[*wajue caifu*] (*to seek fortune*)、挖掘潜力[*wajue qianli*] (*to exploit potential*), since 财富[*caifu*] (*wealth*) and 潜力[*qianli*] (*potential*) weakens concrete time and space, which   exactly displays stylistic attributes of prosody.

2.3.4   Nominalization

In Chinese, monosyllabic verbs possess an obvious action attribute while disyllabic verbs can be transferred into [-V]. For example, 保[*bao*]/保证[*baozheng*] (*to guarantee*):

(5) 保/保证　　　你　　一　　　学　　　就　　　会
　　bao/baozheng　*ni*　*yi*　*xue*　*jiu*　*hui*
　　to guarantee　you　as soon as　learn　then　grasp
　　to guarantee that you can grasp it as quickly as you learn it

Besides, 保证[*baozheng*] (*to guarantee*) can be used as a noun, for example:

(6) 安定　　团结　　是　　我们　　取得　　胜利　　的　　保证。
　　 anding　 *tuanjie*　 *shi*　 *women*　 *qude*　 *shengli*　 *de*　 *baozheng.*
　　 stability　 unity　　be　　our　　 get　　 victory　 DE　 guarantee
　　 Stability and unity is the guarantee of our victory.

Another example of 编[*bian*]/创作[*chuangzuo*] (*to create*) can be taken. Chinese people can say编话剧[*bian huaju*]/创作话剧[*chuangzuo huaju*] (*to write a play*), and they can also say 一部划时代的创作[*yibu huashidai de chuangzuo*] (*a landmark work*).

2.3.5　Lexicalization of Monosyllabic Verbs

Some monosyllabic verbs, firmly associated with other components, will become lexicaliazational structures, and that they cannot be substituted. For instance, 表达 [*biaoda*] (*to express*) is exemplified in the group of 表[*biao*]/表示[*biaoshi*] (*to express*), but 表达[*biaoda*] (*to express*) itself is a word, so表示[*biaoshi*] (*to express*) can not substitute 表达[*biaoda*] (*to express*). This situation always occurs among monosyllabic verbs.

2.3.6　Extended Meanings of Disyllabic Verbs

Some disyllabic verbs have extended meanings, so they cannot be substituted by the corresponding monosyllabic verbs. For example, 报[*bao*]/报销[*baoxiao*] (*apply for reimbursement*):

(7) 药　　费　　已经　　　　报/报销　　　　了。
　　 yao　 *fei*　 *yijing*　　 *bao/baoxiao*　　 *le.*
　　 medicine　 fee　 already　 apply for reimbursement　 ASP
　　 The medicine fee has already been applied for reimbursement.

However, 报销[*baoxiao*] (apply for reimbursement) has extended meanings, such as,

(8) 桌　　上　　的　　菜　　他　　一　　个　　人　　全　　报销　　了
　　 zhuo　 *shang*　 *de*　 *cai*　 *ta*　 *yi*　 *ge*　 *ren*　 *quan*　 *baoxiao le*
　　 Table　 LOC　 DE　 dish　 he　 one　 CL　 person　 all　 finish ASP
　　 He ate up all the dishes on the table.

In this circumstance, 报销[*baoxiao*] cannot be substituted by 报[*bao*].

2.3.7　Other Part of Speech

Some disyllabic verbs can change their part of speech in different contexts, such as 比 [*bi*]/比较[*bijiao*] (*to compare*).

(9) 这　　两　　件　　衣服　　比/比较　　起来,　　颜色　 是　 这　 件　　好。
　　 zhe　 *liang jian*　 *yifu*　 *bi/bijiao*　 *qilai,*　 *yanse*　 *shi*　 *zhe*　 *jian*　 *hao.*
　　 these　 two　 CL　 cloth　 compare　 COMP,　 color　 be　 this　 CL　 good
　　 This one is better in color when compared.

In fact, 比较[*bijiao*] (*to compare*) can also be used as an adverb. For example,

(10) 这　　篇　　文章　　写　　得　　　比较　　好。
　　 zhe　 *pian*　 *wenzhang*　 *xie*　 *de*　　 *bijiao*　 *hao.*
　　 this　 CL　 article　 write　 DE　　 comparatively　 good
　　 This article is comparatively good.

2.3.8   Others

Parallel structures of some monosyllabic and disyllabic verbs fail them to substitute. 修[*xiu*]/修补[*xiubu*] (*to repair*): 修桥补路[*xiu qiao bu lu*] (*to mend the bridges and the roads*), and 擦[*ca*]/摩擦[*moca*] (*to rub*): 摩拳擦掌[*mo quan ca zhang*] (*be eager for doing something*) are typical examples. Meanwhile, some disyllabic verbs, such as辞 [*ci*]/辞职[*cizhi*] (*to resign*): 他已经辞了职[*ta yijing ci le zhi*] (*he has resigned*), can be used as separable words, and this sort of monosyllabic-disyllabic verbs cannot be substituted either. Table 3 will show the amount of these kinds of verbs.

Table 3. Type and distribution of non-interchangeable verbal monosyllabic and disyllabic synonyms

type	item	number	proportion
(1)	Collocation of monosyllable and disyllable words	158	27.3%
(2)	Embedded compounding monosyllabic morphemes	54	9.3%
(3)	Collocation objects	190	32.8%
(4)	Nominalization of disyllable verb	62	10.7%
(5)	Lexicalization of monosyllable verb	59	10.2%
(6)	Extended meaning of disyllable verb	12	2.1%
(7)	Disyllable verb with other part of speech	6	1.0%
(8)	Others	38	6.6%
	Total number	579	100%

3   Prosodic Factors of Non-interchangeable Verbal Synonyms

3.1   Correlation Analysis of Non-interchangeable Verbal Synonyms and Prosody

Except for the 5th item "lexicalization of monosyllabic verbs", the 6th item "extended meanings of disyllabic verbs" and the 8th "others", 470 examples are related with prosody. The details are shown as follows:

Table 4. Prosodic analysis of non-interchangeable verbal monosyllabic and disyllabic synonyms

	type	item	number	proportion
Related with prosody	(1)	Collocation of monosyllabic and disyllabic words	158	27.3%
	(2)	Embedded compounding monosyllabic morphemes	54	9.3%
	(3)	Collocation objects	190	32.8%
	(4)	Nominalization of disyllable verbs	62	10.7%
	(5)	Disyllabic verbs with other part of speech	6	1.0%
	Total number		470	81.1%
Not related with prosody	(6)	Lexicalization of monosyllable verbs	59	10.2%
	(7)	Extended meaning of disyllable verbs	12	2.1%
	(8)	Others	38	6.6%
	Total number		109	18.9%
Summary			579	100%

3.2   Verb-Object Collocations and Limitation of Prosodic Conditions

According to Feng(2006), disyllabic verbs generally cannot dominate monosyllabic composition, such as种树[*zhong shu*]——*种植树[*zhongzhi   shu*]——种植树木 [*zhongzhi   shumu*] (*to plant trees*), 读报[*dubao*]——*阅读报[*yuedu   bao*]——阅读 报纸[*yuedu   baozhi*] (*to read newspaper*).

Therefore, monosyllabic verbs in verb-object collocations of "monosyllabic verb + monosyllabic object" cannot be substituted by disyllabic verbs. 158 examples (27.3% of the whole) are in the corpus data, such as:

保[bao]/保持[baochi] (to keep): 保温[bao wen]/*保持温[baochi wen]/保持温度 [baochi wendu] (to keep the temperature constant);

保鲜[baoxian]/*保持鲜[baochi xian]/保持新鲜[baochi xinxian] (to keep fresh).

吃[chi]/吸收[xishou] (to absorb): 这种纸不吃墨[zhe zhong zhi bu chi mo]/*这种 纸不吸收墨[zhe zhong zhi bu xishou mo] (this kind of paper doesn't absorb ink well);

愁[chou]/忧虑[youlü] (to worry): 不愁吃[bu chou chi]/*不忧虑吃[bu youlü chi] (free from worrying about not having food to eat), 不愁穿[bu chou chuan]/*不忧虑穿 [bu youlü chuan] (free from worrying about not having clothes to wear);

产[chan]/出产[chuchan] (to produce): 产棉[chan mian]/*出产棉[chuchan mian] (to produce cotton), 产煤[chan mei]/*出产煤[chuchan mei] (to produce coal)), 产大 豆[chan dadou]/出产大豆[chuchan dadou] (to produce soy), 产大理石[chan dalishi]/出产大理石[chuchan dalishi] (to produce marble).

3.3   Embedded Compounding Monosyllabic Morphemes

Feng (2006) defined the "embedded compounding monosyllabic morpheme" as monosyllabic word used in a disyllabic template. Huang (2012) further pointed out, monosyllabic word used in a disyllabic template is a new kind of language phenomenon in Modern Chinese. This kind of monosyllabic words is also constrained by syntax and prosody. On the one hand, it is syntactically free. On the other hand, in daily life, from the aspect of prosody, these monosyllabic words should be used in a disyllabic template formally and gracefully. Thus, it is not easy for monosyllabic verbs to be substituted by corresponding disyllabic verbs.

It is true for disyllabic words used as a couplet. We can say 到达北京[daoda Beijing] (to arrive at Beijing), 到达首都[daoda shoudu] (to arrive at the capital), 到达法 国[daoda Faguo] (to arrive in France), but we cannot say *到达京[daoda jing] (to arrive at Beijing), *到达都[dadao du] (to arrive at the capital), *到达法[daoda fa] (to arrive in France).

54 words (9.3% of the whole) cannot be substituted because of limitations of embedded compounding monosyllabic morphemes and disyllabic words used as a couplet.

3.4   Grammar Attribute of Prosody: Concrete Space-Time and Weakening Concrete Space-Time

Concrete space-time displayed by monosyllabic verbs and weakening concrete space-time manifested by monosyllabic verbs constitute the grammar attribute of prosody. Thus, these two kinds of verbs have different collocation objects. Monosyllabic verbs prefer to be associated with specific words while disyllabic verbs prefer abstract nouns. Since as many as 190 (32.8%) paired non-interchangeable monosyllabic-disyllabic verbs are caused by this attribute, discussions are to be made one by one.

3.4.1   Concrete Space-Time Possessed by Monosyllabic Verbs

15 verbs with the hand-radical characters from *ShuoWenJiezi* (*Analytical Dictionary of Characters*) are chosen. They are:

持[*chi*](*to hold with the palm*), 拏[*na*](*to hold with the hand*), 拑[*qian*](*to carry something under one's arm*), 摰[*zhi*](*to hold with the fingers*), 操[*cao*](*to hold with only one hand*), 握[*wo*] (*to hold with two hands*), 擽[*lie*](*to hold the hair*), 揮[*dan*] (*to dust*), 攝[*she*](*to take in*), 捦[*qin*](*to seize*), 搏[*bo*](*to seize, to strike*), 撲[*she*] (*to sort out the stalks used in divination*), 挾[*xie*](*clasp under arm, hold to bosom*), 挈[*qie*](*to lead by hand*), 據[*ju*](*to occupy*).

These characters vividly demonstrate concrete space-time of monosyllabic verbs.

3.4.2   Weakening Concrete Space-Time Possessed by Disyllabic Verbs

Concrete space-time possessed by verbs becomes less accessible after verbs are nominalized, and this is called weakening concrete space-time, such as:

(11) 随着   市场   的 扩大,   产品   销售   已 不   成   问题。
     suizhe shichang de kuoda ,   chanpin xiaoshou yi bu cheng wenti.
     with   market   DE expansion, product sale   already NEG become problem
     With the expansion of the market, it's no problem in product distribution.

市场的扩大[*shichang de kuoda*] (*the expansion of the market*) is not restrained by time, condition and mode since its specific word symbols such as time, place, mode and degree are removed. It is weakening concrete space-time that makes the collocation object of disyllabic verbs abstract. Therefore, they cannot be replaced by monosyllabic words freely.

3.5   Nominalization of Disyllabic Verbs

In this research, 62 disyllabic verbs (10.7% of the whole) can also be nominalized. There are two ways to check whether these verbs can be nominalized: it has already been marked as a noun in the dictionary, and when applied in utterances it can function as a noun, such as采购[*caigou*] (*to purchase*). It can be used like:

(12) 采购   设备   采购   机器
     caigou   shebei   *caigou   jiqi*
     to purchase equipment   to purchase machine
     to purchase equipments   to purchase machines
     While it can also used as noun:

(13) 他　在　食堂　　当　　采购。
　　　ta　zai　shitang　dang　caigou.
　　　he　in　the canteen　as　　purchaser
　　　He works as a purchaser in the canteen.

创作[*chuangzuo*] (to create) can be taken as another example:

(14) 他　创作　了　一　部　话剧.　（创作[*chuangzuo*] used as a verb）
　　　ta　chuangzuo　le　yi　bu　huaju.
　　　he　create　　ASP one　CL　play
　　　He wrote a play.

(15) 一　部　划时代　的　　创作（创作[*chuangzuo*] used as a noun）
　　　yi　bu　huashidai　de　chuangzuo.
　　　one　CL　landmark　DE　work
　　　a landmark work

Linguists, such as Lü(1942,1952), Zhu(1985) and Chen(1987), have described nominalization of verbs for a long time. Feng(2009) even pointed out that a disyllabic format is the necessary condition and the syntactical marker for modern Chinese verbs to transfer to nouns or multifunctional words. Wang (2009) further verified that prosodic morphology of disyllabic words can nominalize verbs. The author for this paper found out that generally these nominalized disyllabic verbs do not have time-space feature. Namely, without time, place, means, etc., they have an abstract meaning.

4　Conclusion

It can be illustrated in this paper that prosodic morphology plays a vital role in unsubstitutable verbal synonymys, from the perspective of interchangeability of Chinese verbal monosyllabic and disyllabic synonymys.

First of all, collocations for monosyllabic and disyllabic verbs are very important in the fact that when they have the same meaning and similar pragmatic use, nearly a quarter of unsubstitutable examples are caused by the prosodic collocation of monosyllabic words and disyllabic words.

Secondly, embedded compounding monosyllabic morphemes and disyllabic words used as a couplet restrict some collocation elements in monosyllabic words or disyllabic words. It also makes 10% paired monosyllabic-disyllabic verbs non-interchangeable.

Thirdly, grammar attribute of Chinese prosodic is the most important factor in non-interchangeability due to the differences caused by collocation objects. This attribute failed 30% paired verbs to substitute each other, because monosyllabic verbs possess the concrete space-time while disyllabic verbs possess the weakening concrete space-time, resulting in different collocation objects.

The last one is nominalization of disyllabic verbs. In other words, 10% non-interchangeabilites are produced by the attribute of [-V] manifested by disyllabic verbs.

Acknowledgment. The study is supported by the Beijing Language and Culture University scientific research project (The central university basic scientific research business special fund project) (Grant No. 13YBG11), and the Youth Elite Project of Beijing Language and Culture University.

References

Chen, N.: Enlargement of Modern Chinese Noun Colligation. Studies of the Chinese Language (5) (1987). (in Chinese)

Cheng, J., Xu, X.: A Study on the synonymous monosyllabic and disyllabic verbs in HSK word list. Journal of Chinese Teaching in the World (4), 43–57 (2004). (in Chinese)

Feng, S.: Expressions of Written Chinese, Vol. 1. Beijing Language and Culture University Press, Beijing (2006). (in Chinese)

Feng, S.: On Chinese Prosodic Word. Social Sciences in China (1), 161–176 (1996). (in Chinese)

Feng, S.: On Chinese Nature Foot. Studies of the Chinese Language **262**, 40–47 (1998). (in Chinese)

Feng, S.: On Principles. Mechanisms and Teaching of Register and Grammar. Series of Lectures in Minzu University of China (2013). (in Chinese)

Feng, S.: Prosodic, Register and Chinese Teaching. Lectures in Beijing Language and Culture University (2013). (in Chinese)

Huang, M.: Prosodic Syntax of monosyllabic words used in a disyllabic template. Beijing Language and Culture University Press, Beijing (2012). (in Chinese)

Lü, S., Zhu, D.: Speech on Chinese Grammar and Rhetoric. Liaoning Education Press, Shenyang (1952). (in Chinese)

Lü, S.: Chinese Grammar Outline. Commercial Press, Beijing (1942). (in Chinese)

Wang, L.: Zhe ben shu de chu ban–Case Study of Chinese Prosody. Chinese Prosody Seminar in Chinese University of Hong Kong (2013). (in Chinese)

Wang, Y.: On Grammar Mechanism of Predicative Constituent's Nominalization in Formal Written Chinese. TCSOL Studies **50**(3), 72–78 (2013). (in Chinese)

Zhang, B., Fang, M.: Functional Studies of Chinese Grammar. Jiangxi Education Press, Jiangxi (1996). (in Chinese)

Zhang, G.: Different Function Between Monosyllable Verbs and Dissyllable Verbs Used as Syntactic Components. Journal of Huaibei Coal Industry Teachers' College (Philosophy and Social Sciences) (3), (1989). (in Chinese)

Zhang, G.: Difference Collocation Function between Monosyllable Verbs and Dissyllable Verbs. Journal of Shanghai Normal University (1), (1990). (in Chinese)

Zhu, D.: Lexical verbs and nominal verbs in modern written Chinese. Journal of Peking University (Philosophy and Social Sciences) (3), (1989). (in Chinese)

Semantic Derivation of the "吃 *[chi] (eat)* + Object" Idiom in Mandarin, Taiwanese and Hakka

Xiangyun Qiu[✉]

Graduate Institute of Taiwan Literature, National Changhua University of Education,
Changhua, 500 Taiwan
chuss@cc.ncue.edu.tw

Abstract. *"吃 [chi] (Eat)"* in chinese is a high-frequency verb. It can be found in modern chinese *"吃 X"* idiom commonly. This paper summarizes the semantic interaction between the verb *"吃"* and its object constructed in Madarin, Taiwanese and Hakka, and analysizes the types of its object first, the differences and similarities between "typical objects" and "non-typical objects" are also discussed. The process of deriving the meaning of the verb *"吃"* is also analyzed within the framework of the cognitive metaphor, metonymy, and the prototype theory, in order to highlight the characteristic representations of Taiwan's languages.

Keywords: Taiwan's Languages · *吃[chi](eat)* + object · Idiom · Semantic derivation · Metaphor · Metonymy

1 Introduction

The word *"吃 [chi] (eat)"* in chinese is a high-frequency verb, which is commonly seen in the construction of *"吃 + object"* idiom in modern chinese: two-word idioms such as *"吃醋* （eat vinegar; jealous）*, three-word idioms such as *"吃豆腐 (eat bean curd; make a pass at someboby)"*, etc.. In view of the grammatical structure, *"吃 (eat)"* is a transitive verb, which is assumed to be followed by a food noun in the patient-object position, however, many of the collocates are not related to food, such as *"吃力 (eat strength; struggle)"*, adjectives such as *"吃苦 (eat bitterness; suffering)"*. Of which the semantic complexity of *"吃"* is far beyond the original meaning.

The counterpart of Modern chinese *"吃 [chi]* in ancient Chinese is *"食 [shi]"*. Starting from the Six Dynasties to the Tang Dynastry, *"食 [shi]* , *喫 [chi]* , *吃 [chi]"* are used in a alternative way. However, *"食 [Sh]"*, instead of *"吃 [chi]"*, is still used in Taiwanese and Hakka, preserving the treasure of ancient chinese. This paper uses Madarin chinese Dictionary and Hakka Dictionary by the Ministry of Education as the langage database to discuss *"吃 X"* construction, the semantic derivation of *"吃 "* as a verb and the types of the following object (X) in the perspective of cognitive semantics and prototype theorys.

© Springer International Publishing Switzerland 2014
X. Su and T. He (Eds.): CLSW 2014, LNAI 8922, pp. 31–42, 2014.
DOI: 10.1007/978-3-319-14331-6_4

2   The Structural Relationship of "吃 + object" in Mandarin and Hakka

Two kinds of objects follow the verb "吃 " in chinese: food nouns called "regular objects" or "typical objects" and non-food nouns called "irregular objects" or "non-typical objects" :

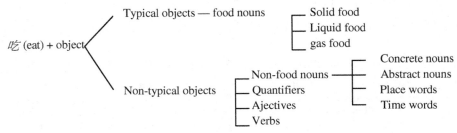

Fig. 1. The types of the object in "吃 X"

To compare the structural relationship of the verb "吃" and the object in Taiwan's Mandarin, Taiwanese and Hakka, the respective representations can be seen as follows:

2.1   "吃 + Typical Object"

"吃" means chewing solid food and swallowing it, and the following object is supposed to be something solid and edible. However, from this type of "吃 X" idioms, we can see:

A. Food nouns following "吃" in Mandarin are the solid while those in dialects are either the solid or the gas, showing the local and global semantic differences of "吃"

In Mandarin, "吃" usually refers to the solid and edible food, eg. "吃飯 (eat rice; have a meal); only few words go with liquid food such as "吃奶 (eat milk; sucking breast)" etc.. But there are more collocates of "吃" related to liquid food in Taiwanese and Hakka, for example, "吃水 (eat water; drink water),吃酒 (eat wine; drinking), 吃茶 (eat tea; drink tea)", etc.. where "吃", has carried an extended meaning of drinking. Moreover, "吃" even goes with the gas such as "吃煙 (eat smoke; smoke), 吃毒 (eat posion; drug abuse)", where "吃" has another extended meaning of inhaling, those are not seen in Mandarin. As studies show,"吃" in Taiwanese and Hakka refers to both drinking and inhaling: "吃" in the Tang Dynasty in terms of eating can be followed either by the object in solid form or that in liquid form (Chen, 2013: 87). There are also "食/吃漿 (eat paste; soak)" and "食/吃哚水 (eat mouth water; rely on eloquence)" in Taiwanese (Rulong Li and Haijiang Xie 2004). Thus, despite the fact that "吃" followed by liguid and gas words in modern chinese has been rare, "吃" in

Taiwanese and Hakka has revealed the phenomenon of semantic extension in that they carry boarder meanings than Mandarin and also inherit and retain the usage of ancient chinese.

B. "吃" is followed by a food noun in Mandarin and dialects but often used metaphorically

Although many "吃 X" idioms are connected to food terms, in general, they do not refer to the eating itself but are used to describe other events or situations. The "吃 X 飯 *(eat X rice)*" idiom is one of the most widely used terms in this case. For example, "吃閒飯 (eat free rice; doing nothing to earn one's keep), 吃白飯 (eat white rice; eat without paying), 吃軟飯 (eat soft rice; live off a women), 吃現成飯 (eat ready rice; enjoy the fruits out of the other people's labour)" in Mandarin all refer to enjoying but never doing any work; "吃衙門飯 (eat government office rice; receive a salary from the government), 吃洋飯 (eat foreign rice; live off foreigners),吃公家飯 (eat public rice; receive a salary from the government)" refer to living off a specific profession; others like "吃牢飯 (eat prison rice; do time in prison), 吃子孫飯 (eat offspring rice; eat the rice of future generations), 吃大鍋飯 (eat big pot rice; eat rice from the same pot)", etc.. In addition to "吃 X 飯", there are other idioms carrying both original and metaphorical meanings. For instance, in Mandarin "吃鴨蛋 *(eat duck eggs)*" means scoring zero; "吃醋 *(eat vinegar)* "means being jealous; "吃錯藥 (eat wrong medicine)" means acting strange and "吃黑棗(eat black dates)" means getting shot. In Taiwanese, "吃菜" is not just about eating vegetables but generally refers to a vegetarian; "吃重鹹 (eat heavy salty)" refers to enjoying flirting with women and "吃胖餅(eat plump cake)"is pronounced the same as 碰壁 (touch the wall), meaning a rebuff in Mandarin.   In Hakka, "沒吃鹽 (not eat salt) "implies no strength; "吃酒 (eat wine)" could be attending wedding; "吃甜茶 (eat sweet tea)"is engagement; "吃糜(eat porridge)" refers to an easy job. However, "吃豆腐" is used metaphorically as teasing or sexual harassment in Mandarin but as intimacy in Taiwanese. "吃油" refers to oil consumption in Mandarin but it also refers to oil obsorbing in Hakka. Also, others like "吃人(eat people; bully), 吃土 (eat dust; loser), 吃屁 (eat fart; flatter), 吃貨 (eat goods; secretly buy cheap stocks)" do not mean literally but have metaphorical implications.

2.2   "吃 + Non-Typical Object"

Any X that is not a food noun in "吃 X" structure is categorized as a "non-typical object" (In Hongyin Tao 2000).   The comparison of the structural relationship of the verb "吃" and the object in Mandarin, Taiwanese and Hakka can be seen as follows:

A. Non-food, concrete nouns following "吃" include words about places, tools, methods, subjects, results, etc..

"吃" *is* followed by a place object such as "吃餐廳 (eat restaurant; eat out) or "吃館子 (eat restaurant; eat out) "; by a tool or method object such as   "吃火鍋 (eat hot pot; block shot), 吃罐頭 (eat cans; eat canned food), 吃大碗公 (eat a big bowl; eat a lot)", "吃頭路 (eat head road; doing a job or making a living)" in Taiwanese and Hakka; by a subject object such as "吃甜頭 (eat sweet head; draw benefits), 吃貨 (eat goods; quietly buying cheap stocks), 吃公款 (eat public money; embezzle public funds), 吃釘子 (eat nails; encountering obstruction), 吃螺絲 (eat screws; a slip of the tongue during a live broadcast)", or by an object as a brand name such as "吃麥當勞 (eat at McDonald), 吃肯德雞 (eat at KFC), 吃安非他命 (eat amphetamines), 吃嗎啡 (eat morphine)", and "食/吃桌 (eat table; attending wedding, 吃錢(eat money; corruption), 吃人(exploitation), 吃家己 (eat yourself; umemployed), 吃生腳 (eat new legs; bullying newcomers)" in Taiwanese; by a result object such as "吃敗仗 (eat lost war; defeat), 吃棍子 (eat sticks; get hit with a stick), 吃耳光 (eat ear light; a slap in the face), 吃拳頭 (eat a fist; get punched), 吃黃牌 (eat a yellow card; getting a warning due to a foul play)" and "吃屎 (eat shit: it is similar to a curse word "Go to Hell."), 吃紅單 (eat a red ticket; getting a traffic ticket), 吃秤頭 (eat scale head; refers to playing tricks)" in Taiwanese and "吃屁卵 (eat fart egg; making efforts but getting nothing in return" in Hakka.

B. "吃" is followed by an abstract noun
There are 吃案 (eat a case; cover up), 吃力 (eat strength; laborious), 吃驚 (eat strength; laborious), 吃味(eat taste; jealous), 吃電 (eat power; power consumption), 吃價 (eat price; lower the price), 吃虧 (eat deficit; suffer losses), 吃大補帖 (eat a big post; eat prescribed chinese medicine), 吃老本 (eat capital; live off one' old gains/a吃evement), 吃排頭 (eat suffering; being scolded), 吃官司 (eat lawsuit; be sued), 吃重罪 (eat felony; commit a felony), 吃偏方 (eat falk prescription; take folk medicine), 吃勞保 (eat labor insurance; join labor insurance)" in Mandarin; "食/吃老本 (eat capital; live off one' old gains) ; 食/吃色(eat color；refers to dyeing), 食/吃命 (eat name; taking one's place or having a false reputation), 食/吃名聲 (eat reputation; rely on the reputation)" in Taiwanese, all carry the meaning of relying on. "吃電 (eat power; power consumption)), 吃價 (eat price ; lowering the price) in Hakka. Among which "吃" does not carry the meaning of eating itself; instead, it creates other verb meanings such as "to embezzle, to consume, to accept, to encounter, and to rely on."

C. "吃" is followed by a place or time word
  There are premises or place words such as "吃館子 (eat restaurant; eat out), 吃餐廳 (eat restaurant; eat out), 吃公家 (eat public organizations; receive a salary from the government), 吃四方 (eat four directions; enjoy food everywhere), 吃八方 (eat eight directions; popular or take benefits everywhere) in Mandarin, and in 吃廟堂 (eat government; receive a salary from the government)", "吃大飯店 (eat big hotel; eat an expensive meal)" in Taiwanese and Hakka. For time words, there are "吃宵夜 (eat late night; eat midnight snack)" in Mandarin, "食/吃晝 (eat daytime; have lunch) in Taiwanese, "食/吃朝 (eat morning; have breakfast), 食/吃晝 (eat daytime; have lunch)、食/吃夜 (eat night; have dinner) "in Hakka, where three meals in the morning, at noon and at night are described seperately.

D.   "吃"   is followed by an ajective

"吃" can be followed by a color ajective such as   "吃紅 (eat red; share benefits), 吃黑 (black eats black; con within a con) or by a quality adjective such 吃素 (eat vetetable; vegetarian), 吃苦 (eat bitterness; suffer), 吃香 (eat aroma; popular), 吃重 (eat heavy; arduous), 吃腥 (eat fishy; adulterous), 大吃小 (big eats small; of bullying), 吃軟不吃硬 (eat soft not eat hard; persuaded by reason but not be cowed by force)" , etc.. Also "食/吃燒 (eat heat; eat something hot) , 食/吃冷 (eat cold; eat something cool)" and "食/吃涼 (eat cool; eat something cool), 吃平安 (eat peace; eat to get blessing) , 食/吃伯公福 (eat uncle blessing; get blessing from an earth god)" in Taiwanese and Hakka. Status adjectives include "吃驚 (eat deflated; frustrated), 吃緊 (eat tight; tense situation) " in Mandarin, "食/吃豐沛 (eat abundant; eat a rich meal) " in Taiwanese and Hakka respectively. Meanwhile, in Taiwanese, "食/吃老 (eat old)" refers to getting old; "食/吃傖 (eat vulgar) is bullying honest people, "食/吃便 (eat convenient)" or "食清領便" (eat clear collect convenient) " *means living on the labor of others.*

E.   "吃"   is followed by a verb

Examples include "吃租 (eat rent; live on rent) " in Mandarin，"吃補 (eat supplement; eat medicinal food),吃拜拜 (eat pray; have a feast after worship)" in Taiwanese and "食/吃釣, 食/吃料理 (eat dishes; have a meal) , 食/吃月給 (eat monthly salary)" in Hakka, of which "食/吃月給" is derived from Japanese, meaning making a living on a regular monthly salary. Songlin Chen (2012: 54) suggests that "吃 "with a meaning of suffering in Modern chinese can be used in "吃 + a verb" idioms such as "吃虧 (eat deficit; suffer losses), 吃驚 (eat surprise; feel surprised), and in "吃 + a noun" idioms such as "吃棒子 (eat stick; beat with a stick), 吃官司 (eat lawsuit; involve in a lawsuit), 吃罪 (eat crime; bear the blame) "and "吃釘子 (eat nails; encounter obstruction)". He also addresses that the three definitions of "吃", eating, getting and sufferring, are associated with the development from an active voice of "eating" to a passive voice of "suffering".

F.   "吃" can be followed by measure words, quantifiers and shape-based classifiers in Taiwanese and Hakka

The object can be a quantifier, for example "食/吃七碗 (eat seven bowls; eat a lot) "in Taiwanese, or a shape-based classifier such as "食/吃大碗 (eat big bowl; eat a big meal), 吃兩口 (eat two bites; take a bite)" . *And* "食/吃大垤 (eat big anthill)" in Hakka refers to eating the food prepared by the bereaved family, further showing its unique characteristics of culture and language. In addition, "吃" can be followed by only measure words in Taiwanese and Hakka, for instance, "食/吃百二 (eat hundred two)" in both dialects refering to longevity.

Accoriding to Hongyin Tao (2000: 26), the patient of the verb "吃" has been extended in two directions: one is about the non-typical food patient, which can be treated as an object, eg. "吃奶 (eat breast; sock the breast), 吃水 (eat water;

drink water), 吃油 (eat oil; oil consumption), 吃湯 (eat soup; eat soup), 吃酒 (eat wine; drink alcohol)"; the other is about the edge of the argument structure (eg. Premises), which is also seen as the patient, for instance, "吃利息 (eat interests; earn interests), 吃家裡 (eat home; live off your family), 吃批評 (eat criticism; suffer criticism)", thus forming the extension of the "吃" argument structure. The above findings can be reflected in Hongyin Tao's suggestion (2001), "The more frequently the verb is used, the more unstable the argument structure is built."

3   The Verb "吃/食" Metaphors in Mandarin and Hakka Have Evolved into Polysemous Representations

The semantic performance of the "吃 X" idiom is very diverse whether in Mandarin, Taiwanese or Hakka. For example, there are 9 senses of the "吃" idiom in Madarin chinese Dictionary by the Ministry of Education, including "chew and swallow, inhale, take one's chess pieces or cards when playing, engulf, be responsible, bear, suffer, bother, and consume.". Nevertherless, as the Dictionary 1) does not provide a comprehensive perspective, 2) the senses are listed scattered, and 3) other expressions of "吃" in dialects have not yet been discussed, this paper further discovers another 17 senses of "吃", such as "absorb, drink, try to experience, experience, enjoy, accept and gain, occupy, fasten, depress, rely on, bully, work to make a living, erotic relationship between men and women, grow to survive, abusive language" etc., in which those of "吃" rarely used in Mandarin but often used in Taiwanese and Hakka include inhaling as "吃煙 (eat smoke; smoke)", the match between the upper and lower part as "吃不緊 (eat not tight; not match well)", pressing lower as "吃價 (eat price; lower the price)", encouraging as "食/吃氣 (eat gas; bear anger)" and survival as "食/吃百二(eat hundred two; longevity)". Among these words, "食/吃志(eat ambition; ambitious) "and "食/吃氣" with the meaning of encouraging are special usage only seen in Taiwanese, which also indicates that "吃" in Mandarin has extended its original meaning of "吃/食" to a more complicated and diverse usage, showing greater semantic diversity.

Why is the verb "吃/食" characterized with such a complicated polysemy? The complicated senses of the verb "吃/食" do not come out of nowhere, instead, the conversion and extention of their meanings result from metaphors and metonymy. According to Bi Rong Huang (2010), the concept of human words represents the original concept how humans perceive the world, which takes a central and basic position in the vocabulary system. Human cognition starts from their body experience. To use body as our gelstalt reference prototype can help us to build new concepts (G. Lakoff &M. Johnson: 1980). With conceptual metaphors, we use our most familiar experience to shape the perception of the unknown, abstract or complex concept for the outside world, accordingly expanding the scope of lexical semantics. Metaphor highlights the "similarity" between two things placed side by side with a "analog strategy," while metonymy is based on its "proximity", highlighting part of characteristics of a whole thing with a "focus strategy" to emphasize the message, quickly showing the meaning intended to convey. The following discusses how "吃" phrases have extended to other semantic categories due to metaphor.

3.1   The Metaphorical Phrases of *"吃"*

In view of different kinds of food following *"吃"*, their obvious similarities in terms of the shape, nature, function or other aspects may cause the agent's cognitive association and then generate a metaphorical implication. By using concrete food to imply abstract food, for instance, the "*吃* + concrete food" term as *"吃飯* (eat rice; have a meal) "may extend to the "*吃* + abstract food" terms such as *"吃軟飯* (eat soft rice; live off a women), *吃白飯* (eat white rice; eat without paying), *吃閒飯* (eat free rice; lead an idle life), *吃現成飯* (eat ready rice; enjoy the fruits out of the other people's labour), *吃閉門羹* (eat closed door soup; be left out), *吃定心丸* (eat hear-shooting pill, give assurance), *吃了秤砣* (eat metal weights; determined), *吃 大補帖* (eat a big post; eat prescribed chinese medicine)", etc.. The latter derives from the former's metaphorical association.

Metaphorical phrases highlight the similarities between things in terms of their form or nature. The features in metaphorical similarities of "*吃*" phrases are as follows:

A. The highlights of similar shapes: eg." *吃鴨蛋* (eat duck eggs; score zero), *吃 黑 棗* (eat black dates; get shot)".
B. The highlights of similar nature: eg. *"吃豆腐* (eat bean curb; make a pass at a woman), *啞巴吃黃連* (a dumb eat coptis; unspeakable suffering)".
C. The highlights of similar functions: eg. *"吃定心丸* (eat hear-shooting pill, give assurance), *吃大補帖* (eat a big post; eat prescribed *吃*nese medicine)".

The interaction between the verb and the following object has showed a phenomenon of metonymy. All the complicated meanings derive from the prototype category of "eating" for *"吃"* through a metaphorical process. Many of the "*吃* + object" idioms have shifted from their typical meaning of "eating" for *"吃"* to other polysemous words after layers of metaphor and metonymy. *"吃"* originally means eating something edible and later is mapped into other abstract things through metaphor implication; for example, *"吃"* has derived its meaning from the mouth's eating action, eg. *"吃鴨蛋* (eat duck egg; score zero)" , to the metaphorical implication of the mouth's speaking action, eg. *"吃螺絲* (eat screws; a slip of the tongue)" , and futher to the metaphor of the action received by the body, eg. *"吃悶 棍* (eat stuffed stick; be set up) or the abstract meaning of "live on" such as *"吃頭 路* (eat head road; do a jogb) "and" *吃自己* (eat yourself; live on yourselt)" in Taiwanese and Hakka. Meanwhile, as *"吃"* carries the meaning of having something into the stomach, it derives the meaning of digestion as "*吃不消* (eat not digest; unbearable) "or that of taking the result as *"吃敗仗* (eat lost war; defeat)". These words have formed a metaphorical relationship due to the characteristic correlation between each word.

The cognitive framework for *"吃* " in chinese seems to have formed a unique *"吃食* "structural metaphor. As is pointed out by Lakoff & Johnson (1980), structural metaphors allow us to use one highly structured and cleared delineated concept to structure another, and use the specific terms for elaborating a concept to elaborate another. Most of people organize and understand the abstract concept through the concept of "吃", where the "similarity" is the structural transformation function between each system (Xiao-fang Yin & Zhi-peng Ren, 2003: 79), thus forming a big structucral metaphor. The forgoing "吃" metaphors mentioned in view of host structure, in addition, have formed a structural metaphor of *"X is eating"* as the following representations:

A. **Inhaling and absorbing is eating:** eg. "吃墨 (eat ink; absorb ink), 吃油 (eat oil; absorb oil)", etc..

B. **Engulfing and devouring is eating:** eg. "吃錢 (eat money; corruption), 黑吃黑 (black eats black; con within a con), 吃回扣 (eat commission; take commission), 天狗吃月 (dog star eats the moon; lunar eclipse), 大小通吃 (big small all eat; make a clean sweep) ", etc.. The further derivation includes the metaphorical implication of "sinking is eating", eg. 吃水線 (eat water depth; the minimum depth of water a ship or boat can safely navigate)" in Mandarin

C. **Consuming and wasting is eating:** eg. 吃力 (eat strength; struggle), 吃電 (eat power; power consumption), 吃油 (eat oil ; absorbing oil)", etc..

D. **Accepting, enjoying and suffering is eating:** eg. "吃味 (eat taste; jealous), 吃醋 (eat vinegar; jealous), 吃馬屁 (eat horse ass; enjoy being flattered), 吃軟不吃硬 (eat soft not eat hard; persuaded by reason but not be cowed by force)" , etc.. The metonymy of "enjoying is eating" derives from "accepting is eating," for example, "吃香(eat aroma; popular), 吃軟飯 (eat soft rice; live off a women)" , etc.. If "accepting" is seen as negative, the metonymy of "suffering is eating" is formed in the examples such as   "吃驚 (eat surprise; feel surprised), 吃虧 (eat deficit; suffer losses), 吃苦(eat bitter; suffering), 吃重 (eat heavy; arduous), 吃皮子 (eat plank; beaten with a plank), 吃竹子 (eat bamboo; beaten with a stick), 吃 拳頭 (eat a fist, get punched), 吃巴掌 (eat a palm; get slapped), 吃耳光 (eat ear light; a slap in the face), 吃釘子 (eat nails; encounter obstruction), 吃罪名 (eat crime name; bear the blame), 吃官司 (eat lawsuit; be sued)", ect..

E. **Obtaining and getting is eating:** As eating allows the body to obtain nuitrition, thus the result of the action is mapped into the metonymical implication of "getting is eating" , for example, 吃鴨蛋 (eat duck egg; score zero), 吃敗仗 (eat lost war; defeat), 吃閉門羹 (eat closed door soup; be left out)", etc..

F. **Experiencing and going through is eating:** The "experiencing" meaning derives from "trying and experiencing", for example, "吃墨水(eat ink water; educated), 吃洋墨水 (eat foreign ink water; study abroad), 吃苦頭 (eat suffering; suffer), 偷吃禁果 (eat the forbidden fruit; a sexual activity)", etc..

G. **Relying on and living on is eating:** "Living on someone or off something", eg. "吃父母 (eat parents; live off parents), 吃自己(eat yourself; live off yourself), 吃公家 (eat public organizations; receive a salary from the government), 吃老本 (eat capital; live off one' old gains/achievement), 吃勞保 (eat labor insurance; join labor insurance), 吃公家飯 (eat public rice; receive a salary from the government), 吃頭路 (eat head road; do a job), 吃名聲 (eat reputation; rely on the reputation)" in Taiwanese and Hakka.

H. **Bullying is eating:** Deriving from "eatting up and depressing down", eg. "吃人 (eat people; bully), 大吃小 (big eats small; of bullying), 吃價 (eat price; lower the price) in Hakka", etc..

I. **Mat吃ng is eating:** As "chewing" is the coordinated action of upper and lower teech, eating has the meaning of "the matching of upper and lower parts" such as (*Lun Zi*; wheel*) 吃不緊 (eat not tight; not match well)" in Hakka.

J. **Sexual activity between men and women is eat:** As "食色性也" (eat, appearance, nature; by nature, we desire food and sex) and "秀色可餐 (beauty appearance can eat; be beautiful enough to forget the hunger)", "食(eat) "and "色 (sex)" are categorized into the same realm of nature. The action of eating is similar to sexual behavior between men and women, thus eating has been used as a euphemistic metaphor for sexual behavior between men and women, for example, "偷吃腥 (secretly eat fishy; adulterous), 吃豆腐 (eat bean curd; make a pass at someboby), 吃花酒 (eat flower wine; drink by the company of prosititutes)", etc..

K. **Surviving is eating:** This type of idioms is frequently seen in Taiwanese and Hakka such as "吃百二 (eat hundred two; longevity)" referring to wishing people for a long life.

The "吃" metaphorical words are all based on the similarities or correlations between the new thing and the "吃" action, which can be elaborated by the theory of prototype category: since the "吃" words use mouth's chewing and swallowing as the prototype, and later have the family similarity of *He, Xi and Tun* (drinking, inhaling and swallowing), the "吃" metaphor can also be used in *Yao, He, Xi* and *Tun* (biting, drinking, inhaling and swallowing) words. Furthermore, the result of "吃" is the body accepting the food, so those words such as *Jiu Shou, Xiang Shou, Cheng Shou, Zao Shou* and *Ai Shou* (accepting, enjoying, bearing, suffering and enduring) are all similar to "吃" in meaning, where the source domain is mapped into the target domain. The "吃" metaphorical words can be analysed by prototype category theory: the collection of many meanings formed by conceptual metaphor is a large conceptual scope, of which there are both central and edge semantic features. Many of them are the result of diffussion "radiating" outward from the central metaphor, leading to a process of semantic derivation.

3.2 The Metonymical Words of "吃"

The grounding of metonymic concepts involves physical or causal associations (Lakoff & Johnson 1980). In this sense, metonymy substitutes one entity for another entity only when there is an internal association between two entities, i.e. two entities from the same cognitive domain.

The variety of categories of metonymy can be further summarized as three types (Jian-Shiung Shie, 2008: 55):

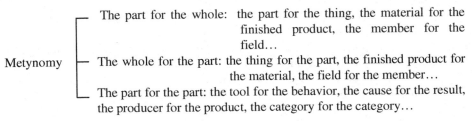

Metynomy
— The part for the whole: the part for the thing, the material for the finished product, the member for the field…
— The whole for the part: the thing for the part, the finished product for the material, the field for the member…
— The part for the part: the tool for the behavior, the cause for the result, the producer for the product, the category for the category…

Fig. 2. The Categories of Conceptual Metonymy (Hsiangyun 吃u, 2011)

Metonymy is grounded from a proximy of the same domain. The related categories are showed as below:

A. **The metonymy of the kitchenware and tableware used when eating:** the metonymy of kitchenware includes "吃大鍋飯 (eat big pot rice; eat rice from the same pot) , 吃小灶 (eat small stove; give special care)" and the metonymy of kitchenware includes" 吃大碗 (eat big bowl; eat a big meal)", etc..

B. **The metonymy of eating places:** the metonymy of place includes "吃館子 (eat restaurant, eat out), 靠山吃山 (near mountain eat mountain, those living on the mountain live off the mountain) " while that of direction includes "吃四方 (eat the world; monks collectining alms everywhere) , 吃八方 (eat eight directions; popular or take benefits everywhere)", etc..

D. **The metonymy of eating time:** the metonymy of time includes "吃宵夜 (eat nights; eat midnight snacks) in Mandarin and   "食吃朝 *(eat morning; eat breakfast),* 食吃晝 *(eat daytime; eat lunch), and* 食吃晝 *(eat night; eat dinner)* " in Hakka.

E . **The metonymy of eating source object:** the metonymy of people includes "吃父母 (eat parents; live off parents), 吃自己 (eat yourself; live off yourself)" ; the metonymy of things inclues "吃利息 (eat interests; earn interests), 吃勞保 (eat labour insurance; join labor insurance)", etc..

As the "吃 *(eat)*" verb involves the action, process, method, result, tool, place, time, nature, feeling and other aspects, the semantic derivation comes from the metaphor or metonymy of highlighting a certain aspect.

One thing worth mentioning: some think that the representations of eating places as" 吃食堂 (eat restaurant; eat out), 吃館子 (eat restaurant; eat out) , 吃公家 (eat public organizations; receive a salary from the government) "can be seen as eating at a certain palce. However, in view of cognitive patterns and mapping method, it should be the metonymy of "the place for the content," where the place food produced is closely associated with the content of food, thus naturally being used to refer to the food from the place (Ya-Ning Nie, 2008: 113).

4   Conclusion

Given those examples mentioned above, we can see how complicated and diverse the semantic derivation is for the "吃 (eat)" category of the mouth eating verbs in Taiwan's Mandarin, Taiwanese and Hakka:

A. **The interaction and association between the structure and semantic derivation of the "吃 (eat)" verb and its following objects**
With a broad experience for eating food, the metaphorical approach by using 吃 to map the abstract thing will be more diverse and complicated.

B. **In the process of semantic derivation of "吃 (eat)", conceptual metaphor plays a key role in the mechanism**
With the approach of cognitive metaphor and prototype theory, it will be easier to explore and elaborate the process of semantic derivation of eating verb. Also the various representations of metaphor and metonymy are summarized to discuss the polysemous development from concrete to abstract meaning of the "吃" verb through metaphorical implication. The object of "吃" verb has also made a generalization from the "+concrete" to the "-concrete" through metaphorical implication, highlighting the importance of metonymy and metaphor in the cognitive and semantic extention.

C. **The "吃 X" idioms are characterized with cultures of thinking**
The comparison of the usage of Mandarin, Taiwanese and Hakka dialects can further understand the different levels of cultural heritage. For instance, "吃錢" (eat money; corruption) in Mandarin reflects the bureaucratic culture; "吃重鹹" (eat heavy salty; enjoy flirting with women) in Taiwanese reflects the euphemistic culture; "吃大垤 (eat big anthill; eat the food prepared by the bereaved family)" in Hakka reflects funeral culture. If we can explore the ethnic cognition and cultural concept implied, by observing the cognitive patterns of Taiwanese people speaking in Mandarin and Hakka to correctly grap their semantic features, it will be more helpful for future language teaching or cultural analysis.

As we can see from those metaphorical and metonymic examples for the sourse domain of "吃 (eat)", the metaphorical derivatives are not presented in a fragmented and scattered way; instead, there is a system of organized structure between them, forming a "structural metaphor". By spreading the various types and areas of eat experience, the related bodily sensations, emotions, actions and places to enjoy will be naturally experienced. The full range and multi-level experience of eating is the derivative basis of meaning. Expanding from the body's "small universe" to the outside "big universe", the whole world seems to become a cognitive world in human's physical perception.

References

[1] Lakoff, G., Johnson, M.: Metaphors we live by. University of Chicago Press, Chicago (1980). Shi-zhe Chou(Annotation). Linking Publishing, Taipei (2006)

[2] The Ministry of Education, Hakka Dictionary. http://hakka.dict.edu.tw/hakkadict/index.htm

[3] The Ministry of Education, Madarin chinese Dictionary. http://dict.revised.moe.edu.tw/

[4] The Ministry of Education, Taiwanese Dictionary. http://twblg.dict.edu.tw/holodict_new/index.html

[5] Chen, S.-l.: From Active Voice "Eating" to Passive Voice "Suffering"-The Semantic Change of Verb 吃 in Chinese. Journal of Chinese Language Teaching **9**(1), 52–73 (2012)

[6] Chen, S.-l.: The Study of 喫 and 吃 -Based on chinese Character Etymology. Journal of Chinese Language Teaching **10**(2), 63–89 (2013)

[7] Huang, B.-R.: Observing Semantic Cogniton from the Meaning Distribution of Body Words. Journal of Shanghai University (Social Science Edition) **17**(6), 118–125 (2010)

[8] Xie, H., Li, R.: A Contrastive Study On the Glosseme "eat" among chinese Dialects. Language Science **3**, 96–104 (2004)

[9] Nie, Y.-N.: On Cognitive Models and Characteristics of Chinese Metaphors and Metonymies of "Eating" in Terms of Embodied Realism. Journal of Hunan University (Social Sciences) **22**(2), 113–117 (2008)

[10] Tao, H.: "Eating" and Emergent Augument Stucture. Language Science **3**, 21–38 (2000)

[11] Shie, J.-S.: A Cognitive Linguistic Account of Conventional Metonymies in Contemporary Mandarin Chinese in Taiwan. Journal of Humanities and Social Sciences **4**(1), 55–67 (2008)

[12] Ying, X.-F., Ren, Z.-P.: Structural Metaphor: Rationale and Pragmatic Nature from a Systematic Perspective. Journal of TienJin University (Socail Sciences) **3**, 279 (2003)

On the Lexical Meaning of Conditional Connectives in Chinese

Yan Jiang(✉)

The Hong Kong Polytechnic University, Hong Kong, China
ctyjiang@polyu.edu.hk

Abstract. This paper examines some common logical notions, their explicit encoding in English and in Chinese, their representations in logic, and their semantic characterizations. Detailed treatments are given to the analysis of *the necessary condition* and the counterfactual protasis-inducer *'yàobúshì'* (if-not-be) in Chinese. Factors affecting the comprehension of these terms are explored in detail. Given that the characterization of the necessary condition is a rather familiar topic, the novel aspect of this study lies in the analysis of *'yàobúshì'*, which is characterized here as an explicit counterfactual marker taking on a proposition which is both *veridical* and a *falsifying contingent*.

Keywords: Chinese conditionals · Chinese counterfactuals · Veridicality · Contingency

1 Preambles

It goes without saying that logical notions and formalisms can help sharpen semantic characterization of natural language. In this regard, the study of Chinese conditionals provides an ideal testing ground. At present, the question of how conditionality is encoded in Chinese is still not well understood. For the few cases and constructions that have received more investigations, conscious effort in applying logical tools to their analysis could provide rigour, generality, simplicity and more justifications, leading to more mature theoretical accounts. On the other hand, as presented in [1], there is the special branch of logic called *conditional logic*, which has as its primary concern the logical and semantic properties of conditional sentences in natural language. Given that most insights in conditional logic have been reached with English as its focal object of investigation, it is high time that more treatments to Chinese conditionals were provided, so that new and richer findings can be obtained. What is more, the study of conditionals has brought up many related issues in the philosophy of language, such as the metaphysics of possible worlds, probability, logic in conversation, causality and contingency, etc., so much so that it is claimed that "one is likely to learn more philosophy from a thorough study of conditionals than from any other philosophical topic" [2]. To what extent can the study of Chinese conditionals shed light on these issues from its unique angle? Answers will emerge as findings accumulate.[1]

---

[1] It is worth pointing out that Chinese conditionals should also be studied along the cognitive lines, involving empirical psychological investigations. But that is too big a topic that cannot be treated here.

© Springer International Publishing Switzerland 2014
X. Su and T. He (Eds.): CLSW 2014, LNAI 8922, pp. 43–54, 2014.
DOI: 10.1007/978-3-319-14331-6_5

Following the above route of investigation, this paper examines some common logical notions as exemplified by their explicit encoding in Chinese. Section 2 starts with an introduction of the established treatment of the Necessary Condition in propositional logic, moving on to its realization in Chinese as compared with English, followed by a discussion on conditional perfection in Section 3. Section 4 presents a description of 'yàobúshì'/if-not-be/ (要不是) as the typical explicit counterfactual conditional marker in Mandarin Chinese. Section 5 utilizes the notion of *veridicality* in analyzing the counterfactuals led by 'yàobúshì'. Section 6 examines the notion of *contingency* and puts forward the view that Chinese explicit counterfactuals led by 'yàobúshì' are *falsifying contingents*.

2 Transposition and the Representation of the Necessary Condition[2]

Modus Ponendo Ponens (MPP) and Modus Tollendo Tollens (MTT) are two sides of the same coin, because they are reliant on one same truth table, that of the conditional connective $\rightarrow$. Given the truth-conditions of the arrow functor, to make the conditional true when the protasis is known to be true, the apodosis has no choice but to be true, yielding MPP as a deductive schema. To make the conditional true when the apodosis is known to be false, the protasis has to be false. Hence the deductive schema MTT. This relationship can be captured by applying Transposition to (1), resulting in (2):

(1) $P \rightarrow Q$
(2) $\sim Q \rightarrow \sim P$

Transposition provides the key to the representation of the Necessary Condition given that the Sufficient Condition is adequately represented by (1). For Chinese not only has conditionals headed by the Sufficient Conditional marker 'zhǐyào...jiù' (只要......就), but also ones headed by the Necessary Conditional marker 'zhǐyǒu...cái' (只有......才), mirroring the distinction between the English 'so long as' and 'only if'.[3] The key to representing the Necessary Conditional is to apply Conversion to (1), yielding (3).

(3) $Q \rightarrow P$

(3) is in fact no different from the Inversion of (1), given here as (4), as (4) can be obtained from (3) through Transposition. But to apply Inversion directly to (1) would commit the fallacy of Negating the Protasis, while applying Conversion to (1) can be a valid yet restricted move, as it poses no harm to sound deduction and has literally turned the original formula into a different one – one that captures the Necessary

---

[2] For similarity and difference between Transposition and Contraposition, cf. Talk: Contraposition (Wikipedia) http://en.wikipedia.org/wiki/Talk:Contraposition (accessed May, 2014).

[3] The treatments of "if" and its Chinese equivalents will appear later in this section, which have been deliberately held back due to their ambivalent nature over the Necessary and the Sufficient.

Condition. The relevant examples of the Sufficient Condition in English and Chinese are listed as (5) - (9), and those of the Necessary Condition, as (10) – (13).[4]

(4) ~P → ~Q

(5) <u>So long as</u> we scatter it, thought force is of little use to us, but as soon as we are prepared to take the trouble necessary to harness it, all knowledge is ours.[5]

(6) <u>So long as</u> men can breathe or eyes can see/So long lives this, and this gives life to thee. (William Shakespeare, Sonnet 18: Shall I compare thee to a summer's day)

(7) <u>Zhǐyào</u> shǐyòng zhèzhǒng xǐdíjì, <u>biàn</u> kě xǐdé gàngànjìngjìng。 (<u>只要</u>使用这种洗涤剂, <u>便</u>可洗得干干净净。) "*So long as this lotion is used, the washing can be properly done.*"

(8) <u>Zhǐyào</u> bǎ qiú chuán gěi duìyǒu, tāmen <u>jiù</u> néng défèn。 (<u>只要</u>把球传给队友, 他们<u>就</u>能得分。)"*So long as the ball is passed to the teammates, they can score.*"

(9) <u>Zhǐyào</u> nǐ liǎndàn zhǎng dé háisuàn guòdéqù, nǎpà yīgè zì yě bú rènshí, <u>yě</u> zhàoyàng néng dāng yǎnyuán。 (<u>只要</u>你脸蛋长得还算过得去, 哪怕一个字也不认识, <u>也</u>照样能当演员。)"*So long as you are pretty, you can be an actor, even if you are illiterate.*"

(10) Nothing terrible will befall if you eat a piece of pizza — <u>only if</u> you exist on a diet of nothing but pizza.[6]

(11) We all agree that small stores are important, but they can remain viable <u>only if</u> they can carry out their trading on Sundays.

(12) Yǒude rén zhǔzhāng, biǎntáotǐ yī fāyán jiù bǎ tā qiēchú, yǐmiǎn zàochéng rìhòu de máfán。 qíshí, zhèzhǒng zuòfǎ guòyú cǎoshuài, <u>zhǐyǒu</u> zài búdéyǐ de qíngkuàng xià <u>cái</u> kǎolǜ qiēchú biǎntáoxiàn。 (有的人主张, 扁桃体一发炎就把它切除, 以免造成日后的麻烦。其实, 这种做法过于草率, <u>只有</u>在不得已的情况下<u>才</u>考虑切除扁桃腺。) "*Some proposed to cut off tonsil as soon as it has an inflammation, but this is a rash decision. Operation is considered only if no other cures can be found.*"

(13) Yóuyú zhèlǐ de shùmù shífèn chóumì, <u>zhǐyǒu</u> pīnmìng de xiàng shàng zhǎng cáinéng zuìdà xiàndù de jiēshòu dào yángguāng, yīncǐ, zhèlǐ de shùmù yībān dōu hěn zhí 、hěn gāo, shì shàngděng de jiànzhù cáiliào。 (由于这里的树木十分稠密, <u>只有</u>拼命地向上长, <u>才</u>能最大限度地接受到阳光, 因此, 这里的树木一般都很直, 很高, 是上等的建筑材料。) "*As woods here are dense, trees can get optimal sunlight only if they grow upward as much as possible. That is why trees here are usually all very straight and tall, making them ideal construction products.*"

---

[4] All Chinese examples are taken from CCL Corpus, Beijing University, at http://ccl.pku.edu.cn:8080/ ccl_corpus/

[5] Example taken from A.K. Kamath (2007) *Think Positive: Things Will Go Right*. Lotus Press. Chapter 1.

[6] Examples (10)-(11) are taken from British National Corpus, at http://www.natcorp.ox.ac.uk/

In all the above natural language examples, we use P to represent the protasis and Q, the apodosis, and translate the conditional words 'so long as', 'only if', '*zhǐyào...jiù*' (只要……就) and '*zhǐyǒu...cái*' (只有……才) into the arrow connective. Then the Sufficient Condition is represented by (1), and the Necessary Condition, by (3). For ease of reference, the translations are presented as follows:

(14) So long as P, Q $\Rightarrow$ $P \rightarrow Q$

(15) Q only if P $\Rightarrow$ $Q \rightarrow P$

(16) *Zhǐyào* P, *jiù* Q $\Rightarrow$ $P \rightarrow Q$

(17) *Zhǐyǒu* P, *cái* Q $\Rightarrow$ $Q \rightarrow P$

3   Semantic Underdeterminacy and Conditional Perfection

The conditional relations hitherto discussed can be further utilized to represent conditional sentences in English led by the more common 'if' connective, and its counterparts in Chinese, such as 'rúguǒ' (如果), 'yàoshì' (要是), 'jiǎrú' (假如), and 'ruò' (若). These *iffy* connectives can be used to compose sentences that are semantically underdetermined, denoting either the Sufficient Condition or the Necessary Condition, or even the Necessary & Sufficient Condition, as shown in the following: [7]

(18) You can pay by cash or by cheque. If you pay by cash you will normally obtain a receipt as proof of payment. [the Sufficient]

(19) If you are found guilty, the trial enters into its next very complicated part — the sentencing phase. [the Necessary]

(20) If the assessor is not fluent in ASL, an interpreter needs to be used to effectively convey communication during the interview process. [the Necessary & Sufficient]

(21) Zài zhègè dǎoyǔ de hǎibīn , yǒu yīpiàn chǎng 800mǐ 、 gāo 18mǐ de jiébái shāqiū 。 rén zǒu zài shāqiū shàng , shāzǐ jiù huì fāchū wāng wāng de gǒujiào shēng 。 yòng shǒu cuō shāzǐ , yěnéng fāchū tóngyàng de shēngyīn 。 rúguǒ zài shāqiū shàng xùnsù bēnpǎo , hái néng tīng dào dǎléi sì de shēngyīn 。 (在这个岛屿的海滨，有一片长800米、高18米的洁白沙丘。人走在沙丘上，沙子就会发出汪汪的狗叫声。用手搓沙子，也能发出同样的声音。如果在沙丘上迅速奔跑，还能听到打雷似的声音。) "*In the beach area of this island, there is a white sand dune stretching 800m long with a height of 18m. If someone walks on the dune, the sands will emit barking sounds. If one rubs sands with his hands, he will hear the same kind of sound. If someone runs quickly on the dune, the sands will even emit sounds like thunder.*" [the Sufficient]

(22) 1 9 2 9 nián, déguó fāshēng kōngqián yánzhòng de jīngjì wēijī, rénmín qúnzhòng kùnkǔ bùkān 。 xītèlè lìyòng zhègè jīhuì, dàochù jìnxíng qīpiàn xuānchuán, chuīxū rúguǒ tā shàngtái, nénggòu xiāomiè shīyè, měigè rén dōu

---

[7] Examples (18)-(20) are taken from IntelliText Corpora, at http://smlc09.leeds.ac.uk/itweb/htdocs/Query.html

yǒu gōngzuò hé miànbāo 。 xǔduō shòupiàn de qúnzhòng zhīchí le xītèlè, déguó lǒngduàn zīchǎnjiējí fēnfēn chūqián zhīchí nàcuìdǎng 。（１９２９年，德国发生空前严重的经济危机，人民群众困苦不堪。希特勒利用这个机会，到处进行欺骗宣传，吹嘘如果他上台，能够消灭失业，每个人都有工作和面包。许多受骗的群众支持了希特勒，德国垄断资产阶级纷纷出钱支持纳粹党。）*"In 1929, Germany experienced an unprecedented economic crisis that badly affected people's lives. Hitler seized this opportunity to spread deceitful propaganda all over the country, boasting that if he came to power, unemployment would be eliminated and everyone would have job and bread. Many people were taken in and chose to support Hitler. The German monopoly capitalist class also gave money to support the Nazi Party."* [the Necessary]

(23) Dìèr nián , tā shàng zòu dàoguāng dì , lìzhǔ jìnyān 。 tā zhǐchū , rúguǒ tīngrèn yāpiàn dàliàng shūrù zhōngguó , nàme , zài shù shínián hòu, zhōngguó bújǐn "jǐ wú kě yǐ yùdí zhī bīng ", érqiě "wú kě yǐ chōngxiǎng zhī yín" 第二年，他上奏道光帝，力主禁烟。他指出，如果听任鸦片大量输入中国，那么，在数十年后，中国不仅 "几无可以御敌之兵"，而且 "无可以充饷之银". *"In the ensuing year, he wrote to the Tao-Kuan Emperor, pleading him to ban opium. He pointed out that if opium was allowed to be imported into China in huge quantities, then in a matter of several decades, China would almost have no soldiers to resist external invasions, nor money to pay for military expenditure."* [the Necessary]

(24) Rúguǒ nǐ shì gāo jū dǐngbù de shǎoshù rén, nǐ jiù yōngyǒu le nǐ xiǎng yào de yīqiē , cáifù 、 quánwēi 、 hūfēnghuànyǔ 、 zuǒyòuféngyuán 、 shēngsèquǎnmǎ ; rúguǒ nǐ bú zài zhèxiē rén zhīliè , nǐ jiù méiyǒu tài duō jiàzhí.（如果你是高居顶部的少数人，你就拥有了你想要的一切，财富、权威、呼风唤雨、左右逢源、声色犬马；如果你不在这些人之列，你就没有太多价值。）*"If you are one of the few at the very top, you will have everything you want: fortune, authority, having everything in your command, leaving nothing undone, and enjoying every conceivable form of luxury. If not, then you are a nobody. "*[the Necessary & Sufficient]

Proper logical representation would not be a problem, as is already shown in the last section. The real issue is when to use which, and whether we should take "if" and its equivalents to be an inherently ambiguous functor. In some current versions of inferential pragmatics, proliferation of ambiguity is to be avoided as much as possible. Hence the Sufficient Condition is taken to be the basic meaning of "if"-conditionals, which can sometimes be strengthened to the stronger Necessary & Sufficient Condition. Conditional Perfection thus conceived is to be governed by pragmatic principles. In relevance-theoretic pragmatics, for example, the literal meaning of a sentence cannot be directly gleaned from the logical form, which is the compositional meaning of the sentence. Since LF is underdetermined, it needs to be developed in all directions so as to obtain the full-fledged literal meaning, yielding what is called *explicature* in relevance theory. Hence, Conditional Perfection can be viewed as a process of *explicating*, from the Sufficient Condition to the Necessary & Sufficient one. But when to explicate the LF of an if-conditional and to what extent? This is governed by the Principle of Relevance, to the satisfaction of the language user who can get an optimally relevant interpretation of the conditional statement.

No matter how Conditional Perfection actually works, it turns the Sufficient Condition into the Necessary & Sufficient Condition, i.e. the *iff* relation, to be translated into the bi-conditional $\leftrightarrow$. However, if a language user hears a conditional and interprets its meaning as the Necessary Condition only, he should choose to represent the "If P, Q" sentence as "$Q \rightarrow P$", rather than "$P \rightarrow Q$". Without adopting the ambiguity strategy, the solution seems to be to use Conditional Perfection in a different sense, which is to explicate through conversion, while the standard Perfection involves adding the Necessity Condition on top of the Sufficient Condition.

With dedicated conditional markers, the Sufficient, the Necessary, and the Necessary & Sufficient conditions can be easily distinguished. But when an all-neutral *iffy* word is used, the language user has to resort to his knowledge of the world to determine which exact relation is involved. As pointed out in [3], there can be a set of conditions that are jointly sufficient without being individually necessary, and there can also be a set of conditions that are individually necessary without being jointly sufficient. It is also a familiar scenario when discussing non-monotonic logic that a monotonic conditional inference may not hold when some additional and contradictory premises are smuggled in, sometimes against our prescribed understanding of the background knowledge of the world. Hence, even when we take some conditionals as communicating the Necessary Condition, we may be ignoring many common-sense assumptions whose truth is taken for granted. Otherwise, we may never know when a condition is really the Necessary Condition, as shown in the following example:

(25) Jīnshǔ yě huì "píláo"! bú xìn, kěyǐ shìshì : yòng shǒu xiǎng lāduàn yīgēn
     tiěsī , bú kěnéng 。 rúguǒ nǐ láihuí wānqǔ tiěsī , fǎnfù wānshé , tiěsī jiù
     duàn le 。 zhèzhǒng zài wàilì zuòyòng xià de pòhuài xiànxiàng , kēxué
     shàng jiù jiào zuò píláo 。(金属也会"疲劳"!不信，可以试试：用手想拉
     断一根铁丝，不可能。如果你来回弯曲铁丝，反复弯折，铁丝就断了。
     这种在外力作用下的破坏现象，科学上就叫做疲劳。) "*Metal can also
     'fatigue'! If in doubt, you can give it a try: Try to snap a wire by hand pull. It
     won't work. But if you bend it back and forth repeatedly, it will break. This
     structural damage caused by external loading is called metal fatigue in ma-
     terial science.*"

(25) can be taken as a case of the Sufficient Condition. Bending the iron wire will make it break, but it can also be cut by pliers. (25) can be taken as the Necessary Condition for breaking an iron wire *by hand only*. However, such descriptions involve a *ceteris paribus* assumption, that other things are held constant. What if the iron wire happens to be as resilient as a copper wire? Then it refutes the above Sufficient Condition. What if the iron wire is as crisp as a thin incense stick? Then the above Necessary Condition, i.e. repeated bending, will not be needed. It depends also on the mutual understanding that the agent is willing to keep on bending the wire, that he has enough stamina to do that, that he will not stop bending in order to attend to some

more urgent agenda items, that bending the wire as such will not cause damages and will therefore not invite interference from others, and that there will not be an earthquake or landslide or big flood at the place, etc., etc. All these may contribute to the set of sufficient conditions, and many could be necessary conditions. But most will be ignored because they constitute the general background knowledge which guarantees the performance of human rational behaviors. Given a certain situation, things happen in their usual way. If something new takes place, then *ceteris paribus*, other things will follow, in their predicted ways. Similar considerations led Sanford to claim that "[n]ecessary condition and sufficient condition are not purely technical terms" [4:179], because their explications involve accessing intrinsic properties of the propositions involved, i.e. the content, whereas purely technical terms only possess extrinsic properties, what can be established purely in terms of formal properties. Taken in this light, exclusive disjunction is not a purely technical term either, but Boolean conjunction, inclusive disjunction, and material implication are purely technical due to their extrinsic properties and their lack of intrinsic ones.

But conditionals with explicit relation markers are different. So long as you hit 'zhǐyào...jiù' (只要……就), 'zhǐyǒu...cái' (只有……才), or 'dāngqiějǐndāng' /if and only if/ (当且仅当), you take the speaker to be communicating the Sufficient, the Necessary, or the Necessary & Sufficient Condition. It is the speaker's choice, the speaker's perception of the scenario, which you can accept without querying.

4   Explicit Counterfactual Conditionals

The above discussions have centered around indicative conditionals. When we look at subjunctive conditionals or counterfactuals, Chinese and English diverge considerably. English uses fake-tense to encode explicit counterfactuality, while Mandarin Chinese only makes use of a few lexicalized constructions to encode explicit counterfactuality. Some examples are give below.

(26) If war had not broken out, they would have married, but when the Kleibers were sent away to prison-camp, her last hope of love and security collapsed; that was when she left the Island and went up West.[8]

(27) Dāngchū , wǒ cóng diànyǐngyuàn cízhí láidào běijīng de shíhòu , jiālǐrén jí tóngshì 、 péngyǒu jiù jílì fǎnduì 。 yàobúshì wǒ yìng xià yītiáo xīn , gēnběn jiù cí bú liǎo zhí , gèng lái bú liǎo běijīng 。 (当初, 我从电影院辞职来到北京的时候，家里人及同事、朋友就极力反对。<u>要不是</u>我硬下一条心，根本就辞不了职，更来不了北京。) *"Initially, when I quit my cinema job to come to Beijing, my family members, colleagues and friends were all deadly against it. Had I not made up my mind, I would not have been able to resign, nor would I have been able to come and make it in Beijing. "*

---

[8] From British National Corpus.

(28) 1:0, zhōngguó zúqiúduì yíng de gòu xuán de, bǐsài jìnxíng de yě gòu xié
      de 。 yàobúshì Hǎo Hǎidōng nà yǒudiǎn yùnqì de jìnqiú , píngjú kěndìng huì
      zhāo lái búmǎn hé fēiyì 。 suǒyǐ , shuǎng bú qǐlái 。 (1:0, 中国足球队赢得
      够悬的, 比赛进行得也够邪的。<u>要不是</u>郝海东那有点运气的进球,平局肯
      定会招来不满和非议。所以, 爽不起来。) "*One: Nil. The Chinese football
      team won a very close match with real good luck. Had it not been for Hao
      Haidong to score that lucky goal, a tie would surely have incurred dissatis-
      faction and complaints. That is why nobody took it with a light heart.*"

(29) Xīlà dàibiǎotuán suī shì zuìhòu yīgè rùchǎng, dàn huòdé de zhǎngshēng shì
      zuì jiǔ 、 zuì rèliè de。 zhè bú qíguài, yīnwéi tāmen shì dōngdàozhǔ ,
      guānzhòng méiyǒu lǐyóu lìnxī zìjǐ de zhǎngshēng。 zhídé yītí de shì, xīlà
      dàibiǎotuán cóng zhǔnbèi rùchǎng dào ràochǎng yīzhōu duō hòu, gòng dédào
      le 18 fēn 2 miǎo zhōng de zhǎngshēng , yàobúshì zhǔchírén dǎduàn, hěn
      nánshuō gǔzhǎng néng chíxù dào shēnme shíhòu 。 (希腊代表团虽是最后
      一个入场,但获得的掌声是最久、最热烈的。这不奇怪,因为他们是东道
      主, 观众没有理由吝惜自己的掌声。值得一提的是,希腊代表团从准备入
      场到绕场一周多后,共得到了18分2秒钟的掌声, <u>要不是</u>主持人打断,很难
      说鼓掌能持续到什么时候。) "*Although the Greek delegation was the last
      to enter the stadium, they won the longest and loudest round of applause.
      This is hardly surprising, as they represented the host country and the spec-
      tators had no reason to save on their applause. It is worth pointing out that
      the Greek delegation won an applause lasting for 18 minutes and 2 seconds,
      from the time they prepared to enter the stadium to the end of one lap's
      march. Had it not been for the ceremony presenter who put the cheers to an
      end, it would have been hard to tell how long the applause could last.*"

In the above examples, 'yào bú shì', though internally complex, behaves exactly
like a conditional functor. It is used as a single lexical item, different from the compositional meaning of 'yàoshì…bú'/If … not/"要是… 不. 'yàoshì…bú' is not an
explicit marker of counterfactual conditionals, because it can also form indicative
conditionals. 'yàoshì…bú' parallels "If … not" in English, but 'yào bú shì' seems to
be remotely equivalent to the English "Had it not been for …".

'Yào bú shì' is internally complex for a special reason. It takes on a proposition P,
which should be about a state or event that is both true and real, and returns a protasis
P* which is counterfactual. Here, negation obviously plays a vital role, but negation is
only one necessary condition, not a sufficient one. In the 'yàoshì…bú' construction,
which also forms a protasis, negation works as well, but the resulting protasis does
not have to be contrary to fact.

Harbsmeier [5] claimed that 'wēi'/if not/ (微) in Pre-Qin classical Chinese is en-
tirely limited to counterfactual usage, saying that the noun mentioned after 'wēi' must
refer to something that is presupposed to have been non-existent. The examples he
gave were 'wēi fū rén zhī lì'/Without that person's help/(微夫人之力……), and 'wēi
fū zǐ zhī fā wú fù yě'/But for the Master's lifting the veil for me/ (微夫子之发吾覆也)
(both being nominalized sentences, the marker being 之) as well as 'wēi tàizǐ yán'
/Had it not been for (you) the Prince's words…/ (微太子言) (nominalized without

a nominalization marker). Here, Harbsmeier seemed to have made a mistake. What is presupposed should be something that must be *existent*, which is related to the nominalized event after 'wēi'. This is also the property of 'yào bú shì', which can be taken as the modern version of 'wēi'. So the proposition led by 'yào bú shì' should be about an event that has already happened, and established as true. What is more, it should not be some proposition about abstract, general, timeless states. This can be established through both introspection and corpus search. Try to create a 'yào bú shì' counterfactual with abstract ideas, the resulting conditional is bound to be weird. What also tend to be anomalous are 'yào bú shì' counterfactuals containing a proposition with an extra layer of negation. To say the least, they are difficult to process.

How can the above characterizations of 'yào bú shì' be sharpened?

5   Veridicality

One viable notion to adopt is *veridicality*, which has recently been re-developed in the works of Giannakidou. Giannakidou & Mari [6] provides the most updated definition of (*subjective*) *veridicality* as "truth judgments depending on what epistemic agents know or believe to be true, and other factors in the context relating to the epistemic status of individuals." This definition distinguishes itself from some other, older definitions of (*objective*) *verdiciality* and (*perceptive*) *veridicality*, which are not so distinguishable from related notions like *realis* and *factivity*. [9]

Guided by this new definition, 'yào bú shì' can be characterized as an operator taking a veridical proposition: what the agent knows or believes to be true. We can also call 'yào bú shì' a *veridical operator*. A similar operator in Mandarin is 'zǎo zhīdào …' /Early know… / (早知道) which however, is not a conditional connective:

(30) Dǎ guò zhèzhǒng shōufèi diànhuà de háizǐ zài zhīdào zìjǐ gěi jiātíng zàochéng zhème dà de sǔnshī hòu, wǎngwǎng yě hòuhuǐ : "dāngshí zhǐshì tú yīshí gāoxìng, juédé xīnxiān 、 hǎowán。 rúguǒ zǎo zhīdào yào jiāo zhème duō qián , wǒ yě jiù bú huì dǎ le 。"(打过这种收费电话的孩子在知道自己给家庭造成这么大的损失后，往往也后悔："当时只是图一时高兴，觉得新鲜、好玩。如果<u>早知道</u>要交这么多钱，我也就不会打了。") *Those children who had made such pay-phone calls, after learning about the huge phone bills incurred for their homes, were often full of remorse: 'I made the phone call only because I was curious and thrilled. Had I known it would cost that much, I would not have called at all'.*

(31) Tā xiàng xiāoxié tóngzhì kūsù shuō : "yàoshì zǎo zhīdào shàngdāng shòupiàn, wǒ jiù bú gàn le。 xiànzài nòng dé yīshēn máfán, xiōngdì jiěmèi dōu bú xiàng rèn, hái jīyā le yīdàduī méi tuīxiāo chūqù de chǎnpǐn , wǒ qù zhǎo shuí ā ?" (她向消协同志哭诉说："要是<u>早知道</u>上当受骗，我就不干了。现在弄得一身麻烦，兄弟姐妹都不相认，还积压了一大堆没推销出去的产品，我去找谁啊？") *She told staff at Consumer's Association in tears, 'Had I known it was a fraud, I would not have got involved. Now I am*

---

[9] Cf. Giannakidou & Mari [6] for comparisons between these notions and for formal characterization of the newly defined notion.

all troubles. My brothers and sisters have all turned away from me. And I am stuck with loads of unsold goods. Whom can I turn to?' "

(32) Cóngqián yǒu yīgè rén chī shāobǐng。dìyīgè shāobǐng méiyǒu chī bǎo, zài mǎi dìèrgè。zhídào zuìhòu dìsāngè luòdù cái bǎo le。nàrén kāishǐ hòuhuǐ qǐlái, shuō: zǎo zhīdào dìsāngè shāobǐng bǎo dùzǐ, hébì huāqián chī qiánmiàn liǎnggè? (从前有一个人吃烧饼。第一个烧饼没有吃饱, 再买第二个。直到最后第三个落肚才饱了。那人开始后悔起来, 说: 早知道第三个烧饼饱肚子, 何必花钱吃前面两个？) *"Once upon a time, there was a man eating sesame-seed cakes. Having taken one, he was still hungry. So he bought another one, and the third one. Then he was full but started to regret, 'Had I known the third one would make me full, I wouldn't have spent money on the first two!'* "

Corpus findings immediately reveal that 'zǎo zhīdào' is not to be treated on a par with 'yào bú shì'. As 'zǎo zhīdào' can follow 'rúguǒ' or 'yàoshì', it is not to be taken as a conditional functor itself. Jiang & Wang [7] uses the notion of *antiveridicality* to characterize the behavior of the Shanghainese me51hau3 /*Much-preferred...*/ (蛮好......) as a counterfactual *desiderative*. Some relevant examples are quoted below:

(33) Mehau   ganggang   cen   ditik   qi   nao ![10]
     Much-preferred just-now   take   underground go   EM-SMP
     蛮好刚刚乘地铁启孬！
     (EM-SMP = emotive sentence-final particle)
     "It would have been much better that we took the underground at the time.
     刚才要是坐地铁去就好了。"

(34) Mehau   nong   ganggang   vyao   gang   bak   yi
     Much-preferred you   just-now   do-not   tell   to   him

     tin   nao.
     hear   EM-SMP

     蛮好侬刚刚勿要岗摆伊听孬！
     "It would have been much better that you did not let him/her know (that) at the time.
     你刚才要是不告诉他就好了。"

6 Contingency

Subjective veridicality constitutes one necessary condition for the use of 'yào bú shì', but it still does not capture the intuition that 'yào bú shì' does not take on abstract propositions like science or math laws, even though they can be subjectively established as truth. In Armstrong [8], non-abstract counterfactuals are given the name *contingent counterfactuals*: "Contingent counterfactual claims are often to be found

---

[10] As tone sandhi in Shanghainese is very complicated, it is customary for non-phonetic studies to omit tones in example sentences.

in ordinary discourse, for instance, 'If you had not put your foot on the brake so promptly just then, there would have been a nasty accident.'" Talks of *historical contingencies* are also frequently encountered: "What if there had been no American War of Independence? What if Ireland had never been divided?   What if Britain had stayed out of the First World War? What if Hitler had invaded Britain or had defeated the Soviet Union? What if the Russians had won the Cold War? What if Kennedy had lived? What if there had been no Gorbachev?" [9]

However, *contingency* seems to be a rather slippery term in philosophy. A consultation of philosophical literature reveals that all counterfactual hypotheses are about contingencies, and so are all conditional hypotheses. One other useful source is Rescher [7], in which he distinguishes between *falsifying* and *truthifying* causal counterfactuals. Falsifying counterfactuals hypothesize what actually did happen had not happened, whereas truthifying counterfactuals hypothesize what did not actually happen had happened. According to Rescher, historical counterfactuals of the falsifying type "are in general retrospectively cause-determinative in nature" and "generally address the preconditions for an actual occurrence". Such counterfactuals are less speculative and more situation-bound. This rightly fits the characterization of 'yào bú shì' counterfactuals. So what follows 'yào bú shì' can now be re-characterized as a proposition which is both veridical and a falsifying contingent. This is the conclusion we can reach at the present research stage.

7   Looking Ahead

The use of 'yào bú shì' counterfactuals only constitutes one kind of Chinese counterfactual conditionals, but it is the most prominent explicit counterfactual conditional in Mandarin. Implicit counterfactual conditionals involve inference and subtle lexical cues. That is a complicated issue that will have to be addressed elsewhere. [11]

Acknowledgements. I thank fellow members of Chinese counterfactual discussion group for thought-provoking discussions: Leo Kam-ching Cheung (philosopher), Leung-fu Cheung (mathematician), Thomas Hun-tak Lee (linguist and psycholinguist), and Kai-yee Wong (philosopher), all based at the Chinese University of Hong Kong. I also thank my former Ph.D. students Chuansheng He, Maggie Yuying Wang and Eddy Chun Wing Wong for working with me on topics on conditionals. Last but not the least, I thank the anonymous reviewer for helpful suggestions on the penultimate version.

References

1. Nute, D., Cross, C.B.: Conditional Logic. In: Gabbay, D.M., Guenthner, F. (eds.) Handbook of Philosophical Logic, vol. 4, pp. 1–98. Springer, Heidelberg (2002)
2. Bennett, J.: A Philosophical Guide to Conditionals. Oxford University Press, Oxford (2003)

---

[11] Cf. Wang [11].

3. Swartz, N.: The Concepts of Necessary Conditions and Sufficient Conditions. Unfinished lecture notes, Department of Philosophy, Simon Fraser University. http://www.sfu.ca/~swartz/conditions1.htm
4. Sanford, D.H.: If P, Then Q: Conditionals and the Foundations of Reasoning, 2nd edn. Routledge, London (2003)
5. Harbsmeier, C.: Language and Logic in Traditional China. Cambridge University Press (1998)
6. Giannakidou, A., Mari, A.: Future and Universal Epistemic Modals: Reasoning with Non-veridicality and Partial Knowledge. Ms. (2014)
7. Jiang, Y., Wang, Y.: Counterfactual Subjunctive Assertions in Shanghai Dialect. To appear in Commemorative Essays on the 120th Birthday of Professor Y. R. Chao
8. Armstrong, D.M.: Truths and Truthmakers. In: Schantz, R. (ed.) What is Truth?. Walter de Gruyter, Berlin (2002)
9. Ferguson, N.: Virtual History: Towards a 'chaotic' theory of the past. In: Ferguson, N. (ed.) Virtual History: Alternatives and Counterfactuals. Basic Books, New York (1999)
10. Rescher, N.: Conditionals. The MIT Press, Cambridge (2007)
11. Wang, Y.: The Ingredients of Counterfactuality in Mandarin Chinese. China Social Science Press, Beijing (2013)

Combination of Mandarin Chinese Verb "xiě" and Nouns from the Perspective of Generative Lexicon Theory

Qiang Li[✉]

Department of Chinese Language and Literature, Peking University, Beijing, China
leeqiang2222@163.com

Abstract. The semantic combination and generation do not always obey Frege's Principle. In many cases, the meaning of the whole structure is beyond the sum of its constituents' meaning. Under the guideline of the generative lexicon theory, through retrieving relevant corpora, this paper investigates the collocation of Chinese verb "写"(xiě, write) and nouns on the basis of qualia roles, semantic types and relevant compositional mechanisms, and illustrates that the combination of the verb "xiě" and nouns is complex. Besides, irregular objects of the verb "xiě" will be discussed. Qualia roles can provide a new explanation for the irregular objects of the verb "xiě".

Keywords: Generative lexicon theory · xiě · Qualia role · Semantic type · Compositional mechanism · Irregular object

1   Introduction

Combination between words, especially the semantic generation, has been the issue of the generative lexicon theory. In order to explain the inconsistent phenomenon of semantic combination, Pustejovsky (2006) put forward the table below to show the relationship between semantic types of nouns and compositional mechanisms.

Table 1. Semantic types of nouns and compositional mechanisms

	Type Selected		
Argument Type	Natural	Artifactual	Complex
Natural	Sel/Acc	Intro	Intro
Artifactual	Exploit	Sel/Acc	Intro
Complex	Exploit	Exploit	Sel/Acc

This research is sponsored by the National Social Science Fund Major Project "Chinese parataxis characteristic research and large knowledge base and corpus construction under the background of international Chinese language education" (Approval No. : 12&ZD175). We hereby express our sincere thanks.

© Springer International Publishing Switzerland 2014
X. Su and T. He (Eds.): CLSW 2014, LNAI 8922, pp. 55–65, 2014.
DOI: 10.1007/978-3-319-14331-6_6

The table shows that, when the target semantic type of nouns following verbs conflicts with the source semantic type, some mechanisms are needed to realize semantic combination. Besides, certain corresponding relationship exists between semantic types and compositional mechanisms. For instance, Sel/Acc only occurs in the case that the target semantic type is identical with the source semantic type; exploitation occurs in the case that the target semantic type is a component of the source semantic type. Besides, when the target semantic type is richer than the source semantic type, intro can be effective.

Wang & Huang (2010) made a careful investigation into the combination of Chinese verb "看"(kàn, look at) and nouns with the generative lexicon theory, and found that the compositional mechanisms of "kàn" and nouns are much more complex than the situation described in table 1. On the basis of the findings in Wang & Huang (2010), this paper makes a deep investigation into the combination of the verb "xiě" and nouns, and discusses the irregular objects of the verb "xiě".

2   Theoretical Background

To illustrate semantic generation and explain lexical combination, Pustejovsky (1991, 1995) designed a set of framework describing the qualia structure of nouns, which contains four levels of semantic knowledge.

(1)Constitutive role which describes the relationship between an object and its components;
(2)Formal role which describes properties of an object that are different from other objects in greater cognitive domain;
(3)Telic role which describes function and purpose of an object;
(4)Agentive role which describes how an object is produced.

These four roles are an encyclopedic knowledge of objects, reflecting different dimensions of objects referred by nouns. However, Pustejovsky (2001, 2006, and 2011) and Pustejovsky & Jezek (2008) pointed out that not all nouns own these four qualia roles. Hence, they divide nouns into three types as follows:

(1)Natural type which relates to formal role and constitutive role. For instance, rock/water/rabbit/sky;
(2)Artifactual type which relates to agentive role and telic role. For instance, doctor/mother/chair/table/knife;
(3)Complex type which is composed of natural type and artifactual type. For instance, book/newspaper/magazine[1].

---

[1] Take "book" for example. In Chinese, we often say "尽信书则不如无书"(If you believe all in books, it is better to have no books.). In this sentence, the former "书"(book) refers to knowledge in books, while the latter "书"(book) refers to a physical object.

On the basis of these three types, Pustejovsky (2001, 2006, and 2011) and Pustejovsky & Jezek (2008) illustrated the compositional mechanisms of verbs and nouns as follows:

(1) Pure Selection (Type Matching): the type a function requires is directly satisfied by the argument;

(2) Accommodation: the type a function requires is inherited by the argument;

(3) Type Coercion: the type a function requires is imposed on the argument type. This is accomplished by either:

①Exploitation: taking a part of the argument's type to satisfy the function;

②Introduction: wrapping the argument with the type required by the function.

This paper discusses the combination of the verb "xiě" and nouns on the basis of the semantic types of nouns, qualia roles and the compositional mechanisms, and respectively investigates selective restrictions of different meanings of "xiě" on its objects, illustrating that the combination of "xiě" and nouns is complicated.

3   Combination of "xiě" and Nouns

This paper focuses on four kinds of meanings of "xiě", and refers to: Modern Chinese corpus of Peking University and Chinese corpus of language committee[2]. Meanwhile, we also query related cases with the help of Baidu and Google search engine.

3.1   "xiě": Write with Tools

3.1.1   "xiě"+ Artifactual Type

(1) Pure Selection

"数字"(number), "汉字"(character), "英语"(English), "阿拉伯语"(Arabic), "标题"(title), "名字"(name), "字母"(letter) and "邮政编码"(code) can combine with "xiě". The semantic information of these nouns contains "字" (character). Hence, they can follow "xiě" directly and satisfy the semantic requirement of "xiě". The compositional mechanism of "xiě" and these nouns is pure selection.

(2) Artifactual Exploitation

Although some nouns do not contain the abstract content, they can still be objects of "xiě". For instance, "毛笔" (brush), "钢笔" (pen) and "铅笔" (pencil). This is because they all have the telic role "xiě". They can be expressed as:

     Phys $\otimes_{\text{telic}}$ write：毛笔 (brush), 钢笔 (pen), 铅笔 (pencil)

---

[2] The Website of modern Chinese corpus of Peking University:
     http://ccl.pku.edu.cn:8080/ccl_corpus/

   The Website of Chinese corpus of language committee:
     http://www.cncorpus.org/

As the telic role "xiě" and "字" (character) are psychologically closely linked, "字" (character) can be activated by "xiě". "写毛笔／钢笔／铅笔" (write with a brush/pen/pencil) means "写毛笔字／钢笔字／铅笔字" (write brush character/pen character /pencil character).

(3) Dot Introduction

Some nouns only mean substance. For instance, "黑板" (blackboard), "白板" (whiteboard), "稿纸" (manuscript paper), "卡片" (card), "条幅" (banner) and "纸条" (note). All these nouns can be objects of "xiě". When these nouns follow "xiě", information property can be added to them by dot introduction. These nouns seem to be complex nouns[3]. On one hand, they are substantial entity; on the one hand, they have information property.

(4) Qualia Introduction

When "楷书" (regular script), "宋体" (Song typeface) and "草书" (cursive script) are in combination with "xiě", meaning of "字" (character) is added to these nouns. "Xiě" introduces the visible formal role "字" (character) into these nouns so as to realize semantic combination. These nouns can be represented as:

Abstract $\otimes_{formal}$ character: 楷书 (regular script), 宋体 (Song typeface), 草书 (cursive script)

"写楷书／宋体／草书" (write regular script/Song typeface/cursive script) means "写楷书字／宋体字／草书字" (write characters of regular script/Song typeface/cursive script).

3.1.2 "xiě"+Complex Type

(1) Dot Exploitation

①*Information property can be exploited*

For instance, "考卷" (exam paper) and "试卷" (exam paper). They can refer to physical objects or information on an exam paper. That is to say, they are complex nouns[4]. When they follow "xiě", information can be exploited. "写试卷／考卷" (write exam paper) means "在试卷／考卷上写字" (write words on a piece of exam paper). Similarly, "写匾额" (write plaque) only means "在匾额上写字" (write words on a plaque).

---

[3] The reason we say "seem" is that "黑板(blackboard)/稿纸(manuscript paper)/纸条(scrip)" only stand for physical objects, and they do not have information property. Information property generates in the specific context. Hence, these nouns do not belong to the complex type.

[4] For instance, in the sentence "老师正在看试卷"(Teachers are looking at answers given by students.), "试卷"(exam paper) obviously does not mean a physical paper, but means information or content.

3.2   "xiě": Write Articles or Books

3.2.1 "xiě"+Artifactual Type

(1) Pure Selection

Nouns which contain information property can be objects of "xiě". For instance, "碑文" (inscription), "歌词" (lyric), "誓词" (oath) and "文章" (article). These nouns can directly satisfy the semantic requirement of "xiě". Hence, they are in combination with "xiě" through pure selection.

(2) Qualia Introduction

Some abstract nouns like "法律" (law), "历史" (history) and "马克思主义" (Marxism) can also follow "xiě". For instance,

① 写 诗 这种 活动 比 写 历史 更 富于 哲学 意味。

　　write poem this activity than write history more rich philosophy meaning

　　"Writing Poetry is richer than writing history in philosophical meaning."

② 农民 革命军 却 也 曾 拿 它 来出布告，写

　　farmer revolutionary army but also ever catch it make bulletin write

法律，宣传 一些 在当时 有 进步 意义 的 思想。

　　law propagandize some then have progressive meaning de thought

"However, revolutionary army of farmers had also made bulletin with it, written books about law, and propagandized some progressive thought at that time."

③ 毛泽东同志 和 其他 共产主义者 写 马克思主义 的 著作，也
Mao Zedong and other Communist write Marxism de books also
还是 用的 这 一套 文字。
still use this kind character

"This kind of character is still used in books written by Mao Zedong and other Communists."

When these nouns are objects of "xiě", the formal role can be introduced into them. For example, in "写法律" (write law), "法律" (law) becomes a physical object. "写历史" (write history) and "写马克思主义" (write Marxism) are the same cases. These nouns can be represented as:

　　Abstract $\otimes_{formal}$ phys：法律 (law), 历史 (history), 马克思主义 (Marxism)

(3) Artifactual Exploitation

According to Pustejovsky & Jezek (2008), the agentive role in nouns of artifactual type can be exploited, which is called artifactual exploitation. For instance, "西游记" (Journal to West), "三国演义" (War among Three Kingdoms) and "红楼梦" (Dream of Red Mansions) can refer to novels and teleplays, whose agentive role are respectively "xiě" and "拍" (make). In "xiě+N", the agentive role "xiě" of these nouns can be exploited so as to realize the semantic combination. These nouns can be represented as:

literature ⊗_{agent} write："西游记"(Journal to West), "三国演义"(War among Three Kingdoms), "红楼梦"(Dream of Red Mansions)

3.2.2 "xiě"+Complex Type

Nouns like "散文" (prose), "小说" (novel), "诗歌" (poem) and "自传" (autobiography) are complex nouns, which are composed of physical property and information aspect. For instance, on one hand, they can follow classifiers like "摞 (luò), 沓 (dá), 册 (cè), 本 (běn)", which illustrates that they mean physical objects; on the other hand, they can follow classifiers like "部 (bù), 章 (zhāng), 首 (shǒu), 篇 (piān)", which illustrates that they mean information. The verb "xiě" and these nouns are combined by dot exploitation.

① *Information property can be exploited*
For instance, "写了(一部)散文(write a essay)/写了(一章)小说(write a chapter of novel)/写了(一首)诗歌(write a poem)/写了(一篇)自传(write an autobiography)". Besides, when some complex nouns are composed of event and information like "歌曲" (song), "戏曲" (play), "悲剧" (tragedy) and "喜剧" (comedy)[5], information property contained in these nouns is also exploited to satisfy the semantic requirement.

②*Physical Manifestation can be exploited*
For instance, "写了(一摞)散文(write several essays)/写了(一本)小说(write a novel)/写了(一册)诗歌(write a volume of poem)/写了(一本)自传(write an autobiography)". In these phrases, the physical manifestation of the nouns is exploited.

③ *Both information property and physical manifestation can be exploited*
Some complex nouns like "书" (book), "信" (letter), "专著" (monograph), "通知" (notice), "对联" (couplet) and "稿件" (manuscript) are composed of physical manifestation and information property. In the semantic interpretation of the structure "xiě+N", both physical manifestation and information property can be exploited by "xiě". The verb "xiě" is a creative verb, and the nouns following it usually contain the meaning of result. Take "写信" (write a letter) for example. When the content in the letter has been written, the physical object "letter" appears.

---

[5] These nouns contain temporality. For example, "五分钟的歌曲"(a song of five minutes), "一个小时的戏"(a drama of an hour). Besides, they can be modified by verbal measure words like "一出/**场**悲剧/喜剧"(a tragedy/comedy).

3.3 "xiě": Describe

3.3.1 "xiě"+Natural Type

(1) Pure Selection/Accommodation

Nouns like "自然" (nature), "山" (mountain), "水" (water), "花" (flower) and "大海" (sea) can follow the verb "xiě". They can directly satisfy the semantic requirement of "xiě". The common semantic feature of these nouns is that they all have external visual cues and can be available for people to enjoy or observe. Besides, "女人" (woman), "男人" (man) and "孩子" (child) can follow "xiě" by accommodation, because the objects of "xiě" can be some traits of people. For instance, "女人的容貌" (woman's appearance) and "男人的体格" (man's body) can be seen or observed; "孩子的性格" (child's character) cannot be seen but can be felt.

3.3.2 "xiě"+Artifactual Type

(1) Accommodation

According to Pustejovsky (2008), nouns of artifactual type are composed of head type and tail type, which are connected by tensor type $\otimes$. For instance, "beer" can be represented as: liquid$\otimes_{Telic}$drink. When the head type is exploited only, compositional mechanism is accommodation. The head type "human" of nouns referring to people like "爸爸(father), 妈妈(mother), 外公(grandpa), 外婆(grandma)" and nouns referring to status like "政委(political commissar), 厂长(factory director), 保姆(babysitter), 总统(president)" is exploited to realize combination with "xiě". The head type "physical object" of nouns like "工厂 (factor), 长城 (Great Wall)" is exploited to realize combination with "xiě". Meanwhile, the head type "abstract object" of nouns like "事迹 (deed), 爱情 (love), 亲情 (kinship), 婚姻 (marriage)" is exploited to realize combination with "xiě". The head type of all these nouns is exploited to combine with "xiě" so as to realize semantic combination.

3.3.3 "xiě"+Complex Type

(1) Dot Exploitation

For example, "学校" (school) refers to a building or an institution, which can be seen in the contrast of "盖学校" (build a school) and "办学校" (run a school). "学校" (school) which follows the verb "盖" (build) means a building, while "学校" (school) which follows the verb "办" (run) means an institution. When "学校" (school) combines with "xiě", "写学校" (write school) can both mean "describe the building and scenery in school" and "describe the school life", which is realized by exploiting the two different semantic facets of "学校" (school). In the former case, the meaning "building" is exploited, and in the latter case, the meaning "institution" is exploited. However, in most cases, the meaning "institution" is common as shown in the following examples:

《学苑》　这本　杂志是　写　学校　　的。
Xueyuan   this   magazine is   write school de

"*'Xueyuan' is to describe the school life.*"

近年来　写　　学校　　的　作品　也　　有　　进步。
Recently write school de article also have progress

"Recently articles describing the school life are also progressing."

3.4   "xiě": Write Program

3.4.1 "xiě"+Artifactual Type

(1)Pure Selection
This meaning of "xiě" is not common, which mostly appears in the domain of computer science. Nouns like "程序" (program), "算法" (algorithm) and "C语言"(C language) can combine with "xiě" through pure selection.

4   Qualia Roles and Irregular Objects of the Verb "xiě"

Chinese is a kind of parataxis language, and the tolerance on collocation between words is big. As a result, many verbs can take irregular objects. Xing (1991) called these irregular objects "replace-nominal object". According to him, regular objects of verbs only include target objects, and other kinds of objects all belong to "replace-nominal object". Through the discussion in section 3, we can find that the first meaning of "xiě" can bring irregular objects, namely "write with tools". Here three cases are included:

① instruction: 写毛笔, 写钢笔, 写铅笔(write characters with a brush/pen/pencil)
②manner: 写楷书, 写宋体, 写草书(write characters of regular script/cursive script/Song typeface)
③ location: 写黑板, 写稿纸, 写纸条(write characters on a blackboard/a piece of manuscript paper/a note)

Why can the verb "xiě" take these nouns as its objects? We think qualia roles can provide an explanation.

1. The telic role of "毛笔" (brush), "钢笔" (pen) and "铅笔" (pencil) is "xiě", and "字"(character) can be activated by "xiě", which has been tested by some psychological experiments. For instance, Altmann (1999) and Warren & McConnell (2007) have pointed out that concepts of relevant nouns are included in the lexical knowledge of verbs. When people process the verbs, information about nouns can also be evoked. Then we can predict that nouns like "毛笔" (brush), "钢笔" (pen) and "铅笔" (pencil) have strong relationship with the concept of "字"(character) through the telic role "xiě". Hence, people can transform the regular expression "用 (use)+ 工具

(instruction)+动作 (activity)+对象 (object)" into the irregular expression "动作 (activity)+工具(instruction)", which the concept of "字"(character) is implied. Besides, the verb "xiě" is just the telic role of "毛笔" (brush), "钢笔" (pen) and "铅笔" (pencil), which can provide a condition for these nouns to act as objects of "写"(write). This can be shown in the following figure 1.

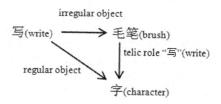

Fig. 1. Combination of the verb "写"(xiě, write) and "毛笔"

2. "楷书" (regular script), "草书" (cursive script) and "宋体" (Song typeface) are originally abstract nouns, referring to different ways of writing. They all have the formal role "字" (character). That is to say, the concept of "字" (character) is contained in the semantic information of these nouns. Hence, they can combine with "xiě". Wang (2000) pointed out that "写宋体" (write Song typeface) actually means "写宋体字" (write characters of Song typeface), which illustrates that "宋体" (Song typeface) refers to "字" (character). This can be shown in figure 2.

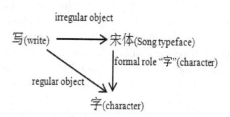

Fig. 2. Combination of the verb "写"(xiě, write) and "宋体"

3. Like the case of "毛笔" (brush), "钢笔" (pen) and "铅笔" (pencil), the telic role of "黑板" (blackboard), "稿纸" (manuscript paper) and "纸条" (note) is "xiě"[6], which can make them connected with "字" (character). Hence, the concept of "字" (character) can be psychologically activated by "黑板" (blackboard), "稿纸" (manuscript paper) and "纸条" (note). The regular form "在黑板/稿纸/纸条上写字" (write characters on a blackboard/a piece of manuscript paper/a note) can be compressed into "写黑板/稿纸/纸条" (write blackboard/manuscript paper/note). This case can be shown as follows.

---

[6] "写"(write) is the basic telic role of "稿纸"(manuscript paper) and "纸条"(note). Besides, for specific purpose, "稿纸"(manuscript paper) can also be folded and "纸条"(note) can also be pasted.

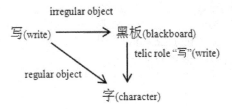

Fig. 3. Combination of the verb "写"(xiě, write) and "黑板"

Xing (1991) pointed out that the existential condition of "replace-nominal object" is that there must be triangle contact among the replace-nominal object, the regular object and the verb. Otherwise, the structure "V+N" cannot be established. Actually, from the perspective of qualia roles, the qualia role of the replace-nominal object activates or contains the semantic information of the regular object. For instance, the telic role "xiě" of "黑板" (blackboard) and "毛笔" (brush) activates the default object "字" (character). The formal role of "楷书" (regular script) is "字" (character). Therefore, if a verb carries replace-nominal objects, then it actually means that there is a connection between the verb and the regular objects.

5   Conclusion

This paper makes a detailed investigation into the combination of the verb "xiě" and nouns. The semantic types of these nouns are mostly the artifactual and the complex ones, while the natural type is rare. The compositional mechanisms involved are pure selection, accommodation, artifactual exploitation, dot introduction, dot exploitation and qualia introduction. Thereinto, pure selection can be seen on any meaning of "xiě" and its objects. Especially when "xiě" combines with nouns of the artifactual type, pure selection is more obvious. Dot exploitation exists in the combination of first three meanings of "xiě" and complex nouns. Besides, other compositional mechanisms are sporadic. In addition, this paper discusses the combination of "xiě" and its irregular objects. Qualia roles of the object nouns, especially the telic role and the formal role, can explain the formation of the unconventional structure "xiě+N".

Reference

1. Altmann, G.: Thematic role assignment in context. Journal of Memory and Language **41**(1), 124–145 (1999)
2. Pustejovsky, J.: Construction and the Logic of Concepts. In: Bouillon, P., Busa, F. (eds.) The Language of Word Meaning, pp. 91–123. Cambridge University Press (2001)
3. Pustejovsky, J.: Type theory and lexical decomposition. Journal of Cognitive Science **6**, 39–76 (2006)
4. Pustejovsky, J.: Coercion in a general theory of argument selection. Linguistics **49**(6), 1401–1431 (2011)

5. Pustejovsky, J., Jezek, E.: Semantic Coercion in Language: Beyond Distributional Analysis. In: Lenci, A. (ed.) Distributional Models of the Lexicon in Linguistics and Cognitive Science (2008). Special issue of Italian Journal of Linguistic

6. Song, Z.: The Latest Development of Generative Lexicon Theory. Yuyanxue Luncong **44**, 202–221 (2011). (in Chinese)

7. Shan, W., Chu-Ren, H.: Compositional Operations of Mandarin Chinese Perception Verb "kàn": A Generative Lexicon Approach. In: PACLIC 24 Proceedings (2010)

8. Warren, T., McConnell, K.: Investigating effects of sectional restriction violations and plausibility violation severity on eye-movements in reading. Psychonomic Bulletin & Review **14**, 770–775 (2007)

9. Wang, Z.: The Cognitive Investigation on "吃食堂" (eat in refectory). Language Teaching and Linguistic Studies **2**, 59–64 (2000). (in Chinese) ("吃食堂"的认知考察,《语言教学与研究》第2期59-64页)

10. Xing, F.: Observation on Object-Introduction in Chinese. Chinese Teaching in the World **2**, 76–84 (1991). (in Chinese) (汉语里宾语代入现象之观察,《世界汉语教学》第2期76-84页)

The Mechanism Behind Idioms' Meaning Extension

Hongyan Liu[1(✉)], Peicui Zhang[2], and Baopeng Ma[3]

[1] Hebei Finance University, Baoding, China
{chlhy_youxiang,zhangpeicui,mabaopeng1234}@163.com
[2] Henan University, Kaifeng, China
[3] China University of Mining and Technology, Xuzhou, China

Abstract. Meaning extension is an important mechanism by virtue of which new idioms are produced. Guided by the Principle of Economy, language users reanalyze the meanings of original idiomatic expressions, their semantic focus and the construction of their components, thus get a different explanation of the original idioms based on a new understanding of their literal meanings, which eventually lead to the semantic evolution.

Keywords: Idioms · Extended meaning · Reanalysis · Principle of Economy

Idioms are formed with two or more words with a certain structure. There are some idioms that can still have proper syntagmatic and semantic relation for its components when understood on the basis of their literal meanings, which gives rise to "changes of application", a phenomenon of "reinvesting forms with new meaning". [1]. When this phenomenon is conventionalized, it is then called "changes of development". There are still other names in academic circles for this phenomenon, such as "literal understanding of the idioms", "inverse extension", and so on.

Language evolution results from the join forces of external motivation and the internal mechanism. The same is equally true for the phenomenon of "reinvesting forms with new meaning". Communication needs constitute the external motivation, which is reflected by the phenomenon of the lexical vacancy (with meaning but no lexical form). The accommodation of the linguistic system provides the internal mechanism. In this paper, we will focus on the detailed investigation of the internal mechanism.

The changes of the component meaning, the syntagmatic relation between the components, and the semantics nucleus of the components constitute the main factors for the phenomenon of "reinvesting forms with new meaning".

1 New Understanding of the Components of the Idioms

If the components of an idiom get totally different meanings, the idiom itself will accordingly get a new literal meaning, which results in the semantic evolution of the idiom. The change of the meaning of each component lies in the polysemy, the semantic change, and the substitution of the components, the disappearance of the linguistic origin and so on.

© Springer International Publishing Switzerland 2014
X. Su and T. He (Eds.): CLSW 2014, LNAI 8922, pp. 66–74, 2014.
DOI: 10.1007/978-3-319-14331-6_7

1.1   Polysemy of the Components

The ancient Chinese had a relatively small vocabulary, so the words were often extended in meaning to express new concepts about new products or social life styles, which made the polysemic words a common phenomenon. The components of some idioms had a bundle of meanings, so if the idiom was understood on the basis of a different meaning of the components, it would get a new meaning accordingly, which would meet the requirement of certain communicative needs. And the new meanings of the idioms were established through constant use. It is a synchronic phenomenon that the polysemy of the components leads to semantic evolution of the idioms, while the polysemy of the components was achieved through a diachronic process. Take "一丝不挂" as an example. Originally "一丝不挂" meant "the fish was not trapped by the fishing line", as shown in (1):

(1) 一丝不挂，竿木随身。（《楞严经》）

Then Buddhists took it as "not bothered by the secular world." The idiom thus got its original meaning, as shown in (2):

(2) 一丝不挂鱼脱渊，万古同归蚁旋磨。（宋黄庭诗）

However, "一丝不挂" gradually became a fixed idiom, with a broad meaning "to get rid of or be detached from", as shown by (3), and this became the literal meaning of the idiom.

(3) 放闸老兵殊耐冷，一丝不挂下冰滩。（宋杨万里诗）

The idiom got the meaning "naked" in the following literatures, which was the extended meaning of the idiom.

Retrieving CCL corpus of Modern Chinese [2], we get a total of 196 entries in the synchronic use of the idiom in modern Chinese, among which 33 entries have the original meaning, 1 entry has the literal meaning and 162 entries have the extended meaning (with reference to *The Grand Chinese Dictionary* [3] and *Contemporary Chinese Dictionary* (sixth edition) [4]).

The key factor to the semantic evolution of "一丝不挂" is the polysemic word "丝". In the literal meaning of the idiom, "$丝_1$" refers to "the fine thread-like silk" and it means "fishing line" in idioms. "$丝_2$" is a meaning more frequently used. It means "silk" and the "textile made of silk". With a powerful association, language users derive the "$丝_2$" from "$丝_1$". This component of the idiom can be easily understood with the meaning "$丝_2$", which means "with clothes on" to describe someone "naked." Therefore the meaning "being naked" fills up the semantic vacancy, which becomes established as an extended meaning through constant use.

Not only the polysemic monosyllabic component but also the polysemic disyllabic component of the idioms leads to semantic evolution. For example, the semantic evolution of the idiom "风流人物" [*fengliu renwu*] is caused by the polysemic disyllabic word "风流".

1.2   The Semantic Change of the Components

The diachronic semantic change of the components is also one reason for the different understanding of the components.

1.2.1   Ancient and Modern Meaning

The semantic evolution lies in the diachronic development of the component meaning, which refers to a phenomenon in which the idiom was understood with a new modern meaning in place of the ancient meaning. Comparatively speaking, "ancient" and "modern" means the difference in times, with "ancient" referring to an earlier time and "modern" a later time. In general, the "ancient meaning" is rarely used in Modern Chinese, and it is only occasionally used in fragment of the Modern Chinese for certain stylistic purpose. Language users are more familiar with the "modern meaning". When understood with the "modern meaning" for its components, the idiom will get a new literal meaning, and further derive a new extended meaning.

Take "姗姗来迟" as an example. It first appeared in the Han Dynasty:

(4) 是邪，非邪？立而望之，偏何姗姗其来迟！（《汉书·外戚传上·孝武李夫人》）

Originally, it was used to describe a "walking manner", and then it became established as an idiom, to describe "women's slow and calm walking manner." This is the literal meaning of the idiom, as shown in (5):

(5) "小兰如芙蓉女儿，明秀无匹，姗姗来迟，媚不可言。（清无名氏《帝城花样·小芗传》）

In the subsequent literature, "姗姗来迟" usually meant "being failed to arrive at the appointed time, or being late", which was the extended meaning of the idiom.

(6) 那时唐卿、珏斋也都来，只有荜如姗姗来迟，大家只好先坐了。（《孽海花》五）

The difference between the ancient and modern meaning of "迟" caused the semantic evolution of the idiom "姗姗来迟". "迟$_1$" means "to walk slowly", which is the ancient meaning. "迟$_2$" means "being late", which is the modern meaning. Language users are more familiar with "迟$_2$", so they gradually replace "迟$_1$" with "迟$_2$" in the understanding of idioms with this word, which caused the semantic evolution.

The difference between the ancient and modern meaning of the disyllabic components of the idioms can also lead to semantic evolution. For example, the semantic evolution of the idiom "体贴入微" lies in the different ancient and modern meaning of "体贴". Probably, each component of the idioms has different ancient and modern meanings. For example, the semantic evolution of the idiom "良心发现" is caused by the difference between the ancient and modern meaning of "良心" and "发现".

1.2.2   Disyllabification

The disyllabification of Chinese lexicon can also cause the semantic change of the component meaning of idioms. Idioms are usually composed of monosyllables which are the roots of Chinese and have specific and independent meanings. The two in some idioms are related with each other and can constitute a disyllabic word in Modern Chinese. The two monosyllables and the disyllabic word are the same in form, but they have different meanings. The new idiom is easier to be understood if the two syllables are taken as a disyllabic unit, which can lead to semantic evolution of the idioms.

> (7) 自非早杜乱萌，大施拯救，则逃亡相继，万一穷极无聊，铤而走险，是又为延庆之续矣。（明吴牲《柴庵疏集·九·西安北界被贼残伤急行赈济疏》）

The syntactic structure of the idiom "穷极无聊"is "穷*极+无*聊" ("+"connects two relatively independent parts, while "*"connects two components which are closely related), "穷" and "极" form a complementary phrase with an adjective as the center, while "无聊" is an endocentric phrase with the verb as the center. "穷极无聊" describes "an extremely poor life", which is the original meaning of the idiom.

> (8) （谭绍闻）先二日还往街头走走，走的多了，亦觉没趣。穷极无聊，在店中结识了弄把戏的孙海仙。（《歧路灯》四四）

In the subsequent literature, "穷极无聊" means "too bored to do anything", which is the extended meaning of the idiom.

The semantic change of the idiom "穷极无聊" is caused by the disyllabification of "无" and "聊". Originally "聊" meant "to depend on". "无" and "聊" often occured together with the meaning "to have nothing to depend on". When "无" and "聊" became a disyllabic word "无聊", they got a new meaning "to be bored because of idleness." In Modern Chinese, it has become a very high-frequency word according to the *Lexicon of Common Words in Contemporary Chinese (draft)* [5].

"聊" with the meaning "to depend on" in Modern Chinese is used in a formal style and with a very low frequency. Language users are more familiar with the word "无聊" and tend to reconsider the idioms with more familiar meanings and structures. In addition, the meaning of "无聊"in the idiom with extended meaning becomes more prominent, while the meaning of "穷" is weakened. So the disyllabification and the shift of semantic center together changed the semantic meaning of the idioms.

1.3   Substitution of Meanings

Substitution of new meanings means to re-explain the idiom with new meanings of the components, hence getting an extended meaning of the idiom based upon the new literal meanings of the components, which sometimes happens merely because of the popularization of certain classical words [6].

> (9) 吴公差强人意，隐若一敌国矣！（《东观汉记·八·吴汉传》）

The syntactic structure of "差强人意" is "差*强+人*意"，in which "差" and "强" constitute a verb-centered phrase, while "人" 和 "意" constitute a noun-centered phrase. "差强" and "人意"constitute a "V+O" idiom. "差强人意" originally meant "to encourage or excite people", for instance, .

> (10) 太祖喜曰："李万岁所言，差强人意。"（《周书·李远传》二五）

Then, "差强人意"meant "to be satisfying", which was the first extended meaning of the idiom.

> (11) 奉常差强人意，但觉亦欠子细商量，甚恨前此匆匆，不能甚款也。（《朱文公集·四八·答吕子约》）

Then, "差强人意" got the meaning "to be satisfying in general", which is the second extended meaning.

(12) 2003年该站比赛冠军、威廉姆斯车队车手蒙托亚此次表现差强人意，仅名列第五。

Retrieving CCL corpus of Modern Chinese [1], we can get 77 entries of "差强人意" in Modern Chinese, among which 53 entries have the original meaning and the first two extended meanings, and 24 entries have a new meaning(the third extended meaning)—"not satisfying because of the bad situation."

Ostensibly, the form of "差强人意" remains unchanged; however, it has changed indeed. The form of this idiom with the first extended meaning is "差(chā)强(qiáng)人意" which is called the original form. Here "差"is an adverbial with the meaning "a little, slightly", and "强" is verb with the meaning "to be inspired, excited". The idioms "殊强人意"、"甚强人意" are variants of the original form. The components "殊"、"甚" and "差" are in the same position and similar in meaning, i.e. "very". The form of this idiom with the second and third extended meaning is "差(chà)强(qiǎng)人意", which is called the later form. Here "差" is an adjective with the meaning "bad, not good enough", "强" is an adverbial, meaning "barely". Language users are more familiar with the later form because of its high frequency in daily use. Consequently, when we do not have a careful study of the meaning of the idiom, we may pick up a new (but not correct) meaning for it.

Sometimes the substitution of meanings occurs with the substitution of the components of the same pronunciation or with the evolution of the lexicon. For example, both the form and pronunciation of the word "错" of the idiom "铸成大错" are substituted. "正经" of the idiom "一本正经" is substituted in form, and also is a disyllabic word changed from two syllables.

1.4   De-etymologization

De-etymologization refers to the practice that language users tend to understand the meaning of an idiom from the literal meanings of the components without considering the etymology. Zhu Chuhong tries to offer account from the perspective of context [7]. The "context" defined by Mr. Zhu and the "etymology" are similar but not the same terms. The "context" refers to the language environment in which the idiom was created. "Etymology" refers to the special meaning of the idiom when the content of the idiom is mapped onto the form. It is more proper to use "etymology" than "context". The main reason for language users disregarding the etymology is their strangeness to the etymology because of the development of the time. Consider the following example:

(13) 宁武子，邦有道则知，邦无道则愚。其知可及也，其愚不可及也。（《论语·公冶长》）

"愚" in (13) means "to pretend to be ignorant in a disadvantageous situation," it is a praise of the power of Ning Wuzi in politics from Confucius. "愚不可及" can be understood as "very wise", which is the original meaning of the idiom. In Modern Chinese, however, "愚不可及" is a negative expression with the meaning "very stupid", as in (14), which is the extended meaning of the idiom.

(14) 那个叫做里瓦雷兹的倒霉蛋昨天把这篇愚不可及的文章提交给了委员会。
(CCL)

The original meaning of the idioms includes semantic meanings which cannot be got from the literal meanings of the components. "愚" is endowed a special meaning. The semantic meanings are due to the etymology of the idioms. And the extended meanings of the idioms are just from the literal meanings of the components with no influence from the etymology.

2   Changes in the Combination of the Components

Once the combination relationship of the components has changed, new denotation will be generated, thus causing the semantic change of idioms. The above change refers to the changes in analyzing the grammatical structures of idioms and manifests itself in two aspects, namely the segmentation of components and the qualitative determination of components.

2.1   Different Segmentation of Components

Idioms in Chinese usually consist of two or more components. One idiom can sometimes be segmented into different syntactic structures, which will yield different combination relationships between the components.

Here in this example, "花朝月夕" [*hua zhao yue xi*], literally denoting "mornings with bloomy flowers, and nights with bright moon", is frequently used to mean "wonderful time with fine scenery".

(15) （威）招纳文人，聚书至万卷。每花朝月夕，与宾佐赋咏，甚有情致。（《
旧唐书·罗威传》）

While in this example, "花朝月夕" [*hua zhao yue xi*] actually refers to "Flower Festival celebrating the birthday of all flowers on the 15th day of the 2nd lunar month" and "mid-autumn festival on the 15th of the 8th lunar month", as shown in (16):

(16) 盖花朝月夕，世俗恒言。二八两月为春秋之中，故以二月半为花朝，八月
半为月夕也。（明田汝成《熙朝乐事》）

When the original meaning is to be expressed, the components of this idiom are all monosyllabic words, thus indicating the syntactic structure "花*朝+月*夕". However, when the derived meaning is desired, the components fall into two disyllabic words, namely "花朝" [*hua zhao*] and "月夕" [*yue xi*]. Both are proper names.

According to the old folk customs, fifteenth of the 2nd lunar month is the birthday of flowers —hence acquiring the name "花朝" [*hua zhao*]. As is recorded in the book *Meng Liang Lu* written by Wu Zimu of the Southern Dynasty, "the customs of Zhejiang area have 15th of the 2nd lunar month celebrated as the flower festival. is the reason is that the day, in the middle of the spring, is considered as a time for all sorts of flowers to come into bloom and also the prime time for sightseeing." The day called "月夕" [*yue xi*] refers solely to the Mid-Autumn Festival. Also in this book, Wu Zimu says "the 15th of the 8th lunar month is in the middle of autumn and hence called the mid-autumn.

During that night, the moon is notably brighter than it normally is. That day is also called "月夕" [*yue xi*]. Different segmentations of the components will result in different combination relations, from which different denotations have derived. These denotations have further generated different derived meanings, thus causing the semantic change of idioms.

2.2   Different Qualitative Determination of Components

Qualitative determinations actually define the components segmented out each time from the idioms. The basis for the definition is the grammatical relations between two components. Any change in the grammatical relations will lead to the semantic change of idioms. Consider the following example:

(17)   犹冀玄当洗濯胸腑，小惩大诫，而狼心弗革，悖慢愈甚。（《魏书·恒玄传》）

Here, "小惩大诫" [*xiao cheng da jie*] can be understood with the original meaning as "the minor offense imposed on someone so as give him a lesson and prevent him from serious blunders". In the later literature, "小惩大诫" [*xiaocheng dajie*] referred to "either mild or severe punishment", as shown in (18):

(18)   亦有调停两和怿，反复无常旋构隙。小惩大诫终何益。（清黄安涛《打怨家》诗）

In expressing the original meaning, "*cheng*" is a verb and means "to punish". "*jie*" is also a verb and means "to warn". The syntactic structure of this idiom is a compact structure of a complex clause. Therefore, the idiom means "using mild punishment to prevent bigger mistakes".

Being used to express the derived meaning, both "惩" [*cheng*] and "戒" [*jie*] are nouns, denoting "punishment" and "warning" respectively. Thus, "小惩" [*xiao cheng*] refers to mild punishment while "大戒" [*da jie*] means harsh punishment. The idiom is a coordinate phrases, with its syntactic structure being "小*惩+大*诫".

In the semantic evolution of this idiom, "惩" [*cheng*] and "戒" [*jie*] are converted from nouns into verbs, causing the idiom's original compact structure of a complex clause changing into a nominal structure of coordination. Due to the approximately corresponding relationship between lexical meaning and grammatical meaning, the conversion between nouns and verbs is a widespread phenomenon. There are still many lexical meanings and grammatical relations of Ancient Chinese remained in idioms. So for them, the changes in part of speech of their components are relatively common.

The same idiom can have different etymologies which will make the form of this idiom bear different grammatical relations.

(19)   而后酌量经帑，制定薪津，亦先忧后乐也。（钱基博《辛亥江南光复实录》）

"先忧后乐[1]" [*xian you hou le*] first appeared in *Da Dai Li Ji* compiled in the West Han Dynasty, and meant "if people are worried about their business and then strive for it, they shall enjoy the success of it; if people are indulged in enjoyments and leave their business unfinished, they will end up worrying about the failure of it".

The idioms can be interpreted as "only by hard working first can people harvest success and happiness at last".

(20)　然先忧后乐之志，海内固已信其有弘毅之器。（《宋史·范仲淹论传》）

While "先忧后乐₂" [*xian you hou le*] originate from *Account of Yueyang Building* written by Fan Zhongyan of Song Dynasty, it means "then, when they were happy? They would say, 'to be first to worry about the affairs of the state and the last to enjoy oneself'". The idiom actually means "to be the first to worry about the affairs of the state and to be the last to enjoy oneself."

The syntactic structure of "先忧后乐₁" is a compact structure of a conditional complex clause and can be divided into two parts, namely "to worry first" and "to enjoy last". The former is the prerequisite of the latter while the latter is the results after accomplishing the former. However, "先忧后乐₂" is the contracted form of "to be the first to worry about the affairs of the state and to be the last to enjoy oneself". Different etymologies have given rise to different meanings and different syntactic structures of the same idiom.

3　Changes in the Semantic Focus

Different components make different contributions to the meanings of an idiom. The components serving as the basis of expressing or deriving meanings have a prominent role within the idioms and serve as the semantic focus, while other comparatively marginal components are, of course, not the focus. However, the focus of meaning of idioms can change with the time, which will definitely result in different interpretations of idioms. Consider the following example:

(21)　无情六合乾坤里，颠鸾倒凤，撑霆裂月，直被消磨。（金元好问《促伯丑奴儿·学闲闲公体》）

In this example, "颠鸾倒凤" originally refers to "the inversion of the order". However, "颠鸾倒凤" can be used to imply the sexual intercourse between men and women, thus it has derived another meaning, as shown in (22):

(22)　小生得到卧房内，和小姐解带脱衣，颠鸾倒凤，同谐鱼水之欢，共效于飞之愿。（元王实甫《西厢记》）

The idiom focuses on "颠倒" [*diandao*] (to put upside down) when it comes to the literal sense. In this respect, the words "鸾" [*Luan*] (male phoenix) and "凤" [*Feng*] (female phoenix) are weaker in presenting their senses and could be easily replaced by other words, such as " Dian San Dao Si", without affecting the comprehension of the idiom. When it comes to the extended meaning, however, the idiom puts its emphasis on "Luan" and "Feng", together with "Dian" and "Dao" to express an extended meaning. "Luan" and "Feng" are divine birds from the legend, which are used to represent couples. In *Lasting Words to Awaken the World* of the Ming Dynasty, it says "the happy couples may fight, while the foes may unite." Besides, a lot of idioms tend to use "鸾" and "凤" to refer to a couples, for example, "鸾凤和鸣" [*Luan Feng He Ming*] (harmony in marriage), "镜分鸾凤" [*Jing Fen Luan Feng*] (a couple part), and so on and so forth. By combining "鸾凤" (to refer to couples) and "颠倒" (to refer to the action) and via mediating of imagination, the extended meaning of the idiom "Dian Luan Dao Feng" is constructed.

4   Conclusion

To interpret idioms based on their lexical and syntactic forms is usually considered improper. However, this phenomenon of reinvesting forms with new meaning is not unjustified and is a result of the internal mechanism of human language.

Firstly, the interpretation of idioms with reference to their forms is essentially a reanalysis and reinterpretation of idioms based on their components. In the process of construing familiar idioms, language users tend to perform this task by taking a holistic view. For those unfamiliar ones, however, they tend to understand it part by part. If there are more than one option for them to understand the components of an idiom (in terms of their meaning and inter relations), reanalysis might occurs, and new literal meaning might thus be obtained.

Secondly, the Economy principle plays an essential role in the understanding of an idiom. In accordance with their mental lexicon, language users tend to interpret an idiom of archaic or unusual meaning with respect to common understandings. Specifically, it means to replace the obscure meaning with concrete meaning, mapping the familiar concrete concepts onto strange and abstract ones.

Acknowledgments. We would like to express our sincere gratitude to Dr. Shaoshuai Shen for helping us to polish earlier drafts of the current paper. We also wish to acknowledge the anonymous reviewers for their valuable comments. The study is jointly supported by the Humanities and Social Sciences by the Ministry of Education (14YJC740115), and Social Science Foundation of Henan Province (2014CYY011).

References

1. Shi, C.: On Changes of Application and Development of Idioms. Chinese Language Learning (6), 37–43 (2006). (in Chinese)
2. Chinese corpus of Peking University. http://ccl.pku.edu.cn:8080/ccl_corpus/. Accessed frequently from October 10, 2013 until now
3. Luo, Z.: The Grand Chinese Dictionary. Shanghai Lexicographical Publishing House, Shanhai (1986). (in Chinese)
4. Language Research Institute, Chinese Academy of Social Science. Contemporary Chinese Dictionary, 6th edn. The Commercial Press, Beijing (2012). (in Chinese)
5. China's National Linguistics Work Committee: Lexicon of Common Words in Contemporary Chinese (draft). The Commercial Press, Beijing (2008). (in Chinese)
6. Su, B.: Popularization of Some Classical Words. Language Planning (1), 27–28 (1993). (in Chinese)
7. Zhu, C.: A New Perspective on Idioms' Unusual Meaning Extending. Language and Culture Press, Beijing (2010). (in Chinese)

A Cognitive Grammar Approach to Relative Antonyms

Fengmei Ren[✉]

School of Foreign Languages, Henan University, Kaifeng 475001, China
renfm070608@163.com

Abstract. The semantic meaning of relative antonyms *AB* is the absolute construal and relative construal of the properties of the object concerned, with the normal quantity being the reference point. When *A* which denotes higher salience or *B* which denotes lower salience appears individually in usage events, *A* is used in priority to *B*. The cognitive motivation lies in prominence, and the properties which enjoy a higher cognitive prominence are represented in priority to those which enjoy a lower cognitive prominence. When *A* and *B* co-occur in usage events, the difference in the lexical categories of *AB* (adjectives, nouns and adverbs) is motivated by their different semantic profiles.

Keywords: Relative antonyms · Construal · Cognitive prominence · Semantic profile

1 Introduction

Leech (1983) defined "an antonymic relation" as "the opposite or contrastive semantic meaning existing between one word and another" and "antonyms" as "words that have opposite or contrastive meanings". In *Modern Chinese Dictionary* (5th edition), "antonyms" are defined as "words that have opposite meanings". Antonyms are classified into absolute antonyms and relative antonyms (Lehrer1985; Leech 1983; Croft& Cruse 2004). The former type refers to a pair of antonyms whose semantic meanings are exclusive and there does not exist a transitional state between the states they refer to, for instance, *true/false*, *dead/alive* and *married/single*, etc. in English and 生[*sheng*](*alive*)/死[*si*](*dead*) and真[*zhen*](*true*)/假[*jia*](*false*), etc. in Chinese are absolute antonyms; while the latter refers to a pair of antonyms whose meanings are opposite but not exclusive, for instance, *big/small*, *tall/short*, *old/young*, *heavy/light* and *good/bad*, etc. in English and 高[*gao*](*tall*)/低[*di*](*short*), 好[*hao*](*good*)/坏[*huai*](*bad*) and 胖[*pang*](*stout*)/瘦[*shou*](*slim*), etc. in Chinese are relative antonyms. Antonyms are popular in Chinese language use. The following are some examples.

(1)这种蘑菇有多大？——直径4米多，重达100千克 。
Zhezhong mogu you duo da? ---Zhijing 4 mi duo, zhong da 100 qianke.
This kind of mushroom how big? ---Diameter 4 meters more, heavy to 100 kilograms.
'How **big** is this kind of mushroom? ---It has a diameter of more than 4 meters and is as **heavy** as 100 kilograms.'

X. Su and T. He (Eds.): CLSW 2014, LNAI 8922, pp. 75–84, 2014.
DOI: 10.1007/978-3-319-14331-6_8

(2) 在非洲，有一种常被误认为昆虫的蜂鸟，身长不足2厘米，只有2克重。

Zai Feizhou, you yizhong chang bei wu renwei kunchong de fengniao, shenchang buzu 2 limi, zhiyou 2 ke zhong.

In Africa, there is a kind of often mistaken for hummingbird, body long less more than 2 centimeters, only 2 grams heavy.

'In Africa, there is a kind of hummingbird often mistaken for an insect, whose body is less than 2 centimeters **long** and as **heavy** as only 2 grams.'

(3) 他家的客厅有多大？ ---8平方。

Ta jia de keting you duo da? ---8 pingfang.

His house's sitting room how big? ---8 square meters.

'How **big** is the sitting room in his house? ---8 square meters.'

From the corpus including the above examples, we discover that speakers tend to use a relative antonym denoting a higher scale rather than one denoting a lower scale when they describe the properties (height, size, weight, etc.) of an object. For instance, speakers prefer to say *How big /long/heavy is ...* rather than *How small/short/light is....*This inclination in language use can be seen in both English and Chinese as is shown in sentences (1)-(3). In sentence (3), for instance, a sitting room with a size of 8 square meters is not considered a big one, yet, when peopole ask about its size, they prefer to say "他家的客厅有多大？" [*Tajia de keting you duo da?*] (*How **big** is the sitting room in his house?*) rather than "他家的客厅有多小？"[*Tajia de keting you duo xiao?*] (*How small is the sitting room in his house?*) The preference of a relative antonym denoting a higher scale to one denoting a lower scale can also be seen in other languages besides Chinese and English. For instance, in French, people prefer to say "*Comment est cela **lourd**?*" (*How **heavy** is this ?*) rather than "**Comment est cela léger?*" (*How light is this ?*). In Russian, people prefer to say "*Как **высоко** это здание ?* " (*How **tall** is the building ?*) rather than "*Как низко это здание?* "(*How short is the building ?*) Similarly, the minority group in China speaking Uyghur language ask about the width of a river by "*bu dɛrjaniŋ kɛŋliki qantʃɛ?*" (*How wide is the river?*) instead of "*bu dɛrjaniŋ tarliqi qantʃɛ?* "(*How narrow is the river?*) (Cited from Zhang Ling 2013). This inclination to use a relative antonym to denote the scale of an object works unless there is a preassumption. For instance, in a specific situation, the speaker and the listener both know that the river is very narrow, then "*How narrow is the river?*" is acceptable.

Based on our observation of Chinese relative antonyms, we find that Chinese speakers (like other language speakers) have an inclination to use a relative antonym denoting a higher scale rather than one denoting a lower scale when describing the properties of an object. What cognitive motivation, then, lies behind such an inclination prevalent in Chinese as well as in other languages?

Further observation of Chinese relative antonyms leads us to the discovery that Chinese relative antonyms can not only be used individually but in pairs as can be seen in the following instances (4)-(9).

(4) 当时规定自一品至七品，在不同颜色的官服上要分别绣上大小不同的花朵。

Dangshi guiding zi yipin zhi qipin, zai butong yanse de guanfu shang yao fenbie xiu shang daxiao butong de huaduo.

At that time rule from the first rank to the seventh rank, in different colors official uniforms must embroidery big small different flowers.

'At that time, it was ruled that uniforms for officials from the first to the seventh rank must have embroidered flowers of different **sizes**.'

(5) 莫斯科，是一座有800多年历史的名城。它建立在7个**高低**起伏的山丘上，整个城 市就像一个大蜘蛛网。

Mosike,shi yizuo you 800 duonian lishi de mingcheng. Ta jianli zai 7-ge gaodi qifu de shanqiu shang, zhengge chengshi jiu xiang yige da zhizhuwang.

Moscow is a having 800 more years historic famous city. It built on 7 high low winding hills, the whole city just like a big spider net.

'Moscow is a famous city with a history of more than 800 years. It is built on 7 hills of different **heights**, and the whole city is just like a big spider net.'

(6) 好风好雨好时节，枯木逢春，又从一边生出一株幼桑来，现已有碗口**粗细**。

Haofeng haoyu hao shijie, kumu fengchun, you cong yibian shengchu yizhu you sang lai, xian yi you wankou cuxi.

Good wind good rain good season, withered wood meeting spring, from one side grow a young mulberry, now has bowl thick and thin.

'With the favorable spring wind and rain, a young mulberry grows from one side of the withered tree, and now the **size** of its trank is as big as the mouth of a bowl.'

(7) 皇上认为高允太不识**好歹**，吆喝一声，叫武士把他捆绑起来。

Huangshang renwei gaoyun bushi haodai, yaohe yisheng, jiao wushi ba ta kunbang qilai.

The emporor thought Gao Yun didn't know goodness and badness, shouted once, ordered the soldiers to fasten him.

'The emporor thought that Gaoyun din't know what was good for him, and shouted to order the soldiers to fasten him with a rope.'

(8) 嘴都说破了，老王**高低**不答应。

Zui dou shuopo le, lao Wang gaodi bu daying.

Mouth even speak damaged, elderly Wang high and low didn't agree.

'Despite my exhausting persuasion, elderly Wang refused to agree **anyway**.'

(9) 孩子**死活**都不去幼儿园。

Haizi sihuo dou buqu youeryuan.

The kid dead and alive not go to the kindergarten.

'The kid would not go to the kindergarten **anyway**.'

From the above instances, we can see that the lexical category of Chinese relative antonyms used in pairs can be adjectives as in (4)-(5), nouns as in (5)-(7), as well as adverbs as in (8)-(9). This is one of the features of Chinese as we see that in the English versions of these Chinese sentences, their equivalent expressions are single words. In English, people incline to describe the properties of an object with an individual adjective or individual noun deriving from an adjective. For instance, when asking about the length of a rope, people say "How **long** is the rope? /What's the **length** of the rope?" This paper does not intend to make a comparative study of relative antonyms in Chinese and other languages, instead, the author intends to have a closer observation of Chinese with some other languages as references. Why, then, can relative antonyms in Chinese used in pairs be realized syntactically as different lexical categories? And what cognitive mechanism is working behind the change in their lexical categories?

With the above questions in mind, the author reviewed literature and found profound research achievements in the study of relative antonyms. Researchers abroad are mostly concerned about the classification and markedness of antonyms. Among these researches, Lehrer (1985) studied antonyms with markedness theory. Leech (1983) classified antonyms into absolute antonyms and relative antonyms from the perspective of semantics. Croft & Cruse (2004) devoted one whole chapter in their book *Cognitive Linguistics* to the classification of relative antonyms, namely, monoscalar antonyms and biscalar antonyms. Researchers at home are mostly concerned about the markedness of relative antonyms. Wang Mingyu (2004) studied the markedness of relative antonyms from the perspective of semiotics and proposed that relative antonyms have an asymmetric relationship between the two contrastive components. Li Shukang (2010) studied the marked models of English antonymic adjectives with prototype theory being the theoretical guidance, and proposed that the marked and unmarked lexical items in every pair of relative antonyms form a semantic category, the unmarked lexical item corresponding to the prototypical members of the category, while the marked lexical item corresponding to the marginal members of the category. Bao Wenshu & Guo Rui (2012) made a comparative study of the markedness of the English and Chinese antonymic adjectives. Niu Baoyi (2007) studied relative antonyms *tall* and *short* with cognitive prominence theory being theoretical guidance, and proposed that priority of high salience is the cognitive motivation of the tendency in relative antonym use. From the above literature review we notice that the research questions raised previously in this paper have not been answered. Therefore, this paper attempts to explain them with construal and prominence thought in cognitive grammar and cognitive gestalt theory.

2   Construal and Prominence

According to cognitive grammar, meaning equates with conceptualization (Langacker, 1991: 4). The semantic meaning of an expression (or its predication) not only lies in the conceptual content it represents, but in the contrual of the conceptual content (Langacker, 1991: 4). The same conceptual content can be construed in many different ways, and every way of construal represents one meaning (Langacker 1991: ix). Construal is the major part of language (Croft & Cruse 2004: 73). It is a human ability to imagine and describe the same situation in different ways. As a basic cognitive ability of human beings, it is the speakers' conceptualization of an object's nature, features and behavior from different perspectives (Langacker, 1987: 140). Construal can be realized as prominence, attention, perspective and the ability of comparison (Croft & Cruse 2004). In the process of construal, the content with higher prominence catches   attention more easily and is often taken as foreground in the construed situation; while the content with lower prominence does not catch attention easily and is often taken as   background or reference in the construed situation (Talmy 2001: 76). The content with higher prominence is used more frequently than that with lower prominence. For instance, the same content "the relative location of a mountain and a temple" can be construed differently because of their different prominence in the construal process. The two objects of construal, "the mountain" and "the temple", have different prominence in the speaker's cognitive processing activity. When the speaker says "山上有座庙" [*Shanshang you zuo miao.*] (*There is a temple on the top of the mountain*), he is taking "the mountain" as a reference point to describe the location of "the temple", and therefore "the temple" receives more attention. "庙下有座山" [*Miao xia you zuo shan.*] (*There is a mountain under the temple.*) is not acceptable to an average speaker, for the reason that in terms of prominence, "the temple" receives the speaker's attention more easily and gets more prominence in his cognitive processing of the situation, and therefore is taken as the foreground information; while the prominence of "the mountain" is relatively lower, and catches less attention from the speaker and receives less prominence in his cognitive processing, therefore, it is taken as the background information or reference. The former expression "山上有座庙" [*Shanshang you zuo miao.*] (*There is a temple on the top of the mountain*) in which "the temple" is more prominent is used more frequently, while the latter expression "庙下有座山" [*Miao xia you zuo shan.*] (*There is a mountain under the temple.*) in which "the mountain" is more prominent is used less frequently.

Based on the above thought, we use *AB* to stand for relative antonyms.The semantic meaning of *AB* is the integration of the two construals with the normal quantity being the reference point. The feature of a construed object more prominent than the normal quantity is construed as *A*; while the feature of a construed object less prominent than the normal quantity is construed as *B*. The semantic construal is the projection of cognitive prominence onto language. We will apply this idea to the explanation of the research questions raised in the previous part of this paper.

3   The Construal of Relative Antonyms

Croft and Cruse (2004) classified construal into absolute construal and relative construal. Take "高/低" [*gao/di*] (*tall/short* or *high/low*) as an example. When we say "Yao Ming is 2.26 meters tall", we have an absolute constual of Yao Ming's height which is accurately measured with a tool. When we say "Yao Ming is very tall", we have a relative construal of his height by taking the normal height of Chinese males (1.75 meters or so) as a reference. In contrast, when we say "Pan Changjiang is very short", we have a relative construal of Pan's height by taking the normal height of Chinese males as a reference, only in the other direction of the scale. From the perspective of semantics, relative antonyms are an integration of two construals of an object's certain properties. Croft & Cruse (2004) explained this kind of monoscalar system with a figure (see Fig. 1).

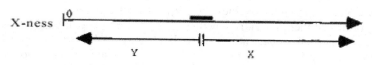

Fig. 1. (Croft & Cruse 2004: 173)

In Fig. 1, *X-ness* means a monoscalar property of a certain object, such as height or length. It is represented by the arrow directing to the right, with "0" at the left end being the starting point. The arrow directing to the right means the overall scale which can be infinitely large. It corresponds to absolute construal (e.g. Yao Ming's height, 2.26 meters.) along which every point represents a specific quantity. The bold short line above this arrow means the normal quantity, for instance, the normal height of a common Chinese (1.75 meters or so). The short arrows X and Y below the long arrow mean the two relative construals of an object's certain property with the normal quantity being the reference point in two opposite directions.   The arrow Y directing to the left means that the quantity of the construed property is lower than the normal quantity (for instance, Pan's height is lower than an average Chinese male's height), while the arrow directing to the right means the scale of the construed property is higher than the normal quantity. From this figure, we can see that every point in the arrow standing for absolute construal corresponds to a specific scale, for instance, 1 cm, 3 kg, 850 tons, etc., and therefore, every point in the arrow standing for relative construal is included in absolute construal.

As is pointed out in the introduction of this paper, of the two components of a relative antonym, A standing for a higher scale is more frequently used than B standing for a lower scale. The cognitive motivation leading to such an inclination of relative antonym usage is cognitive prominence. Based on the observation of human cognitive tendency, cognitive linguistics proposes that for a certain object, the property of a higher scale attracts more human attention, is more prominent in cognitive processing and more easily constued, and when projected onto language, it is processed as figure (or foreground)   and enjoys a priority when being represented in language; the property of a lower scale catches less attention, is less prominent in cognitive processing and is contrued less easily, and when projected onto language, it is processed as ground (or background) and does not enjoy a priority when represented in language (Langacker, 1987: 120). The choice of an object as figure or ground is influenced by many factors. In cognition, an object or the property of an object that is construed with a higher scale (such as a tall man) is more prominent in cognitive processing and enjoys a priority when represented in language, that is to say, it is expressed in a front position of a sentence when described in language. That explains why speakers incline to say sentences like "他家的客厅有多大？ " [*Tajia de keting you duo da?*] (*How big is the sitting room in his house?*)   instead of "他家的客厅有多小？ " [*Tajia de keting you duo xiao?*] (*How small is the sitting room in his house?*)

4   The Lexical Category of Relative Antonyms: Semantic Prominence

Different from the definition of lexical categories in terms of structural distribution analysis, cognitive grammar defines the major lexical categories such as nouns and verbs according to their semantic functions. According to cognitive grammar, lexical categories are not individual entities, but a kind of symbolic structure just like other grammatical categories. The grammatical category of an expression is not determined by its conceptual content, but by its profile (Langacker, 2008: 98). Language expressions can be classified into two types, namely, nominal expressions and relational expressions. The conceptual content of the two can be the same, while their respective construal and their profiles may be different (Langacker 1987, 1991, 2008). In cognitive grammar, a noun represents a thing, and its semantic profile is a region that is prominent in a cognitive field.   Relational expressions can be classified into process-es and atemporal relations according to the temporal factor. A process is represented by a verb, while an atemporal relation is represented either by an adjective, an adverb, an infinitive, a preposition or a participle. The difference between these two types of expressions lies in their different ways of mental scanning. A process is an outcome of sequential scanning and its conceptualization is dynamic, while an atemporal rela-tion is an outcome of summary scanning which produces a cognitive gestalt that is triggered holistically. For instance, the verb *cross* and the preposition *across* are both construal of the same conceptual content "from one side of an object to the other side", but the ways they are conceptualized are different, the former is a dynamic conceptualization of a situation through sequential scanning which scans the changes in the situation from one state to another, while the latter is a summary scanning of all the component states of a dynamic process and the result is a complex concept. The difference between these lexical categories is owing to the different nature of their focal participants, namely, trajector and landmark. A noun profiles a thing that occu-pies a region in a cognitive field. Its semantic structure is represented in Fig. 2, and the circle in it represents a region in a cognitive field. An adjective and an adverb both profile a relation that has only a trajector. An adjective has an object as its trajector, and its semantic structure is represented in Fig. 3, and the circle in it represents the trajector in this relation, the arrow represents the property of the trajector that is con-strued, *n* represents the normal quantity of the property, the dotted line in bold type means that the quantity of the trajector's property of is higher (it can be lower) than the normal quantity. An adverb is different from an adjective in that it has a relation as its trajector which has its own trajector and landmark. Its semantic structure is seen in Fig. 4.

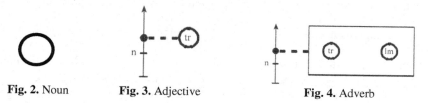

Fig. 2. Noun   **Fig. 3.** Adjective   **Fig. 4.** Adverb

We now apply these thoughts to explain the different lexical categories of relative antonyms.   According to the defining of lexical categories in cognitive grammar, the difference in the lexical categories of the relative antonyms is motivated by their dif-ferent semantic profiles. Take "高低" [*gaodi*] (*high and low*)   for instance.

(10) a. 只见远处的山丘高低起伏, 连绵不断。

   Zhijian yuanchu de shanqiu gaodi qifu, lianmianbuduan.
   Only see the distant hills high and low, endless.
   'We can only see the endless hills in the distance, some are high, and some are low.'

   b. 这座楼高低和那座楼差不多。

   Zhe zuo lou gaodi he na zuo lou chabuduo.
   This building height and that building almost.
   'This building is almost of the same **height** as that one.'

c. 孩子高低不上幼儿园。
Haizi gaodi bu shang youeryuan.
The kid gaodi not go to the kindergarten.
*'The kid wouldn't go to the kindergarten **anyway**.'*

In (10a), "高低" [*gaodi*] (*high and low*) has a semantic profile, i.e., the hills, which is the trajector of the atemporal   relation. The expression "高低" means that the height of the hills is higher or lower than the normal height of a hill on the monoscale. Its semantic structure can be seen in Fig. 5. The circle in it represents the trajector, i.e., the hills, which is the profiled and foregrounded object which is being conceptualized. The solid line represents the relation with only one trajector, that is, the property of "高" [*gao*] (*high*) and "低" [*di*] (*low*) in the monoscale are prominent in cognitive processing. The dotted line represents the property of the hills' height which is not prominent on the monoscale. The two properties "高" [*gao*] (*high*) and "低" [*di*] (*low*) which are prominent in cognition activates the speaker's conceptualization of all the points of height of these hills, therefore, a cognitive gestalt of the hills' height is formed. In the cognitive processing, all the hills in sight as the trajector are being construed and conceptualized instead of the high ones and the low ones only.

In (10b), "高" [*gao*] (*high*) and "低" [*di*] (*low*) represent the two prominent points of height of the construed object (the building), and these two points are foregrounded, the overall scale between the higher point denoted by "高" [*gao*] (*high*) and the lower point denoted by "低" [*di*] (*low*) is profiled and is construed as an abstract region in cognitive processing, therefore it is realized in language as an abstract noun. Its semantic structure is seen in Fig. 6. The dotted circle in it means the object (*this building*) which is not profiled in cognition, but it provides a cognitive access to the construal of the height of the building. The solid line means that the two regions that the object (*this building*) occupies in the cognitive field of height are profiled, and the two profiled regions activate the whole scale of height, including every point in this scale.

Sentence (10c) is different from (10a) only in that the trajector in (10c) is a relation "孩子（不）上幼儿园" [*Haizi (bu) shang youeryuan.*] (*The kid wouldn't go to the kindergarten.*) which has its own trajector and landmark. It is the scope of degree that is profiled. Its semantic structure is seen in Fig. 7. The square in it represents the trajector "孩子（不）上幼儿园" [*Haizi (bu) shang youeryuan.*] (*The kid wouldn't go to the kindergarten.*) which is a process with its own trajector "孩子" [*haizi*] (*this kid*) and landmark "幼儿园" [*youeryuan.*] (*the kindergarten*). Both the solid and dotted lines represent the relation between the trajector "孩子（不）上幼儿园" [*Haizi (bu) shang youeryuan.*] (*The kid wouldn't go to the kindergarten.*) and its degree: the solid lines mean the two degrees represented by "高" [*gao*] (*high*) and "低" [*di*] (*low*) are profiled in cognitive processing, and the dotted lines mean that the degrees they represent are not profiled. The bold line between the two points "高" and "低" means that these two profiled regions of degree activate the whole scale of degree between them, and thereby a cognitive gestalt of the degree to which the trajector "孩子（不）上幼儿园" works. The gestalt of the degree includes every point (region) in this scale, thus the metonymic meaning (*anyway*) of "高低" is derived.

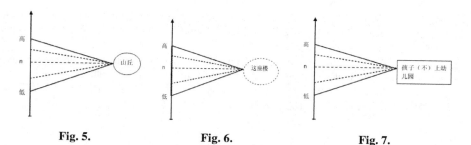

Fig. 5.   **Fig. 6.**   **Fig. 7.**

5   Conclusion

Based on a careful observation of Chinese corpus in comparison with other languages, this paper studied the inclination in the use of Chinese relative antonyms and their different lexical category realizations when used in pairs. · It proposed that the semantic meaning of a relative antonym is the absolute or relative construal of an object's property in terms of a scale with the normal quantity being the reference point. When used individually, the relative antonym denoting a higher scale enjoys a priority. The cognitive motivation lies in that the property with higher prominece receives more attention in cognitve processing and is represented in language prior to the property with lower prominence. When used in pairs, the relative antonym is realized differently in terms of its lexical category, and its different lexical categories in different usage events is motivated by the different semantic profie as well as the function of cognitive gestalt.

References

1. Bao, W., Guo, R.: A comparison of the markedness of anti-sense adjectives between English and Chinese based on Prototype Theory. Journal of Guizhou University (Social Sciences) (1), 146–149 (2012). (in Chinese)
2. Croft, W., Cruse, D.: Cognitive Linguistics. Oxford University Press, Cambridge (2004)
3. Langacker, R.W.: Foundations of Cognitive Grammar, vol. I. Stanford University Press, California (1987)
4. Langacker, R.W.: Foundations of Cognitive Grammar, vol. II. Stanford University Press, California (1991)
5. Langacker, R.W.: Cognitive Grammar: A Basic Introduction. Oxford University Press, New York (2008)
6. Leech, G.: Semantics. Penguin, Harmondsworth (1983)
7. Lehrer, A.: Markedness and antonymy. Journal of Linguistics **21**, 397–429 (1985)
8. Li, S.: Prototypical effects in markedness of English adjective antonyms. Journal of Beijing University of Aeronautics and Astronautics (Social Sciences Edition) (1), 98–102 (2010). (in Chinese)
9. Niu, B.: Salience priority: A cognitive study of relative antonym s like *tall-short*. Foreign Language Research (2), 46–52 (2007). (in Chinese)
10. Talmy, L.: Toward a Cognitive Semantics: Concept Structuring Systems, vol. I. The MIT Press, Cambridge (2000)

11. Wang, M.: The markedness of language semiotics and its expression in antonyms. Foreign Language Research (3), 1–10 (2004) (王铭玉. 语言符号的标记性及其在反义词偶中的体现. 外语学刊, (3), 1–10 (2004)). (in Chinese)
12. Zhang, L.: On the anti-sense and asymmetry of antonymic adjectives in the Uygur language. Journal of Southwest University for Nationalities (Humanities and Social Sciences) (5), 179–182 (2013) (张玲. 维吾尔语反义形容词不对称现象解析. 西南民族大学学报 (人文社会科学版) (5), 179–182 (2013)). (in Chinese)

Instantiations of the Generation Mechanism of A-not-A Question in Chinese and Some Relevant Syntactic Issues

Yuan Tian[1(✉)] and Jie Xu[2]

[1] School of Chinese Language and Literature, Wuhan University, Wuhan, Hubei, China
hntianyuan@gmail.com
[2] Department of Chinese, University of Macau, Taipa, Macau, China
Xujie007@gmail.com

Abstract. Different subtypes of A-not-A question in Chinese are all generated through the mechanism of "Positive-Negative Reduplication" (and "Deletion") with different restrictions and conditions, which can provide explanations for many basic commons and characteristic among these subtypes of A-not-A question and some relevant interrogative sentences. The generation abilities of A-not-A question among the different constructions are variable. And the generation mechanisms of A-not-A question and "K-VP" question play important role in issues on the confusion of classification, mixed sentence in dialects and whether it can be embedded.

Keywords: A-not-A question · Generation mechanism · Instantiation

1 Introduction

Different nationalities use different methods to express interrogative category. The syntactic structures of Han nationality to express interrogative category mainly include yes-no question, constituent question, disjunctive question and A-not-A question. A-not-A question is the most special one among the four questions from the angle of linguistic typology. Besides the languages of minority nationalities in the south of China and languages in South and Southeast Asia, A-not-A question is rare in other languages of world. (Wu 2008) So it becomes a hotpot in the research of Chinese grammar, and different schools do systemic and multi-angle researches on it. Differ from traditional descriptive grammar's focusing on the classification of A-not-A question, (Fan 1982, Zhu 1985, Tang 1981 and Wu 1990 etc.) generative grammar scholars concentrate on its generation mechanism. From 1950s or 1960s on, domestic and overseas Chinese researchers began their studies on the generation process of A-not-A question from both theories and practices. (Wang 1967, Huang 1988, Huang et al. 2009, Xu and Tian 2013).

As a special Chinese question expression, A-not-A question are very common in mandarin, Chinese dialects and some minority languages in China. Generally, A-not-A question consists of three basic subtypes: "A-not-A", "A-not-AB" and "AB-not-A". These subtypes of A-not-A question have certain similarities, while the differences of syntactic features and distribution in dialects become the important issues the generative grammar scholars focus on when they discuss the generation mechanism, so these subtypes are usually treated differently according to their characteristics.

© Springer International Publishing Switzerland 2014
X. Su and T. He (Eds.): CLSW 2014, LNAI 8922, pp. 85–98, 2014.
DOI: 10.1007/978-3-319-14331-6_9

In the researches focused on the generation mechanism of A-not-A question, "Conjunction Reduction" by Wang (1967), "Modular Approach" by Huang (1988) and Huang et al. (2009) had more important influence. Wang (1967) proposed that various forms of A-not-A question and disjunctive question are both resulted by the successive optional application of reduction process. However, this analysis has obstacles on the "Directionality Constraint", "Principle of Lexical Integrity" and "Principle against Preposition-Stranding".

Huang (1988) and Huang et al. (2009) believed that the two subtypes of A-not-A question: "V-not-VP" and "VP-not-V" should be distinguished and should be treated as the results of different generation mechanisms. The base form of "A-not-AB" is a simple sentence with an interrogative inflectional category with [+Q] feature, which is reflected as reduplication in the phonetic form (Reduplicate the initial component first, and then turn the same component in the latter into negative form). While "AB-not-A" is resulted from deletions of the base form which has coordinate predicates (The two items of this coordinate predicates structure are connected through an empty "还是[haishi](or)" with [+Q][A-not-A] feature). This analysis is effective to distinguish two subtypes of A-not-A question according to two different deriving mechanisms, and it really can explain the differences of the two subtypes to a certain extent. But it focused too more on their differences than similarities, and it seemed too complex. (Xu and Tian 2013)

2   Reduplication (and Deletion)--The Unified Generation Mechanism of "A-not-A" Question

Based on the past studies concentrated more on their different characteristics, Xu and Tian (2013) paid more attention on the common similarities of three basic subtypes of A-not-A question and taking their respective characteristics into account at the same time, proposing that the generation mechanism of A-not-A question should be treated in unified analysis instead of in separated way, and put forward that "reduplication (and deletion)" can deal with the generation issues of all subtypes of A-not-A question. The simple and effective two-step operation can not only reflects the common similarities but also deals with the differences among subtypes of A-not-A question.

The operations related to the generation mechanism of the three subtypes: "A-not-A", "A-not-AB" and "AB-not-A" are only "Reduplication" and "Deletion". The limited operation of "Reduplication" and "Deletion" can generate all subtypes of A-not-A question.

Reduplication, as the compulsory operation induced by grammatical features, is used to check the interrogative feature[1]. Reduplication is the Positive-Negative Reduplication operation of relevant components in the predicate-initial position [2].

---

[1] Interrogative category can be achieved through many forms. In Chinese, there are two processing methods of interrogative category-- "interrogative modal particle adjoining" and "positive-negative reduplication", and the relevant grammatical mechanism will choose one from these two processing methods when it meets interrogative category. Chinese positive-negative reduplication is a dynamic process of interrogative category. (Xu 2000,2001).

[2] The So called predicate-initial position is the initial of the predicate in Chinese sentence. More about predicate-initial position can be seen in Xu (2006) , Xu and Li (2010).

The reduplication could refer to the whole predicate (the whole verb phrase or adjective phrase), the first one or several syllables of the verb or adjective. Both "A-not-A" and "A-not-AB" can be generated just through "Positive-Negative Reduplication" ("X-not-X"), the only difference between them is the scope of reduplication. If X is the whole predicate(AB), the output is "AB-not-AB"; If X is the first one or several syllables of the verb or adjective, the output is "A-not-AB". Differ from these two subtypes; the generation of "AB-not-A" also needs "Deletion".

Deletion is motivated by some pragmatics features, so it is the optional operation. After the reduplication of the whole predicate(AB), we can get a whole "AB-not-AB" form, and then we could do the deletion to the last part of the second B of "AB-not-AB" then get the "AB-not-A". Reduplication is syntactically motivated to check the interrogative features, so it is compulsory. While deletion is pragmatically motivated, and it is just the deletion of some parts which are not essential. As to the extent of deletion, it depends on speaker's pragmatics mind and context.

The proposal, using "reduplication (and deletion)" to deal with "AB-not-A" and "A-not-AB" which is put forward by Xu and Tian (2013), is more simple and direct, and can solve the existing issues and explain the differences between "AB-not-A" and "A-not-AB". Basically speaking, the reason of these differences is that the operation conditions of reduplication and deletion are different. Reduplication does not need to obey "Principle of Lexical Integrity" and "Principle against Preposition-Stranding", but deletion must obey them. Therefore, "A-not-AB" which is only referring to reduplication procedure need not obey "Principle of Lexical Integrity" and "Principle against Preposition-Stranding", while "AB-not-A" referring to reduplication and deletion must.

3 The Instantiation of Unified Generation Mechanism of Reduplication (and Deletion)

According to Xu and Tian (2013), all subtypes of Chinese A-not-A question are the outputs of executing reduplication (and deletion) operations in different ways. This simple operational program actualizes in different ways in different sentences. Next we will explain the instantiation of A-not-A question under "Positive-Negative Reduplication (and deletion)" analysis with examples like verbs and adjectives of single syllable, verbs and adjectives of double syllables, verbs of single syllable with object and verbs of double syllables with object.

3.1 Verb and Adjective of Single Syllable

The verbs and adjectives of single syllable just refer to "Positive-Negative Reduplication" in the generation of "A-not-A" question. There is no need and not possible to execute deletion. After reduplication, basic "A-not-A" question is formed.

(1)　　　你　　看不看？

　　　　　Ni　　kan-bu-kan

　　　　　You　look- not-look

　　　　　Do you look at it or not?

(2)   他   帅不帅？

Ta   shuai-bu-shuai

He   handsome-not-handsome

Is he handsome or not?

3.2   Verb and Adjective of Double Syllables

(3)   a.   你   喜欢不喜欢？

Ni   xihuan-bu-xihuan

You   like-not-like

Do you like it or not?

b.   你   喜不喜欢？

Ni   xi-bu-xihuan

You   li-not-like

Do you like it or not?

c.   *你   喜欢不喜？

Ni   xihuan-bu-xi

You   like -not-li

Intended reading: *Do you like it or not?*

(4)   a.   她   漂亮不漂亮？

Ta   piaoliang-bu-piaoliang?

She   beautiful-not- beautiful?

Is she beautiful or not?

b.   她   漂不漂亮？

Ta   piao-bu-piaoliang?

She   beau-not- beautiful?

Is she beautiful or not?

c.   *她   漂亮不漂？

Ta   piaoliang-bu-piao?

She   beautiful-not- beau?

Intended reading: *Is she beautiful or not?*

Through "Positive-Negative Reduplication", Verb and adjective of double syllables can directly generate two subtypes: "A-not-A" and "A-not-AB". There are two situations. The first is the reduplication of the whole verb "喜欢[*xihuan*](*like*)", leading to the basic form "AB-not-AB" ((3a) "你喜欢不喜欢[*ni xihuan bu xihuan*](*Do you like it or not?*) "; the second is the reduplication of the first syllable of verb "喜欢

[*xihuan*](*like*) " leading to the subtype of "A-not-AB" (（3b） "你喜不喜欢[*ni xi bu xihuan*](*Do you like it or not?*) ". After reduplication, we can do deletion theoretically, but the output of deletion must meet the conditions of "Principle of Lexical Integrity" and "Principle against Preposition-Stranding". (3c) "*你喜欢不喜[*ni xihuanbuxi*](*Do you like it or not?*)" cannot be generated directly through duplication, because the two units besides the negative component are not the same, it does not follow the basic requirement of "X-not-X" reduplication. So it can only be got through deletion after "Positive-Negative Reduplication". But "喜[*xi*](*li(ke)*)"is not a whole word that can be used alone, it is just a part of the word "喜欢[*xihuan*](*like*)", it disobeys the "Principle of Lexical Integrity", so (3c) is ungrammatical. The generation of adjective A-not-A question in (4) has the same problem with (3). So, verb and adjective of double syllables can only generate two subtypes: "A-not-A" and "A-not-AB".

3.3   Single-Syllable-Verb with Object

（5）   a.   你   吃早饭不吃早饭？

             Ni   chizaofan-bu-chizaofan?

             You   eat breakfast -not- eat breakfast

             Do you have breakfast *or not?*

       b.   你   吃不吃早饭？

             Ni   chi-bu-chizaofan?

             You   eat -not- eat breakfast

             Do you have breakfast or not?

       c.   你   吃早饭不吃？

             Ni   chizaofan-bu-chi?

             You   *eat breakfast-not-eat*

             Do you have breakfast or not?

（6）   a.   她   买书不买书？

             Ta   maishu-bu-maishu?

             She   buy the book not buy the book

             Does she buy the book or not?

       b.   她   买不买书？

             Ta   mai-bu-maishu?

             She   buy not buy the book

             Does she buy the book or not?

       c.   她   买书不买？

             Ta   maishu-bu-mai?

             She   buy the book not buy

             Does she buy the book or not?

After the reduplication and deletion of the VO phrase, the three subtypes of A-not-A question could be generated. Taking "买书[*mai shu*](*buy book*)" as the example.

(7)   a.   他   买书。

Ta   maishu

He   buy book

He is buying the book.

b.   他   买书不买书？

Ta   maishu bu maishu

He buy book not buy book

Does he buy the book or not?

c.   他   买书不买？

Ta   maishu bu mai

He   buy book not buy

Does he buy the book or not?

d.   他   买不买书？

Ta   mai bu maishu

He   buy not buy book

Does he buy the book or?

First, after the "Positive-Negative Reduplication" of the whole VP "买书 [*maishu*](*buy the book*)" in (7a), (7b)"他买书不买书[*ta maishu bu maishu*](*Does he buy the book or not?*) ("AB-not-AB") " is generated. If continue to operate deletion, the second object "书[*shu*](*book*)" can be deleted, then (7c) "你买书不买[*ni maishu bu mai*](*Do you buy the book or not?*)("AB-not-A")" is generated.

If at the first step "Positive-Negative Reduplication", only the verb "买[*mai*](*buy*)" in the VO phrase "买书[*maishu*](*buy book*)" is reduplicated, (7d)"你买不买书"[*ni maibumaishu*](*Do you* buy the book *or not?*)("A-not-AB") is generated.

3.4   Verbs of Double Syllables with Object

(8)   a.   你   认识他。

Ni   renshi ta

You   know him

You know him.

b.   你   认识他不认识他？

Ni   renshi ta bu renshi ta?

You   know him not know him

Do you know him or not?

c. 你   认识他不认识？
    Ni   renshi ta bu renshi?
    You   know him not know
    Do you know him or not?

d. *你   认识他不认？
    Ni   renshi ta bu ren
    You   know him not kn-
    Intended reading: *Do you know him or not?*

e. 你   认识不认识他？
    Ni   renshi bu renshi ta?
    You   know not know him
    Do you know him or not?

f. 你   认不认识他？
    Ni   ren bu renshi ta?
    You   know him not know him
    Do you know him or not?

The A-not-A generation of double-syllables-verb with object is basically the same with the single-syllable-verb. After the two steps "Positive-Negative Reduplication" and "Deletion", all three subtypes of A-not-A question can be generated. Taking the double-syllables-verb "认识[*renshi*](*know*)" as the example, the generation procedure of all three subtypes of A-not-A question are displayed in (8). There are three types of reduplication at the first step "Positive-Negative Reduplication", which lead to different subtypes of A-not-A question.

First, after the "Positive-Negative Reduplication" of the whole VP "认识他[*renshi ta*](*know him*)" in (8a) , (8b)"你认识他不认识他"[*ni renshi ta bu renshi ta*](*Do you know him or not?*) ("AB-not-AB") is generated. Then we can do the deletion. After deleting the second object "他[*ta*](*he*)", which is same with the first object, (8c)"你认识他不认识"[*ni renshi ta bu renshi*](*Do you know him or not?*)("AB-not-A") is generated. Meanwhile, if the verb "认识[*renshi*](*know*)" is the word we reduplicate at the first step "Positive-Negative Reduplication", then we can get (8e) "你认识不认识他"[*ni renshi bu renshi ta*](*Do you know him or not?*)("A-not-AB").

The A-not-A generation of double-syllables-verb with object construction and single-syllable-verb with object construction are not totally the same. Besides reduplicate the whole VP (8b) and the whole Verb (8e), the double-syllables-verb can only reduplicate the first syllable of the verb to produce A-not-AB (8f), which disobey the "Principle of Lexical Integrity". And this is the form the single-syllable-verb will never have. (8e) "你认识不认识他[*ni renshi bu renshi ta*](*Do you know him or not?*)" represent the A-not-AB(I) type, (8f) "你认不认识他[*ni ren-bu renshi ta*](*Do you know him or not?*)" represent the A-not-AB(II) type. Other thing is that referring to the AB-not-AB through reduplication, theoretically, we can both delete the second object and the last syllable of the latter verb. But (8d) "*你认识他不认[*ni renshi ta bu ren*]

(*Do you know him or not?*)" is not tenable. As it is said in the former context, the reason is that the deletion must obey the "Principle of Lexical Integrity".

The A-not-A subtypes generated by these four types of constructions can be seen as Table 1.

Table 1. Subtypes of A-not-A Question Generated by Four Types of Constructions

SUBTYPES / FOUR CONSTRUCTIONS	"A-not-A"	"A-not-AB(I)"	"AB-not-A"	"A-not-AB(II)"	Total
verb and adjective of single syllable	+				1
verb and adjective of double syllables	+	+			2
single-syllable-verb with object	+	+	+		3
double-syllables-verb with object	+	+	+	+	4

We can see two relevant but different phenomena as follows from Table 1.

First, these four constructions are different on the ability of generating A-not-A question. Among them, double-syllables-verb with object has the strongest ability of generation, and then come single-syllable-verb with object, verb and adjective of double syllables, and verb and adjective of single syllable. Both double-syllables-verb with object and single-syllable-verb with object can produce all three basic subtypes of A-not-A question, but the former can produce A-not-AB (II) which disobeys the "Principle of Lexical Integrity"; verb and adjective of double syllables and verb and adjective of single syllable can produce two subtypes and one subtype respectively. So, different components and constructions have different abilities on the generation of A-not-A question, and verb and adjective of double syllables is stronger than verb and adjective of single syllable, those with object are stronger than ones without object.

Secondly, it can also reflect that these subtypes of A-not-A question have different restrictions on the components and constructions to generate A-not-A question. The "AB-not-A" question has more restrictions than other subtypes. This is due to the operation "Deletion" it referring to, which has to meet more conditions than the operation "Positive-Negative Reduplication".

4   The Comparison Between the Generation Mechanism of "A-not-A" Question and that of Relevant Interrogative Sentences

The generation mechanism of Reduplication (and Deletion) can deal with the generation of all subtypes of A-not-A question, but it is useless to other interrogative sentences. The generation mechanisms of four basic question types in Chinese are different. In Chinese, the methods of pronunciation, interrogative words and syntax are used to express interrogation. As to constituent question, disjunctive question and yes-no question, A-not-A question, the main methods of interrogative expression they depend on are related with lexicon and grammar respectively. The interrogative expression of constituent question and disjunctive question depend on the interrogative pronoun and the conjunction "还是[*haishi*](*or*)" with [+Q] feature, while yes-no question and A-not-A question depend on grammatical methods, "Interrogative Modal's Adjoining" and "Positive-Negative Reduplication".

When we need to express interrogation, one of grammatical operation ("Interrogative Modal's Adjoining" and "Positive-Negative Reduplication") could be chosen or just use pronunciation. The only restriction is when the sentence already has a word with the feature [+Q], it do not need more grammatical operations (Xu 2001). That is to say, anyone of the word with the feature [+Q], "Interrogative Modal's Adjoining" and "Positive-Negative Reduplication", can be used to check the interrogative features so it has no need to choose more than one. Otherwise, it will go against the economic principle of language, meanwhile the sentence will be not tenable because of the focus problem. And this can also explain why more than one of these four interrogative expressions cannot exist in one sentence normally (11)(12).[3]

(9) 你   想看书？

　　　Ni   xiang kanshu

　　　You   want to read books

　　　Do you want to read the book?

(10) 你   想看什么   吗？[4]

　　　Ni   xiang kan shenme   ma

　　　You   want to read what   Q

　　　What do you want to read?

(11) *你   看不看书   吗？

　　　Ni   kan-bu-kan shu   ma

　　　You   read-not-read book   Q

　　　Intended reading: *Do you want to read the book?*

(12) *你   看书还是看电影   吗？

　　　Ni   kanshu haishi kandianying ma

　　　You   read book or see movie   Q

　　　Intended reading: *Do you want to read or go to cinema?*

There are more interrogative expressions in Chinese dialects. As to A-not-A question, besides the three basic subtypes "A-not-A", "A-not-AB" and "AB-not-A", some other expressions in dialects are also classified into A-not-A question. Shao (2010) pointed out "VP-neg-VP", "VP-neg" and "K-VP" questions are the basic subtypes of A-not-A question in dialects. "K-VP" question has gained a lot of attention ever since

---

[3] There are some special sentences which contain more than one interrogative expression. For example, Xing (1987) proposed that there is a dual-interrogative sentence which contains both constituent question and yes-or-no question. When several interrogative components exist in the same sentence, generally one component will express interrogation mainly while the other one is redundant and will express something like mood and modal. So, we can choose one of the interrogative points in the sentence to answer.

[4] Here "什么[shenme] (what)" is no longer a interrogative pronoun, while it makes a general reference, or we can treat one interrogative point as redundancy.

Zhu (1985) talked about it, the classification of which is the focus of the discussion. Now there are mainly three opinions about the classification of "K-VP" question: scholars represented by Zhu (1985) insisted it belongs to A-not-A question; scholars represented by Li (1990) and Liu (1991) proposed that it is yes-or-no question; scholars represented by Xu and Shao (1998) identified it as "A-not-A--yes-or-no question", because it has common with yes-or-no question in structure and with A-not-A question in function. On the basis of formal syntax theory, Xu (2011) proposed that "K-VP" question is the result of "adjoining" operation at the "predicate-initial position". It is a special grammatical phenomenon which is independent from both A-not-A question and yes-or-no question. This is no final conclusion till now, instead of entangled with its classification, the similarities and differences of generation mechanism between A-not-A question and "K-VP" question will be discussed in this part.

The similarities and differences between A-not-A question and "K-VP" question are to some extent due to their generation mechanisms; According to the X-bar Theory, all structures are endocentric constructions and the character of the head decides that of the whole structure, therefore the head is decisive in the whole sentence. The heads of the sentence representative formula IP and CP are C (Complementizer) and I (Predicate-initial) respectively in Chinese. Influenced by the Head-position Parameter, C (Complementizer) is at the initial or final of the sentence, and with I position, these three positions constitute the three key positions which are sensitive to sentential functions. C position and I position are both the key positions to the interrogative sentences. As to A-not-A question and "K-VP" question, I position is key. The "Positive-Negative Reduplication" of A-not-A question operates at I (predicate-initial) position, while K-components of the "K-VP" question are adjoined to the I (predicate-initial) position.[5] Both of them are the result of grammatical operations at I (Predicate-initial) position and they are same in checking interrogative features, so they have common similarities in the way to answer and the distributions of modals (Zhu 1985).

In addition, A-not-A question and "K-VP" question have obvious differences on embedding ability. A-not-A question usually can be embedded as subject or object, while "K-VP" question in dialects usually cannot be embedded.

(13)   他来不来   不重要。

Ta lai-bu-lai   buzhongyao

He come-not-come   *not important*

Whether he comes or not is not important.

(14)   父母最关心   孩子健不健康。

Fumu zuiguanxin   haizi jian-bu-jiankang

Parents most care   child hea-not-healthy

The thing the parents care most is whether the child is healthy or not.

---

[5] Yes-or-no questions and "KVP" question are the results of the "Interrogative Modal's Adjoining". The difference is that "K-components" in "KVP" question are at predicate-initial position which is in the middle of the sentence, but "ma" is at C position which is at the final of the sentence. The hierarchy syntactic position of "吗(ma) [Q]" is higher than "K-components". This influences the differences on whether they can be embedded.

(15)   河南永城话Yongcheng dialect, Henan province（Xu 2011）

    a.   他可支持　　关系不大。

        Ta ke zhichi   guanxi buda

        He Q support   importance not big

        Whether he support me is not important.

    b.   我不在乎　　他可支持。

        Wo bu zaihu   ta ke zhichi

        I　not care   he Q support

        I do not care whether he supports me.

(16)   合肥话Hefei dialect, Anhui Province（Zhu 1985）

    a.   随你可去。

        Sui ni ke qu

        follow you Q go

        Whether to go or not depends on you.

    b.   随便可洗都行。

        Suibian ke xi douxing

        Casual Q wash both OK

        Whether to wash or not is OK.

There is a special phenomenon about A-not-A question and "K-VP", which is the "K-VP -not-VP" question in the modern vernacular novels and dialects like Wu dialect.

(17)   安徽东流话 Dongliu Dialect, Anhui Province（Zhu 1985）

    可　香不香？

    Ke　xiang-bu-xiang

    Q　fragrant-not- fragrant

    Is it fragrant?

(18)   汕头话 Shantou Dialect, Guangdong Province（Shi 1990）

    你　岂参加唔？

    ni　qi canjia wu

    you　Q join not

    Do you join?

These are the mixed sentences of A-not-A and "K-VP" expressions existing in Wu dialects, southwestern mandarin and Xiajiang mandarin (Zhu 1985). The special part of it is the two operations of "interrogative modal's adjoining" and "Positive-Negative Reduplication" used in one sentence to express interrogation.

(19) *你   看不看书   吗？

　　　Ni   kan-bu-kanshu   ma

　　　You   read-not-read book   Q

Intended reading: Do you read books?

(20)   可   香不香？

　　　Ke   xiang-bu-xiang

　　　Q   fragrant-not- fragrant

Is it fragrant?

These two sentences are both generated through the operation of "Interrogative Modal's Adjoining" and "Positive-Negative Reduplication". The sentence (19) in mandarin is not tenable, while sentences like (20) exist in some dialects. Zhu (1985) pointed out it a mixed sentence of new structure and old structure in the development of language and it is the result of dialects influencing on each other. Besides, we think that the grammatical feature of "K-components" which is different from "吗[*ma*](*Q*)", offers the syntactic possibility for the existence of the mixed sentence.

As we mentioned above, IP and CP have two sentential heads: C (complementizer) and I (predicate-initial position), they are sensitive to the sentential functional category. Both "K-components" and "吗[*ma*](*Q*)" are interrogative modal words adjoined to the sentence, but the important difference between them is their syntactic position. "K-component" is at the predicate-initial position, but "吗 [*ma*](*Q*)" is at the complementizer position which is at final of the sentence. According to the hierarchical structure, C (complementizer) position is higher than I (predicate-initial) position. The hierarchy structure decides the scope. Therefore, interrogative modal word "ma", which has a higher hierarchy in the sentence, has an absolute strong influence. And "K-component", which is at I position, might be a auxiliary interrogative word or express not very strong interrogative mood or other modalities, so it can serve with other interrogative methods.

5   Conclusion

The operation of reduplication (and deletion) with different restrictions which are not ad hoc, proposed by Xu and Tian (2013), can deal with the generations of all A-not-A question subtypes. It not only can reflect the common similarities of the three subtypes, but also can explain the differences among them. Moreover, it can deal with the similarities and differences between A-not-A question and some other relevant interrogative sentences.

Based on this generation mechanism analysis, after compare, we find that different components and structures have different abilities on generating A-not-A question. Double-syllables-verb with object has the strongest ability of generation, and then come single-syllable-verb with object, verb and adjective of double syllables, verb and adjective of single syllable. Verb and adjective of double syllables is stronger than verb and adjective of single syllable, those with object are stronger that ones without object.

It can also reflect that different subtypes of A-not-A question have different restrictions on the components and structures to generate A-not-A question. "A-not-A" subtype has the least restrictions, and then comes "A-not-AB", while "AB-not-A" has the most restrictions.

In Chinese, we can use pronunciation, lexical words and grammar to express interrogation. The grammatical operations mainly consist of "Interrogative Modal's Adjoining" and "Positive-Negative Reduplication". The four basic questions use different methods to express interrogation, but the number of methods chosen are restricted. "K-VP" question in dialects and A-not-A question have similarities and differences, so lots of arguments on their classification arise. Both similarities and differences are related with their generation mechanism. "K-VP" question is the result of "interrogative modal adjoining" at the "predicate-initial position", while A-not-A question is the result of "Positive-Negative Reduplication" at the "predicate-initial position". Both of them are the result of grammatical operations at "predicate-initial position" to check interrogative features, so they have common similarities in the way to answer and the distributions of modal words. And different operations have also relevant with the respective characteristics of the two question types. There are always confusions between yes-or-no question and "K-VP" question. Yes-or-no question are also the result of "interrogative modal adjoining", but it is at C position which is at the final of the sentence and its hierarchy is higher than I position which is at the predicate-initial position. So there are differences between their abilities of being embedded.

References

1. Huang, C.-T.J.: Logical Relations in Chinese and Theory of Grammar. Ph.D. diss., MIT (1982)
2. Huang, C.-T.J., Li, Y.-H., Li, Y.: The Syntax of Chinese. Cambridge University Press, New York (2009)
3. Wang, W.S.W.: Conjoining and Deletion in Mandarin Syntax. Monumenta Serica **26**, 224–236 (1967)
4. Fan, J.: On the patterns of Yes-No Questions. Studies of the Chinese Language **171**, 426–434 (1982). (in Chinese)
5. Liu, D.: The Question Word and the "可VP" pattern in the Suzhou Dialect. Studies of the Chinese Language **220**, 27–33 (1991). (in Chinese)
6. Li, X.: On the A-not-A Questions. In: Linguistics and Chinese Teaching. Beijing Language and Culture College Press, Beijing (1990). (李小凡.也谈反复问句.语言学与汉语教学,北京:北京语言学院出版社 (1990)) (in Chinese)
7. Shi, Q.: The A-not-A Questions in Shantou Dialect. Studies of the Chinese Language **216**, 182–185 (1990). (施其生.汕头方言的反复问句.中国语文 (3) (1990)) (in Chinese)
8. Shao, J., et al.: The Comparative Study on the Interrogative Category in Chinese Dialects. Jinan University Press, Guangzhou (2010). (邵敬敏等.汉语方言疑问范畴比较研究.广州:暨南大学出版社 (2010)) (in Chinese)
9. Tang, T.: The Study on interrogative sentences in Mandarin. The Journal of the Normal University **26**, 219–277 (1981). (汤廷池.国语疑问句研究.师大学报 (26) (1981)) (in Chinese)
10. Wu, Z.: On Methods of Combination and Splitting of A-not-A Questions and "可" Questions. Linguistics Study **19**, 58–67 (1990). (in Chinese)

11. Wu, F.: The Origin of the Interrogative Construction "A-not-A" in the Languages in Southern China. Minority Languages of China **169**, 3–18 (2008). (in Chinese)
12. Xing, F.: On Special Yes-no Questions in Modern Chinese. Language Teaching and Linguistic Studies **34**, 73–90 (1987). (in Chinese)
13. Xu, J.: "Reduplication" as a Grammatical Device and "Interrogation" as a Grammatical Category. Chinese Linguistics **2**, 6–18 (2000). (in Chinese)
14. Xu, J.: Grammatical Principles and Grammatical Phenomena. Peking University Press, Beijing (2001). (徐杰.普遍语法原则与汉语语法现象.北京:北京大学出版社 (2001)) (in Chinese)
15. Xu, J.: Three Sensitive Positions in a Sentence and Question—A Cross-Linguistic Perspective. In: Shan, Z., Lu, J. (eds.) Studies on Chinese Philology 2005, pp. 223–234. China Social Sciences Press, Beijing (2005). (徐杰.句子的三个敏感位置与句子的疑问范畴—跨语言的类型比较. 载单周尧、陆镜光主编语言文字学研究, 北京:中国社会科学出版社 (2005)) (in Chinese)
16. Xu, J.: Sentence Head and the Predicate-Initial Position. Chinese Linguistics **15**, 51–61 (2006). (in Chinese)
17. Xu, J., Li, Y.: The "Predicate-Initial" Position in Chinese and Relevant Syntactic and Theoretical Issues. Chinese Language and Literature Research **1**, 98–107 (2010). (徐杰,李莹.汉语"谓头"位置的特殊性及相关句法理论问题.汉语言文学研究 (3) (2010)) (in Chinese)
18. Xu, J., Zhang, Y.: The Nature of "Ke(可)-VP" Interrogatives in Some Chinese Dialects. Chinese Linguistics **34**, 60–70 (2011). (in Chinese)
19. Xu, J., Tian, Y.: A Unified Account for 'A-not- AB' and 'AB-not- A' Questions and Some Relevant Syntactic Issues. Contemporary Linguistics **15**, 379–392 (2013). (in Chinese)
20. Xu, L., Shao, J.: The Study on Shanghai Dialect Grammar. East China Normal University Press, Shanghai (1998). (徐烈炯,邵敬敏.上海方言语法研究.上海:华东师范大学出版社 (1998)) (in Chinese)
21. Zhu, D.: Two Types of Yes-or-no Questions in Chinese. Studies of the Chinese Language **184**, 10–20 (1985). (in Chinese)

A Reanalysis of Chinese Passive with a Retained Object

Juan Wang Villaflor[1(✉)] and Ying Li[2]

[1] Hawaii Language Center, Honolulu, Hawaii 96822, USA
juanv@hawaii.edu
[2] Schools of Foreign Languages, Central China Normal University,
Wuhan, 430079 Hubei, China
liying20110126@126.com

Abstract. This paper holds that Chinese passive with a retained object is not derived as a result of possessor raising, but from the passivization of the rob-type double object construction (DOC) with the two objects having the possessive semantic relationship. This rob-type DOC can be regarded as a DOC with characteristics of a low applicative, where the head Appl introduces the indirect object as its specifier and the direct object as its complement. The passivization of the rob-type DOC leads to only the movement of its direct object, and thus produces the so-called passive with a retained object. This analysis can provide solutions to the problems left behind by the Possessor Raising Analysis.

Keywords: Chinese passive with a retained object · Possessor raising · The rob-type DOC · Low applicative construction

1 Introduction

Chinese has a unique passive construction: the passivized verb can still take an object after passivization; additionally, the subject and the retained object have a possessive relationship. The possessive relationship includes not only the "possessor-possessee" relationship, but also the "whole-part" and the kinship relationship. This construction is known as the passive with a retained object. Examples are shown in the following:

(1) Zhang San bei   Li Si toule   yige   qianbao.
  Zhang San BEI   Li Si steal-LE one-CL wallet
  "Zhang San's wallet was stolen by Li Si."

(2) Wang Wu bei   dadiaole   liangge menya.
  Wang Wu BEI beat-fell-LE two-CL front teeth
  "Wang Wu's two front teeth were knocked out."

The current work is partially supported by the Research Committee of University of Macau (Standard Research Grant MYRG172(Y2-L3)-FSH11-XJ), China National Social Sciences and Humanities Research Council (Research Grant for Young Scholars (12CYY051). We also thank the two reviewers and professor Jie Xu for their valuable comments and suggestions, and also Brent Pack for helping revise the paper.

© Springer International Publishing Switzerland 2014
X. Su and T. He (Eds.): CLSW 2014, LNAI 8922, pp. 99–111, 2014.
DOI: 10.1007/978-3-319-14331-6_10

(3) Wang Mian bei   shale   fuqin.

　　Wang Mian BEI kill-LE father

　　"Wang Mian's father was killed."

Chinese passive with a retained object is generally explained by the Possessor Raising Analysis, a type of NP-movement, in which the possessor subject moves from the object position and leaves behind the possessee in the presence of the passive morpheme *bei*. This analysis is so widely acknowledged that some even call this kind of passive "the possessor raising construction".

In this paper, we aim to make a reanalysis of the passive with a retained object. We will claim that this kind of passive construction is not derived as a result of possessor raising, but from the passivization of the rob-type DOC with the two objects having a possessive relationship. The passivization of the rob-type DOC only allows for its direct object to move to the subject position and thus produces the passive with a retained object.

This paper is structured as follows. In section 2, we will present the Possessor Raising Analysis and list its challenges. In section 3, we will point out that the underlying D-structure for the passive with a retained object is the rob-type DOC, which leads us to make a proposal in section 4 as to the syntactic derivation of the passive with a retained object and the case received by the retained object. Section 5 is the conclusion.

2   The Possessor Raising Analysis and Its Challenges

In the passive constructions, in the presence of the passive morpheme *bei*, the transitive verbs tend to behave like unergative verbs. Unergative verbs do not assign external thematic roles, thus in the D-structure, they only take internal objects but never the external subjects. Therefore, the subjects in all the passive constructions are taken to be generated in the object position, and then move from the object position to the subject position. It is because in the passive with a retained object construction the subject and the retained object have a possessive relationship that Xu (1999, 2001) first points out that its D-structure is "*bei* V+NP1 de NP2", where *de* is the syntactic marker for the possessive construction in the object position. The possessor NP1 then moves from the object position to the subject position, and the passive with a retained object takes shape. The derivational process is shown in the following by taking (1) as the example.

(4) a. bei Li Si toule **Zhang San de yige qianbao**   (D-structure)

　　b. **Zhang San$_i$** bei Li Si toule t$_i$ yige qianbao   (NP1 movement)

　　c. Zhang San bei Li Si toule yige qianbao.   (S-structure)

Here the NP1 movement is also known as "the possessor raising". The Possessor Raising Analysis is widely accepted among Chinese scholars. The disputes, however, are on the motivation of the NP1 movement and the case received by the retained object. We will only discuss three representative viewpoints below.

The first was held by Xu (1999, 2001) that the NP1 movement is driven by case. The passivization leads to the loss of the case-assigning ability of the transitive verb. In order to satisfy the Case Filter of the NPs in the sentence, there are two options: one is to move the whole post-verbal NP phrase "NP1 de NP2" to the subject position, thus producing the commonly seen passive construction; the other is to only move NP1, thus generating the passive with a retained object. The retained object NP2 receives a special case—the partitive case, assigned by the passivized verb[1]. The concept of the partitive case was borrowed from Finnish, where the object of the verb receives either the accusative case or the partitive case. The question is why Chinese would work the same way as Finnish.

Later on, Han (2000) denied the existence of the partitive case by stating that NP1 already receives the possessive case from the head noun NP2 before its movement. Therefore, the reason for NP1 movement is not to receive case itself, but to gain case for the whole NP phrase in the object position. After NP1 moves to the subject position, it receives the nominative case from the sentence head I and then passes the case to the retained object through the chain linking NP1 and its trace. Note that if this is the case, the NP1 actually receives both the possessive case and the nominative case. This is not going to work as it is against the universal rule—The Case Filter. In addition, it is proposed by the generative grammar that the movement is a more costly syntactic operation and should be driven by self-interest. However, as we can see in Han's proposal, NP1 movement is obviously not driven by its own interest.

Wen & Chen (2001) discussed the motivation of NP1 movement under the theoretical framework of Minimalist Program. They advocated that NP1 movement is not driven by case, but by feature-checking requirement. To be specific, the functional sentence head I has a strong [D] feature and demands that NP1 with the same [D] feature move to the specifier position of IP for feature checking. However, they did not discuss who assigns the case to the retained object and what it is.

Besides from the disputes within the analysis, there still remain some problems that were identified in previous literature (see Sun & Wu, 2003; Pan & Han, 2005; Shen, 2006; An, 2007). We will make only a summary of the problems here.

First, the Possessor Raising Analysis violates the Left Branch Condition (LBC) put forward by Ross. The LBC stipulates that no NP on the left branch of another bigger NP may be extracted from this bigger NP. The Chinese language observes this constraint, as indicated by the following example that *Zhang San*, the possessor of the NP phrase in the object position, is prohibited from moving out of the NP.

(5) a. Wo kanjianle Zhang San de   baba.

    I   see-LE   Zhang San DE father

    "I saw Zhang San's father."

  b. *Zhang San$_i$, wo kanjianle [t$_i$ baba].

---

[1] It is pointed out that Chinese passivized verbs have a different case-assigning ability from those in English. They are still able to assign internal case even if undergoing passivization.

Second, it is still not clear as to what case is assigned to the retained object. The partitive case fails to provide a satisfying answer. As shown in Finnish, the partitive case signifies the indefinteness, thus any NP that receives this case is an indefinite NP. In other words, definite NPs and universal quantificational NPs are excluded from receiving the partitive case. However, it is observed by Pan & Han (2005) that in Chinese passive with a retained object construction, definite NPs and universal quantificational NPs do appear in the retained object position as shown in the following examples, which signals that the partitive case cannot be assigned to the retained object.

(6) Xiaoma bei toule   nage qianbao hou, zhenggeren   biande jusangle.

Xiaoma BEI steal-Le that-CL wallet   after   whole person become depress-LE

"After Xiaoma's wallet was stolen, he became depressed."

(7) Bei huile   qiaoliang, gaidiqu de jiaotongyunshu xiangdang kunnan.

BEI destroy-Le bridge   this area DE transportation   rather   difficult

"This area's transportation became rather difficult as its bridge was destroyed."

(Pan & Han, 2005:6)

Third, it is hard to explain where the possessive marker *de* goes after NP1 movement. Xu (1999, 2001) provided two hypotheses: one is that it does not even exist in the D-structure; the other is that it is deleted at the same time when NP1 moves to the subject position. Han (2000) held that *de* shows up in the D-structure and disappears in the S-structure. These explanations cannot hold water as *de* is considered as a functional category and a functional category cannot simply disappear or be deleted in a random way, which is inconsistent with linguistic theories and also poses problems for language acquisition in a way.

Last but not the least, it also seems difficult to explain the difference between English and Chinese with regard to the passive with a retained object construction. As we know, English does not have this kind of construction. It requires the whole object to move to the subject position to form the general passive. What causes the difference? Is it because in English the passivized verb is unable to assign case? Why is that? These problems remain unresolved.

3   The D-structure for the Passive with a Retained Object

As stated above, there are disputes and problems about the Possessor Raising Analysis even though it is widely acknowledged and accepted. In this section and the following, with an aim to resolve the disputes and the problems, we attempt to make a reanalysis of the passive with a retained object construction.

According to the Possessor Raising Analysis, the D-structure for the object of the passivized verb in the passive with a retained object construction is "NP1 *de* NP2", which is built upon the possessive semantic relationship between the subject and the retained object in the surface structure. This, however, boils down to one question: is the semantic possessive relationship necessarily realized as the *DE* construction (NP1 *de* NP2) in syntax? In other words, is the semantic possessive relationship only correspondent to the syntactic *DE* construction? The answer, undoubtedly, is NO!

The *DE* construction is only one of the syntactic realizations of the semantic possessive relationship. This relationship may also be realized as two parallel grammatic units in syntax, for instance, the double subject or topic construction[2].

(8) Nake   shu   yezi da.

that-CL tree   leaf big

"That tree's leaves are big."

(9) Ta xinyan'er buhuai.

he heart-eye not bad

"His heart is not bad. (He has a good heart.)"

In the examples, the two NPs in the subject position are in parallel grammatical positions. This point can be illustrated more clearly in Korean and Japanese in which the two NPs in the subject position are equally case-marked.

(10) Chinkwu-ka son-i   aphu-ta. (Korean)

friend-Nom hand-Nom hurt

"The friend's hand got hurt."

(11) Mary-ga   kao-ga   kawaii. (Japanese)

Mary-Nom face-Nom cute

"Mary's face is cute."

Furthermore, in Chinese rob-type DOC, the double objects also have the possessive relationship. For example:

(12) Ta   toule   lingju   yizhi   lao muji.

She steal-LE neighbour one-CL old hen

"She stole an old hen from the neighbour."

(13) Xiaotou qiangle   ta   wubaikuai   qian.

the thief rob-LE   him   five hundred-CL money

"The thief robbed him of five hundred yuan."

Additionally, in Chinese complement clause (also known as another De construction[3]), the possessor NP and the possessee NP can occur respectively in the subject and

---

[2] This construction is quite disputable. Some consider the two parallel NPs in the subject position as two subjects, one is "the big subject" and the other is "the small subject". Those who take Chinese as a topic-prominent language regard the two NPs as two topics. There are even some holding that one is a subject and the other is a topic. No matter what the nature of the two NPs is, the point is that they are in parallel grammatical status.

[3] The Chinese DE can be realized as three different functional words morphologically. "de1" constitutes the possessive construction and is used between the head noun and its modifiers, as shown in examples (4) and (5). "de2" is used between the head verb and its modifiers. "de3" is used after the main verb to introduce the complement.

the complement positions. In the following examples (14) and (15), the subjects "ta" and "haizi", and the components "yanjing" and "lian" in the complement positions have the possessive relationship.

(14) Ta   kude   yanjing dou zhongle
    She cry-DE eye   both swollen-LE
    "She cried so hard that both of her eyes are swollen."

(15) Haizi xiade   lian dou baile
    Child frighten-DE face all white-LE
    "The child was frightened that his face turned white."

The Possessor Raising Analysis can only be used to explain the passive with a retained object where the subject and the retained object have a possessive relationship, it cannot help to explain other passive constructions where the subject and the retained object do not have a possessive relationship, such as sentences below.

(16) Zhexie zhenguide yishupin   bei ta   suisuibianbiande songle   ren.
    these precious-DE artistic artifact BEI him casually-DE   present-LE people
    "These precious artistic artifacts were given away to other people by him."

(17) Na   yidong fangzi bei Wang laoban geile   qingren.
    that one-CL house BEI Wang boss   give-LE lover
    "That house was given by Boss Wang to his lover."

(18) Wo bei renjia   kaile   yige   da wanxiao.[4]
    I   BEI other people play-LE one-CL big joke.
    "I was played a big joke by the others."

(19) Ta bei women youle   yimo.[5]
    he BEI us   amuse-Le one humor
    "He was amused by us. (Lit. He was played a humor by us)"

For sentences like (16) and (17), we certainly won't say that they are derived as a result of possessor raising because it is not difficult to see that they are the passive constructions of the give-type DOC, in which the direct object moves while the indirect object stays. But for sentences like (18) and (19), most scholars tend to see them as fixed patterns, whose derivations are beyond the syntactic rules. That's also why they have never been given much attention. In view of the syntactic structure, together with the passive construction we have been talking about, these are all passives with retained objects constructions. However, theoretically, they are derived from different sources.

---

[4] "kai wanxiao (play jokes)" is an idiomatic verb phrase in Chinese. In this passive construction, they are broken down as two components.

[5] "youmo" (humor, humors)" is an inseparable phrase in Chinese, they are also broken down in this passive construction.

Are they really different constructions that have no relations? Or could it be that the theoretical analysis is going the wrong way?

Considering those examples above, we argue that the D-structure for the passive with a retained object is "*bei* V+ NP1 NP2". In other words, the possessive relationship is realized as double objects, two parallel grammatical units. In the process of passivization, one object NP1 moves to the subject position and the other object stays. Again taking (1) as the example, we will show the derivational process as the following.

(20) a. bei Li Si toule **Zhang San yige qianbao**   (D-structure)

　 b. **Zhang San**ᵢ bei Li Si toule **t**ᵢyige qianbao   (NP1 movement)

　 c. Zhang San bei Li Si toule yige qianbao   (S-structure)

To be more specific, the D-structure of the passive with a retained object is the rob-type DOC. The rob-type DOC is usually regarded as a different type of DOC from the give-type DOC. It is constructed with verbs like "qiang (rob)", "tou (steal)", "pian (swindle)", "chi (eat)", "da (beat)", "na (take)", as seen in examples (12) and (13). The two objects in the rob-type DOC normally have the possessive relationship, thus the passivization of examples (12) and (13) brings exactly the passives with retained objects where the subjects and the retained objects have the possessive relationship.

(21) Lingju   bei ta toule   yizhi   lao muji.

　　 neighbor BEI him steal-LE one-CL old hen

　　 "The neighbour's hen was stolen by him."

(22) Ta bei   xiaotou qiangle wubaikuai   qian.

　　 he BEI   thief rob-LE five hundred-CL money

　　 "His five hundred yuan was stolen by the thief."

Sentences like (18) and (19) can be restored to a DOC, as seen in the following. This DOC, by nature, is similar to the rob-type DOC and can be taken as an extended type of the rob-type DOC. As noted by Huang (2007), the rob-type DOC is not constrained by verbs with a semantic meaning of robbing or stealing; any ditransitive verbs that are able to take the agent, the affectee, and the patient arguments can form the rob-type DOC.

(23) Renjia   kaile wo yige wanxiao.

　　 other people play-LE me one-CL joke

　　 "The others played a joke on me."

(24) Women youle   ta yimo.

　　 we   amuse-LE him one-humor

　　 "We amused him. (Lit. We played him a humor.)"

Although we hold that the passive with a retained object is derived from the rob-type DOC, not all the rob-type DOCs can be passivized, as shown in the following examples. This has something to do with the semantic meaning associated with the passive construction. In general, the subject of the passive construction denotes the affectee by the event, or the experiencer of the event.

(25) a. Wo maile shudian yiben   shu.

      I   buy-LE store   one-CL book

      "I bought a book from the store."

   b. *Shudian bei wo   maile   yiben   shu.

      store   BEI me buy-LE one-CL book

      "The store was bought a book by me."

(26) a. Ta duguo   Lu Xun wupian zawen.

      he read-PST Lu Xun five-CL essay

      "He read Lu Xun's five essays."

   b. *Lu Xun bei ta   duguo   wupian   zawen.

      Lu Xun BEI him read-PST five-CL essay

      "Lu Xun was read five essays by him."

4   The Syntactic Derivation of the Passive with a Retained Object

The previous section pointed out that the passive with a retained object is derived from the movement of the indirect object of the rob-type DOC under passivization. In fact, the movement can only be the indirect object instead of the direct object. In this section, we are mainly going to answer two questions: what is the motivation for the movement of the indirect object? Why does only the indirect object move?

Compared with the typical give-type DOC, the rob-type DOC is not truly a DOC as its indirect object is not an obligatory component in the sentence. In other words, the rob-type verbs can go without the indirect object and take only one object. For instance, the following make perfect grammatical sentences:

(27) Xiaotou qiangle wubaikuai   qian.

     thief   rob-LE five hundred-LE money

     "The thief robbed five hundred yuan."

(28) Ta toule   yizhi   lao muji.

     She steal-LE one-CL old hen

     "She stole one old hen."

In the give-type DOC, the give-type verbs must take two objects, otherwise, the sentences are ungrammatical. Therefore, we can say that the give-type verbs are real ditransitive verbs while the rob-type verbs are mono-transitive verbs. The rob-type DOC is formed by adding one more argument to the rob-type verb and thus changing its valency. In this sense, the rob-type DOC is a DOC with the characteristics of the applicative construction that has been found in many languages. Actually, in recent years, Tsai (2009) and Sun (2010) have put forward similar opinions.

The applicative construction is a productive construction in Bantu languages, with overt marking in the verbal complex that allows a participant normally encoded as an oblique to realize as a core object. The applicatives may have the effect of increasing the valency of a verb. As shown in the following examples, in Chichewa and Kinyarwanda, the obliques like the instrument and the location can be realized as the core arguments of the verbs.

(29) Fisi   a-na-dul-ir-a   mpeni chingwe.   (Chichewa)

hyena Agr-Pst-cut-Appl-Asp knife   rope

"The hyena had cut the rope with the knife."

(30) Umwaan   y-a-taa-ye-mo   a-maazi igitabo.   (Kinyarwanda)

child   Agr-Pst-throw-Asp-Appl   CL-water book

"The child had thrown the book into the water."

(Baker, 1988:238)

Inspired by Marantz (1993), the recent literature abounds in discussions of languages of different families whose ditransitive constructions behave like the applicative construction (see Pylkkänen, 2008:16-45 for English, Finnish and Japanese; McGinnis, 2001:1-14 for Albanian, Icelandic and Italian; Gervo, 2003: 51-80 for Spanish; Constanta & Rivero, 2007:212-217 for Romanian). Pylkkänen's (2008) distinguished two different types of applicative constructions: the high applicative, which denote a relation between an event and an individual, syntactically attaching above the VP, and the low applicative, denoting a relation between two individuals, syntactically attaching below VP. She also takes the following properties as diagnostics for identifying whether a language instantiates the high or low applicative: (i) only high applicative heads can combine with stative verbs; (ii) only high applicative heads combine with unergatives. Chinese rob-type DOC is consistent with Pylkkänen's definition of the low applicative construction because neither the intransitive verb like "pao (run)" nor the static verb like "xihuan (like)" can occur in this DOC.

(31) *Ta paole   lingju   yizhi   ji.

She run-LE neighbor one-CL chicken

"She ran one chicken of the neighbor."

(32) *Ta xihuan lao popo   wuwan   mian.

He like   old grandama five-CL noodles

"He likes old grandma five noodles."

Therefore, in the rob-type DOC, the head Appl introduces the direct object as the complement and the indirect object as the specifier. Still taking (1) as the example, we show its D-structure as the following:

(33)

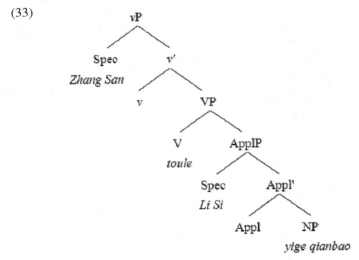

We will explain why and why only the indirect object NP1 moves under the theoretical framework of Minimalist Program. Chomsky (1999, 2000) proposed that syntactic derivations undergo semantic and phonological interpretation in incremental chunks or phases. Phases can be headed by C, D or by active, theta-assigning v. Once a phase is complete, movement and agreement operations can target its head and constituents in its edge—adjuncts and specifiers, but cannot target constituents in its domain (complement).

According to McGinnis (2001), different semantic properties of an applicative head affect not only phrase structure, but also phase structure. In other words, a high applicative head is a phase head, while a low applicative head is not, and the phasehood is responsible for the asymmetries in passivizing A-movement. In the low applicative, the phase head is v, which has an EPP feature and can attract the constituents in its domain to move to the edge. There are two constituents in the domain of the phase: the indirect object NP1 and the direct object NP2. It is stipulated by Relativized Minimality that only the constituent within the domain that is closer to the landing point is entitled to move. The indirect object NP1 is relatively closer than the direct object NP2 and thus is entitled to move. This is shown in the following diagram.

Other related questions are: who assigns case to NP2 after NP1 movement? And what is the case? In our analysis, NP2 does not receive case from the verb. Once being passivized, the verb loses its ability to assign case. NP2 actually receive the accusative case from the applicative head, which can be supported by the evidence from other languages. Chinese is not the only language that has the passive with a retained object, Korean and Japanese also have this kind of construction. The morphological case-markings in these two languages clearly indicate that the retained object receives the accusative case.

(34)

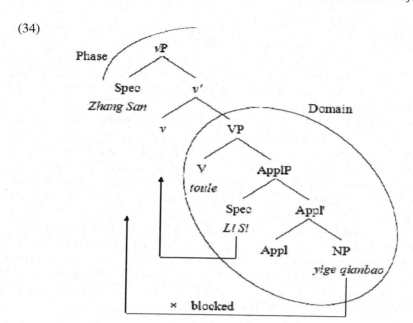

(35) John-ka son-ul   cap-hi-ess-ta.   (Korean)
    John-Nom hand-Acc catch-Pss-Pst-Decl
    "John was caught by hand."

(36) Taroo-ga Tanaka-niyotte atama-o tatak-are-ta.   (Japanese)
    Taroo-Nom Tanaka-Prep head-Acc Pat-Pss-Pst
    "Taroo was patted on the head by Tanaka."

5   Conclusion

In this paper, we make a reanalysis of the passive with a retained object. We hold that the passive with a retained object construction is not derived as a result of the possessor raising, but from the passivization of the rob-type DOC in which the two objects have a possessive relationship. The rob-type DOC is a DOC with characteristics of a low applicative, in which the head Appl introduces the indirect object as its specifier and the direct object as its complement. In the low applicative, the phase head is not Appl but v, which has an EPP feature and can attract the constituents in its domain to move to the edge. According to Relativized Minimality, only the indirect object NP1 is entitled to move to the edge. Thus the passivization of the rob-type DOC leads to only the movement of the indirect object NP1 and thus the passive with a retained object is generated. This analysis can resolve the problems left behind by the Possessor Raising Analysis.

First, the violation of LBC. In our framework, what moves is not the possessor noun, but the indirect object, thus it does not violate LBC.

Second, the case received by the retained object. By illustrating examples from Japanese and Korean, we proved that the retained object receives the accusative case from the head Appl, but not the partitive case from the passivized verb, which avoid the problems caused by the partitive case.

Third, the DE problem. We hold that the D-structure for the object in the passive with a retained object construction is not the possessive construction with "de", but the double object construction. Therefore, "de" has never existed in our analysis.

Lastly, the difference between English and Chinese with regard to the passive with a retained object. We say that Chinese passive with a retained object is derived from the rob-type DOC, since English does not have the rob-type DOC and naturally does not have the passive with a retained object.

Meanwhile, our analysis can provide a unified explanation to the passive with a retained object where the subject and the retained object have a possessive relationship and the passive with a retained object where the subject and the retained object do not have a possessive relationship as shown in examples (16) to (19). We can simply say that all these passive constructions are derived from the DOC, specifically, the give-type DOC and the rob-type DOC respectively.

References

1. An, F.: Theta-role Theory and the Raising of Superior Element in Possessive Noun Phrase (in Chinese). Journal of PLA University of Foreign Languages **3**, 11–17 (2007)
2. Baker, M.: Incorporation: A theory of grammatical function changing. University of Chicago Press, Chicago (1988)
3. Chomsky, N.: Derivation by phase. MIT Occasional Papers in Linguistics 18. Department of Linguistics. MIT (1999)
4. Chomsky, N.: Minimalist inquiries: The framework. In: Martin, R., Michaels, D., Uriagereka, J. (eds.) Step by Step: Essays on Minimalist Syntax in Honor of Howard Lasnik. MIT Press, Cambridge (2000)
5. Diaconescu, C.R., Maria, R.L.: An applicative analysis of double object constructions in Romanian. Probus **19**, 209–233 (2007)
6. Cuervo, M.C.: Datives at Large. Ph.D. dissertation. Massachusetts Institute of Technology, Cambridge (2003)
7. Han, J.: A Study of Possessor Raising Movement in Relation to Case Theory (in Chinese). Modern Foreign Languages **3**, 261–272 (2000)
8. Huang, C.T.J.: Thematic Structure of Verbs in Chinese and their Syntactic Projections (in Chinese). Linguistic Sciences **4**, 3–21 (2007)
9. Kikushima, K.: High and middle applicatives in Japanese: adversity causatives and v-te kureru construction. Japanese Studies **3**, 1–22 (2013)
10. McGinnis, M.J.: Variation in the phase structure of applicatives. In: Rooryck, J., Pica, Pierre (eds.) Linguistic Variations Yearbook, pp. 105–146. John Benjamins, Amsterdam (2001)
11. Pan, H., Han, J.: The Syntax of Surface Unaccusative Constructions (in Chinese). Studies in Language and Linguistics **3**, 1–13 (2005)
12. David, P.A.: Applicative Construction. Oxford University Press, Oxford (2007)

13. Pylkkänen, L.: Introducing Arguments. The MIT Press, Massachusetts (2008)
14. Shen, J.: The Generative Mechanism of Sentences Like Wangmian died father: Sentence Generation by Blending in Chinese (in Chinese). Studies of the Chinese Language **4**, 291–300 (2006)
15. Wei-Tien, T.: High applicatives are not high enough: A cartographic solution. Paper presented at the 6th Workshop on Formal Syntax & Semantics, National Taiwan Normal University, Taipei (2009)
16. Sun, J., Wu, Y.: A Reanalysis of "Possessor Raising Movement" (in Chinese). Linguistic Sciences **6**, 46–52 (2003)
17. Sun, T., Li, Y.: Licensing Non-core Arguments in Chinese (in Chinese). Studies of the Chinese Language **1**, 21–33 (2010)
18. Wen, B., Chen, Z.: An MP Approach to Possessor Raising in Chinese (in Chinese). Modern Foreign Languages **4**, 412–416 (2001)
19. Xu, J.: Some Theoretical Issues of the Two Types of Chinese 'retained object' Constructions (in Chinese). Contemporary Linguistics **1**, 16–29 (1999)
20. Xu, J.: Grammatical Principles and Grammatical Phenomenon. University Press, Beijing (2001)

Quantitative Research on the Origins of Contemporary Chinese Vocabulary Based on *The Great Chinese Dictionary*

Xueyang Liu[1], Bin Li[1,2(✉)], Yingjie Zhang[2], and Liu Liu[1]

[1] School of Chinese Language and Literature,
Nanjing Normal University, Nanjing 210097, China
liuxueyang1220@163.com, liuliu1989@gmail.com
[2] State Key Lab for Novel Software Technology,
Nanjing University, Nanjing 210023, China
{lib,zhangyj}@nlp.nju.edu.cn

Abstract. The evolution of the Chinese vocabulary is one of the indispensable parts of the research on the history of the Chinese language, and is the basis of clarifying the origins of contemporary Chinese vocabulary. For lack of the high-quality and large-scale diachronic corpus, the overall evolutionary process of the Chinese vocabulary is hard to demonstrate and the quantitative-analytical description of the Chinese lexical evolution still remains a problem. *The Great Chinese Dictionary* records over 490,000 senses of both ancient and contemporary words. By manually labeling the historical period of the example sentences for every sense in the dictionary, a diachronic Chinese lexical database was built. Then we probed into the distributions of the number and word length of contemporary vocabulary in each historical period. Eventually, we estimated the correlation between the number of words and their age by regression analysis.

Keywords: *The Great Chinese Dictionary* · Contemporary vocabulary · Quantitative analysis · Glottochronology

1 Introduction

Dynamics, as one of the essential features of language, is reflected in each language element, especially in the vocabulary. For instance, in contemporary Chinese vocabulary (which refers to all the words having been used until today since 1949), some words once entered but later disappeared from Chinese lexical system, such as "红卫兵(*Red Guards*)" and "大跃进(*Great Leap Forward*)", which showed the history of the Great Cultural Revolution; some words appeared in a certain period of China's history and stay in use until today with some changes of their original lexical meanings like "白 (*white*)" and "红 (*red*)". In this paper, we probe into the evolution of the Chinese vocabulary with both of these two types of words.

Contemporary words are the final state in the evolution of the Chinese vocabulary, so the research on the differences between contemporary words and those of the

© Springer International Publishing Switzerland 2014
X. Su and T. He (Eds.): CLSW 2014, LNAI 8922, pp. 112–123, 2014.
DOI: 10.1007/978-3-319-14331-6_11

former periods is the main focus in the study of Chinese language history. By comparing the syllabic number of contemporary words with that of ancient Chinese vocabulary, several researchers have found the inevitable trend that monosyllables developed into polysyllables [1, 2]. Some comparisons have been done from the semantic aspect, intended to describe or explain the semantic changes [3, 4]. These researches have explored the rudimentary thread and the internal regularities of some words or some types of words, however, they were deficient in the overall view of the evolution of the Chinese language. Meanwhile, due to the lack of database to get the statistical data of the whole history of the Chinese vocabulary evolution, qualitative analysis rather than quantitative-analytical method was often used in such researches.

The quantitative-analytical method has been emphasized and applied in the research of vocabulary [5-9]. On the one hand, it can expand new fields in the study of vocabulary, and on the other hand, it can re-examine, review and confirm the existing theories as well as the present viewpoints of vocabulary [10]. The application of it in the study of the Chinese vocabulary history is supported by the increase of corpus resources based on the real texts. However, because of the great difficulties in collecting, arranging and refining the real texts of each period in the Chinese history, it is still a problem to conduct the study of the Chinese language history at present. Faced with such inevitable difficulties, the dictionary containing the diachronic developing information of vocabulary is of great use for speculating the evolution of Chinese vocabulary.

Contemporary Chinese vocabulary is closely related to our daily life. We concern about not only its present, but also its history. In which periods the words emerged? What influence have the changes of dynasties exerted on the vocabulary system? What regularities will be shown by the distributions of each contemporary word's length in different periods? These questions still remain unanswerable due to the shortage of positive data or evidences. This paper is to conduct the study on the basis of the quantitative analysis of the dictionary database so as to attain the descriptive analysis of the history of contemporary Chinese vocabulary.

2   Data Resources

The analysis materials in this paper are all the contemporary words recorded by the example sentences in *The Great Chinese Dictionary* [11], which is a historical Chinese dictionary containing a large number of both ancient and modern words. It traces back to the origins of every word in order to reveal its whole development: it presents the example sentences of not only the earliest emergence of each sense of the word but also its diachronic development in different dynasties. However, *The Great Chinese Dictionary* does not record all the historical period of each example sentence, which actually is indispensible for this study; therefore, we need to make a supplement. We manually made use of Duxiu Knowledge Base (http://www.duxiu.com/) and other web resources such as Baidu Encyclopedia and Wikipedia to obtain the comparatively accurate time of each example sentence. To simplify the understanding of the changing over 3000 years, we divided the whole Chinese language history into fifteen periods based largely on dynasties as illustrated in Table 1.

Table 1. The periods and their time span in labeling the period information

Period	Start	End
先秦(*Pre-Qin*)	20th century BC	221 BC
秦(*Qin*)	221 BC	206 BC
汉(*Han*)	206 BC	220 AD
三国(*Three Kingdoms*)	220 AD	280 AD
晋(*Jin*)	265 AD	420 AD
南北朝(*Southern & Northern*)	420 AD	589 AD
隋(*Sui*)	581 AD	618 AD
唐(*Tang*)	618 AD	907 AD
五代十国(*Five Dynasties & Ten Kingdoms*)	907 AD	979 AD
宋金(*Song & Jin*)	960 AD	1279 AD
元(*Yuan*)	1206 AD	1368 AD
明(*Ming*)	1368 AD	1644 AD
清(*Qing*)	1616 AD	1911 AD
民国(*Republic of China*)	1912 AD	1949 AD
当代（*Contemporary*）	1949 AD	1986 AD

By collating and arranging this information, we set up a database which stores all the words recorded in *The Great Chinese Dictionary* and their respective related information such as morphology, senses and example sentences. Each row of data represents the information of each sense of one word in *The Great Chinese Dictionary*. According to statistics, *The Great Chinese Dictionary* has recorded 336,164 words and 493,772 senses, among which 39,972 senses don't have example sentences. After ignoring this smaller part, we altogether obtain more than 450,000 senses with their historical period (including more than 310,000 words and 880,000 example sentences). In this database, there are 33,845 contemporary words sharing 38,449 senses and 43,863 example sentences.

3　The Period Distributions of Contemporary Words and Senses

Contemporary vocabulary is the product of the ever-lasting accumulation of all the preceding words in the history. Then, when did those 33,845 contemporary words and their 38,449 senses which have been recorded in *The Great Chinese Dictionary* appear, and during which periods were they being used? What is the relationship between the form and use of the words as well as senses and the period? A macroscopic research on the above-mentioned questions can help to clarify the developing thread of Chinese vocabulary, verify and supplement the research results of the history of the Chinese language.

3.1   The Use of Contemporary Words and Senses in Former Periods

The contemporary words always appeared in one period from Pre-Qin to Contemporary Era and are kept in use until today, the total number of the use of contemporary words and senses reflects the contribution of each period to them. The gap in the sum of the use from two adjacent periods also reflects the variation degree between different periods. For all the contemporary words in the database, we have counted their total number in every period. Nevertheless, due to the limitation of the dictionary, the database does not provide all the example sentences which senses used in real texts, so it is a big problem to recognize that the use of senses is successive or isolated. In consequence, based on different assumptions, we have different demonstrates of the use of contemporary words and senses.

Assumption One: *If the dictionary has given the example sentences, we can assume that this specific word or sense has been used in the period which the example sentences belong to.*

Fig. 1 provides a description of the use of contemporary words and senses in former periods.

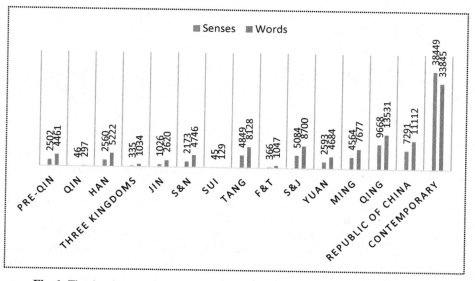

Fig. 1. The development of contemporary words and senses under Assumption One

It is very clear that the contribution of the words from different periods to contemporary words presents a fairly great fluctuation; especially from Republic of China to Contemporary Era, the sum of words and senses both had substantial changes. However, the number of words are not accurate; thus, in some certain periods like Qin, Three Kingdoms, Five Dynasties and Ten Kingdoms, Sui Dynasty which all had relatively short time span and the real texts were difficult to obtain, the sum of the words and senses may appear less than that of the actual situation.

Besides, the number of words is more than that of senses in Fig. 2, it's because that the words are more stable than the senses in use. The words can be used in a long time but the senses cannot. The comparison between the number of words and senses in the figures below can also be explained by this reason.

Assumption Two: *If The Great Chinese Dictionary has provided the example sentences only from one period, this word or sense can be regarded as the unique one of this period; if the dictionary has given the example sentences from more than one period, this word or sense can be regarded as being used from the earliest period to the latest.*

Fig. 2 provides a description of the use of contemporary words and senses in former periods under this assumption.

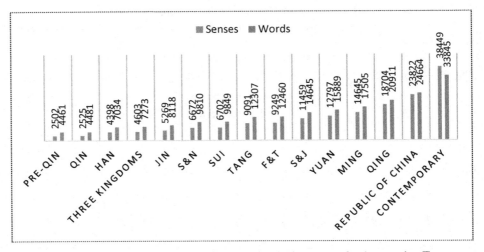

Fig. 2. The development of contemporary words and senses under Assumption Two

Fig. 2 shows the total number of words and senses each period owned. Similar to Fig. 1, the great differences between Republic of China and Contemporary Era demonstrate the necessity of the study on contemporary words and senses. But the words and senses are not simply in use, and also cannot be used again after being discarded from the language. In this sense, this assumption may have exaggerated the contributions of the periods to vocabulary.

As a result, neither of the previous two assumptions can really reflect the true appearance of the vocabulary evolution; but we do find the trend of the general accordance of contemporary words and senses during these periods, and we also find the great changes from Republic of China to Contemporary Era. What's more, Assumption One can be considered to represent the minimum number of distributions of contemporary words in different periods while Assumption Two as the maximum one. So far, we have achieved the general and interval understanding of how the words and senses have been in use during these fifteen periods, which is great progress compared to the previous study.

3.2   The Emergence of Contemporary Words and Senses in Former Periods

The previous parts have revealed the fact that contemporary words and senses do exist in these periods, then, where does this fact come into being? We tried to analyze the earliest period in which contemporary words and senses emerged, that's to say, to analyze the total increasing number of them. Fig. 3 shows the distribution of the increasing number of words and senses appearing in each period.

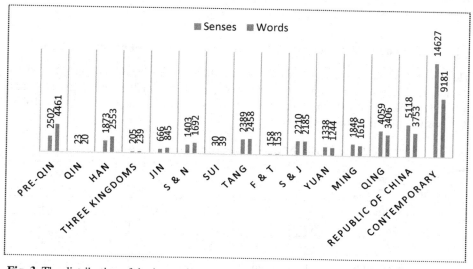

Fig. 3. The distribution of the increasing number of words and senses appearing in each period

The study on the history of the Chinese language indicated that there are four historic stages which witnessed the large numbers of new words and significantly improved the development of vocabulary. The first stage is the vocabulary inputting from Western Regions in Han dynasty. The second is the influence of Buddhism in Southern and Northern Dynasties and Tang Dynasty. The third is the vocabulary inputting from the West countries around the Reform Movement of 1898 in Qing Dynasty, and the last is the influence of Socialist culture after 1949 in Contemporary Era. All the four stages have contributed to the development of vocabulary in history, but their contributions are not the same. Wang Li (1980) compared the influence of the four stages: the influence of the Modern Chinese is greater than that of Buddhism, and the influence of Buddhism is greater than the culture of Western Regions. The above conclusion is also proved in Fig. 3 that the increasing number of new words in Qing Dynasty is far greater than that in Tang or Han Dynasty. It also indicates that the sum of new words emerging in Republic of China is less than that in Contemporary Era and is more than that in Qing Dynasty. The break out of the May Fourth Movement was suggested as a significant factor which influenced the number of new words in Republic of China.

4   The Period Distributions of Contemporary Words' Length

When tracing them back to the former periods, we have found the great variations in the number of contemporary words and senses in different periods. But as for the new emergence or the use of them, the words both represented similarities in the same period. Then, does the number of the syllables, as another feature of a word, represent the same tendency in the period distributions? To answer this question, we described from two aspects.

4.1   The Length Distributions of Contemporary Words in Former Periods

The numbers of vocabulary in each period and different length were obtained to show the length differences in former periods. Because of the small number of the words whose lengths are more than 4, we regard them as a whole to take into account. Table 2 shows the statistical results.

Table 2. The number of vocabulary in each period and word length

Length / Dynasty	1	2	3	4	>4	Average Length
Pre-Qin	1495	2693	22	227	24	1.80
Qin	283	14	0	0	0	1.05
Han	1515	3435	40	213	19	1.82
Three Kingdoms	451	548	4	28	3	1.63
Jin	837	1693	14	70	6	1.75
S & N	1233	3313	34	158	8	1.82
Sui	41	78	4	5	1	1.81
Tang	1629	5999	96	375	29	1.92
F & T	359	632	18	36	2	1.75
S & J	1663	6187	174	624	52	2.00
Yuan	937	3095	202	402	48	2.07
Ming	1380	5314	252	661	70	2.07
Qing	1828	9288	633	1665	117	2.20
Republic of China	1494	7393	939	1185	101	2.21
Contemporary	2258	23296	3606	4261	424	2.35

Horizontally speaking, although monosyllables were predominant in Pre-Qin Dynasty, not all of them can stay in use until today. In contrast, the numbers of disyllables staying in use until now are greater than that of monosyllables. But compared with the later periods, the rate of monosyllables in Pre-Qin Dynasty is the biggest. It can also be proved by the data that the average length of the words which can stay in use to Contemporary Era is slightly less than 2.

Vertically speaking, Han, Tang, Song and Qing Dynasty make a greater contribution to contemporary monosyllables; Tang, Song and Qing Dynasty also contribute to contemporary disyllables more significantly; Qing Dynasty and Republic of China make a greater contribution to trisyllables and four-syllable words. In another word, the period closer to Pre-Qin Dynasty makes bigger contribution to monosyllables, while the period closer to Contemporary Era contributes more to disyllables, so as far as the average length of words is concerned, with the development of the society, the average length of words increased gradually.

4.2   The Length Distributions of Newly-Emerging Words in Former Periods

The differences of each period's vocabulary are not only shown on the numbers of newly-emerging words, but also the length distribution. In Fig. 4, we take the periods as X-axis and the number of newly-emerging contemporary words as Y-axis. The colored bars represent the distribution of word's length of 1, 2, 3 and 4 in order.

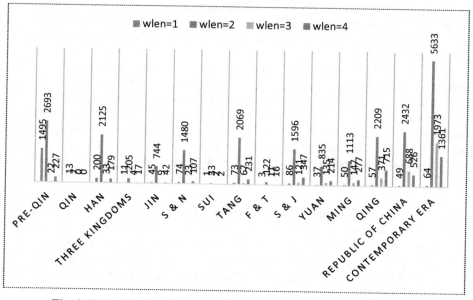

Fig. 4. The length distributions of newly-emerging words in former periods

Fig. 4 shows the length distributions of newly-emerging contemporary words in each period as well as the changing tendency of newly-emerging words' length in different periods. On one side, from the aspect of the diachronic development of vocabulary, the number of monosyllables increased slowly while those of disyllables increased outstandingly. This phenomenon could be explained by the economy of Chinese vocabulary: with the plenty of monosyllables created by the former periods, people began to take advantage of the existing monosyllables to create disyllables so that they could avoid the trouble of memorizing the ever-increasing numerous monosyllables. On the other side, we can also find the significant differences of word length distributions in a certain period. Take Pre-Qin and Contemporary Era as an example, the numbers of newly-emerging disyllables staying in use until today are greater than monosyllables both in Pre-Qin Dynasty and Contemporary Era, but new disyllables increased greatly, trisyllables and four-syllable words ranked second and the newly-emerging monosyllables scarcely increased in Contemporary Era. In conclusion, this kind of quantitative analysis has presented a simple, direct and effective inspection in the differences of the length distributions in each period.

5   The Discussion of Regularities in Vocabulary Evolutions

The quantitative-analytical study on the vocabulary resources of *The Great Chinese Dictionary* can not only reveal the development of Chinese vocabulary in different periods, verify and supplement the research results of the history of the Chinese language, it can also speculate the period of Chinese vocabulary through calculations of the vocabulary evolution, that is to say, setting up the correlation between the number of the words and their historical period. In this sense, the study can discover the regularities in vocabulary evolution, which the study on the history of the Chinese language cannot accomplish.

In the 1950s, M. Swadesh, an American linguist, measured the time interval between the ancient languages and the modern ones they developed into by the statistical method [12, 13], which is also called glottochronology. He calculated the retention rate of words for about 1,000 years by comparing with 200 core words of different languages and cultures and he found the percentage of the words' retention is a constant between 0.72 and 0.85 reflecting the elimination of semantically unstable words. At last, he got the formal representation of vocabulary periods.

$$\ln r = \ln c / t \qquad (1)$$

Take English as an example, "c" is equal to 0.85, "r" represents the retention rate of words compared to the list of 200 core words, "t" is the gap of time between the ancient language and modern language. By calculating its "r", we can roughly make sure how old this specific ancient language is. However, some scholars are skeptical about this method: they argued that the correlation between ancient and modern languages cannot verified only by relying on the relationship between the different number of vocabulary [14]. In spite of the queries, glottochronology made an assumption that the two languages being compared are related and the time is achieved based on the similarities of the number of two languages, which is in accordance with our study, so this method provided a meaningful reference to research on the development of the Chinese vocabulary.

We use the number of words in each period in assumption one in section 3.1 to calculate the retention rate of words r. The time before the present t can also be calculated by the span between the time *The Great Chinese Dictionary* edited and the time it used. The relation between t and r is shown in Fig. 5.

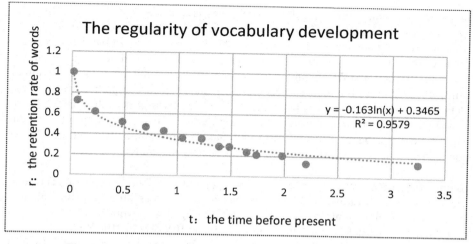

Fig. 5. The Regression Analysis of the Vocabulary Development Data

Fig. 5 directly indicates the relationship between t and r by regression analysis. Firstly, we used correlation analysis and got a conclusion that the variation t has a significant negative correlation with r (R=-0.88). Then, regression analysis was used to analyze the experimental data in order to get a formula reflecting the correlation between t and r. Lastly, we got a nonlinear regression equation representing the regularity of Chinese vocabulary development:

$$r = -0.16 \ln t + 0.35 \qquad (2)$$

The coefficient of determination R^2 is equal to 0.96, which is nearly close to 1, so this function is good to reflect the correlation between t and r. Consequently, we can use it to conjecture the time t when r is known.

6   Conclusions and Future Work

Due to the difficulties in building a large scale of annotated corpus with real texts, studies on the history of the Chinese vocabulary always focus on the description of vocabulary in a specific book or during a certain period in history. Our study makes up for these defects, to a certain extent, with the database based on *The Great Chinese Dictionary* and other web resources as supplements. It systematically reflects the development of vocabulary during a long period from Pre-Qin Dynasty to Contemporary Era, especially the development of contemporary vocabulary in former periods. It can also be used for the investigation into the regularities of the vocabulary evolution.

However, dictionary resources cannot be a replacement of real texts; the use of dictionary is only a compromise, due to the shortage of real ancient texts remaining at present. There is much more work to carry on so as to obtain the relatively accurate development of the Chinese vocabulary. Firstly, the corpus being under construction of the real texts in Pre-Qin, Han Dynasty and other periods can be used as supplements for the words including morphology and example sentences in the database. In this way, the corpus can not only enlarge our database, but also make the content more comprehensive. Secondly, we should further analyze the database, such as describing the pronunciations, semantic and morphological features of all the words in different periods, in a hope to get the delicate conclusion of the evolution of Chinese vocabulary. Finally, we need to take into account comprehensively all the factors like the internal ones of language itself, the external ones of the society, history and culture and the use of language as well, by which we can explore the reason why Chinese vocabulary changed and try to make use of computers to set up calculation models so as to forecast the evolution of Chinese vocabulary.

Acknowledgments. We are thankful for the hard work of Zhou Shunan, Qu Tanchun, Ma Yan, Li Yue, Ji Zhiwei and other students, who were searching the historical period of each example sentence. This work is the staged achievement of the projects supported by National Social Foundation of China (10&ZD117, 10CYY021) and the research base of Philosophy and Social Sciences for Universities in Jiangsu (2010JDXM023).

References

1. Zhao, K.Q.: The Study of Ancient Chinese Vocabulary (古代汉语词汇学). The Commercial Press, Beijing (2005). (in Chinese)
2. Wang, L.: Chinese Language History Draft (汉语史稿). Zhong Hua Press, Shanghai (2004). (in Chinese)
3. Jiang, S.Y.: Preliminary Exploration of the Historical Development of the Meaning and Vocabulary System of Chinese Language. Journal of Peking University (Philosophy and Social Sciences) **43**(4), 84–105 (2006). (in Chinese)
4. Zhao, Q.: Research on Rules of Lexical Semantic Change and Cognitive Motivation of Chinese Body Nouns. PhD Thesis at Beijing Language and Culture University (2007). (in Chinese)
5. Su, X.C.: The semantic trend of studies of contemporary Chinese vocabulary (当代汉语词汇研究的大趋势——词义研究). Journal of Guangdong Education Institute, 38–42 (1994). (in Chinese)
6. Su, X.C.: The Realization of Statistical Method in the Study of Vocabulary (词汇计量及实现). The Commercial Press, Beijing (2010). (in Chinese)
7. Su, X.C.: A Quantitative Study of Chinese Vocabulary (汉语词汇计量研究). Xiamen University Press, Xiamen (2001). (in Chinese)
8. Li, B., Xi, N., Feng, M., Chen, X.: Corpus-Based Statistics of Pre-Qin Chinese. In: Ji, D., Xiao, G. (eds.) CLSW 2012. LNCS, vol. 7717, pp. 145–153. Springer, Heidelberg (2013)
9. Xiang, X.: The Study of Polysyllabic Words in Classic of Poetry (《诗经》里的复音词), Linguistics Review (The 6th). The Commercial Press, Beijing (2010). (in Chinese)
10. Su, X.C.: Computational Methods' Functions in Chinese Vocabulary Studies and Statistical Methods for Frequency. Yangtze River Academic (2), 118–124 (2007). (in Chinese)
11. The Great Chinese Dictionary 2.0 [CD]. The Commercial Press, Hong Kong (2005). (in Chinese)

12. Swadesh, M.: Lexico-statistic Dating of Prehistoric Ethnic Contacts: with Special Reference to North American Indians and Eskimos. Proceedings of the American philosophical society **96**(4), 452–463 (1952)
13. Feng, Z.W.: Studying Language by Quantitative Methods. Foreign Language Teaching and Research (Bimonthly) **44**(2), 256–269 (2012). (in Chinese)
14. Campbell, L.: How to Show Languages are related: Methods for Distant Genetic Relationship. The Handbook of Historical Linguistics. Blackwell Publishing, UK (2003)

The Ergativization of the Verb "死"[si](Die) in Chinese Language History

Yichen Zhang[✉]

Department of Chinese, FAH, University of Macau, Macau, China
zhangyichen1212@163.com

Abstract. This paper investigates the Ergativization of the Chinese verb "死"[si](die)（the same below）in Chinese Language History based on the Ergativization theory of Lemmens (1998). Ergativization refers to the process of transitive or intransitive verb entering the ergative structure. The semantic change of verbs led to change of syntactic structure, and "死" experienced the evolution from intransitive verb to semi intransitive verb from ancient Chinese to modern Chinese. Its original syntax structure "死+relational object" in the Qin and Han Dynasty also changed into "V+死+object". The "死+object" structure appearing after the Song Dynasty made the verb "死" turn into a real Ergative verb.

Keywords: Unaccusative verb · Ergativization

1 Introduction

In modern Chinese, "死"[si]（die）is an intransitive verb, but sometimes, it appears with an object. E.g.

- 一个 人　死了　　　　死 了 一个人　　　　王冕　　死 了 父亲
  One person die -ed　　die -ed　one person　Wangmian　die -ed　father

According to the Unaccusative Hypothesis of Perlmutter (1978), it is believed that "死" is an unaccusative verb. The final subject of unaccusative verb is its initial object, i.e. the subject in surface structure is the logical object in deep structure, while the final subject of unergative verb is its initial subject, which means that the subject in surface structure is exactly the subject in deep structure. On the surface, the three examples above show three different types of structure, namely:

- NP+"死"　　　　　　　"死"+NP　　　　　　NP$_1$+"死"+NP$_2$

However, from the perspective of generative grammar, all of them are derived from one and the same deep structure, i.e. unaccusative verb "死" generates basic form "死+NP" (Xu Jie, 1999, 2001). In Chinese, unaccusative verb can be used in surface unaccusative sentence, i.e. the unique argument in position of underlying object can also be in the same position in surface structure. Han Jingliang and Pan Haihua (2005)

© Springer International Publishing Switzerland 2014
X. Su and T. He (Eds.): CLSW 2014, LNAI 8922, pp. 124–133, 2014.
DOI: 10.1007/978-3-319-14331-6_12

called sentence structure that can reflect the unaccusative attribute of verb in surface syntactic structure as "surface unaccusative constructions". Common sentences of this type include existential verb sentence , non-causative verb sentence with corresponding causative form , and passive sentence , e.g.

- 来   了   客人   沉   了 三艘 船   被   偷   了 一辆 摩托车

  come -ed   guest   drop -ed three ships Passive verb steal -ed one motorcycle

Correspondingly, typical unaccusative verb in Chinese can be divided into three categories: (1) verbs conveying existential meaning, such as "死(die), 来(come), 落 (fall)" ; (2) verbs with causative meaning, such as "开(turn on), 沉(sink), 掉(drop)"; (3) "被"(PASSIVE VERB).

For the latter two categories of unaccusative verb, some scholars argue that they are evolved from transitive verbs, which is called ergativization. Pan Haihua and Han Jingquan (2005) included causative verbs into derivative unaccusative verbs. In fact, the non-causativization of verb is to derive unaccusative verb from causative transitive verb, which can be called unaccusativization of verb, namely, ergativization. Deng Siying (2008) argued that "被" (passive verb) should be an unaccusative verb. The "ergativization" applied to Chinese passive sentence analysis refers to a syntactic process of turning transitive verbs into intransitive verbs. After ergativization, the subject of verb cannot be agent, while an accusative case of the verb that can be assigned is "eaten", and the original ability of assigning accusative case for object as internal argument disappears.

This essay puts forward a different concept of "ergativization". Lemmens (1998) defined it in this way: the process of transitive or intransitive verb entering the ergative structure is called "ergativization". Therefore, "ergativization" may happen to not only transitive verb but also intransitive verb. The first category of unaccusative verbs with existential meaning mentioned above were not ergative verb at the very beginning, but experienced the evolution from intransitive verb to semi intransitive verb. The semantic change led to the change of syntactic structure and they finally entered the ergative structure to turn into real ergative verbs. This paper takes unaccusative verb "Si" for example to investigate its ergativization from three aspects such as the semantic change of verbs, the selection of subject and the tense of minor sentences.

2   The Ergativization of Chinese Verb "死"

2.1   Semantic Evolution of "死"

Perlmutter argued that the non-ergativization and the unaccusativity of verb are rooted in semanteme but reflected in syntax. The semantic evolution of verb is an important reason for its ergativization. Davidse (1992) also pointed out the importance of semanteme when describing ergativization. However, Davidse's description of ergativization was just limited to "controlled" intransitive verbs and he held that a non-instigatable intransitive verb cannot be ergative, such as "faint, stumble and die". The development of "starve" provides an evidence for the ergativization of "uncontrollable" intransitive verbs. Lemmens presented the process that the semantic change of intransitive verb "starve" leads to its ergativization. In primary ancient English literature, "starve" referred to a prolonged death caused by hungry, coldness, sadness or chronic disease, and the resulting metaphorical meaning indicates a kind of extreme pain or desire. According to statistical data of ancient English, this phenomenon appeared at the end of the 16th century and continued in the 17th century. After "starve", "for, of" etc. appeared to indicate the emphasis on sufferers. In modern English, "for" does not have to appear any longer, which means that the meaning of "starve" further specialized into "to die for, or suffer extremely from, lack of food" from the 17th century to now. Nevertheless, in figurative usage, "for" is generally added to express "desire, yearn", such as "a company starving for cash".

Semantic change was also accompanied by syntactic structure. Since then, "starve" began to appear in double-argument structure:

- He...also sterued them for honger and cold, so that many died.(OED,1560)

- Who abuseth his cattle and starues thme for meat(OED,1573)

- In steede of consuming and staruming your euil, you giue it nourishment(OED,1581)

The above is a typical example of the ergativization of intransitive verb. As a non-instigatable verb, "starve" originally meant "to die". However, the development from "loss" to "prolonged death" created semantic condition for the appearance of "instigator". That is to say, "starve" gradually turned to be a semi intransitive verb indicating "lead to death". Although ergativization might be an extended usage at the very beginning, as ergative mode was gradually established, verb lost its connection with intransitive verb, thus becoming a mature ergative verb. And so, semantic extension lays the foundation for the extension of syntactic structure.

Similar to "starve" in English, Chinese verb "死" also experienced the transformation from an intransitive verb to a semi intransitive verb. The following will give an illustration according to the semantic change of "死" from ancient Chinese to modern Chinese.

2.1.1   "死+ Relational Object"

Li Zuofeng (1983) studied six works in close ages, including *The Commentary of Zuo*, *The Analects of Confucius*, *Mencius*, *Chuang Tse*, *Hsun-Tzu*, and *The Book of Rites*. He selected several intransitive verbs to observe their usage and get statistical figures, shown in the table below:

It can be seen from the above table that "Transitive: Intransitive" of "死" accounts for a small proportion and it is an obvious intransitive verb. From semantic perspective, "死+ Object" contains three meanings:

Example	Without Object and Complement	With Causative Object	Transitive: Intransitive	With Relational Object	Act as Predicate
灭 (beat)	19	115	6.0:1	0	135
败 (lose)	32	111	3.5:1	0	147
伤 (hurt)	15	52	3.5:1	0	73
绝 (extinct)	4	11	2.8:1	0	16
止 (stop)	77	83	1.1:1	2	175
出 (come out)	84	30	1 : 2.8	41	215
下 (come down)	29	7	1:3.5	29	66
退 (go back)	66	10	1:6.6	7	84
怒 (angry)	83	13	1:6.4	8	105
堕 (drop)	9	1	1:9	0	11
死 (die)	172	4	1:43	37	263

- 其北陵, 文王之所辟风雨也，必死是间。（《左·僖三十二年》）

The north mountain is a place where King Wen avoid the storm, (you) will die in two mountain gorge.

- 然子死晋国, 子孙必得志于宋。（《左·定六年》）

However, if you died for visiting Jin , your descendant would be successful in Song.

- "死吾父而专于国，有死而已"。（《左·襄二十一年》）

(He) killed my fater and collect dictatorship, so　（I ）have to die.

"死" in first two examples is followed by relational object. In the first example, it means place, while the second example shows the "motive usage" of "死', which is common in literatures of pre-Qin period, indicating reason and purpose. In general ancient Chinese grammar books, the direct various relations between verb and object included causative usage, conative, and motive usage, which was called "relational object". The location of object in Chinese contains not only a variety of essential components, but also tool, material, way, place, time and some non-core components that are difficultly generalized by current semantic roles. These components were not originally the core argument of verb, but sometimes they can hold the position of surface object. However, they can enter neither the deep structure nor the ergative structure. "The causative usage in the third example can be rarely seen, for 'die something' of 'die for something' holds the formal position of causative 'die something', while '杀'[sha]（kill） holds the semantic position of the causative usage of '死'. This kind of situation appeared for four times in nine books, so it can be said that '死' was a typical intransitive verb in pre-Qin period." (Mei Zulin, 1991)

2.1.2 "V Si+NP"

It is believed that the transformation from intransitive verb to semi intransitive verb is a typical manifestation of the ergativization of verb "死", while its semi intransitive verb transformation started with the appearance of "Si" acting as verb-resultant predicate-complement complement.

In the period of two Han dynasties, "transitive verb + intransitive verb" compound verbs such as "压死"(*crush to die*) and "烧死" (*burn to die*)appeared, but predicate-complement structure with object behind appeared late. Ōta Tatsuo (1958) used verbs "死" and "杀" to test the time when verb-complement structure appeared in ancient Chinese, i.e. before the Sui Dynasty, verb was followed by "死" instead of "杀", and in the Tang Dynasty, there were more examples of "死". Therefore, he argued that causative compound word (verb-complement structure) appeared in the Tang Dynasty. Mei Zulin (1991) "V死" was followed by object to act as verb-complement structure until the 5th century, so he believed that verb-complement structure appeared in the Six Dynasties.

Wu Fuxiang (2000) put forward that during the Six Dynasties, due to the transformation of "杀" from transitive verb to intransitive verb, "S $_{performative}$ + V$_1$+ 杀+ O" had turned from serial verb construction to verb-complement structure, in which, "杀" acted as the result complement of "死". Since the grammatical attribute (intransitive) and lexical meaning ("(living beings) lose their life") of " 杀 " in "S $_{performative}$ + V$_1$+ 杀+ O" are the same as that of intransitive verb "死", "死" started holding the position of "杀" in "S performative + V$_1$+ 杀+ O", thus forming T"S $_{performative}$ + V$_1$+ 死+ O". This kind of example appeared in the Six Dynasties and gradually increased in the Tang Dynasty.

- 是邻家老黄狗，乃打死之。(幽明录，太平广记卷四三八引)

  He beat the neibor's old dog to death.

- 律师，律师，扑死佛子耶。(开天传信记，太平广记卷九二引)

  The noble buddhist is swatting the son of buddha.

- 主人欲打死之。(广古今五行记，太平广记卷九一引)

  The master wants to beat it to death.

Regarding the "V 死" in pre-Qin and two Han Dynasties, it has two patterns, namely, "S $_{non-performative}$ +V$_1$ +死" and "S $_{performative}$ +V$_1$ +死". In the first pattern, the object of "V$_1$ 死" was preposed to act as receptor subject. In such kind of sentence, "V$_1$ 死" cannot be followed by object. In the second pattern, both "V$_1$" and "死" are intransitive verbs, and since intransitive verb is of semantic "introversion' and functional intransitivity, "V$_1$ 死" cannot be followed by object either.

2.1.3   "死+ NP" and "NP₁+ 死+ NP₂"

After the Ming and Qing Dynasties, a large number of "死+ NP" sentences appeared. In the meantime, a special construction "NP₁+ 死+ NP₂" also appeared. Grimshaw (1990) said, "The identity of aspect of unaccusative argument enables it to become internal argument and makes it in object position rather than subject position of deep structure." This is the further development for the semi intransitive transformation of "死". At that time, unaccusative verb had already entered the ergative construction. E.g.

● 孔明亦自言一年死了几多人，不得不急为之意。（《朱子语类》卷第一百三十六）

   Kong Ming also said many people died this year, so he had to think about it.

● 寨内原有二十四人，死了晁盖一个，只有二十三人。（《大宋宣和遗事亨集》）

   Originally the population of the village is 24, now Chao Gai died, so only 23 people left.

● 又闻氏连次不来哭禀，两个差人又死了一个，只剩得李万，又苦苦哀求不已。（《三言二拍·喻世明言》）

   (He)heard Mrs Wen cried the intrinsic no more, and one of the two policeman died, the other Li Wan beg piteously for mercy.

2.2   The Semantic Property of NP in "死+ NP"

As mentioned before, the deep structure of "NP+ 死", "死+ NP" and "NP₁+ 死+ NP₂" is "死+ NP" in Chinese, the semantic change of verb "死" is closely related to the semantic property of "NP", to investigate the ergativization "死", the semantic meaning of NP must be studied, and the NP that can enter the ergative construction should also meet some conditions. In general, if the unaccusative verbs express the non-subject willingness of the object referred to by the argument or describe the involuntary event of the state/place of these objects, semantically, "theme" or "patient" argument is selected as its subject. In the deep structure, they used to be the object of a sentence.

2.2.1   The Animacy of NP

Dixon (1994) put forward that S, A, and O are universal syntactic-semantic primitives. A indicates transitive subject in underlying structure, O indicates transitive object in underlying structure, and S indicates intransitive subject in underlying structure. The subject S of single-argument clauses in Chinese does not always selects A, but S often selects O. In Chinese, that when S tends to perform the function of A or O is generally determined by the controllability. It is argued that this "tendency" is related to the animacy of nouns. Dixon (1994) summarised "Norminal Hierarchy", i.e. "the norminal hierarchy from the perspective of functionally tending to A instead of O" is:

   The first personal pronouns> the second personal pronouns>demonstrative pronoun, the third personal pronouns> proper nouns> common nouns

That is to say, the higher the animacy of a noun is, the more likely it is to act as agent, which means that the function of this noun tends to A; the lower the animacy of a noun is, the less likely it is to act as agent, which means that the function of this noun tends to O. In other words, the higher the animacy of a noun is, the more likely it is to tend to controlled verb; the lower the animacy of a noun is, the more likely it is to tend to non-person-description verb and non-instigatable verb. According to division, "死", as a "non-instigatable verb" (Yuan Yulin, 1991), its subject S should tend to a low-animacy noun, but in fact, it is the opposite. In "NP +死", NP is of extremely high animacy, meaning "experience, suffer". Zhu Xingfan (2005) argued that in "小虫死了 (the insect died), 兔子来了(the rabbit came)", intransitive verbs "死, 来" have causative meaning. He also argued that "死" in "王冕死了父亲"(Wang Mian's father died) has two arguments and its causative role is realized via syntactic method. In specific, the sentence contains invisible light verbs. As event predicates of sentence, light verbs choose agent as their specifier and they determine if the event structure of sentence is "causative" or "agent". The paper does not discuss whether light verb exists or not, but it can be said that an "instigator" or "causer" indeed exists in the ergativization of "死", to let "死" transform from a complete non-instigatable intransitive verb to a semi intransitive verb with causative meaning.

2.2.2   The Semantic Relation Between NP1 and NP2

For a very special structure "NP₁+死+NP₂", it is generally believed that there is posses possessive and affiliation relation between NP₁ and NP₂. Guo Jimao (1990) called this kind of sentence as "possessor-subject-possessum-object sentence". He depicted subject, object, predicate verb and the characteristic of its usage of "了 [le], 着[zhe], 过[guo]"based on subsection. Besides, he also made a comparison between this sentence pattern and two related sentence patterns, to reach a conclusion that such sentence pattern as "猎人死了一只狗" (The hunter's dog died)is similar to "猎人的狗死了" (The hunter's dog died) in respect of semantic structure and similar to "猎人杀了一只狗"(The hunter killed a dog) in respect of syntactic structure. There is a stable "possessive/affiliation" relation] between subject and object, but there is not direct semantic relation between subject and predicate verb, and object is the agent of verb. All verbs are unidirectional verbs (intransitive verbs). These studies undoubtedly deepen our knowledge of related sentence patterns. With excellent study value, they lay a good foundation of linguistic fact for analyzing the essence of problem.

2.3   Tense and Aspect Study of "死+ NP"

Delancey (1981) put forward that the pattern of divisive ergativization is aspect division, i.e. ergative form is related to perfective aspect and past tense, and accusative form is related to imperfective aspect or past tense and future tense. He said, "Ergative morphology is related to perfective aspect or past tense, and accusative morphology is related to imperfective aspect or present tense or future tense." Take Gujarati for example:

- Ranesh   pen   khərid-t-o   hə-t-o.

   (positive) (negative) buy-imperfective aspect-positive auxiliary verb- imperfective aspect-positive

   'Ramesh was buying the pen.'

- ranesh-e   pen   khərid-y-i.

   (positive)-ergative   buy-perfective-negative

Although Chinese is a language with unformatted mark, in "死+ NP", unaccusative verb "死" is often followed by auxiliary verbs such as "了[le], 过[guo]" to indicate the meaning of past tense, and if they are deleted, it will not work, e.g.

- 他 死 一个 孩子 了*   他 已经   死   一个   孩子   了

   He die one child -ed*   He already die   one   child   -ed

- 他 死 一匹 马*   他 死 过 一匹 马

   He die one horse*   He die -ed one horse

Li Zuanniang (1987) pointed out that verbs meaning disappearance and verbs meaning appearance are actually used to indicate some change, so "了[le]" is indispensable in this kind of sentence. Guo Jimao (1991) also paid attention to the use of auxiliary verbs such as "了[le], 着[zhe], 过[guo]" in possessor-subject sentence.

In addition to meaning "appearance, disappearance", unaccusative verb with existential meaning also indicates "experience, suffer". Thus, it is closely combined with auxiliary verbs such as "了[le], 过[guo]" indicating past perfect tense, which is a reflection of ergative form in Chinese and as well the semantic foundation for the ergativization of unaccusative verb.

3   The Ergativization of English Unaccusative Verb "die"

In modern English, "die" is also an intransitive verb. Lemmens described in his book the ergativization tendency of "die", "...in such gradual sensible death...God dies away in us, as I may say, all human satisfaction, in order to subdue his poor creatures to himself." (OED, 1748) He argued that "God" was obviously an "instigator" in that age by directing quoting "all human satisfaction to die away". "Although the ergativity of 'die' is not established, its ergativization tendency has already existed."

We hold that English verb "die" has ergativization, just like Chinese verb "Si", for "die" can also be followed by cognate object. Cognate object means that NP central word of object is the nominalization form of event or state expressed by verb, which is not only completely the same as verb semantically, but also the same or similar to verb formally. Kuno & Takami (2004) mentioned examples of unaccusative verbs with cognate object, e.g.

- Mark twain died a gruesome death.
- The tree grew a century's growth within only ten years.
- The stock market dropped its largest drop in three years today.

From the examples above, it can be seen that in addition to "die", verbs that can be followed by cognate object such as "grow" and "drop" also belong to intransitive verbs with existential meaning. It can be speculated that similar to Chinese, such kind of verbs in English also have ergativization process in history of language and their ergative structure is gradually coming into being.

4   Conclusion

The appearance of Chinese ergativization is the manifestation of creativity in linguistics. This paper applies the theory of ergativization to investigating the ergativization process of "死" – a modern Chinese intransitive verb with existential meaning in history of Chinese. Different from the other two kinds of Chinese intransitive verbs, "死" experienced a semantic evolution from intransitive verb to semi intransitive verb from ancient Chinese to modern Chinese. The semantic change of verb led to change of syntactic structure, and its syntactic structure also changed from "死+ Relational Object" in the Qin and Han Dynasties to "V+ 死+ Object" in the Six Dynasties. "死+ Object" appearing after the Song Dynasty enabled verb "死" to become a real ergative verb (or unaccusative verb). The aspect of unaccusative argument enabled it to become an internal argument and hold the position of object instead of subject in the deep structure. Although ergativization might be an extended usage at the very beginning, with the gradual establishment of ergative pattern, verb lost its connection with intransitive verb and turned into a mature ergative verb. After investigating the semantic meaning of verb "死", this paper discusses the semantic property of NP in "死了+NP" and special sentence pattern "NP1+死了+NP2", to indicate that the main standard of semantic preference is the animacy and possessive relationship of noun phrase. Chinese is mark-free language, but verb "Si" must be added by auxiliary verbs such as "了, 过" indicating past tense, which is also a form of ergativization. It can be speculated that other Chinese verbs with existential meaning also have ergativization in history, which is reflected in three aspects such as the semantic change of verb, the semantic property of main noun phrase, and tense and aspect of minor sentence. In ergativization structure, underlying intransitive subject S sometimes tends to perform the function of A and sometimes tends to perform the function of O (A indicates transitive subject in underlying structure and O indicates transitive object in underlying structure), which proves that Chinese is neither pure ergative language nor pure accusative language but a language with special divisive ergativity. Further studies on this subject will be carried out in the future.

References

1. Davidse, K.: Transitivity/Ergativity: The Janus-headed Grammar of Actions and Events. In: Davies, M., Ravelli, L. (eds.) Advances in Systemic Linguistics, pp. 105–135. Printer Publishers, London (1992)
2. Delancey, S.: An Interpretation of Split Ergativety and Related Patterns. Language **57**, 626–657 (1981)

3. Dixon, R.M.W.: Ergativity. Cambridge University Press, New York (1994)
4. Lemmens, M.: Lexical Perspectives on Transitivity and Ergativity: Causative Constructions in English. John Benjamins Publishing Company, Amsterdam (1998)
5. Grimshaw, J.: Argument Structure. MIT Press, Cambridge (1990)
6. Kuno, S., Takami, K.: Functional Constrains in Grammar: On the Unergative-unaccusative Distinction. John Benjamins, Amsterdam (2004)
7. Deng, S.: Ergativization and Chinese Passive Sentences. Chinese Language **4**, 291–301 (2004)
8. Deng, S.: Rethink of Chinese Passive Sentences Analysis. Contemporary Linguistics **4**, 208–319 (2008)
9. Guo, J.: Possessor-subject Possessee-object Sentence. Chinese Language **1**, 24–29 (1990)
10. Li, Z.: Existential Sentence of Appearing-type and Disappearing-type Verbs. Linguistic Researches **3**, 21 (1987)
11. Li, Z.: Chinese Intransitive Verbs and Their Causative Usage in the Pre-Qin Period. Linguistics Review, 117–144 (1983)
12. Mei, Z.: View the Development of Verb-complement Structure Based on "Verb Sha" and "Verb Si" in the Han Dynasty – the Neutralization of "Agent-patient" Relations of Words Since the the Middle Ancient Times. Linguistics Review (1991)
13. Pan, H., Han, J.: Studies on the Syntax of Surface Unaccusative Constructions **9**, 1–13 (2005)
14. Wu, F.: On the Origin of Verb-complement Structure "V Si O". Research on Ancient Chinese Language **3**, 44–48 (2000)
15. Xu, J.: Two Sentences with Retained Object and Related Syntactic Theoretical Problems. Contemporary Linguistics **1**, 16–29 (1999)
16. Xu, J.: "Transitivity" Features and Related Four Types of Verb. The Study of Language 3 (2001)
17. Yuan, Y.: Imperative Sentences and Category of Verbs. Chinese Language **1**, 10–20 (1991)
18. Zhu, X.: Light Verbs and Chinese Intransitive Verbs with Object. Modern Foreign Languages **8**, 221–231 (2005)

Grammaticalization and Subjectivization of "Po"

Haifeng Yang[✉]

School of Politics and Administration, Wuhan University of Technology,
Wuhan, Hubei, People's Republic of China
yanghaifengtl@163.com

Abstract. This paper investigates the grammaticalization of "po" on the basis of a survey on examples from Chinese classic works, and finds that: 1) the use of "po" shifted from an adjective to a degree adverb and a scope adverb; 2) the use of "po" shifted from an objective scope adverb to a modal adverb. This paper focuses on the syntactic environment that triggered the grammaticalization of "po" and how it became a functional word. The increasing subjectivity of this functional word is also discussed.

Keywords: "Po" · Grammaticalization · Subjectivization · Show

1   Introduction

"Po"[1] as a degree adverb first appeared in *Historical Records*[2] , and became popular in the Middle Ages. In view of its grammatical function, "po" is an atypical degree adverb[3]. Though there is not much academic research on it, "po" is covered in many treatises and dictionaries. We can read that "po means the tilting of one's head" in *ShuoWen JieZi*[4], that "po means little" in *Guangyashigu two*, and that "po means not enough since ancient times" in *Chinese Grammar Theory* by Wang Li. "Yan is a little proficient at interpreting *The Book of Rites*, but not performing rituals and ceremonies." (*RulinLiezhuan of Historical Records*) When it is used as a modifier, its meaning is the same as "shao"[5]. For example, "I would like to learn some of the ancient rituals and integrate them with those of the Qin's."(Shu SuntongLiezhuan of Historical Records") When the predicate includes a 目的位(objective position), "po" seems to modify the scope of this目的位(objective position). For instance, "颇采古礼"(*po cai gu li*, learn some old rites)means "learn some of the ancient rituals". Sometimes, "po" can be used in descriptive sentences. For example, "pojia"[6] is equivalent to good

---

[1] "po" is the pinyin for the Chinese character "颇".

[2] Written by Sima Qian, a great Chinese historian, in about 95 B.C.

[3] Hong Chengyu(1997)*The Degree adverb of "Po" in* Historical Records, Journal of capital normal university.

[4] A dictionary about words and expressions compiled by Xu Shen (58-147), a famous Chinese linguist.

[5] The pinyin for the Chinese character 稍.

[6] Pinyin for Chinese character 颇佳.

X. Su and T. He (Eds.): CLSW 2014, LNAI 8922, pp. 134–142, 2014.
DOI: 10.1007/978-3-319-14331-6_13

enough（not very good）in English and assez bon（not tres bon）in French. I don't think that the interpretation of "po" as "shen ye"[7] in*zhengzitong*is appropriate. Judged from thousands of years of language habits, "po" just means dissatisfaction or humbleness, and it has never been used for hyperbole[8]. TatsuoOhta says in *Chinese Historical Grammar* that "po" means "shen ye", "shao ye"[9]. However, I don't think it is correct that "po" indicates strength and weakness at the same time. I believe it is simply used to show direction and has nothing to do with strength or weakness[10]. Hong Chengyu investigated the semantic issues of "po" used in *Historical Records* as a degree adverb, and he made a clear statement that "po", at least until the Tang Dynasty, only means semantic weakness of degree. Gao Yuhua investigated a variety of usages of "po" in middle ancient Chinese, and analyzed their origins and historical development[11]. Generally speaking, however, the present relevant researches are not systematic enough and fail to clearly reveal the historical development of po's meaning. Thus, this paper focuses on an analysis of its syntactic environment, how it became a functional word and its increasing subjectivity as well.

2   The Grammatical Meaning and Characteristics of "Po"

On the basis of a careful study of many usages of "po" and the researches done by scholars and professionals, this paper divides the usages of "po" into three categories: degree adverb, scope adverb, and interrogative adverb, according to po's semantic and functional features.

2.1   The Usages of "Po" as a Degree Adverb

A degree adverb indicates the degree that some quality, state or action can reach. And the degree is exactly what the semantic features of a degree adverb mean. According to the statistics on the examples taken from Chinese classic works, such as *Historical Records, Discourses Weighed in the Balance, Book of Han,* there are two types of usage in this case.

A. "Po" is used before a verb or adjective, indicating low degree, equivalent to "a little" or "slightly. For instance:

（1）往冬时，为王使于楚，至莒县阳周水，而莒桥梁颇坏，信则揽车辕未欲渡也。(*wang dong shi ,wei wang shi yu chu,zhi juxian yangzhoushui,er ju qiaoliang po huai,xin ze lan cheyuan wei yu du ye;* Last winter, I was sent to the Kingdom of Chu as an envoy and came to the Yangzhou River in Ju County.On seeing the bridge

---

[7] Pinyin for Chinese character 甚也.

[8] TatsuoOhta, Chinese language historical grammar(in Chinese). Peking University Press, Beijing (1987).

[9] Pinyin for Chinese character 稍也.

[10] Wang Li（1951）Theories on Chinese Grammar, Commercial Publishing House.

[11] Gao Yuhua（2001）A *Study of the Adverb Po in the Middle Ancient Chinese,* Journal of Wenzhou Normal College.

was slightly damaged, I held the shafts of the carriage to stop the horse.) (BianqueCanggongLiezhuan of Historical Records)

(2) 斯则坐守信言师法，不颇博览致咎也。(*Si ze zuo shou xin yan shifa,bu po bolan zhi jiu ye;* This is because they are just too convinced of their mentors' interpretations of the books, but reluctant to read a little more themselves.) (Xieduan in Discourses Weighed in the Balance)

(3) 涉浅水者见虾，其颇深者察鱼鳖，其尤甚者观蛟龙。(She qian shui zhe jian xia,qi po shen zhe cha yu bie,qi you shen zhe guan jiaolong; Those who step into the shallow water see only the shrimps; those who enter the deep water the fish and turtles; while those who come into the far deep water the flood dragons.)(Bietongin Discourses Weighed in the Balance）

These two types of usage are quite common.

B. "Po" is used before a verb or adjective, indicating high degree, similar to "very" or "quite". On this usage, scholars have always disagreed with each other. Zhou Bingjun (1981), Yang Bojun(1992), LvYaxian(1992) and other scholars believe that this usage is originally used in *Historical Records*. Xiang Xi（1993), Gao Yuhua (2001) believe that it is originally used in the Eastern Han Dynasty(25-220), and Hong Chenyu(1997) claims that it's not used until the Tang Dynasty （618-907). The following example is quoted from *LishengLujiaLiezhuan ofHistorical Records*.

(4) 及诛诸吕，立孝文帝，陆生颇有力焉。(*Ji zhu zhu lv,li xiaowendi,lusheng po you li yan*; The trusted people of Lv were all killed and Xiaowen Emperor was crowned, to which Lu Jia had contributed a lot.)

Some scholars think that "po" in this sentence means high degree, while others argue that "po" indicates low degree. Considering the context of the this sentence, I think "po" means "very" or "quite" instead of "a little" or "slightly". My support lies in what's written in *Record of Lujia and Volume 43, Record of Lujia too, in the Book of Han*. It is said that when the Liu reign was under great threat, Lu Jia mediated so much by first establishing agreement between the ruling class and the army and then affecting the whole upper class of the Han Dynasty, which helped to lay a solid foundation of getting rid of the Lv Group and restoring the Liu's reign. The "po" in "陆生颇有力焉"(*lusheng po you li yan;* Lu Sheng has contributed a lot)can only mean "hen" or "shen", instead of "lue" or "shaowei".

Here are two more such examples quoted from *Historical Records*.

(5) 绛侯得释，盎颇有力。(Jianghou de shi, ang po you li; Marquis Hou was released as a result of Ang's great help.)（Yuan Ang Chao Cuoliezhuan）

(6) 廷尉乃言贾生年少，颇通诸子百家之书。(Tingwei nai yan Jiasheng nian shao,po tong zhuzibaijia zhi shu; Tingwei recommended that Jia, as a young man though, was quite proficient at the books of the Hundred Schools of Thought.) （Qu Yuan liezhuan)

It is worth noting that when it represents high degree, "po" can be used only in the sentences of strong comparison, as examples (4) and (5) above have shown; when it indicates low degree, things are just the opposite, namely, it can never be used in comparative sentences, as examples (1) and (2) above have indicated.

2.2   The Usages of **"Po"** as a Scope Adverb

The Scope adverb, a subcategory of adverb, is typically used to indicate the scope that a notional element belongs to, or used as the constraint of a verbal element. More importantly, a scope adverb is mainly used to reveal the universality of the relevant things within a certain scope or the individuality of the members within some scope. Therefore, we say a scope adverb is used to limit some scope. In light of the statistics on the usages of "po" in *Historical Records, Discourses Weighed in the BalanceBook of Han*, "po", as a scope adverb, is equivalent to "jie", and can be translated into "quan" or "dou".[12] Here are some examples :

（7）其后岁余，骞所遣使通大夏之属者皆颇与其人俱来，于是西北国始通于汉矣。(*Qi hou sui yu, qian suo qian shi tong daxia zhi shu zhe jie po yu qi ren ju lai, yushi xibeiguo shi tong yu han yi;* One year later, more than half of the envoys to the Country of Xia and others sent by Zhang Qian returned to the Han Dynasty with all their followers in that country. Countries in the northern western region, from then on, began to establish relationships with the Han Dynasty.) (Dayuanliezhuan*of*Historical Records)

（8）蔡盗取三顷，颇卖得四十余万。(*Cai dao qu sanqing,po mai de sishi yu wan;* Cai took three qins of the land and sent them secretly for more than 400,000 taels of silver.) (*Shiji,LiGuangzhuan of Historical Records*)

（9）昔晋氏丧乱，颇由祖尚虚玄，胡贼遂覆中夏。(*Xi   jinshi sang luan, po you zu shang xu xuan,huzei sui fu zhongxia;* Zhongxia was overthrown just because of JinShi's ancestors' obsession in Taoism. （*Nanshi,He Shang zhizhuan*)

"Po", as a scope adverb, was first used in Ancient Chinese, and then became heavily used in late Western Han Dynasty. Until after Eastern Han Dynasty, "dou" emerged. Dou is an equivalent of "po" as a scope adverb in meaning. Thus, the two words coexisted and competed each other for quite some time.

2.3   The Usages of **"Po"** as an Interrogative Adverb

Used before a verb or verbal phrase, "po" can function as an interrogative adverb, meaning guess or question. This usage was ever discussed by KoujirouYoshikawa, a Japanese scholar in Chinese, *On Chinese Essays*, republished in 1966, Zhumo Study.

"Po", as an interrogative adverb, is often used together with "bu","fou", or "wei" [13]in the form of "po + vp+bu/fou/wei", of which the "po+vp+bu" pattern is most widely used. In this situation "po" is used to help tone down but not tone up. The function of "po" is just opposite to other interrogative adverbs like "jing", "ding" or "zhong" . It is roughly the same as "ke" that is used in modern Chinese interrogative sentences. [14]Here is an example sentence "po is like ke" from the 18th volume of

---

[12] Jie, quan, and dou are pinyin for Chinese characters 皆，全 and 都 respectively.

[13] bu, fou, and wei are pinyin for Chinese characters 不，否 and 未 respectively.

[14] Jing, ding, zhong and ke are pinyin for Chinese characters 竟，定，终 and 可 respectively.

Yiqiejingyinyi by Hui Lin. This usage can be dated back to *Zhongbenqijing*[15] written in the Eastern Han Dynasty. A large use of "po" can be seen in the Wei, Jin, South and North Dynasties, especially in Buddhist Scriptures. This wide use lasted to the Tang Dynasty and appeared occasionally in the writings of the Song Dynasty. Here are some examples from *Diamond Sutra*[16].

（10）（秦译）须菩提白佛言、世尊颇有众生得闻如是言说章句生实信不？

(*xu puti bai fo yan,shizun po you zhongsheng de wen ru shi yan shuo zhangju sheng shi xin fou;* Xu Puti asked the Buddha, "in the future, when people are lectured these profound tenets, will they have a true belief in them?")（*Zheng Xin xi you fen*）(Qin translation)

（11）（玄奘译）诸豫流者颇作是念我能证得豫流果不？(*zhu yu liu zhe po zuo shi nian wo neng zheng de yu liu guo fou;* For you people who have been in the field, do you have the idea that you can justify the result of being a follower?) (*Zheng Xin xi you fen*) (Xuanzang Translation)

Examples of this type can be seen in the translated works of Diamond Sutra. As for the reason why such kind of sentence pattern appeared, ShinjoMizutani claims that "po...bu" pattern is employed to make the interrogative mood more apparent.

In addition, "po" can also be used in yes-no interrogative sentences, echoes other interrogative words like "hu", "ye", etc. However, there are not many of this kind of examples. For instance:

（12）吴王颇知学乎？(*Wuwang po zhi xue hu;* Is King Wu a learned man?) (*Sanguozhi,wuzhi*)

（13）沙门，颇见我四部之众耶？(*Shamen,po jian wo sibu zhi zhong ye;* Shamen, Do you see my army in Sibu?)（The Arranged Works of Hinayana Sutra）

In the Tang Dynasty, "po" was still used as an interrogative adverb and was mainly used in repetitive questions containing "vp+bu"structure. Different from Han Wei and Six Dynasties, "fou" is more often used than "bu" at the end of the repetitive questions, and more examples can be found in yes-no questions. For instance ;

（14）庾信是大罪人，见此受苦, 汝见庾信, 颇识否?(*Yuxin shi da zuiren,jian ci shou ku,ru jian yuxin,po shi fou;* Yuxin is undergoing his penalty as a criminal here. Do you know him?) (Tai Ping GuangJi, Fayuanzhulin)

（15）尔等颇识我否？(*Erdeng po shi wo fou;* Do you know me well?) (*Jiutangshu,fengangzhuan*)

Occasionally, we can read some sentences with "xie(邪)" at the end. For instance:

（16）子颇知有寒山子邪？(*Zi po zhi you hanshanzi ye;* Do you know a man called Han Shan zi?)（*Xian zhuanshiyi*）

The sharp increase of "fou" and decrease of "bu" at the end of sentence shows that the division of the two words became gradually clear.

---

[15] DuanGaiying *A Historical Study on the Questions with "Po" and the year whenzhuanji baiyuanjing was translated,* Journal of Southwest University of Science and Technology, 2001.

[16] Shinjo Mizutani. *A Study of Po in the Traditional Semantic Perspective.* Studies on the History of the Chinese Language, Sanxingtang, 1994.

After the Mid-Tang Dynasty, the use of "vp+bu?" structure decreased, and that of "po+vp+wu?" increased. According to the statistics made by Jiang Lansheng, all the relevant sentences are in the form of "po+vp +wu?" in *YouyangZazu*by DuanChengshi. For instance:

（17）向客，上帝戏臣也，言泰山老师，颇记无？(*Xiang ke,shangdi xi chen ye,yan taishan laoshi,po ji wu;* The guest, an official for the God, said that you are the reincarnation of Taishan. Do you still remember that?) (volume 2)

（18）刘四，颇忆平昔无？(*Liusi,po yi ping xi wu; Liu Si, do you remember the past?*)（volume 15）

"Po" as an interrogative adverb can seldom be found in the literature and materials in the Song Dynasty, though it didn't die out.

（19）外间百姓颇相信否？(*Waijian baixing po xiangxin fou;* Do the mass people believe in it?)（Ye Mengde,*Shilinyanyu*)

3   The Grammaticalization and Subjectivization of "Po"

Shuo Wen JieZi says "po means the tilting of one's head."DuanYuzhu annotates "something tilting". "po" was originally a state adjective, and had its meaning changed in the course of historical development. The following is a review of such changes.

3.1   Minimum Cognitive Structure and Minimum Lexical Meaning Structure

3.1.1 The Generalization of Meaning

Lexical meaning is the result of cognitive conceptualization, abstracted from human being's experience of the physical world. Human being's metaphorical competence enables themselves to describe changes across domains, usually from concrete domain to abstract domain. "po" is a state adjective. It was originally used to express the direction that one's head tilted toward. If it had been used merelyin such a concrete domain, the application scope of "po" would have been very narrow. This was not in line with the tendency of polysemy of Chinese characters, and could not help people to express themselves well. In the process of language development, people changed their focus from the word's original conceptualized things to part of its meaning, namely, tilting toward one side. Therefore, the application scope of this meaning got expanded and generalized. A lot of adjective pos can be found in Chinese classic works.

(20) 举贤而授能兮，循绳墨在不颇。(*Ju xian er shou neng xi,xun sheng mo zai bu po;* To run the country well, we should get the really capable people, no matter rich or poor, and to implement strictly the laws.)（The Songs of Chu）

(21) 以劳受禄，则民不幸生，刑罚不颇，则下无怨心，名正分明民不惑于道。(*Yi lao shou lu,ze min bu xing sheng,xingfa bu po,ze xia wu yuan xin,ming zhengfenming min bu huo yu dao;* To reward people matching their contributions, they will have a willing life; to implement the penalties in accordance with the laws, the people will not complain; with good institutions and responsibilities, the people will cast no doubt as to how to run the country.)（*Juncheng, Guan Zi*)

(22) 婼将与季氏讼, 书辞无颇 。(*Ruo jiang yu jishi song,shu ci wu po;* Ruo would launch a lawsuit against Jishi. Be fair when writing the indictment.) (*ZuoZhuan*)

These three examples show that po's meaning shifted from the tilting of one's head to the tilting of all the physical things in this world, and then to people's poor or evil morality. Due to the expansion of po's event domain, its function of an adjective referring to a concrete thing became weaker and weaker, which resulted in the generalization of po's meaning.

3.2   Development of Po's Syntactic Structures

In the process of po's changing from a notional word to a functional word, semantic meaning is the basis, and the development of the syntactic structure plays a decisive role. After generalization of its semantic meaning, po's syntactic position in a sentence becomes very flexible, and it can be used as many syntactic constituents. The generalization of its meaning is the first step of how it became a functional word. The change from a notional word to a functional word could not have happened except that "po" had been used together with an adjective.

3.2.1   "Po+A" Structure

The wide use of this structure might appear in the Pre-Qin period, and this structure is a good breeding ground for degree adverbs. According to the research on relevant materials, there are 54 pos in *ZuoZhuan* all together. 36 of them are in the form of "po+A" structure, 10 pos are noun phrases and the other 8 are modified by adverbs. In this structure, "po" is used as adverbial. In spite that it has changed to be a functional word, "po" still has adjective features in a certain degree[17]. So we say "po" is not a real adverb in this case, for example:

(23) 刑之颇类, 狱之放纷, 会朝之不敬, 使命之不听, 取陵于大国 。(*Xing zhi po lei,yu zhi fang fen,hui chao zhi bu jing,shi ming zhi bu ting,qu ling yu da guo;* Orders are made inappropriately and not implemented strictly; penalties are made unfairly; messy lawsuits, meetings without proper manners are conducted. All these lead to the abuse by the powers and the chaotic lives of the mass people, yet everything remains unrevealed. And all of the above are my faults.) (*Zhaogong* 16)

Gradually, the large use of "po" as an adverbial led to the weakening of po's function as a notional word, and the strengthening of its function of objective quantification, and thereby "po" became a degree adverb.

When "po" indicates low degree, "po" is equivalent to "lue". Since "lue" means "jie, quan, or xi", "po" also can mean quan. This is "相因生义"(*Xiang yin sheng yi;* Mutually Affected Semantic Generation of Two Words) (Jiang Shaoyu 1989). For this, Liu Qi makes a clear point in his *Zhuzibianlue*, "po, originally meant 'Lue', while 'Lue' means 'Xi', so they mean the same." This fact reflects the tendency of how the meaning of natural language extends, namely, a concept comes from people's knowledge of the real world, and then extends to the understanding of the possible world.

---

[17] Adjective features here refer to grammatical characteristics of adjectives.

3.2.2 "Po+Bu/Wei/Fei" Structure

The formation of "po" as a scope adverb means that "po" can inevitably be used as universal quantification for negative proposition. Therefore, it is often used before negative words such as "bu", "wei", "fei". "po" should still be regarded as a scope adverb in a negative sentence, even though NP, which is to be quantified, appears before "po" and "po" may sometimes contain the meaning of subjective mood. For example:

（24）是时财匮, 战士颇不得禄矣 。(*Shi shi cai kui,zhanshi po bu de lu yi;* At the time the country was poverty stricken and many of the soldiers couldn't get their pay.) （Ping zhunshu of Historical Records）

（25）南越、东瓯咸伏其辜, 西蛮北夷颇未辑睦。(*Nanyue,dongou xian fu qi gu,ximan beiyi po wei ji mu;* In the year of 110 A.D, the Emperor decreed, "the rebels in the South and the East have both been suppressed, while those in the West and the North are still active."） （*Wudiji of the Book of Han*）

However, as NP, the object to be quantified, is more and more implicit in deep structure in negative sentences, po's function as a universal quantifier began to deteriorate, and its subjective modality increased. Thus "po" emerged as a modal adverb to strengthen the negative mood.

3.2.3 "Po+VPhu/ye" Structure

This structure mainly appeared after the Han, Wei and Six Dynasties, for instance:

(26) 吴王颇知学乎？(*Wuwang po zhi xue hu;* Is King Wu a learned man?) (*Sanguozhi,wuzhi*)

（27）沙门, 颇见我四部之众耶？(*Shamen,po jian wo sibu zhi zhong ye;* Shamen, Do you see my army in Sibu?) （The Arranged Works of Hinayana Sutra）

The subjectivization of "po" deepened. That is to say, it can be put after the subject to modify sentence rhyme. It can also be put at the beginning of the sentence, and echoes the modal particle used at the end of a sentence. Shi Jinsheng (2003) states that the location of sentence components has close link with their degree of subjectivization. Usually, the components with high degree of subjectivity are put at the outer place of the sentence, and the components with low degree of subjectivity are put at the inner place. The change of po's position from the middle to the beginning of a sentence reflects that its subjectivity deepens.

4   Conclusion

Based on a close and thorough description of the usages on the adverb "po", and from a cognitive perspective, this paper analyses the chronological changes of "po" and is concluded as follows:

(1) In the Western Han Dynasty, the adverb "po" has two usages, high and low, in terms of degrees, which can be indicated in the appropriate sentences. "po", when used to refer to high degrees, can only be used in the sentences carrying sharp con-

trasts in conversations; when used to refer to low degrees, it can be used in other sentences rather than in those with sharp contrasts.

(2) When used as an interrogative adverb, "po" is not for strengthening the tone, but alleviating it, meaning "a little".

(3) The formation of "po", is a result of both, syntactically, its adjacent context and semantically, the generalization of meanings. That is to say, the specific meanings of "po" has been abstracted and extended, some of its notional element got lost, and its usage range broadened.

From the discussions above, we can draw a conclusion that the grammaticalization process of "po"is often accompanied by the subjective permeation of its speakers, which meanwhile is also a process of its subjectivization.

References

1. Wang, L.: Historical grammar of Change. The Commercial Press, Beijing (2001). (in Chinese)
2. Ohta, T.: Chinese language historical grammar. Peking University Press, Beijing (1987). (in Chinese)
3. Lv, X.: The development from the pre Qin to Han degree adverbs. Journal of Peking University **5**, 61–68 (1992)
4. Cheng, X.Q.: Study of dissyllabic words in the *Lnuheng*, pp. 262–340. Shandong Education Press, Shandong (2010). (in Chinese)
5. He, L.S.: Characteristics of the grammar of the *Shiji*, pp. 1–261. Shandong Education Press, Shandong (1992). (in Chinese)
6. Wu, F.X.: Studiesonthe grammar of the *Dunhuangbianwen*, pp. 1–497. Yuelu Publishing House, Hunan (1996). (in Chinese)
7. Yang, B.J., He, L.S.: Grammar and evolution of oldChinese, pp. 122–125. Language Publishing House, Beijing (1992). (in Chinese)
8. Yang, H.: What Thought from *Luokao*. Reading and Writing **4**, 32 (2007). (in Chinese)
9. Gao, Y.H.: A Study of the Adverb Po in the Middle Ancient Chinese. Journal of Wenzhou Normal College (2001) (1)
10. Hong, C.Y.: The Degree adverb of "Po" in Historical Records. Journal of Capital Normal University (1997) (1)

On *chi:* Its Gestalt and Collocations

Huibin Zhuang[1(✉)], Yichen Zhang[2], Xiangling Li[1], Shaoshuai Shen[1],
and Zhenqian Liu[3]

[1] Henan University, Kaifeng, China
`{Zhuanghuibin, lixiangling1978}@163.com`
[2] University of Macau, Macau, China
`zhangyichen1212@163.com`
[3] Shandong University, Jinan, China
`levinliu1964@163.com`

Abstract. Starting from the collocations of *chi* "to eat" with those animal-associated food names, the paper discusses the gestalt of *chi*. The study shows that the gestalt of *chi* includes not only the chain links of "putting food into mouth", "chewing" and "swallowing", but also the links of "source of food", "cooking", "digesting", "absorbing", etc. The collocations of *chi* and its transitivity and meaning are all essentially related with its gestalt link(s). A detailed discussion of the gestalt of *chi* is helpful in the understanding of its collocations, semantics and expressions.

Keywords: *chi* · Gestalt · Collocation · Transitivity

1   Introduction

We will start our discussion with the collocation of *chi* and those animal-associated food names. As an interesting phenomenon in Chinese, when talking about eating animal-derived food, the language users may say *chi niu rou* "to eat beef", *chi zhu rou* "to eat pork", and *chi gou rou* "to eat dog meat", but they cannot say **chi niu* "to eat an ox", **chi zhu* "to eat a pig", and **chi gou* "to eat a dog".On the contrary, they may say *chi laoshu* "to eat a mouse", *chi she* "to eat a snake", *chi mazha* "to eat a grasshopper", and *chi mayi* "to eat an ant", but rarely can they say *chi laoshu rou* "to eat mouse meat", *chi she rou* "to eat snake meat", *chi mazha rou* "to eat grasshopper meat", and *chi mayi rou* "to eat ant meat". Besides, to some animal-associated expressions, both ways are acceptable, for example, *chi ji (rou)* "to eat chicken".

Some people might explain this phenomenon in the following way: a smaller animal can be put into the mouth and swallowed directly, but a bigger one cannot be put into the mouth unless being cut into pieces. For example, a pig cannot be put into the mouth, but an ant can. This account, at the first glance, seems to be sensible; however, once considered carefully, counterexamples are pervasive. For example, in everyday life, we hear people talking about *chi ji* "eat chicken" frequently, but in a broad sense, a chicken is too big to be put into the mouth. Then how can we explain this phenomenon?

© Springer International Publishing Switzerland 2014
X. Su and T. He (Eds.): CLSW 2014, LNAI 8922, pp. 143–152, 2014.
DOI: 10.1007/978-3-319-14331-6_14

2   The Gestalt and Meaning of *chi*

If we replace *chi* with *kao* "roast" or *zhu* "boil", the two most basic ways by means of which the ancient people cook, an appropriate explanation can be achieved. Generally speaking, animal-derived food can be cooked in two ways: 1. to cook wholly, e.g., to roast or boil a mouse, a chicken, or many ants as a whole; 2. to cook partially, e.g., animals such as, pig, horse, wolf, etc. are too big to be roasted or boiled, and need to be cut into pieces before cooking.[1] When those two ways are mapped into language, two categories are obtained: smaller animals that can be cooked directly might become the objects of *chi* "to eat", for example, *chi laoshu* "to eat a mouse", *chi mazha* "to eat a grasshopper"; bigger animals, are hard to cook without being cut into pieces, therefore, only their parts can be collocated with *chi* "to eat", for instance, *chi gou rou* "to eat dog meat", and *chi zhu shetou* "to eat pig tongue". In this sense, when people discuss the collocations of *chi* "to eat" with animal-associated food names, they actually talk about the ways of cooking instead of the event of eating.

The fact that the collocation of *chi* "to eat" with animal-associated food names, obviously, are closely related to the ways of cooking in reality indicates that there are certain rationale in language using, namely iconicity [1-2]. Language is a mirror of the world, and it is structured in line with reality. More importantly, it shows that the ways of cooking are probably included in the gestalt of *chi* "to eat". That is, *chi* "to eat" includes not only the chain links of "putting food into mouth", "chewing" and "swallowing", but also some other links such as "ways of cooking" and so on. All these links together make up the whole link chain that *chi* "to eat" represents. Before moving on to talk about other related issues, we will have a careful examination of the gestalt of *chi* "to eat" first.

What is gestalt? According to the Gestalt psychology, the mind forms a global whole with self-organizing tendencies, which means people tend to complete the incomplete forms subconsciously. Consider the following picture:

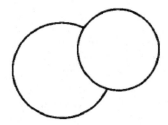

People tend to believe that this picture is composed of two circles, because the circle is a gestalt [3], by virtue of which people can feasibly make up the gap. It is natural for people to understand the world according to their experiences.

Generally, gestalt is applied by people not only to understand the things around them, but also the processes they perceive. According to Cognitive Grammar, the

---

[1] Interestingly, *kao ru zhu* "to roast suckling pig" and *kao ru yang* "to roast suckling lamb" seem to be exceptions. However, if we think that a suckling pig/lamp is small enough to be cooked as a whole, we can understand it without any problem.

function of a verb is to profile a process [4]. Since a process means a dynamic continuity, it might be understood as an integration of a series of links (Of course, there are processes which are homogeneous from the very beginning to the end. In this case, we think that it consists of numerous homogeneous links). Usually, the absence of some links does not affect our understanding of the process. Take *chi* "to eat" as an example. The gestalt-links of it should not only include "putting food into the mouth", "chewing" and "swallowing", but also "source of food", "ways of cooking", "digesting", "absorbing", etc. This can be shown as below: [2]

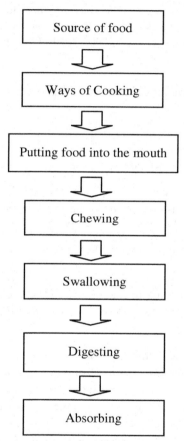

Chart 1. Gestalt-links of *chi* "to eat"

Obviously, few events can cover the whole the range of this link. As a usual case, an action that involves only part of the link might still be called *chi* "to eat". For example, the most frequent event in everyday life is *chi fan* "to have dinner", which

---

[2] Note that we are talking about "human's eating of animals", instead of "animals eating animals"; otherwise, the links will change slightly. For example, the links "source of food" and "ways of cooking" might be changed into "hunting".

involves three most frequent links, i.e., "putting into mouth", "chewing", and "swallowing", which is shown in the following context:

—tā zài chī shénme? (What is he eating?)
—tā zài chī mántou. (He is eating steamed bread.)

Due to the fact that *chi fan* "have dinner" is the most frequent action in human life, above three links can be regarded as the basic or canonical ones. Even for those links, in many occasions, a *chi* "eating" event might not involve all of them. For example, *chi yaopian* "literal reading (hereafter abbreviated as lit): to eat pill; to have pill" does not have the link of "chewing", and *chi kouxiangtang* "lit: to eat gum; to chew gum" does not involve swallowing. In spite of this, people still use *chi* "to eat" to refer to those actions, because it is the gestalt that helps to make the links. Besides, instead of the basic ones, *chi* "to eat" frequently involves some other links, which can be shown in the following context:

Zhàngfu: jīntiān wǎnfàn chī shénme? (Husband: What shall we have for dinner?)

qīzi: chī mǐ ba? nǐ zuò háishì wǒ zuò? (Wife: Rice? Who cook it?)

zhàngfu: nǐ zuò ba. (Husband: Can you do it?)

Obviously, *chi* "to eat" in this example focuses on the cooking link.

The fact that the most basic links of *chi* "to eat" are "putting into the mouth", "chewing", and "swallowing" does not imply that a *chi* event need to involve basic links every time when it is employed. In many occasions, an event is called *chi* "to eat" but involves none of the links. For example, *chi laoben* "lit: to eat savings; to rely on one's laurels", which actually involves the link "source of food". The reason for this event's being named *chi* "to eat", obviously, is that the gestalt helps to make up the missing links.

Now we will examine the entries of the item *chi* in the *Contemporary Chinese Dictionary* [5] (6th edition), and try to find out the link(s) each entry involves one by one. There are 8 entries under the item *chi* in the *Contemporary Chinese Dictionary* (sixth edition), as shown below:

①to put food into the mouth, chew and swallow it (including sucking and drinking), for example, *chi fan* "to have dinner" | *chi nai* "lit: to eat milk; to suck milk" | *chi yaopian* "lit: to eat pills; to take pills";

②to live on a particular thing, for example, *chi laoben* "lit: to eat savings; to rely on one's laurels" | *kao shan chi shan* "lit: t close to mountain and eat mountain; to live on the mountain when you live in the mountain area";

③to absorb (liquid), for example, *daolin zhi bu chi mo* "lit: Daolin paper does not eat ink; Daolin paper does not absorb ink";

④to eliminate (mostly in military or chess games), for example, *chi diao diren yi ge tuan* "lit: to eat up a regiment of the enemy; to eliminate a regiment of the enemy" | *na ju chi ta de pao* "lit: to eat his cannon with you chariot; to annihilate his cannon with your chariot[3]";

---

[3] The word "cannon" and "chariot" are the names used for the chess pieces of the Chinese chess.

⑤to bear, for example, *chi de xiao* "lit: to be able to eat up; bearable" | *chi bu zhu* "lit: to eat but not hold; cannot bear";

⑥to suffer, for example, *chi kui* "lit: to eat loss; to suffer loss" | *chi jing* "lit: to eat surprise; to be surprised" | *chi piping* "lit: to eat criticizing; to be criticized";

⑦to waste, for example, *chi li* "to be laborious" | *chi jin* "to entail much effort";

⑧to be subject to (mostly commonly in pre-modern colloquial), for example, *chi ta chixiao* "lit: to eat his smear; to be laughed by him".

It is obvious that of all those entries, only the first one has tight connection with the basic links, i.e., "putting into mouth", "chewing", and "swallowing". The other entries, however, bear no significant relation to those links. Consequently, a question arises naturally concerning the reason why those entries can be all categorized into *chi* "to eat".

With the gestalt-chart of *chi*, all the eight entries can be accounted for, as shown below:

Entry ① involves the basic link(s), i.e., "putting into mouth", "chewing" and "swallowing";

Entry ② involves the link "source of food";

Entry ③ involves the link "absorbing";

Entry ④ involves the links "putting into mouth", "chewing" and "swallowing" (which also involves a process of metaphorization [6].

Entry ⑤ involves the link "digesting" (which also involves a process of metaphorization);

Entry ⑥ involves the links "putting into mouth" and "swallowing" (which also involves a process of metaphorization);

Entry ⑦ involves the link "absorbing" (which also involves a process of metaphorization;

Entry ⑧ involves the links "putting into mouth" and "swallowing" (which also involves a process of metaphorization.

The above analysis shows that those entries all involve certain link(s) of the gestalt of *chi,* and are categorized as *chi accordingly.*

3   The Collocations of *chi:* Further Exploration

In the above analysis, we can see that owing to the different link(s) involved, *chi* "to eat" acquires different meanings in different context, and therefore has different collocations, for example, *chi fan* "to have a meal", *chi laoben* "to rely on one's laurels", chi mo "to absorb ink", *chi de xiao* "to be bearable", *chi kui* "to suffer losses", *chi li* "to be laborious", and *chi ta chixiao* "to be laughed by him". Albeit catching certain characteristics of *chi,* this explanation is not delicate enough for people to well understand the collocations. A further exploration is required for the gestalt of *chi* to eat"; however, concerning the limitation of space, we will focus on the analysis of *chi*'s collocation with nouns, so as to give a clue to the whole range of the phenomenon.

It is not unusual for an action to cover only certain portions of the link. For example, when we talk about *chi xiaozao* "lit: to eat small kitchen; to have the food cooked individually", we focus mainly on the ways of cooking, and when we talk about *chi shitang* "lit: to eat canteen; have a meal in the canteen" and *chi fanguan* "lit: to eat restaurant; to have meal in the restaurant", we focus mainly on the place of cooking where the links "cooking", "putting into mouth", "chewing" and "swallowing" get involved. Therefore, in order to study the collocations of *chi,* we need to examine each link in detail.

We will start from the link "source of food". To meet the purpose of convenient communication, language users may emphasize different aspects in varied situations. Thus we have *chi shan* "lit: to eat mountain; to live on the mountain" that emphasizes the location or place where the food is obtained; we also have *chi huilu* "lit: to eat bribery; to take bribery" that emphasizes the way the food is obtained (in a metaphorical sense); and we also have *chi zhe zhang yu wang* "lit: to eat this fishing net; to live on this fishing net" that emphasizes the tool by which food is obtained.

Moving on to examine the "cooking" link, we have *chi ditan* "lit: to eat roadside stall; to have a meat at roadside stall" when the location of cooking is the focus. We also have *chi xiaozao* "lit: to eat small kitchen; to have the food cooked individually", *chi dongbei luandun* "to have northeast stew", and *chi mala tang* "to have tingling spicy hot pot" when the way of cooking is the focus. When the cooking tool is the focus, we might have *chi xiao guo* "lit: to eat small wok; to have the food cooked with a small wok". When the ingredient is the focus, we have *chi ji* "to eat chicken", *chi laoshu* "to eat a mouse", *chi zhu rou* "to eat pork", and *chi gou rou* "to eat dog meat".

When it comes to the link of "putting into mouth", we have *chi da kou* "totake a big mouthful"[4] that focuses on the manner, *chi shouzhitou* "lit: to eat finger; to suck a finger" that focuses on the object (it involves the link "putting into mouth" but not "chewing" and "swallowing"), *chi qingdiao/chi qifen* "lit: to eat atmosphere; to eat something for the atmosphere" [7] that focuses on the environment, *chi da wan* "lit: to eat big bowl; to have a meal with a big bowl", *and chi kuaizi* "lit: to eat chopsticks; to have a meal with chopsticks" [5] which focus on the tool.

For the link "chewing", we still employ *chi* to refer to *chi ganzhe* "to eat sugarcane; to chew sugarcane", *chi kouxiangtang* "lit: to eat gum; to chew gum" when we just perform the act of chewing instead of swallowing.

With respect to the link of "swallowing", we have *chi jiaonang* "lit: to eat capsule; to take capsule" that focuses on the swallowing tool; and *chi yaopian* "lit: to eat pill; to take pills" when we swallow without chewing.

---

[4] http://msn.tv.sohu.com/u/vw/24079311

[5] One day, two famous linguists had dinner together. Prof. Zhang Hongming said to Prof. Li Yafei, "Ni jiu chi zhe shuang kuaizi ba 'lit: you eat this pair of chopsticks; you can use this pair of chopsticks'." (See Syntax of Chinese [8], p.70).

As for the links "digesting" and "swallowing", most of the collocations are conceptualized in a metaphorical way, for example, *chi li* "lit: to eat strength; to be laborious", *chi mo* "lit: to eat ink; to absorb ink", etc.[6]

The above analysis can be summarized as the following table:

Table 1. A detailed analysis of *chi* with its nominal collocations

	Location	Ways	Tool	Object	....
Source of food	*chi shan* "to live on the mountain"	*chi huilu* "to take bribery"	*chi zhezhang yuwang* "to live on this fishing net"	—	....
Cooking	*chi shitang* "to have a meal in canteen"	*chi xiaozao* "to have the food cooked individually"	*chi xiaoguo* "to have the food cooked with a small wok"	*chi zhurou* "to eat pork"	....
Putting into mouth	—	*chi da kou* "to take a big mouthful "	*chi da wan* "to have a meal with a big bowl"	*chi shouzhitou* "to suck a finger"	....
Chewing	—	—	—	*chi kouxiang tang* "to chew gum"	....
Swallowing	—	—	*chi jiaonang* "to have capsule"	*chi yaopian* "to take pills"	....
Digesting	—	—	—	—	....
Absorbing	—	—	*chi li* "to be laborious"	*(zhi) chi mo* "(of paper) to absorb ink"	....

---

[6] It is necessary to note that although some collocations belong to certain links of *chi*, the whole phrases might be metaphorized again, and obtain a kind of idiomatic meaning. For example, *chi doufu* "to eat tofu" can mean "to flirt" [9].

From Table 1, we can find that *chi* can collocate with different nouns.The constructions formed in those ways have their rationales, and can be account for through a detailed study of *chi*. The common practice in the received wisdom that treats the phrases such as, *chi fanguan* "lit: to eat restaurant; to have a meal at restaurant", and *chi fu mu* "lit: to eat parent; to live on parents", as marginal constructions reflects an ignorance of the gestalt of *chi*, and of taking only those parts, such as, basic links of "putting into mouth", "chewing" and "swallowing", as the whole. There are certain occasions where *chi* involves links that are not any of those three basic ones, such as *chi shitang* "to eat at the canteen", and there are also occasions where *chi* involves only one or two of the basic links, for example, *chi ganzhe* "to chew sugarcane" and *chi kouxiangtang* "to chew gum" do not involve the link "swallowing". Therefore, we cannot deny the fact that all the *chi*s can be put into the gestalt of *chi* and called *chi*.

4   On the Transitivity of *chi*

It has been pointed out by Xu [10],

> Verb is a big family. On the one hand, it consists of a continuum which ranges from verbs with strong transitivity to those with weak transitivity; on the other hand, a verb may demonstrate different transitivity in different context....

This insightful opinion can be understood in the following way: when used in varied situations and contexts, *chi* may involve different links; therefore, the transitivity it demonstrates will be different accordingly, for example, in a situation that involving link "origin of food", *chi* represents a weaker transitivity than in those involving basic links, such as, "putting into mouth", "chewing", and "swallowing"., This can be elaborated more specifically as the following: the former involves only location, way of cooking, tool, but not object, which is supported by the fact that if *chi* involves only those aspect but not the object in the links of "putting into mouth", "chewing", and "swallowing", its transitivity will be less strong.

Therefore, it can be concluded thattransitivity is closely related to the links involved in different situations. In a situation with non-canonical links where a NP that collocates with a verb is not its object, the transitivity of the verb will be hidden. Even in a situation involving canonical links but under the same condition, the transitivity of the verb cannot be triggered. Only when the situation involves the basic links and the noun in the collocation functions as the object, the transitivity can be triggered. In other words, the two factors, i.e., whether a situation involves the canonical link(s) and whether the noun in the collocation is the object of the verb, are essential in judging the extent of the transitivity.

From this perspective, a further step will bring us a completely new view on the transitivity, which is that if a verb does not have a proper object in its canonical links, the transitivity of the verb cannot be triggered, and then the verb will be treated as an intransitive verb, such as *shui* "to sleep", *ku* "to cry", etc. In certain situations where transitivity is partially triggered, it might take some "objects", which can be shown by *shui diban* "to sleep on the floor", *Zhu Geliang ku Zhou Yu* "lit: Zhu Geliang cried

Zhou Yu; Zhu Geliang cried on Zhou Yu's death". If a verb has its object in the canonical links, its transitivity will be triggered completely, and this verb may be called transitive verb, for example *chi* "to eat", *sha* "to kill", etc.

There are also situations where the object and the location are the same or have the almost same status. For example, in *pa shan* "to climb mountain", both the location and object are *shan* "mountain"; and in *wa jinzi* "to dig gold", *wa yecai* "to dig wild vegetables" [11]. Although *jinzi* "gold" and *ye cai* "wild vegetable" are not the true objects (patient) of *wa* "dig", a strong transitivity of the verb can be observed. In Chinese, we have a lot of expressions like this, such as, *suo suo* "to lock the lock" and *suo men* "to lock the door", *tanzou gangqin* "to play the piano" and *tanzou quzi* "to play the tune", *la che* "to pull a cart" and *la mei* "to load and transport coals", *pian ren* "to cheat someone" and *pian qian* "lit: to cheat money; to cheat someone for money", etc. Among those pairs, it is hard to decide which one is more transitive than the other one. Therefore, after the long-term development and evolution of verbs, certain components of the verb, such as, the location, result, goal, and agent, has acquired strong patient features [12].

5   Conclusion

Starting from the collocation of *chi* with animal-associated food names, the paper discusses the gestalt process of *chi*. The result shows that the gestalt process of *chi* includes the links such as, "source of food", "cooking", "putting into mouth", "chewing", "swallowing", "digesting", and "absorbing". Among these links, "putting into mouth", "chewing" and "swallowing" are the most basic ones. In order to give a plausibleaccount for *chi*, especially its meanings, collocations and transitivity, we have studied the gestalt links of *chi* in detail. Generally speaking, when the situation involves the basic links and a noun in the collocation functions as the object of the verb, the transitivity can be triggered completely.

Acknowledgments. We would like to express my sincere gratitude to Zhijian Wang, Fengmei Ren, Limei Yang, Tian Li, and Qian Liu for their inspiration, guidance, and/or revision of the argument in this paper. The usual disclaimers apply. The study is jointly supported by the Humanities and Social Sciences by the Ministry of Education (14YJC740115), and Social Science Foundation of Henan Province (2014CYY011).

References

1. Jacobson, R.: Quest for the Essence of Language. Diogenes **45**, 23–31 (1965)
2. Greenberg, J.H.: Some Universals of Grammar, with Particular Reference to the Order of Meaningful Elements. In: Greenberg, H. (ed.) Universals of Language, pp. 73–113. MIT Press, Cambridge (1966)
3. Anderson, J.: Cognitive Psychology and its implications. W.H. Freeman and Co., New York (1985)

4. Langacker, R.W.: Cognitive Grammar: A Basic Introduction. Oxford University Press, New York (2008)
5. Language Research Institute, Chinese Academy of Social Science: Contemporary Chinese Dictionary (6th edn.). The Commercial Press, Beijing (2012). (in Chinese)
6. Lakoff, G., Johnson, M.: Metaphors We Live By. The University of Chicago Press, Chicago (1980)
7. Sun, T., Li, Y.: Licensing non-core arguments in Chinese. Studies of the Chinese Language (1), 23–35+97 (2010). (in Chinese)
8. Huang, C.-T.J., Li, Y.-H., Li, Y.: The Syntax of Chinese. Cambridge University Press, New York (2009)
9. Her, O.-S.: Grammatical Representation of Idiom Chunks. Paper Presented at the 8th Annual Conference of the International Association of Chinese Linguistics, Melbourne, Australia (1999)
10. Xu, S.: Stereotypical relation: the study of syntactic construction. Journal of Foreign Langues (2), 8–16 (2003). (in Chinese)
11. Xing, F.: hanyu binyu dairu xianxiang zhi guancha [the way for objects to be introduced in Chinese]. Chinese Teaching in the World (2), 76–84 (1991). (in Chinese)
12. Tan, J.: Semantic synthesis, the evolution of word meanings and the objects of verbs. Studies of the Chinese Language (2), 99–108 (2008). (in Chinese)

The Nature of *men* and Its Co-occurrence with Numeral Expressions in Mandarin Chinese

Ying Zhang[✉]

School of Humanities, Anqing Normal University, Anqing 246133, Anhui, China
zhangying0491@163.com

Abstract. In the construction "numeral expression + NP+ *men*" which can be further analyzed as "[numeral expression + NP]+ *men*", *men* is a functional word with the function to denote a large quantity. In Chinese, *men* is used to meet the pragmatic requirements rather than the syntactic ones. Whether to use *men* or not depends on the speaker's subjective wishes. In certain cases, due to the Economy Principle, numeral expressions and *men* can not co-occur.

Keywords: *men* · Numeral expression · Economy Principle · The co-occurrence restriction

1   Introduction

Abundant literature can be found on the morpheme 们 [*men*](*MEN*) and its co-occurrence with numeral expressions. However, the nature and function of 们 [*men*](*MEN*) in the construction are still not very clear.

As the first step in our account, consider the following sentence in Chinese:

(1) 皇帝　　　亲自　　　　带着　　一群　　最高贵　　　　的
　　　Huangdi　qinzi　　　daizhe　yi-qun　zuigaogui　　de
　　　emperor　on his own　lead　one-CL　the noblest　DE
　　　骑士　　们　　来　　了。
　　　qishi　men　lai　le
　　　knights　MEN　come　LE

'The emperor himself came with a group of the noblest knights.'

There are different views regarding the legitimacy of 们[*men*](*MEN*) in the sentence above. As noted in Jiang Fuxing (1999), 们[*men*](*MEN*) should be deleted here. However, Zhang Yisheng (1999) argues that the co-occurrence of NP-*men* (eg. 骑士们[*qishi men*](knights)) and numeral expressions containing collective classifier (eg. 一群[*yiqun*](*a group of*)) in Chinese is a language redundancy phenomenon, since 们 [*men*](*MEN*) is to emphasize the preceding noun as a group. It is worth noting that the article is accompanied by the editor's note, which says that "一群最高贵的骑士们 (*a group of the noblest knights*)" is well-formed, but it is no longer used nowadays.

© Springer International Publishing Switzerland 2014
X. Su and T. He (Eds.): CLSW 2014, LNAI 8922, pp. 153–160, 2014.
DOI: 10.1007/978-3-319-14331-6_15

In the current research, I would like to have a more detailed examination of the co-occurrence of 们[*men*](*MEN*) and numeral expressions, and attempt to identify what the nature of 们[*men*](*MEN*) is.

2   The Syntactic Structure of "Numeral Expression + NP + *men*"

The series of papers by Xing Fuyi (1965) has discussed the co-occurrence of 们 [*men*](*MEN*) and numeral expressions. As he points out, numeral expressions include: quantifiers containing indefinite collective classifier (eg. 一群[*yiqun*](*a group of*)), quantifiers containing indefinite numbers (eg. 几位[*jiwei*](*some*)), and pro-forms containing universal quantificational meaning (eg. 所有[*suoyou*](*all*)), examples are given in (2)[1].

(2) a. 一群 　　 "刘翔迷" 　　　 们

　　　 yi-qun 　 LiuXiangmi 　　 men

　　　 one-CL 　 Liu Xiang's fans 　 MEN

　　　 '*a group of Liu Xiang's fans*'

　 b. 几位 　　　 老帅 　　　　 们

　　　 ji-wei 　　 laoshuai 　　　 men

　　　 several-CL 　 senior commanders 　 MEN

　　　 '*several senior commanders*'

　 c. 所有 　　 孩子 　 们

　　　 suoyou 　 haizi 　 men

　　　 all 　　　 children 　 MEN

　　　 '*all the children*'

For the purpose of easy discussion, the co-occurrence of 们[*men*](*MEN*) and numeral expressions is represented as "numeral expression + NP+ *men*" below.

From the corpus data, we find that 们[*men*](*MEN*) co-occurs with "number+ classifier + NP" expressions in most cases. And based on the classifiers listed by Li Xingjian (2010), the classifiers that co-occur with们[*men*](*MEN*) include 班[*ban*](*a group of*), 帮[*bang*](*a bunch of*), 拨[*bo*](*a group of*), 堆[*dui*] (*a bunch of*), 队[*dui*](*a queue of*), 个 [*ge*](*individual unit*), 伙 [*huo*](*a crowd of*), 列 [*lie*](*a row of*), 名 [*ming*](*individual unit*) , 排[*pai*] (*a row of*), 批[*pi*](*a group of*), 群[*qun*](*a group of*), 位[*wei*](*individual unit*), 些[*xie*](*a number of*). For instance,

(3) a. 一班 　　　 朝气蓬勃， 　　 锐意改革 　　　　　 的 　　 领导 　　 们

　　　 yi-ban 　　 zhaoqipengbo 　 ruiyigaige 　　　　　 de 　　 lingdao 　 men

　　　 one-CL 　 vigorous 　　　　 determined reformist 　 DE 　 leader 　 MEN

　　　 '*a group of vigorous and reform-minded leaders*'

---

[1] All examples are mainly taken from the Modern Chinese Corpus compiled by the Center for Chinese Linguistics of Peking University (CCL Corpus).

b. 一帮　　　小顽童　　　们

   yi-bang　xiaowantong　men

   one-CL　little brat　　MEN

   'a bunch of naughty children'

c. 十几个　　　妈妈　　　们

   shiji-ge　　mama　　men

   a dozen-CL　mother　MEN

   'a dozen mothers'

d. 几十名　　　　参将　　　　们

   jishi-ming　　canjiang　　men

   dozens of-CL　army officers　MEN

   'dozens of commanders'

e. 一些　科学家　们

   yi-xie　kexuejia　men

   one-CL　scientist　MEN

   'some scientists'

Chu Zexiang (2000) and Huang et al. (2009) have pointed out that all the numeral expressions in the examples above denote an indefinite quantity, and most scholars are in favor of this view. However, we find that the numeral expressions denoting definite quantity can also co-occur with 们[*men*](*MEN*). The following example from Xinhua News Agency(2004) illustrates this.

(4) 76岁　　　的　　上海市民　　　　蔡觉新　　为　他　5个

   76sui　　　de　　shanghaishimin　Cai Juexin　wei　ta　wu-ge

   76-year-old　DE　Shanghai citizen　name　　for　he　five

孙辈　　　　的　　孩子　　们　　　每人　　　　存了

sunbei　　　de　　haizi　　men　　meiren　　　cun-l e

grandchildren　DE　children　MEN　per person　save-LE

一张　　　200元　　的　　生肖存单。

yi-zhang　200yuan　de　　shengxiaocundan

one-CL　　RMB200　DE　　a bank deposit slip

'Cai Juexin, a 76-year-old Shanghai citizen, opened a bank account and deposited RMB 200 for each of his five grandchildren.'

It should be noted that the co-occurrence of 们[*men*](*MEN*) with the numeral expressions denoting definite quantity is quite rare.

Also note that in Chinese a bare noun cannot occur in these patterns at all, *五个 孩子们[*wu ge haizi men*] (*five children*) is unacceptable.

Logically, the structure of "numeral expression + NP+ *men*" is either "[numeral expression + NP] + *men*" or "numeral expression + [NP+ *men*]". There is evidence, however, that the former is more adequate. I will elaborate on this conclusion below.

Shi Yuzhi (2002) claims that numeral expressions have [- definite] feature, and *men*-contained phrases have [+ definite] feature. That is, *men*-contained phrases and numeral expressions exhibit semantic mismatches. Therefore, the sequence "numeral expression + NP+ *men*" has the following structure:

(5)   [Numeral expression + NP]+ men

(5) is the structure for the typical phrases with 们[*men*](*MEN*) such as [一些科学家]们(*some scientists*).

This can be proved by means of substitution method. Take 一些科学家们 (some scientists) as an instance. If we replace 科学家们[*kexuejia men*] (*some scientists*) with 他们[*tamen*](*they*), the phrase *一些他们[*yi-xie tamen*] (*some they*) will be ungrammatical. It is mainly because that 他们[*tamen*](*they*) with [+ definite] feature[2] and the numeral expressions with [- definite] feature exhibit semantic mismatches. The test shows that the numeral expressions cannot be combined with *men*-contained phrases directly.

3   The Nature and Function of *men*

One question we need to address is what the role of 们[*men*](*MEN*) in Mandarin Chinese. Obviously, 们[*men*](*MEN*) is not used to meet the requirements of syntax since whether to use们[*men*](*MEN*) or not does not affect the legitimacy of the structure. This observation is supported by the contrast in the following examples:

(6) a. 这班　　　毛贼娃儿
　　　zhe-ban　　maozeiwa'er
　　　this-CL　　bandit (contemptuous term)
　　　'*this group of bandits*'

　　b. 这班　　　毛贼娃儿　　　　　　　们
　　　zhe-ban　　maozeiwa'er　　　　　men
　　　this-CL　　bandit (contemptuous term)　　MEN
　　　'*this group of bandits*'

The two examples, with the same semantic content, come from the same paragraph in a novel and only differ in the use of 们[*men*](*MEN*).

In addition, it should be noted that phrases without 们[*men*](*MEN*) are used more often in corpus. Why do we need 们[*men*](*MEN*)? Our answer is that 们[*men*](*MEN*) is used to meet the pragmatic requirements.

---

[2] 他们(they) have [+ definite] feature. In Chinese, when the subject is indefinite, the sentence must be saved by the existential 有[*you*](*have*). When a number expression is in the subject position, the sentence is more acceptable if 有(have) occurs, such as 有一个人去北京了 (*A man went to Beijing*). See Huang et al. (2009) for the related discussion. In contrast, 他们(they) in the subject position cannot add 有[*you*](*have*), that is, *有他们知道这件事(*Someone knows anything about it*) is unacceptable.

To illustrate this point, let's analyze the nature of 们[men](*MEN*) first. Roughly speaking, the literature on 们 [men](*MEN*) presents two main views: (a) 们 [men](*MEN*) is a collective marker (see Yuen Ren Chao,1979); (b) 们[men](*MEN*) is a plural morpheme (see Xing Fuyi,1996/2000). As noted by Huang et al. (2009), problems arise no matter we analyze 们[men](*MEN*) as a plural marker or as a collective marker. On the one hand, 们[men](*MEN*) is only attached to a human noun or a pronoun[3], unlike the typical plural suffix –s in English, which can be suffixed to nouns quite productively, such as books vs.*书们[shu men] (*books*); On the other hand, it is not acceptable to attach 们[men](*MEN*) to definite demonstrative expressions to form expressions such as "这/那个人们[zhe/na-ge ren men] (*this/that person*)" which tend to mean "this/that person and the others".

Based on the phenomena discussed above, we may speculate that the larger the number is, the greater the possibility of the co-occurrence of 们[men](*MEN*) and numeral expressions could be, but the data showed otherwise. Take Chinese classifier 名[ming](*individual unit*) for example, the following are examples showing their co-occurrence:

(7) a. 几名　　　　中央委员　　　　　　　们
       ji-ming   zhongyangweiyuan   men
       several-CL central committee members   MEN
       '*several central committee members*'

   b. 十几名　　　　　　不屈　　的　劳工　　们
       shiji-ming   buqu   de   laogong   men
       more than a dozen-CL unyielding DE   labor   MEN
       '*more than a dozen unyielding labo rs*'

   c. 这　一百几十名　　　　　　老头、　儿童　　和
       zhe   yibaijishi-ming   laotou   ertong   he
       this   more than one hundred- CL   old man   child   and
       青壮年　　　　　们
       qingzhuangnian   men
       young adults   MEN
   '*more than one hundred old men, children and young adults*'

In CCL corpus, we did not find the examples of the co-occurrence of 们[men](*MEN*) and such large numbers as一千[yiqian](*one thousand*),一万[yiwan](*ten thousand*).

According to examples above, we assume that whether to use 们[men](*MEN*) or not depends on the speaker's subjective wishes. If the speaker wants to express a large number, he would attach 们[men](*MEN*) to the numeral expression to emphasize the

---

[3] In Chinese, 猫们[mao men](*cats*) , 狗们[gou men] (*dogs*) are the anthropomorphic attitude to animals. See Xing Fuyi (1996/2000) for details.

quantity. Even if a numeral expression expresses small quantity objectively, such as 几个[ji-ge](*several*), 十几个[shiji-ge](*more than a dozen*), 几十个[jishi-ge](*dozens of*), when the speaker assumes them large, he tends to add 们[men](*MEN*). By contrast, if a numeral expression shows large quantity objectively, such as 几千个 [jiqian-ge](*thousands of*), 几万个[jiwan-ge](*tens of thousands of*), and the hearer and the speaker tend to have the same judgment, the speaker will no longer use 们 [men](*MEN*) to emphasize the quantity in view of the Economy Principle.

With the analysis above, the instances we have discussed earlier (such as (4)/(6b)) become understandable.

Example (4) is from a news report, the reporter wants to illustrate that the deposit slip was very popular in the year of the Monkey, and he takes Cai Juexin's family for example. Cai juexin has five grandchildren and he opened one bank account for each of them, the reporter thinks that the word 5个(*five*) denotes a large quantity and the number five covers every member of the family's third generation, therefore, 5个孙辈的孩子[wu-ge sunbei de haizi](*five grandchildren*) can be suffixed with 们[men](*MEN*).

The cases in (6a-b) are from the following sentences, the phrases of our concern are marked in bold face: "李哥, 你怎么不下令呀? 难道连这班毛贼娃儿也害怕么?派我去吧,即令捉不到黑虎星本人,只要杀他个落花流水,也让这班毛贼娃儿们知道知道厉害,乖乖儿把抢去的东西送回,以后车走车道,马行马路,井水不犯河水。(姚雪垠《李自成》)" (Brother Lee, why haven't you ordered? Are you afraid of this group of bandits? Please send me on mission, even if I can not catch Black Tiger Star, at least I will let them know the force of us and let them obediently send back what they have taken from us. Later on, they mind their business, and we'll mind ours. (Yao Xueyin , Li Zicheng))

It is clear that 这班毛贼娃儿 (this group of bandits) and 这班毛贼娃儿们 (this group of bandits) have the same semantic content. The speaker tends to claim that he can lead his army to its victory over the enemy easily, so he uses 们[men](MEN) to emphasize the large quantity of the enemy in order to show off his ability.

In short, 们[men](MEN) is a functional word, its role is to emphasize a large quantity subjectively.

4   The Co-occurrence Restriction

Nevertheless, there are two situations in which 们[men](*MEN*) cannot co-occur with the numeral expressions even if the speaker regards the quantity very large:

(a)   Certain numeral-classifier pairs may be reduplicated as ABB, such as 一列(*a row of*) →一列列(*many lines of*). In general, the reduplication patterns are not compatible with 们[men](*MEN*), as in (8):

(8) a. 一列列　　　军人　　(*们)

yi-lielie　　　junren　　(*men)

one- repeat CL　soldier　(*MEN)

'*many lines of soldiers*'

b. 一队队   学生   (*们)

    yi-duidui   xuesheng   (*men)

    one- repeat CL   student   (*MEN)

    'many groups of students'

c. 一排排   干部   (*们)

    yi-paipai   ganbu (*men)

    one- repeat CL   cadre (*MEN)

    'many rows of cadres'

(b) When the classifier is preceded by an adjective denoting a large quantity, 们 [men](MEN) cannot be used, as in (9):

(9) 一大群   看热闹   的   市民   (*们)

    yi-da-qun   kanrenao   de   shimin   (* men)

    one-large-CL   rubberneck   DE   citizen   (*MEN)

    'a large group of rubberneckers'

It is well known that the reduplication of the numeral-classifier pair[4] and the adjectives such as 大[da](large) can also denote a large quantity. They both have the same grammatical function as 们[men](MEN). According to the Economy Principle, the form with same grammatical function should be used only once.

However, there are rare instances when the language redundancy phenomenon appears, for example:

(10) 一队队   着装整齐   的   公安

     yi-duidui   zhuozhuangzhengqi   de   gong'an

     one-repeat CL   dress tidily   DE   policeman

     交警   们

     jiaojing   men

     traffic policeman   *MEN

     'many groups of tidily dressed policemen and traffic policemen'

In (10), the reduplication pattern 一队队(many group of) and 们[men](MEN) co-exist.

5   Conclusion

In this article I have re-examined the nature of 们[men](MEN) in Mandarin Chinese and its co-occurrence with numeral Expressions.

In Chinese, both numeral expressions denoting indefinite quantity and those denoting definite quantity can co-occur with 们[men](MEN). Of course, it is undeniable

---

[4] On the reduplication of the numeral-classifier pair, see Li Yuming (1996).

that the co-occurrence of 们[*men*](*MEN*) with the numeral expression denoting definite quantity is quite rare, and the reason is still unclear.

I conclude that the interior structure of "numeral expression + NP + men" is "[numeral expression + NP] + men". 们[*men*](*MEN*) is a functional word which is used to emphasize a large quantity. Whether to use 们[*men*](*MEN*) or not depends on the speaker's subjective judgment. However, 们[*men*](*MEN*) is not compatible with those forms denoting large quantity due to the economy principle. Logically, the speaker can only estimate the definite things, and that is why a phrase with 们[*men*](*MEN*) demonstrates [+ definite] feature.

Turning back to (1), I suggest that it is a grammatical sentence, and similar expressions are still available in Modern Written Chinese.

References

1. Chao, Y.R.: A Grammar of Spoken Chinese, p. 125. The Commercial Press, Beijing (1979). (in Chinese)
2. Chu, Z.: Mutual Repulsion between Numerals and Plural Markers. Minority Languages of China **5**, 58–64 (2000). (储泽祥: 数词与复数标记不能同现的原因.《民族语文 **5**, 58–64 (2000)) (in Chinese)
3. Huang, C.-T.J., Li, Y.-H.A., Li, Y.: The Syntax of Chinese, pp. 307–311. Cambridge University Press, Cambridge (2009)
4. Jiang, F.: Men should be deleted in a Chinese sentence. Verbalism **3**, 24 (1999). (江复兴: 这个"们"应删去.《咬文嚼字 **3**, 24 (1999)) (in Chinese)
5. Zhang, Y.: Whether men should be deleted or not in a Chinese sentence. Verbalism **8**, 31–32 (1999). (张谊生:这个"们"该不该删.《咬文嚼字 **8**, 31–32 (1999)) (in Chinese)
6. Li, Y.: The meaning of reduplication. Chinese Teaching in the World **1**, 10–19 (1996). (**李宇明**:论词语重叠的意义.《**世界汉语教学 1**, 10–19 (1996)) (in Chinese)
7. Li, X.: Modern Chinese Classifiers Standard Dictionary. Hebei Education Press, Shijiazhuang (2010). (**李行健主编**.《现代汉语量词规范词典》,**石家庄:河北教育出版社** (2010)) (in Chinese)
8. Shi, Y.: On the interaction of syntactic structure and lexical markers—the effect of the expression of definiteness on Chinese syntax. Contemporary Linguistics **1**, 25–37 (2002). (in Chinese)
9. Wang, C.: Men-drop in numer+ classier+ NP' expressions. Language Planning **7**, 9–10 (1995). (**王灿龙**. "们"在**数量名**组合中的脱落.《语文建设 **7**, 9–10 (1995)) (in Chinese)
10. Xing, F.: More on the co-occurrence of men and the numeral expression. Studies of the Chinese Language **5**, 365–366 (1965). (**邢福义**.再谈"们"和表数词语并用的现象.《**中国语文 5**, 365–366 (1965)) (in Chinese)
11. Xing, F.: The Chinese Grammar, p. 239. Northeast Normal University Press, Changchun (1996, 2000). (**邢福义**.《汉语语法学》,长春:东北师范大学出版社, p. 239 (1996/2000)) (in Chinese)

A Study on the Causative Alternation from a Non-derivational Perspective

Daran Yang[✉]

PLA University of Foreign Languages, Luoyang, China
coolydr@163.com

Abstract. The previous studies on the causative alternation can be divided into the derivational and non-derivational approaches. The cross-linguistic facts show that the former fails to provide an adequate account of the relationship between the causative and unaccusative alternates. However, the latter approach also faces some problems. In this paper we abandon the former and make a revision to the latter based on the theory proposed by Huang *et al.*(2009). We argue that the causative and unaccusative variants share one and the same root which conceptualizes different types of events and selects different eventive light verbs, resulting in two lexical items with different ways of argument realization.

Keywords: The causative alternation · Non-derivational perspective · Eventive light verbs

1   Introduction

Verbs with flexible ways of argument realization are called "variable behavior verbs"(Borer 1994). A typical example of them is the so-called "change-of-state verbs", which can be used either transitively or intransitively, as shown in (1):
(1) a. Pat broke the window.
   b. The window broke.
In (1a), *break* in its causative use takes an external argument and an internal one. In (1b), the external argument disappears and the internal one moves to the subject position, resulting in the ergative(or unaccusative) use of *break*. These alternating ways of argument realization displayed by verbs like *break* is called "the causative alternation".[1]

The causative alternation has been the subject of much discussion in linguistic theory. The focus of debate is on the relationship between the causative and unaccusative alternates. Most of the previous studies take on a derivational approach, assuming a direct derivational relationship between the two variants. In recent years, however, some scholars adopt a non-derivational approach, which argues against any direct

---

[1]   *break* in (1b) is also called "the inchoative verb" or "the anticausative verb", thus the causative alternation is also termed as "the causative/inchoative alternation" or "the anticausative alternation"(Levin and Rappaport Hovav 1995).

© Springer International Publishing Switzerland 2014
X. Su and T. He (Eds.): CLSW 2014, LNAI 8922, pp. 161–169, 2014.
DOI: 10.1007/978-3-319-14331-6_16

derivational relationship and posits a common base for the two alternates. This paper is in favor of the latter approach based on the cross-linguistic facts. However, there are still some problems for the previous non-derivational studies and we will put forward a new analysis from the non-derivational perspective built on the theory proposed by Huang *et al.*(2009).

2   Literature Review

In this section, we will present the main ideas and the major drawbacks of the derivational and non-derivational approaches respectively.

2.1   The Derivational Approach and Its Problems

Proponents of the derivational approach hold that in the causative alternation, one alternate is derived from the other in the Lexicon by certain lexical rules. But they differ in which alternate is basic and which one is derived. Dowty(1979), Williams(1981) and Pesetsky(1995), among others, claim that the causative alternate is derived from the unaccusative one in that the former denotes an accomplishment which is composed of an achievement denoted by the latter. Dowty(1979: 206) proposes that the unaccusative *break* in (2) undergoes a causativization process, i.e. the addition of an eventive predicate CAUSE to the semantic decomposition.

(2) $break_{unacc}$: $\lambda x[\text{BECOME broken}(x)]$
        +CAUSE $\downarrow$

    $break_{caus}$: $\lambda x \lambda y[(y) \text{ CAUSE [BECOME broken}(x)]]$

With regard to linguistic facts, some unaccusative verbs in English have no causative counterparts, which seems to prove they are basically monadic. Example (3) is from Gu (1996: 7):

(3) a. The guests arrived.

    b. *The party arrived many guests.

If the unaccusative *arrive* in (3a) is assumed to derive from its causative counterpart, at least (3b) should be a legitimate structure, which is, however, contrary to the fact. It follows that the direction of derivation should be from the unaccusative alternate to the causative one and the latter is not always licit.

In contrast to the causativization analysis, many studies claim that verbs showing causative alternation are inherently dyadic predicates which undergo a detransitivization process, deriving the unaccusative variant (Chierchia 1989; Levin and Rappaport Hovav(hereinafter L&R)1995, 2005; Reinhart 2002). L&R(1995: 83) propose a bi-eventive analysis of causative verbs whereby their lexical semantic representations(LSR) consist of a causing subevent and a central subevent connected by CAUSE. The argument "causer" is associated with the causing subevent and the theme with the central one. When the causative verb changes into the unaccusative variant, the causer is lexically bound in the mapping from LSR to argument structure(AS) and cannot be projected into the syntax. This is illustrated in (4):

(4) the unaccusative *break*

LSR: [[x DO-SOMETHING] CAUSE [y BECOME BROKEN]]

Lexical binding ↓   Linking rules ↓

AS: Ø   <y>

L&R(1995: 85-86) observe some restrictions for English change-of-state verbs in their intransitive uses, which seems to prove the detransitivization analysis is on the right track. For example, *cut* in (5) only has a transitive use and lacks an unaccusative variant and *break* in (6) can be used intransitively only for certain choices of internal arguments.

(5) a. The baker cut the bread.

 b. *The bread cut.

(6) a. He broke his legs/the contract/ the world record.

 b. His legs/*The contract/ *The world record broke.

In recent years, the rationale of the derivational approach has been questioned by many based on the cross-linguistic facts(Haspelmath1993; Alexiadou *et al.* 2006; Schäfer 2009). The first problem concerns the morphological form of the alternation. Generally speaking, derived forms are supposed to be morphologically marked. So if the unaccusative form is basic, as the causativization view claims, the causative form is expected to be morphologically marked, and vice versa. However, both patterns can be found cross-linguistically (Haspelmath1993).

(7) a. causative marking:

  Georgian: *duy-s*   'cook(unaccusative)'

     a-duy-ebs   'cook (causative)'

 b. unaccusative marking:

  Russian: *katat'-sja*   'roll(unaccusative)'

     katat'   'roll(causative)'

Furthermore, there are some languages in which both variants are morphologically marked, forming non-directed alternations. The Japanese example (8) can illustrates this:

(8) *atum-aru* 'gather(unaccusative)'

 atum-eru 'gather(causative)'

The second problem concerns cross-linguistic differences in verbal and selectional restrictions. On the one hand, it is true that English unaccusative verbs such as *arrive* and *exist* have no causative variants, but their counterparts in such languages as Japanese allow the alternation. The example below is from Matsumoto(2000).

(9) a. Takushi-ga   genkan-ni   tsui-ta.

  taxi-NOM   front door-GOAL arrive-PAST

  The taxi arrived at the front door.

 b.Untenshû-ga takushi-o genkan-ni   tsuke-ta.

  driver-NOM taxi-ACC front door-GOAL arrive-PAST

  The taxi driver brought (his) taxi to the front door.

On the other hand, although English verbs like *break* can only select certain types of subjects and verbs like *cut* and *kill* have no unaccusative variants, there are no such restrictions for their counterparts in such languages as Greek. Example (10) is from Alexiadou *et al.*(2006) .

(10) a. O Petros/o sismos   skotose ti   Maria
        Peter/the earthquake killed   the   Mary
        Peter/the earthquake killed Mary.
    b. I   Maria skotothike (apo/ me ton sismo)
        the Mary killed   by/with the earthquake
        Mary killed (by/with the earthquake).

These facts show both the causativization and detransitivization views do not fare satisfactorily with respect to the issue of verbal/selectional restrictions. The evidence for the directional approach is far from convincing.

2.2   The Present Non-derivational Studies and Their Problems

In view of the problems facing the derivational approach, some scholars argue for a non-derivational analysis, assuming a common base for the alternating verbs.(Piñón 2001; Alexiadou *et al.* 2006; Schäfer 2009, 2010). If the LSR of causative verbs involves three predicates CAUSE, BECOME and STATE, the sentence 'John opened the door again.' is supposed to have three readings. However, von Stechow(1995) observes that it only has restitutive and repetitive readings just as their unaccusative counterparts. Given this fact, Kratzer(2005) and the subsequent works (Alexiadou *et al.* 2006; Schäfer 2010) argue for the same event composition for both causatives and unaccusatives and they differ only in the presence vs. absence of *Voice*.

(11) a. The door opens
        [CAUSE [the door √OPEN]]
    b. John opens the door
        [John [*Voice* [CAUSE [the door √OPEN]]]]

As shown in (11), the causative and unaccusative variants of *open* have and only have the CAUSE predicate in their event composition and the causative alternation is in essence a *Voice* alternation.

Since the two variants come from a common base, there is no need to distinguish the basic form from the derived one and the cross-linguistic differences in morphological marking and verbal/selectional restrictions do not pose a threat to the non-derivational approach. However, the previous non-derivational studies still face some problems. First, the *Voice* projection seems to have only syntactic function of introducing external arguments and no concrete eventive semantics. To integrate it into the event composition of causative verbs may result in a blending of syntactic units and event predicates. Second, if the two variants have one and the same CAUSE predicate in their event composition, then how can we determine the events denoted by them are externally or internally caused? In addition, the previous studies claim CAUSE can take part in the syntactic operations by introducing internal arguments, but   this function has been questioned by many other scholars(Lin 2004; Ramchand 2008 among others).

3   A New Analysis Based on Huang *et al.*(2009)'s Theory

In this section, we will put forward a new non-derivational analysis of the causative alternation based on Huang *et al.*(2009), which can make some improvement on the previous studies. First we briefly introduce Huang *et al.*'s theory and then present our analysis.

3.1   An Brief Account of Huang *et al.*'s Theory

Huang *et al.*(2009) put forwards a new theory of argument realization based on the theory of Hale and Keyser(1993) and the Light Verb Syntax of Lin(2001). According to Huang *et al.*, a lexical verb is composed of a lexical root √ which conceptualizes a set of events *e* and a few light verbs(Lv) which indicate the event type of *e* by sifting the information on the participants of *e*, which directly determines the nature of the event type. The theory is presented in detail as follows:

(12) V ∈ { (√), [Lv1 √], [Lv2 √], [Lv2 [Lv1 √]] } , √ stands for a verb root.

(13) a. Lv1 manifests the type of event without an external cause and is approximately described as "enter S(state)" or "enter R(esult)". The participant that enters the state or relation is interpreted as Theme.

   b. Lv2 manifests the type of event with an external cause which is approximately described as "bring about a dynamic E(event)" or bring about R". The external cause, interpreted as Agent or Originator, is implicated by Lv2 but not conceptualized as part of the event.

   c. Other intrinsic participants of E, S and R are manifested as optional or obligatory theta-roles, as determined by √.

   d. The choice of an Lv must not conflict with the type of event already coded in √.

   e. Participant-information resulting from above must satisfy the theta-criterion.

   According to this theory, the root √ contains information about participants and other relevant factors for the event. An Lv does not add any meaning to √ but only spells out the event type conceptualized in √. Likewise, a theta-role like Theme is not provided by Lv1 but is simply selected by Lv1 because it is the participant in the Lv1-types of event. That is to say, the theta-roles a given V must have are fundamentally determined by the type of event already encoded in √. For example, in English conceptualization, events of laughing and crying necessarily have an originator, so √*laugh* and √*cry* only are only compatible with Lv2 which implicates an external Agent role. In contrast, Chinese consider those events as either ones with an originator or involuntary outbursts of emotions, hence √*xiao*'laugh' and √*ku*'cry' in Chinese are compatible with either Lv1 or Lv2. The lexical semantic structures(LSSs) of these verbs are given below:

(14) a. laugh: [Lv2 √*laugh*]
    b. cry: [Lv2 √*cry*]
(15) a. xiao 'laugh': [Lv2 √*xiao*] or [Lv1 √*xiao*]
    b. ku 'cry' : [Lv2 √*ku*] or [Lv1 √*ku*]

3.2   A New Non-derivational Analysis of the Causative Alternation

From Huang *et al.*'s theory, we can see that variable-behavior verbs arise from the ambiguity of the event types that a verb root encodes and the compatibility of the root with different Lvs. If a root conceptualizes more than one type of events, it has the options of combining with Lv1 or Lv2, or both, resulting in different configuration in the LSS of the verb. We argue that the verbs undergoing the causative alteration are formed by the roots of this type. The causative and unaccusative variants share a common verb root, which conceptualizes different types of events and thus combines with different Lvs, resulting in two lexical verbs with different argument realization.

Let's take the verb *open* as an example to illustrate our point. In human conceptualization, the event of opening may be indentified as an event that simply comes about without emphasizing any external factor. In this regard, √*open* can conceptualize the type of event which happens without an external cause and is compatible only with Lv1, which implicates an internal Theme role. On the other hand, the event of opening can also be brought about by an external cause. That means √*open* can also conceptualize the type of event with an external cause, resulting in both Lv1 and Lv2 inside the verb's LSS. In brief, the same root √*open* can combine with Lv1 or both Lv1 and Lv2 to form different LSSs, which in turn determines the different argument structures for the verb. This is illustrated as below:

(16) a. open₁   LSS: [Lv1√*open*]

AS: V <Theme>

e.g. The door opened.

b. open₂   LSS: [Lv2 [Lv1√*break*]]

AS: V <Agent, Theme>

e.g. Bill broke the vase.

The above two verbs differ only in the presence vs. absence of Lv2 in their LSSs, but there is no direct derivational relationship between them. To be more exact, open₂ is not derived by adding an Lv2 to the LSS of open₁; neither is open₁ derived by taking Lv2 away from the LSS of open₂. According to our analysis, neither Lv1 nor Lv2 can be separated from the LSS of a verb since they are only a linguistic "spell-out" of the event type coded in √, not something that is totally independent of the semantics of √. In this sense, our analysis is also carried out from a non-derivational perspective as we take the two variants to come from one source, i.e. the root √, which, combined with different Lvs, constitutes two independent lexical verbs with different argument realization.

However, our analysis has some important differences from the previous non-derivational studies. First, although Lv2 is similar to CAUSE in terms of event semantics, their distinction is clear-cut in that the former adds no extra meaning to the root, nor does it participate in any syntactic operations as the latter does. The LSS of a verb only contains eventive light verbs and excludes the components such as *Voice* which make no contribution to the semantic composition of the verb. In this sense, there will no mixing of syntactic and semantic components.

Second, the previous studies stipulate the same event composition for both variants, but in our view, the two variants stem from one root which conceptualizes different types of event. Whether the event encoded by a root is internally caused or externally caused can be clearly seen from the Lvs that the root is combined with.

Our analysis not only solves the problems faced by the previous non-derivational studies, but also gives a satisfactory explanation of the cross-linguistic differences in morphological marking. We assume that a lexical word is morphologically made up of a root and functional morphemes. The functional morphemes are often realized as affixes in languages, serving as a marker indicating the event types of verbs. The same verb root can be inflected with different affixes, forming different lexical items. For instance, the Georgian verb root √*duy* can take on different affixes, forming a causative verb and an unaccusative one respectively. See example (7a), repeated in (17):

(17) *a-duy-ebs*   'cook (causative)'
     duy-s   'cook(unaccusative)'

In (17), the causative alternate is morphologically more complex than the unaccusative one, but they have no direct derivational relationship whatsoever because the suffix −*eb* is by no means a functional morpheme in itself. In our view, the two alternates are derived from one source, i.e. the verb root √*duy*. The causative variant is formed by adding both a prefix *a-* and a suffix −*ebs* to the root while the unaccusative variant is formed by adding a suffix −*s*. Neither of the two variants is derived from the other.

The Japanese example (8)(repeated in (18)) can be explained in a similar vein.

(18) *atum-aru* 'gather(unaccusative)'
     atum-eru 'gather(causative)'

Both of the variants are morphologically marked and there is no telling which one is the basic. In our view, they both stem from a common root √*atum* which is inflected with different morphemes, forming two independent lexical items.

As for those languages with impoverished inflections such as English and Chinese, since they have no overt functional morphemes to mark verbs of various event types, we may sometimes get confused between the lexical verbs and their roots(e.g. *break* and √*break*) and between the variants of a verb(e.g. the causative and the unaccusative variants of *break*). If our analysis for the fully-inflected languages is on the right track, the two variants of the same form in English or Chinese can be regarded as a single root which takes on different covert functional morphemes, as shown in (19) and (20). Ø1 and Ø2 stand for the covert affixes marking the unaccusative and causative verbs.

(19) a. the accusative *break*=√*break*+Ø1
     b. the causative *break*=√*break*+Ø2
(20) a. the accusative *chen* 'sink'=√*chen*+Ø1
     b. the causative *chen* 'sink'=√*chen*+Ø2

4   Summary

In this paper, we adopt a non-derivational perspective for the analysis of the causative alternation. However, in view of the problems in the previous non-derivational studies, we argue that the causative and unaccusative variants share a common verb root, which conceptualizes different types of events and thus combines with different Lvs, forming two lexical verbs with different argument realization. The cross-linguistic differences in morphological marking are due to the diversified forms(overt vs. covert) of functional morphemes combined with a root across languages. In this sense, our analysis is consistent with Chomsky's assumption that languages are universal in lexical roots and the computational system but differ only in the visible elements such as functional morphemes.

References

1. Yang, G.: Generative Syntax and Some Properties of Verbs in the Lexicon. Foreign Linguistics **3**, 1–16 (1996). (in Chinese)
2. Alexiadou, A., Anagnostopoulou, E., Schäfer, F.: The Properties of Anticausative Cross-linguistically. In: Frascarelli, M. (ed.) Phases of Interpretation, pp. 187–211. Mouton de Gruyter, Berlin (2006)
3. Borer, H.: The Projection of Arguments. In: Benedicto, E., Runner, J. (eds.) Functional Projections. University of Massachusetts Occasional Papers, vol. 17, pp. 19–47. University of Massachusetts, Amgerst (1994)
4. Chierchia, G.: A Semantics for Unaccusative and Its Syntactic Consequences. Ms, Cornell University (1989)
5. Dowty, D.: Word Meaning and Montague Grammar. D. Reidel Publishing Company, Dordrecht (1979)
6. Hale, K., Keyser, J.: On Argument Structure and the Lexical Expression of Syntactic Relations. In: Hale, K., Keyser, J. (eds.) The View from Building 20: Essays in Linguistics in Honor of Sylvain Bromberger, pp. 53–109. The MIT Press, Cambridge (1993)
7. Haspelmath, M.: More on the Typology of Inchoative/Causative Verb Alternation. In: Comrie, B., Polinsky, M. (eds.) Causatives and Transitivity, pp. 87–120. John Benjamins, Amsterdam (1993)
8. Huang, C.T., Li, Y.H., Li, Y.F.: The Syntax of Chinese. Cambridge University Press, Cambridge (2009)
9. Levin, B., Rappaport, H.M.: Unaccusativity: At the Syntax-lexical Semantics Interface. The MIT Press, Cambridge (1995)
10. Levin, B., Rappaport, H.M.: Argument Realization. Cambridge University Press, Cambridge (2005)
11. Lin J.: Event Structure and the Encoding of Arguments: The Syntax of the Mandarin and English Verb Phrase. PhD. Dissertation. The MIT Press, Cambridge (2004)
12. Lin, T.-H.: Light Verb Syntax and the Theory of Phrase Structure. PhD. Dissertation, University of California, Irvine (2001)
13. Matsumoto, Y.: Causative Alternation in English and Japanese: a Close Look. English Linguistics **17**, 160–192 (2000)
14. Piñón, C.: A Finer Look at the Causative-inchoative Alternation. In: Hastings, R., Jackon, B., Zvolenszky, Z. (eds.) Proceedings of SALT 11. CLC Publications, Ithaca (2001)
15. Pesetsky, D.: Zero Syntax. Experiencers and Casacades. The MIT Press, Cambridge (1995)

16. Ramchand. C.: Verb Meaning and the Lexicon: A First-Phase Syntax. Cambridge University Press, Cambridge (2008)
17. Reinhart, T.: The Theta System-an Overview. Theoretical. Linguistics **3**, 229–290 (2002)
18. Schäfer, F.: The Causative Alternation. Language and Linguistics Compass **2**, 641–681 (2009)
19. Schäfer, F.: The Syntax of (Anti-)Causative. John Benjamins, Amsterdam (2010)
20. Williams, E.: Argument Structure and Morphology. The Linguistic Review **1**, 81–114 (1981)

The Processing of Dummy Verbs in Semantic Role Labeling

Mengxiang Wang[1,2], Yang Liu[2], and Houfeng Wang[2(✉)]

[1] Teachers' College of Beijing Union University, Beijing 100011, China
[2] Institute of Computational Linguistics, Peking University, Beijing 100871, China
{wmx1984,liuyang,wanghf}@pku.edu.cn

Abstract. Semantic Role Labeling (SRL) generally focuses on the verbs, while the Dummy Verbs as a special category, often appear in front of the verbs structure, resulting in the form of verb-object structure. Based on this, in some semantic resources, the Dummy Verbs are always treated as the key verbs, and then to label semantic roles. However, their meanings do not contain action, and their existence is just for grammar, not for semantics, therefore, they should be treated differently from general verbs in the process of semantic roles labeling. This paper aims to filter the dummy verbs that only play the role in the syntax, and make the real core components of the sentence fell on the corresponding key verb, so as to analyze the semantic components correctly. At the same time it also can make contribute to the SRL of PMT (Peking University Multiview Chinese Treebank).

Keywords: Dummy verbs · Semantic Role Labeling · Multi-view Chinese Treebank

1 Introduction

Let's see two sentences from the LTP of Harbin Institute of Technology:

(1) 我们　　明天　　进行　对　案件　的　调查。
Women mingtian Jinxing dui anjian de diaocha
We tomorrow Jinxing on case de investigation
We will have an investigation on the case tomorrow.

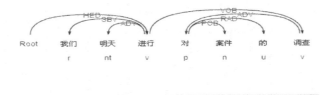

(2) 对　这些　困难　要　予以　克服。
Dui zhexie kunnan yao yuyi kefu
On these difficulties yuyi overcome

X. Su and T. He (Eds.): CLSW 2014, LNAI 8922, pp. 170–180, 2014.
DOI: 10.1007/978-3-319-14331-6_17

These difficulties must be overcame

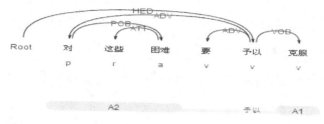

(A0、A1、A2 are the arguments of verbs)

Both sentences were based on the dummy verb as "jinxing(进行)" and "yuyi（予以）" as the center for the grammar analysis and semantic role labeling (SRL). This kind of SRL has two problems: Firstly, the definition of core verbs dose not conforms to the sentence meaning. As we all know, the first step of semantic role labeling is to confirm the predicate, this is the premise of the semantic role labeling (SRL). If the core verbs were wrong, it would be impossible to make the semantic role labeling correct. Though from the syntactic formation, both sentences can be understood as the form that core verbs followed by verbs as object. Though from the perspective of syntactic formation, this is correct as both verbs are followed with verb objects, while from the perspective of semantics, the "have" and "be" is meaningless, the actual meaning of those two sentences is "we are going to investigate this case tomorrow" and "overcome those difficulties". So, the core verbs of the two sentences is "investigate" and "conquer" and the "case" and "difficulties" are the "Patient." of "investigate" and "overcome " .

Secondly, it is likely some verbs will be regarded as arguments, such as "investigation（调查）" and "overcome（克服）" become the "patient". This is not conforming to the general way that we usually used in SRL that is only nouns are endowed with semantic roles. In fact, we can find the similar issues when we study other Treebank. Such as, in Chinese Propbank, in the processing of words as "jinxing（进行）" and "yuyi(予以)", there are the same problems exist as dependency Treebank in HIT. The difference is the object after the verb is labeled as "noun",such as:

(3) 对　发生　的　灾害　　事故　及时　进行　　补偿
　　 Dui　fasheng　de　zaihai　　shigu　jishi　jinxing　buchang
　　 On　happen　de calamity　accident betimes jinxing　compensation
　　 Have compensation of the calamity accident that happens"

The Chinese Propbank processed this internal data as following:

```
on ( dui )            对 P   (PP*PP) - * * * *
happen ( fasheng )    发生 VV   (VP*VP) 发生 * * (V*V) *
de ( de )             的 DEC  * - * * * *
calamity ( zaihai )   灾害 NN   (NP* - * * (A0* *
accident ( shigu )    事故 NN   *NP) - * * *A0) *
betimes ( jishi )     及时 AD   (ADVP*ADVP) - * * * (AM-ADV*AM-ADV)
jinxing ( jinxing )   进行 VV   (VP*VP) 进行 * * * (V*V)
compensation ( buchang )  补偿 NN  (NP*NP) - * * * (A1*A1)
。 PU  * - * * * *
```

One of the reasons is related to the standard of the part-of-speech tagging, another reason is the words followed the verb "jinxing(进行)" is generally a gerund, it can be noun and verb at the same time, so it will be labeled as NP naturally. Though in this way, the "compensation (补偿)" can be the argument of "jinxing (进行)" and conforms to the principle of SRL, while in the deep sentence meaning, it hasn't reflected the actual semantic relationship of the sentences but interfered by the syntactic formation.

The reason as why these problems exist is because the existence of verbs like "jinxing(进行)"and "yuyi(予以)" makes the real core verb act as object and its function has been erased formally which has caused some interference in semantic analysis. In some sense, verbs as"jinxing(进行)"and "yuyi(予以)" is the noise in the process of SRL, this paper is to deal with this special situation, thus to ensure the accuracy of the analysis of semantic role and provide some support for the improvement of semantic role labeling of PMT in the future.

2   The Characteristics and Selections of Dummy Verbs

2.1   The Characteristics of Dummy Verbs

Scholars as Lv (1980), Zhu (1982) Zhou (1987), Li (1990) etc. have made researches on characteristics of dummy verbs. Dummy verbs also known as function verbs etc, it has the characteristics that common verbs do not have.

In view of the formal, dummy verbs usually followed by VP as object. For example, "Jinxing Jiaoxue(进行教学)" (it means teach a lesson) while common verbs followed by NP as object"Da ren (打人) " (it means beat someone) . Certainly, it doesn't mean the dummy verbs can not followed by NP as object, Du (2010) has made an statistics of the specific situation of the object followed after some dummy verbs in " People's Daily of 2001, as below:

Dummy verbs	Jinxing (进行)	JiaYi (加以)	Yuyi (予以)	Geiyi (给以)	Jiyu (给予)	Zhiyi (致以)
Total	21403	875	1422	40	2481	254
No Object	1792 (8.37%)	0	0	0	19 (0.76%)	0
Followed NP	531 (2.48%)	0	0	1 (2.5%)	77 (3.10%)	46 (18.11%)
Followed VP	19080 (89.15%)	875 (100%)	1422(100%)	39 (97.5%)	2385 (96.14%)	208 (81.89%)

From the data above we can see though the dummy verb can be followed by NP as object, while the proportion is very limited and in most situations, it is followed by VP.

In view of the Semantics, dummy verbs doesn't have the actual semantics of an action, the semantics has been virtualized as it followed by object and it has no impact on the sentence meaning when it is deleted. The major sentence meaning is expressed by the object that followed, for example, "Mingtian(tomorrow) Jinxing(进行) Bisai(competion)" (Tomorrow competition), it doesn't change the sentence meaning when we delete the verb "Jinxing(进行)". Therefore, we can say, the existence of dummy verbs is not for sentence meaning but based on the grammar forms.

However, what need to be mentioned is it is not all dummy verbs are meaningless, such as "Bisai Zhengzai Jinxing（比赛正在进行）", (The competition is ongoing) and the "Jinxing（进行）" (ongoing) here has its actual meaning and can not be deleted.

2.2   The Selections of Dummy Verbs

There are not many dummy verbs, but the linguistics fields don't have a clear argument for their quantity and range.. On the basis of Grammatical Knowledge Dictionary of Peking University, this paper has combined the common opinions in linguistics fields; it is believed that there are seven dummy verbs as "Jinxing(进行), Jiayi（加以）, Yuyi（予以）, Geiyi（给以）, Jiyu（给予）, Zhiyi（致以）, You（有）".

Among this, "You（有）" is not a specialized dummy verb, because "you （有）" can indicate the actual meaning as "have", and it is very common to be followed by NP. We still choose "you(有)" as dummy verb for 2 reason: one is "you(有)" have some characteristics of dummy verb. It can be followed by VP, on that time, the main verb will focus the VP, while the "you(有)" has been virtualized and it has no impact on the sentence meaning when it is deleted. For example:

(4) 我　　（有）　说过　　那句　　话　　吗?
　　Wo　you　shuoguo　naju　hua　ma
　　I　have　said　that　sentence?

When "you(有)" was deleted, the sentence meaning didn't change.

Reason two is that the number and frequency of "you(有)" in corpus are both relatively high, and so do the situation followed by VP. We investigated the test data of Chinese Propbank(260,000 words). We found that "you(有)" appears 7350 times, followed by VP 989 times. The usage ratio as a dummy verb is not high, only 13.5%, but the total number is still considerable. On the other hand ,the proportion of "you(有)+NP" is much higher. In this case, we put you "(有)" into a separate category, as a special dummy verb.

Besides "(有)", other words are not always regarded as the dummy verbs. For example:

(5) A. 会议　　进行　　了　七天
Huiyi   jinxing le   qitian
Meeting   is ongoing   7 days

B. 他　　一只手　　给予，　一只手　　　索取
ta yizhishou   jiyu,   yizhishou   suoqu
He one hand   to give,   one hand   to get

In these 2 sentences, the verbs "jinxing(进行)"and "jiyu(给予)" have their own meaning "ongoing" and "give". In this case, they can not be regarded as dummy verbs at this time.

In common, people usually distinguished this situation by meaning, but for computer only can distinguish them by form. Through the study we found their connected components can be used to distinguish them. When it connected to VP, its lexical semantic will weaken (like example (4)), but if it followed by NP or no Object, its lexical semantic will not weaken (like example(5)).

So the following component is VP or NP is to decide these 7 words can be used as dummy verbs or used as general verbs.

3   The Standard of Part-of-Speech Tagging Followed by Dummy Verbs

Generally speaking, dummy verbs are followed by VP. While currently, in some tree-bank, the Part-of-Speech tagging of the object following dummy verbs is not accurate and uniform. On the contrary, in some corpus the rate for dummy verbs (Except "You"(有)) followed by NP is much higher than VP, For example, According to the Part-of-Speech tagging method, the paper has made a statistics of the dummy verbs (except "You"(有)) of the 260,000 words test data in Propbank:

Dummy verbs	Jinxing(进行)	Jiayi (加以)	Yuyi(予以)	Jiyi(给以)	Jiyu(给予)	Zhiyi(致以)
Total	2161	32	160	1	261	7
Followed NP	1168 (54.0%)	18 (56.25%)	92 (57.5%)	1 (100%)	188 (72.0%)	2 (28.6%)
Followed VP	542 (25.1%)	14 (43.75%)	43 (26.9%)	0	40 (15.3%)	5 (71.4%)

The reason for this kind of situation is mainly because most of the constituents that followed dummy verbs are gerund or conversion word, while all these are labeled as N. for example, "Jinxing Chuban", (进行出版/publish), Jiayi Jiandu" (加以监督/supervision) " Jiyi Zhichi"(给予/Support". the "出版" (Chuban –publish), "监督" (Jiandu- supervision)and "支持" (Zhichi- support) has been labeled as N. Besides, we have selected the gerund verb lists of **Grammatical Information Dictionary** and compared those verbs with the NP component followed by dummy verbs in Chinese Propbank, the specific statistic data is as following:

Dummy VERBS	进行(JINXING)	加以(JIAYI)	予以(YUYI)	给以(GEIYI)	给予(JIYU)	致以(ZHIYI)
FOLLOWED NP	1168	18	92	1	188	2
GERUND	1134 (97.1%)	18 (100%)	92 (100%)	1 (100%)	139 (73.9%)	2 (100%)

The above statistics indicate that in the Labeling system of Chinese Propbank, the part-of-Speech tagging of gerund verb followed by the dummy verbs are processed as N. Similar problems exist in the current PMT of Perking University.

We can say, the issue of the processing of the constituents followed by dummy verbs is the common issue of most Tree-bank and the reason is currently the common Tree bank processed dummy verbs as core verbs. The solution to avoid this is to do something in the part-of-Speech tagging. If one is a verb and another followed word is labeled as Noun then there is no doubts the core of the sentence would be the verb. If one is verb and the followed word is also a verb then, the followed constituent is very likely to become the core of the sentence. This is conforms to the rules of the linguistics as "the followed constituent of dummy verbs usually is the core of the sentence's meaning". What we need to do is to label the speech of the word. If the word followed is NP, then there is no doubts the dummy verbs is the core of the whole sentence. If the dummy verbs are followed by gerund, then it can be processed as V. we can compare these 2 sentences:

(6) A 她 给予   了   我   生命
     Ta Jiyu   le   Wo   Shengming
     She   give(Jiyu)V   me   Life(N)
    B 我们   要 给以   鼓励
     Women   yao jiyu   guli
     We   will jiyu(V)   encourage(N/V)

In Chinese, "life(生命)" always be a noun, but "encourage(鼓励)" will be gerund word, In our mind, the gerund word "encourage(鼓励)" followed by dummy verb need be labeled as "V".

Though the judgment of speech of gerund is controversial in the grammar field, but the paper believes, from the perspective of SRL, once the followed word after dummy verb is gerund, then it should be labeled as V instead of N. The reason is, semantically, the judgment of these words preferred to verb and the characteristics to express an action is more obvious than the dummy verb, so it is very likely to become the core constituent of the sentence. Generally, the core of the sentence is the predicate. Therefore, so it is more reasonable to process the gerund followed by dummy verb as V semantically. For example, in the auto-segmentation system of Harbin Institute of Technology, the gerund is processed as V, the only difference is the VP followed by the dummy verb is not processed as core predicate.

4   Discussion of Semantic Role Labeling of the Constituent Followed the Dummy Verb

4.1   The Semantic Role Labeling when Followed by VP

When the dummy verb is followed by VP, then the core of the semantic is in the part behind. Therefore, in the process of specific semantic role labeling, we must filtering the dummy verb with reduced semantic meaning and assign the semantic roles according to the relations between the followed verbs and argument to enhance the accuracy of the semantic role labeling. Such as:

(7)　　A 我们　　　要　对　这个人　　　加以　　防范
　　　　Women　　Yao dui　Zhegeren　Jiayi　Fangfan
　　　　We　　　Will dui　This man　Jiayi　precaute
　　　　B 我们　　　要　　防范　　　　这个人
　　　　Women　　Yao　Fangfan　　Zhegeren
　　　　We　　　will　precaute　　this man

Their SRL should be the same that is. (Agent+ 防范precaute +Patient)

4.2   The Semantic Role Labeling when not Followed by VP

When it is not followed by VP, the dummy verb would be general verb, and the SRL is due to the concrete dummy verb, because the different dummy verbs take different semantic role.

According to the statistics above, only can the "Jinxing(进行), Jiyu（给予）, You（有）" can take the NP, other dummy verbs hardly take NP as object, so we just discuss these 3 words:

i. For "Jinxing(进行)", when it is used as a general verb, it means "ongoing" or "making". Strictly speaking, it does not belong to the action verbs. For the accuracy of semantic role, the following NP can't be simply labeled as "Agent" or

"Patient", but "Experiencer" and "Theme". Because the verb "Jinxing(进行)" can transform between"NP$_1$+V+NP$_2$"and"NP$_2$+V". For example:

(8) A 公司   正在   进行   一个 会议 →
     Gongsi   zhengzai jinxing yige huiyi→
     Company   is   making a   meeting →
     Experiencer   jinxing(进行) Theme(semantic role)

     →B一个   会议   正在   进行
     → Yige   huiyi zhengzai   jinxing
     → A   meeting is   making
     Theme   jinxing(进行)   (semantic role)

Wang(2013) pointed out that if a verb can transform between "NP1+V+NP2"and"NP2+V", the NP1 role will be "Experiencer", and the NP2 will be "Theme".

ii. For "Jiyu(给予)", when it is used as a general verb, it means "give" (action verb) , so its semantic roles this time can match "give" 's frame:"Agent+give+ （Dative) +(patient)". Let's see the case(6A) above:

她   给予   了   我   生命
Ta   Jiyu   le   Wo   Shengming
She   give(Jiyu) V   me   Life(N)

SRL will be "She[Agent] give(给予) me[Dative] life[Patient]".

iii. For "you(有)", its usage is complex。 We first need to consider the format"you(有)+N+Adj", because at this moment , "you(有)" is not a verb strictly as Lin (1993) 、Xu （2000) said, but preposition, Such as the below sentence, the "you(有)" like the preposition "like":

(9)"这 花   开得   有   碗口   那么 大"
   Zhe hua kaide you   wankou name da
   Flower   open   like   bowl   big
   (the flower is so big like bowl)

At this point, we should filter out the"you(有)", let the "open(开)" as the core, control the argument "flower （花) ", whose semantic role is "Agent".

In addition, when "you(有)" followed by NP, there will be 2 situations. One is meaning possess, the relative semantic roles are "possessor + possession". The other usage often appears in the existential sentences, indicating "exist", the relative semantic roles are "Location/Time+ Existent". For example:

(10) A. 我 有   一支   笔
        Wo you   yizhi   bi
        I   have a   pen
        Possessor+have+possession (Semantic roles)
     B. 山上   有   个   庙
        Shanshang   you   ge   miao
        Mountain   exist a   temple
        Location +exist+ Existent (Semantic roles)

C. 周日　　　有　　　手术
Zhouri　　you　　shoushu
Sunday　exist　operation
Time +exist+ Existent (Semantic roles)

In a word, during SRL, the dummy need to do filtering. If there is a "dummy verb + VP" or "you(有)+NP+ Adj", the "dummy verb" or "you (有)+NP" should be erased. If dummy verb do not followed by VP, then according to below:

Verbs	Semantic role matching
Jinxing (进行)	Experiencer+ Jinxing(进行)+Theme；Theme+进行
Jiyu (给予)	Agent+ Jiyu (给予)+ (Dative) +(Patient)
You (有)	"Possessor+ You (有)+Possession"；"Location/Time+ You (有)+Existent"

Need to be pay attention to is the filtering of dummy verb applies only to the semantic category, or just to SRL. Because the SRL reflects the deep semantic relations between verbs and nouns, so it is not necessary to take the some form or syntax factors into consideration. Erasing some non-practical meaning verbs is useful for clearing the relation between verbs and nouns and determining the real core verb. But to the view of syntax, the dummy verb is essential. For example, in case (1), if the dummy verb "jinxing(进行)" was erased, the semantic will not be changed, but syntactically, "jinxing(进行)" must exist, otherwise this sentence is out of grammar and unable to convince.

5   Experiment and Conclusion

In order to illustrate the effect of dummy verbs to the accuracy of SRL, we use the data of PMT 1.0. The data are artificial double blind annotated, so the accuracy is relatively high. But the PMT 1.0 only do the syntactic analysis, there is no SRL, so that is in line with the requirements of our experiment. We select 10000 sentences and correct the part of speech tagging with our standard and rules. In SRL process, we pay attention to screening and filtering on the dummy verbs. For example:

(11)

公司　通过　　电子仪器　对 这家 住户　进行　日夜　　　　监视

Gongsi　tongguio　dianziyiqi　dui zhejia　zhuhu　jinxing　riye　　jianshi

Company through electronic device dui this family jinxing day and nigh monitoring

In syntactic analysis tree structure, this sentence is take the verb "jinxing(进行)" as the core, arguments are "company(公司N)、 family （住户N）、 monitoring （监视V） ", but in semantic analysis, the verb "jinxing(进行) have no meaning, which should be erased in, and "monitoring(监视)" should be the predicate. SRL is output as "company/N/[AGENT(施 事)], electronic device/N/[INSTRUMENT （工具）], family/N/[TARGET （对象）],monitor/V/", as shown in bellow:

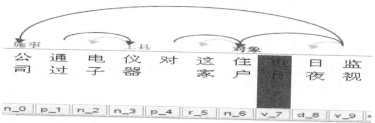

After the statistics, in the corpora 10000 sentences, there are 1810 sentences with dummy verbs, accounting for 18.1% of the total, and the ones need to erase dummy verbs are 616 cases, accounting for 6.2% of the total. The specific distribution is as follows:

Dummy verbs		Jinxing（进行）	JiaYi（加以）	Yuyi（予以）	Geiyi（给以）	Jiyu（给予）	Zhiyi（致以）	You(有)
Total		372	20	26	0	38	18	1336
Need erased	Followed VP	318	20	26	0	29	18	173
	"you(有)" +N+Adj	-	-	-	-	-	-	12

The erased processing of 616 dummy verbs can enhance the accuracy of 6.2% predicate labeling, which also improves SRL..These features of dummy verbs can only improve the accuracy of SRL in those sentences with dummy verbs, and do not affect the sentences without dummy verbs.

Then, we combine the above ideas and do the SRL in the 1810 cases; we make a statistics about the SRL in 2 kinds of situation:

SRL	precision	Recall	F
Some dummy verbs erased	91.7%	95.5%	94.1%
Some dummy verbs not erased	73.7%	76.0%	74.8%

To sum up, in the current SRL process, the features of dummy verbs were not taken into account in various semantic resources. The dummy verbs with their own characteristics can easily become the process noise to the SRL, if we can distinguish and filter them under the premise of right part of speech tagging and syntactic analysis, there will be a good help to the predicate labeling and SRL. When the dummy verb followed by VP, we should take VP as the core and to label its relative semantic role. When it is not followed by VP, the dummy verb would be general verb, and the SRL is due to the concrete dummy verb, because the different dummy verb take different semantic role, we can only choose "Experiencer+Theme", "Agent+(Dative)+(Patient)", "Possessor+Possession" or "Location/Time+ Existent" as the arguments' semantic role matching. But for the length limit, we can't discuss specific labeling method, also failed to summarize the characteristics of VP which following dummy verbs, this will be the future work.

Acknowledgment. This research was partly supported by National Natural Science Foundation of China (No.61370117,61333018), Major National Social Science Fund of China (No.12&ZD227) and National High Technology Research and Development Program of China (863 Program) (No.2012AA011101).

References

[1] Du, Q.: A Tentative Study on Dummy Verbs of Contemporary Chinese Language. Master thesis, Shanghai Normal University, Shanghai (2010). (in Chinese)

[2] Liu, Y.: Dummy Verbs and Their Object. Journal of Southwest University for Nationalities (Humanities and Social Science) (5) (2004). (in Chinese)

[3] Lv, S.: Xian Dai Han Yu Ba Bai Ci. The Commercial Press, Beijing (1980). (in Chinese)

[4] Lin, T.: Discussion about Preposition "you (有)". YinDu Journal (1993). (in Chinese)

[5] Li, L.: Verbs in Modern Chinese. China Social Sciences Press, Beijing (2000). (in Chinese)

[6] Lin, X., Wang, L., Sun, D.: Modern Chinese verb Dictionary. Beijing Language and Culture University Press, Beijing (1994). (in Chinese)

[7] Lian, L., Hu, R., Yang, C.: Shallow semantic parsing based on Chinese Penn Treebank. Journal of Application Research of Computers (3) (2008). (in Chinese)

[8] Peng, D.: On "Jingxing (进行)"、 "geiyi (给以)" and Their Object. Journal of Jinan University (1987). (in Chinese)

[9] Wang, M., Liu, Y., Wang, H., Zhang, L.: The Acquisition of Chinese Ergative Verbs and the Verification of Relevant Rules in Semantic Role Labeling. In: Liu, P., Su, Q. (eds.) CLSW 2013. LNCS, vol. 8229, pp. 173–180. Springer, Heidelberg (2013). (in Chinese)

[10] Xu, Z.: On you (有) As a Preposition. YinDu Journal (2000). (in Chinese)

[11] Yu, S.: The Grammatical Knowledge-base of Contemporary Chinese—A Complete Specification. Tsinghua University Press, Beijing (1998). (in Chinese)

[12] Zhou, G.: The classification of Dummy verbs. Journal of Chinese Language Learning (1) (1987). (in Chinese)

Categorization and Intensity of Chinese Emotion Words

Jingxia Lin[1] and Yao Yao[2]([⊠])

[1] Division of Chinese, Nanyang Technological University, Singapore, Singapore
`jingxialin@ntu.edu.sg`
[2] Department of Chinese and Bilingual Studies, The Hong Kong Polytechnic
University, Hung Hom, Hong Kong
`ctyaoyao@polyu.edu.hk`

Abstract. Despite the increasing interest in studying Chinese emotion words, there has been no reliable references in the published literature on the category (e.g. *happiness, anger*) and intensity (e.g. low, high) of emotion words in Chinese as perceived by native speakers. This study is the first to collect and analyze average language users' perception of emotion category and intensity of Chinese emotion words. Results of this study will serve as an important reference for future research on language and emotion.

Keywords: Chinese emotion words · Emotion category · Emotion intensity

1 Introduction

In recent years, the research on Chinese emotion words and expressions has enjoyed increasingly high popularity and wide application in the fields of both linguistics and artificial intelligence (especially in automatic sentiment analysis; see [1], [2], among others). However, a fundamental problem in this line of research is the lack of reliable, widely-accepted ratings of emotion category (e.g. *happiness, anger*) and emotion intensity (e.g. low, high) for Chinese emotion words. Existing studies computed the measures either from a few researchers' judgment or automatic computation ([3], [4], [5], [6]), neither of which can accurately represent the perception of average language users (cf. [5], [7], [8]). This study aims to fill the gap by collecting laymen's ratings of emotion category and intensity of Chinese emotion words from a large-scale online survey. In the current paper, we report results of the first stage of the study.

2 Data and Procedure

Design of the current study mainly follows Strauss and Allen's [8] survey of English emotion words.

© Springer International Publishing Switzerland 2014
X. Su and T. He (Eds.): CLSW 2014, LNAI 8922, pp. 181–190, 2014.
DOI: 10.1007/978-3-319-14331-6_18

2.1 Data and Design

A total of 374 Chinese emotion words are taken from Xu and Tao ([4], cf. [6], [8])[1] and randomly divided into four word lists. To control for rating reliability, each list also includes two or three words repeated within the list, two words repeated across all the lists and one pseudoword (几几) resulting in 98 items on each list. Table 1 shows all the repeated items within or across the lists.

Table 1. Repeated items for testing rating reliability

厌倦, 悲痛	Repeated within list 1
担忧, 丧气	Repeated within list 2
惊惧, 惊喜	Repeated within list 3
愤慨, 愁闷, 惦念	Repeated within list 4
开心, 愤怒	Repeated across all lists
几几	Made-up word across all lists

2.2 Participants and Procedure

Participants are 92 native Chinese speakers (mostly university students) from Mainland China. Each participant is randomly assigned to work on one word list adminis-tered on the Google Form platform. For each test item, the participant's task is to choose the most appropriate emotion category from seven basic emotion categories ([8], [4], [6]): *happiness* (喜), *sadness* (哀), *anger* (怒), *fear* (惧), *surprise* (惊), *anxiety* (焦虑), *disgust* (厌恶). If none of the basic emotion categories is appropriate, the participant may choose from the other three options: *other emotions* (其他情感类型), *neutral/emotionless* (中立/无情感色彩), and *unfamiliar with the word* (不理解词义). If the word is recognized as a true emotion word (i.e. one of the seven basic categories or other emotions), the participant also needs to rate its emotion intensity on a 7-point scale (1=basically no emotion; 7=very strong emotion).

It should be noted that the 374 test words not only cover typical emotion words (e.g., 开心, 愤怒) but also words whose emotional content is arguable (e.g., 对不住, 痒痒; cf. [6]). Furthermore, the test materials also include words that are less commonly used or only used in certain dialectal regions (e.g., 背悔, 来劲). Thus, it is up to the participants to decide whether or not the test words are truly emotion words. The participants can choose *neutral/emotionless* (中立/无情感色彩) if they think a certain test word does not express any emotion, or *unfamiliar with the word* (不理解词义) if they do not understand the meaning of a test word.

The number of participants assigned to work on each word list is given in Table 2. On average, each word is rated by 21.1 participants (s.d. = 3.3).

---

[1] Xu and Tao's (2003) list has 390 words in total. Our study excludes 16 monosyllabic words that are listed as category names in Xu and Tao ([4]), e.g., 喜 and 悲.

Table 2. Number of participants for each list

Word list	Number of participants
List 1	27
List 2	22
List 3	21
List 4	22

3 Results

3.1 Reliability

Rating reliability within the rater is measured by the rating consistency of words repeated within the word list. For each intra-list word ($n = 9$), we first calculate the percentage of participants that rate the two occurrences of the word with the same category. On average, each item is rated consistently by 75% of the participants (range: 55% - 100%). Furthermore, correlation tests show that six out of the nine intra-list repetition items have consistent intensity ratings (correlation coefficient > 0.5) between the two occurrences and these six items cover all four lists (see Table 3). Taken together, these results indicate that the participants are in general quite consistent when rating emotional category and intensity.

The second type of rating reliability is the consistency across raters. Since each participant only works on one word list, word items repeated across lists (开心, 愤怒) are used to gauge rating consistency across different rater groups. All four groups of participants unanimously ($>85\%$) categorized 开心 and 愤怒 as words of *happiness* and *anger*, respectively. Furthermore, T-test results show that the intensity ratings of 愤怒 did not vary significantly across lists (all $p > 0.05$). Cross-list differences did exist in intensity ratings of 开心, but the range of variation was small (between 4.3 and 5.5 on the 7-point scale) and in all four lists, 开心 was recognized as a high-intensity emotion word (see section 3.2 for the classification of emotion intensity). The repeated pseudoword, 几几, is recognized most often as *unfamiliar* across groups (48.2 - 68.2%), followed by

Table 3. Correlation coefficient of the intensity ratings of items repeated within lists

Word repeated twice within a list		Correlation coefficient
List 1	厌倦	0.12
	悲痛	0.82
List 2	担忧	0.78
	丧气	0.57
List 3	惊喜	0.40
	惊惧	0.62
List 4	愁闷	0.74
	愤慨	0.62
	惦念	0.41

neutral/emotionless (13.6 - 22.2%). Altogether these two categories accounted for more than 70% of the ratings in all four groups. Compared with the English study, the Chinese pseudoword was less reliably recognized as a non-word (i.e. unfamiliar), probably because the Chinese pseudoword 几几 is associated with real words such as 磨磨叽叽 and 叽叽喳喳 by the participants.

3.2   Categorization and Intensity Results

For each test word, we calculate the emotion categories with the highest and second highest percentage of raters as the primary and secondary emotion categories. Following Strauss and Allen [8], we divide the test words into two groups: *representative* emotion words and *blended* emotion words. Representative emotion words are defined as those whose primary emotion category is agreed by more than 70% of the raters and therefore can be considered as highly representative of the primary category, e.g., 开心 (*happiness* by 100%) and 厌倦 (*disgust* by 96.3%, *sadness* by 3.7%). Blended emotion words are those whose primary category is voted by no more than 70% of the voters and therefore express a mixture of more than one emotion type, e.g., 狂乱 (the two most-often-rated categories are *other emotions* by 31.82% and *anxiety* by 22.73%) and 懊恼 (the two most-often-rated categories are *anger* by 33.33% and *sadness* by 29.63%).

Raw intensity ratings for true emotion words (i.e. primary category is one of the seven basic emotion types or other emotions) are averaged across all raters and then broadly classified as *high* (average intensity rating > 4) and *low* (average intensity < 4). By using a less fine-grained intensity scale, we reduce potential problems associated with within- and inter-rater inconsistencies. Category and intensity information of all the representative emotion words (n = 139) is listed in the Appendix.

4   Discussion

4.1   Findings of the Current Study

As discussed above, current results from the survey generate a list of words that are highly representative of each emotion category (see Appendix for more). Table 4 below further presents a list of words that are unanimously voted (100%) into one emotion category and thus can be considered as core members of the category.

The results of this study also suggest that words with lower intensity tend to be *blended* with multiple emotions. As shown in Table 5 below, emotion words with high intensity have roughly equal chances to be representative of an emotion category or blended. However, when emotion intensity is low, the odds of being *representative* against *blended* is even lower than 1:4.

This study also finds six words that are rated as other emotions by more than 70% of the participants: 怜惜 (86.36%), 吝惜 (80.95%), 惭愧 (74.07%), 羞涩 (71.43%), 激昂 (71.43%), 羞怯(70.37%). These ratings indicate that the seven emotions of this study (*happiness* 喜, *sadness* 哀, *anger* 怒, *fear* 惧, *surprise* 惊,

Table 4. Highly representative emotion words

Category	Words voted by all participants into the category
disgust	腻烦, 讨厌
sadness	哀伤, 悲伤, 悲恸
happiness	赞赏, 欢乐, 欢欣, 乐意, 快乐, 愉悦, 喜悦, 欢娱, 欢快, 欢愉, 高兴, 惊喜, 欣喜, 喜欢, 欢
anger	愤怒, 忿怒, 暴怒
surprise	诧异, 吃惊, 惊疑, 惊愕, 震惊
fear, anxiety, neutral, unfamiliar	NA

Table 5. Counts of representative and blended emotion words in different intensity conditions

	High intensity	Low intensity
Representative	118	21
Blended	116	88

anxiety 焦虑, *disgust* 厌恶) may not be sufficient to categorize emotions, and thus serve as a reference for the long-debated question regarding what emotion is primary or basic (cf. 24 categories in Xu and Tao [4], five in Lee [6], and six in Turner [9], [10]).

4.2 Comparison with Previous Studies

Among others, Lee [6] also publishes a Chinese emotion word list, divided into five basic emotions (*happiness, sadness, anger, fear,* and *surprise*) and complex emotions as well as three intensity categories (high, moderate, and low). The emotion words in Lee [6] also come from Xu and Tao [4]. However, the categorization of emotion type and intensity in Lee [6] mainly followed Turner's ([11]) emotion classification model for English by mapping Chinese emotion words to the English emotion taxonomy. There are two potential problems with this approach. First, it can be hard (if not impossible) to find precise equivalents of emotion words across languages; second, even if cross-language mapping based on lexical meaning can be established, the corresponding words may carry different emotional connotation, resulting in nuanced differences in the perception of emotional content by language users. When compared with the word list in Lee [6], the current study reveals both similarity and significant differences. Take words of happiness in Lee [6] as an example. Lee [6] lists 37 emotion words in the *happiness* category, among which four are labeled as low intensity, four as high intensity and 29 as moderate intensity. Our results show that while the majority of these words are indeed categorized as representative of *happiness* (i.e. agreed by more than 70% of the raters) in our study, nine items fall into the *blended* category. Furthermore, four items are rated as *happiness* by less than half of the raters: 怡和 (27.27%), 晓畅 (36.36%), 闲适 (40.91%), 放松 (45.45%). More differences are revealed when comparing intensity classification. While the words labeled as low-intensity in Lee [6] do receive a low average rating of 2.98 in our study, the high- and moderate-intensity items were rated with 4.78 and 4.72, respectively. A follow-up T-test revealed that the high- and moderate-intensity items are rated with similar intensity in our study ($p > 0.1$). In other words, the high- and moderate-intensity items in Lee's study are shown to be very similar in intensity in our study.

5   Conclusion and Future Studies

To summarize, we report the first study to collect and analyze laymen's ratings of emotion category and emotion intensity of Chinese emotion words. Results of this study will serve as an important reference for future research on language and emotion, for instance, the possible relations among emotion category, emotion intensity, and the tones of the Chinese emotion words ([12]).

In the next stage of the study, we will recruit more participants and also take into consideration factors that may affect perception of emotion words, including gender, age, and region (Mainland China, Hong Kong, and Singapore).

References

1. Li, S., Wang, Z., Lee, S.Y.-M., Huang, C.-R.: Sentiment Classification with Polarity Shifting Detection. In: 2013 International Conference on Asian Language Processing (IALP), pp. 129–132. IEEE, Urumuqi (2013)
2. Xu, G.: The Construction and Application of Chinese Sentiment Lexicons. PhD dissertation, Peking University (2012)
3. Chang, L.-L., Chen, K.-J., Huang, C.-R.: Alternation across Semantic Field: A Study of Mandarin Verbs of Emotion. In: Yung, O.-B. (ed.) Special Issue on Chinese Verbal Semantics. Computational Linguistics and Chinese Language Processing, vol. 5(1), pp. 61–80 (2000)
4. Xu, X., Tao, J.: The Study of Affective Categorization in Chinese. In: 1st Chinese Conference on Affective Computing and Intelligent Interaction, Beijing (2003)
5. Xu, L., Lin, H., Zhao, J.: Construction and Analysis of Emotional Corpus. Journal of Chinese Information Processing 22(1), 116–122 (2008)
6. Lee, S.Y.-M.: A Linguistic Approach to Emotion Detection and Classification. PhD dissertation, the Hong Kong Polytechnic University (2010)
7. Nabi, R.L.: The Theoretical versus the Lay Meaning of Disgust: Implications for Emotion Research. Cognition and Emotion 16(5), 695–703 (2002)
8. Strauss, G.P., Allen, D.N.: Emotional Intensity and Categorisation Ratings for Emotional and Nonemotional words. Cognition and Emotion 22(1), 113–133 (2008)
9. Turner, J.H.: The Evolution of Emotions in Humans: A Darwinian - Durkheimian Analysis. Journal for the Theory of Social Behaviour 26, 1–34 (1996)
10. Turner, J.H.: Human Emotions: a Sociological Theory. Routledge, NewYork (2007)
11. Turner, J.H.: On the Origins of Human Emotions: A Sociological Inquiry into the Evolution of Human Affect. Stanford University Press, California (2000)
12. Yao, Y., Lin, J., Huang, C.-R.: Lexicalized Emotion? - Tonal Patterns of Emotion Words in Chinese. In: 25th North American Conference on Chinese Linguistics, Ann Arbor (to appear)

Appendix: Emotion Intensity and Category of Representative Emotion Words

Table 6. Emotion intensity and category of representative emotion words

Word	N (# of raters)	Intensity (broad)	Primary Category	Secondary category
乐意	27	High	喜	—
乐	27	High	喜	—
喜悦	22	High	喜	—
喜欢	27	High	喜	—
开心	27	High	喜	—
快乐	22	High	喜	—
惊喜	21	High	喜	—
愉悦	21	High	喜	—
欢乐	21	High	喜	—
欢娱	27	High	喜	—
欢快	21	High	喜	—
欢愉	21	High	喜	—
欢欣	21	High	喜	—
欢	27	High	喜	—
欣喜	21	High	喜	—
高兴	22	High	喜	—
热爱	27	High	喜	其他情感类型
爽心	26	High	喜	不理解词义
兴奋	22	High	喜	其他情感类型
欢喜	20	High	喜	焦虑
欢悦	21	High	喜	惊
喜爱	21	High	喜	—
得意	21	High	喜	其他情感类型
畅快	26	High	喜	其他情感类型
幸福	20	High	喜	中立
快慰	20	High	喜	不理解词义
自豪	22	High	喜	中立
欢畅	22	High	喜	其他情感类型
满意	21	High	喜	中立
顺心	27	High	喜	其他情感类型

Table 6. (*continued.*)

Word	N (# of raters)	Intensity (broad)	Primary Category	Secondary category
舒畅	21	High	喜	其他情感类型
珍视	26	High	喜	其他情感类型
痛快	21	High	喜	其他情感类型
得志	27	High	喜	其他情感类型
舒坦	27	High	喜	其他情感类型
舒服	26	High	喜	其他情感类型
快活	22	High	喜	其他情感类型
来劲	22	High	喜	中立
赏识	21	High	喜	其他情感类型
推崇	25	High	喜	其他情感类型
景慕	24	High	喜	其他情感类型
珍爱	27	High	喜	其他情感类型
钟爱	21	High	喜	其他情感类型
亢奋	25	High	喜	其他情感类型
赞赏	18	Low	喜	–
舒心	21	Low	喜	其他情感类型
可心	19	Low	喜	不理解词义
喜欢	21	Low	喜	中立
欣慰	20	Low	喜	其他情感类型
可意	26	Low	喜	不理解词义
称意	18	Low	喜	中立
称心	20	Low	喜	其他情感类型
忿怒	27	High	怒	–
暴怒	21	High	怒	–
愤懑	21	High	怒	厌恶
生气	22	High	怒	厌恶
激愤	26	High	怒	其他情感类型
愤怒	24	High	怒	厌恶
愤慨	22	High	怒	其他情感类型
忿恨	21	High	怒	厌恶
窝火	27	Low	怒	焦虑
吃惊	21	High	惊	–
惊愕	21	High	惊	–
惊疑	26	High	惊	–
震惊	20	High	惊	–
惊讶	21	High	惊	哀
愕然	27	High	惊	其他情感类型
惊骇	21	High	惊	不理解词义
惊诧	21	High	惊	惧
惊惶	27	High	惊	焦虑

Table 6. (*continued.*)

Word	N (# of raters)	Intensity (broad)	Primary Category	Secondary category
惊奇	20	High	惊	其他情感类型
惊慌	20	High	惊	惧
诧异	25	Low	惊	—
畏惧	22	High	惧	其他情感类型
恐惧	22	High	惧	惊
怕	27	High	惧	其他情感类型
畏怯	27	High	惧	其他情感类型
害怕	21	High	惧	惊
焦急	27	High	焦虑	其他情感类型
焦虑	22	High	焦虑	惧
心焦	21	High	焦虑	其他情感类型
焦炙	26	High	焦虑	不理解词义
着急	21	High	焦虑	惊
忧虑	19	High	焦虑	哀
焦躁	26	High	焦虑	其他情感类型
心急	21	High	焦虑	其他情感类型
烦燥	21	High	焦虑	厌恶
担忧	20	High	焦虑	惊
烦躁	20	High	焦虑	其他情感类型
担忧	20	High	焦虑	惊
烦躁	20	High	焦虑	其他情感类型
烦	21	High	焦虑	厌恶
发愁	20	High	焦虑	哀
不安	21	Low	焦虑	惧
烦恼	22	Low	焦虑	其他情感类型
烦闷	20	Low	焦虑	厌恶
挂虑	19	Low	焦虑	其他情感类型
烦心	27	Low	焦虑	厌恶
腻烦	27	High	厌恶	—
讨厌	27	High	厌恶	—
厌恶	21	High	厌恶	哀
厌烦	22	High	厌恶	焦虑
反感	22	High	厌恶	焦虑
鄙视	21	High	厌恶	哀
厌倦	27	High	厌恶	哀
鄙薄	25	High	厌恶	其他情感类型
憎恶	21	High	厌恶	怒
蔑视	27	High	厌恶	其他情感类型
轻蔑	21	High	厌恶	其他情感类型
鄙夷	25	High	厌恶	其他情感类型

Table 6. (*continued.*)

Word	N (# of raters)	Intensity (broad)	Primary Category	Secondary category
瞧不起	21	High	厌恶	中立
敌视	22	High	厌恶	怒
哀伤	27	High	哀	–
悲伤	27	High	哀	–
悲恸	22	High	哀	–
哀痛	21	High	哀	–
悲哀	22	High	哀	其他情感类型
伤心	27	High	哀	厌恶
哀愁	26	High	哀	怒
悲怆	20	High	哀	不理解词义
沉痛	21	High	哀	中立
苍凉	21	High	哀	中立
哀怨	21	High	哀	厌恶
悲痛	26	High	哀	厌恶
悲切	20	High	哀	其他情感类型
伤感	20	High	哀	中立
哀戚	20	High	哀	不理解词义
悲凄	20	High	哀	其他情感类型
悲凉	21	High	哀	其他情感类型
沮丧	22	High	哀	焦虑
心酸	21	High	哀	其他情感类型
悲壮	20	High	哀	其他情感类型
绝望	21	High	哀	焦虑
感伤	22	Low	哀	其他情感类型
遗憾	21	Low	哀	其他情感类型
惭愧	26	High	其他情感类型	哀
激昂	19	High	其他情感类型	喜
怜惜	20	Low	其他情感类型	中立
吝惜	18	Low	其他情感类型	中立
羞涩	17	Low	其他情感类型	中立
羞怯	23	Low	其他情感类型	中立

Lexical Semantic Restrictions on the Syntactic Representation of the Semantic Roles of Pinjie Class

Zhen Tian and Shiyong Kang[✉]

Key Laboratory of Language Resource Development and Application of Shandong Province and School of Chinese Language and Literature, Ludong University, Yantai, China
kangsy64@163.com

Abstract. Based on semantic roles, this paper describes the building process of the Database of Lexical Semantic Constraints on the Syntactic Representation of the Semantic Role Instrument (LSCI). All the head words of optional arguments in the annotated corpus of Chinese text books of primary and middle schools are extracted and then tagged with semantic categories, syntactic categories and semantic roles. Based on this database, we investigate the semantic roles of instrument, material, manner, cause and goal, and quantify the dependency strength of semantic categories on syntactic positions.

Keywords: Semantic role · Pingjie class · Syntactic category · Lexical meaning

1 Introduction

The syntactic representation of semantic role mainly focuses on investigating the interface between syntax and semantics, or how deep semantic cases are mapped into surface syntactic constituents. Semantic roles can be organized into a hierarchy with several levels. According to the relationship between the semantic role and predicate verb, we can classify semantic roles into two types: core semantic roles and peripheral semantic roles. The relationship between the core semantic roles (i.e., agent and patient) and the predicate verbs is very tight, and most of the core semantic roles are indispensable for corresponding predicate verbs. This type of semantic roles usually appear as subject or object. The relationship between peripheral semantic roles (i.e., instrument and manner) and the predicate verbs is much looser. Much research on semantic role focused on core semantic roles, while few researches have paid attention to the syntactic representation of peripheral semantic roles.

We focus on investigating the semantic roles of Pingjie class, which is a subset of the peripheral semantic roles. Specifically, the Pingjie class contains five semantic roles, e.g., instrument, material, manner, cause and goal. Generally, the occurrence of actions is often relying on some tools, materials and in some

© Springer International Publishing Switzerland 2014
X. Su and T. He (Eds.): CLSW 2014, LNAI 8922, pp. 191–197, 2014.
DOI: 10.1007/978-3-319-14331-6_19

Table 1. Tagset of Syntactic Categories

tag	syntactic category
S	subject
P	predicate
O	object
A	attribute
D	adjective
C	complement
J	pivotal
S	subject
T	independent chunk

way. The five roles have similar semantic and syntactic features. Thus, we call them semantic roles of Pingjie class.

Supported by the National Social Science Foundation of China (*Study on the Semantic Structure of Modern Chinese Sentence Based on Large-scale Annotated Corpus*), we have built the Syntactic and Semantic Corpus of Modern Chinese. Based on this corpus, we investigated the mapping rules from sentence semantic structure to syntactic categories and semantic categories, and found that the semantic categories of the arguments impose restrictions on their syntactic functions. From this perspective, [1] explored the lexical semantic restrictions on the syntactic representation of core semantic roles, and concluded the rules and characteristics of th mapping from semantic roles to syntactic categories. The experimental results of [10] also show that lexical semantic features have effect on the semantic role labeling task and so demonstrated the usefulness of the construction of a database of lexical semantic restriction. Through the annotation of lexical semantic information, syntactic and semantic information, we can establish relationship between syntactic categories and predicate-argument structures through lexical semantic information, and so may help automatic semantic role labeling.

2   The Construction of LSCI

The annotated corpus of Chinese text books of primary and middle schools contains 0.7 million Chinese characters, which belong to 15,835 sentences. We designed 24 semantic roles and 8 syntactic categories, and annotated the syntactic structure and semantic structure for each sentence according to the designed framework. The semantic role tagset and syntactic category tagset are shown in Table 1 and 2, respectively.

Annotated Instance: (*2788*)[S 我/r]D[D 有些/d[P 懊悔/v]V[O 自己/r 的/u 莽撞/an ▲] C 了/y。

(*2788*)[S I/r]D[D some/d[P regret/v]V[O myself/r de/u rush/an ▲] C le/y。

Based on the annotated corups, we extracted these sentences that contain any of the semantic roles of Pinying class. The numbers of sentence instances for

Table 2. Tagset of Semantic Roles

tag	semantic roles	tag	semantic roles	tag	semantic roles
S	agent	S	isa	P	place
D	subject	F	part	A	direction
L	possessor	T	dative	E	scope
Y	coagent	B	SourceWhole	C	cause
O	patient	I	instrument	G	goal
K	object	M	material	N	quantity
Z	causer	Q	manner	J	standard
R	result	H	time	W	basis

Table 3. Lexical semantic restriction instances of the semantic role "instrument"

ID	SenNum	NHD	SC_NHD	PV	SC_PV	marker	SS_Pat
1	35	眼(eye)	Bk03	望(lool)	Fc04		SIPV
2	86	手(hand)	Bk08	攀(climb)	Fa03	用(with)	DIPV
3	259	话(word)	Dk11	安慰(comfort)	Hi35	以(with)	DIPV
4	269	铅笔(pencil)	Bp16	画(draw)	Hg19	用(with)	DIPV
5	1907	字母(letter)	Dk05	代表(represent)	Hi14	用(with)	DIPV

instrument (I), material (M), manner (Q), cause (C) and goal (G) are 301, 42, 551, 232 and 118, respectively. We consider the semantic category of the head word of each semantic role and predicate verb as the semantic category of the whole structure. To do this, we tagged each head word with a semantic category according to Tongyicicilin (compiled by Jiaju Mei).

Based on this annotated corpus, we used the extracted information to build LSCI and so can explore the influence of semantic features of nominal structures on the syntactic distribution of semantic roles of Pingjie class. With extracted information, we construct a table for each semantic role. Each table contains fields of ID, sentence number (SenNum), nominal head word (NHD), semantic category of NHD (SC_NHD), predicate verb (PV), semantic category of verb (SC_PV), case marker (marker), syntactic-semantic pattern (SS_Pat). For instance, Table 3 is a part of the table for the semantic role "instrument".

In Table 3, "SenNum" denotes the sentence number in the annotated corups, through which we can read the context of the sentence. "NHD" and "PV" denote the head words in the phrases acting as the semantic roles of Pingjie class and the corresponding predicate verb, respectively. "Syntactic-semantic pattern" denotes the lexical semantic frame formed by NHD and PV. For instance, in the pattern of SIPV, "S", "I", "P" and "V" denote syntactic category "subject", semantic role "goal", predicate verb and the function of the verb. In these patterns, the part of PV is constant.

Table 4. Mapping laws from semantic roles to syntactic categories

Syntactic Category (Sentence Pattern)	Count
Instrument-Adverbial (DIPV)	266
Instrument-Subject (SIPV)	26
Instrument-Pivotal (JIPV)	3
Instrument-Object (OIPV)	9
Material-Adverbial (DMPV)	38
Material-Subject (SMPV)	3
Material-Object (PVOM)	1
Manner-Adverial (DQPV/PVDQ)	609
Manner-Complement (CQPV)	1
Manner-Subject (SQPV)	4
Cause-Adverial (DCPV/PVDC)	214
Cause-Object (PVOC/OCPV)	6

3   The Relation Between the Lexical Semantic Meaning and Syntactic-semantic Meaning of the Semantic Roles of Pingjie Class

3.1   Sentence Pattern

A certain type of semantic role usually chooses a certain type of sentence pattern. We refer to this phenomenon as syntactic coordination. Based on the annotated corups, we get the mapping laws from semantic roles to syntactic categories.

From Table 4, we may find that the semantic roles of Pingjie class can appear at many syntactic positions, while the probabilities are quite different. We refer to the syntactic positions with relatively higher as regular coordinations and others as irregular coordinations. Obviously, the regular coordinations of Pingjie class are adverbial positions, and complement, subject and object are all irregular coordinations.

3.2   Formal Marker

Markedness is one of the characteristics of Pingjie class. Most instances of the Pingjie class with regular coordinations co-occur with a preposition. These prepositions can be classified into following types.

a. The first type of prepositions are usually used to introduce the semantic role of cause. This type of prepositions include "以(with), 通过(through), 趁(while), 顺着(along), 靠(on), 随着(with), 凭(by), 迎着(towards), 经(through)". Among this types of prepositions, "以(with)" and "用(with)" are most popular. They account for over 80% of the instances of this types of prepositions (shown in Table 5). Note that "以(with)" is ambiguous in Chinese.

b. The second type of prepositions are usually used to introduce the semantic role of instrument. This type of prepositions include "为(for), 被(by), 把(ba), 以(with), 由(by), 给(for)".

Table 5. Instance counts in the annotated corpus for the first type of prepositions

prepositions	Count
趁(while)	4
以(with)	60
通过(through)	38
借(by)	1
顺着(along)	2
靠(on)	14
随着(with)	17
凭(by)	1
经过(through)	4
用(with)	53
随(along with)	20
趁着(while)	3
当着(facing)	2
迎着(towards)	1
按照(according to)	1
经(through)	9

c. The third type of prepositions, including "用(with), 靠(on)", are used to introduce the semantic role of material (shown in Table 6).

d. The fourth type of prepositions, including "为(for), 为了(for)", are used to introduce the semantic role of goal.

e. The fifth type of prepositions, including "因为（because of）, 由于(because of)". Among this type of prepositions, "因为(because of)" is most popular and it accounts for about 22.35% (shown in Table 7).

Table 6. Instance counts in the annotated corpus for the third type of prepositions

prepositions	Count
用(with)	27
拿(with)	2
靠(with)	1
以(with)	1
由(with)	1

3.3 Characteristics of the Lexical Semantic Restrictions on Mapping from Semantic Roles to Syntactic Categories

In *Tongyicicilin*, about 70,000 Chinese words are classified according to semantic categories. It contains 12 top and 94 second categories. The 12 top categories are A[human], B[object], C[time and space], D[abstractions], E[feature], F[action], G[mental activity], H[activity], I[phenomenon and state], J[correlation], K[auxiliary], L[honorific].

Table 7. Instance counts in the annotated corpus for the fifth type of prepositions

prepositions	Count
因为(because of)	40
为了(for)	11
由于(because of)	37
为(for)	1
因(since)	13
之所以(the reasons why)	1
为什么(why)	39
怎么(why)	21
出于(because of)	13
为何(why)	3

Based on the analysis on the annotated corpus, we arrive at the following selectional preference ("$>$" denotes the left category has higher preference than the right one).

For the semantic role of manner, K>D>E>B>H>I>A>=C=G>F>J;

For the semantic role of cause, E>I>H>D>G>J>F>K>A>B;

For the semantic role of goal, H>E>A=B>I>D>G>J>F;

For the semantic role of instrument, B>D>C>J>G>E;

For the semantic role of material, B>D.

4   Conclusion

From analysis on LSCI, we found that the selection restriction of semantic categories on the semantic roles of Pingjie class is much more strict than that on the core semantic roles, including agent and patient. This observation agrees with our presupposition. The selection restriction is associated with not only sentence patterns, but also the prepositions used to associate nouns with predicate verbs. Though analysis on the large-scale annotated corpus, we explored the lexical semantic restrictions on semantic roles and so prepared knowledge base for word sense disambiguation and entailment recognition.

Acknowledgments. We thank the anonymous reviewers for their constructive comments, and gratefully acknowledge the support of the National Social Science Foundation of China (No.12BYY123).

References

1. Zhou, M., Kang, S.: The Construction and Application of the Database of Lexical Semantic Constraints on the Syntactic Representation of Semantic Roles. Chinese and Oriental Languages Information Processing Society, Singapore (2010). (in Chinese)

2. Gao, R.: Study on the Semantic Role of Instrument Based on Juwei. Bulletin of Chinese Language Teaching **7**, 148–153 (2011). (in Chinese)
3. Chen, C.: Study on the Semantic Layer of Modern Chinese. Xuelin Press, Shanghai (2003). (in Chinese)
4. Gong, Q.: The Position of Word Sense in Joint Analysis of Syntax and Semantics. Linguistic Researches **4** (1996). (in Chinese)
5. Li, L.: Sentence Patterns of Modern Chinese. Commercial Press, Beijing (1986). (in Chinese)
6. Lu, J.: On the Analysis of Semantic Orientation: Chinese Linguistics Symposium (1). Beijing Language University Press, Beijing (1997). (in Chinese)
7. Kang, S., Xiaoxing, X., Ma, Y.: Semantic Category Constraints on the Syntactic Representation of Agent and Patient. Chinese and Oriental Languages Information Processing Society, Singapore (2010). (in Chinese)
8. Jianming, L.: On Interface Between Syntax and Semantics. Journal of Foreign Languages **3**, 30–35 (2006). (in Chinese)
9. Pan, H.: Lexical Mapping Theory and Its Application in Chinese. Modern Foreign Languages **4**, 1–16 (1997). (in Chinese)
10. Shao, Y., Sui, Z., Yunfang, W.: Chinese Semantic Role Labeling Based on Lexical Semantic Features. Journal of Chinese Information Processing **6**, 3–10 (2009). (in Chinese)
11. Sun, D., Li, B.: Study on the Cohesion of Lexical-semantic and Syntactic-semantic in Verb-core Structures. Applied Linguistics **1**, 134–141 (2009). (in Chinese)
12. Wang, B.: On the Relationship Between the Lexical Meaning of Verbs and Their Argument Realization. Chinese Linguistics **1**, 76–82 (2006). (in Chinese)

Syntactic Distribution of Motion Agents' Concept from the Redundancy of Leg Nouns

Li Meng[✉] and Xiangnong Li

College of Liberal Arts of Central China Normal University,
Wuhan 43000, China
mengli_xy08@163.com

Abstract. This article uses the theory of lexicalization typology of motion event to study the sentences of body movement, and arguing that the occurrence of N_{leg} is not only the result of the pragmatic effect, but also the result of the combined effect of the semantic differences among leg verbs and construction meaning of the sentence which meets the principle of syntactic-semantic harmony. We find that the semantic role of leg nouns in self-contained motion is figure and patient and that the self-contained motion is atypical in syntactic and semantic representation.

Keywords: Leg nouns · Leg verbs · Self-contained motion · Syntactic distribution

1   Introduction

(1) 他 （） 闻了闻，觉得周围有股清香的味道。 *(He smelt and felt that there was fragrant smell around.)*

(2)他 （） 伸了伸。 *(He stretched.)*

It can be seen that in the sentences above, the disappearance of "鼻子 *(nose)* " or "手 *(hand)* " has different effect on sentence and that the occurrence or disappearance of bodily noun is part of the study of bodily sentence. The study of bodily sentences started long time ago and it has two main interests: the bodily noun's syntactic position and semantic role in the bodily sentence, and the occurrence and disappearance of bodily nouns in sentences. Scholars have made many achievements in these two aspects, but still have to solve some other problems:

I. The bodily noun's semantic role is mainly judged by its syntactic position (Li 1986, Xing 1986, Ma 2003), and a deep study of the relevant sentence categories and the relations between these sentences is not available;

II. Some scholars (Yuan 1994, Wang 2001, Shu 2008) have proved the redundancy of bodily nouns from perspectives of " semantic connotation", " semantic activation "

I really appreciate that Mr. Shi Wenlei from Zhejiang University and Mr. Li Yunbing from Chinese Academy of Social Sciences have offered me great guidance and materials for this article. I myself am responsible for the possible mistakes in the article.

X. Su and T. He (Eds.): CLSW 2014, LNAI 8922, pp. 198–210, 2014.
DOI: 10.1007/978-3-319-14331-6_20

and so on; some (Wu 2003, Wang 2001, Shu 2008) discuss the conditions needed by the co-occurrence of bodily nouns and bodily verbs[1] from the perspective of the new information constituent occurring before bodily nouns for distinguishing, and Wang (2004) and Liu (2010) have studied it respectively from the perspectives of " the pan-spouse match " and syllable requirement. We, however, propose that these explanations cannot cover all the situations in N_{leg} redundancy. Examples are as follows:

(3) 在小组讨论时, 不时有学生腿跪到椅子上, 身子趴到桌子中间。我们应多给他们宽容, 笑着扶他坐好远比命令式的效果要好 。（百度网页 《信任宽容——给学生驰骋的空间与力量》）*(While in group discussion, some students often kneel their knees on their chairs, bending over their tables. We shall be tolerant with them, and it is much better to help them sit back to the chair than to give an order. (Baidu website, Trust and Tolerance——Give Students Space and Power to Fly))*

(4) 然而脚刚要踹上屁股时, 那人腰一拧, 身子一侧 韩生的这一脚登时踹了个空。（新浪网 《盗墓物语》）*(While he was just stamping the foot on his hip, the man twisted his waist and inclined himself; Han Sheng thus stamped on nothing. (Sina, Grave Robbing Legend))*

Most of the previous researches focus on hand verbs, while researches on other bodily verbs are few. We find that different bodily verbs perform differently in terms of the above two problems. Meng (2010) tried to explain the sentences with leg verbs from the perspective of the internal semantic differences of leg verbs, but some problems still need to be settled.

In view of the current researches mentioned above, the paper takes leg verb (henceforth V_{leg}) sentence as a cut, and mainly focuses on the spatial sentence and the situation change sentence[2], trying to use Talmy's lexicalization typology of motion event (1985, 1991) to explain the reason for leg nouns (henceforth N_{leg}) and V_{leg}' s co-occurrence and hoping to provide some useful help to the research of bodily sentences. Based on the Center for Chinese Linguistic PKU's Corpus and network corpus, the author selects texts that have a stronger sense of spoken language in different times and builds up a N_{leg}'s co-occurrence corpus which has about 23,500 example sentences with 1,100,000 characters. According to the practical example sentences, the paper comes to the conclusion as follows:

(1) The occurrence of N_{leg} is not only the result of the pragmatic effect, but also the result of the combined effect of the semantic differences among V_{leg}s and construction meaning of the sentence, which meets " the principle of harmony between meaning and syntax " ;

(2) In self-contained motion, usually N_{leg}s occur as an object and its semantic role is figure and patient;

---

[1] In recent years, there are some studies of the subcategories of "Bodily verbs" , such as "Hand verbs" , "Mouth verbs" and so on. "leg verbs are the ones that express the movement or dynamic state done with leg or foot" (Meng 2009), We abbreviate these verbs as V_{leg}, and the nouns of this kind as N_{leg}.

[2] Considering the limit of the length of an article, we will not discuss the sentence of " agent-patient meaning " carefully, besides being in case of need.

(3) The atypical syntactic and semantic embodiment of self-contained motion is as follows: time constituent cannot occur freely and semantic categories of path and ground are few; meanings of syntactic structure such as spactial meaning, situation-change meaning , and agent-patient meaning are all atypical.

2 V_{legs}' Classification and Self-contained Motion's Atypical Property

(5) 他从家里走到学校。 *(He walked from home to school.* (translational motion))
(6) 他踩在凳子上。 *(He stepped on the stool.* (self-contained motion))
(5') *他的[脚]从家里走到学校。 *(His feet walked from home to school.)*
(6') 他的[脚]踩在凳子上。 *(His feet stepped on a stool.)*

Examples (5) and (6) respectively represent two different motion events, the former belonging to translational motion and the latter self-contained motion. According to the scope of figure's displacement, Talmy (2000) divides the motion events into two categories: Translation motion, and Self-contained motion. Translation motion refers to after some time-point, the entire mobile has moved from one location to another. Self-contained motion refers to the figure motion that is limited in the scope of one's body or its entirety and whose translational position does not change in terms of the reference relation between the figure and the environment around after some time. Self-contained motion includes rotation such as rolling and revolving, oscillation such as swaying, vibration and tremble, dilation such as expansion and contraction, and so on (Shi 2014).

In recent years, there are many achievements in the research of motion event, mostly focusing on the translational motion event, which is not related to the atypical property of self-contained motion event (Shi 2014). We, however, finds that a study of self-contained motion will help solve many problems with the bodily sentence, such as examples (5') and (6'). The main research field of the paper is limited to the self-contained motion and internal event[3] in translational motion.

2.1   The Classification and Syntactic Feature of V_{legs}

Talmy's lexicalization typology of motion event includes four main factors: figure, ground, motion and path. In addition, there are still manner and cause. Path is considered as the basic factor to determine the frame of motion and as the main standard to classify linguistic typology depending on the choice of main verb or adjunct word.

When uttering a sentence, language users have a certain inclination in choosing the factors above and the grammatical form. To study the morphological syntactic distribution from a semantic perspective is a direction of the lexicalization typology

---

[3] Tenny and Pustejovsky (2000) divide events into internal ones and external ones. The former refers to the displacement or the change of state, the latter refers to the cause or agent which results in the internal event (quoted from Shi (2014)).

research (Shi 2011). Next, we'll take the semantic difference in the V_{leg}s as a cut to deal with the problem of occurrence and disappearance of N_{leg} in leg motion event:

Group A

a   b

我走了三个多小时了。 →*我[的脚]走了三个多小时。

(I have been walking for more than three hours. →*My [feet] have been walking for more than three hours.)

我骑马骑了很长时间。 →*我[的腿]骑马骑了很长时间。

(I have been riding a horse for a long time. →*My [legs] have been riding a horse for a long time.)

我跑了很长时间。 →*我[的腿]跑了很长时间。

(I have been running for a long time. →* My [legs] have been running for a long time.)

Group B

a   b

我踩在墙上。 →我[的脚]踩在墙上。

(I step on the wall. → My [feet] stepped on the wall.)

我跪在地上。 →我[的腿]跪在地上。

(I kneel on the ground. →My [legs] kneel on the ground.)

我踢在门上。 →我[的脚]踢在门上。

(I kick the door. → My [foot] kicks the door.)

We classify these V_{leg}s into two categories and define them as follows:

Body-involved verb: the leg movement it refers to is in accordance with the motion of the whole body, namely, the leg movement is just "my " whole movement. Verbs of this kind have the meanings of [-leg separate motion], such as "蹦 [beng] $(hop^1{}_1)$, 骑$_1$ [qi] $(ride^1{}_2)$, 跑$_1$ [pao] $(run^1{}_1)$, 蹚$_1$ [tang] *(walk in water)*, 跳$_1$ [tiao] $(jump^1{}_{1,2})$, 站$^1{}_1$ [zhan] $(stand^1{}_1)$, 走 [zou] $(walk^1{}_1)$ " and so on, that are shown as " $V_{body\text{-}involved}$ ";

Leg-only verb: the movement it refers to involves only leg, and the leg movement is not in accordance with the situation of whole body. Verbs of this kind have the semantic meaning of [+leg separate motion], such as "站$^1{}_1$ [zhan] $(stand^1{}_1)$, 踩 [cai] $(tread^1{}_1)$, 蹬$_2$ [deng] $(pedal^2{}_2)$, 跪 [gui] *(kneel)*, 跨$_1$ [kua] *(stride over/into)*, 迈$^1{}_1$ [mai] $(stride^2)$, 踏$_1$ [ta] *(step on)*, 踢 [ti] $(kick^1{}_{1,2})$, 踹[chuai] $(trample_1)$" and so on, these verbs are shown as" $V_{leg\ only}$ ". [4]

These verbs in Group A are $V_{body\text{-}involved}$, indicating translational motion; the ones in Group B are $V_{leg\text{-}only}$, indicating self-contained motion. In the sentence with translational motion, time constituent can be used while N_{leg} cannot; in the sentences with self-contained motion, space constituent is used and N_{leg} can occur. Though $V_{leg\ \text{-}only}$ sometimes can co-occur with time constituent, the motion internality is not homogeneous.

---

[4] This article takes expressions' meaning in *the Dictionary of Modern Chinese (6th version)* as the object of study. We mark the meanings which are in the scope of our study in the lower right corner of these V_{leg}s, such as "走$_1$", and homographs in the top left corner, such as "站$^1{}_1$". These meanings in English language are consulted with *LONGMAN Dictionary of Contemporary English (4th version)*.

For example, "他踩了一会儿 *(He kept treading for some time)*, 他踢了很久*(He kept kicking for a long time.)* ". These two sentences refer to the situation after the end of motion, or the repeating of motion, instead of a separate motion.

In a word, we can confirm a principle of the co-occurrence of V_{leg} and N_{leg}: usually $V_{body\text{-}involved}$ does not occur with N_{leg}, and $V_{leg\text{-}only}$ can occur with N_{leg}. Then, the reason why the two types of verbs incline to occur in two different types of sentence structures will be discussed.

2.2　$N_{leg\text{-}only}$ and Spactial Meaning of Sentence Pattern

The two big categories motion and event respectively correspond with time and space. Langacker (1987) defined "event " as "the position change of an entity during a unit of time ". People conceptualize motion event with the cognitive operation of sequential scanning (Li 2012).

What V_{body} involved refers to is a kind of typical translational motion; time constituent can occur in its sentence freely and the path and ground information is rich. For example:

(7)烈日下，他已经走了两个小时了。（时间）*(Under the burning sun, he has been walking for two hours.(time))*

(8)他从（离开）学校（起点）走到（往到）家里（终点），要走过（经越）一个报亭（界标），还要沿着（维度，一维线）河边（介质）走一段。*(If he walks home (goal) from (departure) school (source), he needs to pass (traversal) a newspaper stall(milestone), and then walks a short distance along (dimension, one-dimension line) the bank (medium).)*

(9)他向（矢量）学校（终点）跑去。*(He ran for (vector) the school (goal).)*

(10)等他走进（维度 三维容器）教室（终点）时，已经上课了。*(By the time he walked into (dimension; three-dimension container) the classroom (goal), the class had begun.)*

What $N_{leg\text{-}only}$ indicates with time constituent is not a separate motion event, which has been discussed in Section 2.1. The path constituents can be "在 [zai] " and "到 [dao] ", standing for " to leave for "; some verbs can also be added with "进 [jin]" standing for " dimension ", and "向 [xiang]" standing for vector, while ground constituents always stand for "goal " with few semantic categories. For example:

(11) 他（的脚）跪/踹/踢/踩/蹬到（往到）墙上（终点）。*(His （foot） kneels /stamps /kicks/ treads/ steps on the wall (goal).)*

(12) 他（的脚）踩进（维度）水里（终点）。*(His (feet) stepped into(dimension) the water(goal).)*

(13) 他（的脚）向（矢量）我（终点）踢过来。*(His (foot) kicks at (vector) me (goal).)*

Zhang (2009) believes that the construction of " V+在+处所（*V+at+location*) " refers to a typical completed situation event, paying no attention to the motion process and emphasizing the space location and situation of the event.

The participants of event, especially their site of participant become the objects that attract most attention. We find that like "在", the other paths such as "到" and "进" that can co-occur with $V_{leg-only}$ also highlight the spacial relation between figure and ground when the motion ends. In contrast, the path and ground information of $V_{body-involved}$ highlight the process of the motion event.

2.3   Principle of Syntactic-Semantic Harmony in the Spacial Meaning of Ruling

According to the modern Chinese corpus, the co-occurrence of the V_{leg} and N_{leg} is mainly the spacial meaning pattern of " $N_{leg}+V_{leg}+path+ground$ " and branch corresponding narration formed by other clauses, such as (3),(4) and (14):

(14)她不再作声，看着他离开床，十分艰难地站起来，他的腿踩入雨水，然后弯着腰走了出去。（余华《夏季台风》）*(She spoke no more, watching he leave the bed, stand up with great difficulty, and his feet step into the water, and walk out while bowing. (Yu Hua, Summer Typhoon))*

In the examples above, the descriptions of leg situation are completed not independently but by contrasting with other parts of the body. Examples are "腿踩 [tui cai] *(leg step)* " and "腰弯 [yao wan] *(waist bow)* " in (14), "腿跪 [tui gui] *(leg kneel)* "and "身子趴 [shenzi pa] *(body grovel)* " in (3), "脚踹 [jiao chuai] *(leg stamp)* " and "腰拧，身子侧 [yao ning, shenzi ce] *(waist twist, body ncline)* " in (4). In such narrations, why is N_{leg} expected to occur? We hold that it is for the sake of the harmony between meaning and syntax.

Semantic harmony means that when many events are being narrated, the motion of each event is basically in accordance with the required semantic role. For example, there can be " agent1-motion1 ", " agent2-motion2 " in a event; in the narration of two or more events, when the semantic roles chosen by events are basically the same, the harmony and accordance between previous and latter meanings can be achieved, the semantic connection among events can be highlighted, and cognitive harmony and better cognitive effect can be aroused. Syntactic harmony refers to the form's accordance of many events at grammatical surface, such as " subject 1- predicate 1; subject 2 - predicate 2 ", " attributive 1 - head word 1; attributive 2 - head word 2", and so on.

Syntactic harmony is the form's representation of semantic harmony; when the harmonious semantic constituents in the event are expressed in an harmonious sentence pattern, the harmonious correspondence between meaning and syntax is achieved and so is the better expression effect in pragmatic aspect. In the examples above, when the harmonious expression of meaning and syntax is not achieved, the accepting degree will be lowered greatly. For example:

(3')不时有学生[腿]跪到椅子上，身子趴到桌子中间→？不时有学生跪到椅子上，身子趴到桌子中间 *(Sometimes some students' [knees] kneel on their chairs, bending over their tables. →? Sometimes some students kneel on their chairs, bending over their tables)*

(4')[脚]刚要踹上屁股时，那人腰一拧，身子一侧→？刚要踹上屁股时，那人腰一拧，身子一侧 (*[The foot] was just stamping on his hips, the man twisted his waist and inclined himself.* →? *[The foot] was just stamping on his hips, the man twisted his waist and inclined himself*)

(14')他的[腿]踩入雨水，然后弯着腰走了出去→？他踩入雨水，然后弯着腰走了出去 (*His [feet] step into water, and he walks out while bowing.* →? *He steps into water, and he walks out while bowing*)

Lu (2010) proposes that " the principle of semantic harmony " is the basis of rhetoric and that the harmonious collocation among the clauses is the demand of speech expression. Thus, we believe that the principle is a basic of the co-occurrence of N_{leg} and V_{leg}. In the corpus we collect, about half of N_{leg}'s occurrence belongs to such branch correspondence narration.

In a word, the co-occurrence of N_{leg} and V_{leg} is related with the specific meaning of the verb, which satisfies the demand of syntactic-semantic harmony of the whole text.

3   Situation Change's Meaning and Subject-Object Translocation

As related above, scholars judge the semantic role mainly from the perspective of its syntactic position; while treating the same motion event, they make different judgments of bodily nouns when the sentence form changes. For example, Li (1986) describes in detail three kinds of " bodily behavior sentences ", believing that sentences of this kind are special and that when preceding a verb, bodily nouns usually occur with personal nouns to form an attributive structure and thus they shall be treated as the agent of the sentence, and when they are put behind verbs, they are patients. Next we will discuss this question:

3.1   The Sentence Meaning of the Situation Changes

We express these two structures as A. $N_{human}+V_{body}+N_{body}$, B.$N_{human}+N_{body}+V_{body}$. This article mainly discusses self-contained motion event. Together with the study of the leg verb sentences, the author holds that the transformation sentences have several features as follows:

I. Not every sentence can be transformed parallelly; the verbs in sentences are usually " hidden transitive verb ", such as "张 [zhang] (*open*), 伸 [shen] (*stretch*), 眨 [zha] (*wink*)", which can constitute separable words with the bodily nouns after; if the verbs are transitive, the sentences usually have ambiguity when transformed.

(15) a. 他的手伸向远方。(*a.His hand stretched out toward a distant place.*)

　　*b. 他伸手向远方。(*b. He stretched out his hand toward a distant place.*)

(16)　a. 他的手伸了伸。(*a. His hand stretched.*)

　　　b. 他伸了伸手。(*b. He stretched out his hand.*)

(17) a. 他瞪着一双小绿豆眼睛 。(a. He glared with his small mung bean-like eyes.)

？b. 他一双小绿豆眼睛瞪着（某物） 。(? b. His small mung bean-like eyes glared at (something).)

(18) a. 他踢了踢脚。(a. He kicked with his feet.)

？b. 他的脚踢了踢（某物） 。(? b. His feet kicked (something).)

II. The sentences that can be transformed parallelly usually have the changing situation meaning and the grammatical form of the transitive predicate may be " V + adj." and the semantic reference of complement is directed to N_{body}; hidden transitive verbs may have forms like " V (了/一) [le/yi] V ", for example:

(19) a.他的嘴反倒张不开了。(His mouth could not open instead.)

b.他反倒张不开嘴了 。（He could not open his mouth instead.)

(20) a. 他的脚踩肿/疼了。(His feet swelt /ached while stamping.)

b. 他踩肿/疼了脚。 (He stamped and his feet swelt/ached.)

The adjectives "开 [kai] (open), 肿 [zhong] (swelt), 疼 [teng] (painful) " in the examples above respectively refer to Norgan "嘴 [zui] (mouth), 脚 [tui] (leg)", indicating the changing situation of body organs. In example (15) and (16), the verbs are both "伸[shen] (stretch)" , but the former is used in the sentence indicating movement and thus cannot be transformed parallelly; the structure " V (了) V " has meaning of attempt and the situation meaning of repetition in short time, such as example (16) and examples like "眨了眨眼 [zha le zha yan] (wink eyes),眼眨了眨 [yan zha le zha] (eyes wink); 撅一撅嘴 [jue yi jue zui] (pout one's mouth), 嘴撅一撅 [zui jue yi jue] (mouth pouts)" . However, the structure " V (了) V " cannot be formed by transitive verbs, otherwise it has ambiguity when the sentence has N_{body} as its subject, such as example (18).

Xu (2004) believes that as to some verbs " the patient object often moves to the position of subject in the surface structure", and that we can say that verbs of this kind's "transitiveness is hidden and potential, and they can thus be called as 'hidden transitive verbs' ". At the same time, this kind of verbs can be followed by one noun phrase at most, which is 'patient', such as "死 [si] (die), 塌[ta] (collapse) ... 走 [zou] (walk) ". The words "张, 伸, 眨" mentioned above are typical hidden transitive verbs and because of its non-typical transitiveness, they can only be followed by one patient object. Therefore, when bodily nouns work as the subject, the use of " V (了) V " won't produce ambiguity as if other patients are omitted. Transitive verbs such as "踩 [cai] (tread), 踢 [ti] (kick), 踹 [chuai] (stamp), 瞪 [deng] (glare) " are, however, different and have two arguments; if N_{leg} is at the position of subject, it will tacitly approve that there must be another noun working as object.

3.2 N_{leg}'s Semantic Role in Subject-Object Translocation Sentence

In the sentence with meaning being changed by the situation, N_{body} mainly works as an object. We choose six groups of examples with subject-object translocation, namely "踹

脚 [chuai jiao] *(stamp feet)*, 脚踹 [jiao chuai] *(feet stamp)*; 蹲腿 [dun tui] *(squat on legs)* , 腿蹲 [tui dun] *(legs squat)*; 迈脚 [mai jiao] *(lift feet)*, 脚迈 [jiao mai] *(feet lift)* "and so on, as key words to collect all the relevant sentences in CCL corpus and study their frequency of use. We find that whether it is in ancient Chinese or in modern Chinese, Category A with N_{body} as the object takes up the biggest percentage.

A 踹脚：B脚踹——现汉1：0，古汉2:0 ；

A蹲腿：B腿蹲——现汉3：2，古汉3:0 ；

A迈脚：B脚迈——现汉7：3，古汉2:0 ；

A踢脚：B脚踢——现汉26：7，古汉7:3 ；

A举手：B手举——现汉1227：37，古汉129:1 ；

A眨眼：B眼眨——现汉82：1，古汉211:1

(A stamp feet: B feet stamp -- modern Chinese1:0, ancient Chinese 2:0

A squat on legs: B legs squat -- modern Chinese 3:2, ancient Chinese 3:0

A lift feet: B feet lift -- modern Chinese 7:3, ancient Chinese 2:0

A kick feet: B feet kick -- modern Chinese 26:7, ancient Chinese 7:3

A raise hands : B hand raises -- modern Chinese 1227:37, ancient Chinese 129:1

A wink eyes : B eyes wink -- modern Chinese 82:1, ancient Chinese 211:1)

In the subject-object translocation sentences of this kind, N_{leg} of Category A are at the object position in deep structure. Xu (2004) holds that the universal principle of noun movement is " up-ward and ascending" instead of "down-ward and descending ". Similarly, the "把" sentence is transformed from verb-object structure. Zhang (2002) proposes that object is put in advance because of a pragmatic choice and that when N_{body} becomes the viewpoint of narration, "把" moves it up and makes it much closer to the subject. When N_{leg} of Category B is the subject, it can confirm the scope of situation change; if V is transitive, N_{leg} cannot be omitted.

In a word, the case of " Subject-object translocation " is the sentence of "situation change"; and whether in terms of the syntactic and pragmatic rules or number of examples, N_{leg} mainly works as an object and is always patient in semantic role.

There is a kind of sentence of " agent-patient meaning ", as well as these two kinds discussed above, for example: "他用脚踢墙。 *(He kick the wall with his feet.)* " The sentence has some characteristics as follow : object of this sentence is patient rather than location; the structures in which N_{leg} occurs, present the manner meaning integrally, such as "用+N腿 *(use/with+ N_{leg})* ,用+修饰语+N腿 *(use/with+ modifier+N_{leg})*,'V₁N腿V腿' 中的 'V₁N腿'", so N_{leg} is not typical in present it; the occurrence and disappearance of N_{leg} are free, and the kinds of these sentences of $V_{leg-only}$ are richer than $V_{body-involved}$'s. When N_{leg} occurs, the former has three kinds, that are" N人+的+N腿+V唯腿+路径+受事 *(N_{person}+的+N_{leg}+$V_{only-leg}$+path+patient)*、 N人+用 +N腿+V唯腿+路径+受事 *(N_{person}+use/with+N_{leg}+$V_{only-leg}$+path+patient)*、 N人+V₁N腿+V唯腿+ 受事 *(N_{person}+ V₁N_{leg}+N_{leg}+$V_{only-leg}$+patient)* ", the latter has one, that is " N人+用 +N腿+V涉身+准受事 *(N_{person}+use/with+N_{leg}+$V_{body-involved}$+ quasi-patient)* ". When N_{leg} disappear, The former is " N人+V唯腿+路径+受事 *(N_{person}+$V_{only-leg}$+path+patient)*" , the latter is " N人+V涉身+准受事 *(N_{person}+$V_{body-involved}$+ quasi-patient)*". Because of the limit of this article, the author will discuss this issue in another article carefully.

4   Semantic Role, Syntactic Disappearance and $N_{leg}s'$ Occurrence

4.1   The Semantic Role of N_{leg}

The agent and figure are concepts in different cognitive frames. Shen (1999) lists the typical features of the agent: liveness, cause, autonomy, dominance and obviousness. In the sentence with both N_{human} and N_{leg}, N_{human} has the typical feature of the agent while N_{leg} doesn't. But the figure doesn't have specific demands for liveness. It can be either an independently moving object or an passively moving object under influence.

(21)他走了。（自位移）　(*He has gone.* (self-movement))

(22)他把球踢走了。（他位移）　(*He kicked the ball away.* (forced movement))

The figure "他 [ta] *(he)*" in self-movement in the example has relatively high liveness and the features of the agent; in (22), the figure in forced movement is "球 [qiu] *(ball)*", and the agent is "他".

Based on the analysis throughout the whole article, we summarize the semantic role related to N_{leg} as follows: (1) the agent in sentence is always N_{human}; (2) the figure in the sentence with $V_{body\text{-}involved}$ is always N_{human}; (3) in the sentence with both $V_{leg\text{-}only}$ and N_{leg}, the figure is N_{leg}, but when N_{leg} disappears, the figure is N_{human}; (4) in the sentence with situation change meaning, figure and patient are both N_{body}.

4.2 $N_{leg}s'$ Occurrence and Disappearance

We count the main sentences related to self-movement above and get five $V_{body\text{-}involved}$ sentences, two of which may have no N_{leg} and three of which have, and seven $V_{leg\text{-}only}$ sentences, two of which may have no N_{leg} and five of which have.

According to the data above, some sentences may have no N_{leg}: there are two in all $V_{body\text{-}involved}$ sentences, making up 40% of the five sentences of this category; there are two in $V_{leg\text{-}only}$ sentences, making up 28.57% of the seven sentences of this category. The data indicate that compared with $V_{body\text{-}involved}$, N_{leg} tends to occur in $V_{leg\text{-}only}$ sentences.

Sometimes the sentences must occur with N_{leg}: there are two in $V_{body\text{-}involved}$ sentences, making up 66.7% of the 3 N_{leg} sentences of this category; there is one in $N_{leg\text{-}only}$ sentences, making up 20% of the five N_{leg} sentences. These data show that when there is N_{leg} in $V_{body\text{-}involved}$ sentence, it usually has semantically true value, which is demanded by logic and mandatory; in $V_{leg\text{-}only}$ sentences, the disappearance and occurrence of N_{leg} are free.

Through the analysis of all kinds of relative sentences, we find that when N_{leg} occurs in different $V_{leg\text{-}only}$ sentences, it is harmonious with its sentence meaning: in the sentences with spacial meaning, the nature of N_{leg} as a noun is harmonious with the highlight of the intimate spacial meaning; in the sentences with situation change meaning, N_{leg} is the necessity for sentence to confirm the scope of situation change; in the sentences with agent-patient meaning, the manner (instrument) meaning of N_{leg} is harmonious with the occurrence of patient object required by the instrument in the sentence. To sum up, the occurrence of N_{leg} in sentence has a certain tendency, which is related to the category of V_{leg} and to the sentence meaning.

5   Self-Contained Motion's Atypical Syntactic-Semantic Representation

The paper takes V_{leg} as a point of cut and relates the syntactic and semantic phenomenon of the non-typicalness of self-contained motion. Except that "the sentences with V_{leg} cannot have time constituents freely and the categories of the path, ground are few", the spacial meaning, agent-patient meaning and situation change meaning of the V_{leg} sentences don't express typical motion events.

Many   " V_{leg}+在+location " sentences indicate spacial meaning instead of the time of non-motion; the situation change meaning of verb resultative structure is the metaphor and expansion of the typical motion meaning, whose event is change (Song 2007) ; "用+N_{leg} " sentences mainly indicate agent-patient meaning and self-contained motion is usually integrated in them and the percentage of sentences indicating the percentage only self-contained motion is very small.

6   Conclusion

This article uses the occurance and disappearance of leg nouns in self-contained motion as a cut to argue the viewpoint that the semantic role of N_{leg} is defined by the redundant components and the construction meaning of the sentence where V_{leg} and N_{leg} co-occur and to introduce the comprehensive causes of the appearance of N_{leg} and its semantic role in the sentence. Also, the atypical syntactic and semantic embodiment of self-contained motion is discussed by comparing self-contained motion with translational   motion.

The occurance of bodily nouns in the bodily sentence is of typological significance. Hu (2005, 2009) believes that constituents such as main body, instrument and modifier in the vocabulary of ancient-middle age Chinese have the tendency of deriving from hiddenness to occurance. Shi (2011) proposes that the transformation of manner from hiddenness to occurance is the manifestation of the Chinese's transformation from V style language to S style language and that Chinese has derived from a language that emphasizes path to one that emphasizes manner. Based on the statistics of corpus data, we are trying to discuss whether the disappearance and occurance of N_{leg} are following this tendency in Chinese grammar and its possible phenomena, which we will relate in another paper.

References

1. Hu C.: From hiddenness to appearance I – on a basic change in medieval vocabulary. In: Lu, J. et al. (eds.) Essays on Linguistics 2005. vol. 31, pp. 1–21. Commercial Press, Beijng (2005). (胡敕瑞. 从隐含到呈现(上)——试论中古词汇的一个本质变化.语言学论丛. 北京: 商务印书馆 (31), 1–21 (2005)) (in Chinese)
2. Hu, C.: From hiddenness to appearance II – on a basic change in medieval vocabulary). In: Lu, J. et al. (eds.) Essays on Linguistics 2009, vol. 38, pp. 99–127. Commercial Press, Beijing (2009). (胡敕瑞. 从隐含到呈现(下)——词汇变化影响语法变化.语言学论丛. 北京: 商务印书馆, vol. 38, pp. 99–127 (2009)) (in Chinese)
3. Li, L.: Modern Chinese's Sentential Patterns, pp. 145–149. Commercial Press, Beijing (1986). (李临定. 现代汉语句型. 北京: 商务印书馆, pp. 145–149 (1986)) (in Chinese)
4. Li, X.: Comment on the Concept Frame Theory in Spacial Motion Event. Foreign Language Education 33, 21 (2012). (李雪. 空间移动事件概念框架理论述评. 外语教学 33 卷, 21 (2012)) (in Chinese)
5. Liu, C.: Omitting and Redundance of Attributive Nouns and Part Nouns—a Contest between Economy Principle and Rhythm Demand. Studies in Language and Linguistics 30, 93–97 (2010). (刘春卉. 属性名词与部位名词的省略与冗余——经济原则与韵律要求 的较量.语言研究 33卷, 93–97 (2010)) (in Chinese)
6. Lu, J.: The Base of Rhetoric – Principle of Semantic Harmony. Contemporary Rhetoric (1), 13–20 (2010). (陆俭明. 修辞的基础——语义和谐律. 当代修辞学 (1), 13–20 (2010)) (in Chinese)
7. Meng, L.: Research on the Problem of Disappearance and Occurrence of Partner Leg Nouns. Journal of Language and Literature Studies (9), pp. 30–37 (2010). (孟丽. 配偶腿 部名词的隐现问题研究. 语文学刊 (9), 30–37 (2010)) (in Chinese)
8. Ma, H.: A Study of Bodily Action Sentences. Journal of Zhejiang Normal University (social science version) 28, 27–29 (2003). (马洪海. 论身体行为句式. 浙江师范大学学报(社会科学版 28卷, 27–29 (2003)) (in Chinese)
9. Shi, W.: Guowai Xuejie dui Cihua Leixingxue de Taolun (Discussion in the Foreign Academy on Lexicalization Typology). Journal of PLA University of Foreign Languages 34, 14 (2011). (史文磊. 国外学界对词化类型学的讨论. 解放军外国语学院学报 34卷, 14 (2011)) (in Chinese)
10. Shi, W.: Diachronic Change of the Lexicalization Pattern of Elements in Motion Event in Chinese. In: Lu, J. et al. (eds.) Essays on Linguistics 2011 vol. 43, p. 20. Commercial Press, Beijng (2011). (史文磊. 汉语运动事件要素词化模式的历时演变.语言学论丛. 北京: 商务印书馆, vol. 43, p. 20 (2011)) (in Chinese)
11. Shi, W.: Evolution of Lexicalization Pattern of Motion Events: A Case Study from Chinese, pp. 6, 8, 70. Commercial Press, Beijing (2014). (史文磊. 汉语运动事件要素词化类 型的历时演变. 北京: 商务印书馆, pp. 6, 70 (2014)) (in Chinese)
12. Shu, D.: Renzhi Yuyixue (Cognitive Semantics), p. 132. Shanghai Foreign Language Education Press, Shanghai (2008). (束定芳.认知语义学. 上海: 上海外语教育出版社, 132 (2008)) (in Chinese)
13. Talmy, L.: Lexicalization patterns: Semantic structure in lexical forms. In: Shopen, T. (eds.) in Language Typology and Syntactic Descriptionm, vol. 3, pp. 57–149. Cambridge University Press, Cambridge (1985)

14. Talmy, L.: Path to realization: A typology of event conflation [A]. In: Sutton, L.A., Johnson, C., Shields, R. (eds.) In: Proceeding of the 17th Annual Meeting of the Berkely Linguistic Society, pp. 480–519. Berkeley Linguistics Society Press, Berkeley (1991)
15. Talmy, L.: Toward a Cognitive Semantics, vol. 2. MIT Press, Cambridge (2000)
16. Wang, J.: Hanyu Shengming Fanchou Chulun (The Animate Category of Chinese Language). p. 263. Huadong Normal University Press, Shanghai (2004). (王珏. 汉语生命范畴初论.上海: 华东师范大学出版社, p. 263 (2004)) (in Chinese)
17. Wang, Z.: Gongju Dongci jiqi Xiangguan Jufa Yuyi Jiegou (Instrument Verb and Its Relative Syntactic, Semantic Structure). In: Shi, Y. (eds.) From Semantic Information to Typological Study, p. 134. Beijing Language and Culture University Press, Beijing (2001). (王占华. 工具动词及其相关的的句法、语义结构. 从语义信息到类型比较. 北京:北京语言文化大学出版社, 134 (2001)) (in Chinese)
18. Xing, F.: Chinese Grammar. pp. 77–78. Dongbei Normal University Press, Changchun (2002). (邢福义. 汉语语法学. 长春: 东北师范大学出版社, pp. 77–78 (2002)) (in Chinese)
19. Xu, J.: Principle of Universal Grammar and Chinese Grammatical Phenomena. p. 32, 36, 44. Peking University Press, Beijing (2004). (徐杰. 普遍语法原则与汉语语法现象. 北京: 北京大学出版社, pp. 32, 36, 44 (2004)) (in Chinese)
20. Yuan, Y.: Hanyu Dongci de Peijia Yanjiu (Research on the Coordination Valence of Chinese Verbs), pp. 109–115. Jiangxi Education Press, Nanchang (1998). (袁毓林. 汉语动词的配价研究. 南昌: 江西教育出版社, pp. 109–115 (1998)) (in Chinese)
21. Zhang, B.: Pragmatic Property of Agent Role. Studies of The Chinese Language 2002 (6), 486 (2002). (张伯江. 施事角色的语用属性. 中国语文 (6), 486 (2002)) (in Chinese)
22. Zhang, G.: Verb Scalar Value and Meaning Emergence in "在+location " Construction. Studies of The Chinese Language (4), 347–356 (2009). (张国宪. "在+处所"构式的动词标量取值及其意义浮现. 中国语文, (4), 347–356 (2009)) (in Chinese)

Investigate into the Cognitive Motivation of the Derivative Meaning of Words: The Case of *Luojuan*

Qingshan Qiu(✉)

School of Chinese Language and Literature, Hubei University,
Wuhan, People's Republic of China
qiuqs313@163.com

Abstract. Taking the "裸捐(*Luojuan*; nakedly donate)" as an example and insisting on CCMO(Cognition-Combinatory Meaning Outlook, CCMO), this paper has completed the new segmentation and description on the structure of word meaning, and holds that the structure of word meaning constituted by the three elements, that is "referent meaning(RM), attribute meaning(AM) and feature-value meaning(FVM)", and this paper also hold that the strong expressive power of word meaning dues to the varied possibilities of the combinations among the elements of meaning's structure. The different assignments and combinations of the elements of meaning's structure have brought about the new derivations of word meaning. And the psychology of cognitive metaphor plays an important and basic role in the different assignments and combinations of three elements of the meaning's structure. Taking three elements of the meaning's structure of "裸捐 (*Luojuan*; nakedly donate)"as an example, its feature-value meanings are different each other, and based on the figurative abstraction and the cognitive metaphor, those different feature-value meanings all have been unified and symbolized as a symbol of "裸(*Luo*; nakedly)", which led to the richness and magic beauty of the meaning of "裸捐(*Luojuan*; nakedly donate)".

Keywords: "裸捐(*Luojuan*; nakedly donate)" · Sphere structure of word meaning(SSWM) · Cognitive metaphor · Cognition-combinatory meaning outlook (CCMO)

1 Introduction

Yan Xiong(2005) pointed out that the word *Luojuan* has five meanings, and they are:

(1) unreservedly donate (the initial popular meaning),
(2) empty promise, acting in bad faith (the rapid nascent meaning),
(3) only donate cash, do not donate supplies,
(4) when make a donation, not use red bag and check, but donate directly the cash,
(5) not donate a penny (section (3), (4) and (5) are possible and potential meaning).

Yan Xiong thought about the possible reasons of the word *Luojuan* has five meanings, but did not give clear and systematic answers. He thought that the second and first meaning of *Luojuan* is very different, even irrelevant, but from the literal meaning

© Springer International Publishing Switzerland 2014
X. Su and T. He (Eds.): CLSW 2014, LNAI 8922, pp. 211–218, 2014.
DOI: 10.1007/978-3-319-14331-6_21

to the implication meaning is so natural, almost one word can make people understand. As long as there are certain users, the second meaning of *Luojuan* will be very popular. The meanings of *Luojuan* so rich that people feel one word can so agilely and uninhibitedly extend new meanings. The evolution and update of language, the new derivation and transformed of word meaning, these are psychological association, or combustion role of context, or combination ability of language's elements, the reason may be difficult to determine. [1]

Based on Yan Xiong's think and doubt, this paper continues to investigate the cognitive motivation and metaphor mechanism of the meaning's rapid change and mass produce of *Luojuan* and its same kind words. From the angle of the meaning's generation and reception, this paper explains the reasons for one word can so agilely and uninhibitedly extend new meanings, and constructs the mode of the meaning's generation and reception of *Luojuan* and its same kind words.

2   A Description of the Meaning Structure of *Luojuan*

Luojuan is a compound word made up of two morphemes, and the two morphemes are "*Luo*" and "*Juan*". *Juan* is a morpheme represented "action", and is head theory in the construction of word meaning, and is the starting point of cognitive processes. *Luo* is a morpheme represented "specific cognitive outcomes", and is modifier in the construction of word meaning, and is the terminal point of cognitive processes. The process that people understand the meaning of *Luojuan* is a cognitive process. About the cognitive process, Qingshan Qiu(2010, 2012) thought that a cognitive process is composed of three elements, that is, referent, attribute, feature-value. So a least cognitive process also includes three elements, that is, to determine a cognitive referent, to determine an attribute of this referent, to determine a feature-value of this attribute.[2-4] We know that the cognitive process (or least cognitive process) included three elements is a structurized cognitive structure (or least cognitive structure) in essence. The cognitive structure can be formulated as follows :

- cognitive structure= 【referent + attribute + feature-value】
- least cognitive structure = 【(one)referent+(one)attribute+(one)feature-value】

We know that, in the process of cognitive practice, selecting a cognitive referent is the starting point of the cognitive process, and determining an attribute of this referent is the midpoint of the cognitive process, and determining a feature-value of this attribute is the terminal point of cognitive processes. That needs to be noted, as corresponding relationship and matching relations among these three elements, "referent, attribute, and feature-value", so that the three elements all can respectively act as actually the starting point, the midpoint and the terminal point of their cognitive process. But, no matter which elements acts as the starting point, "from the starting point to the terminal point", such a cognitive process will not change. Take *Luojuan* as an example, the process that people grasp and understand the meaning of *Luojuan* is a cognitive process. Obviously, this process also has these three elements, that is, "referent, attribute, and feature-value". The *Juan* is the starting point of cognitive process, acting as a cognitive referent; *Luo* is the terminal point of cognitive process, acting as the feature-value matched with an attribute. Specifically speaking, *Juan* that people first designate is a cognitional referent represented "action", is the starting point where the cognitive activities continue to go on, and *Juan* represented "action" has many attributes, for instance, agent, object, way, time, place, results etc., these are the attributes of *Juan* and are also the angles that people use to grasp and understand the *Juan*. "Attribute" is the midpoint of cognitive process, and it fills the role of the association of the starting point and the terminal point in the cognitive process. Every attribute of *Juan* represented action there has many feature-values, for example, the agent attribute there has many feature-values matched their attributes such as He、 Zhangsan、 Lisi、 School etc.. After determining these three elements of cognitive process of *Juan*, and according to the cognition-combination rule of "midpoint" associates with "starting point" and "terminal point", we can use language sign to express the results of cognitions that we have gotten in the process of the cognitive activities. Because this cognitive process contains a lot of least cognitive process, and each least cognitive process will produces a cognitive result, cognitive results can be expressed through many least cognitive processes and the formula. The concrete expressions are as follows:

(a)cognitive construction of *Juan*= 【referent(*Juan*, action) +attribute (all attributes) +feature-value (all feature-values)】
(b)least cognitive construction of *Juan*1= 【referent (*Juan*, action) +attribute (agent) +feature-value (he)】
(c)least cognitive construction of *Juan*2= 【referent (*Juan*, action) +attribute (object) + feature-value (*Luo* : What things do not donate)】
(d)least cognitive construction of *Juan*3= 【referent (*Juan*, action) +attribute (result) + feature-value (*Luo* : All things have donated)】
(e)least cognitive construction of *Juan*4= 【referent (*Juan*, action) +attribute (way) + feature-value (*Luo* : Nakedly donate)】
(f)least cognitive construction of *Juan*N= 【referent (*Juan*, action) + attribute (......) + feature-value (*Luo* : ......)】

In the cognitive process, when we connect three points such as the starting point, midpoint and terminal point, these three least cognitive structures, above (c)、 (d) and (e), can be respectively formulated as follows:

(c1)least cognitive construction of *Juan*2= 【starting point (referent-*Juan*) + midpoint (attribute-object) + terminal point (feature-value-*Luo*)】
(d1)least cognitive construction of *Juan*3= 【starting point (referent-*Juan*) + midpoint (attribute-result) +terminal point (feature-value-*Luo*)】

(e1)least cognitive construction of *Juan*4= 【starting point (referent-*Juan*) + midpoint (attribute-way) + terminal point (feature-value-*Luo*)】

We know that normal people have some cognitions and the economy principle of language influences linguistic communication, so when people express the cognitive results by language symbol, they will generally keep "attribute" factor of the cognitive structure out of the surface structure of combinations of the linguistic symbols. Thus, after when we verbally symbolized the above c1, d1 and e1, and hid the "attribute" factor (midpoint) of the cognitive structure for highlight the "starting point" and "terminal point" elements, we got the linguistic symbol string of *Luojuan*. The specific process as shown below:

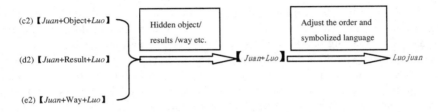

Fig. 1. The cognitive process of *Luojuan*

The above analysis shows that we use metaphor to represent the feature-value in the cognitive process of *Juan*, which makes the different feature-values (for example: unreserved donation, not donate a penny, etc.) matched with different attributes (for example: object, result, way, etc.) to have the same linguistic expressions, that is *Luojuan*. That is to say, the combination structure of *Luojuan* implied a variety of cognitive structures with many attributes as the intermediate points. This is the cognitive motivation of rich and agile meaning of *Luojuan*. We get cognitive explanation about the ambiguity of *Luojuan* from the perspective of metaphor.

In a word, we describe the semantic structure of *Luojuan* from the three factors, these three factors are "referent, attribute, and feature-value". The "referent" (*Juan*, action) is the factor of the starting point, and the "attribute (there are many)" is the factor of the midpoint, and the "feature-value (there are many)" is the factor of the terminal point. As long as we complete a least cognitive process, and there have a new word to reflect it. The attributes of *Juan* are very many, and the feature-values matched with each attribute are also very many, and there are a variety of combination forms among the starting point, the midpoint, and the terminal point. This is the reason why *Luojuan* can extend new meanings so agilely and uninhibitedly. When we abstract and summarize the numerous cognitive outcomes (feature-values) got by many least cognitive processes, we unified use one word *Luo* to express many cognitive outcomes, in this way, and *Luojuan* is produced. In fact, the word *Luojuan* is born in the cognition process of *Juan* and after collecting many least cognitive processes, its rich meanings (polysemy) is due to this.

3   The Generation and Reception Mode of Meanings of *Luojuan*

Seeing the "referent meaning(RM), attribute meaning(AM), feature-value meaning(FVM)" as the three elements of meaning structure, and basing on the above description, we construct the generation and reception mode of the meanings of *Luojuan* as follows:

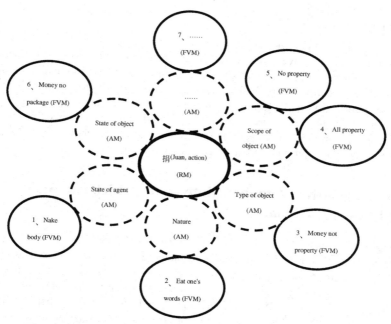

Fig. 2. The generation and reception mode of the meaning of *Luojuan*

Fig.2 shows that people can understand the action *Juan* (the thick and solid line circle represents the cognitive referent in fig.2) from many angles (the dotted line circle represents the attributes in fig.2), such as "state of agent、 state of object、 nature、 type of object、 scope of object etc.". From every perspective (attributes) of cognition to cognitive *Juan*, we can get a lot of feature-values (the thin solid line circle represents the feature-value in fig.2) matched the attributes. With stringing the thick solid line circle and each thin solid line circle and dotted line circle together, we can complete a least cognitive process. According to the cognition-combination rule of the "midpoint" associates with "starting point" and "terminal point", we can use language sign to express the cognition results that we have gotten in the process of the cognitive activities, and we can get a structural model, that is:

● 【terminal point(feature-value)+*midpoint(attribute)*+starting point(referent)】
(Italics represent the hidden elements in the structural model)

Then we verbally symbolized the structural model, and we can get the following 6 forms of the linguistic structure:

(1) naked body to donate,
(2) fail to keep faith to donate,
(3) only the money no property to donate,
(4) to donate all the property,
(5) no property to donate,
(6) no package and directly to donate cash.

That needs to be noted, because the many feature-values of the many attributes of cognitive referent *Juan* have some common features, with using the way of metaphor and a language sign *Luo*, people express these common features, so the above 6 forms of the linguistic structure are verbally symbolized and unified into *Luojuan*. Thus, the *Luojuan* is a collection of large number forms of cognition-semantics combinations, which is the cognition-semantics root of the so agile and uninhibited meanings of *Luojuan*. The reason of so rich meanings of *Luojuan* is the diversity of combinations of cognition-semantics based on the metaphorical thinking.

4   The Cognitive Metaphor Motivation of Rich and Agile Meaning of *Luojuan*

According to the generative model of word meaning, this paper increased the meaning of *Luojuan* from five to six kinds, namely to increase the meaning of "naked body to donate". That needs to be noted, because of the social ethics and rhetoric pragmatic psychology, it is generally difficult to accept the social reality of "naked body to donate", and people think that it is vulgar and uncivilized. In real life, perhaps really does not exist the facts of "naked body to donate", but from a view of theory, same as 裸 捐 (Luojuan; naked body to donate), 裸 奔(Luoben; naked body to run)、裸 购 (Luogou; naked body to buy)、裸 跪(Luogui; naked body to kneel)、裸 浴 (Luoyu; naked body to bath)、裸 睡(Luoshui; naked body to sleep) and so on, all can exist in the language.

The basic meaning of *Luo* is that adult men and women only use or not use cloths to cover the private part of body, and it extends to the body in nature's garb, no covered. Therefore, I tend to think that literal meaning of *Luojuan* is "nakedly donate", and this is the foundation of new derivation of word meaning. Based on the boost of the cognitive psychology, the conceptual domains of "the human body without cover" projects onto the conceptual domains of "other things without cover", this makes the meaning of *Luojuan* very agile and rich. Specifically say, if the uncovered body of human be called the "naked body", so the uncovered money (cash) can be called "naked money". This is the cognitive metaphor foundation of the meaning generation of *Luojuan* 6 (donate money without red bag or a check, but directly submit cash). Similarly, if a person's body without clothes and possessions go to donate, the result is that this person has not a penny to donate or not property to donate. And then from the objective to the subjective, this is the cognitive metaphor foundation of the meaning generation of *Luojuan* 5 (don't want to donate a penny). If a man donates his all clothes and belongings, so naturally he is naked. This is the cognitive metaphor foundation of the meaning generation of *Luojuan* 4 (unreserved donation). If one person only has money and has not clothes and don't go to buy clothes, so naturally he is naked. This is the cognitive metaphor foundation of the meaning generation of *Luojuan* 3 (only donate cash, do not donate supplies). The reason that a person is naked, because no cloth covering his body. From no clothing cannot cover the body to the bushwa cannot be achieved, this is the mapping results of the cognitive metaphor. This is the cognitive metaphor foundation of the meaning generation of *Luojuan* 2 (empty promise, acting in bad faith).

In short, from the perspective of cognition, the derivation and newborn of meanings of *Luojuan* is the result of that the understanding of cognitive metaphor of *Luojuan* is pluralistic and open. And from the perspective of meaning's structure, the derivation and newborn of meanings of *Luojuan* is the result of that the understanding of the structural elements of the meanings (attribute meaning and feature-value meaning) is pluralistic and open. Finally, under the drive of CCMO and SSWM, the specific assignment of three elements of meanings (referent meaning, attribute meaning and feature-value meaning, especially the attribute meaning and feature-values meaning) are different. This forms the different combination structure of language. Based on the figurative abstraction and the cognitive metaphor, those different feature-value meanings all have been unified and symbolized as a symbol of *Luo*, which led to the richness and magic beauty of the meanings of *Luojuan*.

5   Conclusions

About the possible reasons of the new derivation and transformed of word meaning, Yan Xiong (2005) think that this is the psychological association, or the combustion role of context, or the combination ability of language's elements, the reasons may be difficult to determine. [1] In the possible reasons, the author of this paper thinks that the psychological association and the combination ability of language's elements are the most fundamental reasons and are also the most credible reasons. The combustion role of context is the social external reason, and it is based on the first two reasons. The psychological association belongs to the scope of cognitive metaphor, since metaphor is an important way of the derivation and newborn of word meaning and it is the basic psychological behavior, language behavior and cultural behavior. From the view of language, metaphor is ubiquitous, and the world is a metaphorical world. The combination ability of language's elements is actually the combination ability of semantic elements, because the lexical meaning is the core element of language, and hides in the deep of language symbols, and determines the surface symbols combinatory of language's elements. The combination ability of the semantic elements embodies in the matching ability among the three kinds of semantic structure elements (referent meaning, attribute meaning, feature-value meaning).

In modern Chinese, other words of *Luojuan* class such as "裸 奔 (Luoben)、裸 购 (Luogou)、裸 视 (Luoshi)、裸 照 (Luozhao)、裸 戏 (Luoxi)、裸 替 (Luoti)、裸

播 (Luobo)、裸 葬 (Luozang)、裸 卖 (Luomai)、裸 考 (Luokao)、裸 辞 (Luoci)、裸 恋 (Luolian)、裸 爱 (Luoai)、裸 婚 (Luohun)、裸 奏 (Luozou)、裸 妆 (Luozhuang)、裸 装 (Luozhuang)、裸 治 (Luozhi)、裸 疗 (Luoliao)、裸 退 (Luotui)" and so on, all like *Luojuan*, they have very rich phenomenon of the new derivation and transformed of word meaning. [5-10] The strong derived and rapid transformed ability of word meaning of the words of *Luojuan* class, just right explains that the CCMO and SSWM has the basic restrictive function for people to understand and use words.

Acknowledgements. This study is supported by the Youth Project of the National Social Science Foundation of China (Project No.:12CYY057) and the Youth Project of the Humanities and Social Sciences Foundation of Hubei Provincial Department of Education (Project No.:14Q005).

References

1. Xiong Y.: The Rapid Change of Luojuan Meaning. Rhetoric Study **2**, 80 (2005). (in Chinese)
2. Qiu Q.S.: Preliminary Exploration to the Reception Model of Chinese Word Sense. Journal of Hubei University (Philosophy and Social Science) 39(6) 124–127 (2012). (in Chinese)
3. Qiu Q.S.:The Influence of Lexical Connotation on Sentential Ambiguity——Case Studies on "Trousers" and "Skirt". In: Proceedings of the 11th Chinese Lexical Semantic Workshop, pp. 97–101. COLIPS Publications, Singapore (2010)
4. Qiu Q.S.: A Study of Contemporary Chinese Word Meaning Based on Syntax-Semantics Interface. Wuhan University Library, Wuhan (2010). (in Chinese)
5. Chen, Q.L.: The Cognitive Analysis of *Luoguan* and *Luokao*. Journal of North China University of Water Resources and Electric Power (Social Science) **2**, 120–122 (2009). (in Chinese)
6. Shao, C.: The Recognition of "*Luo X*" Word Family. Rhetoric Study **2**, 88–91 (2009). (in Chinese)
7. Wang, C.W., Lei, L.R.: Derivation and Generation of Meanings of "*Luo X*" New Words in Contemporary Popular Media. Southeast Communication **3**, 122–125 (2009). (in Chinese)
8. Yang, H.: What Thought from Luokao. Reading and Writing **4**, 32 (2007). (in Chinese)
9. Zhang, H.: To Talk about Luokao. Language Planning **10**, 55 (2006). (in Chinese)
10. Zhou, Z.L.: A Variety of Luoben. Language Planning 2, 54 (2006). (in Chinese)

Applications on Natural Language Processing

A Rule-Based Method for Identifying Patterns in Old Chinese Sentences

Youran Liu[(⊠)] and Dan Long

School of Liberal Arts, Central South University, 932 Lushan South Road,
Changsha 410083, Hunan, China
youranl@acm.org, longdan2001@163.com

Abstract. This paper introduces a simple method for the recognition and collection of Old Chinese sentence patterns. Based on the manual tagging of the part of speech of high frequency words, other words and sentence patterns can be recognized automatically under this method. The experimental results show that with reasonable pre-selected terms, the recognition accuracy rate of content words, especially nouns and verbs, reaches as high as 86.29% on average; several sentence patterns can be recognized with accuracy rate higher than 95%. In this way, the method can not only be used to simplify the manual recognition and collection of Old Chinese, but also be used as an auxiliary approach in natural language processing for Old Chinese.

Keywords: Sentence patterns · Old Chinese · Part-Of-Speech tagging

1 Introduction

Drawing on the merits of research methods and techniques in Descriptive Linguistics and Statistical Linguistics, this paper makes some exploration in the grammatical features and sentence structures of Old Chinese. It attempts to set up terms which can be used to recognize the part of speech (POS) of Old Chinese words based on its vocabulary and grammatical features, so as to do POS tagging and sentence pattern collection on the corpus tagged by this method. Based on this design, we used Python scripts to implement it with 23 pre-Qin dynasty narrative texts as the untagged corpus. We made several test samples to verify the accuracy of POS in the untagged words and count the tagging coverage rate of the entire text according to the tagging amount and sentence patterns.

Compared with Modern Chinese, Old Chinese has a smaller vocabulary and simpler grammar rules. Firstly, single-character words are in the majority while non-single-character words are nominal and highly-related, which can be noticed with the help of 2-grams statistics (according to the statistical results for Middle Chinese, the majority of its vocabulary is single-character words [1]). In addition, the occurrence rates of most words in Old Chinese are relatively low. In our research, the tagging

Gratitude to the revised suggestions offered by the CLSW 2014 anonymous reviewers.

X. Su and T. He (Eds.): CLSW 2014, LNAI 8922, pp. 221–230, 2014.
DOI: 10.1007/978-3-319-14331-6_22

coverage rate of the entire text reached 77.4% after tagging the top 500 high frequency words in the entire test corpus. Secondly, from the perspective of syntax, some vocabularies and grammar features in Old Chinese are unique and typical such as function words, prepositions and double object structures. Therefore, with the help of rules of sentence patterns and grammar features, the possible alternatives of the POS of untagged words can be worked out.

It is highly costly to tag the syntactic structure of the entire corpus with Statistical Linguistics methods. The method presented in this paper only requires a small amount of manual labor in words tagging—by reasonably tagging high frequency words, the possible POS of untagged words can be ascertained with the help of rules of sentence pattern. The method we introduced is based on this rationale, highly operable, and well-matched with the nature of language.

2   Method Design and Implementation

2.1   Overview

For convenience, we need to definite some important concepts widely used in this paper:

Definition 1. Sentence Pattern: a sequence combined with POS collections or characters, which could not be split into smaller ones[1].

Example1:

$p = [(pos\_tag_1, max\_occurrence_1),...,(pos\_tag_n, max\_occurrence_n)]$ is a sentence pattern p of length n. Of which pos_tag_i is POS or character on position i, $max\_occurrence_i$ is the maximum word length on position i.

[['N', 2], ['V']][2] is a subject-predicate structured sentence pattern with the maximum nouns length 2, such as "书曰 (*the book said*)", "子来 (*the someone came*)".

[['V', 1], ['on', 1], ['N', 2]] is a sentence pattern with preposition "于 (*yu*)", such as "盟于晋 (*league in Jin*)", "朝于王 (*pilgrim to the king*)".

[['N', 2], ['V', 1], ['N', 2]] is a SVO sentence pattern such as "师伐陈 (*the army attacked Chen*)", "秦伯伐晋 (*the king of Qin attacked Jin*)".

Definition 2. Sentence Pattern - String similarity *similarity (p, s, Tag)*:

Suppose p is a sentence pattern, s is a natural language string, and *Tag* is a set of part of speech tags[3].

String $s = \{c_1, c_2, c_{|s|}\}$.

---

[1] Generally they are considered as single sentence and phrase.
[2] See word annotation instruction below.
[3] *Tag[c]* is the POS of character *c*. For example, *Tag ["之 (zhi)"] → {F, AD, PR, CON}*. We will use this notation in the following.

Sentence pattern $p=[(pos\_tag_1, max\_occurrence_1),...,(pos\_tag_{|p|}, max\_occurrence_{|p|})]$

and function $match(pos\_tag, c) = \begin{cases} 1 \ if \ Tag[c] = pos\_tag \\ 0 \ if \ Tag[c] \neq pos\_tag \end{cases}$.

Define the Sentence Pattern-String similarity as:

similarity$(p, s, Tag) = Opt(\sum_{i=1}^{|s|} match(pos_{tag_{i'}}, c_i))$, where $i' \leq$ min $(i, |p|)$, and

for $match(pos'_{tagi}; ci) ... + match(pos'_{tagj}, cj) + \cdots + match(pos_{tag|p|}, c|s|)$, we always have $i' \leq j'$.

Example 2:
$p = [['N', 2], ['V', 1], ['N', 2]]$,
$s = $ 卫人立晋$(the\ person\ of\ Wei\ made\ the\ Jin\ to\ be\ king)$,
$Tag = \{'$卫$(Wei)' = \{'N', 'V'\}, '$人$(person)' = \{'N'\}, '$晋$(Jin)' = \{'N'\}\}$,
    Where

$match(pos\_tag_1, c_1) + match(pos\_tag_1, c_2) + match(pos\_tag_2, c_3) + match(pos\_tag_3, c_4) = 3$,
    And

$match(pos\_tag_1, c_1) + match(pos\_tag_2, c_2) + match(pos\_tag3, c3) + match(pos\_tag3, c4) = 2$.

According to the definition of sentence pattern-string similarity, *similarity (p; s; Tag) = 3*.

Method implementation includes two steps:
1. Part-Of-Speech tagging

(a) Manual POS tagging: Count each word's occurrences in corpus and tag the high frequency words.

(b) Automatic POS tagging: Automatically tag those words which were not tagged in procedure (a).

2. Recognition and collection of sentence patterns

2.2   POS Tagging

2.2.1   Manual Part-Of-Speech Tagging
Before collecting sentence patterns, the POS of characters should be categorized; thus, the first task is to do POS tagging in the text. According to Zipf's Law [2], given some corpora of natural language utterances, the frequency of any word is inversely proportional to its rank in the frequency table. Therefore, to cover as many sentence patterns as possible with less tagging amount, high frequency words should be tagged.

Single characters' occurrences are counted and displayed in table 1. Based on the statistical results, characters to be tagged are chosen in descending order. Those characters chosen to be tagged can be divided into the following types[4] (for tagging),

---

[4] This categorization standard is also used in the following POS tagging and sentence pattern collection.

according to their grammatical function in the sentence, and with the "pre-Qin Chinese words tagging norms"[3]and "sentence/words categorization"[4]as reference:

Content words(C): Noun (N), Verb (V), Adjective (A), Pronouns (P), Numeral (Q)

Function words (F): Adverbs (AD), Prepositions (PR), Conjunctions (CON), Modal (M), Interjection (I)

The frequency of function words in Old Chinese is higher than that of content words. After tagging the top 500 high frequency words in the test corpus, most function words have been tagged[5].

The tagging result of the text is displayed in table 2.

Table 1. Frequency of characters

character	frequency	appearance
之(zhi)	0.03728	7403
子(zi)	0.02534	5033
曰(yue)	0.01893	3759
不(bu)	0.01852	3678
也(ye)	0.01840	3655
以(yi)	0.01741	3458
公(gong)	0.01730	3436
而(er)	0.01584	3147

Table 2. Text tagging format

character	frequency	POS
之(zhi)	7396	F,AD,PR,CON
子(zi)	5015	C,N,P
曰(yue)	3758	C,V
不(bu)	3676	F,AD
也(ye)	3652	F,M,AD
以(yi)	3451	F,PR,C,V
公(gong)	3434	C,N
而(er)	3143	C,P,V,F,CON

2.2.2   Automatic POS Tagging

In our test, the tagging coverage of the entire text—*ZuoZhuan*—have reached 85.61% after the tagging of high frequency words. However, it is still not enough to collect all the occurrences of a certain sentence pattern. Given the different lengths of sentence patterns to be collected, it requires tagged text span to be continuous. Therefore, the

---

[5] See amount of function words in (He Leshi, 1999).

POS of untagged words should be inferred and automatically tagged so as to effectively collect certain sentence patterns.

According to the rule that the part of speech of a character is determined by its syntactic function, we may ascertain its POS if a character bears the same grammatical function in many different sentences which belong to different sentence patterns. Hence, there comes the rationale of automatic tagging: for an untagged character c, if it appears in a sentence as the only one untagged character, c may bear the grammatical function of the position it stands. If c has this grammatical function in all the sentences where it appears, we hold that c has this function. Given that a character's POS is determined by its grammatical function, the POS of c, thus, can be ascertained.

Steps of automatic tagging are as follows：

1. Set a set of sentences *{P}* and text *T*, for an arbitrary sentence *s* in *T*, sentence pattern *p* in *{P} and the set of tagged characters' POS W*, if a Sentence Pattern-String Similarity *similarity* (p, s, W) =|s|-1, that is to say there is only one character in *s* which doesn't belong to the POS set of *p*, then the sentence *s* might belongs to sentence pattern *p*. In text *T*, find all sentence *s* which might belong to *{P}*. Made set *{S}* as the collection of all the sentences which might belong to *{P}* in text T.

2. For all *s* belonged to {S}, we define the set {S, c} as the collection of all the sentences *s* in {S} with the untagged character *c*.

3. Set threshold *threshold* and POS sets *{U}* for all text, suppose that $POS(c; s)$ is the POS of character *c* in *s*. If there is $|\{POS(c,s) = u | c \in s \in S, u \in U\}| \geq threshold$ |, then *u* is the POS of *c*, and the solutions of u is the final tagging result of *c*.

Example 3:

If P = [['N',2],['V',1],['N',2]] , *T=*{"卫侯如晋 (*the king of Wei went to Jin*)", "叔孙豹如宋 (*Shusun Bao went to Song*)", "叔弓如宋 (*Shu Gong went to Song*)"} , *W={*"叔 (*shu*)"={'N'}, "孙 (*sun*)"={'N'}, "豹 (*bao*)"={'N'}, "宋 (*Song*)"={'N'}, "卫 (*Wei*)"={'N','V'}, "侯 (*prince*)"={'N'}, "晋 (*Jin*)"={'N'}} , threshold = 0.3, then the automatic tagging procedure should be as following:*

1. For a sentence pattern in *P*, similarity(['N',2],['V',1],['N',2]], "卫侯如晋 (*the king of Wei went to Jin*) ",*W*) = 3,similarity(['N',2],['V',1],['N',2]], "叔孙豹如宋 (*Shusun Bao went to Song*) ",*W*) = 4, similarity(['N',2],['V',1],['N',2]], "叔弓如宋 (*Shu Gong went to Song*) ",*W*) = 2; *S=*{"卫侯如晋 (*the king of Wei went to Jin*) " , "叔孙豹如宋 (*Shusun Bao went to Song*) "}.

2. Here the untagged character is *c=*"如 (*went to*) " , {S, c} = {S}.

3. POS("如 (went to) ", "卫侯如晋 (*the king of Wei went to Jin*)") ='V',POS("如 (*went to*) ", "叔孙豹如宋 (*Shusun Bao went to Song*) ") ='V' , 'V' ∈ *U*, so $Tag\big[$"如(*went to*)"$\big] \in \{'V'\}$.

2.3 Sentence Pattern Recognition and Collection

Sentence pattern set is made before and then certain sentences are collected in accordance with these patterns. The sentence pattern set does not need to be the same with the one chosen in the process of automatic tagging.

According to the definition of sentence pattern, sentences belonging to one sentence pattern[6] share the following tips:

1. Words/characters in the same position belong to the same POS category;
2. Words/characters in the same position have the same grammatical form.

The recognition and collection of sentence patterns consists of the following steps:

1. Set up the sentence pattern set $\{P\}$ to be collected and list all the patterns in this set by length in descending order.

2. Set the sentences to be statistic as $\{S\}$, *tagged characters'* POS set as W. For a sentence s in S, if *similarity* $(p, s, W) = |s|$, then s belongs to the sentence pattern p and hence need to be recorded.

3 Testing

3.1 Testing Preparation

The Python programming language is used to implement the method and the source code and testing samples are released on Github[7] in conformity with GPL.

3.1.1 Corpus Selection and Preprocessing

Those corpora used in the test are Old Chinese narrative and historical texts[8] which were selected from public domain and manually collated. To ensure that the statistical results could explicitly reflect the general grammatical features of Old Chinese, the following 23 pre-Qin Dynasty Old Chinese texts are selected:春秋公羊传 (*The Kungyang Commentaries of the Spring and Autumn Annals*),春秋谷梁传 (*The kuliang Commentaries of the Spring and Autumn Annals*),春秋左氏传 (*the Zuo's Commentaries of the Spring and Autumn Annals*),公孙龙子 (*Gongsun Longzi*),管子 (*Guanzi*),国语 (*Discourse of the States*),韩非子 (*Hanfeizi*),道德经 (*Tao Te Ching*),礼记 (*The Book of Rites*),论语 (*The Confucian Analects*),吕氏春秋 (*Lv's Spring and Autumn Annals*),孟子 (*The Works of Mencius*),墨子 (*Mozi*),山海经 (*ShanHaiChing*),商子 (*Shangzi*),孙子兵法 (*The Art of War*),荀子 (*Xunzi*),仪礼 (*Courtesy*),战国策 (*Stratagems of the Warring States*),周礼 (*Zhou Li*),周书 (*Zhou Shu*),周易 (*The Book of Changes*),庄子 (*Zhuangzi*).

---

[6] Here, sentences belonging to the same pattern are similar to "narrowly isomorphic" in Reference 4 (Zhu Dexi, 1992).

[7] http://github.com/gestapolur/GEKIKO.

[8] Compared with poetry, narrative and historical text are more typical in Old Chinese.

3.1.2   Sentence Pattern Setting and Testing Criterion

Common Old Chinese sentence patterns are selected for automatic POS tagging and sentence pattern statistics referring to the sentence patterns in "*The Syntax study on Zuozhuan*"[4], including conventional Subject-predicate Sentence, "VP + '于(*yu*)' + noun" structure, "VP + preposition + NP" structure, "VP+ 者(*zhe*)" structure etc.

In automatic tagging test, words are selected from the tagged verbs, nouns, and adjectives for accuracy calculation and analysis, 200 words from each POS group (if the number is less than 200, then all are selected).

In collecting and analyzing the sentence patterns, for each sentence pattern, 100 test outputs randomly selected are used to compute the accuracy rate. 50 sentences of the pattern above are sorted out from the corpus, and the number of those which belong to the 100 outputs is taken as the recall rate of the sentence pattern. Sentence pattern checking is completed with the help of some teachers and students of the Chinese Department, then the results are reviewed and the statistics analysis is performed.

3.2   Result

3.2.1   Automatic POS Tagging Testing

The main factors affecting POS tagging are the amount of tagged text and the amount of the sentence patterns considered, therefore testing samples are chosen in accordance with the two factors. And the input of each testing sample includes tagged characters' POS set and sentence pattern set. The largest tagged characters' POS set (containing 500 most frequently used words) is selected as the initial tagged set, and the common sentence patterns are selected as sentence pattern set for testing.

In the maximum tagged characters' POS sets, most of the function words are tagged. The coverage reaches 77.41% after the common words are also tagged. Therefore automatically tagging aimed mainly at nouns, verbs and adjectives and the tagging results are as follows.

Table 3. Automatic POS tagging test

POS	symbol	manually tagged amount	automatic tagged amount	precision
Nouns	N	332	3686	99%
Verbs	V	250	2090	92%
Adjectives	A	93	13	11.3%

To sum up, nouns and verbs have more distinct grammatical features than other POS categories in sentence patterns commonly used in Old Chinese.

3.2.2   Sentence Pattern Testing

Two rounds of tests according to the differences of tagged corpus are performed. Firstly, we collected sentences patterns without the help of automatic POS tagging. Then, sentences patterns are collected again under automatic POS tagging. Results of two tests are compared and there are some representative patterns selected as an illustration.

Table 4. Result without automatic POS tagging

pattern	description	frequency	amount	precision	recall
[['V', 1], ['于(yu)', 1], ['N', 1]], [['N', 2], ['V', 1], ['于(yu)', 1], ['N', 2	V+'于(yu)'+N	828	519	98.25%	18%
[[' 以(yi)', 1], ['V', 1], ['N', 2]]	'以(yi)'+VP	889	714	97%	84%
[[' 使(shi)', 1], ['V', 1], ['N', 2]]	'使(shi)'+VP	518	376	80%	28%
[['PR', 1], ['N', 2], ['V', 1], ['N', 2]]	Prep+ N+VP	1698	821	95%	16%
[['N', 2], ['A', 1]]	N+Adj	603	518	96%	32%
[['N', 2], ['V', 1], ['N', 2]]	N+VP	13614	10951	4%	2%

Table 5. Test result with automatic POS tagged corpus[9]

pattern	occurrence	amount	precision	recall
[['V', 1], ['于(yu)', 1], ['N', 1]] [['N', 2], ['V', 1], ['于', 1], ['N', 2]]	2712	1789	99.25%	22%
[[' 以(yi)', 1], ['V', 1], ['N', 2]]	1484	1341	95.5%	84%
[[' 使(shi)', 1], ['V', 1], ['N', 2]]	1507	1194	75%	30%
[['PR', 1], ['N', 2], ['V', 1], ['N', 2]]	1698	821	86.5%	16%

The result in Table 4 shows that the selection of sentence pattern has great impact on precision. Besides, it could be seen from the results of all the tested texts that multi-syllable words also have impact on the test results. Although multi-syllable words are only a small part in the Old Chinese texts, their occurrence frequencies in some sentence patterns are high. For example, in such pattern as" '使 (shi)'+VP", the multi-syllable words are of much significance due to their frequent occurrence. From the wrongly tagged cases it could be known that some errors are caused by the confusion of monosyllable words and multi-syllable words. For example, "以与君周旋 (to socialize with someone)"is regarded as sentence pattern"以与（V）I君周（N）". There are some other errors resulted from the indiscrimination of words' functions in the linear scan of the text. For example, "老臣病足 (There was something wrong with the old courtier's feet)"is matched by an "N+V+N" pattern as "老（N）臣（N）病（V）足（N）", but "老"should be tagged as an adjective. To get the right result"老（A）臣（N）病（V）足（N）", semantic analysis is needed.

---

[9] The "noun + adjective" pattern in the second round of testing did not change it is not listed. And the average precision in this round is 86.29%.

After automatic POS tagging, the automatically tagged nouns and verbs which have higher tagging precision and manual pre-tagged words were selected as tagged corpus for sentence pattern recognition and collection. According to the testing result, adding tagged nouns and verbs to those sentence patterns which have high accuracy rate in the first place would not bring the rate down, but rather in some cases even pushed it up. In the second round of testing, for the convenience of comparison, the same sentence patterns were selected.

It can be seen from the test result in Table 5 that after adding automatic POS tagged nouns and verbs, the precision don't change greatly on the part of those patterns with high precision in the first test.

4   Conclusion

The proposed method intends to use grammatical features of Old Chinese in automatic POS tagging and sentence pattern recognition. Compared with either the Statistical Linguistics approach which needs to label the whole text or the manual method, this proposed method only needs to tag   those frequently used words to get a reasonable correct automatic POS tagging and statistical result. It improves the efficiency of tagging and sentence pattern recognition, and also reduces the factors which may cause artificial errors. And it is more convenient to adjust model to linguistic rules and is considerably consistent with the practical use of language, which is conducive to demonstrating grammatical features from the macro level and getting a syntax overview of the text hence the easiness of comparing grammatical features of text diachronically.

Compared with the Statistical Linguistics approach, this method relies on a correct understanding of Old Chinese grammatical features, so it is difficult to set the pattern rules for the sentences with unobvious grammar rules. Generally, it is more efficient to combine the Statistical Linguistics approach with linguistic rules; however, further research is required. Additionally, the participle, which signifies much to the accuracy rate, has not been considered in this paper. Therefore further improvement is also needed in this regard.

References

1. Liu, J., Song, Y., Fei, X.: The construction of a Segmented and Part-of-speech Tagged Archaic Chinese Corpus: A Case Study on *Huainanzi*. Jounal of Chinese Information Processing **27**(6), 6–15 (2013). (in Chinese)
2. Manning, C.D., Schütze, H.: Foundations of Statistical Natural Language Processing. The MIT Press (1999)
3. Min, S., Bin, L., Xiaohe, C.: CRF Based Research on a Unified Approach to Word Segmentation and POS Tagging for Pre-Qin Chinese. Journal of Chinese Information Processing **24**(2), 39–45 (2010). (in Chinese)

4. Xiechu, G.: The Syntax study on *Zuozhuan*. Anhui Education Press, pp 1–70 (1994) (管燮初. 《左传》句法研究. 合肥: 安徽教育出版社 (1994)) (in Chinese)
5. He, L.: The research of function words in *Zuozhuan*. Commercial Press (2004). (何乐士. 《左传》虚词研究. 北京: 商务印书馆 (2004)) (in Chinese)
6. Zhu, D.: Lecture Notes on Grammar. Commercial Press (2010). (朱德熙. 语法分析讲稿. 北京: 商务印书馆 (2010)) (in Chinese)
7. Fu, Y.: Non-grammatical genders and Poetic syntax variation. Foreign Language Education 2, 15-25 (1992). (in Chinese)

Semi-supervised Sentiment Classification with Self-training on Feature Subspaces

Wei Gao[1(✉)], Shoushan Li[1], Yunxia Xue[1], Meng Wang[2], and Guodong Zhou[1]

[1] Natural Language Processing laboratory, School of Computer Science and Technology, Soochow University, Suzhou, China
{wei.gao512,shoushan.li,yunxia.xue}@gmail.com
[2] School of Humanities, Jiangnan University, Wuxi, China

Abstract. In sentiment classification, labeled data is often limited while unlabeled data is ample. This motivates semi-supervised learning for sentiment classification to improve the performance by exploring the knowledge in unlabeled data. In this paper, we analyze the possibility and the difficulty of semi-supervised sentiment classification and indicate that noisy features may be the main reason for badly influencing the performance. To overcome this problem, we propose a novel self-training approach where multiple feature subspace-based classifiers are utilized to explore a set of good features for better classification decision and to select the informative samples for automatically labeling. Evaluation over multiple data sets shows the effectiveness of our self-training approach for semi-supervised sentiment classification.

Keywords: Sentiment Classification · Semi-supervised Learning · Self-training

1   Introduction

Sentiment classification aims to predict the sentimental orientation (e.g., positive or negative) of a document or a sentence towards a given topic (Pang et al., 2002; Turney, 2002; Wilson et al., 2009). This study has been extensively explored in the natural language processing (NLP) community (Pang and Lee 2008; Liu, 2012). Up to now, the dominating approach to sentiment classification is based on supervised learning methods where labeled data are employed to train a machine learning-based classifier for automatic classification. However, one big problem of such approach is its high dependence on a large amount of labeled data which is expensive and time-consuming to obtain. To overcome this obstacle, an alternative approach is to employ semi-supervised learning methods, which exploit unlabeled data readily available (Dasgupta and Ng, 2009; Li et al., 2010).

On one side, in principle, an unlabeled document could be helpful for semi-supervised learning because the text expressing sentimental information sometimes contains abundant and redundant features to make the classification decision. Consider the following review from the product-review corpus for sentiment classification (Blitzer et al., 2006):

© Springer International Publishing Switzerland 2014
X. Su and T. He (Eds.): CLSW 2014, LNAI 8922, pp. 231–239, 2014.
DOI: 10.1007/978-3-319-14331-6_23

Example 1: *This brand is the worst quality that I have purchased. I would avoid this brand.*

This review contains two strong indicators (called good features), i.e., "*worst quality*" and "*avoid this brand*", for predicting the review as negative. Assume that a trained classifier has already possessed the classification knowledge for predicting "*worst quality*" but have no idea about "*avoid this brand*". Once the review is correctly predicted and added into the labeled data for further learning, the classifier is then likely to contain the classification knowledge for predicting "avoid this brand". Therefore, when we iteratively label the unlabeled documents and use them to retrain the classifier, it is possibly to introduce helpful knowledge inherent in the unlabeled documents. This process is exactly a typical implementation of semi-supervised learning named self-training (Yarowsky, 1995; Abney, 2002). Intuitively, this approach should be effective for semi-supervised sentiment classification since the information of many documents is often abundant and redundant for predicting categories, that is, there are usually more than one good features for predicting the category label. Unfortunately, traditional self-training has been reported to be rather poorly-performed for semi-supervised sentiment classification in previous studies. For example, as reported by Li et al. (2010), self-training is one of the worst approaches for semi-supervised sentiment classification. It is interesting to explore the reasons for such failure of self-training in semi-supervised sentiment classification.

On the other side, an unlabeled document could be harmful for semi-supervised classification because the text sometimes contains much noisy information (i.e. failing to express any sentimental information). Consider another review from the product-review corpus for sentiment classification:

Example 2: *I used a 25 pack of these doing DVD backups. And the last 5 or so failed. I thought it was my software. So I got new software. Guess what? My first disc out of the new package of 25 that I bought failed, too.*

There are totally six sentences in this review. But only two of them express a clear negative meaning while the other four sentences, e.g., "*I thought it was my software*", merely express some facts. Once this review is correctly predicted as a negative sample by the classifier and added into the labeled data, the features in the fact-expressing sentences are considered as informative features for predicting the negative category. Actually, they are noisy features which are not beneficial for sentiment classification. Of course, when the labeled data is abundant, the classifier is certainly able to distinguish the noisy and good features. However, when the labeled data is very limited, as the case in the semi-supervised learning setting, the noisy features are prone to badly affecting the classifier. Therefore, the noisy features may become one of the main reasons for the failure of self-training in semi-supervised sentiment classification.

Therefore, it is possible to improve semi-supervised sentiment classification if we can alleviate the impact of the noisy features. One straightforward way is to only pick the opinion-expressing sentences and add them into the labeled data. Unfortunately, the task of predicting whether a sentence is opinion or fact-expressing is not trivial, even as difficult as the task of sentiment classification itself.

In this paper, we address the above problem from a new perspective of good features. The intuition is that although opinion sentences may be difficult to extract, we can find a way to select a set of good features and employ these good features, instead of the whole set of features, to make the classification decision. Specifically, we randomly split the whole feature space into several disjoint feature subspaces and train several subspace classifiers to classify the unlabeled data. For each sample, the subspace classifier providing the maximum posterior probability of belonging to one certain category (negative or positive) is assumed as the one owning a set of good features. This assumption is reasonable because good features (expressing opinions) are normally more connected to the corresponding category and thus yield higher posterior posterior probability. Each sample is decided using the subspace classifier returning the maximum posterior probability. In this way, each sample is classified using only a set of good features instead of the whole feature set and the bad effect from noisy features can be largely reduced. Evaluation on several publicly available real-world data sets demonstrates the superiority of our proposed approach over traditional self-training approach and other alternatives.

The remainder of this paper is organized as follows. Section 2 overviews the related work on semi-supervised sentiment classification. Section 3 explores the distribution of opinion- and fact- expressing sentences. Section 4 proposes our feature subspace-based semi-supervised approach for sentiment classification. Section 5 evaluates our approach. Finally, Section 6 gives the conclusion and future work.

2   Related Work

While supervised learning methods for sentiment classification have been extensively studied (Cui et al., 2006; Riloff et al., 2006) since the pioneer work by Pang et al. (2002), the studies on semi-supervised sentiment classification are relatively rare.

Dasgupta and Ng (2009) integrate several technologies, such as spectral clustering, active learning, transductive learning, and ensemble learning, to conduct semi-supervised sentiment classification. Li et al. (2010) propose a co-training algorithm with personal and impersonal views for semi-supervised sentiment classification. Zhou et al. (2010) propose a novel semi-supervised learning approach called Active Deep Networks.

Unlike all of above studies, our semi-supervised learning approach is based on self-training which is much easier to implement and language independent. More importantly, this simple yet effective approach impressively outperforms both traditional self-training and the state-of-the-art.

3   Distribution of Opinion- and Fact-expressing Sentences

As mentioned in Introduction, we distinguish two kinds of sentences in the sentimental text: one containing good features, which make unlabeled samples possibly helpful, and the other containing noisy features, which make unlabeled data possibly harmful. To better illustrate, we examine the distribution of both opinion- and fact-expressing sentences in a public data set, collected by Blitzer et al. (2006), which contains four

Table 1. Average numbers of all sentences, opinion sentences and fact sentences in each document.

Domain	#All Sentences	#Opinion Sentences	#Fact Sentences
DVD	9.58	4.84	4.74
Kitchen	5.88	3.69	2.19

domains including book, DVD, electronic, and kitchen appliances. Since annotating a sentence as either opinion- or fact-expressing is very time-consuming, we only manually annotate 1000 documents (500 negative and 500 positive ones) in each of two domains, DVD and Kitchen. Table 1 shows the average numbers of all, opinion and fact sentences in each document of the two domains. From this table, we can see that averagely, 50-60% of the sentences in each document are opinion-expressing. This means the abundance and redundance of both good and noisy features.. Specifically, we find that DVD contains much more fact sentences than opinion sentences compared to Kitchen. Interestingly, this might be a good explanation to the story of using semi-supervised learning, which is shown to be much more difficult in DVD than Kitchen, as reported in previous studies (Li et al., 2010; Zhou et al., 2010).

4   Feature Subspace-based Self-training

One straightforward way to alleviate the impact of noisy features is to only pick the opinion-expressing sentences. Unfortunately, the task of predicting whether a sentence is opinion or fact-expressing is not trivial, even as difficult as the task of sentiment classification itself. Alternatively, this paper attempts to determine a set of good features for each sample. In this way, each sample is classified using only a set of good features instead of the whole feature set and the bad effect from noisy features can be largely reduced.

This section describes our feature subspace-based semi-supervised approach for sentiment classification.

4.1   Feature Subspace-based Classification

A machine learning-based classifier seeks a predictor that maps an input vector x to the corresponding class label y. Generally, the predictor is trained on a finite set of labeled examples (X, Y) where set $X = (X_1, X_2, ..., X_n)$ means n labeled samples, and sample X_i is denoted as $X_i = (x_{i1}, x_{i2}, ..., x_{im})$ with x_{ij} the weight of the corresponding feature w_j ($j=1,2,...,m$). In sentiment classification, the bag-of-words model is often adopted where the features are the containing words and the weights are the Boolean or tf values of the features.

When a feature subset, i.e., $F^S = \{w_1^S, ..., w_r^S\}$ ($r < m$), is used to represent the documents, the original m-dimensional feature space is reduced to an r-dimensional feature subspace. In this way, the modified training data $X^S = (X_1^S, X_2^S, ..., X_n^S)$, denoted as subspace data, consists of r-dimensional samples $X^S = (x_{i1}^S, x_{i2}^S, ..., x_{ir}^S)$ $(i = 1, ..., n)$, and a classifier trained with the subspace training data is called a subspace classifier.

As mentioned in Introduction, in semi-supervised sentiment classification, exploiting the whole feature set as the feature set to train the classifier is problematic due to the limited number of the labeled data and the abundance of noisy features. Therefore, we split the whole feature set into θ disjoint feature subsets and train multiple subspace classifiers. Then, we employ the subspace classifier with the highest confidence to predict each unlabeled text, ignoring other classifiers, assuming the former containing good features and the latter suffering from noisy features.

Formally, the whole feature set is split into θ disjoint feature subspaces F_k^S ($k=1,2,..., \theta$) and each of them is adopted to train a subspace classifier C_k^S. In the iteration of sample selection process in self-training, each subspace classifier C_k^S $(k = 1,2,...,\theta)$ assigns a unlabeled sample (denoted as x) a posterior probability vector $\vec{P}(x_k)$:

$$\vec{P}(x_k^S) = < p(c_1 | x_k^S), p(c_2 | x_k^S) >^t \tag{1}$$

Where $p(c_1 | x_k^S)$ and $p(c_2 | x_k^S)$ denote the probabilities that the k-th subspace classifier predicts the sample as c_1 and c_2, representing negative and positive categories, respectively.

The posterior probability belong to each category is determined by the maximum one among all the posterior probabilities, i.e.,

$$p(c_1 | x) = \max_k \{p(c_1 | x_k^S)\} \tag{2}$$

and,

$$p(c_2 | x) = \max_k \{p(c_2 | x_k^S)\} \tag{3}$$

Finally, the category of a sample is the one which has the bigger posterior probability, given as follows:

$$\begin{aligned} Assign \quad y \to c_1 \quad if \quad & p(c_1 | x) > p(c_2 | x) \\ Otherwise \quad & y \to c_2 \end{aligned} \tag{4}$$

4.2   Self-training

Self-training is a commonly used approach for semi-supervised learning (Yarowsky, 1995; Abney, 2002). The main idea of this approach is to firstly train a classifier with a small amount of labeled data and then iteratively retrain it by adding most confident unlabeled samples as new labeled data.

Given multiple subspace classifiers, the traditional self-training can be modified by using multiple subspaces to measure the confidence of unlabeled samples and make the category prediction. Figure 1 illustrates our modified self-training algorithm.

Input:
$\qquad$ Labeled data L
$\qquad$ Unlabeled data U
Output:
$\qquad$ New classifier C
Procedure:
$\qquad$ Loop for N iterations until $U = \phi$

(1). Randomly split the whole feature set into θ disjoint subsets F_k^S (k=1,2,..., θ)

(2). Learn θ subspace classifier C_k^S (k=1,..., θ)

(3). Use all C_k^S to classify the samples from U

(4). Choose n most confidently-predicted negative samples A^- where the confidence is measured by formula (2) and the automatically-labeled category is determined by formula (4)

(5). Choose n most confidently-predicted positive samples A^+ where the confidence is measured by formula (3) and the automatically-labeled category is determined by formula (4)

(6). Add them into L, i.e., $L = L + A^- + A^+$

(7). Remove A^- and A^+ from U, i.e., $U = U - A^- - A^+$

Use the updated data L to train a classifier C

Fig. 1. The algorithm of feature subspace-based self-training

5　　Experimentation

5.1　　Experimental Setting

Data Setting: The data contains English reviews from four domains: Book (B), DVD (D), Electronics (E) and Kitchen (K) appliances[1] (Blitzer et al., 2007). Each domain contains 1000 positive and 1000 negative labeled reviews. We randomly select 20% instances in each domain as the test data, and select 5% and 10% instances in each domain as the initial labeled data sets, respectively. The remaining instances are used as the unlabeled data.

Features: Each review text is treated as a bag-of-words and transformed into binary vectors encoding the presence or absence of word unigrams.

---

[1] http://www.seas.upenn.edu/~mdredze/datasets/sentiment/

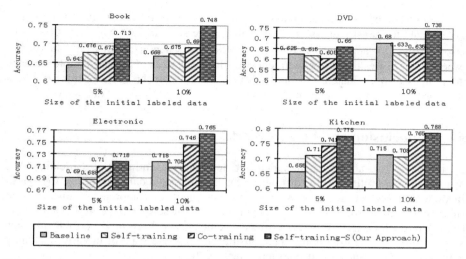

Fig. 2. Performance comparison on document-level semi-supervised sentiment classification, self-training, co-training and our approach

Classification Algorithm: The maximum entropy (ME) classifier implemented with the public tool, Mallet Toolkits[2]. The posterior probabilities belonging to different categories are also provided in this tool.

5.2   Experimental Results

In our experiment, we implement following approaches for comparison:

➢ **Baseline:** Train the ME classifier with only the initial labeled data (without using any unlabeled data).

➢ **Self-training:** Traditional self-training that employs the whole feature space for classification.

➢ **Co-training:** For comparison, we also implement the state-of-the-art for semi-supervised sentiment classification, the co-training algorithm with personal and impersonal views (Li et al., 2010).

➢ **Self-training-S:** Our approach as shown in Figure 2. In the implementation, the top 2 informative samples are selected for manual annotation in each iteration (n=2). As for the subspace number θ, we set it to 5.

Figure 2 shows the performances of these approaches. From this figure, we can see that, compared to the baseline, our approach is clearly superior with average improvement of more than 6% across all the four domains. Although co-training outperforms traditional self-training, it performs worse than our self-training approach in all domains. Especially, in DVD, co-training fails to improve the performance while our self-training approach changes the situation.

---

[2] http://mallet.cs.umass.edu/

The number of feature subspaces θ, is an important parameter in our approach. To evaluate the sensitiveness of this parameter, we set it to 2, 3, 4, 5, 6, 8, 10 and 15 respectively. Our approach is consistently effective when θ is set to the values between 3 and 8. Besides, the effectiveness of different sizes of chosen samples in each iteration is also evaluated and our approach is shown to be robust across different sizes (n=1,2,3,4,5). The detailed discussion of the results is omitted due to space limit.

6   Conclusion and Future Work

In this paper, we address semi-supervised learning in sentiment classification. We analyze the possibility and the difficulty of using unlabeled data to improve the classification performance and propose a novel semi-supervised approach, named feature subspace-based self-training by modifying traditional self-training with feature subspace-based classifiers. Empirical studies demonstrate that our proposed approach significantly outperforms traditional self-training and the state-of-the-art co-training approach for semi-supervised sentiment classification.

Acknowledgments. This research work has been partially supported by three NSFC grants, No.61375073, No.61300152 and No.61273320, one National High-tech Research and Development Program of China No.2012AA011102, one General Research Fund (GRF) project No.543810 and one Early Career Scheme (ECS) project No.559313 sponsored by the Research Grants Council of Hong Kong, the NSF grant of Zhejiang Province No.Z1110551.

References

1. Abney, S.: Bootstrapping. In: Proceedings of ACL 2002, pp. 360–367 (2002)
2. Blitzer, J., Dredze, M., Pereira, F.: Biographies, Bollywood, Boom-boxes and Blenders: Domain Adaptation for Sentiment Classification. In: Proceedings of ACL 2007, pp. 440–447 (2007)
3. Craven, M., DiPasquo, D., Freitag, D., McCallum, A., Mitchell, T., Nigam, K., Slattery, S.: Learning to Extract Symbolic Knowledge from the World Wide Web. In: Proceedings of AAAI 1998, pp. 509–516 (1998)
4. Cui, H., Mittal, V., Datar, M.: Comparative Experiments on Sentiment Classification for Online Product Reviews. In: Proceedings of AAAI 2006, pp. 1265–1270 (2006)
5. Dasgupta, S. Ng, V.: Mine the Easy, Classify the Hard: A Semi-Supervised Approach to Automatic Sentiment Classification. In: Proceedings of ACL-IJCNLP 2009, pp. 701–709 (2009)
6. Joachims, T.: Transductive Inference for Text Classification Using Support Vector Machines. In: Proceedings of ICML 1999, 200–209 (1999)
7. Kullback, S., Leibler, R.: On Information and Sufficiency. Annals of Mathematical Statistics **22**(1), 79–86 (1951)
8. Li, S., Huang, C., Zhou, G., Lee, S.: Employing Personal/Impersonal Views in Supervised and Semi-supervised Sentiment Classification. In: Proceedings of ACL 2010, pp. 414–423 (2010)
9. Li, S., Wang, Z., Zhou, G., Lee, S.: Semi-supervised Learning for Imbalanced Sentiment Classification. In: Proceeding of IJCAI 2011, 1826–1831 (2011c)

10. Liu, B.: Sentiment Analysis and Opinion Mining (Introduction and Survey). Morgan & Claypool Publishers (May 2012)
11. Pang, B., Lee, L., Vaithyanathan, S.: Thumbs up? Sentiment Classification using Machine Learning Techniques. In: Proceedings of EMNLP 2002, pp. 79–86 (2002)
12. Pang, B., Lee, L.: Opinion Mining and Sentiment Analysis: *Foundations and Trends*. Information Retrieval **2**(12), 1–135 (2008)
13. Riloff, E., Patwardhan, S., Wiebe, J.: Feature Subsumption for Opinion Analysis. In: Proceedings of EMNLP 2006, pp. 440–448 (2006)
14. Turney, P.: Thumbs up or Thumbs down? Semantic Orientation Applied to Unsupervised Classification of reviews. In: Proceedings of ACL 2002, 417–424 (2002)
15. Wilson, T., Wiebe, J., Hoffmann, P.: Recognizing Contextual Polarity: An Exploration of Features for Phrase-Level Sentiment Analysis. Computational Linguistics **35**(3), 399–433 (2009)
16. Yarowsky, D.: Unsupervised Word Sense Disambiguation Rivaling Supervised Methods. In: Proceedings of ACL 2005, pp. 189–196 (1995)
17. Zhou, S., Chen, Q., Wang, X.: Active Deep Networks for Semi-Supervised Sentiment Classification. In: Proceeding of COLING 2010, Poster, pp. 1515–1523 (2010)

The Effect of Modifiers for Sentiment Analysis

Xin Kou[✉]

Department of Chinese Language and Literature, Peking University, Beijing, China
snjdkx@163.com

Abstract. Modifiers can affect sentiment orientation. A modifier can change the intensity and polarity of a sentiment word. This paper focuses on the modified polarity. We analyse five hundred comments on goods from the web, and find three features of modifiers which play important roles in sentiment anlysis: *intensity*, *negation* and *implicit polarity*. We also discuss the polarity and intensity of sentiment words with multi-modifiers. Finally we propose a method to calculate the sentiment orientation of the collocations of modifiers and sentiment words.

Keywords: Sentiment analysis · Modifier · Intensity · Polarity

1 Introduction

The task of sentiment analysis is to identify positive and negative opinions, emotions and evaluations. Recent researches have focused on polarity and intensity of texts. In identifying the sentiment orientation of a sentence, the most important and widely used way is to extract sentiment words from the sentence.[1,2,3] If the sentiment words are positive, like *happy* and *delight*, the sentence is classified as positive. Sentiment words can be used to express speakers' attitude and emotion. They can present and determine the polarity of a sentence, e.g. *like/hate* and *comfortable/disgusting*. Though it is easy to distinguish the polarity into positive, negative and neutral classes, the accuracy of sentiment analysis will be impaired without the information about emotional intensity. Therefore, a number of studies focus on the intensity of sentiment words. A representative one into Chinese sentiment words is the *Affective Lexicon Ontology of Dalian University of Technology*.[4,5] This ontology divides sentiment words into seven degrees according to their polarity and intensity. However, the object of sentiment analysis is the text, and all the sentiment words are actually constituents of sentences. In a sentence, there are a number of complex factors that can affect the polarity and intensity of sentiment words, of which the most common one is the modifier of a sentiment word. For example:

不　喜欢
NEG like
I *don't like it.*

太　　好　　了

© Springer International Publishing Switzerland 2014
X. Su and T. He (Eds.): CLSW 2014, LNAI 8922, pp. 240–250, 2014.
DOI: 10.1007/978-3-319-14331-6_24

very good   ASP
Very good.

喜欢 (*like*) is an absolute positive word. When it combines with a negation word, the whole phrase turns into negative.

In this paper, we confine a modifier to the word that modifies a sentiment word and affects the polarity or intensity of sentiment, including 比较 (*relatively*), 很 (*very*), 太 (*too*), 不 (*NEG*), 没有 (*NEG*), etc. They can enhance or reduce intensity, and even change the polarity of the sentence. We use online comments about mobile phones as analysis data in this paper.

Previous research has stressed the importance of modifiers in sentiment analysis. Wang et al. suggest that the collocations of sentiment words and modifiers should be studied to improve the accuracy of phrase-level sentiment analysis.[6] Yao & Lou use the term *Modified Polarity* to describe the modifier's effect on sentence or phrase's sentiment.[7] In addition, they point out that the statistic method would separate sentiment words from the syntactic context and lead to the wrong judgement of intensity and polarity. Chen summarizes the rules of how the polarity and intensity of phrases changing with some negation words and adverbs of degree.[3] Pan studies different adverbs to explain their infulence on changing intensity, and then assigns value to them for calculation.[8] Gu differentiates derogatory adverbs from other ones because they (including 太(*too*), 过 (*too*), 偏 (*too*), etc.) can transform a positive phrase to a negative one.

Though modified polarity has received much research attention, there are still questions. Multi-modifiers are common in Chinese, e.g.

不   很   好
NEG very good
Not very good.

有点 太 大 了
a bit   too big ASP
A bit too big.

How to calculate the polarity and intensity of collocations containing more than one modifiers is not clear. Besides, how different modifiers change the sentiment orientation has not been clearly described. This paper tries to solve these problems.

2   Common Collocation

Most combinations of modifiers and sentiment words belong to common collocations. In this type of collocations, a modifier has only one feature, i.e. either intensity or negation. If the modifier is a degree word, it has the intensity feature, and its value is either Hight ([H]) or Low ([L]). If the modifier is a negation word, it has the negation feature, and its value is Negation ([N]). In this part, we will construct a *Sentiment Orientation Continuum* involving the intensity and polarity of various common collocations. This continuum is the measure of sentiment orientation, and we will put all the different collocations of modifiers and sentiment words into the continuum.

2.1   Degree Word

A degree word can affect the intensity of the phrase and does not change the polarity. We can describe the rules by the formulas below:

$$\text{Degree word + Positive word = Positive} \tag{1}$$

$$\text{Degree word + Negative word=Negative} \tag{2}$$

$$\text{Degree word + Neutral word =Neutral} \tag{3}$$

In terms of intensity, the degree word with a [H] feature will make the phrase's intensity higher, and vice versa. For example, 很好 (*very good*) is more positive than 好 (*good*), and the latter is more positive than 比较好 (*relatively good*). The same rule applies to negative words. We conclude the rules as (4) and (5):

$$\text{Degree word[H] + Positive/Negative word = More Positive/Negative} \tag{4}$$

$$\text{Degree word[L] + Positive/Negative word = Less Positive/Negative} \tag{5}$$

Accroding to the formulas (1) to (5), we can construct a continuum with positive and negative polarities. Different types of collocations can find their positions in the continuum:

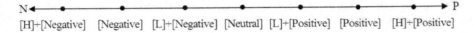

N ◄————•————————•————————•————————•————————•————————•————————•————► P
[H]+[Negative]   [Negative]   [L]+[Negative]   [Neutral]   [L]+[Positive]   [Positive]   [H]+[Positive]

Fig. 1. The Sentiment Orientation Continuum

2.2   Negation Word

From Fig. 1., we find that the phrase composed of a degree word and a sentiment word has the same polarity as the sentiment word itself. As we have pointed out, however, the addition of a negation word will turn the polarity to the other side. Therefore, we can obtain Eq. (6) and Eq. (7) as follows:

$$\text{[N] + Positive word = [Negative]} \tag{6}$$

$$\text{[N] + Negative word = [Positive]} \tag{7}$$

A number of studies have documented the influence of negation words on sentiment orientation. However, the negation words change not only the polarity but the intensity of the phrases with sentiment words. In Mandarin and some other languges, the negation does not change a word to its antonym; instead, it changes the polarity and weakens the intensity[9]. For example:

外形　　　　不　　　好看。
Appearance　NEG　good-looking
The appearece is not good-looking.

我　不　喜欢　这　款　手机。
1st NEG like   this CL mobile phone.
I don't like this mobile phone.

不好看 (*not good-looking*) doesn't mean 难看 (*bad-looking*), especially in comments of goods. In fact, the negation here can weaken the intensity of negative evaluation.

Therefore, we know that negation words can change both the polarity and the intensity of the collocations of negtion words and sentiment words. The position of these collocations can be presented as follows in a simplified continuum:

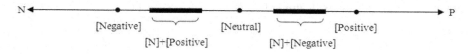

Fig. 2. Collocations with Negation Words in Sentiment Orientation Continuum

We should note that the continuum in Fig. 2. only presents the positions of the most typical types, i.e. the negation of positive words and negative words. In other phrases we have suggested in 2.1, i.e. the collocations of degree words and sentiment words, the influence of negation on polarity and intensity remains.

3   Implicit Polarity

Though most degree words only change the intensity of phrases, some of them are functionally identical to negation words because they also change the polarity. In exsiting studies, however, they are categorized as common degree words. In this section we will view this kind of modifiers as a new calss: modifiers of implicit polarity, and divide them into sub-categories according to their different features.

3.1 *Si* - type

In Mandarin, some modifiers can not modify certain sentiment words, i.e. the modification is conditional. A number of modifiers cannot be combined with positive words in general, and, if they co-occur with positive words pragmatically, the whole phrases will become negative and ironic. The members of this category are:

- 死[*si*] (*deadly*), 要命[*yaoming*] (*really*), 要死[*yaosi*] (*deadly*), 齁[*hou*] (*awfully*), 有些[*youxie*] (somewhat), 有一些[*youyixie*] (*a bit*), 些微[*xiewei*] (*slightly*), 过[*guo*] (*too*), 过头[*guotou*] (*too*), 过于[*guoyu*] (*too*)

We use 死[*si*] to name this type. The feature of these words is to express negative sentiment, regardless of the polarity of the sentiment words they modify. Yet in terms of intensity, they function just as common degree words. They affect the intensity with their inherent intensity feature, e.g.

好   得   要死
good AUX deadly
Deadly good.

有些   时尚
somewaht stylish
Somewhat stylish.

要死 (*deadly*) and 有些 (*somewhat*) express negative evaluations to the targets. If speakers use these modifers, they mean the targets deviate form their expectation. On the other hand, the intensity of the expressions is based on the inherent intensity feature of the modifiers, as [H] feature of 要死 (*deadly*) and [L] of 有些 (*somewhat*).

3.2   *Wubi* – type

Unlike si-type, modifiers we are to discuss in this section can combine with positive words, and maintain the positive polarity of the whole phrase like common degree words. If the modified words are neutral, however, these modifiers will turn the phrases to negative. These words are:

- 无比[*wubi*] (*incomparably*), 异常[*yichang*] (*singularly*), 至极[*zhiji*] (*extremely*), 之极 [*zhiji*] (*extremely*), 出奇 [*chuqi*] (*strangely*), 怪 [*guai*] (*unusally*), 格外 [*gewai*] (*especially*)

This type is named *wubi* (无比). When they are used to modify a positive word in comment texts, they always reflect the speakers' pleasant surprise.

无比   喜欢
incomparably like
Incomparably like.

In contrast, if they are combined with neutral words, the targets are meant to be unexpected and unsatisfying:

异常   大
singularly big
Singularly big.

3.3   *Tai*-type

太[*tai*] (*too*) is a special adverb in Mandarin. It has been much disscused in the existing literature. Researchers have discovered that when 太 (*too*) modifies positive words, the phrase can be either positive or negative. [10,11,12] For example:

太 简朴 了
too plain ASP
Too plain.

太 漂亮　　了
too beautiful ASP
Too beautiful.

In these examples, 简朴 (*plain*) is a positive word in Chinese according to traditional values, and 漂亮 (*beautiful*) is also positive. However, 太简朴了 (*too plain*) is considered as a negative evaluation, meaning someone or something is beyond a proper standard; while 太漂亮了 (*too beautiful*) is positive, with a higher degree than 漂亮 (*beautiful*) itself.

The factor leading to this interesting phenomenon is the intensity of the word that 太 (*too*) modifies, as Zheng[13] has pointed out. The paper classifies the sentiment words modified by 太 (*too*), and finds that the words like 简朴 (*plain*) are closer to neutral sentiment and words like 漂亮 (*beautiful*) are more positive.[13] So we believe the intensity of the positive word can determine whether a 太 (*too*) phrase is positive or not. When 太 (*too*) collocates with neutral words or negative words, the collocation is negative.

3.4 *Juedui*-type

Unlike the above three types, 绝对[*juedui*] (*absolutely*) always make a neutral phrase positive.

绝对　　　大
absolutely big
Absolutely big.

绝对 (*absolutely*) is used to express the speaker's satisfaction with some featrue of the target. If 绝对 (*absolutely*) modifies a neutral word, this positive meaning presents. With positive or negative words, 绝对 (*absolutely*) only strengthens the intensity.

All the modifiers discussed in this section not only affect the intensity but also change the polarity of the phrase. The change of polarity caused by these modifiers is not the same as that by negation words. Negation words are analytic, while these modifiers are more implicit, i.e. the difference between them is that they change the polarity syntactically or pragmatically. Yuan porposes the *"Model of Umbrella"*, using an umberlla metaphor for the implicit expression.[14] He argues that if a word can endow meaning to a structure pragmatically other than semantically or syntaxically, the word has an implicit feature.[14] The modifiers in this section conform to this defination. So we use *implicit polarity* to name this feature, and call the modifiers which have the feature *implicit polarity modifiers*. The implicit polarity modifiers can be divided into four types, i.e. *si*-type, *wubi*-type, *tai*-type, *juedui*-type, which are marked as [A], [B], [T], [J] respectively.

4   Muti-Modifiers

A sentiment word can have mutiple modifiers. According to our data, double modifiers is the most common. Degree words, implicit modifiers and negation words can modify sentiment words together. We will discuss how different multi-modifiers impact the polarity and intensity.

All the collocations have hierarchies in language. In the case of multi-modifiers, the closer a modifier is to the sentiment word, the easier it combines with the word first.

很　不　清楚
very NEG clear
Very unclear.

不是 非常 耐用
NEG very durable
Not very durable.

有点 太 时尚 了
a bit too stylish ASP
A bit too stylish.

很不清楚 (*very unclear*) has two modifiers: the degree word 很 (*very*) and the nagation word 不 (*NEG*). 不 (*NEG*) collocates with the sentiment word 清楚 (*clear*) first, and 不清楚 (*unclear*), as we have pointed out, is negative with a weaker intensity. The phrase is combined with 很 (*very*) then, whose intensity is [H]. The whole phrase becomes negative and has a comparably high intensity. The same pattern is also used in 不是非常耐用 (*not very durable*) and 有点太时尚了 (*a bit too stylish*).

5   The Calculation of Modified Polarity

In section 2 and 3, we have summarized three features of modifiers that can affect polarity and intensity. They are:

- Degree Feature: [H] and [L];
- Negation Feature: [N];
- Implicit Feature: [A], [B], [T] and [J].

We collect modifiers from several word lists, including Hownet[15], the list of Mandarin adverbs[16] and the list of negation words[17]. We have labled 143 modifiers with these three features.

The values of sentiment words are necessary if we want to construct a model to caculate the collocations of modifiers and sentiment words. There are many good resources for us to use, and in this paper we choose Dai[18]. She discribes sentiment words by coordinate axis. The x-axis represents polarity and intensity. Polarity is represented by plus or minus corresponding to positive or negative sentiment orientation. The intensity is divided into three degrees respectively in positive and negative polarity. Therefore we can use seven numbers to discribe the polarity and intensity of sentiment words: negative words have values from -1 to -3 with receding intensity; positive words are from 1 to 3 with enhancing intensity; and neutral words are 0. The y-axis is the activition of a sentiment word, and we will not use this feature in this calculation model. The examples in her model are as follows,

愉悦 (*pleasure*) (3, 0)
焦虑 (*anxiety*) (-2, 3)

Based on the sentiment word resources we have chosen, different modifiers can be assigned. In this paper, our assignment of different features is:

- [H]= 1.5;
- [L]= 0.5;
- [N]= -0.5;

Implicit modifier is a class of modifiers, and the feature of implicit polarity is not involved in computation, so we do not need to mark them numerically. We represent a modifier by coordinate, so a modifier can be written as *Modifier (x, y)* . The x-axis shows the degree feature and negation feature, as we have mentioned in section 2, a word will not have these two features at the same time, since we have classifed the negation words and degree words. The y-axis shows the implicit polarity feature, and if a modifier is not a implicit modifier, then y=0. For example,

不 (*NEG*) (-0.5, 0)
很 (*very*) (1.5, 0)
太 (*too*) (1.5, T)
些微 (*slightly*) (0.5, A)

We can calculate the sentiment of the phrases with modifiers and sentiment words using our labeled vocabulory resources. If a sentiment word is *SentimentWord (x1, y1)*, the word modified it is *Modifier (x2, y2)*, then:

```
If y2=0,
ModifiedPolarity=x1*x2;
```

If the modifier is a common modifier, we can just calculate the new intensity by *x1*x2*, and the polarity is decided by x1.

But when the modifier is an implicit modifier, they differ in their types. According to our analysis in section 3, we can compute them as follows:

```
If y2≠0,
  If y2=A,
    If x1=0,
      then ModifiedPolarity=-x2;
    If x1≠0,
      then ModifiedPolarity=-|x1*x2|;
    If y2=B,
      If x1=0,
        then ModifiedPolarity=-x2;
      If x1≠0,
        then ModifiedPolarity=x1*x2;
    If y2=T,
```

```
If x1=3,
   then ModifiedPolarity=x1*x2;
If x1<0 or 0<x1<3,
   then ModifiedPolarity=-|x1*x2|;
If x1=0,
   then ModifiedPolarity=-x2;
If y2=J,
   If x1=0,
      then ModifiedPolarity=x2;
   If x1≠0,
      then ModifiedPolarity=x1*x2
```

Fig.3. shows how to calculate a collocation of a modifier and a sentiment word in a flow chart:

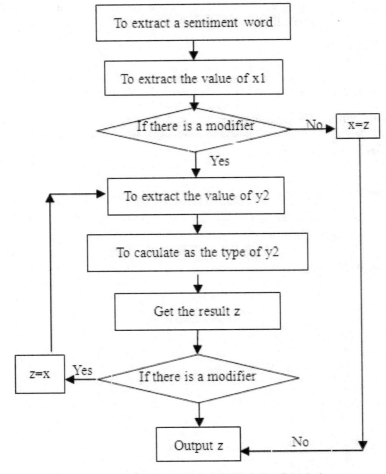

Fig. 3. The Flow Chart of Modified Polarity Calculation

6   Conclusion

In this paper, we have provided evidence to prove that modifiers can change the intensity and polarity of sentiment words in Mandarin. Considering the influence of modifier in sentiment analysis, the traditional means that extracts the polarity and intensity of sentiment words is no longer effective, especially in the phrase-level sentiment analysis. We have porposed that the intensity of modifiers and negation words can respectively change the intensity and polarity of the collocations of modifiers and sentiment words. Besides we have found that there are four classes of modifiers which can change not only intensity but polarity. We call them modifiers of implicit polarity. Intensity, negation and implicit polarity are the three features that affect the sentiment orientation of the collocations of modifiers and sentiment words. Based on the existing sentiment words annotation, we have assigned value to these features and made them computable. We hope the analysis of modifiers in this work can be contributive to the phrase-level sentiment analysis.

References

1. Turney, P.D.: Thumbs up or thumbs down?: semantic orientation applied to unsupervised classification of reviews. In: Proceedings of the 40th Annual Meeting on Association for Computational Linguistics (ACL), Philadelphia, pp. 417–424 (2002)
2. Wilson, T., Wiebe, J., Hoffmann, P.: Recognizing Contextual Polarity in Phrase-Level Sentiment Analysis. In: Proc. of Human Language Technologies Conference/Conference on Empirical Methods in Natural Language Processing (HLT/EMNLP 2005), pp. 347–354 (2005)
3. Chen, J.M.: The Construction and Application of Chinese Emotion Word Ontology. (Master Thesis) Dailian University of Technology, Dalian (2008). (in Chinese)
4. Affective Lexicon Ontology of Dalian University of Technology, Information reaserch laboratory, Dalian
   http://ir.dlut.edu.cn/EmotionOntologyDownload.aspx?utm_source=weibolife (2014)
5. Xu, L.H., Lin, H.F., Zhao, J.: Construction and Analysis of Emotional Corpus. Jouranl of Chinese Information Processing 22(1), 180–185 (2008). (in Chinese)
6. Wang, Z.M., Zhu, X.F., Yu, S.W.: Research on Word Emotional Evaluation Based on the Grammatical Knowledge-base of Contemporary Chinese. International Journal of Computational Linguistics and Chinese Language Processing 10(4) 581–592 (2005). (in Chinese)
7. Yao, T.F., Lou, D.C.: Research on Senmantic Orientation Distinction for Chinese Sentiment Words. In: The 7th Information Control Conference of Chinese, Wuhan (2007). (in Chinese)
8. Gu, Z.J., Yao, T.F.: Extraction and Discrimination of the Evaluated Object and Its Orientation. Jouranl of Chinese Information Processing 26(4), 91–97 (2012). (in Chinese)
9. Shi, Y.Z.: The Symmetry and Asymmetry between Affirmation and Negation. Beijing Language and Culture University Press, Beijing (2001). (石毓智.肯定和否定的对称与不对称. 北京: 北京语言大学出版社 (2001)) (in Chinese)
10. Lu, F.B.: The Study of Adverb Tai: the Question of Conbination of the Three Dimensions of Syntax, Semantics and Pragmatics in Teaching Grammar of Chinese as a Foreign Language. Chinese Teaching in the World 2, 74–81 (2000). (in Chinese)

11. Pan, F.M.: Sentiment Analysis of Online Reviews Based on Semantic Collocation (Master Thesis) Dailian University of Technology, Dalian (2009). (in Chinese)
12. Shao, J.M.: Dynamic Change of *Tai* Modifying Adjectives. Chinese Language Learning **1**, 3–12 (2007). (in Chinese)
13. Zheng, T.G.: Normality Degrees and the Meaning of *Tai+P* Phrases. Language Teaching and Linguistic Studied **2**, 48–55 (2005). (in Chinese)
14. Yuan, Y.L.: On the Semantic Levels and Overflow Conditions of the Implicit Negative Verbs in Chinese. Studies of the Chinese Language **2**, 99–113 (2002). (in Chinese)
15. Hownet, http://www.keenage.com (2013)
16. Zhang, Y.S.: Studies of Mandarin Adverbs. Xuelin Publishing House, Shanghai (2000). (张谊生.现代汉语副词研究. 上海: 学林出版社 (2000)) (in Chinese)
17. Kou, G.Z.: Research in Sentiment Strength Fuzziness with Opinion Mining General Framework. (Doctor Thesis) Wuhan University, Wuhan (2010). (in Chinese)
18. Dai, C.C.: The Study in Semantics, Syntax and Pragmatics of the Sentiment Adjectives (Courses Thesis) Peking University, Beijing (2013). (戴辰忱.情感体验性形容词的语义语用及句法研究.北京大学中文系本科生学年论文 (2013)) (in Chinese)

Word Relevance Computation for Noun-Noun Metaphor Recognition

Yuxiang Jia[1]([✉]), Hongying Zan[1], Ming Fan[1], Shiwen Yu[2], and Zhimin Wang[3]

[1] School of Information Engineering, Zhengzhou University, Zhengzhou, China
{ieyxjia,iehyzan,iemfan}@zzu.edu.cn
[2] Key Laboratory of Computational Linguistics, Peking University, MOE, Beijing, China
yusw@pku.edu.cn
[3] College of Chinese Studies, Beijing Language and Culture University, Beijing, China
wangzm000@gmail.com

Abstract. Metaphor in languages is an analogy-based meaning transfer phenomenon that impacts on question answering, machine translation and other tasks requiring deep semantic analysis. Noun-noun metaphor is a common type of metaphor and is studied in noun-noun semantic analysis. Lexical knowledge bases are important knowledge source for metaphor recognition and understanding. This paper proposes a method to compute word relevance for noun-noun metaphor recognition with the help of a lexical knowledge base, which shows good performance in the experiments. Furthermore, we investigate the representation of metaphor in lexical knowledge bases and its impact on the construction of lexical knowledge bases.

Keywords: Metaphor Recognition · Noun-noun Metaphor · Word Relevance · Lexical Knowledge.

1 Introduction

Metaphor, in essence, is a basic cognitive tool for human beings to understand new things by analogy to known ones [1]. Manifested in natural languages, (linguistic) metaphor is a kind of expression describing one thing in terms of another to enhance the accuracy and effectiveness of the expression. When describing one thing of the target domain, the meaning of the word of the source domain changes. For example, in the metaphorical expression "知识的海洋" (*the ocean of knowledge*), "海洋" (*ocean*) is metaphorically used to describe "知识" (*knowledge*), and its meaning analogically changes from the literal meaning, water area, to an abstract one.

According to the part of speech of the metaphorically used word, linguistic metaphor can be classified into different subtypes, like nominal metaphor, verb metaphor and adjective metaphor. Nominal metaphor also has some subtypes, including referential nominal metaphor and noun-noun metaphor. The form of referential nominal metaphor is "N是N", where N denotes a noun, and "是" (*be*) is a copula. For example, "人生是旅行" (*life is a journey*) is a referential nominal metaphor. The form of

© Springer International Publishing Switzerland 2014
X. Su and T. He (Eds.): CLSW 2014, LNAI 8922, pp. 251–259, 2014.
DOI: 10.1007/978-3-319-14331-6_25

noun-noun metaphor is "N+N" or "N的N", like "人事地震" (*personnel earthquake*) or "知识的海洋" (*the ocean of knowledge*).

Compared with literal expressions, the understanding of metaphorical expressions is more complex and needs deep semantic analysis. Metaphor is pervasive in natural languages and its processing will enhance natural language processing tasks like question answering and machine translation. Metaphor processing contains two steps, metaphor recognition and metaphor understanding. Metaphor recognition is to identify metaphorical expressions from real text and metaphor understanding is to interpret a metaphorical expression with a literal expression and discover the conceptual mapping under the metaphorical expression. From the view of noun-noun semantic analysis, noun-noun metaphor should be recognized and treated specifically. This paper studies the recognition of noun-noun metaphors and proposes an effective lexicon-based word relevance computation method for metaphor recognition.

The rest of this paper is organized as follows. Section 2 introduces related work. Section 3 shows the representations of metaphor in different lexical knowledge bases and its impact on the construction of lexical knowledge bases. Section 4 introduces the proposed word relevance computation method and two other methods for comparison. Section 5 gives experiments and analysis. Conclusion and future work are given in section 6.

2   Related Work

Metaphor recognition is a two-class, metaphor or not, classification problem and can be treated with machine learning methods. Wang et al. [2] proposed a supervised machine learning method to recognize Chinese noun phrase metaphors, utilizing contextual information but omitting collocation information inside the noun phrases. To reduce the labor of human annotation, Shutova et al. [3] proposed a clustering method to recognize English verb metaphors by expanding a metaphor seed set with clustered verbs and nouns.

Another category of methods recognizes metaphors by collocation analysis usually based on some semantic knowledge bases, which can be built manually or through automatic knowledge acquisition. Jia and Yu [4] proposed a method to recognize Chinese verb metaphors based on automatically acquired selectional preference knowledge. Krishnakumaran and Zhu [5] recognized English referential nominal metaphors with hypernym relations in WordNet. Jia and Yu [6] computed semantic distance through CiLin [7] and semantic relations through HowNet [8] to recognize Chinese referential nominal metaphors. Yang [9] used CiLin and a collocation database to recognize Chinese noun-noun metaphors. Feng et al. [10] computed word relevance through Wikipedia to recognize Chinese referential nominal metaphors. Word concreteness and abstractness information can also be applied to metaphor recognition [11].

Machine learning methods provide a unified framework for the recognition of all kinds of metaphors, but they usually need tagged corpus for training the models. Collocation analysis methods are relatively easier to implement but different semantic knowledge bases may be needed for different kinds of metaphors. These two categories of methods can be combined through incorporating collocation analysis results into the machine learning framework to leverage the merits of both.

Compared with referential nominal metaphors, less work has been done on the recognition of noun-noun metaphors. The exploitation of lexical knowledge bases is not enough. Take HowNet for example, only concept definitions have been exploited while semantic hierarchies, concept concreteness and other properties in the knowledge base are not used. So we study the recognition of noun-noun metaphors and try to utilize lexical knowledge bases more extensively.

3 Metaphor and Lexical Knowledge Bases

Metaphor is a main reason of the emergence of new words and new senses. Thus metaphors are reflected in many lexical knowledge bases. Metaphorical senses and metaphorical examples are represented in the Modern Chinese Dictionary, the most reputable Chinese dictionary, with the indicator "比喻" (*metaphor*) and the symbol "◇" respectively. Su and Zhao [12] investigated the metaphor distribution in the Modern Chinese Dictionary (the 2nd edition) and found that 2086 words have metaphorical senses and 402 words have metaphorical examples and they together count 4.43% (2488/56147) of the dictionary vocabulary.

Table 1. Metaphor thought in HowNet

Sememe	Example words	Definition
head|头	房檐 'eaves'	part|部件,%building|建筑物,head|头
heart|心	发动机 'engine'	part|部件,%vehicle|交通工具,heart|心
	中央处理器 'CPU'	part|部件,%computer|电脑,heart|心
body|身	根茎 'rhizome'	part|部件,%plant|植物,body|身
	山脊 'ridge'	part|部件,%land|陆地,body|身
bone|骨	支柱 'pillar'	part|部件,%building|建筑物,bone|骨
	班子 'organized group'	part|部件,%organization|组织,bone|骨
base|根	地基 'ground'	part|部件,%building|建筑物,base|根
	山脚 'foot of a hill'	part|部件,%land|陆地,base|根
limb|肢	枝条 'branch'	part|部件,%plant|植物,limb|肢
leg|腿	车轮 'wheel'	part|部件,%LandVehicle|车,leg|腿
wing|翅	机翼 'wing'	part|部件,%aircraft|飞行器,wing|翅,*fly|飞
mouth|口	大门 'gate'	part|部件,%building|建筑物,mouth|口
eye|眼	窗户 'window'	part|部件,%building|建筑物,eye|眼
nerve|络	走廊 'corridor'	part|部件,%building|建筑物,nerve|络
tail|尾	结尾 'ending'	part|部件,&event|事件,tail|尾
skin|皮	被罩 'quilt cover'	part|部件,%tool|用具,#sleep|睡,skin|皮
flesh|肉	案情 'case'	part|部件,%fact|事情,flesh|肉,#police|警
hair|毛	树叶 'leave'	part|部件,%plant|植物,hair|毛

HowNet, an important electronic lexical knowledge base, defines and organizes concepts using metaphor thought. In HowNet, concepts are defined with sememes. Sememes are some core concepts that make hierarchical taxonomies. There is a class of sememes named SecondFeature, including arms and legs of human beings, organs of animals and plants, etc. Using these familiar and concrete sememes to analogically define other unfamiliar and abstract concepts is just the thought of metaphor. Table 1 shows some examples of such definition. The first column shows sememes of SecondFeature. The second column shows example words. The third column shows the definition of corresponding word which is a combination of sememes (See [8] for detailed specification of definitions). For example, eaves are defined as the head of a building and engine is defined as the heart of a vehicle. We can see the systematic mapping from the domain of human beings to the domain of buildings from definitions using "head|头" for "屋檐" (*eaves*), "bone|骨" for "支柱" (*pillar*), "mouth|口" for "大门" (*gate*), "eye|眼" for "窗户" (*window*), and "nerve|络" for "走廊" (*corridor*). We can also see using concrete concepts to define abstract concepts from definitions using "tail|尾" for "结尾" (*ending*) and "flesh|肉" for "案情" (*case*).

4   Word Relevance Computation for Metaphor Recognition

The semantic relation of the two component nouns is important to decide whether a noun-noun phrase is a metaphor or not, although contextual information is needed sometimes. The two nouns in a noun-noun metaphor usually come from two different concept domains and thus their semantic relevance tends to be small. Based on this hypothesis, we can use word relevance for metaphor recognition.

Corpus-based methods and knowledge-based methods are two categories of methods for word relevance computation. Corpus-based methods measure word relevance based on word co-occurrence information in the corpus and a frequent co-occurrence usually corresponds to a larger word relevance value. Knowledge-based methods measure word relevance based on certain lexical knowledge base, considering the structure and semantic properties of the knowledge base, and the positions of the words in the knowledge base. For noun-noun metaphor recognition, the knowledge-based word relevance computation methods have advantages. Firstly, for corpus-based methods, if a noun-noun metaphor frequently occurs in the corpus, then the word relevance of the two component nouns will be large which conflicts with the hypothesis. Secondly, when human recognizes a metaphor, the literal meaning of the word is actually known. The literal meaning may be lost in the real text but kept in hand crafted lexical knowledge bases and thus can be exploited by knowledge-based methods for metaphor recognition.

We propose a HowNet-based word relevance computation method Rel_{hownet}. HowNet represents concept or word sense using the combination of sememes. With hypernym relations, sememes form several sememe trees, like Entity, Event, Attribute and Attribute Value. For the convenience of computation, we add a root to those trees and form the only tree of all sememes.

In metaphor, similarity exists between two different concepts. A word may have several senses and a sense may be a combination of several sememes. We define word relevance between two words as the maximum value of the relevance of all sememe of all senses of the two words.

As is shown in formula 1, the word relevance is defined as the maximum relevance of all senses of the two words.

$$\text{Rel}_{\text{hownet}}(W_1, W_2) = \max_{i=1..Mc, j=1..Nc} \text{Rel}_{\text{hownet}}(C_i, C_j) \tag{1}$$

As is shown in formula 2, the relevance of sense is defined as the maximum relevance of all sememes of the two senses.

$$\text{Rel}_{\text{hownet}}(C_1, C_2) = \max_{i=1..Ms, j=1..Ns} \text{Rel}_{\text{hownet}}(S_i, S_j) \tag{2}$$

The relevance of two sememes is defined as formula 3 and the value is between 0 and 1. $pathlen(S_1, S_2)$ is the shortest path between the two sememes in the sememe tree. It equals to the sum of path length to their least common parent.

$$\text{Rel}_{\text{hownet}}(S_1, S_2) = 1 - \frac{pathlen(S_1, S_2)}{pathlen(S_1, Root) + pathlen(S_2, Root)} \tag{3}$$

For comparison, we consider the similarity measure Rel_{liu} [13] and a Cilin-based method $\text{Rel}_{\text{cilin}}$. Rel_{liu} is defined as formula 4. It is a linear combination of four types of similarity, the first sememe, other basic sememes, relation sememe and relation symbol. Parameters β_i are weights of the four similarities, among which the weight of the first sememe is the largest (See [13] for details of the parameters).

$$\text{Rel}_{\text{liu}}(C_1, C_2) = Sim(C_1, C_2) = \sum_{i=1}^{4} \beta_i Sim_i(C_1, C_2) \tag{4}$$

But for some concepts, the first sememe is not very representative. Rather, the meaning of the concept is better represented by other sememes. Then the word relevance computed by Rel_{liu} is not reasonable. For example, in table 2, the first sememes "attribute|属性" and "part|部件" are not so representative. The relevance computed by Rel_{liu} of "价格" (price) and "魅力" (charm) is 0.592 while "大门" (gate) and "貂皮" (marten) is 0.675, which are unreasonably large.

Table 2. Word definition examples of HowNet

Word	Definition
价格 'price'	attribute|属性,price|价格,&physical|物质,commercial|商
魅力 'charm'	attribute|属性,ability|能力,&attract|吸引|
大门 'gate'	part|部件,%building|建筑物,mouth|口
貂皮 'marten'	part|部件,%animal|兽,skin|皮,?material|材料

In CiLin, words are classified into five levels of classes. Every top level class corresponds to a five level concept hierarchy tree, where parent node is hypernym of child node and all words are in the leaf nodes. For convenience of computation, we add a root to those trees and form a complete tree. CiLin-based word relevance is the same with formula 1 and the sense relevance is defined as formula 5.

$$\text{Rel}_{\text{cilin}}(C_1, C_2) = 1 - \frac{pathlen(C_1, C_2)}{pathlen(C_1, Root)) + pathlen(C_2, Root))} \qquad (5)$$

The level 5 leaf nodes correspond to word sense C_i (i=1,2). $pathlen(C_1, C_2)$ is the same with that in formula 3, where $pathlen(C_i, Root)$=5 (i=1,2). $pathlen(C_1, C_2)$ takes value from the set {0,2,4,6,8,10} and the scope of $\text{Rel}_{\text{cilin}}$ is [0,1].

5   Experiments and Analysis

According to our hypothesis, the word relevance is prone to be smaller for a metaphorical expression than a literal expression. For a rule-based metaphor recognition method, we can set a threshold firstly. If the word relevance of the two nouns is smaller than the threshold, then it is a metaphor. Otherwise it is literal. Here we design a simplified experiment. For a target noun, we choose a literal noun-noun phrase and a metaphorical noun-noun phrase. If the word relevance of the literal nouns is larger than that of the metaphorical nouns, then the target noun is correctly predicted. Otherwise it is wrongly predicted. In other words, if the relevance difference of the literal nouns and the metaphorical nouns is larger than 0, then the target noun is correctly predicted. Otherwise it is wrongly predicted. As is shown in table 3, we have 33 target nouns and make 33 pairs of noun-noun phrases, a literal one and a metaphorical one. In each noun-noun phrase, the second noun is the target noun. Take the target noun "舞台" (*stage*) for example, the first noun-noun phrase "芭蕾舞台" (*ballet stage*) is a literal expression and the second noun-noun phrase "历史舞台" (*stage of history*) is a metaphorical expression.

Table 3. Noun-noun phrases in the test set

芭蕾舞台	历史舞台	大门钥匙	问题钥匙	西瓜种子	生命种子
房屋支柱	经济支柱	凤凰翅膀	理想翅膀	耕地土壤	腐败土壤
肝动脉	交通动脉	国家海洋	知识海洋	海潮风暴	金融风暴
海底隧道	时间隧道	公路桥梁	友谊桥梁	小儿心脏	祖国心脏
水泥道路	致富道路	院子大门	北京大门	妈妈怀抱	祖国怀抱
寒暑风雨	人生风雨	啤酒泡沫	价格泡沫	海洋风浪	政治风浪
村庄田野	希望田野	病人脉搏	市场脉搏	运动员脚步	春天脚步
鱼脊梁	民族脊梁	奶油蛋糕	市场蛋糕	钢铁火花	思想火花
大门门槛	就业门槛	桥梁工程师	灵魂工程师	图书大厦	科学大厦
水泥台阶	发展台阶	火车车轮	历史车轮	婴儿摇篮	文明摇篮
河口港湾	爱港湾	桃树花朵	祖国花朵	战斗阵地	舆论阵地

We have three relevance computation methods, Rel_{hownet}, Rel_{liu}, and Rel_{cilin}. The metaphor recognition results of the three methods are shown in figure 1 to 3. The x-axis is the index of the test nouns from 1 to 33. The y-axis is the relevance difference between the literal nouns and the metaphorical nouns. If the y-axis value of a test noun is positive, then the noun is correctly predicted. Otherwise it is wrongly predicted. So a figure with more positive y-axis values denotes a better result. Comparing the three figures, we can see that our method Rel_{hownet} achieves better performance than the other two methods.

For a clear comparison, we define a measure, *accuracy*, as the division of the number of correctly predicted test nouns and the total number of test nouns. Table 3 gives the comparison of the three methods. "rel.dif." is short for "relevance difference" and the second column is the number of test nouns with positive relevance difference. In other words, the second column is the number of correctly predicted test nouns. Both the third and the fourth columns are considered as numbers of wrongly predicted test nouns. It shows that our method Rel_{hownet} achieves the highest accuracy of 0.818.

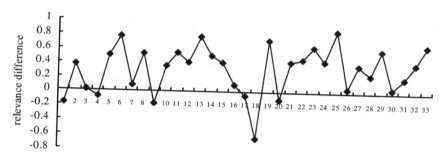

Fig. 1. Result of Rel_{hownet}

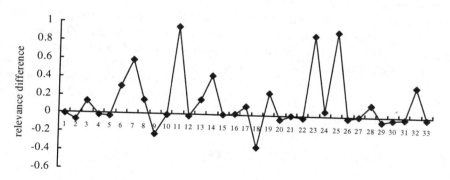

Fig. 2. Result of Rel_{liu}

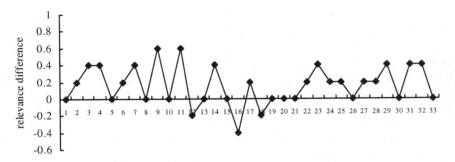

Fig. 3. Result of Rel_{cilin}

The relevance difference for many test nouns are zero in Rel_{cilin}. The reason may lie in the simpler structure and knowledge representation of CiLin than HowNet, which makes it unable to differentiate literal noun-noun phrase from metaphorical noun-noun phrase. However, wrongly predicted cases in Rel_{hownet} like 4, 9 and 17 are correctly predicted in Rel_{cilin}. It is a signal that the combination of the two lexical knowledge bases may further improve the metaphor recognition performance.

Table 4. Results of metaphor recognition

	rel.dif.>0	rel.dif.=0	rel.dif.<0	accuracy
Rel_{hownet}	27	0	6	0.818
Rel_{liu}	17	1	15	0.515
Rel_{cilin}	18	12	3	0.545

Experiments show that, making good use of lexical knowledge bases to compute word relevance can help recognize noun-noun metaphors. However, in some cases, word relevance alone is not enough. For example, "知识的海洋" (*the ocean of knowledge*) is a metaphorical expression, but "海洋知识" (*knowledge of ocean*) is not. The word relevance values of the two expressions are the same. Then word order information is needed to improve the recognition method. In some other cases, contextual information is needed for metaphor recognition. Then incorporating word relevance information and contextual information into machine learning framework may be a good choice. We will do further study on the impact of word relevance on a complete metaphor recognition system.

6   Conclusion and Future Work

This paper proposes a word relevance computation method for noun-noun metaphor recognition, which shows good performance in experiments. We also investigate metaphor representation in lexical knowledge bases and its impact on lexical knowledge base building. We believe that lexical knowledge has great impact on metaphor processing and utilizing such knowledge extensively can improve the performance of metaphor processing. In the future, we will incorporate word relevance information and contextual information into the machine learning framework, and build a complete system for noun-noun metaphor recognition and understanding.

Acknowledgments. This work is partially supported by grants from the National Natural Science Foundation of China (No.60970083, No.61170163, No.61272221, No.61402419), the National Social Science Foundation of China (No.14BYY096), the China Postdoctoral Science Foundation (No.2011M501184), the Postdoctoral Science Foundation of Henan Province (No.2010027), the Open Projects Program of Key Laboratory of Computational Linguistics (Peking University), Ministry of Education, China (No.201301), the 863 Project (No.2012AA011101) and Science and Technology Key Project of Science and Technology Department of Henan Province (No.132102210407).

References

1. Lakoff, G., Johnson, M.: Metaphors We Live By. University of Chicago Press (1980)
2. Wang, Z., Wang, H., Duan, H., Han, S., Yu, S.-W.: Chinese Noun Phrase Metaphor Recognition with Maximum Entropy Approach. In: Gelbukh, A. (ed.) CICLing 2006. LNCS, vol. 3878, pp. 235–244. Springer, Heidelberg (2006)
3. Shutova, E., Sun, L., Korhonen, A.: Metaphor Identification Using Verb and Noun Clustering. In: Proceedings of COLING, pp. 1002–1010 (2010)
4. Jia, Y.X., Yu, S.W.: Unsupervised Chinese Verb Metaphor Recognition Based on Selectional Preferences. In: Proceedings of PACLIC, pp. 207–214 (2008)
5. Krishnakumaran, S., Zhu, X.J.: Hunting Elusive Metaphors Using Lexical Resources. In: Proceedings of the ACL Workshop on Computational Approaches to Figurative Language, pp. 13–20 (2007)
6. Jia, Y.X., Yu, S.W.: Nominal Metaphor Recognition Based on Lexicons. Journal of Chinese Information Processing 25(2), 99–104 (2011). (in Chinese)
7. Che, W.X., Li, Z.H., Liu, T.: LTP: A Chinese Language Technology Platform. In: Proceedings of COLING: Demonstrations, pp. 13–16 (2010)
8. Dong, Z.D., Dong, Q.: HowNet and the Computation of Meaning. World Scientific (2006)
9. Yang, Y.: Computational Model of Chinese Metaphor Recognition and Interpretation. Dissertation of Xiamen University (2008). (in Chinese)
10. Feng, S., Su, C., Chen, Y.J.: Approach to Recognizing Chinese Nominal Metaphor Based on Online-Encyclopedia. Computer Systems and Applications 10, 8–13 (2013). (in Chinese)
11. Turney, P., Neuman, Y., Assaf, D., Cohen, Y.: Literal and Metaphorical Sense Identification through Concrete and Abstract Context. In: Proceedings of EMNLP, pp. 680–690 (2011)
12. Su, X.C., Zhao, C.Y.: The Form of the Metaphorical Meaning and the Exegesis of the Metaphorical Meaning. Journal of Hangzhou Teachers College (Humanities and Social Sciences) 5, 67–71 (2001). (in Chinese)
13. Liu, Q., Li, S.J.: Word Similarity Computing Based on How-net. International Journal of Computational Linguistics and Chinese Language Processing 7(2), 59–76 (2002). (in Chinese)

Learning Semantic Similarity for Multi-label Text Categorization

Li Li, Mengxiang Wang, Longkai Zhang, and Houfeng Wang[⊠]

Key Laboratory of Computational Linguistics,
Peking University, Ministry of Education, Beijing, China
{li.l,wmx1984,zhanglongkai,wanghf}@pku.edu.cn
http://klcl.pku.edu.cn/

Abstract. The multi-label text categorization is supervised learning, where a document is associated with multiple labels simultaneously. The current multi-label text categorization approaches suffer from limitations when the expensive labelled text data is little but the unlabelled text data is abundant, because they are unable to exploit information from unlabelled text data. To address this problem, we learn the word semantic similarity by deep learning using the unlabelled text data, and then incorporate the learned word semantic similarity into current multi-label text categorization approaches. We conduct experiments with the *Slashdot* and *Tmc2007* datasets, and these experiments demonstrate our proposed method will greatly improve the performance of current multi-label text categorization approaches.

1 Introduction

In traditional single-label text categorization, a document is associated with a single label. The multi-label text categorization is concerned with learning from documents associated with multiple labels simultaneously. In recent years, the multi-label text categorization attracts increasing attentions [5,11,14]. The multi-label text categorization methods are distinguished into two categories in [13] , namely 1) algorithm adaptation methods and 2) problem transformation methods. Algorithm adaptation methods adapt traditional single-label text categorization algorithms for multi-label text categorization problems. Problem transformation methods transform a multi-label text categorization problem into one or more traditional single-label text categorization problems. Problem transformation allows greater flexibility since it abstracts away from a specific classifier. A lot of current problem transformation methods, for example *Ensemble Classifier Chain* (ECC) [8] and RAndom K labEL (RAKEL) [15], produce the state-of-the-art performance. This paper focuses on the problem transformation methods.

The multi-label text categorization, like the traditional single-label text categorization, suffers from the well-known limitations when the labelled data is small. For example, since *sunshine* is semantically similar to *sunlight*, these two words should share the similar weight values. However, due to the small labelled

X. Su and T. He (Eds.): CLSW 2014, LNAI 8922, pp. 260–269, 2014.
DOI: 10.1007/978-3-319-14331-6_26

data, the word *sunlight* has been observed rarely (or never) in the training set and the word *sunshine* has been observed enough times in the training set. The weights of these two words will be very different. To address this problem, we present a semi-supervised deep learning method for multi-label text categorization. This method learns the word semantic similarity using deep learning and then incorporates the word semantic similarity into the supervised classification model with word semantical regularization. The word semantical regularization will make the weights of semantically correlated words close, even if one of them has not been observed in the training set. We conduct experiments with *Slashdot* and *Tmc2007* datasets under two evaluation metrics. The dataset *Slashdot* is concerned about science and technology news categorization, which predicts multi labels given article titles and partial blurbs mined from Slashdot.org. The *Tmc2007* dataset is concerned about safety report categorization, which is to label aviation safety reports with respect to what types of problems they describe. These experiments demonstrate our proposed method will improve the performance of multi-label text categorization approaches.

The remainder of this paper is organized as follows. We learn the word semantic similarity from the unlabelled textual data using deep learning in section 2. Section 3 introduces how we incorporate word semantic similarity into multi-label text categorization using regularization. Experiments with various multi-label datasets and evaluation measures, which demonstrate the effectiveness of our presented semi-supervised learning method, are introduced in section 4. Section 5 concludes this paper by summarizing our work.

2   Learn Word Semantic Similarity with Deep Learning

In this section, we learn word semantic similarity with deep learning. Deep learning is part of a broader family of machine learning methods based on learning representations. Deep learning typically uses artificial neural networks. The levels in these learned statistical models correspond to distinct levels of concepts, where higher-level concepts are defined from lower-level ones, and the same lower-level concepts can help to define many higher-level concepts [1].

In natural language processing, a lot of deep learning researchers attempt to learn continuous distributed vector representations of words [2, 4, 7]. Unlike the traditional one-hot representation, the continuous distributed vector representation of a word is a real-valued vector. It usually looks like $[0.792, 0.109, -0.542, ...]$ with 50 or 100 dimensions. The semantic similarity between two words can be measured with the cosine similarity of corresponding word vector representations.

We learn continuous distributed vector representations of words by *continuous Skip-gram* [6]. The continuous Skip-gram algorithm is an efficient deep learning method for learning high-quality distributed vector representations that capture a large number of precise semantic word relationships. The continuous

Skip-gram builds a classification problem, which inputs each current word to a log-linear classifier with continuous projection layer, and predicts words within a certain range before and after the current word. By minimizing the loss function of the classification problem with a word based on another words in the same sentence, the continuous Skip-gram learns continuous distributed vector representations of words.

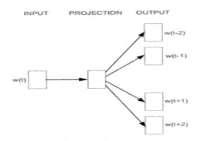

Fig. 1. Archtecture of continuous Skip-gram

To learn the word distributed vector presentations, we need a large corpus of unlabeleed text. For the *Slashdot*, we crawl about 40M article titles and partial blurbs from Slashdot.org[1], which contains 75,012 article titles and partial blurbs. For *Tmc2007*, we use the raw text data of this dataset (both training and test dataset). The raw text data is about 25M, which contains aviation safety 21,519 reports. We download it online[2].

After deep learning, we can compute semantic similarity between each word pair in the vocabulary of *Slashdot* or *Tmc2007* with the cosine similarity of word vector representations as semantic similarity. The word *systems* is important since the dataset *Slashdot* is concerned about science and technology news. We shows the the cosine similarity between *systems* and other words in *Slashdot* in Table 1. The five words most cosinely similar to the word *systems* are *devices*, *technologies*, *system*, *applications* and *networks* in this table, which are semantically similar to *systems*. Hence, the table shows Deep learning can investigate the word semantic similarity in *Slashdot*. The dataset *Tmc2007* is concerned about security reports categorization where the word *assault* is important. Table 2 shows the cosine similarity between word *assault* and other words in *Tmc2007*. Similarly, the table shows that deep learning also can investigate the word semantic similarity in *Tmc2007*.

With the computed semantic similarity, we build the semantic similarity matrix $\mathcal{L}$, where $\mathcal{L}_{i,j}$ is the semantic similarity value between the i-th word and the j-th word in vocabulary.

---

[1] http://www.slashdot.org
[2] http://web.eecs.utk.edu/events/tmw07/

Table 1. The cosine similarity between word *systems* and other words in *Slashdot*

word1	word2	cosine similarity
systems	devices	0.744
systems	technologies	0.680
systems	system	0.680
systems	applications	0.671
systems	networks	0.585
...	...	...
systems	selling	-0.170
systems	making	-0.173
systems	mention	-0.174
systems	discussed	-0.175
systems	favoriate	-0.197

Table 2. The cosine similarity between word *assault* and other words in *Tmc2007*

word1	word2	cosine similarity
assault	attack	0.674
assault	harass	0.386
assault	route	0.374
assault	fire	0.332
assault	advance	0.331
...	...	...
assault	correct	-0.137
assault	troubleshoot	-0.138
assault	direct	-0.140
assault	strong	-0.141
assault	head	-0.142

3   Incorporate Word Semantic Similarity

In this section, we show how to incorporate the word semantic similarity into supervised classification models, which are used in problem transformation methods of multi-label text categorization

For the prediction model, we mainly consider regularized linear models, e.g., support vector machines, logistic regression. The model is represented with a p-dimensional weight vector $\boldsymbol{w}$ and an intercept b. The classification prediction is setting a threshold θ on $\boldsymbol{w}^T + b$. To learn $\boldsymbol{w}$ and b, we minimize a loss function on the training set plus a regularization term on $\boldsymbol{w}$:

$$\underset{\boldsymbol{w},b}{\text{argmin}} \frac{1}{n} \sum_{i=1}^{n} loss(y_i, \boldsymbol{w}^T x_i + b) + \lambda \boldsymbol{w}^T \boldsymbol{w} \tag{1}$$

where λ is the regularization coefficient which balances the loss function and the regularized term.

To incorporate the word semantic similarity prior into supervised classification models, we replace the original regularized term $\lambda w^T w$ with the new one $\lambda w^T \mathcal{L} w$, where $\mathcal{L}$ is the word similarity matrix.

$$\underset{w,b}{\operatorname{argmin}} \frac{1}{n} \sum_{i=1}^{n} loss(y_i, w^T x_i + b) + \lambda w^T \mathcal{L}^{-1} w \qquad (2)$$

All regularized linear models, include logistic regression and linear SVM, in the form of Eq.(5) can be solved with the following three steps [10]. First, transform the training instances by

$$\bar{x}_i = \mathcal{L}^{-\frac{1}{2}} x_i \qquad (3)$$

Second, a standard liner model is learned

$$\underset{\bar{w},b}{\operatorname{argmin}} \frac{1}{n} \sum_{i=1}^{n} loss(y_i, \bar{w}^T \bar{x}_i + b) + \lambda \bar{w}^T \bar{w} \qquad (4)$$

finally, obtain the optimal solution by

$$w = \mathcal{L}^{-\frac{1}{2}} \bar{w} \qquad (5)$$

The method of incorporating the semantic similarity into supervised learning is similar to the method proposed in [16]. The difference is that we incorporate the semantic similarity into supervised learning in multi-label problem transformation, while the method proposed in [16] incorporates the semantic similarity into the standard classifcation problem.

4 Experiments

4.1 Datasets

The evaluations are done on two textual datasets. The first dataset is the *Slashdot* dataset, introduced in [8]. It is concerned about science and technology news categorization, which predicts multi labels given article titles and partial blurbs mined from Slashdot.org. The second dataset is *Tmc2007*, introduced in [11]. It is concerned about safety report categorization, which is to label aviation safety reports with respect to what types of problems they describe. Both of them can be found online[3,4].

Table 3 shows these multi-label datasets and associated statistics. $|D|$ denotes the size of the entire dataset, $|L|$ denotes the number of labels, Distinct denotes the number of distinct labelings. The measure label cardinality *Lcard*, which is one of the standard measures of "multi-label-ness", defined as follows, introduced in [13].

---

[3] http://meka.sourceforge.net/
[4] http://mulan.sourceforge.net/datasets.html

Table 3. Multi-label datasets and associated statistics

dataset	$|D|$	$|X|$	$|L|$	Distinct	Lcard
Slashdot	3782	1079	22	156	1.18
Tmc2007	28596	500	22	1341	2.16

$$Lcard(D) = \frac{\sum_{i=1}^{|D|} \sum_{j=1}^{|L|} y_j^i}{|D|}$$

where D denotes the entire dataset, l_j^i denotes the j-th label of the i-th instance in the dataset.

4.2 Method Setup

In the word semantic similarity learning phase, we use *word2vec* [12], an efficient implementation of the continuous Skip-gram algorithm, to learning the continuous distributed vector represenations of words. The code of *word2vec* is available online[5]. The dimension of word continuous distributed vector is set to 200 and the window of learning is set to 5.

In the supervised learning phase, *five-fold cross validation* is employed. To validate effectiveness of our method, we incorporate the semantic similarity into ECC and RAKEL to improve their performance. ECC and RAKEL are simple but state-of-the-art methods. For ECC, ensemble iterations are set to 10 and the label orders are generated randomly. ECC subsamples 80% of training set for one individual model. For RAKEL, we set parameter size of the subset of labels $k = 5$, the number of iterations m=$|L|$. LR is utilized as the base classifier model in ECC and RAKEL since LR is a simple but efficient classificaton model. ECC and RAKEL incorporated with the word semantic are referred to as ECC-r (ECC with word semantic similarity regularization) and RAKEL-r. All methods are implemented in Matlab 2012b.

Note that these models produce real-valued predictions, $p_1, p_2, ..., p_{|y|}$. A threshold t needs to be used to determine the final multi-label set y such that $l_j \in y$ where $p_j \geq t$. We select threshold t, which makes the $Lcard$ measure of predictions for the training set is closest to the $Lcard$ measure of the training set [8]. The threshold t is determined as follows, where D_t is the training set and a multi-label model H_t predicts for the training set under threshold t.

$$t = \underset{t \in [0,1]}{\text{argmin}} |Lcard(D_t) - Lcard(H_t(D_t))| \tag{6}$$

4.3 Evaluation Metrics

We use the two most famous and important multi-label evaluation metrics: hamming loss and 0/1 loss.

---

[5] https://code.google.com/p/word2vec/?

The Hamming Loss is ratio of misclassied instance-label pairs to total instance-label pairs. It is introduced in [9] and defined as follows.

$$HammingLoss = \frac{1}{|D||L|} \sum_{i=1}^{|D|} |S_i \Delta Y_i| \tag{7}$$

where S_i is the prediction label set for the i-th instance in testing dataset, and Y_i is the true label set. Let Δ denote the symmetric difference of two sets, equivalent to XOR operator in Boolean logic. Lower is better.

The 0/1 Loss [3], is known as the exact match measure as it requires any predicted set of labels Y to match the true set of labels S *exactly*. The 0/1 Loss is defined as follows:

$$0/1Loss = \frac{1}{|D|} \sum_{i=1}^{|D|} I(S_i = Y_i) \tag{8}$$

where $I(true) = 1$ and $I(false) = 0$. Lower is better.

4.4   Results

Comparion with the Original Methods. We compare the methods incorporated word semantic correlations(ECC-r, RAKEL-r) with the original methods (ECC, RAKEL). We set the regularization coefficient to 0.001, which is a common regularization coefficient value for the $\ell2$ regularization term. Table 4 shows the performance of different methods. The methods incorporated word semantic similarity win over the original methods in all cases, except Rakel and Rakel-r achieve highly similar performance on the *Slashdot* dataset in terms of hamming loss. The improvements are for the most part statistically significant.

Table 4. Performance of each method in terms of different evaluation metrics. Lower is better.

	Slashdot		Tmc2007	
	hammingloss↓	0/1 loss↓	hammingloss↓	0/1 loss↓
ECC	0.063	0.857	0.064	0.732
ECC-r	**0.061**	**0.808**	**0.062**	**0.721**
RAKEL	0.046	0.783	0.061	0.701
RAKEL-r	0.046	**0.755**	**0.059**	**0.689**

Regularized Coefficient Influence. Because the regularization coefficient λ in Eq.(1) and Eq.(2) is the critical parameter. Our experiments show ECC vs ECC-r, RAKEL vs RAKEL-r with different regularization coefficients. The regularization coefficient λ varies in $\{0.01, 0.005, 0.001, 0.005, 0.0001\}$. Figure 2 and Figure 3 show the performance of each method on different datasets with different regularized coefficients. Methods incorporated with word semantic similarity

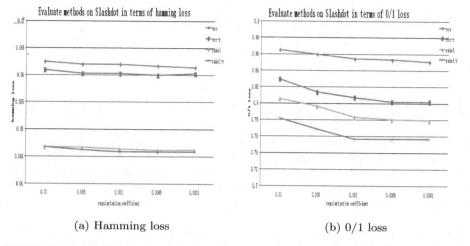

(a) Hamming loss

(b) 0/1 loss

Fig. 2. Performance of each method with different regularized coefficients λ in terms of different evaluation metrics on the *Slashdot* dataset. Both of two evaluation metrics are better when lower.

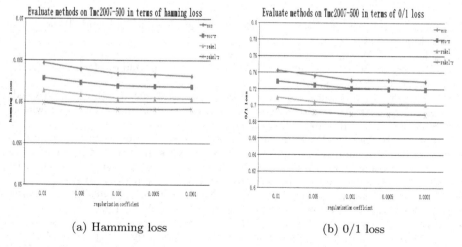

(a) Hamming loss

(b) 0/1 loss

Fig. 3. Performance of each method with different regularized coefficients λ in terms of different evaluation metrics on the *Tmc2007* dataset. Both of two evaluation metrics are better when lower.

almost win over the corresponding original methods clearly on the *Slashdot* and *Tmc2007* datasets under the two important and famous evaluation metrics. The only exception case is that Rakel and Rakel-r achieve highly similar performance on the *Slashdot* dataset in terms of hamming loss.

5   Conclusion

The current multi-label text categorization approaches are unable to exploit information from unlabelled text data. To address this problem, in this paper, we learn the word semantic similarity by deep learning from the unlabelled text data, and then incorporate the learned word semantic similarity into current multi-label text categorization approaches. We conduct experiments with the *Slashdot* and *Tmc2007* datasets, and these experiments demonstrate our proposed method improves the performance of current multi-label text categorization approaches under two famous evaluation metrics.

Acknowledgments. This research was partly supported by National High Technology Research and Development Program of China (863 Program) (No. 2012AA011101), National Natural Science Foundation of China (No.61370117,61333018), Major National Social Science Fund of China (No. 12&ZD227) and China Postdoctoral Science Foundation (No. 2013M530456).

References

1. Bengio, Y.: Learning deep architectures for ai. Foundations and Trends® in Machine Learning **2**(1), 1–127 (2009)
2. Collobert, R., Weston, J., Bottou, L., Karlen, M., Kavukcuoglu, K., Kuksa, P.: Natural language processing (almost) from scratch. The Journal of Machine Learning Research **12**, 2493–2537 (2011)
3. Ghamrawi, N., McCallum, A.: Collective multi-label classification. In: Proceedings of the 14th ACM International Conference on Information and Knowledge Management, pp. 195–200. ACM (2005)
4. Huang, E.H., Socher, R., Manning, C.D., Ng, A.Y.: Improving word representations via global context and multiple word prototypes. In: Proceedings of the 50th Annual Meeting of the Association for Computational Linguistics: Long Papers, vol. 1, pp. 873–882. Association for Computational Linguistics (2012)
5. Katakis, I., Tsoumakas, G., Vlahavas, I.: Multilabel text classification for automated tag suggestion. In: Proceedings of the ECML/PKDD (2008)
6. Mikolov, T., Chen, K., Corrado, G., Dean, J.: Efficient estimation of word representations in vector space (2013). arXiv preprint arXiv:1301.3781
7. Mikolov, T., Yih, W.-T., Zweig, G.: Linguistic regularities in continuous space word representations. In: Proceedings of NAACL-HLT, pp. 746–751 (2013)
8. Read, J., Pfahringer, B., Holmes, G., Frank, E.: Classifier chains for multi-label classification. Machine Learning **85**(3), 333–359 (2011)
9. Schapire, R.E., Singer, Y.: Boostexter: A boosting-based system for text categorization. Machine Learning **39**(2), 135–168 (2000)

10. Schölkopf, B., Simard, P., Smola, A.J., Vapnik, V.: Prior knowledge in support vector kernels. In: Advances in Neural Information Processing Systems, pp. 640–646 (1998)
11. Srivastava, A.N., Zane-Ulman, B.: Discovering recurring anomalies in text reports regarding complex space systems. In: 2005 IEEE Aerospace Conference, pp. 3853–3862. IEEE (2005)
12. Mikolov, G.C.T., Chen, K., Dean, J.: word2vec (2013). https://code.google.com/p/word2vec/
13. Tsoumakas, G., Katakis, I.: Multi-label classification: An overview. International Journal of Data Warehousing and Mining (IJDWM) **3**(3), 1–13 (2007)
14. Tsoumakas, G., Katakis, I., Vlahavas, I.: Effective and efficient multilabel classification in domains with large number of labels. In: Proc. ECML/PKDD 2008 Workshop on Mining Multidimensional Data (MMD 2008), pp. 30–44 (2008)
15. Tsoumakas, G., Vlahavas, I.P.: Random k-labelsets: An ensemble method for multilabel classification. In: Kok, J.N., Koronacki, J., Lopez de Mantaras, R., Matwin, S., Mladenič, D., Skowron, A. (eds.) ECML 2007. LNCS (LNAI), vol. 4701, pp. 406–417. Springer, Heidelberg (2007)
16. Zhang, Y., Dubrawski, A., Schneider, J.G.: Learning the semantic correlation: An alternative way to gain from unlabeled text. In: Advances in Neural Information Processing Systems, pp. 1945–1952 (2008)

Latent Semantic Distance Between Chinese Basic Words and Non-basic Words

Shanon Yi-Hsin Lin[✉] and Shu-Kai Hsieh

Graduate Institute of Linguistics, National Taiwan University, Taipei, Taiwan
r00142004@ntu.edu.tw, shukai@gmail.com

Abstract. What determines the "basicness" of words still remains a challenging question in creating basic lexicons and basic wordlists. Since frequency and dispersion seem to be the most dominant criteria, it is questioned that whether contextual factors also help to define the concept of "basicness." From the perspective of the distributional model, meanings are represented through the interaction between words and their contexts. Hence, this research aims to examine an existing wordlist and tentatively take it as the standard of "basicness," trying to seek the differences between "basic words" and "non-basic words" based on their occurrences in different texts. Two experiments were conducted to answer the research questions. The first calculated the "latent semantic distances" between basic words and non-basic words. The second calculated and examined the "near neighbors" of basic word and non-basic words. It has been discovered that basic words tend to occur in more similar texts than non-basic words do; in addition, the near neighbors of basic words tend to be more "basic", too. This research contributes to providing a more "contextual" perspective in exploring "basicness."

Keywords: Basic Lexicon · Basic Word Lists · Latent Semantic Analysis

1   Introduction

Defining or quantifying the "basicness" of words (or core vocabulary) has always been a challenging yet important issue for linguistics, cognitive science, as well as language teaching fields. Since the "basicness" of words could be elaborated from many different perspectives –language acquisition, psycholinguistic or ontological, different kinds of projects have been carried out to generate "basic lexicon" or "basic wordlist." For example, EuroWordnet has been developing the "basic concepts" by mapping the synsets within different languages (Vossen 2002); "basic wordlists" in each language are also created for language teaching or language learning purposes, such as General Service List (Bauman and Culligan 1995) and Academic Word List (Coxhead 2000) in English language.

In creating basic lexicon or wordlists, the most common criteria are frequency and dispersion (Brezina and Gablasova 2013); however, seldom does past literature aim to explore the contextual factors. In the recent years, more and more researchers began to wonder whether "meanings" are stored in our long-term memory as "readymade"

© Springer International Publishing Switzerland 2014
X. Su and T. He (Eds.): CLSW 2014, LNAI 8922, pp. 270–277, 2014.
DOI: 10.1007/978-3-319-14331-6_27

information (Kintsch and Mangalath 2011:347), or are in fact generated through the interaction between words and contexts (Barsalou, 1987). Since contexts play a decisive role in determining the meaning of a word, and a word should be defined by its "company" and "environment" (Firth 1957), it is possible that meanings are actually constructed in contexts instead of being stored in our mental lexicon (Kintsch and Mangalath 2011).From the past research and literature, it is believed that contextual factors may significantly influence the construction of "meaning"; looking into contextual factors may provide new perspectives and shed light on the exploration of word basicness.

Therefore, this research tries to differentiate basic words and non-basic word in terms of their contexts. However, at current stage, there is still no consensus on what determines the basicness of lexical items; what we can do for now is to examine the existing basic concepts or basic words with different perspectives first, attempting to find out other possible factors that might related to word basicness, or the characteristics that basic words tend to possess. Once the characteristics or the patterns are identified, the viewpoint of "basicness" could become more diverse and flexible, and these characteristics may also illuminate how different lexical items behave differently and how people use them in contexts.

2   Literature Review

The construction of basic concepts and basic wordlists has been quite prevalent in every language; from EuroWordnet Basic Concepts (Vossen, Bloksma et al. 1998) to English General Service List (Brezina and Gablasova 2013), Chinese TOCFL wordlists (Chang and Chen 2005), linguists has been dedicated to creating a more "appropriate" and "complete" version of "basic words", which are supposed to reflect the most "basic" and "common concepts" in human mind and their daily language use, also providing better coverage for different texts. Nonetheless, the criteria used to weight lexical items are actually quite subjective in defining the basicness. Since the concept of basicness could be "dynamic" (it may differ with different purposes in use or different text genres), finding out a definite or absolute set of criteria seem to be impossible. Hence, it would be more practical to start from the already-made basic lexicon or basic wordlists and to examine the behaviors of so-called "basic words" and "non-basic words" to see whether there are any patterns or characteristic shared. In addition, previous literature has claimed the importance of "contextual factors" in understanding the word meaning (Harris 1981, Barsalou 1986, Kintsch and Mangalath 2011). With the aim to identifying the different behaviors of basic words and non-basic words, their presence in the contexts should be observed and further analyzed.

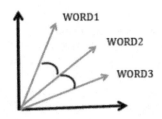

Fig. 1. An example of vectors in LSA

In this paper, we will employ the distributional model of meanings (Turney et al., 2010), which has been a revival of theories and methods for quantifying and categorizing semantic similarities and other properties between linguistic items based on their distributional properties in large samples of language data. According to Distributional Hypothesis (Harris 1954), linguistic items that appear in similar contexts tend to share related meanings; following Distributional Hypothesis, LSA (Latent Semantic Analysis) (Landauer and Dumais 1997) looks into word meanings through their occurrences in texts. LSA is a technique that analyzes the relationships between terms and the texts they occur. Since words occur in similar texts tend to be closer in meaning, LSA calculates word counts in each document and paragraph from representative corpora, putting word counts into different rows, and the columns are the texts they occur; then a huge and sparse matrix is formed. Afterwards, singular value decomposition (SVD) is adopted to simplify the matrix while preserving those significant columns. By doing this, the occurrences of words are represented as different vectors, indicating the "environment structure" of words, and the cosine values between these vectors reflect the similarity of the environments they occur, and further imply their similarity in meaning. For example, in Figure 1, the three words are represented as three vectors after SVD; since the angle of cosine values between word 2 and word 3 is smaller, it could be inferred that word 2 and word 3 are more similar in meaning than word 3 and word 1. Cosine values given in LSA fall between 0 and 1; when values between two terms are close to 1, it means the two terms (which are termed "near neighbors") behave very similarly in texts, and they are supposed to be closer in meaning as well; values close to 0 represent two terms behave very differently in texts, thus less similar in meaning. By examining words and their environments, LSA aims to understand the meaning through contexts instead of words themselves.

LSA has been applied to many different researches. For instance, TASA corpus (Quesada 2007), a corpus containing reading texts for American high-school students, includes 90 thousand different words, which are organized in 44 thousand documents, was constructed into a very huge and sparse matrix to build LSA space, computing the semantic distance among different words. In Chinese research, LSA is also applied to many different projects. For example, Chen & Wang et al. (2009) built large-scale LSA space using Sinica Corpus 3.0, a balanced modern Chinese corpus containing more than 9 thousand documents and 78 thousand words. This project is called Chinese Latent Semantic Analysis (http://www.lsa.url.tw/ modules/lsa/), in which they adopt different weightings and dimensions to build different LSA spaces (Chen, Wang et al. 2009). Chinese Latent Semantic Analysis provides the calculation of pairwise comparison, near neighbors, and also word-to-document LSA spaces, and the computation of semantic distance makes contribution to writing evaluation. Chang and Song (2005) also build an automatic Chinese writing evaluation system with LSA to examine the article abstract writing of elementary school students. In addition, Yeh (2002) creates a LSA space with 100 news documents to process documents abstracts automatically. Most of the application of LSA relates to writing evaluation system, with the help of word-to-document semantic space. On the other hand, word-to-word semantic spaces help us to understand word meanings by providing words that share similar meanings and calculating the semantic distances between words through comparing their occurrences in texts. While understanding word basicness, LSA may provide a new perspective to see how basic words and non-basic words interact in their environments. Therefore, the research questions of this research will be as following:

(1) For basic words and non-basic words, which may tend to occur in similar contexts, and be more similar in meaning?

(2) What are the latent semantic distances between basic words and non-basic words? Does the distance differ with different part-of-speech?

(3) Is there any shared pattern between the near neighbors of basic words and non-basic words? For example, do the near neighbors of basic words tend to be basic, too?

3   Methodology

In order to answer the questions above, this research takes TOCFL wordlists (a Chinese wordlists) as the standard in choosing basic words and non-basic words. TOCFL is a leveled wordlist for foreign learners of Chinese (http://www.sc-top.org.tw/chinese/download.php). There are five levels in TOCFL wordlist and 8000 words in total (Chang 2005).

The words are ranked according to their weighting values, which comes from the mapping between CKIP wordlist (Sinica Academia Corpus Study Group 1998), CPT2002 wordlist (Chang 2002), HSK1992 wordlist (National Chinese Teaching Leading Group 1992) as well as frequency counts in Sinica Corpus and Chinese elementary textbooks (For more detailed elaboration, please refer to Chang 2005). The 500 words in beginner level are selected as "basic words" in this research. Although they are selected as the "top 500" basic word only because of frequency accounts, they might still represent "basicness" in a sense since they appear in almost every Chines wordlists. The other 7500, on the other hand, are the candidates for "non-basic words" for this research. In later analysis, beginner level to fluent level is named as level 1 to level 5 to show their difficulty levels.

3.1   Experiment 1

In order to compare the interaction within basic words and within non-basic words, the cosine values among basic words and non-basic words are calculated. The cosine values are obtained from Chinese Latent Semantic Analysis (http://www.lsa.url.tw/modules/lsa/), which consists of 49021 words and 9277 documents from Academia Balanced Sinica Corpus. Once the vector space is created, LSA R package (Fridolin 2011) provides an easy-to-use function for pair-wise cosine values calculation as shown in the following screenshot..

```
> cosine(NewMatrix["晚上",], NewMatrix["電影院",])
             [,1]
[1,] 0.4374268
```

Fig. 2. The Screenshot of Cosine Function

By putting two terms, "night" and "movie theater" as examples, into the cosine function, LSA package returns the cosine value, which is 0.4374 in this example, of the two target terms. We first mapped basic words and non-basic words with the 49021 words in Chinese LSA to make sure the selected basic words and non-basic words do occur in the 9277 documents; next, nouns and verbs are singled out respectively, for part-of-speech may also influence word meanings. Finally, we have four different groups of words: basic nouns, basic verbs, non-basic verbs, and non-basic nouns, and from each group we choose 100 words through random sampling. Later, among the 100 words in each group, the cosine value of each word with other words in the group are calculated through pairwise comparison (total 4095 combinations); by doing this, the semantic distances among all the words in each group are obtained, and then we may compare the interaction within basic verbs, basic nouns, non-basic verb, and non-basic nouns through the mean values of their semantic distances. When the cosine value between two terms is higher, the two terms are more similar in meaning, and this may imply closer semantic distances; on the contrary, low cosine values suggest less similar in meaning and farer semantic distances.

3.2   Experiment 2

To examine the shared traits between the near neighbors of basic words and non-basic words, we first extract all the near neighbors of each basic word and non-basic word, which are the words that have the highest cosine value with the target words. For example, the near neighbors of "movie" are "directors" and "film". This means that the two words tend to occur in the similar context as "movie" does.

```
Results:

1 電影 1.000 [dian4 ying3] movie/film
2 導演 0.930 [dao3 yan3] direct/director (film etc.)
3 影片 0.905 [ying3 pian4] film/movie
```

Fig. 3. The Screenshot of Chinese LSA Near Neighbors

In this part, we first separated all the words on TOCFL wordlist into four groups: basic nouns (nouns in level 1), basic verbs (verbs in level 1) and non-basic nouns (nouns in level 2-5), non-basic verbs (verbs in level 2-5). Next, we calculated and extracted the near neighbors whose cosine values are higher than 0.9. After we obtained all the near neighbors, we further examined their difficulty levels to see the difficulty level distribution of each group.

4   Results and Discussion

In this section, the results of the two experiments will be presented, as well as the implication of the results.

4.1   Experiment 1

According to the results, it is discovered that the semantic distances among basic verbs are the closest. The average cosine value among the 100 basic verbs is 0.6659. We can see from Figure 4 that the cosine values mostly range from 0.6 to 0.8, and this suggests that they actually occur in very similar texts. On the other hand, the average cosine value among basic nouns is 0.4368, lower than that of basic verbs. Compared with basic words, non-basic words tend to have even lower cosine values. The average cosine values among the 100 non-basic verbs is 0.3691, which is a little higher than that of the 100 non-basic nouns with its values falling to 0.3391.Again, it could be seen from Figure 4 that verbs tend to occur in more similar environment than nouns do. Furthermore, if we compare cosine values of basic words with non-basic word, we can see that basic words tend to share more similar texts than non-basic words do, for their cosine values are higher. Next, it is found that non-basic words are less similar in meanings, and the semantic distances among non-basic words are farer, for they less appear in similar environment. On the contrary, basic words are inclined to occur in more similar environments, and this indicates that they are more similar in meaning, and the semantic distances among basic words are closer. Additionally, it seems that verbs share more similar environment than nouns do.

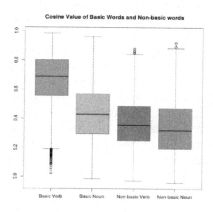

Fig. 4. The Box Plot and Bar Plot of the Cosine Values and Latent Semantic Distance of the Four Groups

4.2   Experiment 2

According to the results of the second experiment, in which all the near neighbors of the four groups are calculated and examined, it is discovered that the near neighbors of basic words tend to be basic words, too, while the near neighbors of non-basic words tend to be non-basic words. We can see from the following Figure 5 that among all the near neighbors of basic nouns and basic verbs, the percentages of level-1 words are the highest. On the contrary, among all the near neighbors of non-basic nouns and non-basic verbs, the percentages of level-4 words are the highest.

This suggests that words of the same level tend to occur in similar contexts; that is to say, basic words tend to co-occur and be dominant in certain contexts, while non-basic words would co-occur and be dominant in other different contexts.

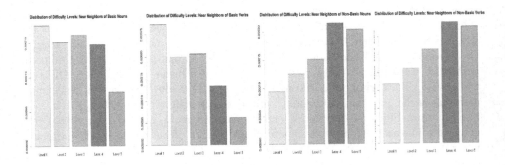

Fig. 5. The Percentage of the Near Neighbors of the Four Groups

5   Conclusion and Future Work

The results shown above suggest that basic words in TOCFL may be a group of words that more often appear in similar contexts. Non-basic words, on the other hand, less occur in similar contexts since the cosine value among them is lower. Furthermore, the near neighbors (words occurring in similar contexts and possess similar meaning) of basic words are also basic in nature, while those of non-basic words tend to be more advanced.

It seems that basic word and non-basic word do behave differently and possess different characteristics in terms of their occurrence in contexts. Therefore, future work may explore deeper to see the "basicness" of words in terms of collocations. Moreover, the patterns or characteristics of these collocates should also be probed into to see word basicness in a different way.

References

1. Barsalou, L.W.: Are there static category representations in long-term memory? Behavioral and Brain Sciences **9**(04), 651–652 (1986)
2. Bauman, J., Culligan, B.: General service list. ms (1995). http://www.jbauman/gsl.html
3. Brezina, V., Gablasova, D.: Is There a Core General Vocabulary? Introducing the New General Service List. Applied Linguistics (2013)
4. Chang, L.: A preliminary approach to grading vocabulary and patterns of Chinese as a second language. National Science Council Research Report (NS-92-2411-H-003 -045) (2004)
5. Chang, L., Chen, F.: hua2yu3 ci2hui4 fen1ji2 chu1tan4. (On Chinese Lexicon Levels). The Sixth Chinese Lexical Semantics Workshop Proceedings (2005). (in Chinese)
6. Chang, L.: dui4ying4 yu2 ou1zhou gong4tong2 jia4gou4 de hua2yu3 ci2hui4 liang4 (On Structuring Chinese Lexicon). Chinese Teaching Research **9**(2), 77–96 (2012). (in Chinese)
7. Chen, M.-L., et al.: The construction and validation of Chinese semantic space by using latent semantic analysis. Chinese Journal of Psychology **51**(4), 415–435 (2009)
8. Coxhead, A.: A new academic word list. TESOL Quarterly **34**(2), 213–238 (2000)
9. Dumais, S.T.: Latent semantic analysis. Annual Review of Information Science and Technology **38**(1), 188–230 (2004)
10. Firth, J.R.: Studies in linguistic analysis. Basil Blackwell, Oxford (1957)
11. Wild, F.: lsa: Latent Semantic Analysis. R package version 0.63-3 (2011). http://CRAN.R-project.org/package=lsa
12. Harris, Z.S.: Distributional structure. Springer (1981)
13. Kintsch, W., Mangalath, P.: The construction of meaning. Topics in Cognitive Science **3**(2), 346–370 (2011)
14. Landauer, T.K., Foltz, P.W., Laham, D.: Introduction to Latent Semantic Analysis. Discourse Processes **25**, 259–284 (1998)
15. National Chinese Teaching Leading Group: Han4yu3 shui3ping2 kao3ci4 hui4yu4 han4zi4 deng3ji2 da4gang1 (The Introduction of Chinese Language Test). Beijing Linguistics Department Published, Beijing (1992). (in Chinese)
16. Quesada, J.: Creating your own LSA spaces. In: Landauer, T.K., McNamara, D.S., Dennis, S., Kintsch, W. (eds.) Handbook of Latent Semantic Analysis, pp. 71–88. Mahwah, Erlbaum (2007)
17. Sinica Academia Corpus Study Group: Lexical Frequency Dictionary. Sinica Academia Chinese Database Group Technical Report CKIP-98-01. Sinica Academia, Taipei (1998a)
18. Turney, D.P., Pantel, P.: From frequency to meanings: Vector space models of semantics. Journal of Artificial Intelligence Research **37**, 141–188
19. Vossen, P., et al.: The eurowordnet base concepts and top ontology. Deliverable D-017, D-34, D-036 (1998)
20. Vossen, P. (ed.): EuroWordNet general document. Technical report. University of Amsterdam, Amsterdam, Version 3, Final, July 1 2002

Manual Investigation on Context for Word Sense Disambiguation

Dan Liu[1]([⊠]), Min Hua[1], Maohua Qian[1], and Xuri Tang[2]

[1] Department of English, Textile University, Wuhan, China
{ellen_liu_2008,jingle11050417}@126.com, sarahq@163.com
[2] Department of English, Huazhong University of Science
and Technology, Wuhan, China
xrtang@hust.edu.cn

Abstract. Context information is of great importance in Word Sense Disambiguation. This paper investigates how window size is involved in the process of Word Sense Disambiguation by developing a way of sense description and manually calculating the window size of context during the process of disambiguation. The sizes of context window are 2.3-1.7 for verbs, 2.4-2.5 for nouns and 1.5-1.7 for adjectives. It is also found that the grammatical categories determine the disambiguation, among which nouns play the most important role. These findings can be used for reference during Word Sense Disambiguation.

Keywords: Sense disambiguation · Sense description · Window value · Word category

1 Introduction

The prevalence of polysemy in natural language inevitably leads to the massive quantity of ambiguity in text language. Word Sense Disambiguation (WSD), therefore, is to recognize the proper sense of ambiguous words in a specific context [1]. Context information, which can help opt for the proper sense of polysemy in the text, may offer clues to the Word Sense Disambiguation. The size of context window and the influence of different word categories provided by the surrounding context are to be discussed in this essay.

2 Literature Review

2.1 Sense Knowledge Base

Generally speaking, dictionary is the common base for Word Sense Disambiguation. However, the senses in the dictionary have the problems such as subtle sense distinction, vague rules of sense differentiation and obscure clues to sense distinction, etc. Kilgarriff commented that the drawbacks, which was mainly due to the restriction of

Sponsored by Program of Chinese Social Science Foundation (Grant No.11CYY030).

© Springer International Publishing Switzerland 2014
X. Su and T. He (Eds.): CLSW 2014, LNAI 8922, pp. 278–285, 2014.
DOI: 10.1007/978-3-319-14331-6_28

the tradition, printed sheet and acceptance on the separation and combination of sense items in the traditional dictionary, limited the practice of word sense analysis [2]; while the new Wordnet established by the cognitive science lab in Princeton University is also subject to criticism owing to its meticulous sense distinction [1]. Hang Xiao [3] is one of the researchers who conducted a series of research concerning this salient problem of dictionary sense knowledge base. His case study is on Contemporary Chinese Dictionary which is the most authorized dictionary in China. The research indicates that the overlapping, separation, inclusiveness and other relationships among the senses of polysemy in the dictionary mainly hindered the accurate distinction of the multiple meanings and resulted in much ambiguity, and these relationships among polysemic senses reduced the accuracy and operability of sense distinction. Consequently, Xiao proposed corresponding methods to comb the relationship among polysemic senses by analyzing the sense relationships to eliminate the ambiguity of meanings. From his research, we obtain the information that it is important to compile better dictionary or establish other sense knowledge base from the clear semantic distinction at the very beginning of the disambiguation research.

2.2 Clues to Disambiguation

Context is the most efficient clue for disambiguation, which refers to the language background of practical language usage and its value in Natural Language Processing reflects in two aspects. On the one hand, context is the base of knowledge in the process of acquisition of natural language, in other words, context itself is knowledge following the inference mechanism; on the other hand, context plays an important role as the supplier of necessary information and resource in solving the usage problem of natural language [4]. Dealing with the collocation of words with different part of speech in the context is of assistance to tremendous decrease of the complexity of Word Sense Disambiguation. The core status of verb in the semantic and syntax system makes its disambiguation research popular. Those researches of verb disambiguation mainly focus on the study of collocation, grammatical function and semantic relation in the field of context information. Jinzhan Lin [5] conducted research on the strategy of polysemous disambiguation from the aspects of grammatical function, semantic relation and usage experience. From the angle of grammatical function, the verb senses were judged by its difference between semantic function and syntax function; from the angle of semantic relation, disambiguation was realized through judging the semantic relation between verbs and other collinear components; from the angle of usage experience, the high probability of correctness was achieved when the sense in common use was taken as the default one.

2.3 Methods of Disambiguation

There are two widely-admitted methods of disambiguation: one is based on dictionary, and the other is based on corpus. The methods can also be classified in terms of the preference of the researchers: one is adopted by the linguistic researchers who attach great importance to the properties of polysemy in order to find out better disambigua-tion solution, and the other is taken by the computational statistics experts who are committed to language usage models through a variety of algorithms. Corpus com-posed of large quantity of samples can be categorized into annotated and non-annotated ones; accordingly, disambiguation methods can be divided into supervised disambig-uation and unsupervised ones. The ultimate proof of Word Sense Disambiguation is the context in the method of supervised disambiguation; in other words, the sense of am-biguous word can be judged in the context through the closest word or several words before or after the ambiguous word. The context chosen in a specific area before or after the ambiguous word is called window [6]. Until now, the size of the window is an influential factor of disambiguation. In this field, the pioneers are the researchers working on English word disambiguation. Martin et al. indicated that if the window size was five, it can supply 95% collocation information [7]; Choueka et al. proposed that if the window size was two, enough information can be obtained to conduct dis-ambiguation [8]. Concerning the research on Chinese words, Song Lu and Shuo Bai weighted context positions by information gain, constructing the function of posi-tion-weight according to weight of context positions and then the function was inte-grated to arrive to the information ratio 85% to define the size of window. They got the most optimized size 8-9 in Chinese [4]. However, they conducted the computa-tional research without any linguistic background.

2.4   Summary

The research in this article is to settle the problem such as meticulous sense distinction, vague clue to sense distinction, so the traditional dictionary cannot be taken as our knowledge base. Instead semantic relations are examined in establishing ground truth word senses by using a fine-grained sense inventory from Hownet, alongside distin-guishing coarse-grained senses and adding the missing senses by the research mem-bers. This research is also to investigate the clues provided by the context from the perspective of semantic relation and collocation in the field of context information. In addition, this research contributes to the computation of the window size, artificial identification of senses and statistics of disambiguation results from a questionnaire. Those are the attempts different from the predecessors in the field of computational statistics.

3   Research Design

The texts in this research, which are already segmented and tagged with part of speech, are from the corpus of People's Daily. The studied words in this research are content words, such as nouns, verbs and adjectives, because they are the carrier of meaning in the texts and are mainly studied in the Word Sense Disambiguation. 24 content words including 11 nouns, 7 verbs and 6 adjectives are selected according to the use fre-from the corpus. (The polysemy from multiple word categories is not included in our research because the cross-category polysemous words are not taken into consideration). The senses of the 24 polysemy are searched in the Hownet and the polysemy themselves are searched in the corpus of People's Daily by using Ultra edit software. The context of each polysemy according to their different senses are copied and stored followed the principle of "i-1".

3.1   Sense Description

The main source of the senses of polysemous words is Hownet, on which the senses are English. The explanation of the senses cannot be copied directly from Hownet because it also has the problems such as sense deletion and meticulous sense distinction. The steps for describing the senses are: first, different senses of the target polysemy are searched in the Hownet, then Baidu online dictionary is used to check whether the senses have deletion (Baidu online dictionary also has the English version of the senses, so comparison can be made), a case in point is adjective 好 (good), the explanation "to show the degree of completion or perfection" listed on the Baidu online dictionary is missing in the Hownet, so this sense is completed when describing the senses of 好 (good). At last, coarse-grained division of senses is achieved by sense description of the four researchers whose mother language is Chinese and second language is English with linguistic background. Take one of the division for example, in the Hownet, the adjective 小 (small) has fine-grained division of 10 senses: "age younger", "less than normal", "low rank", "low voice", "time short", "negligible", "noncritical", "small", "unimportant" and "weak", according to the rules of reducing overlapping, inclusiveness and other relationships, the coarse-grained division of 3 senses is decided by the four researchers after discussion, that is , "unimportant, non-critical, minor", "age younger" and "low voice".

3.2   Questionnaire Design

There are 81 selected sentences in total in the questionnaire, 24 verb polysemy sentences, 30 noun polysemy sentences and 27 adjective polysemy sentences. Each polysemy covers different number of sentences according to different number of senses it contains. Each tested sentence has two parts, one is the material we copy down from the corpus of People's Daily, and the other is the coarse-grained division of senses decided by the research group. One example is listed below:

医学/n 的/u 根本/a 目的/n 应该/v 是/v 保障/vn 人类/n 持续/vd 的/u 健康/an，/w 而/c 健康/a 的/u 概念/n 应/v 是/v "/w 一/m 种/q 躯体/n 、/w 精神/n 与/c 在/p 社会/n 中/f 的/u 完好/a 状态/n "/w 。/w

(the verb 是 (be) is the polysemy to be tested in this sentence)

(*The/art essential/a purpose/n of/p modern/a medicine/n is/v to/p ensure/v the/art sustainable/a health/n of/p human/a beings/n, while/conj the/art concept/n of/p health/n is/v the/art wellbeing/n of/p the/art body/n and/conj mind/n of/p the/art people/n in/p the/art society/n.*)

A) Be B) Exist C) Every D) Suitable

Eg. 1. One question on the questionnaire

The first goal of questionnaire is to test whether the participants can disambiguate the polysemy, in other words, whether they can choose the correct explanations of the polysemous words in the sentences. The questions on the questionnaire are unusual in that the language usage contexts of polysemy are Chinese, while the explanations for polysemy to be chosen are English. We design this questionnaire because it is held that the subjects finish the cognition process of Word Sense Disambiguation when they translate correctly the sense of the polysemy in the context.

The second goal of the questionnaire is to calculate the size of context window. The participants are asked to mark what components in the sentences affect their disambiguation. If they cannot mark the hint words in the sentence, they are asked to write down the clues or reasons they made the decision. The average distance, which is the size of context window, between the target polysemy and the hint words is counted according to the result of the survey.

3.3   Result Calculation

One result of the subjects' selection is the accuracy rate, in other words, the ratio that they make the right choice. Another result is the average distance range. We only take the right choice of explanation into consideration. In one sentence, we count all the hint words which influence the target polysemy, but we choose the highest frequency of them. Take one example to illustrate:

人民日报/nz（5）1948年/t 创刊/v（23），/w 出/v 对/p 开/v 4/m 版/n（12）。

(the verb 出 (*publish*) is the polysemy to be tested in this sentence)

(*People's Daily/nz   started/v   publication/n   in/p   1948/t,   and/conj   it/pron   published/v   in/p   quarter-fold/a   layout/n.*)

Eg. 2. The distance between the hint words and target polysemy

In this sentence, verb 出 (*publish*) is the target verb polysemy, 人民日报 (*People's Daily*), 创刊 (*start publication*) and 版 (*layout*) are the marked hint words. The numbers in the brackets are the frequency marked by the subjects. 创刊 (*start publication*) (23) and 版 (*layout*) (12) are the two hint words obtaining the highest number in this example. Then, the distance range 1-3 words is determined between hint words 创刊 (*start publication*), 版 (*layout*) and target polysemy 出 (*publish*).

Under one type of polysemy sentences, we calculate respective sentence's distance range between target polysemy and hint words. We add all the minimum number of word distances and divide the amount of sentences, at the same time we add the entire maximum number of word distances and divide the amount of sentences, and then the value we obtain is the window value.

We also concern the grammatical categories of the hint words and how they affect the target polysemy disambiguation. In this example, the two hint words 创刊 (start publication) and 版 (layout) influence the sense disambiguation of verb polysemy 出 (publish). We will focus on the verb category of 创刊 (start publication) and noun category of 版 (layout). For all the verb polysemy sentences, we will count how many nouns, verbs, adjectives and other word categories respectively influence the target verb polysemy disambiguation. By counting and ranking hint word's different categories, we obtain different word category's influence on the polysemy disambiguation.

4   Research Results and Analysis

4.1   Results of Annotation

The participants are sophomores in both English majors and non-English majors, 60 questionnaires were delivered and 54 were taken back. Participants' disambiguation of the polysemy verbs obtained 79% precision, polysemy nouns 80% precision and polysemy adjectives an impressive 85% precision. The high accuracy rate shows the high consistency of the choice of the subjects and it may be due to the coarse-grained division of senses adopted in this research. The overlapping, inclusive senses were reduced and the deleting senses were completed in the research through the analysis of the semantic relations among the sense entries. The sense entries are separated from each other and they have clear differentiation. Our research cleanses the clue to the sense distinction and strengthens the operability and the consistency of the sense disambiguation. In addition, coarse-grained classification ensures the description of the senses in common use more easily to be chosen by the subjects, and therefore, it leads to the higher accuracy rate.

4.2   Results of Window Value

The sizes of context window are 2.3-1.7 for verbs, 2.4-2.5 for nouns and 1.5-1.7 for adjectives. It is found that the window size of noun polysemy sentences is larger than the sizes of verb polysemy sentences and adjective polysemy sentences; the words on the left side of the polysemy verbs plays a more important role than the words on the right side; the left word distance and the right word distance is almost equal of the polysemy nouns and adjectives. The average window size is 2-2 for polysemy in the corpus of People's Daily based on the results of respective polysemy type's window values. The value is in great accordance with the results of Choueka at el. [8] and Hughes [9] who stated that the target word's 2-2 position was the best clue to define its meaning. Yarowsky [10] once pointed out nouns has close relationship with the theme of the texts and paragraphs which cover the larger content. As it is obvious, polysemy nouns have a large window value compared with verbs and adjectives because the texts and paragraphs from the corpus of People's Daily have definite theme and they cover a large content.

4.3   Results of Different Categories' Influences

As to the significance of each word category in polysemy disambiguation, we count according to different type of polysemy sentences, the result is as followed:

Noun polysemy sentences   N（48 %）> V（24 %）> A（15 %）> Ad（8%）
Verb polysemy sentences   N（48 %）> V（35 %）> A（8%）=Ad（8%）
Adjective polysemy sentences N（74 %）> Ad（10 %）> V（7%）

We can see nouns play vital role in disambiguating polysemy nouns/adjectives/verbs. The nouns' great influence on polysemy nouns is because of the particularity of the texts as mentioned above. The reason why nouns exert great influence on polysemy verbs in the sentences copied from the corpus is that verbs only appear in two grammatical structures: one is "adverbial+verb+complement" and the other is "subject+verb+object". The more quantity of the latter structure can easily explain the great influence of nouns on polysemy verbs disambiguation. Besides, in terms of the collocation of verbs and the components before and after it, the fixed collocation of nouns and different entries of the polysemy verbs is the most popular one, while adjectives and adverbials can seldom form that fixed collocations. Polysemy verbs disambiguation is realized through judging the semantic relations between verbs and its collinear noun components. Hence, it is easy to understand nouns can be the most influential factor of verbs sense disambiguation. In regard to the sense distinction of the polysemy adjectives, they tend to collocate with the fixed nouns, and vice versa it is no doubt nouns exert the considerable impact on the sense distinction of the polysemy adjectives.

5   Conclusions

The data in our research is from the non-annotated corpus of People's Daily. The sense knowledge in our research is from Hownet combined with Baidu online dictionary and the sense description of four researchers. The accuracy of the subjects' annotation of the questionnaire survey is high and the calculated window size is close to the results of the precedent researchers with computer linguistic background. This is an attempt for the researchers with linguistic background, who provide a new way to calculate the window size from the cognition process of the language users. We explore the way of sense description and calculate the window values of the context during the process of disambiguation based on manual distinction of senses of the polysemy. We find that different word categories have different influence on the disambiguation, among which nouns play the most important role. The findings are of great benefit to the usage of context information during the Word Sense Disambiguation.

Word Sense Disambiguation can be explored and the window size can be obtained through the questionnaire survey. For the future work, we can increase the number of polysemous words to be tested in the survey and interview the subjects to see how they think before they make the choice and what help them to disambiguate the senses in order to explore more about the context information from the angle of language users. The future work will provide new insights for the Word Sense Disambiguation.

Appendix

7 polysomic verbs：是 (*be*) （2） ，有 (*have*) （2） ，要 (*want*) （3） ，为 (*do*) （4） ，出 (*create*) （7） ，让 (*let*) （3） ，做 (*make*) （3） ；
11polysomic nouns：问题 (*trouble*) （3） ，文化 (*culture*) （3） ，思想 (*ideology*) （3） ，关系 (*relation*) （3） ，精神 (*spirit*) （3） ，组织 (*organization*) （3） ，情况 (*situation*) （3） ，历史 (*history*) （3） ，单位 (*unit*) （2） ，水平 (*level*) （2） ，作用 (*function*) （2） ；
6 polysomic adjectives：大 (*big*) （8） ，新 (*new*) （3） ，好 (*good*) （6） ，多 (*multiple*) （3） ，高 (*high*) （4） ，小 (*small*) （3） 。
（The numbers in the brackets are the numbers of the senses.）

References

1. Wu, Y.: A Survey of Chinese Word Sense Disambiguation Resources, Methods and Evaluations. Contemporary Linguistics **2**, 113–123 (2009). (in Chinese)
2. Kilgarriff, A.: I don't Believe in Word Senses. Computers and the Humanities **31**, 91–113 (1997)
3. Xiao, H.: The Sense Relations and Sense Distinction of Polysemes in the Dictionary. Journal of Yunnan Normal University (Humanities and Social Sciences) **1**, 43–48 (2010). (in Chinese)
4. Lu, S., Bai, S.: Quantitative Analysis of Context Field in Natural Language Processing. Chinese J. Computers **7**, 742–747 (2001). (in Chinese)
5. Lin, J., Wang, H.: The Strategies for Sense Disambiguation of Chinese Polysomic Verbs. Journal of Yunnan Normal University (Humanities and Social Sciences) **1**, 55–60 (2010). (in Chinese)
6. Lan, M.: Methods of Word Sense Disambiguation. Science and Technology Information **9**, 478–482 (2010). (in Chinese)
7. Martin, W., Van Sterkenburg, P.: On the Processing of Text Corpus. In: Hartmann, R. (ed.) Lexicography: Principles and Practice, New York, pp. 56–64 (1983)
8. Choueka, Y., Lusignan, S.: Disambiguation by Short Contexts. Computers and the Humanities **19**, 147–158 (1985)
9. John, H.: Automatically Acquiring a Classification of Words [PhD dissertation]. University of Leeds, Paris (1994)
10. David, Y.: One Sense per Collocation. In: Process ARPA Human Language Technology Workshop, Boston, pp. 266–271 (1993)

Conventionalizing Common Sense for Chinese Textual Entailment Recognition

Shengjian Ni[1(✉)], Yichen Chen[2], and Donghong Ji[2]

[1] School of Foreign Languages, Anqing Normal University,
Anqing 246000, Anhui, China
`hijackon@163.com`
[2] School of Computer, Wuhan University, Wuhan 430000, China
`donghong_ji2000@yahoo.com.cn`

Abstract. Textual entailment relations between concrete expressions and abstract concepts such as linguistic functions, attributes of entities and their values, emotions, moods, and situations, scenes, fields, occupations, etc can not be obtained with the help of syntactic transformation or dependency analysis. Usually, it is considered that to obtain these entailment relations common sense is needed, which makes the process of achieving these relations unpredictable. Lexical functions and scripts own the ability to conventionalize the common senses, which makes the recognition of these textual entailments predictable and derivable and thus improves corpus coverage in recognition of Chinese textual entailments.

Keywords: Textual Entailment Recognition (RTE) · Common sense · Lexical function (LF) · Script · Conventionalization

1 Introduction

It has been pointed out that *recognition of textual entailments* (RTE for short) is the core of most *natural language processing* (NLP for short)[1]. If the truth of one text snippet (the entailed text snippet, called "hypothesis"(H for short)) comes from the truth of another text snippet (the entailing one, called "text"(T for short), then it can be said that there is *textual entailment* (TE for short) relationship between theses two text snippets, e.g.,

(1)a. 男：停 车， 停 车 ！ 对 不 起 ， 请 出 示 您 的 驾 驶 执 照．
   (Man: Stop, stop! Excuse me, your driving license, please.)
   女：请 您 高 抬 贵 手 ， 放 过 我 这 一 次 吧 ！ *(Woman: I beg your leniency, please, let me get away this time!)*(T)
   问：说 话 的 两 个 人 很 可 能 是 什 么 关 系 ？ *(Question: What might be the relationship between the two speakers?)*
   A. 警 察 和 嫌 疑 犯 *(a policeman and a suspect).* B. 交 警 和 司 机 *(a traffic policeman and a driver).*
   C. 收 费 员 和 司 机 *(a tollman and a driver).* D. 门 卫 和 司 机 *(a gatekeeper and a driver)*

© Springer International Publishing Switzerland 2014
X. Su and T. He (Eds.): CLSW 2014, LNAI 8922, pp. 286–295, 2014.
DOI: 10.1007/978-3-319-14331-6_29

b. 答：B. 即 " 说 话 的 两 个 人 很 可 能 是 交 警 和 司 机 ".(*Answer: B, i.e. "The two speakers might be traffic policeman and a driver.*)(H)

This example tells us that we can get (1)b from (1)a, i.e. (1) entails (1)b or (1)b is entailed by (1)a and there is entailment relationship between (1)a and (1)b. Specifically speaking, the relationship between (1)a and (1)b belongs to the TE relation of concrete expressions and the abstract concept of occasion (judgment).

Existing studies usually recognize TE relations from the perspectives of word relations, syntax transformation, or dependency analysis. Nevertheless, these methods are not applicable in finding out the TE relations between many text snippets, as is exemplified in the above example. TE relations between these text snippets that can not be digged out by existing methods includes: TE relations between concrete expressions/utterances and such abstract concepts as meta-linguistic functions, entity attributes and their values, feelings, and moods, occasions, scenes, fields, professions, etc. These TE relations between concrete expressions and abstract concepts account for about 30% of all the TE relations, according to existing corpus the author owns.

The excavation of these entailment relations between concrete expressions and abstract concepts usually involves common sense and is thus considered to lack predictability or derivability. To compensate for this disadvantage, this paper tries to introduce lexical functions and scripts to help dig out these TE relations between concrete expressions and abstract concepts as are mentioned above. Studies shows that lexical functions and scripts both have the ability to conventionalize common sense during the process of finding out TE relations between text snippets.

In this study, conventionalization is understood as follows:

Utilizing lexical functions, image schemata, etc to find out the inevitability of common sense that are usually considered as haphazard, endowing common sense with certain structure(s)/relation(s), predicability, and derivability.

From this definition, it can be seen that both LFs and image schemata have the capability of conventionalizing common sense. Of all the image schemata, scripts own the main and typical functions of conventionalization. We can refer to Ni and Ji[2] for the concept of script and the following sections starts with the notion of LF, and then it is demonstrated how LFs and scripts show their function of conventionalization during the process of RTE.

2   Lexical Function

As one of the main contents of *Meaning-Text Theory* [3][4], *lexical functions* (LFs for short) are the core means for expressing the many-to-many respondences between meaning(s) and texts and they can effectively replace a lot of transformation work when suitable.Mel'čuk defines LF as follows:

LF is a kind of function used to express particular relations and it related a particular lexical unit with a group of lexical units with similar meaning, and a lexical function can be stated as: $f(L) = \{Li\}$[3]

A lexical unit is the unification of particular meaning and form; and according to the above definition, f expresses specific relation and Li stands for serval lexical units with similar meaning. Every LF expresses a specific sense of a word/linguistic unit; and if a word/linguistic unit has several senses, there will be corresponding number of LFs for it. Clearly, a lexical unit can be a word or other linguistic units bigger than words. Study shows that besides meaning similarity, LFs can also express syntagmatic, paradigmatic, and some logical relations between lexical units.

In this study, LFs are utilized to directly show the corresponding entailment relations between many abstract concepts and concrete language expressions, as is exemplified in the examples in the following sections.

3   LFs and Scripts' Conventionalizing Function in RTE

Conventionalization of common sense starts at the latest in 1970s[5][6][7][8]. Nevertheless, these is a lack of deep or comprehensive study in related perspectives. And this section offers a comparatively overall discussion of the conventionalization function of LFs and scripts in RTE of Chinese.

The entailment correspondences between such abstract concepts as meta-linguistic functions, attributes and their values, and feelings, moods, etc and concrete expressions lack structures or systematicness; and it is suitable to conventionalize the common sense involved in the recognition of these entailment correspondences with help of LFs. Meanwhile, conventionalization of the common sense involved in the recognition of the entailment correspondences between such abstract concepts as occasions, scenes, professions, fields and concrete expressions is suitable to be carried out drawing on scripts, as common sense involved here owns clear structures and systematicness.

3.1   Conventionalization Function of LFs in Chinese RTE

Two kinds of clues can be used in RTE that involves meta-linguistic functions, attributes and their values, and feelings, moods, etc. The first kind of clue is the relations between abstract concepts, such as synonymy, antonymy, hypernymy, etc, e.g., 漂亮 (pretty), 美丽 (beautiful), 英俊 (handsome) all tell us that somebody are good-looking; the second kind of clue is the entailment correspondences between abstract concepts and concrete expressions, which has not be paid attention to and the conventionalization of which is the main content of this subsection.

3.1.1   Conventionalization Function of LFs in Recognizing the Entailment Relations Between Meta-Linguistic Functions and Concrete Expressions

For example,

(2)a. 女：我实在 太 喜欢他 了，就给他 写 了 信，可 是 他 也 不 回 信，每次见了 面 呢，就 像 什么也 没发生过一样，真让人 搞 不懂.(*Woman: I liked him so much that I wrote him, but he did not write back and very time he met me he acted as if that nothing has happened.*)

男：别烦恼了，不 **妨 再 写 信**. (*Man: Don't worry, you might as well write him again.*)(T)

b. 男 的 在 向 女 的 提 建 议. (*The man is offering suggestion to the woman.*)(H)

It can be judged that (2)a entails (2)b. To obtain such a conclusion, one of the key is to decide that 不妨 (*might as well*) has the function of 提 建 议 (*offering suggestion*) ; and this kind of entailment relation can be expressed directly with the following LF:

提 建 议 (*offering suggestion*) == 不 妨 (*might as well*)..., 为 什 么 不 (*why not*)..., 你 觉 得...如 何 ？ (*How about ......*)

This LF means that all these concrete expressions to the right of the equation entail the meta-linguistic function to the left of the equation. This LF is helpful for a computer to decide the entailment relation between (2)a and (2)b.

3.1.2   Conventionalization Function of LFs in Recognizing the Entailment Relations Between Attributes, Their Values and Concrete Expressions

Linguistic ontologies (e.g. taxonomy of HowNet)usually contain only abstract concepts such as attributes and their values and there is a lack of entailment correspondences between these abstract concepts and concrete expressions[9]. However, in listening or reading understanding of language teaching, students are often required to decide the entailment relationship between attributes, their values and concrete expressions, e.g.,

(3)a. 大 山 里 的 村 姑 和 都 市 里 的 小 姐 ， 同 样 有 "沉 鱼 落 雁 之 容 ， 闭 月 羞 花 之 貌". (*Both some countrywomen and some misses from cities have the looks that makes fish and wild geese to fall down, and makes flowers to feel inferior.*)(T)

b. 这 句 话 的 意 思 是 ： 大 山 里 的 村 姑 和 都 市 里 的 小 姐 都 有 很 漂 亮 的.(*This sentence means that both some countrywomen and some misses from cities are beautiful.*)(H)

For a native speaker of Chinese, it is easy to decide that (3)a entails (3)b. It is usually considered that RTE of this example involves common sense, and the process or motivations behind this recognition cannot be made clear with existing RTE methods.

In the taxonomy of HowNet, 相 貌 (*looks*), as an attribute, owns two abstract concepts: 美 (*beautiful*) and 丑 (*ugly*). In (3)b, 漂 亮 (*pretty*) is the a synonym of (貌) 美 (*beautiful*) at an abstract level. The values of looks are abstract concepts, however, these utterances used to express these abstract concepts are usually concrete and embodied, drawing on such cognitive models as metonymy and metaphor[10]. Some of these utterances are indirect, e.g., 沉 鱼 落 雁, 闭 月 羞 花 (she *has the looks that makes fish and wild geese to fall down , and makes flowers to feel inferior*); some of them are direct, e.g. 手 如 柔 荑 ， 肤 如 凝 脂 (*her hands are like soft grass and her skin is like congealed fat*).

To obtain the entailment relationship between these concrete utterances and abstract concepts, we can also construct a LF to conventionalize the entailment relationship:

(貌) 美 (*beautiful*) = = 沉 鱼 落 雁, 闭 月 羞 花, 倾 城 倾 国 (*makes cities and nations fall down, i.e. drop-dead gorgeous*), 手 如 柔 荑 ， 肤 如 凝 脂 ， ......

This LF means that all these expressions to the right of the equation entail/imply that somebody (usually a girl or woman) is (very) beautiful.

3.1.3 Conventionalization Function of LFs in Recognizing the Entailment Relations Between   Abstract Feelings and Concrete Expressions

RTE between abstract feelings and concrete expressions has certain proportion in language teaching, e.g.,

(4) a. 可 惜 的 是, 鸡血 石经三 四 百 年 的开采，产量 日渐稀 少, 现 采 地 已 封 坑, 由 此 引发了 近 年 来鸡血 石 市 价 直线上升. (*It is a pity that after several hundred years of exploitation, the output of oriental jasper is decreasing day by day and now the mines have been shut down, which leads to the fast rise of the prices of oriental jasper.*)(T)
问 : 作 者 的 心 情 是 : A. 欣 慰   B. 气愤   C.遗憾   D. 无 所 谓. (*Question: The mood of the author is : A. Delighted. B. Angry. C. Regretful. D. Indifferent.*)
   b. 答 : 作 者 的 心 情 是遗 憾. (*Answer: The mood of the author is regretful.*)(H)

A native speaker of Chinese can judge with ease the entailment relation between (4)a and (4)b, and for a computer to carry out this task, the following LF should be helpful:

遗 憾 (*Regretful*) = = 可 惜 (*it is a pity*),(非 常) 抱 歉 (*I am very sorry*), 引 以 为 憾 (*deem it regrettable*), 恨 不 相 逢 未 嫁 时 (*regret meeting a true lover only after one's marriage*),...

Similarly, all these expressions to the right of the equation entail the mood of *regretful*.

While analyzing feelings expressed by concrete utterances, we can refer to certain linguistic ontologies, e.g. HowNet. However, linguistic ontologies usually do not offer the correspondent entailment relations between abstract concepts and concrete expressions, which implies that there is a need to overcome this inadequacy and LFs can play an irreplaceable role in this job.

3.2 Conventionalization Function of Scripts in RTE

There are also two kinds of clues that are useful in RTE involving fields, scenes, and occasions, professions: clues between abstract concepts, and clues between abstract concepts and concrete , embodied expressions. The latter clues are the study content of this subsection.

As early as 1970s, some schloars, including Schank & Abelson[7], began to study the conventionalization function of scripts, though there were no related systematic or comprehensive studies.

Study shows that scripts are applicable in conventionalizing the common sense involved in recognizing the entailment relations between fields, scenes, occasions, professions and concrete utterances, as will be exemplified in the following subsections respectively.

3.2.1 Conventionalization Function of Scripts in Recognizing the Entailment Relations Between Fields and Concrete Expressions

In the taxonomy of HowNet, fields belong to the *Secondary feature*, and the entailment relations between certain fields and concrete expressions can be linked through scripts, e.g.,

> (5) a. 中 央电视台 新闻评论部 今 年 3 月开始 推 出 的 《实话实说》 栏目 播 出 后 引 起 了观众 的 极 大兴趣，同时引 起 了 影视评 论界 的关注. (*Great interest of the audience has been aroused since the department of news analysis of CCTV began to release the column Speak the Plain Truth, and meanwhile, the attention of critical circles of Film and Video has also been attracted.*)(T)
>
> b. 《实话实说》是电视栏目. (*Speak the Plain Truth is a TV column.*) (H)

This is a typical example of field judging in RTE and because of the dispersal of related information in different places of concerned text snippet(s), this kind of examples are difficult to be conventionalized by LFs. However, they are suitable to be conventionalized by scripts in many occasions.

Particular words or events of certain fields can be expressed in the form of scripts. As far as the field of TV is concerned, there might be different variants of the TV script. However, in concrete contexts like (5), a general script sketch can be very helpful for RTE, e.g., the following script sketch of TV column from the perspective of audience is crucial for RTE of (5):

Script: TV column
Roles: TV station, the department of news analysis, TV column, audience, *critical circles of TV, TV presenter*, television reporter, ...
Purpose: Making TV column
Scene 1: Preliminary planning
Scene 2: Material preparation
Scene 3: Material arrangement
Scene 4: Broadcasting

This script sketch of TV column can contribute to the computer recognition of the entailment relationship between (5)a and (5)b. Of this script, the following roles play an important role in discriminating the TV column script from other scripts (e.g. scripts of broadcast station): TV station, critical circles of TV, and television reporter, etc. As all these roles are typical of the script of TV column. With the help of this and script and certain algorithm, a computer can decide with ease that (5)a entails (5)b.

Nevertheless, because of the unawareness of cognition, the processes or motivations of TE can not be made clear completely and results of RTE in NLP are probabilistic.

3.2.2 Conventionalization Function of Scripts in Recognizing the Entailment Relations Between Occasions, Scenes and Concrete Expressions

Both *occasion* and *scene* are based on certain physical circumstances. An *occasion* obtains dynamic event(s) and a scene is characteristic of static event(s) or scenery. Both *occasion* and *scene* can be conventionalized by scripts in RTE.

3.2.2.1   Judgment of Occasions. Scripts can describe dynamic events with special logical relations (e.g. Cause-effect relation) and thus they can be motivations in judging occasions, e.g.,

(6)a. 男：一 块 五 两 斤， 又 新 鲜 又 好 吃 啊 ！大 娘， 买 点 儿
　　　回 去 尝 尝 ！ (*Man: One yuan and a half per kilogram, fresh and delicious! Aunt, buy some to have a taste!*)
　　女 ：这 么 贵 呀， 便 宜 点 儿 吧， 一 块 钱 两 斤 ！ (*It is expensive, a little cheap please, one yuan per kilogram!*)(T)
　　b. 我 们 可 能 在 农 贸 市 场 听 到 这 段 对 话. (*We may hear the above conversation in a farmer's market.*)(H)

To help recognizing the entailment relation between (8)a and (8)b, we can construct the following script sketch for farmer's market from the perspective of buyers:

Script: Farmer's market
Roles: Buyers, sellers, vegetables, foods, fixings, money, weighing apparatus, ...
Purpose: Buy foods and fixings for daily use.
Scene 1: Get into a farmer's market
Scene 2: Look for vegetables, foods or fixings wanted, go to certain booths
Scene 3: Asking prices, offering prices, counter offering, determining prices, finishing the trade (here the Commerce_Transaction Frame from the FrameNet project can be embedded.)
Scene 4: Get out of the market.

In scene 3, the importance of asking prices, offering prices,and counter offering are different, and offering prices is the most important and counter offering is of least importance. These meta-linguistic functions in scene 3 can be recognized with the methods demonstrated in 3.1.1.

So far, it can be decided that (6)b may be entailed by (6)a.

Studies show that in suitable situations frames from the FrameNet project can be embedded in scripts as scripts are composed of events which are often expressed in the form of frames. This kind of embedding is of great significance as the FrameNet project is a comparatively mature resource of NLP.

3.2.2.2 Judgment of Scenes. Scripts can also describe static events and act as motivations in judging scenes,e.g.,

(7) a. 这 个 不 大 的 屋 子 里 有 四 张 床， 每 张 床 前 有 一 个 小 书 桌 ， 左 边 两 床 之 间 有 一 个 书 架， 书 架 上 放 满 了 书, 桌 子 上 、 椅 子 上 、 床 上 也 都 是 乱 七 八 糟 的 书 。 屋 角 有 一 个 脸 盘 架， 上 面 放 着 几 个 脸 盆， 最 上 边 的 脸 盆 还 有 一 副 网 球 拍. (*This is not a big room with four beds inside, and in front of every bed there is a little desk; there is a bookshelf between the left two beds and books are squeezed in on the bookshelf; there are all books scattered on desks, chairs, and beds. At the corner of the room, there lies a washbasin rack with some basins in it and there is a tennis racket in the basin at the top.*)(T)
问 : 这 是 什 么 地 方 ？ A. 办 公 室   B. 客 厅   C. 教 室   D. 学 生 宿 舍 (Question: What is this place? A. It is an office. B. It is a saloon. C. It is classroom. D. It a students' dorm.)
    b. 答 : 这 个 地 方 是 D. 学 生 宿 舍. (*Answer: This place is a students' dorm.*)(H)

Dorms are different from other kinds of rooms. By default, if there are several/many beds and appliances of study, living, and sports in a room, it can be decided with great certainty that the room is a dorm. The following script sketch of students' dorm is helpful in deciding the entailment relationship between (7)a and (7)b:

Script: Students' dorm
Roles :   Student(s),   appliances of study, living, and sports
Purpose(s): live, study

This script describe a static scene with no dynamic events. Though there is no single role that can differentiate this scene from others, the combination of several roles can offer us a basically correct decision. With the help of this script and certain algorithm, a computer can make a right decision with little difficulty.

3.2.3 Conventionalization Function of Scripts in Recognizing the Entailment Relations Between Professions and Concrete Expressions

There are also a lot of RTE examples that are based on judgment of professions and motivated by scripts,e.g,

(8) a. 我 们 两 口 子 都 很 忙， ……我 不 坐 班， 白 天 接 待 来 访 的 客 人 和 朋 友, 晚 上 写 文 章 写 到 半 夜, 从 凌 晨 四 点 到 上 午 九 点 是 我 的 休 息 时间。经 常 是 我 还 没 有 起 床, 就 有 人 敲 门 了. (*Our couple are very busy, ...I do not keep office hours, receiving visitors and friends daytime, and writing articles until midnight; my resting time is from four o'clock to nine in the morning. Regularly, there is already someone knocking at the door before I get up .*)(T)

问 ： 我 大 概 是 做 什 么 工 作 的 ？ (*Question: What is the occupation of "I"*)

A. 大 学 教 师 或 作 家 B. 编 辑 或 作 家 C. 大 学 老 师 或 大 夫
　　D. 编 辑 或 大 夫

(A. University faculty or writer.　　B. Editor or writer.
C. University faculty or doctor.　　D. Editor or doctor

b. 答 ： B. 我 大 概 是 做 编 辑 或 作 家. (*Answer: "I" is probably an editor or writer.*)(H)

Occupations vary in many facets, such as workplace, affair, and schedule, etc. Though there might be overlap in these facets, the combination of the contents of these facets offers the possibility to differentiate one occupation from another in concrete contexts. Of course, when there is not enough information, only an ambiguous answer can be offered, as is exemplified by this example.

Similarly, script sketches of university faculty, writer, and editor, doctor are helpful in recognizing the entailment relationship between (8)a and (8)b. As the methods and principles of constructing these script sketches are the same, only the scripts of writer and editor are given as follows.

Script: Writer
Role(s): Writer
Classification: Poets, prosers, novelists, playwrights, etc.
Schools: Romantic, solemn, emotional, graceful and restrained, etc.
Purpose(s): Create literary images/systems and literary world of implication, etc.
Workplace: (Mainly) home, libraries.
People dealt with: Editors, readers, etc.
Schedule: Irregular
The script sketch of editor is much simpler than that of writer:
Script: Editor
Role(s): Editor
Purposes: Editing others' articles or literary works according to the requirements of publishing
Workplace: (Mainly) editorial offices, home, libraries.
People dealt with: Writers, readers, etc.
Schedule: comparatively regular

With the help of concerned scripts (including the above two scripts) that are activated by elements in the involved text snippets and suitable similarity algorithms, a computer can decide that B is the best choice for the above example.

The above examples imply that construction of scripts should take into consideration such factors as the need to understand certain texts and the characteristics of the concerned methods of NLP.

Study shows that script elements own different ability of differentiating one script from another, thus, drawing on these elements, the entailment relations obtained may vary in probability.

4 Conclusion

This paper shows LFs and scripts' conventionalization function of common sense in RTE. In other words, both LFs and scripts have the ability to endow common sense with structures, predictability, and derivability, which should have the potential to increase corpus coverage and further improve the effects of RTE in NLP. To obtain this improvement in practice of RTE, at least two things should be further done in the future. On one hand, further and complete studies on conventionalization of common sense in virtue of LFs and scripts should be carried out; on the other hand, corresponding resources such as corpora of scripts and Chinese Explanatory Combinatorial Dictionary based on LFs should be constructed, which should be a tremendous job. This study also shows that for a linguistic ontology to be applicable in NLP, there is a need to link these abstract concepts of ontologies with concrete expressions, drawing on LFs and image schemata.

References

1. Pazienza, M.T., Pennacchiotti, M., Zanzotto, F.M.: A linguistic inspection of textual entailment. In: Bandini, S., Manzoni, S. (eds.) AI*IA 2005. LNCS (LNAI), vol. 3673, pp. 315–326. Springer, Heidelberg (2005)
2. 倪 盛 俭, 姬 东 鸿. 基 于 图 式 的 文 本 蕴 涵 识 别 初 探. 14 届 汉 语 词 汇 语 义 学 国 际 会 议 论 文 集, 中 国, 郑 州 (2013). (Ni, S., Ji, D.: A Tentative Exploration into Recognition of Textual Entailments Based on Image Schemata. In: Chinese Lexical Semantics Workshop (CLSW-15), Zhengzhou, China (2013))
3. Mel'čuk, I.: Lexical Functions in Lexicographic Description. In: Proc. of the 8th Annual Meeting of Berkeley Linguistic Society (1982)
4. Mel'čuk, I.: Lexical functions: a tool for the description of lexical relations in a lexicon. Lexical Functions in Lexicography and Natural Language Processing **31**, 37–102 (1996)
5. Minsky, M.: Frame-systems. AI. Memo. Mass. Institute of Technology, Cambridge (1974)
6. Schank, R.C.: Identification of conceptualizations underlying natural language. Computer Models of Thought and Language **187**, 247 (1973)
7. Schank, R.: The structure of episodes in memory. In: Bobrow, D., Collins, T. (eds.) Representation and understanding: Studies in cognitive science. Academic, New York (1975)
8. Schank, R.C., Abelson, R.P.: Scripts, plans, and knowledge. Yale University (1975)
9. 萧 国 政, 等. 从 概 念 基 元 空 间 到 语 义 基 元 空 间 的 映 射, 华 东 师 范 大 学 学 报 (哲 学 和 社 会 科 学) (1), 139–143 (2011). (Xiao, G., et al.: Mapping from the Space of Conceptual Primitives to the Space of Semantic Primitives. Journal of East China Normal University (Philosophy and Social Sciences) (1), 139–143 (2011))
10. 张 辉, 卢 卫 中. 认 知 转 喻. 上 海: 上 海 外 语 教 育 出 版 社 (2010). (Zhang, H., Lu, W.: Cognitive Metonymy. Shanghai Foreign Language Education Press, Shanghai (2010))

Scale-Free Distribution in Chinese Semantic Field Network: A Main Cause of Using the Shortest Path Length for Representing Semantic Distance Between Terms

Hua Yang[1,2(✉)], Mingyao Zhang[3], Donghong Ji[4], and Guozheng Xiao[2]

[1] School of Mathematics and Computer Science, Guizhou Normal University,
Guiyang 550001, China
yanghuastory@foxmail.com
[2] College of Chinese Language and Literature, Wuhan University, Wuhan 430072, China
gzxiao@foxmail.com
[3] School of Foreign Languages and Literature, Wuhan University, Wuhan 430072, China
myzhang@whu.edu.cn
[4] School of Computer, Wuhan University, Wuhan 430072, China
donghongji_2000@yahoo.com

Abstract. In large-scale network, using the weighted shortest path length to evaluate the relatedness between two terms is factually infeasible because of the actual time and space consumption, despite the fact that the related classic algorithm runs at complexity of $o(n^3)$. However, in many natural language processing tasks, what we need to do is merely obtain the terms which are most related to a given term rather than obtain relatedness between every pair of terms, which makes it possible for using shortest path length between two terms within a large-scale complex network to evaluate semantic relatedness between two terms. Furthermore, one of the semantic field network's important properties—scale-free distribution of node degree makes it much more feasible to use the shortest path length to evaluate semantic distance between two terms.

Keywords: Semantic field network · Complex network · Semantic relatedness · Scale-free distribution · Shortest path length

1 Introduction

It is often required to measure semantic relatedness, also called semantic distance between two terms in many natural language processing. In most cases, it is required to obtain only the most related terms and evaluate the relatedness between each of the most related terms and a given term. For example, for query expansion technique used in information retrieval, it is necessary and sufficient to obtain the terms having the highest relatedness to the user query, and evaluate the relatedness between the expanded term and the user query. For the above-mentioned problem, most traditional

© Springer International Publishing Switzerland 2014
X. Su and T. He (Eds.): CLSW 2014, LNAI 8922, pp. 296–304, 2014.
DOI: 10.1007/978-3-319-14331-6_30

methods compute the relatedness between every pair of terms and use the process of sorting the numerical value as one indispensible step so as to obtain R terms which are most semantically closed to the related to given source term. Traditional methods are mainly categorized as two: 1) the methods based on manual resources; and 2) the methods based on statistics [1-4]. The former institute rules to compute relatedness between two terms based on linguists' intuition and the structure of the manual resource, such as dictionary or thesaurus [3-10]. The latter retrieve contexts of the two terms based on concurrence information in large-scale corpus, and use the similarity between the two contexts to evaluate relatedness between the two terms [2, 11-15], with the method of evaluating similarity between two contexts based on space distance, set operation, etc.

Chinese semantic field is defined as the semantic system composed of meaning of all Chinese terms. We proposed using complex network to represent this type of semantic system. After modifying the earlier version of network we have constructed, we expect to employ the concept of shortest path length to evaluate the semantic relatedness, i.e. the semantic distance. However, this idea confronts the difficulty while using the classic algorithms for computing shortest path length because of the large scale of the modified version of network. To solve this problem, we analyzed in detail the feature of the original problem and the intrinsic process of the most popular classic algorithms, and found the solution. Furthermore, we discovered that the network's node degree obeys the scale-free distribution, which is another important and contributive factor for lowering real time and space consumption. It is emphasized that the contribution of the network's scale-free distribution is indispensible for the feasibility of the solution. Since question of computability, which is about why we can obtain the shortest path length in such a large-scale network as semantic distance between linguistic units, is often raised by the readers of our previous papers, we will answer it in detail in this paper. Also, it is confirmed that other researchers can use the similar method if the node degree of the network they constructed obeys the scale-free distribution.

This paper is organized as follows. Section 1 introduces the concept of semantic field, especially the association semantic field and presents the construction of semantic field network. Section 2 describes the reason for modifying the original version of network and defines the semantic relatedness between two terms in the modified version of network. Section 3 discusses the solution for obtaining R terms with the top R relatedness, i.e., the lowest semantic distance, to a given term. Section 4 presents the scale-free distribution of node degree of the semantic field network, and explains how it contributes to the feasibility of the found solution.

2   Semantic Field Network

2.1   Concept of Association Field and Construction of Semantic Field Network

Semantic field is defined as a system composed of more than one term's meaning. The concept of association field originated from the idea of term association by Saussure [16, 17]. Ullmann defined the semantic field as a network surrounding the given term. Every term is surrounded by a network and then connects itself to other terms [18][19]. An interesting question is raised by the following example. Given a term "奥 运 会 (ao yun hui, the Olympic Games)" as stimulus, why most people associate it with "金 牌 (jin pai, gold medal) ", "世 界 冠 军 (shi jie guan jun, world champion)", and so on? We hold that this psychological process originated from the common sense of most people, and, indirectly, originated from the widely-used media, including paper, television, web page, and so on. More specifically, the reason is that these terms often co-occur in a given topic-related text, especially as keywords. Another interesting phenomenon is presented in the following examples. If three terms: "刘 翔 (Liu Xiang, a famous hurdler in China) ", "跑 步 (pao bu, running) ", and "冠 军 (guan jun, champion) " are put together, most people will determine that 刘 翔 is the famous hurdler instead of a common person; and "run" is a high level match instead of normal running. Namely, given no syntactic information and precise process of analyzing sememe, we can still understand the meaning of the each term, with more precision than each term alone.

Based on the concept of semantic association field, it can be seen that terms in the same field have higher co-occurrence frequency than otherwise. On the contrary, the higher possibility two terms co-occur, the higher possibility they belong to the same one field. So, it is reasonable to decide whether two terms belong to a field from the viewpoint of possibility rather than from the viewpoint of dualism: the higher co-occurrence frequency for two terms, the higher possibility they belong to the same field. This concept of field is an expanded one and it is a generalized version of semantic field, which is a not so precise compared with the definition in linguistics, but more practical in natural language processing.

2.2   Construction of Chinese Semantic Field Network

Semantic field is defined as the system of term's meaning [20]. A language's semantic field is composed of all terms in the language and the relationship among the terms. We tried to use more than one kind of networks to approximately represent the Chinese term field. The network described in this paper is the best one of the networks employed in our earlier work, which aims at expanding complex query described in natural language for information retrieval task, notated as KTCN-R. The construction process is as follows: 1) extract key terms for all texts in a corpus; 2) for each paragraph of each text, if two key terms of this text co-occur in a paragraph, it is expected that the two terms tend to be in the same field, then add these two terms into KTCN-R with one unidirectional edge between them and attach the new edge a weight value of 1. 3) If that link exits in the KTCN-R, just increase the edge weight by 1 instead of generating a new edge.

After KTCN-R is constructed, an edge, together with the weight attached to it, is used to express the relationship of association. The edge itself means that the two terms involved may have possibility to possess association relationship between them, with the weight evaluating the possibility. In computer science, the node of KTCN-R is merely character string, which is not close to the concept of term meaning. However, as mentioned above, a term can express its own meaning if they are surrounded by the terms around it. Note that we emphasize that the term is a node of the network instead of an isolated element.

A question may be raised that why we places emphasis on using key terms as network nodes. The answer is that two terms in a field do not necessarily possess syntactic relationship or co-occur in a small window, such as a sentence.

2.3 Modification of Network and Definition of Semantic Relatedness Between Two Terms

From the standpoint of graph theory, the lower the numerical value of a shortest path length, the geographically closer between the starting node and the ending node of the path. In KTCN-R, the higher weight attached to an edge, the closer the semantic distance between the two terms involved, which are linked directly by the edge. This fact contradicts the actual meaning of shortest path length in most algorithms for computing the shortest path length, in which low edge weight expresses the concept of closeness. To resolve this contradiction, we modified the weights on the edges of KTCN-R as follows: define MaxEdgeWeight as the maximum of the edge weight of KTCN-R, modified each edge weight as: NewEdgeWeight = MaxEdgeWeight − OldEdgeWeight +1. The modified version of KTCN-R is notated as M-KTCN-R.

After the modification operation, we can define the semantic distance for two terms as the length of the shortest path between the two terms involved which are the starting node and ending node of the path in M-KTCN-R respectively.

3 The Method for Obtaining top Nodes with Lowest Shortest Path Lengths from Source Node

Although the semantic distance is defined for two terms, it is worth discussing how we can obtain R terms which are the most semantically related to a given source term. In a large network, it is never a simple problem that can be easily solved by employing classic algorithms.

3.1 Algorithm Selection and Complexity Analysis

To compute the shortest path length, two classic algorithms can be employed: Floyed algorithm and Dijkstra algorithm [21].

For the general principle of Floyed algorithm, see Ref. [21] for detailed information. The core operation of Floyed algorithm is shown in Formula 1, where k is the numerical notation of the node to be considered while adding a new node into possible paths already obtained, i is the starting node notation of the path, and j is the ending node notation of the path. Implementing Floyed algorithm necessitate a assisting sequence of matrix: $\{ D^{(-1)}, D^{(0)}, D^{(1)}, \ldots, D^{(k)}, \ldots, D^{(n-1)} \}$ where $D^{(-1)}[i][j]$ is the length of the path form   node v_i to node v_j, with no other node in the path except v_i and

v_j themselves, i.e., there is only one edge in the path. Each element in

$D^{(k)}[i][j]=\text{Min}\{\ D^{(k-1)}[i][j]\ ,\ D^{(k-1)}[i][k]+D^{(k-1)}[i][j]\ \}\ (0 \leq k \leq n-1)$ is the length of the path which pass the nodes which has the numerical notations lower than k or equal to k, but not pass the nodes which has the numerical notations higher than k. So, elements in $D^{(n-1)}[i][j]$ is the length of shortest path length between v_i and v_j.

if (D[i][k] + D[k][j] < D[i][j]) D[i][j] = D[i][k]+D[k][j];   Formula 1

Dijkstra algorithm can be used to solve the problem of obtaining shortest path from a given source node, i.e., starting node, to every other node in a network. For the problem of computing all shortest path length between every pair of nodes in a network, it is required to set every node as the source node and call the above process n times, where n is the number of nodes of a network.

If the purpose is to obtain every path for each pair of nodes in a network, both Floyed algorithm and Dijkstra algorithm runs at the complexity of $O(n^3)$. However, even with the complexity of $O(n^3)$, which is an acceptable complexity in algorithm theory, the algorithm is factually infeasible for very large-scale network.

As far as the Floyed algorithm is concerned, it is unacceptable for its space consumption: we investigated the connectivity property of KTCN and found it was highly connected and its largest component contained almost all nodes of the whole network. So, $D^{(n-1)}$ can never be a sparse matrix. If unsigned integer type of C language is employed to represent the notation of each node, about 1900 gigabytes of memory space is required, which is condition difficult to satisfy.

However, for many NLP tasks, it is unnecessary to compute semantic distances for each pair of terms. For example, the aim of query expansion technique used in query expansion is to obtain the terms most related to the user query.

For this kind of tasks, within M-KTCN-R, the algorithm that we need should possess two features: 1) the algorithm can be directed at a given source node; 2) for a given source node, R nodes with the top shortest path lengths to the source node can be found without needing to compute all shortest path lengths, R<<n, where n is the node number of the network. These two requirements lower the time consumption to a great extent. The requirements also negate the usability of Floyed algorithm because no path can be determined as the shortest before the algorithm is finished.

On the contrary, Dijkstra algorithm can obtain R lowest path length beginning with the given starting node, from the lowest one the highest one.

Furthermore, if adjacency multilist is adopted as storage structure for a network, only the nodes which are detected before but not determined as the nearest, should be searched. This intrinsic operation lowers the time consumption further. Consider the average case, the operation of searching R nodes which has the lowest path length to the source node runs at the complexity of $O(R \times <k>)$, where <k> is the average of node degree in the network, which is a complexity much lower than $O(n^3)$.

3.2   Scale-Free Distribution of Node Degree in Semantic Field Network and Its Contribution to the Computability

Original semantic field network, KTCN-R, is constructed from the corpus of simplified Chinese for IR4QA in NTCIR-7. The corpus includes 545,162 news articles [22]. The triple (N, E, W) is used to describe the scale of KTCN-R, where N is the number of nodes, E is the number of edge, W is the sum of all edge weight, of the network. KTCN-R has the scale of (713218, 19042384, 71188915), with the maximum of edge weight of MaxEdgeWeight=10337. As mentioned before, obtaining R nodes which has the lowest path length to the source node runs at the complexity of $O(R \times <k>)$. The average of node degree $<k>=53.3985$, so the complexity of the algorithm is more precisely approximated as $O(53.3985R)$, which is a very low complexity.

Now it is the appropriate time to discuss what scale-free distribution is and how it contributes to the feasibility of using short path length in M-KTCN-R to evaluate the relatedness between two terms. If a network's node degree obeys the highly heterogeneous distribution, i.e., very fewer nodes possess high degree while most nodes possess low degree, the distribution is called scale-free distribution. For the term "scale-free", its original meaning is the absence of noticeable feature for data samples. This property makes great difference between scale-free distribution and normal distribution, for the latter possess a very noticeable numerical feature---expectation, with the samples distributed around the expectation. The closer to the expectation, the more samples are distributed. The concept of scale-free distribution has deeper significance in complex network science, which describes the property of node degree distribution in most complex network of the real world: the lower node degree, the more nodes possess that degree.

Nodes in KTCN-R possess 3808 kinds of numerical value of degree, with the minimum of 1, and maximum of 77214; Distribution of KTCN-R's degree are shown by piecewise function: Fig. 1, Fig. 2, and Fig. 3 are respectively the distribution of nodes with the degree in intervals of (0, 200], (201, 500], (500, 1118). The fourth section of the distribution, which represents the distribution of nodes whose degrees are greater than or equal to 1118, involves the remaining nodes not shown in Fig. 1, Fig. 2, and Fig. 3, with degrees smaller than 10. So, it is summed up that the node degree distribution of KTCN-R obeys scale-free distribution, which, leads to the scale-free distribution of nodes in M-KTCN-R.

In the process of Dijkstra algorithm, for the paths whose lengths are lowest to a given node, the shortest path with the minimum length contains only one edge. The secondly shortest path length will be either one of the following cases: 1) the path is composed of only one edge; 2) the path is composed of the one of the already obtained shortest paths succeeded by only one more edge follows that path. The computation of other shortest path can be deduced analogously.

So, in the process of obtaining a new shortest path length, it is required to read the neighbors of ending nodes of the already obtained shortest path. Due to the scale-free distribution of node degree in M-KTCN-R, it is of low possibility to read large amount of data of the neighbors. So, a conclusion can be drawn that the scale-free distribution of M-KTCN-R results lower time consumption in computation process.

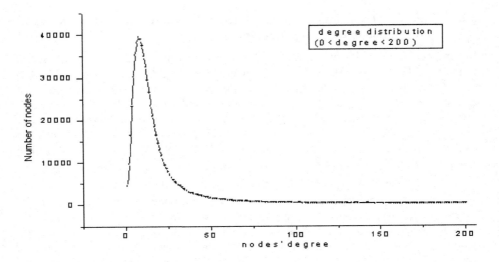

Fig. 1. KTCN-R's node degree distribution in (0, 200]

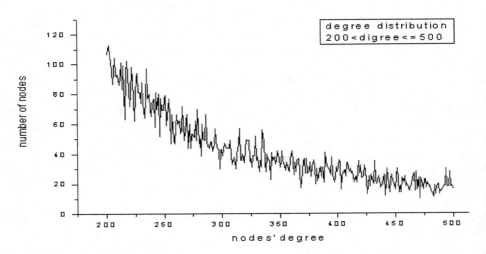

Fig. 2. KTCN-R's node degree distribution in (201, 500]

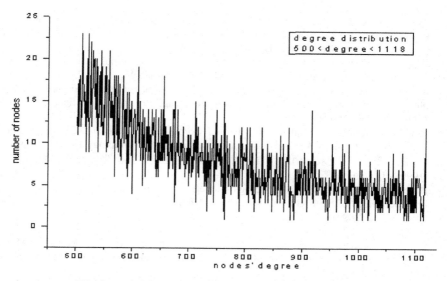

Fig. 3. KTCN-R's node degree distribution in (500, 1118)

4   Conclusion

In large-scale network, using the weighted shortest path length to evaluate the relatedness between two terms is factually infeasible because of the actual time and space consumption. Semantic field network's important property---scale-free distribution of node degree is a contributive factor to makes it feasible to implement the idea of using the shortest path length to evaluate semantic distance between two terms, and leads to the feasibility of obtain most semantically-related terms, which is a subtask of many NLP tasks

Acknowledgement. This paper is supported by Natural Science Foundation Project (61070243), Major Project of Invitation for Bid of National Social Science Foundation (11&ZD189), Guizhou High-level Talent Research Project (TZJF-2010-048), Guizhou Normal University PhD Start-up Research Project (11904-05032110011), Governor Special Fund Grant of Guizhou Province for Prominent Science and Technology Talents (identification serial number "黔省专合字(2012)155号"), and the Chinese Postdoctoral Science Foundation (2013M531730).

References

1. Li, S., Zhang, J., Huang, X., et al.: Semantic computation in a Chinese question-answering system. Journal of Computer Science and Technology **17**(6), 933–939 (2002)
2. Mohammad, S., Hirst, G.: Distributional measures as proxies for semantic relatedness (2005). http://www.cs.toronto.edu/compling/Publications
3. Agirre, E., Rigau, G.: A proposal for word sense disambiguation using conceptual distance. Amsterdam Studies in the Theory and History of Linguistic Science Series **4**, 161–172 (1997)

4. Alvarez, M.A., Lim, S.J.: A Graph Modeling of Semantic Similarity between Words. In: Proceedings of the International Conference on Semantic Computing, pp. 355–362. IEEE Computer Society, Washington, DC (2007)

5. Jiang, J.J., Conrath, D.W.: Semantic similarity based on corpus statistics and lexical taxonomy. In: The Proceedings of ROCLING X, Taiwan (1997)

6. Resnik, P.: Semantic similarity in a taxonomy: An information-based measure and its application to problems of ambiguity in natural language. Journal of Artificial Intelligence **11**(11), 95–130 (1999)

7. Bin, W.: Automatic Alignment of Bilingual Corpus on Chinese and English. Graduate University of Chinese Academy of Sciences (Computer Technology Research Institute) (1999). (王斌. 汉英双语语料库自动对齐研究. **中国科学院研究生院** (计算技术研究) (1999)) (in Chinese)

8. Banerjee, S., Pedersen, T.: Extended gloss overlaps as a measure of semantic relatedness. In: Proceedings of the Eighteenth International Joint Conference on Artficial Intelligence, pp. 805–810 (2003)

9. Patwardhan, S., Pedersen, T.: Using WordNet-based context vectors to estimate the semantic relatedness of concepts. In: Proceedings of the EACL 2006 Workshop Making Sense of Sense-Bringing Computational Linguistics and Psycholinguistics Together, Trento, Italy (2006)

10. Hughes, T., Ramage, D.: Lexical semantic relatedness with random graph walks. In: Proceedings of the Conference on Empirical Methods in Natural Language Processing(EMNLP), pp. 581–589 (2007)

11. Brown, P.F., Della, P.S., Della, P.V., et al.: Word-sense disambiguation using statistical methods, pp. 264–270. Association for Computational Linguistics, Morristown (1991)

12. Budanitsky, A.: Lexical semantic relatedness and its application in natural language processing, Technical Report CSRG390. University of Toronto (1999)

13. Dagan, I., Lee, L., Pereira, F.C.: Similarity-based models of word cooccurrence probabilities. Machine Learning **34**(1), 43–69 (1999)

14. Doan, A.H., Madhavan, J., Domingos, P., et al.: Learning to map between ontologies on the semantic web, p. 673. ACM (2002)

15. Weeds, J., Weir, D.: Co-occurrence retrieval: A flexible framework for lexical distributional similarity. Computational Linguistics **31**(4), 439–475 (2005)

16. Jicheng, L.: Tentative Study on Lexical Cohesive Means in English Discourse. Journal of Foreign Languages. 5, 2 (1986). (林纪诚. 英语语篇中词汇衔接手段试探. **外国语** (**上海外国**语学院学报). 5, 2 (1986)) (in Chinese)

17. Riguang, X.: Semantic Association Field and Translation of Changing Categories of Nouns and Adjectives from Chinese to English. Journal of Xi'an International Studies University 12(4), 84–86 (2004). (夏日光. 语义联想场与名形词类转变的英译. **西安外** 国语学院学报 12(4), 84–86.(2004)) (in Chinese)

18. de Saussure, F.: Course in General Linguistics. The Commercial Press (1980). (索绪尔. **普通**语言学教程. **商务印书馆** (1980)) (in Chinese)

19. Yue, W.: The Principles and Types of Russian Semantic Field Classification. Economic Research Guide (14), 227–228 (2012). (王悦. **俄**语语义场划分的原则与类型. 经济研究 导刊 (14), 227–228 (2012)) (in Chinese)

20. Yande, J.: Chinese Semantics. Peking University Press (1999). (贾彦德. 汉语语义学. **北 京大学出版社** (1999)) (in Chinese)

21. Weimin, Y., Weimin, W.: Data Structure: C language version. Tsinghua University Press (2002). (严蔚敏, 吴伟民. **数据**结构: C 语言版. **清华大学出版社** (2002)) (in Chinese)

22. Tetsuya Sakai, E.: Overview of the NTCIR-7 ACLIA IR4QA Subtask (2008)

Recognition and Extraction of Honorifics in Chinese Diachronic Corpora

Dan Xiong[1], Jian Xu[1], Qin Lu[1(✉)], and Fengju Lo[2]

[1]Department of Computing, The Hong Kong Polytechnic University, Hong Kong, China
{csdxiong,csjxu,csluqin}@comp.polyu.edu.hk
[2]Department of Chinese Linguistics and Literature, Yuan Ze University, Zhongli, Taiwan
gefjulo@saturn.yzu.edu.tw

Abstract. Honorifics in this paper refer to names of official positions and titles of nobility or honor. They can be found in various written records in different periods and have great historical significance. This paper introduces a machine learning system to recognize the honorifics in diachronic corpora. A tagged corpus of four classic novels written in the Ming and Qing dynasties is used to train the system. The system is then used to automatically recognize and extract the honorifics in pre-Qin classics, Tang-dynasty poems, and modern Chinese news. Experimental results show that the system can achieve relatively good results in recognizing the honorifics in the pre-Qin classics and Tang-dynasty poems. This work is an attempt to improve the performance of automatic recognition of honorifics in diachronic corpora. The system can be a helpful tool in the studies on the evolution of honorifics throughout Chinese history.

Keywords: Honorifics · Chinese diachronic corpora · Machine learning algorithm

1 Introduction

Honorifics, defined as names of official position (官職名) and titles of nobility or honor (爵位封號) in this paper, are important elements used for addressing or reference to persons. Scattered in various written records over ancient times, they carry significant historical and cultural information. In the field of natural language processing and its applications, it is of great importance to recognize and extract honorifics effectively. From ancient times to the modern age, some honorifics have been kept throughout Chinese history, yet, many have changed alongside the transformation of political systems and the development of economy and culture.

This work is one of the first attempts to investigate the honorifics in diachronic corpora comprising different styles of written Chinese ranging from pre-Qin classics to modern journalistic text. First, training data is prepared using a tagged corpus of four notable novels written in the Ming and Qing dynasties [1], namely, *Romance of the Three Kingdoms* (《三國演義》), *Water Margin* (《水滸傳》), *The Golden Lotus* (《金瓶梅》), and *A Dream of Red Mansions* (《紅樓夢》). Then, a machine

© Springer International Publishing Switzerland 2014
X. Su and T. He (Eds.): CLSW 2014, LNAI 8922, pp. 305–316, 2014.
DOI: 10.1007/978-3-319-14331-6_31

learning system based on Conditional Random Fields (CRFs) is developed to recognize the honorifics in Chinese diachronic corpora. To evaluate the performance of the system over the honorifics in different styles of Chinese text, we use several classics created during pre-Qin periods as testing data, that is, *The Commentary of Zuo* (《左傳》) and *Discourses of the States* (《國語》), as well as Tang-dynasty poems and modern news (*People's Daily*). This is the first of this kind of work, which is expected to provide reference to other researches related to recognition of named entities from diachronic corpora.

The rest of the paper is organized as follows. Section 2 gives a brief introduction of related work. Section 3 presents the annotation of the data for training. Section 4 describes the machine learning algorithm. Evaluation is given in Section 5. Section 6 is the conclusion.

2 Related Work

In written text, honorifics convey important information on people and their relationships which reflect historical significance. Therefore, when looking at honorifics from the perspective of natural language processing, it is necessary to regard them as a type of named entity. The complexity of the administrative systems and the variety of the honorifics used throughout Chinese history make it more difficult to identify and retrieve them from mass data either manually or automatically. With the transition of dynasties, the number of honorifics has become increasingly large. In modern China, some influential dictionaries on honorifics based on Chinese bureaucratic/administrative systems [2,3,4] are published, which have included as many as more than 20,000 entries. Like other words that are introduced over time as the result of the change in society, some honorifics disappear and new ones are created. Some may still be in use now, yet their meanings have changed completely, such as "博士" (*bóshì, literally Erudite Scholar*), which refers to a doctoral degree in modern Chinese but was an official position for scholars in feudal China. In both historical classics and literary works, not only the honorifics of the current times are extensively used, but also those of earlier ages are frequently quoted. For example, even in modern newspaper *People's Daily*, the official position "宰相" (*zǎixiàng, Prime Minister in feudal China*) is often cited. Therefore, no matter what style of text is processed, the effective extraction of honorifics is essential in natural language applications.

Honorifics are largely ignored in previous work related to the construction of tagged corpus. The study of honorifics based on diachronic corpora is a particularly rare attempt. The specification for modern Chinese corpus annotation commonly used in mainland China [5] simply regards honorifics as common nouns, which are tagged with "/n", such as "省長/n" (*shěngzhǎng/n, the governor of a province*) and "財政部/nt 部長/n" (*cáizhèngbù/nt bùzhǎng/n, Minister of Finance*). The Tagged Corpus of Early Mandarin Chinese constructed by Taiwan's Academia Sinica [6,7] also treats honorifics as common nouns tagged with "Na", such as "李(Nb)御史(Na)" (*Lǐ(Nb) yùshǐ(Na), the Imperial Censor whose surname is Li*). In the Ancient Chinese Corpus [6,8] of Academia Sinica, honorifics are regarded as animate nouns (有生名詞) tagged with "NA1", such as "內史(NA1)[+attr]過(NB1)[+prop]" (*nèishǐ(NA1)[+attr] Guò(NB1)[+prop]*, *Metropolitan Superintendent whose name is Guo*). Collectively, honorifics in all these corpora are treated as common nouns rather than named entities.

In our earlier work on building the diachronic corpora, we realized that some important information might be missed out if honorifics were simply handled as common nouns [1]. Honorifics can be used independently, for instance, "御史" (*yùshǐ, Imperial Censor*), or grouped with personal names, such as "李御史" (*Lǐ yùshǐ, the Imperial Censor whose surname is Li*), or used together with terms of address to show respect, for example, "御史大人" (*yùshǐ dàrén, His Excellency Imperial Censor*). In whatever way they appear in text, honorifics are often used to refer to specific persons and perform the function of named entities. In consideration of this, we treat them as a type of named entity.

3   Classification and Annotation of Honorifics

In consideration of the significance of honorifics, this work regards them as a type of named entity, which is tagged with "/nu" and classified into two subtypes:

- Names of official positions (官職名): including the official positions appointed by governments or military institutions, which are tagged with "/nu1", such as "尚書/nu1" (*shàngshū/nu1, Minister*). This subtype only includes those which are officially appointed. Terms of address, such as supervisor and housekeeper, are studied separately [9].
- Titles of nobility or honor (爵位封號): including the titles granted to members of the aristocracy or bestowed on outstanding persons, which are tagged with "/nu2", for instance, "郡王/nu2" (*jùnwáng/nu2, Prince*) and "貴妃/nu2" (*guìfēi/nu2, Imperial Consort*)

If an honorific is used in combination with a name of a place or an organization, the whole compound term will be bracketed with "[ ]", in which the name of the place or the organization is explicitly annotated, for example, "[戶部/nt 尚書]/nu1" (*[hùbù/nt shàngshū]/nu1, Minister of Revenue, in which "hubu" is a ministry*) and "[臨淄/ns2# 侯]/nu2" (*[Línzī/ns2# Hóu]/nu2, Marquis of Linzi, in which "Linzi" is a place*). During system training, only the official position "尚書" (*shàngshū, Minister*) and the title of nobility "侯" (*Hóu, Marquis*) are treated as honorifics, whereas the organization name "戶部" (*hùbù, ministry*) and the place name "臨淄" (*Linzi*) are regarded as their contextual features.

Since we look at honorifics from the perspective of natural language processing, only those used for addressing or reference are regarded as honorifics in our work. For example, in "司徒/nu1 王允/nr3#" (*sītú/nu1 Wáng Yǔn/nr3#, Minister of the Interior Wang Yun, in which Wang Yun is a personal name and "situ" is his official title*), the official position "司徒" (*sītú, Minister of the Interior*) is tagged as an honorific because it refers to the particular person Wang Yun. While in "出/了/一/個/郎中/缺" (*chū/le/yī/gè/lángzhōng/quē, there is a vacancy for a Vice Minister in the Ministry*), although "郎中" (*lángzhōng*, *Vice Minister*) is an official position, it is regarded as a common noun as it is not used for addressing or reference.

4 Algorithm Design

The four fictional works used as training data were composed during the Ming and Qing dynasties in the style of vernacular Chinese, which is an intermediary between traditional and modern Chinese. In the corpus of the vernacular fictions [1], words are segmented, and named entities including personal names, terms of address, honorifics as well as the names of places, buildings, and organizations are annotated, but part-of-speech (POS) tags are not provided.

Table 1. Examples of feature design

No.	Type of feature	Description	Example
1	C_n (n $= -2,-1,0,1,2$)	The current character, the two ones before it, and the two ones after it	$C_{-2} = 乃(nǎi)$ $C_{-1} = 司(sī)$ $C_0 = 徒(tú)$ $C_1 = 王(Wáng)$ $C_2 = 允(Yǔn)$
2	T_n (n $= -2,-1,1,2$)	The named entity types of the two characters before the current character as well as the two ones after it	$T_{-2} =O$ $T_1 =$nr3 $T_{-1} =O$ $T_2 =$nr3
3	$C_n C_{n+1}$ (n $= -2,-1,0,1$)	bigram	$C_{-2} C_{-1}$ $= 乃司(nǎi\ sī)$ $C_{-1} C_0 = 司徒(sī\ tú)$ $C_0 C_1$ $= 徒王(tú\ Wáng)$ $C_1 C_2$ $= 王允(Wáng\ Yǔn)$
4	$C_{-1} C_1$	The combination of the character before the current character and the one after the current character	$C_{-1} C_1$ $= 司王(sī\ Wáng)$
5	$Punc(C_0)$	Whether the current character is a punctuation	$Punc(C_0 = 徒\ tú)$ $= False$
6	$Num(C_0)$	Whether the current character is a number	$Number\ (C_0 = 徒\ tú)$ $= False$

To extract an honorific, we treat it as a sequential tagging issue and apply the CRFs model [10]. In this model, we can take advantage of different contextual features, including the named entity types, for example, nu, ns, nt and so on. To extract an honorific through the sequence labeling technique, it is necessary to determine the beginning and ending of the honorific. In this case, the CRFs model is used. Let $x = x_1, x_2, \ldots, x_t, \ldots, x_T, 1 \leq t \leq T$ be a sequence of Chinese characters with length T and y be a corresponding sequence of output labels. Each observation x_t is then associated with a label $y_t \in \{\text{B-GZ, I-GZ, B-JF, I-JF, O}\}$, which indicates whether the character x_t is a part of a Chinese honorific. B-GZ indicates the beginning of an official position and I-GZ is the continuation of the official position. O (outside) refers to the fact that the character is not a part of an honorific. Six types of features are added to the CRFs model. In the second type, the tags of named entity types include nr (personal name), na (term of address), ns (place name), nt (organization name), nv (building name), and O (does not belong to any entity type). The CRFs model can make use of the character features and contextual features. The sentence "布/nr2# 视/之/，/乃/司徒/nu1 王允 /nr3# 也" (*Bù/nr2# shì/zhǐ/, /nǎi/sītú/nu1 Wáng Yǔn/nr3# yě; Bu looked back and found it was the Minister of the Interior Wang Yun.*) is taken as an example to illustrate the design of the features, as shown in Table 1. In the examples, the character "徒" (*tú, a part of the honorific Minister of the Interior*) is set as the current character.

For the first and second features, the window size is set to 2. In this work, we have also tested the widow size of 3 and 4. Since the CRFs model has a large number of features, we have to estimate parameters in large quantity. To solve this problem, we adopt the SampleRank algorithm [11]. Previous parameter learning approach [12] requires inferences over the full dataset before the parameters are updated. The SampleRank method solves this problem by performing parameter updates within each step of the Markov Chain Monte Carlo (MCMC) inference [11]. It computes gradients between neighboring configurations in an MCMC chain. When disagreement occurs between model ranking and objective ranking, a higher model score is assigned to the sample that has a lower loss. By so doing, the SampleRank algorithm reduces the number of iterations in parameter estimation.

5   Performance Evaluation and Data Analysis

5.1   Training and Testing Datasets

Four influential Ming-Qing novels are used as the main collection of data for system training. The testing datasets consist of three corpora involving historically significant works of different styles created in different historical times. Tables 2 and 3 show the statistics of the training and testing datasets.

Table 2. Statistics of the training datasets

Times	Text type	Dataset	Size (10,000 characters excluding punctuations)
Ming-Qing dynasties	Vernacular fictions	Romance of the Three Kingdoms	48.25
		Water Margin	75.92
		The Golden Lotus	65.24
		A Dream of Red Mansions	72.95

Table 3. Statistics of the testing datasets

Times	Text type	Dataset	Size
Pre-Qin	Historical classics	The Commentary of Zuo	Full text with 198,800 characters excluding punctuations
		Discourses of the States	Full text with 70,400 characters excluding punctuations
Tang dynasty	Classical Chinese poetry	Poems	142 lines of 126 poems by Li Bai, Du Fu, and Han Yu
Modern China	Modern news	People's Daily	News of January 1998 with 1,605,800 characters excluding punctuations

The four fictions are helpful for system training since they depict many people in official ranks and both real and fictional honorifics are flexibly used for addressing or reference. As honorifics are often used together with other named entities, in the pre-Qin classics and Tang-dynasty poems used for testing, we also annotated named entities including personal names, terms of address, as well as the names of places, buildings, and organizations in accordance with the specification for the novels. Since the *People's Daily* corpus constructed by Peking University [5] is directly used as the testing dataset of modern Chinese and honorifics in the corpus are treated as common nouns, there are no gold answers for the honorifics in this dataset. Table 4 lists the number of the honorifics in the training and the testing datasets, including their category (the same honorific is counted only once) as well as occurrence (all honorifics are counted).

Table 4. Number of the honorifics in the training and testing datasets

Dateset		Name of official position		Title of nobility or honor	
		Category	Occurrence	Category	Occurrence
Training	Romance of the Three Kingdoms	198	2535	39	848
	Water Margin	124	3045	27	121
	The Golden Lotus	132	1671	13	36
	A Dream of Red Mansions	53	202	59	741
Testing	The Commentary of Zuo	119	844	12	2433
	Discourses of the States	49	166	7	165
	Tang-dynasty poems	36	67	20	55
	People's Daily	-	-	-	-

5.2   Experimental Results

Overall Experimental Results. Precision (P), recall (R), and the F-score (F) are applied to evaluate the performance of the system. The FACTORIE system [13] is used to train the CRFs model, and the number of iterations is set to 20. Since the contextual features can affect the performance of the system, we set the window size to 2, 3, and 4, respectively. In other words, setting window size to 2 refers to the fact of using the two characters before and the two after the current character in observation. To assess the efficiency of the algorithm, we also compute the overlapping ratio between the honorifics in the training datasets and those in the testing datasets (the honorifics in the testing datasets are manually tagged as the standard answer for evaluation purpose). The formula for calculating the overlapping ratio is $\frac{|S_1 \cap S_2|}{|S_1 \cup S_2|}$, in which S_1 and S_2 are the respective collections of the honorifics in the two comparative datasets. Since the honorifics in the existing corpus of *People's Daily* were annotated as common nouns, it is not feasible to tag them manually. So, for the *People's Daily* testing data, we only measured its precision by checking the results of our system. Table 5 lists the overall experimental results, in which P, R, and F are the values when F reaches its peak.

Table 5. Overall experimental results

Evaluation item	Dataset	The Commentary of Zuo	Discourses of the States	Tang-dynasty poems	People's Daily
Name of official position	P	68.44%	54.05%	94.44%	21.89%
	R	22.87%	24.10%	25.37%	-
	F	34.28% (Window 4)	33.33% (Window 3)	40.00% (Window 2)	-
	Overlapping ratio	2.16%	1.81%	5.30%	-
Title of nobility or honor	P	79.77%	46.11%	42.86%	6.52%
	R	34.69%	50.30%	21.82%	-
	F	48.35% (Window 2)	48.12% (Window 2)	28.92% (Window 2)	-
	Overlapping ratio	8.18%	6.54%	5.83%	-

As shown in Table 5, the average overlapping ratio between the honorifics in the training datasets and those in the testing datasets is just 4.97% with the maximum of 8.18% only. In the cases of pre-Qin classics and Tang-dynasty poems, the system achieved average precision and recall of 64.28% and 29.86%, respectively, which should be considered quite good results. One main reason is that the honorifics in pre-Qin classics and Tang-dynasty poems are real rather than fictional. In comparison with real honorifics, fictional ones can be grouped and used quite flexibly. For example, in the pre-Qin classics, it is the official position "司空" (*sīkōng, Minister of Public Works*) that achieves the highest precision. In the Tang-dynasty poems, the honorific with the highest precision is "太守" (*tàishǒu, Governor*). Both are real rather than fictional.

Generally speaking, the system achieved relatively low precision in automatically recognizing the honorifics in modern news, only 21.89% and 6.52% for the two categories, respectively. This result, however, can provide reference for other researches related to recognition of named entities in diachronic corpora. The major cause lies in the much greater changes of the official administrative system in modern China. Most honorifics in feudal China have disappeared in modern time. Even if some lexical items are still in use, they do not function as official positions any more, such as "博士" (*bóshì, literally Erudite Scholar, an official position for scholars in ancient China*). Some lexical items in the same surface form are different in semantics and even pronunciation. The word "大夫", which was pronounced as "dàfū" and functioned as an official position in ancient China, while is pronounced as "dàifū" and used to address a doctor now. In such cases, the system cannot recognize the honorifics correctly. Nevertheless, some honorifics in the modern news are still successfully recognized, including the following cases: 1) There is a small number of honorifics which are still being used in modern Chinese with basically the same semantic meaning, such as "参谋" (*cānmóu, Strategist*) and "王后" (*wánghòu, queen, which exists in some countries in the contemporary world*). 2) A few lexical items are used as official titles in both ancient and modern China. Since they have kept the same word form, the system is able to recognize them although the connotations of the words' meaning have changed to some extent. For example, "书记" (*shūjì, Secretary*), which functions as an official position in both classical and modern Chinese, is frequently used in the news and successfully recognized by the system. 3) In modern news, ancient honorifics are quoted sometimes, which can be recognized by the system if they are included in the training datasets.

Since the central issue of our work is named entity, only those used for addressing or reference with specific referents are tagged as honorifics, while others are considered as common nouns. This makes honorifics context-sensitive. As mentioned earlier, there are no POS tags in the training datasets. Therefore, it is very hard for the system to identify whether these kinds of lexical items should be treated as honorifics. For example, in the sentence "司徒/具/徒，/司空/视/途" (*sītú/jù/tú/,/sīkōng/shì/tú; Minister of the Interior dispatches servants, and Minister of Public Works inspects roads*), neither "司徒" (*sītú, Minister of the Interior*) nor "司空" (*sīkōng, Minister of Public Works*) is used for addressing or reference, but they are wrongly extracted by the system as honorifics.

Effectiveness of Varying Window Size for Pre-Qin Classics and Tang-Dynasty Poems. Figures 1, 2, and 3 show the tendencies of the F-scores of the two pre-Qin classics and the Tang-dynasty poems when the window size is set to 2, 3, and 4 respectively. As shown in the figures, the F-scores stabilize after 10 iterations. The digits on the figures indicate the peak of each trend line. In the following figures, NOP is the abbreviation of names of official position, and TNH refers to titles of nobility or honor.

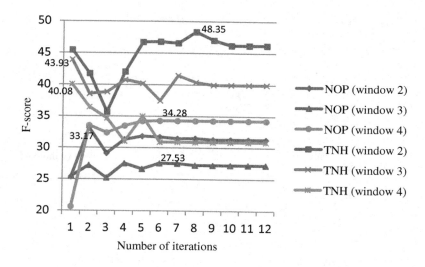

Fig. 1. Tendency of the F-scores of *The Commentary of Zuo*

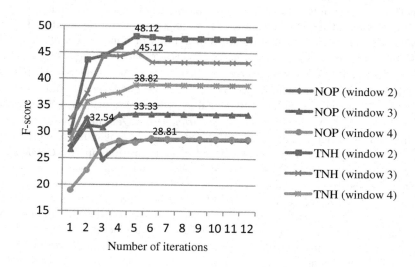

Fig. 2. Tendency of the F-scores of *Discourses of the States*

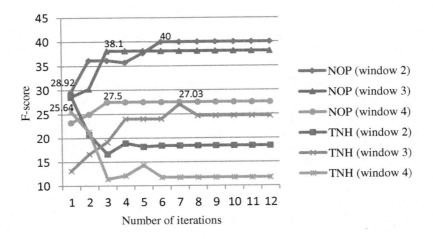

Fig. 3. Tendency of the F-scores of Tang-dynasty poems

As shown in Figures 1 and 2, for the two pre-Qin classics, the system achieves better performance in automatically recognizing the titles of nobility or honor, with an average F-score of 48.24%, than the official positions, with an average F-score of 33.81%. The major cause is that the titles of nobility or honor in the pre-Qin classics are the five ranks of "公" (*Gōng, duke*), "侯" (*Hóu, marquis*), "伯" (*Bó, earl*), "子" (*Zǐ, viscount*), and "男" (*Nán, baron*), which show obvious regularity. Their F-scores reach the peak when the window size is set to 2. This is because the titles of nobility or honor are often used together with the name of the states, such as "[齐/ns1 侯]/nu2" (*[Qí/ns1 Hóu]/nu2, Marquis of Qi, the monarch of the Qi state*). Due to a low overlapping ratio of about 2%, the results of the official positions in the two pre-Qin classics are relatively poor. The F-scores of the official positions in *The Commentary of Zuo* and *Discourses of the States* reach the highest points when the window size is set to 4 and 3 respectively. In other words, the recognition of the honorifics in *The Commentary of Zuo* requires more contextual features in comparison to that of *Discourses of the States*. This is because the former one, focusing on the recording of events, provides more information such as personal name and place name in the context of the honorifics. Making use of these contextual features is helpful for automatic extracting. The interchangeable words and variants in the pre-Qin classics also affect the performance of the system. For example, "大史" (*dàshǐ, Court Historian*), the honorific with the lowest precision in *The Commentary of Zuo*, cannot be recognized since it is written as "太史" (*tàishǐ, Court Historian*) in later periods.

There is no doubt that the style of Tang-dynasty poems is quite different from that of the training datasets. In consideration of the low overlapping ratios of less than 6%, the experimental results of the poems are relatively good. The main reason is that the honorifics in the poems are real and usually used together with personal names. Both categories of honorifics with the highest precision are used in combination with surnames. Since the language of poems is more compact, the F-scores of both official positions and titles of nobility or honor in the poems reach the peak when the window size is 2. Due to the limitation of sentence length and the requirement for rhythm, abbreviated forms are widely used in poems, which is an obstacle of automatic recognition. For example, "平津" (*píngjīn, Pingjin, a place name*) was ever used to replace Marquis of Pingjin.

6 Conclusion

From pre-Qin periods to modern China, the official title system has changed greatly, which results in a large number of honorifics. In different kinds of literature throughout Chinese history, honorifics are extensively used in various forms. Therefore, it is necessary to correctly recognize them when computers are used to process natural languages, especially classical Chinese. This paper presents a machine learning system for automatically recognizing and extracting the honorifics in Chinese diachronic corpora. The corpus used for system training comprises four classic novels written in the Ming and Qing dynasties, in which words are segmented with annotated named entities, but POS tagging is not provided. Sequence labeling algorithms are then applied to automatically recognize the honorifics in two pre-Qin classics, Tang-dynasty poems, and modern news. The datasets used in this work involve texts of different styles created in different ages, ranging from pre-Qin periods to modern China. Although the overlapping ratios between the honorifics in the training datasets and those in the testing datasets are very low and there are no POS tags in the training datasets, the system can still achieve relatively good results in recognizing the honorifics in the pre-Qin classics and Tang-dynasty poems. This work attempts to improve the performance of automatic recognition of honorifics in diachronic corpora covering fictions, historical classics, traditional poems, and modern news, which can provide reference for other work related to extraction of named entities from diachronic corpora. The results are also expected to help the studies on the evolution of honorifics throughout Chinese history. In our future work, POS tags can be added to the training datasets to provide more features for machine learning in order to improve the performance of the system.

Acknowledgments. This work is partially supported by the Chiang Ching-kuo Foundation for International Scholarly Exchange under the project "Building a Diachronic Language Knowledge-base" (RG013-D-09).

References

1. Xiong, D., Lu, Q., Lo, F., Shi, D., Chiu, T.-s., Li, W.: Specification for Segmentation and Named Entity Annotation of Chinese Classics in the Ming and Qing Dynasties. In: Ji, D., Xiao, G. (eds.) CLSW 2012. LNCS, vol. 7717, pp. 280–293. Springer, Heidelberg (2013)
2. Yu, L.N.: Dictionary of Chinese Bureaucracy. Heilongjiang People's Publishing House, Harbin (俞鹿年:中國官制大辭典.黑龍江人民出版社,哈爾濱) (1992). (in Chinese)

3. Zhang, Z.L., Lü, Z.L.: A Comprehensive Dictionary of Official Title System in Imperial China. Beijing Publishing House, Beijing (張政烺,呂宗力:中國歷代官制大辭典.北京出版社,北京) (1994). (in Chinese)
4. Xu, L.D.: A Dictionary of Chinese Official Title System. Shanghai University Press, Shanghai (徐連達: 中國官制大辭典.上海大學出版社,上海) (2010). (in Chinese)
5. Yu, S.W., Duan, H.M., Zhu, X.F., Swen, B., Chang, B.B.: Specification for Corpus Processing at Peking University: Word Segmentation, POS Tagging and Phonetic Notation. Journal of Chinese Language and Computing **13**(2), 121–158 (2003). (in Chinese)
6. Wei, P.C., Thompson, P.M., Liu, C.H., Huang, C.R., Sun, C.F.: Historical Corpora for Synchronic and Diachronic Linguistics Studies. International Journal of Computational Linguistics and Chinese Language Processing **2**(1), 131–145 (1997). (in Chinese)
7. Academia Sinica Tagged Corpus of Early Mandarin Chinese. http://app.sinica.edu.tw/cgi-bin/kiwi/pkiwi/kiwi.sh
8. Academia Sinica Ancient Chinese Corpus. http://app.sinica.edu.tw/cgi-bin/kiwi/akiwi/kiwi.sh
9. Xiong, D., Lu, Q., Lo, F.J., Shi, D.X., Chiu, T.S.: A Corpus-Based Study of Personal Names and Terms of Address in Chinese Classical Novels. Journal of Chinese Information Processing (to be published). (in Chinese)
10. Lafferty, J.D., McCallum, A., Pereira, F.C.N.: Conditional Random Fields: Probabilistic Models for Segmenting and Labeling Sequence Data. In: Proceedings of the Eighteenth International Conference on Machine Learning, pp. 282–289. Morgan Kaufmann, San Francisco (2001)
11. Wick, M., Rohanimanesh, K., Culotta, A., McCallum, A.: SampleRank: Learning Preferences from Atomic Gradients. In: Neural Information Processing Systems (NIPS), Workshop on Advances in Ranking (2009)
12. Wallach, H.: Efficient Training of Conditional Random Fields. In: Proc. 6th Annual CLUK Research Colloquium (2002)
13. McCallum, A., Schultz, K., Singh, S.: FACTORIE: Probabilistic Programming via Imperatively Defined Factor Graphs. In: Advances in Neural Information Processing Systems 22 (NIPS 2009 Proceedings), pp. 1249–1257 (2009)

A Hypothesis on Word Similarity and Its Application

Peng Jin[1(✉)], Likun Qiu[2], Xuefeng Zhu[3], and Pengyuan Liu[4]

[1] School of Computer Science, Leshan Normal University, Leshan 614004, China
jandp@pku.edu.cn
[2] School of Chinese Language and Literature, Ludong University, Yantai 260045, China
qiulikun@pku.edu.cn
[3] Institute of Computational Linguistics, Peking University, Beijing 100871, China
yusw@pku.edu.cn
[4] Applied Linguistic Research Institute, Beijing Language and Culture University,
Beijing, China
liupengyuan@pku.edu.cn

Abstract. A hypothesis is proposed: the semantic distance between the synonyms or near-synonyms should have the same characteristic as the distance in a metrics space. Metrics space is a set where a notion of distance (called a metric) between elements of the set is defined. At the same time, three properties should be held: (i) Identity of Indiscernibles – the distance is zero if and only if the two elements are the same. (ii) Symmetry – The distance between element A and B is equal to the distance between element B and A. (iii) Triangle Inequality – Given three elements A, B and C, the sum of any two pairs' distance is greater or equal to the rest one. The first two properties is reasonable intuitively; as to the last one, we first get the word similarities based on *HowNet* and check whether the synonyms or near-synonyms listed in *Cilin* Extended Edition can satisfy this property. The experiments show that more than 98.5% triples (consists of three synonyms) satisfy the last property – triangle inequality. Fatherly, we detect a large quantity of thesaurus errors according to our hypothesis.

Keywords: Word similarity · Metrics space · *Cilin* · *HowNet*

1 Introduction

Analysis of word sense is a preliminary research in the field of lexical semantics, its main task is to determine the word relationships between words. Generally, similarity is considered as the most important one. Word similarity, quantifying how similar when two words is given, mainly focuses on finding synonymous words, such as *father* and *dad*, or near-synonym, such as *enlarge* and *expand*. A basic task is, given a target word w, ranking the other words according to their similarities to the word w. The general use of word similarity is to alleviate the so-called data sparseness problem, which is an open problem in natural language processing community [1]. It is widely used to smooth the statistical language model [2] as well as improve some commercial systems, such as Bid-term suggestion [3] and query expansion [4].

© Springer International Publishing Switzerland 2014
X. Su and T. He (Eds.): CLSW 2014, LNAI 8922, pp. 317–325, 2014.
DOI: 10.1007/978-3-319-14331-6_32

One important approach for the computation of word similarity is based on thesauruses, which are usually created manually by linguists. A classical example is *WordNet* [5]. It clusters the words related to the same concept into a synset (as a node), and then all nodes are organized by hyponymy as a taxonomy tree. In Chinese, *Cilin* [6] is a resource with similar structure to *WordNet*. A different thesaurus is *HowNet* [7], which defines a concept via a set of {feature, value} pairs rather than a set of synonyms. Although these thesauruses have been compiled by experts taking a long time and contain a large amount of linguistic knowledge, there are still many problems, including the lack of some word senses and incorrect categorization of some word sense. For instance, the originally goal of *Cilin* is avoiding monotonous vocabulary in writing rather than NLP. Since *Cilin* was compiled manually, there exists serious problem of incorrect categorization in it. If we try to solve the problem manually with the help from linguists, it is like looking for a needle in a haystack.

In this paper, we first bring forward a hypothesis, i.e. the semantic distance between the synonyms or near-synonyms should have the same characteristic as the distance in a metrics space. Given three synonyms in a thesaurus, if the semantic distance of a word to the other two words are greater than the distance between the other two words, i.e. violating the property of triangle inequality, it is likely that the word has been incorrectly categorized in the thesaurus.

The rest of this paper is organized as follows: Section 2 introduces the related work. In Section 3, we describe the hypothesis in detail and propose an approach to detect incorrect categorization based on the hypothesis Experiments are demonstrated in Section 4. Finally, we conclude this paper in Section 5.

2   Related Work

2.1   The Methods of Computing Word Similarity

There are two methods for computing the similarity score between two words.

One is based on a handcrafted electronic thesaurus, which is referred to as thesaurus-based method. Considering *WordNet*, two words belong to different synset (two nodes in this semantic tree), (Resnik, 1995) obtained the similarity score according to the numbers of nodes from one word to the other [8]. (Jiang and Conrath, 1997) improved it via taking the depth of nodes into account [9]. (Budanitsky and Hirst, 2006) evaluated these algorithms [10] and (Pederson, 2008) implemented these algorithms in a software tool [11]. To Chinese language, (Liu and Li, 2002) computed the word similarity based on *HowNet* [12]. It should be noted that behind the idea of *HowNet* is completely from *WordNet*, (Dong and Dong, 2002) constructed *HowNet* with the basic element "primitive sememe" [7]. There are totally more than two thousand sememes in this thesaurus, but there are also 8 relationships such as hyponymy and part-whole among the sememes. The word similarity score could be obtained through their sememes' similarity, equation 1 as follows:

$$sim(p_1, p_2) = \frac{\alpha}{\alpha + d} \tag{1}$$

where p_1, p_2 are two sememes, d is the path in the sememes tree and α is an adjustable factor.

If one word has more than one sense (multi concepts in *HowNet*), the maximum one is denoted as the word similarity.

The advantage of this method is finding the semantic similar words given a word w rather than w's associated words. The disadvantage is if w is out-of-vocabulary (OOV), it is impossible to get its similar words and it will not be the others neighbors (we also call similar word as neighbor). What's more, some novel senses will be ignored.

The other way to get the word similarity scores is relying on the large scale corpus, we call it statistics-based method. The assumption behind this method is the co-occurrence words could play a proxy to represent the meaning of target word, so-called "You shall know a word by the company it keeps" [13]. Each word is usually viewed as a vector, each dimension is a co-occurrence word. Then, any metrics such as cosine or K-L divergence could be measured the semantic distance between any two words. (Lin, 1998) used mutual information to improve the computing [14], while an emerging vector represent is based on deep learning and overwhelm the predecessor [15].

The advantage of this method is no need for the thesaurus which is expensive to create and maintenance. The shortcoming is many associated words rather than semantic similar words are selected out.

Both of these two methods denote word similarity score as a proper fraction and the greater value is the more close they are. In this paper, we propose the hypothesis that deeming the semantic distances among synonyms could construct a metric space is exactly according to these scores. In our experiments, we adapt the thesaurus-based method to get these scores. Furthermore, the hypothesis with the scores are applied to find some words are incorrectly categorized in a thesaurus.

2.2   Incorrect Categorization in Thesaurus

Some research were carried out to detect incorrect categorization in a thesaurus. (Qiu et al., 2012) proposed a method for detect incorrect categorization based on distributed word representation [16]. For each given word, the method computes similarity scores between the target word and any other word, and then a KNN classification is used to classify the target word into a category in a given thesaurus. If the given word and another word have been tagged as synonymous words in another thesaurus yet not be classified into a same category in the given thesaurus, the method will take the target word as an instance of incorrect categorization.

3   The Hypothesis

3.1   Metric Space vs. Word Similarity

Metric space is a set, the distance among its elements is defined. Let Ω denote a set, for any three elements in it, x, y, z, d is denoted the distance between two elements. Three properties should be satisfied as follow:

(i) $d(x, y) = 0$ **iff** $x = y$ identity of indiscernibles

(ii) $d(x, y) = d(y, x)$ symmetry

(iii) $d(x, y) + d(x, z) \geq d(y, z)$ triangle inequality

In fact, non-negative $d(x, y) \geq 0$ could be easily deduced the three prosperities.

As far as word similarity are concerned, let $sim(w_i, w_j)$ denote the similarity score between word w_i and w_j. Obviously, it is reasonable to set its value 1 if and only if i equal to j. From the description in section 2.1, it is naturally the systematic is satisfied, i.e. $sim(w_i, w_j) = sim(w_j, w_i)$. If we define $1 - sim(w_i, w_j)$ as these two words' semantic distance and denote it as $dis(w_i, w_j)$, so, there should be $dis(w_i, w_j) = 0$ iff i equal to j. Because $sim(w_i, w_j)$ is symmetry, $dis(w_i, w_j)$ should also be symmetry.

If the word similarity sim is satisfied triangle inequality, their semantic distance dis should be equivalent to satisfied triangle inequality. We proof it as follows: Given three words w_i, w_j, w_k, if $sim(w_i, w_j) + sim(w_i, w_k) > sim(w_j, w_k)$ then,

$$\Rightarrow -sim(w_i, w_j) - sim(w_i, w_k) < -sim(w_j, w_k)$$
$$\Rightarrow -sim(w_i, w_j) - sim(w_i, w_k) + 1 < -sim(w_j, w_k) + 1$$
$$\Rightarrow -sim(w_i, w_j) + dis(w_i, w_k) < dis(w_j, w_k), \text{considering } dis(w_j, w_k) < 1$$
$$\Rightarrow 1 - sim(w_i, w_j) + dis(w_i, w_k) > dis(w_j, w_k)$$
$$\Rightarrow dis(w_i, w_j) + dis(w_i, w_k) > dis(w_j, w_k)$$

3.2   The Application of the Hypothesis

Theoretically, if the hypothesis is true, semantic distance among words should be also satisfied with the three properties: identity of indiscernibles, symmetry and triangle inequality. The first two properties are satisfied according to the description in the above section. To triangle inequality, because the word similarity scores are computed based on thesaurus, the incorrect categorization probably cause it is not satisfied in some condition. We utilize this character to detect the incorrect categorization in the thesaurus.

Given any three words w_i, w_j and w_k, their similarity scores are separately computed as sim_{ij}, sim_{jk} and sim_{ik}. If these three scores are not satisfied with the property of triangle inequality, we suspect there is at least one of these three words are wrongly grouped with its synonyms (in *WordNet*, it is a synset but it is a line in *Cilin*).

We first traverse all synonym sets in a thesaurus (called test thesaurus). A lot of synonym triples (each one consists of three synonyms) are collected. To each triple, three word similarity scores are computed based on the thesaurus-based algorithm. Obviously, another thesaurus is needed, we call it reference thesaurus. When a triple does not comply the property of triangle inequality, it will become a suspect, i.e. there is a word in the triple is incorrectly categorization. And if sim_{ij} is the largest one, the problematic word is probably w_k.

4   Experiments

In this paper, *Cilin* is the test thesaurus and *HowNet* is used as the reference thesaurus. The word similarity is got by the software[1] developed by (Liu and Li, 2002). All parameters are default setting.

4.1   Experimental Setup

There are totally 77,343 words in *Cilin* and they are classed into five levels according their abstract degree. They are arranged into a semantic tree and higher level means more abstract. In the lowest one, there are 17,817 nodes and each node consists of some synonyms they represent the same concept. For example, a node (a line in *Cilin*) "A a 01 A 04= 劳力 (labor) 劳动力 (labor force) 工作者 (worker)", the first capital "A" is the first level code (it denotes the concept of "人" (human being)). From left to right, "a", "01", "A" and "04" is respectively the code for the 2nd, 3rd, 4th and 5th level. "=" means the words listed in this line are synonyms.

Although there are 17,817 lines (synsets) in *Cilin*, there are 4,377 lines contain only one word in it and 4,162 lines contain only two words. Except them, 9,095 lines are experimented. To each line, any three words are formed as a triple, there are totally 79,699,501 triples. In each triple, we extract any two words to form a word pair and get their word similarity by the software. To each word pair, if one of words is not listed in *HowNet*, we denote the similarity -1 because we can't get the similarity score. It is regretted that there are 305,057 word pairs' similar value are -1, and so results in 14,880,874 triples could not be verified by the property of triangle inequality.

4.2   Experimental Results

There are 64,818,627 triples are tested at last. Among them, 64,067,416 triples are satisfied with triangle inequality, they accounts for 98.84%. It shows the third property, triangle inequality, will be satisfied in fact by the overwhelming majority synonym or near-synonym[2]. Table 1 illustrates the results sorted by their first level code in detail.

---

[1] It could be free download from http://www.keenage.com.

[2] It should be noted that only the similarity among synonyms or near-synonyms rather than any words is covered by our hypothesis. In practice, obtaining the dissimilar words nearly make no sense.

Table 1. Statistical Results of Satisfied with Triangle Inequality for *Cilin*

Class	Satisfied	Dissatis-fied	Percentage (%)
A	180,387	6598	3.53
B	1,499,286	40,793	2.65
C	1,643,910	147,729	8.25
D	60,017,108	239,910	0.40
E	270,768	140,738	34.2
F	7,897	7,548	48.87
G	41,833	38,712	48.06
H	80,496	43,736	35.21
I	274,862	42,479	13.39
J	21,407	22,733	51.5
K	29,462	20,235	40.72
L	---	---	---
Total	64,067,416	751,211	1.16

From the above table, the largest number of triples are not satisfied with our hypothesis is class D (abstract). Although there are 239,910 dissatisfied triples, the percentage is the smallest one considering it also has largest number of triples. The largest percentage occurs in the class J (association). Besides it, classes G (mental action), F (action) and K (auxiliary) have larger proportion than the rest. The words in class L (honorific) cannot obtain their similarity score and so, we use "---" to show this case.

4.3   Analysis of Incorrect Categorization

The instances of incorrect categorization in *Cilin* could be divided into three classes:

(1) The test thesaurus *Cilin* contains some ancient word senses, which have been discarded by the reference thesaurus *HowNet*. For example, the word 萌 (sprout) is grouped in the same line with "黎民 (the common people) and 平民 (the populace)" in *Cilin*. In ancient Chinese, it means the common people esp. the non-local people. But the software return the word similarity score between 黎民 and 平民 is 0.8 while the score between 黎民 and 萌 is 0.0489712, at the same time the score between 平民 and 萌 is 0.0397805. This triple is not satisfied our hypothesis because the sum of later twos is less than the first one. So, we suggest remove it from the line. The similar cases are the first and the second row in table 2. Among them the word which is underlined is the problematic word.

(2) The test thesaurus puts some word in wrong place. According to the method described in section 3.2, from the 751,211 triples who are not satisfied inequality, we find 16,613 words are involved in. For example, the word 绍 (a Surname) causes 16,649 triples violate our hypothesis while 典型 (typical) and 焦化 (coking) causes 247 and 16,436 problematic triples respectively. We randomly select 644 suspect triples, inspect them manually, and find 206 ones are indeed incorrect categorization. Table 2 shows some examples.

Table 2. Instances of incorrect categorization in *Cilin*

Category Code	Triples	Similarity Score
Ae09A01	贾 (a surname in Chinese), 经纪人 (broker), 生意人 (businessman)	0.11, 0.11, 1.0
Bh02A44	鸡冠花 (cockscombs), 蓉 (the abbreviation of Chengdu), 紫罗兰 (violet)	0.11, 1.0, 0.11
Cb25A11	长沙 (Changsha), 齐齐哈尔 (Qiqihaer), 典雅 (elegant)	1.0, 0.05, 0.05
Dl01A80	鼻炎 (rhinitis), 黑热病 (kala-azar), 心血管 (angiocarpy)	1.0, 0.13, 0.12
Ed46A01	赫 (conspicuous), 醒豁 (conspicuous), 举世瞩目 (attract world wide attention)	0.77, 0.04, 0.04
Fa08B01	采摘 (pick), 采撷(pick), 摘掉(pick off)	1.0, 0.15, 0.15
Gb08A01	敞亮 (lightandspacious), 领略 (appreciate), 接头 (contact)	1.0, 0.10, 0.10
Hg08C01	模拟 (simulate), 照猫画虎 (simulate), 宪章 (charter)	1.0, 0.07, 0.07
Ih02B14	改道 (divert), 转型 (transform), 体改 (organizational reform)	0.72, 0.04, 0.04
Je04A02	诱 (induce), 诱惑 (induce), 抓住(catch)	1.0, 0.11, 0.6
Ka01A01	颇 (very), 雅 (elegant), 煞 (vicious)	0.66, 0.04, 0.04

In Table 2, "Code" denotes the concept number in *Cilin*; the "similarity score" from left to right is the semantic quantification of the first word and the second one, the first word and the third one, and the second one and third one.

(3) The words in reference thesaurus have been incorrectly categorized. For instance, in the triple (差价 (price differences), 粮价 (grain price), 基价 (basic price)), the word similarity scores from left to right is 0.0521389, 0.0521389 and 1.0. The triple does not satisfy the triangle inequality. This is leaded by the fact that the word 差价 (price differences) is incorrectly classified into the category of 比率 (ratio) in *HowNet*. A similar case is the triple (偏重 (lay particular stress on), 赏识 (appreciate), 推崇 (praise highly)), in which the three similarity scores are 0.347826, 0.0909091 and 0.0963855, respectively. The latter two scores are underestimated.

5   Conclusion and Future Work

In this paper, we propose a hypothesis, i.e. the semantic distance between synonyms or near-synonyms could construct a metric space. It should hold three prosperities: identity of indiscernibles, symmetry and triangle inequality. In particular, in order to verify the third property, we extract 64,818,627 triples from the *Cilin* thesaurus, according to the word similarity scores computed using *HowNet*. 98.84% triples satisfy the property of triangle inequality.

We apply this hypothesis to check incorrect categorization in the *Cilin* thesaurus. From the 1.16% of all triples (the number is 751,221), which do not satisfy our hypothesis, 16,613 words are detected as problematic words. We check a small number of these triples extracted randomly and find out that about 32% of them have been incorrectly categorized. So, our method could reduce the number of words involved with incorrect categorization dramatically from 80 thousand to 16 thousand.

Undoubtedly, the hypothesis should be verified in English language at least in the future. But a more interesting work may be to leverage the hypothesis to filter the associated words from the neighbors automatically computed by these statistical-based algorithms. Our experiments have shown that the similarity score computed through these algorithms could be used to rank the neighbors, as well as remove someone who violates the triangle inequality.

Acknowledgments. This work is partially supported by NSFC (61373056, 61272221, 61103089), Open Projects Program of Key Laboratory of Computational Linguistics (Peking University), Ministry of Education of PRC (No. 201303) and Scientific Research Project of National Language Committee (No. WT125-45). We also thank the reviewers for the valuable comments and advices.

References

1. Lawrence, S., Pereira, F.: Aggregate and mixed-order Markov models for statistical language processing. In: Proceedings of EMNLP, pp. 81–89 (1997)
2. Lee, L.: On the Effectiveness of the Skew Divergence for Statistical Language Analysis. In: Proceedings of Artificial Intelligence and Statistics, pp. 65–72 (2001)
3. Chang, W., Pantel, P., Popescu, A., Gabrilovich, E.: Towards Intent-driven Bid-term Suggestion. In: Proceedings of WWW, pp. 1093–1094 (2009)
4. Gauch, S., Chong, M.K.: Automatic Word Similarity Detection for TREC4 Query Expansion. In: Proceedings of TREC-4, pp. 527–536 (1996)
5. Miller, G.A.: WordNet: A Lexical Database for English. Communication of ACM **38**(11), 39–41 (1995)
6. Mei, J., Zhu, Y., Gao, Y., Yin, H. (eds.): Tongyici *Cilin* [A Thesaurus of Chinese Words]. Commercial Press, Hong Kong (1984)
7. Dong, Z., Dong, Q.: HowNet and the Computation of Meaning. World Scientific Publishing Co. Inc., River Edge (2006)
8. Resnik, P.: Using information content to evaluate semantic similarity. In: Proceedings of IJCAI, pp. 448–453 (1995)
9. Jiang, J., Conrath, D.: Semantic similarity based on corpus statistics and lexical taxonomy. In: Proceedings of ROCLING, pp. 19–33 (1997)
10. Budanitsky, A., Hirst, G.: Evaluating WordNet-based Measures of Lexical Semantic Relatedness. Computational Linguistics **32**(1), 13–47 (2006)

11. Pedersen, T.: WordNet::Similarity (2008). http://wn-similarity.sourceforge.net/
12. Liu, Q., Li, S.: Word similarity computing based on HowNet. Computational Linguistics and Chinese Language Processing **17**(2), 59–76 (2002)
13. Firth, J.R.: A synopsis of linguistic theory, 1930–1955 (1957)
14. Lin, D.: Automatic retrieval and clustering of similar words. In: Proceedings of COLING/ACL, pp. 768–774 (1998)
15. Mikolov, T., Chen, K., Corrado, G., Dean, J.: Efficient Estimation of Word Representations in Vector Space. In: Proceedings of Workshop at ICLR (2013)
16. Qiu, L., Wu, Y., Kang, Y.: Detect Thesaurus Errors Based on Distributional Similarity. Journal of Computational Information Systems **8**(20), 8645–8652 (2012)

Lexical Resources
and Corpus Linguistics

Chinese Near-Synonym Study Based on the Chinese Gigaword Corpus and the Chinese Learner Corpus

Jia-Fei Hong[✉]

National Taiwan Normal University, Taipei, Taiwan
jiafeihong@ntnu.edu.tw

Abstract. The study of Chinese near-synonyms is crucial in Chinese lexical semantics, as well as in Chinese language teaching. Recently, Chinese near-synonyms have become important in teaching Chinese as a foreign language; therefore, it is worthwhile to focus on effective strategies for teaching near-synonyms to Chinese learners, especially in recognizing and using lexical senses for nearly synonymous Chinese words. This study will use the Chinese Gigaword Corpus [1] with the Chinese Word Sketch Engine [2] and the Chinese Learner Corpus (of Written Chinese) [3] to compare the usages of nearly synonymous Chinese words by Chinese learners. This study will focus on two sets of near-synonyms—"*bian4li4*" versus "*fang1bian4*" and "*ren4shi4*" versus "*zhi1dao4*"—as the research objects and discuss their differences in Chinese language teaching.

Keywords: Chinese near-synonyms · Lexical semantics · Chinese teaching, Chinese Gigaword Corpus · Chinese Learner Corpus (of Written Chinese)

1 Introduction

There are approximately 1.4 billion native Mandarin speakers worldwide, and approximately 100 million students are currently learning Mandarin [4], [5], [6]. More than 100 countries and 12,400 schools offer Mandarin courses, including more than 1,100 middle schools in the U.S., where more than 800 colleges also offer Mandarin teaching courses. Therefore, it is crucial to develop and provide scientific empirical teaching materials that adhere to best practices. It is essential that Chinese language teachers utilize a scientific system like Chinese Word Sketch to teach Chinese vocabulary, lexical semantics, and the usage distributions of each pair of nearly synonymous Chinese words to those who are learning Chinese as a second language. This study will compare information about two sets of nearly synonymous Chinese words with the empirical usages by Chinese language learners and investigate their usage errors.

Regarding Chinese vocabulary and near-synonym teaching, there are many different viewpoints and theories; moreover, teaching approaches are manifold. Because the learning achievements of Chinese language learners vary, the goal of this study is to examine Chinese near-synonyms using both a Chinese native speaker corpus and a Chinese learner corpus, and then compare the analyzed data for Chinese near-synonym teaching.

© Springer International Publishing Switzerland 2014
X. Su and T. He (Eds.): CLSW 2014, LNAI 8922, pp. 329–340, 2014.
DOI: 10.1007/978-3-319-14331-6_33

This study will utilize the Chinese Gigaword Corpus with the Chinese Word Sketch Engine to show some usage distributions of two sets of nearly synonymous words. Furthermore, this study also will present a selection of Chinese language learners' usage distributions of these two sets of nearly synonymous words using the Chinese Learner Corpus (of Written Chinese), which was developed by a team led by Hao-Jan Chen (National Taiwan Normal University) [3]. Last, but not least, this study will compare the different usage distributions of the near-synonym words and discuss the empirical errors found.

First this study will explore some related studies in Chinese vocabulary and near-synonym teaching; second, this study will discuss the Chinese Gigaword Corpus, the Chinese Word Sketch Engine, and the Chinese Learner Corpus (of Written Chinese); third, this study will concentrate on "comparison" rather than typical "intuition" and general "comprehension" in Chinese near-synonym teaching; finally, this study will discuss the importance of Chinese near-synonyms and their application in Chinese vocabulary teaching.

2   Previous Studies: Chinese Vocabulary and Near-Synonym Teaching

Vocabulary is an important element of language; unfortunately, it is extremely difficult for Chinese language learners to acquire an extensive vocabulary. Therefore, vocabulary teaching is especially important in Chinese language teaching. However, linguists were not interested in vocabulary acquisition until the early 1980s [7]. Many previous Chinese lexical semantics studies, such as [8], [9], and [10], have been conducted, and there have also been cross-strait lexical differences studies, as in [11] and [12]. In addition, grammatical relations and lexical distributions were discussed in past studies that are related to comparative studies of Chinese lexical semantics and near-synonyms, such as a study on usage differences of "*sheng1* (sound)" and "*ying1* (sound)" [9] and another on usage comparisons of "*qing1chu3* (clear)" and "*ming2bai2* (clear)"[13].

Chinese vocabulary teaching is more complex for Chinese language learners than for Chinese native speakers. In a previous relative study [14], the author mentioned that vocabulary is the core element that connects five key linguistic aspects: phonetic, semantic, grammatical, pragmatic, and culture. These five aspects are included in the construction of a multi-vector network for the Chinese language. Therefore, it is valuable and worthwhile to focus on Chinese near-synonym studies.

Many previous strategies and discussions in studies on Chinese near-synonyms have varied in terms of lexical usages, grammatical information, semantic properties, semantic features, and error analyses [3], [15], and [16]. In addition, learning vocabulary is a process of gradual comprehension and memorization rather than a process of merely reciting a list of words [17].

Because there are no related studies on Chinese near-synonym teaching that compare a Chinese native speaker corpus with a Chinese learner corpus, this study will provide a comparison thereof to demonstrate Chinese native speakers' appropriate usage of Chinese near-synonyms, observe Chinese language learners' empirical usages, and, finally, analyze the latter's usage errors.

3   Chinese Gigaword Corpus and Chinese Word Sketch Engine

The Chinese Gigaword Corpus, version 2.0, was collected from 1990 to 2004. It contains approximately 1.4 billion Chinese characters, including more than 800 million characters from Taiwan's Central News Agency, nearly 500 million characters from China's Xinhua News Agency, and about 30 million characters from Singapore's Zaobao. Before loading the Chinese Gigaword Corpus into the Chinese Word Sketch Engine, all of the simplified characters were converted to traditional characters, and the texts were segmented and POS-tagged using the Academia Sinica segmentation and tagging system [18]. The segmentation and tagging was performed automatically, with automatic and partially manual post-checking. The precision accuracy is estimated to be greater than 95% [19].

The two challenges to corpus-based computational approaches to linguistic analysis are acquiring enough data to show linguistic distributions and designing efficient tools for extracting linguistically significant generalizations from vast amounts of data. The Chinese Word Sketch Engine was developed to facilitate the efficient use of gargantuan corpora [20]. The Sketch Engine (SKE, also known as the Word Sketch Engine) is a novel corpus query system that incorporates word sketches, grammatical relations, and a distributional thesaurus.

The advantage of using the Sketch Engine as a query tool is that it pays attention to the grammatical context of a word, instead of returning an arbitrary number of adjacent words. In order to show the cross-lingual robustness of the Sketch Engine, as well as to propose a powerful tool for collocation extraction based on a large-scale corpus with minimal pre-processing, [19] constructed the Chinese Word Sketch Engine (http://wordsketch.ling.sinica.edu.tw/) by loading the Chinese Gigaword Corpus into the Sketch Engine [21]. All components of the Sketch Engine were implemented, including *Concordance, Word Sketch, Thesaurus,* and *Sketch Difference.*

Fig. 1. Chinese Word Sketch Engine home page

In [2], they mentioned that previous works that contributed significantly to the study of automatic extraction of grammatical relations include work on KWIC [22], the introduction of mutual information [23], and the introduction of relevance measurements [24]. Kilgarriff et al.'s work on Word Sketch Engine (WSE) made a bold step forward in automatic linguistic knowledge acquisition [20] and [25].

In [19], they utilized the Chinese Word Sketch Engine [20] and [21] as the corpus query tool by which grammatical behaviors of two heterogeneous resources could be captured and displayed in a unified Web interface. Therefore, the best way to annotate two heterogeneous corpora to enable them to consistently compare their words' syntactic behaviors through the Chinese Word Sketch Engine is an important concern. The home page of the Chinese Word Sketch Engine is shown below in Figure 1:

In this study, using the "Sketch Difference" function in the Chinese Word Sketch Engine, I will focus on two sets of nearly synonymous words and compare some of their usages and distributions, such as related collocations, argument roles, unique patterns, etc., and examine the differences between the two nearly synonymous words that are commonly used in Chinese near-synonym teaching. The "Sketch Difference" interface is shown in Figure 2 below:

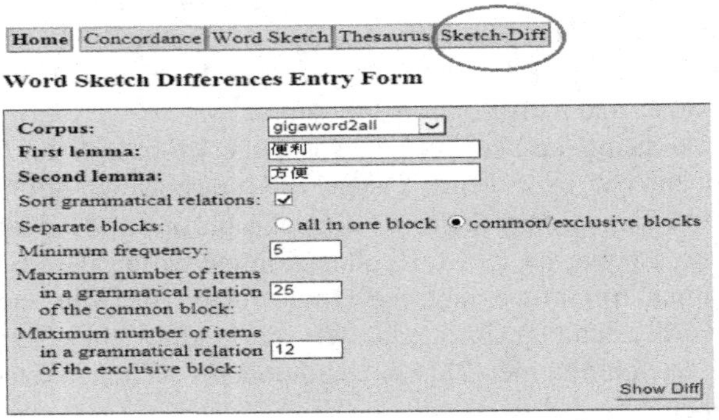

Fig. 2. The "Sketch Difference" interface in the Chinese Word Sketch Engine

"Sketch Difference" is one of the four functions available in the Chinese Word Sketch Engine. This tool's main function is to compare two different words and to show related grammatical constructions and collocation information. Users can compare and study linguistic distributions, usages, and results using this interface. This study will discuss more detail on the comparisons of related words using "Sketch Difference" to obtain usages and distributions in Sections 6 and 7.

4   Chinese Learner Corpus (of Written Chinese)

National Taiwan Normal University (NTNU)'s Chinese Learner Corpus of Written Chinese (http://kitty.2y.idv.tw/~hjchen/cwrite-mtc/main.cgi) is Taiwan's first and largest learner corpus. This corpus was developed by a team led by Hao-Jan Chen from NTNU [3]. It contains writing samples from learners with backgrounds in 40 different native languages, a 300-million-character corpus from learners with different levels of writing abilities, and error marking performed by language professionals, making it the country's largest Chinese Learner Corpus of Written Chinese Errors. In addition, NTNU has compiled Taiwan's only 770,000-character Learner Corpus of Spoken Chinese, which is comprised of native Japanese, Korean, and English-speaking learners. The entire corpus has been transcribed into text files, thus allowing users to listen to recordings online while simultaneously reading the text. These two corpora provide language researchers worldwide the chance to study the pronunciation, grammar, and pragmatics of learners in depth. NTNU has also created a learner vocabulary profile corresponding to the Common European Framework of Reference for Languages (CEFR), developed a set of guidelines to describe the key features of Chinese learners at different levels, conducted research on learners' errors, analyzed learners' use of synonyms and special sentence patterns, and, accordingly, developed a query system for common Chinese sentence patterns and a syntax auto-correct function for common Chinese sentences. The Chinese Learner Corpus Web site is presented in Figure 3 below:

Fig. 3. The Chinese Learner Corpus (of Written Chinese) Web site

5   Research Motivation and Goals

In Chinese lexical semantics, near-synonyms are crucial to learning the language; however, there are many usage errors made by learners. Therefore, it is necessary to teach Chinese language learners to discern the lexical meanings of near-synonyms and apply them in different contexts accurately. In particular, for two nearly synonymous words, it is necessary to understand their different core meanings and use them in different contexts.

For this reason, I will present empirical usages of two sets of nearly synonymous Chinese words using the Chinese Gigaword Corpus (native corpus) and the Chinese Learner Corpus (learner corpus); then, I will examine usages and comparisons as well as study usage errors. In other words, I will point out grammatical information, semantic features, and collocations in the Chinese Gigaword Corpus using the Chinese Word Sketch Engine for Chinese near-synonym teaching. In addition, I will also point out the empirical usages from the Chinese Learner Corpus and compare them. In this way, Chinese language learners can understand the lexical meanings of two nearly synonymous Chinese words, as well as comprehend and apply them correctly in reading and writing.

6   *"Fang1bian4* (Convenient)" and *"Bian4li4* (Convenient)" as Conventionalized by Near-Synonyms

6.1   The Chinese Gigaword Corpus with the Chinese Word Sketch Engine

Using the *"Sketch Difference"* function in the Chinese Word Sketch Engine, I obtained the common patterns of *"fang1bian4* (convenient)" and *"bian4li4* (convenient)" as well as their respective patterns. The patterns of *"fang1bian4"* and *"bian4li4"* can be observed in Figures 4 through 6 below:

方便/便利 gigaword2all freq = 44054/19244

Common patterns

方便	21	14	7	0	-7	-14	-21	便利
Subject 977	366	8.6	0.8	**Modifies** 2121	1378	3.0	0.5	
交通	91	105	33.6 42.2	條件	87	168	23.0 40.2	
生活	27	10	17.4 12.5	交通		113	13.3 37.1	
民眾	26	10	15.3 11.2	時間	82		24.6 3.7	
				地方	75	26	23.5 14.9	
				工具	26	24	22.1 23.2	
				同時	50	33	21.8 19.6	
				優勢	20	31	14.5 20.9	
				管道	18	18	18.2 20.1	
				通道	5	12	9.9 19.0	
				大眾	3	17	7.5 19.0	
				環境	24	42	11.5 18.8	
				金融	12	33	7.1 17.1	
				資訊	8	20	7.8 16.7	
				方式	31	32	14.0 16.5	
				生活	11	24	7.0 14.6	

Fig. 4. Common patterns of *"fang1bian4"* and *"bian4li4"* found with the *"Sketch Difference"* tool

"方便" only patterns

Subject 977	8.6	**Modifies** 2121	3.0
大地	14 22.7	時候	633 70.2
玉米	13 21.4	優點	16 25.3
出行	6 20.0	特點	29 24.2
聯招會	6 16.3	話	30 21.6
市民	15 15.9	途徑	12 14.3
旅客	13 15.4	時機	10 13.9
客戶	9 14.9	方法	14 13.2
遊客	10 14.2	特性	6 12.1
消費者	10 12.9	形式	10 11.2
病人	7 12.1	農地	5 11.0
乘客	6 12.0	做法	8 10.5
大家	8 11.6	自來水	6 10.3

Fig. 5. Patterns of only *"fang1bian4"* found with the *"Sketch Difference"* tool

"便利" only patterns

Subject 366	0.8		Modifies 1378	0.5
職務	16 21.8		通關	8 17.6
貿易	30 21.5		轉機	5 13.4
小時	5 11.1		海	9 12.7
資金	5 7.8		融資	7 12.1
			空間	10 11.8
			前提	5 9.8
			場所	6 9.8
			通訊	6 9.3
			鄉鎮	5 9.2
			位置	5 8.2
			區域	6 8.0
			路	5 7.9

Fig. 6. Patterns of only *"bian4li4"* found with the *"Sketch Difference"* tool

6.2 The Chinese Learner Corpus

Using the Chinese Learner Corpus, I inputted "方便" (*fang1bian4*) and "便利" (*bian4li4*) as keywords and obtain 357 hits and 8 hits, respectively. The results of "方便 (*fang1bian4*)" and "便利 (*bian4li4*)" are shown in Figures 7 and 8 below. In Figure 7, I observed learners' usage errors in empirical sentences, for example, "那杯子是为把『方便』商店的咖啡...." ("That cup is for the convenience store's...."). The correct usage is "那杯子是为把『便利』商店的咖啡...." Regarding usage errors, it is beneficial to use the *"Sketch Difference"* tool in the Chinese Word Sketch Engine to analyze and explore the correct usages of *"fang1bian4"* and *"bian4li4"*.

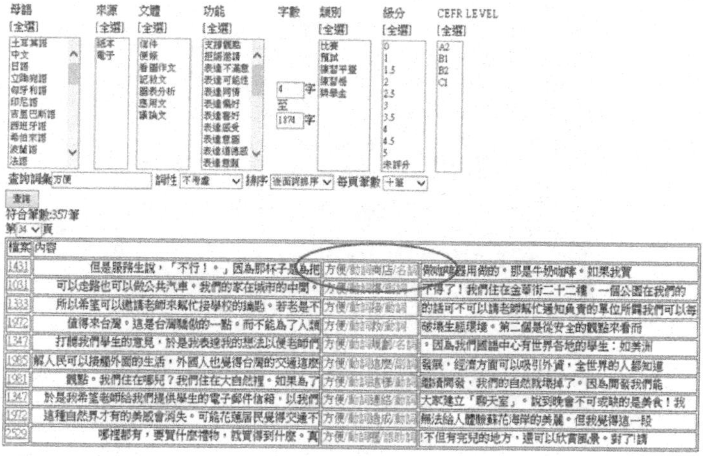

Fig. 7. The usages of *"fang1bian4"* in the Chinese Learner Corpus

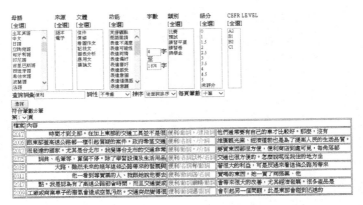

Fig. 8. The usages of "*bian4li4*" in the Chinese Learner Corpus

7 "*Ren4shi4* (Know)" and "*Zhi1dao4* (Know)" as Conventionalized by Near-Synonyms

7.1 The Chinese Gigaword Corpus with the Chinese Word Sketch Engine

With two additional nearly synonymous Chinese words—"*ren4shi4* (know)" and "*zhi1dao4* (know)"—using the Chinese Gigaword Corpus, both the common patterns and the patterns only of "*ren4shi4*" and "*zhi1dao4*", respectively, are shown with the "*Sketch Difference*" function in the Chinese Word Sketch Engine in Figures 9 through 11 below:

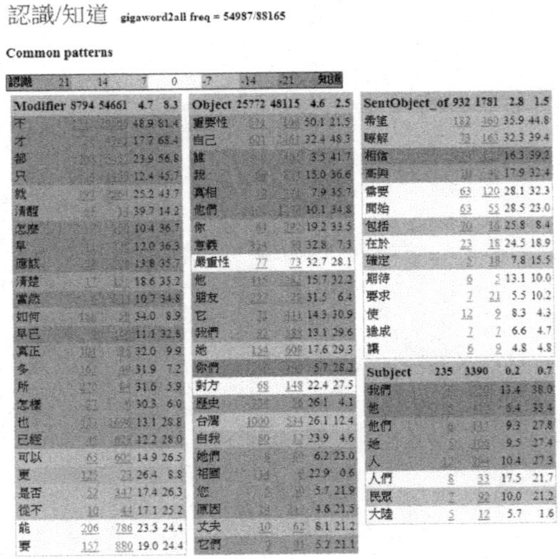

Fig. 9. Common patterns of "*ren4shi4*" and "*zhi1dao4*" found with the "*Sketch Difference*" tool

"認識" only patterns			
PP_對 808 26.7	**PP_從** 41 12.9	**Modifier** 8794 4.7	**Object** 25772 4.6
重要性 35 31.7	觀念 31 41.6	重新 761 57.7	誤區 73 46.0
錯誤 16 25.4		進一步 730 49.3	長期性 70 38.0
危害性 8 25.3		更加 109 40.6	艱巨性 48 36.1
基本 17 23.0		互相 117 38.6	巡迴展 48 32.5
艾滋病 13 20.1		正確 90 37.6	古蹟日 11 32.4
思想 16 17.6		來 612 37.1	危害性 38 32.2
病變 6 17.3		相互 154 36.4	周人 40 31.5
歷史 29 16.5		去 163 31.6	學校系 18 31.0
嚴重性 5 15.3		深刻 45 30.9	緊迫性 31 30.0
意義 13 15.3		全面 132 27.8	基本法 115 29.9
危害 7 14.6		了 220 27.7	形勢 253 29.5
規律 6 14.5		客觀 19 25.8	複雜性 34 28.4

PP_用 7 4.2	**SentObject_of** 932 2.8	**PP_在** 117 1.6	**Modifies** 1428 0.2
建設 5 15.3	有助於 62 38.2	階層 7 21.3	鬼子兵 21 56.4
	促進 58 27.8	形勢 11 21.3	朋友 82 37.6
	有助 15 23.8	時期 5 13.8	基礎 85 28.7
	理解 10 20.5	工作 5 6.9	孫運璿 11 26.8
	自覺 7 16.6	**Subject** 235 0.2	人中 10 22.3
	有待 8 15.6	思想 11 18.5	過程 37 22.1
	持續 15 15.6	高度 8 15.5	老朋友 9 22.0
	有利於 9 14.8	彼此 5 15.2	局限性 5 20.4
	堅持 12 13.3		機會 33 19.5
	旨在 6 12.6		漢字 7 18.4
	不利 6 12.2		黃運交 6 17.6
	涉及 7 10.5		好朋友 5 16.2

Fig. 10. Pattern of only "*ren4shi4*" found with the "*Sketch Difference*" tool

"知道" only patterns			
Modifier 54661 8.3	**PP_從** 49 4.4	**Object** 48115 2.5	**PP_在** 533 2.1
明明 122 51.1	何處 7 29.0	何時 297 45.3	背後 5 15.4
事先 221 39.4		下落 181 37.6	比賽 9 9.4
哪裡 37 32.4		內情 78 35.3	新加坡 6 9.3
無從 26 28.9		答案 120 33.2	飛機 5 9.0
預先 56 27.9		詳情 91 31.1	台灣 11 7.1
不一定 34 24.9		行蹤 78 29.4	情況 6 6.9
大概 22 22.6		名字 125 27.6	時間 5 6.1
未必 22 21.4		事情 180 26.6	中國 11 6.1
怎 14 21.2		去向 44 26.4	地區 10 5.7
即可 71 20.4		何處 47 26.1	美國 7 4.7
早一點 11 20.2		實情 39 26.1	社會 5 4.5
那裡 20 19.7		大勢 31 24.4	大陸 6 4.5

SentObject_of 1781 1.5	**PP_自** 11 1.5	**Subject** 3390 0.7	**Modifies** 1043 0.0
裝作 21 47.8	己身 7 39.8	我 335 46.3	事 150 42.1
怕 49 36.5		大家 148 38.4	事情 52 35.2
急於 28 33.6		你 102 38.1	事實 35 28.2
熟知 16 32.6		誰 61 33.3	邱創煥 11 24.2
知道 60 31.1		您 22 25.8	比例 24 21.0
顯示 74 29.6		你們 21 23.8	東西 14 20.6
偽裝 11 29.5		明眼人 5 19.6	答案 9 20.1
擔心 45 28.1		世人 11 17.6	常識 7 17.7
渴望 18 26.9		一般人 7 16.1	話 15 17.5
懷疑 26 24.8		家人 14 15.9	二二八 6 16.3
樂於 11 23.6		市民 22 14.0	訊息 9 15.7
深怕 8 23.4		別人 9 13.8	消息 19 15.7

Fig. 11. Pattern of only "*zhi1dao4*" found with the "*Sketch Difference*" tool

7.2   The Chinese Learner Corpus

When we conducted the same query for "*ren4shi4*" and "*zhi1dao4*" using the Chinese Learner Corpus, there were 478 hits for "*ren4shi4*" and 1,683 hits for "*zhi1dao4*". These results are shown in Figures12 and 13, respectively. In Figure12, the error sentence is "我剛剛『认识』一家不错的日本餐厅…" ("I know a good Japanese resultant recently.") and in Figure13, the error sentence is "用电邮或MSN连络以后，慢慢『知道』他是怎么样的人" ("You can get to know him through email and MSN."). The correct sentences are "我刚刚『知道』一家不错的日本餐厅." and "用电邮或MSN连络以后，慢慢『认识』他是怎么样的人." Regarding the usage errors, it is also beneficial to use the *Sketch Difference* tool in the Chinese Word Sketch Engine to analyze and explore the correct usages of "ren4shi4" and "zhi1dao4".

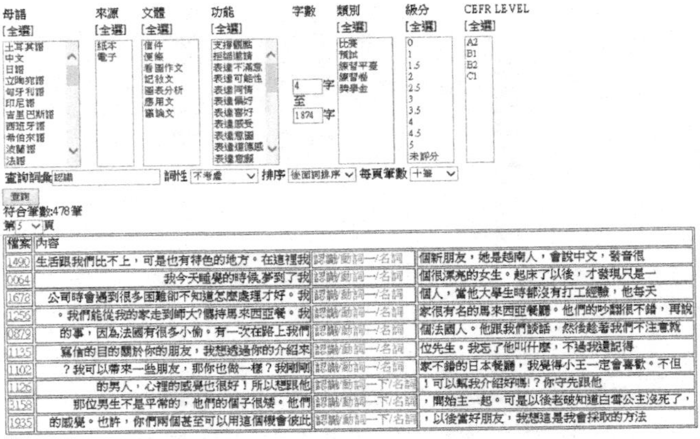

Fig. 12. The usages of "*ren4shi4*" in the Chinese Learner Corpus

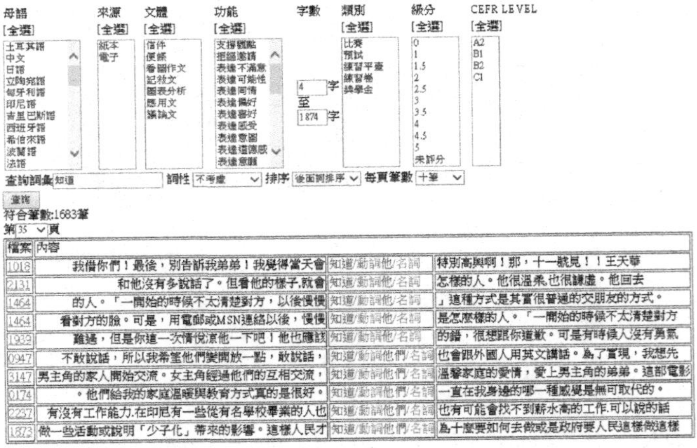

Fig. 13. The usages of "*zhi1dao4*" in the Chinese Learner Corpus

8   Conclusion and Future Work

As far as language learners who are learning Chinese as a second language are concerned, it is crucial to learn the lexical senses of nearly synonymous words, accurately use them in different contexts, and, finally, recognize and comprehend their nearly synonymous senses. It has been found that Chinese vocabulary and near-synonyms are difficult aspects of learning the Chinese language.

This study explored native speakers' Chinese language usage using the Chinese Gigaword Corpus with the Chinese Word Sketch Engine and presented scientific and empirical examples. It also explored Chinese learners' language usage using the Chinese Learner Corpus and discussed their usage errors in depth. Finally, this study compared the differences between native speakers' Chinese language usage and Chinese learners' language usage in order to provide scientific and empirical approaches to learning Chinese vocabulary.

Using both the Chinese Gigaword Corpus and the Chinese Learner Corpus proved useful in extracting related language information. This comparative study of Chinese near-synonyms and its results have provided a breakthrough for Chinese language teaching and learning, as well as for developing Chinese-language materials. In addition, Chinese language learners can extract all possible grammatical information, patterns, and collocations from the Chinese Word Sketch Engine and apply them correctly in speaking and writing; moreover, teachers can explore Chinese learners' most common usage errors in the Chinese Learner Corpus to compare and generalize language usages and differences. Conducting a comparative study of Chinese near-synonyms has proven to be a powerful and scientific method of utilizing corpora to obtain a large amount of empirical data and usage distributions in Chinese language teaching and learning applications. Therefore, based on the learning approach in this study, Chinese language learners can develop greater comprehension of Chinese near-synonyms.

Acknowledgements. This research is partially supported by the "Aim for the Top University Project" and "Center of Learning Technology for Chinese" of National Taiwan Normal University (NTNU), sponsored by the Ministry of Education, Taiwan, R.O.C., and the "International Research-Intensive Center of Excellence Program" of NTNU and the Ministry of Science and Technology, Taiwan, R.O.C., under Grant no. NSC 103-2911-I-003-301.

References

1. Lexical Data Consortium (LDC). Chinese Gigaword Corpus 2.5 (2005). http://www.ldc.upenn.edu/Catalog/CatalogEntry.jsp?catalogId=LDC2005T14
2. Huang, C.-R., Adam K., Wu, Y. et al.: Chinese Sketch Engine and the extraction of collocations. In: Proceedings of the 4th SIGHAN Workshop on Chinese Language Processing, Jeju, Korea, pp. 48–55 (October 14–15, 2005)
3. Wang, Y.-T., Chen, H.-J.H., Pan, I.-T.: Investigation and analysis of Chinese synonymous verbs based on the Chinese Learner Corpus: Example of "bang", "bang-zhu", "bang-mang" and "bian", "bian-de", "bian-cheng". Journal of Chinese Language Teaching **10**(3), 41–64 (2013). (in Chinese)
4. Industrial Development Bureau, Ministry of Economic Affairs (2007)
5. Commonwealth Publishing Group (ed.): Global Views Monthly, Taiwan, Taipei (2011)
6. The Commercial Press (ed.): The World of Chinese, Beijing, China (2010)

7. Paul, M.: The complexities of simple vocabulary tests. In: Brinkman, F.G., van der Schee, J.A., and MCV (1994)
8. Tsai, M.-C.: TONGYANG and XIANGTONG are not YIYANG: The referential differences of "the same" in Mandarin Chinese. Journal of Chinese Language Teaching 7(1), 57–79 (2010). (in Chinese)
9. Huang, C.-R., Hong, J.-F.: Deriving conceptual structures from sense: A study of near synonymous sensation verbs. Journal of Chinese Language and Computing (JCLC) 15(3), 125–136 (2005)
10. Tsai, M.-C., Huang, C.-R., Chen, K.-J., Ahrens, K.: Towards a representation of verbal semantics—An approach based on near synonyms. Computational Linguistics and Chinese Language Processing 3(1), 61–74 (1998)
11. Hong, J.-F., Huang, C.-R.: Cross-strait lexical differences: A comparative study based on Chinese Gigaword Corpus. Computational Linguistics and Chinese Language Processing 9(2), 19–34 (2013). (in Chinese)
12. Hong, J.-F., Huang, C.-R.: A Corpus-based approach to the discovery of cross-strait lexical contrasts. Language and Linguistics 9(2), 221–238 (2008). Taipei, Nankang: Institute of Linguistics; Taipei: Academia Sinica. (in Chinese)
13. Tsai, M.-C.: Jiang "qing1chu3", shui "ming2bai2"—Verbal near synonym, ambiguity and sense division study in Chinese. In: The 3rd Chinese Lexical Semantic Workshop (CLSW 2002). Academia Sinica, Taipei (2002). (in Chinese)
14. Tian, W.-P.: The multi-dimensional properties of vocabulary teaching to foreign students. Chinese Teaching in the World 4, 71–78 (1997). (in Chinese)
15. Hsu, M.-S.: Chinese near synonym study for teaching as second language: Guan1yu2, Zhi4yu2 and Dui4yu2 as examples. In: The 1st California Conference on Chinese Pedagogy, Chapman University, CA (July 5, 2008). (in Chinese)
16. Zhang, B.: Synonymy, near-synonymy and confusable word: A perspective transformation from Chinese to interlanguage. Chinese Teaching in the World 3, 98–107 (2007). (in Chinese)
17. Fang, L.-N.: The strategy research of teaching Chinese as a second language. National University of Tainan: Journal of Humanities and Social Sciences Studies 37, 1–16 (2003). (in Chinese)
18. Huang, C.-R., Chen, K.-j., Chang, L.: Segmentation standard for Chinese natural language processing. Computational Linguistics and Chinese Language Processing 2(2), 47–62 (1997)
19. Ma, W.-Y., Huang, C.-R.: Uniform and effective tagging of a heterogeneous Giga-word Corpus. In: Presented at the 5th International Conference on Language Resources and Evaluation (LREC 2006), Genoa, Italy (May 24-28, 2006)
20. Kilgarriff, A., Pavel, R., Pavel, S., David T.: The Sketch Engine. In: Proceedings of EURALEX, Lorient, France (2004)
21. Kilgarriff, A., Huang, C.-R., Pavel, R., Simon, S., David, T.: Chinese Word Sketches. In: ASIALEX 2005: Words in Asian Cultural Context, Singapore (2005)
22. Sinclair, J.M. (ed.): Looking Up: An Account of the COBUILD Project in Lexical Computing. Collins (1987)
23. Church, K.W., Patrick H.: Word association norms, mutual information and lexicography. In: Proceedings of the 27th Annual Meeting of ACL, Vancouver, pp. 76–83 (1989)
24. Lin, D.: Automatic retrieval, and clustering of similar words. In: Proceedings of COLING-ACL, Montreal, pp. 768–774 (1998)
25. Kilgarriff, A., David, T.: Sketching Words. In: Corréard, M.-R. (ed.), Lexicography and Natural Language Processing. A Festschrift in Honour of B.T.S. Atkins, Euralex (2002)

Semantic Labeling of Chinese Verb-Complement Structure Based on Feature Structure

Bo Chen[(✉)], Chen Lyu, Xiaomei Wei, and Donghong Ji

Computer School, Wuhan University, Wuhan, China
{chenbo,lvchen1989,xiaomeiwei,dhji}@whu.edu.cn

Abstract. Semantic relations are difficult to analyze automatically, especially the semantic relations of Chinese verb-complement structure. In this paper we propose a novel model based on feature structure and apply it to the representation of semantic relations among subjects, verbs, objects, and complements. We focus four different kinds of Chinese verb-complement structures and their semantic relations. We compared the approach we propose with traditional dependency grammars. Feature structure, being recursive undirected graph, facilitates a richer Chinese semantic information extraction when compared to dependency grammar. The results of our analysis show that using feature structures are more suitable for extracting complex semantic relations.

Keywords: Chinese verb-complement sentence · Feature structure · Semantic labeling · Dependency structure · Recursive undirected graph

1   Introduction

Semantic parsing is one of the most difficult tasks in natural language processing, as well as one of the main bottlenecks of large-scale applications of language technology today [1,2,3]. Semantic parsing of Chinese is particularly challenging due in part to flexible word order. Therefore, there is an urgent need to resolve the difficulties of semantic annotation of Chinese sentences, especially for verb-complement structure, complex noun phrases, and so on. In this paper we target the first of these – verb-complement structure.

The verb-complement structure of a prototypical Chinese sentence includes four elements: subject, verb, complement, and object. The semantic relations among the four parts are complex, and include relations linking subject-complement, verb-complement, object-complement, and a triple relating subject-verb-object [4, 5].

It is important, therefore, to find an effective method of annotating and parsing Chinese verb-complement structure. This paper introduces and evaluates a novel model for representing semantics in Chinese using feature structures, and analyzes four different kinds of verb-complement structures. Compared to traditional dependency structure, our model allows a more complete semantic description.

© Springer International Publishing Switzerland 2014
X. Su and T. He (Eds.): CLSW 2014, LNAI 8922, pp. 341–348, 2014.
DOI: 10.1007/978-3-319-14331-6_34

2   Chinese Verb-Complement Structure

2.1   Characteristics of Chinese Verb-Complement Structure

Chinese has a unique verb-complement structure: "Subject + Verb + Complement + Object" (SVCO) or "Subject + Verb + Complement" (SVC). The particle "得" is the formal tag of the structure, as in: "吃 得 饱 [*chi de bao*] (*to eat until full*)", the structure of the phrase is "Verb + Complement". There are also many direct combinations of words in Chinese, such as: "看 完 了 [*kan wan le*] (*to read until the end*)".

As we are focusing on the semantic rather than syntactic relations in Chinese verb-complement structure, we provide a formal description and method of annotation of only semantic relations. Fig.1 shows the main semantic relations of such structure.

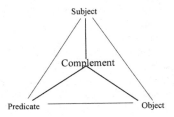

Fig. 1. The semantic relations of Chinese verb-complement structure

The semantic relations of Chinese verb-complement structure include two categories and six subtypes. One category includes relations between the complement and each of the subject, verb, and object. The other category includes the semantic relations among the subject, the predicate, and the object. (1) – (3) are typical sentences with verb-complement structure.

(1) 衣 服　　洗　　干 净　　　　了[1]
　　yifu　　*xi*　　*ganjing*　　*le*
　　clothes　wash　clean
　　The clothes are washed clean.

(2) 衣 服　　洗　　完　　　　了
　　yifu　　*xi*　　*wan*　　*le*
　　clothes　wash　finished
　　The clothes are completely washed.

(3) 衣 服　　洗　　晚　　　　了
　　yifu　　*xi*　　*wan*　　*le*
　　clothes　wash　late
　　The clothes are washed too late.

The syntactic structures of (1) – (3) are described as: "S (*clothes*) + V (*wash*) + C (*adjective*)". In (1) – (3), the subjects and verbs are the same, differing only on the

---

[1] 了 is a function word, which expresses perfective or past tense.

quality of their complements, which are adjectives. And, even though the three sentences have the same syntactic structure, the semantic orientations of their complements are different. In (1), the complement "干 净 (clean)" is related to the subject "衣 服 (clothes)". In (2), the complement "完 (finished)" is related to the perfectiveness of the verb "洗 (wash)". Finally, in (3), the complement "晚 (late)" is related to the time of occurrence of the verb "洗 (wash)". The syntactic similarity of instances of the verb-complement structure masks the differences in their internal semantic relationships.

2.2   Difficulties in Parsing Chinese Verb-Complement Structure

Currently, traditional dependency structure is the main semantic analysis method to parse Chinese [6, 7]. Fig.2 is the typical dependency tree of Chinese verb-complement structure:

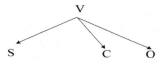

Fig. 2. The dependency tree of Chinese verb-complement structure

If we parse (1) – (3) with a dependency grammar, we will have the same dependency trees, as Fig.3.

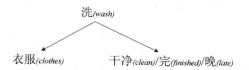

Fig. 3. The dependency trees of (1)–(3)

Dependency grammar approaches cannot fully represent the semantic relations between the subject and the complement.

(4) 小 王　　　　羞　　红　　了　　脸 。
　　xiaowang　　　xiu　　hong　　le　　lian
　　Xiaowang　　shy　　red　　　　　face
　　Xiaowang feels shy and his face turns red.

Fig.4 is the dependency tree of (4).

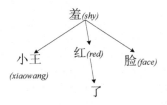

Fig. 4. The dependency tree of (4)

The syntactic structure of (4) is "S (*Xiaowang*)+ V (*shy*) + C (*red*)+O(*face*)". Analyzing (4) according to semantic relatedness and semantic cognition, there are at least 5 word pairs with semantic relations:

[小 王 (*Xiaowang*),   , 羞(*shy*)] ;   [小 王 (*Xiaowang*),   ,脸(*face*)]
[羞 (*shy*),   , 红 (*red*)] ;   [脸(*face*),   ,红 (*red*)] ;
[红 (*red*),   , 了].

Fig.4 is the result of (4) using dependency tree structure. It only represents three semantic relations and omits two others: between the subject "小 王 (*Xiaowang*), and the object "脸 (*face*)", and between the object "脸 (*face*)" and the complement "红 (*red*)". This implies that using traditional dependency structure to parse Chinese verb-complement sentences is not enough to describe all their semantic information, and limits the effectiveness of this approach in many tasks involving processing of Chinese.

3   Feature Structure Theory

Considering the unique characteristics of Chinese, we revised the traditional dependency grammar and proposed a novel method to encode semantic relations based on feature structures, which uses feature triples and, therefore, may be used to describe semantic relations of any number of word pairs [1, 2].

The ultimate purpose of semantic parsing in Machine Translation is to find the semantic relations in a sentence [8]. And this novel approach is highly suited for describing complex semantic relations.

(5) 从   广 州   飞 ,   飞   到   武 汉
cong   Guangzhou   fei   fei   dao   Wuhan
From   Guangzhou   fly   fly   to   Wuhan
Fly from Guangzhou   *Fly to Wuhan*

Taking (5) as example, we show how a set of feature triples of type [Entity, Feature, Value] can easily express its semantic relations:

[飞, 从, 广 州];   [飞, 到, 武 汉].
fly, from, Guangzhou;   fly, to, Wuhan

Feature structure triples can describe a semantic relation and the type of this relation. Every feature triple consists of an entity, a feature and its value. With These triples we can represent the semantic relations by multiple-edged nodes. The formal representation of these triples is a recursive undirected graph. The graph in Fig.5 represents both triples of (5).

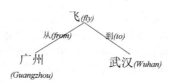

Fig. 5. The feature structure graph of (5)

Using our approach (4) can be represented by the graph in Fig.6.

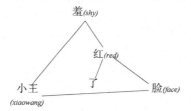

Fig. 6. The Feature structure graph of (4)

In Fig.6, the multi-edged nodes are the subject "小 王 (*Xiaowang*)", the complement "红 (*red*)" and the object "脸 (*face*)". Every node with semantic content has semantic relations with at least two nodes. As shown in Fig.6, our approach can easily describe the entire semantic relations of (4).

Fig. 7 shows an abstract feature structure Graph. Formally, any node of these recursive undirected graphs can itself be a graph [8]. In this way, we allow nesting and multiple correlations.

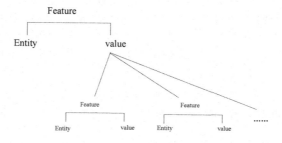

Fig. 7. The feature structure graph

4   Comparing Feature Structure with Dependency Structure

(6) 他   喝   醉   了   酒 。
   ta   *he*   *zui*   *le*   *jiu*
   He   drink   drunk   alcohol

He is drunk.

The syntactic structure of (6) is "S (*he*) + V (*drink*) + C (*drunk*) + O (*alcohol*)". The sentence "他 喝 醉 了 酒 (*He is drunk*)" can be simplified as: "他 醉 了 (*He is drunk*)", in which "醉 (*drunk*)" behaves as predicate instead of being a complement. In Chinese, this sentence structure is common. In "他 醉 了 (*He is drunk*)", "他 (*he*)" and "醉 (*drunk*)" are related as "subject-predicate". For this reason, in the verb-complement structure of (6), the complement "醉 (*drunk*)" should have a semantic relation with the subject "他 (*he*)". (6) can then be described by five triples:

[喝 (*drink*),   , 他(*he*)] ; [喝(*drink*),   , 酒(*alcohol*)] ; [喝(*drink*),   , 醉(*drunk*)] ;
[醉 (*drunk*),   , 他(*he*)] ; [醉(*drunk*),   , 了(*function word*)]

Fig.8 is the feature structure graph of (6).

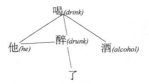

Fig. 8. The Feature structure graph of (6)

(7) 一 个 月   踢   坏   了   三   N   鞋 。
   yigeyue   *ti*   *huai*   *le*   *san*   *shuang*   *xie*
   one month   kick   broken   three   pairs   shoes

He played football so hard that three shoes were broken in one month.

The syntactic structure of (7) is "PP (*one month*) + V (*kick*) + C (*broken*) +O (*three shoes*)". In (7), the complement "坏 (*broken*)" has a semantic relation with the object "鞋 (*shoes*)": subject-predicate. In Chinese, this sentence structure is also very common. The semantic relations in (7) can be described by five triples:

[踢 (*kick*),   , 一 个 月(*one month*)] ; [踢(*kick*),   ,坏(*broken*)] ;
[坏 (*broken*),   , 鞋 (*shoes*)] ; [鞋 (*shoes*), 双(*pair*), 三(*three*)] ;
[坏 (*broken*),   , 了 (*function word*)]

Fig.9 is the feature structure graph of (7).

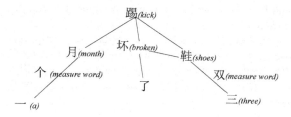

Fig. 9. The Feature structure graph of (7)

We now compare dependency structure with our proposed feature structure approach to parse (6) and (7) in Table 1.

Table 1. Dependency Tree and Feature Graph of (6)–(7)

Dependency Tree	Feature structure Graph
喝(drink) 他(he) 醉(drunk) 酒(alcohol) 了	喝(drink) 他(he) 醉(drunk) 酒(alcohol) 了
踢(kick) 月(month) 坏(broken) 鞋(shoes) 个(measure word) 了 双(measure word) 一(a) 三(three)	踢(kick) 月(month) 坏(broken) 鞋(shoes) 个(measure word) 了 双(measure word) 一(a) 三(three)

In Table 1, the dependency tree approach can represent neither the semantic relation between the subject "他 (*he*)" and the complement "醉 (*drunk*)", nor the one between the object "鞋 (*shoes*)" and the complement "坏 (*broken*)". In the other words, dependency tree approach is lossy, failing to describe complex semantic relations.

Conversely, our proposed model using feature structure triples can easily adapt to the Chinese flexible word order and semantic information by describing semantic relations among any number of word pairs.

5   Conclusion and Future Work

With this paper, we propose "Feature structure" a new approach for semantic description. We compare Chinese verb-complement sentence structures annotated with traditional dependency grammar and Feature structure. The results show that feature structure can better represent complex semantic relations and semantic information.

Feature structure can be represented as a recursive undirected graph, and allows nesting and multiple correlations.

This work lays the foundations, the basic concepts and description feature structure framework. Based on this framework, we have built a large-scale Chinese semantic resource with 30,000 sentences. Our research has been successfully used in relation extraction, event extraction, automatic question & answering as well as the syntactic parsing in machine translation.

Acknowledgment. The work is funded by the following projects: National Natural Science Foundation of China No.61202193, 61202304, the Major Projects of Chinese National Social Science Foundation No.11&ZD189, and the Chinese Postdoctoral Science Foundation No.2013M540593,2014T70722.

References

1. Chen, B., Ji, D.H., Chen, L.: Building a Chinese Semantic Resource Based on Feature structure. International Journal of Computer Processing of Languages, 95–101 (2012)
2. Chen, B., Wu, H., Lv, C., Yang, H., Ji, D.: Semantic labeling of Chinese serial verb sentences based on feature structure. In: Ji, D., Xiao, G. (eds.) CLSW 2012. LNCS, vol. 7717, pp. 784–790. Springer, Heidelberg (2013)
3. Ji, D.H.: Semantic annotation of Chinese phrases using recursive-graph. In: Proceedings of the 38th Annual Meeting of the Association for Computational Linguistics, pp. 101–108. Association for Computational Linguistics, Hong Kong (2000)
4. Gao, Y.: Semantic orientation of resultive construction in modern Chinese: a cognitive semantic perspective. Shanghai International Studies University (2005). (in Chinese)
5. Lyu, S.X.: Semantic analysis of sentences with resultive construction. In: The First International Chinese Teaching Conference (1985). (in Chinese)
6. Zhou, Q.: Annotation Scheme for Chinese Treebank. Chinese Information Processing, 1–8 (2004). (in Chinese)
7. Zhou, M., Huang C.N.: Approach to the Chinese dependency formalism for the tagging of corpus. Chinese Information Processing, 35–53 (1994). (in Chinese)
8. Feng, Z.W.: Machine translation, pp. 412–434. Translation and Publishing Corporation (1998). (in Chinese)

Structurally and Functionally Comparative Analysis of Lexlical Bundles in the English Abstracts of Chinese and International Journals

Gui-ling Niu[(⊠)]

Zhengzhou University, Zhengzhou, Henan, China
mayerniu@163.com

Abstract. The purpose of this paper is to make a comparative analysis of the lexical bundles in the English abstracts of Chinese journals and in those of international periodicals. The most frequently used four-word lexical bundles in the self-made corpus, Chinese-English Parallel Abstract Corpus (CEPAC) [13], were identified and classified structurally and functionally. Results indicate that the lexical bundles in the English abstracts of Chinese journals are structurally incomplete in comparison with those in the texts of international journals. Similarly, in spite of the larger number in type and token, lexical bundles are less varied in form, meaning and function in Chinese journal abstracts. Therefore it is quite necessary to strengthen the richness, diversity and fluency of lexical bundles in Chinese journal English abstracts.

Keywords: Research articles · Abstract · Lexical bundle · Structurally · Functionally

1 Introduction

Phraseology is one of the most prominent research topics in linguistics. The related studies fall into two main categories: theory-driven type and corpus-driven type [21]. The former begins with certain theory model and is mainly concerned with qualitative research, defining and categorizing some research targets. Its limitation lies in its sampling criteria which mainly depend on intuition and psychological salience, lacking the support of the probability or frequency standard of natural language usage [21] Contrary to theory-driven type, corpus-driven phraseology is based on true data and begins with frequency information, with its interests covering varieties of word sequence and the characteristics of their forms and functions [24], ranging from collocation, fixed and semi-fixed expressions, idioms, incomplete word fragments, etc.

2 Lexical Bundle

The term 'lexical bundle' [2] is defined as "sequences of word forms that commonly go together in natural discourse" in the Longman Grammar of Spoken and Written

© Springer International Publishing Switzerland 2014
X. Su and T. He (Eds.): CLSW 2014, LNAI 8922, pp. 349–357, 2014.
DOI: 10.1007/978-3-319-14331-6_35

English, in which the most common recurrent sequences in conversation and academic proses are compared.

'Lexical bundle' is also identified as cluster [17], lexical chunk [18], formulaic sequence [7], lexical phrase [12], phraseology [19], prefab, prefabricated patterns [1], multi-word unit/expressions, MWE [15], recurrent word combination [1], etc. In computational linguistics, it is termed as 'N-gram', in which N stands for the number of words in the lexical bundles.

Recent research in computer analysis of language has revealed a widespread occurrence of lexical patterns in discourse. Pawley and Syder [14] claimed that "lexicalized sentence stems and other memorized strings form the main building blocks of fluent connected speech." Formulaic sequences, as Nattinger and DeCarrico [12] called the recurrent sequence of words, are ubiquitous in language use and they make up a large proportion of any discourse. Alternberg [1] found that 96% of native language discourses conform to certain prefabricated patterns. These data indicate that lexical-bundles are ubiquitous in any discourse, and the co-occurrence of one word with another or others is not by accident.

Numerous linguistic studies have explored either the structural or functional features of this lexical framework. Biber and his students [2][3][4][5][6][7] have conducted continuous study on lexical bundles for years and contributed much to the research of this field, including the taxonomy of lexical bundles and related studies in both spoken and written registers [4][5]. Recurrent word sequences, another name for lexical bundles, have been investigated in several earlier studies [1].

3   Related Research Abroad and at Home

Wray [22] pointed out the two main functions of lexical bundles: 1) the reduction of processing effort; 2) achievement of socio-interactional functions.

Biber & Barbieri's emprical research findings show that lexical bundls are more frequently used in academic oral register than in academic written register; In general, referential functions are the dominant use of lexical bundles in the written university registers [5].

In China, Pu [16] first investigated the patterns of lexical bundles in students' written English based on corpus CLEC; Wei [20] posed a taxonomy of lexical bundles applicable to Chinese English learners by using the data in corpus COLSEC; Besides, Wei [20] also found that a sentence or discourse tends to begin with lexical bundles with certain functions.

In spite of the myriad comparative research targeted to the lexical bundle features in spoken or written academic English [4][5], as well as the research concerning lexical bundles for students in different majors [6] and in the part Introduction in academic articles [8], there is no systematic research regarding the structural and functional difference of lexical bundles between second language RA abstracts and native language RA abstracts based on a large-scale corpus.

This study aims to make a comprehensively comparative analysis between English lexical bundles in Chinese journal papers and those in international journals by using the self-made corpus — Chinese-English Parallel Abstract Corpus (CEPAC) [13]. We intended to explore the lexical bundle features of native language abstracts, to find the non-native language lexical bundle traits in Chinese research articles, and sum up the shortcomings to improve.

4   Research Design

Four-word lexical bundles are the most frequently seen word length [4] .We extracted the four-word recurrent words in the two sub-corpora, CE (English Abstracts Corpus of Chinese journals) and EE (English Abstracts Corpus of International journals), and made corresponding statistics and comparative analysis, by referring to Biber et al.'s [3][4] and Cortes' [6][8] structural and functional taxonomy of lexical bundles, employing the perspective of frequency and using the cluster (N-grams) function in AntConc. Because our study is only concerned with written academic English while Biber et al.'s included both spoken and written English, we deleted those bundles with obvious oral features (eg, "come come come come" in obligation category).

Furthermore, we set a relatively low minimum N-gram frequency, 6, because abstracts belong to written English and hence there are fewer lexical bundles in them compared with oral English. Then with MI value and T-score testing, we removed some clusters that words accidentally co-occurred or only appeared together in less than three abstracts, and we also manually left out those non-discourse attributes or obviously influent word sequences (eg, human wild α synuclein) despite the high frequency, and thus got the final data from the two sub-corpora.

4.1   Structural and Functional Classification of Lexical Bundles

Although lexical chunks look like random word clusters and take no position in linguistics, actually this phenomenon can be reasonablly interpreted structurally and functionally [4]. Lexical bundles are stored as a whole and are the main constituents of texts, serving the function to frame the texts.

4.1.1   Structural Features of Lexical Bundles

In terms of taxonomy of lexical bundles in abstracts, we adopted Biber et al.'s [2] and Cortes' [6] taxonomy and in combination with the bundle features in our self-made CEPAC corpus, we classified lexical bundles into 10 main types structurally (See Table 1).

According to Biber et al. [5], lexical bundles are the main building blocks in discourse and lexical bundles provide a kind of pragmatic 'head' for larger phrases and clauses, where they serve as discourse frames for the expression of new information. Therefore, lexical bundles supply interpretive frames for the developing discourse. For example,

(1) *The aim is to* initiate a debate about whether international consensus can be reached on the content of such a set of standards , and whether a particular set of standards, developed in the Dutch context, is applicable in and relevant to other countries.

Table 1. Distribution of 4-word Lexical Bundles in Corpus CE

Structure	Types		Tokens	
	CE	**EE**	**CE**	**EE**
1.Noun phrase + of	18	19	126	175
2.Noun phrase + post nominal clause fragment	0	3	0	33
3.Other noun phrases	9	3	90	34
4.Prepositional phrase + of	13	15	133	169
5.Other prepositional phrases	18	14	216	156
6.Anticipatory it + Vbe + adj./pp. + (clause fragment)	4	5	29	35
7.Passive + prep. phrase fragment/infinite	9	11	89	101
8.(Modal)Verb/Be + (complement noun /adj. phrase)	20	6	169	51
9. (noun phrase/pronoun) + V + (Complement)	14	25	260	245
10.Others	17	5	158	89
Total	**122**	**106**	**1270**	**1088**

(2) This idea is tested here through experiments investigating *the extent to which* corpus-identified collocations exhibit mental 'priming' in a group of native speakers.

(3) We identified *the ways in which* communication and support within the hybrid community unfolded over a period of time.

As is shown in Table 1, the lexical bundle features in Corpus CE vary greatly from those in Corpus EE. The most prominent features are: First, there are no 'Noun phrase + post nominal clause fragment' 4-word lexical bundles in Corpus CE while there are 'the ways in which, the extent to which, extent to which the' with the frequency of 33 in Corpus EE, which indicates that this structure is underused in CE. Besides, either in the types or total frequencies of lexical bundles in the two sub-corpora, there is a larger number in CE than in EE, but there are much more 4-word clusters which fail to be categorized into the 9 main types and can only be identified as 'others'. In addition, While there are more 4-word lexical bundles in CE, and manifests a higher frequency but bears a relatively single model, in which there are 24 types expressing the significant difference, for instance, 'higher than that of', and many of these bundles are incomplete, for example, 'of verbs has the'. They serve little function in building the context frame; while in contrast, despite the fewer types and lower frequency of lexical bundles in CE, the wider diversity feature is prominent in these bundles and they bear more complete meanings and serve a better function in framing the structure of the other parts of a whole sentence, for example, 'the ways in which' serves the function to connect the whole sentence structure and meaning.

4.1.2   Functional Characteristics of Lexical Bundles

In terms of the functional taxonomy of lexical bundles, we mainly referred to Cortes [6][7][8] and Biber et al. [3][4], and three primary discourse functions were distinguished for lexical bundles in CEPAC: (1) stance bundles, (2) discourse/text organizers, and (3) referential bundles, and the rest bundles are termed as 'others'. As is interpreted by Cortes, stance bundles indicate the speakers' attitude or appraisal to another idea, eg. "I don't know if" , "I think it was"; Discourse /text organizers help to organize discourse or texts, eg. "if you look at" , "on the other hand"; Referential bundles refer to the objective or abstract targets or the text itself or its features, eg. "there's a lot of" , "a little bit more". Referential bundles are mainly used to indicate time, place or the quantity used to introduce a person or an item, for example, "in the present research" , "at the same time".

Both Cortes' and Biber et al.'s structural taxonomies of lexical bundles are mainly based on Halliday's three metafunctions: ideational, interpersonal and organizational functions. In fact, the three core functions can also be subclassified. According to our research needs and by referring to Corts' [6][8] and Biber et al.'s [3][4] taxonomy of lexical bundles, we made the structural taxonomy of lexical bundles as follows:

a. Stance Bundles

a.1. Epistemic stance , eg : may be due to, are likely to be;

a.2. Attitudinal/Modality stance, eg., it is important to, it is necessary to, there is a need to, can be used to;

b. Discourse/Text organizers:

b.1.Topic introduction/focus, eg., in the next section, the rest of the paper is organized as follows, in this study the;

b.2. Topic elaboration/clarification, eg., on the other hand, as well as the;

b.3. Findings / focus, eg., It was found that, The results show that;

c. Referential expressions:

c.1. Identification/focus, eg., one of the most, one of the major;

c.2. Specification of attributes. This kind of lexical bundles can also be subdivided into:

c.2.1. Quantity specification, eg., were randomly divided into, was higher than that;

c.2.2. Framing, eg., the nature of the, in the context of;

c.3. Time, Place and Multi-functional, eg., In the present study, at the same time, at the end of.

That a lexical bundle is categorized into one type doesn't mean that this bundle is applicable to this use only. The functional type of a lexical bundle is mainly determined by its function this bundle serves on most occasions.

As is shown in Table 2, there is a significant difference between the functional lexical bundles in CE and those in EE in many types. First, bundles belonging to epistemic stance, topic introduction/focus and time reference are underused in Corpus CE. Because of the objectiveness of abstracts, there is a very small percentage of Attitudinal/Modality stance which helps to express personal subjective attitude and evaluation in Corpus CEPAC, indicating an obvious academic register characteristics; There are much fewer types and tokens of attitudinal lexical bundles in both the two sub-corpora, CE and EE, compared with Biber et al. [4][5], which investigated the use of lexical bundles in both spoken and written registers (college classroom teaching and textbooks); In Corpus EE, the attitudinal lexical bundles authors used express the authors' relatively objective and modest scientific attitude and stance, for example, 'it is possible to , are more likely to' to introduce an authors' new idea, new information, but to leave some leeway for him/ her to recede in case, and it is more acceptable for readers, for instance,

(4) More specifically, the bilinguals with above-average aptitude were more likely to score within the native range on the GJT than those with below-average aptitude.

Table 2. Distribution of high-frequency 4-word Lexical Bundles in Corpus CE and EE

			CE		EE	
			Tokens	Types	Tokens	Types
STANCE BUNDLES		Epistemic stance	13	2	30	5
	Attitudinal/Modality stance	Desire	0	0	0	0
		Obligation/Directive	0	0	0	0
		Intention/Prediction	0	0	0	0
		Ability	22	2	23	2
DISCOURSE ORGANIZERS	Topic introduction/focus		107	14	401	37
	Topic elaboration / clarification		44	2	58	5
	Research findings/ focus		299	18	226	25
REFERENTIAL EXPRESSIONS	Identification/focus		30	2	32	2
	Specification of attributes	Quantity specification	307	33	27	4
		Framing attributes	342	38	235	23
	Time/place/text reference	Place reference	6	1	30	3
		Time reference	52	3	16	2
		Multi-functional reference (both time and place)	13	2	10	1
OTHER BUNDLES			35	5	0	0
Total			1270	122	1088	106

(5) Results demonstrate that it was possible to identify and build consensus on task types common across workplace domains, and that, given adequate support, graduates

could specify target tasks as a basis for organizing focused, goal-oriented instruction in a context where TENOR was the norm.

The main function of 'Topic introduction/focus' bundles is to introduce the author and lead the readers to the aim and topic of the research, and most of them are supposed to belong to MOVE 'PURPOSE'. This kind of bundles are prominent in Corpus EE and there is a larger percentage in types and tokens, while in CE, there are much fewer types and tokens in the use of this category. This phenomenon agrees with underuse of MOVE 'PURPOSE' in CE [13] and this phenomenon also sheds light on the incompleteness and unbalanced of move distribution in CE, indicating that Chinese journal paper authors lack a clear genre consciousness in abstract writing and Chinese English learners need to enhance the ability to express certain functions with lexical bundles.

Besides, as is shown in Table 2, those bundle types of 'Research findings/ focus' and 'Quantity specification' are significantly overused in CE abstracts, esp. 'Quantity specification' bundles, the tokens of this kind of bundles in CE is 10 times more than those in EE. The usage feature of 'Quantity specification' bundles is closely related to the overuse 'Research findings/ focus' bundles in CE, in that both of them are used to describe the important findings and data features. The tokens of these two types of bundles take up 48% of all lexical bundles in CE abstracts. Although there is a larger bundle token number in CE than in EE, the number of bundle types in CE is less than that in EE. As for 'Quantity specification', despite the absolute high frequency of bundle types, most of them belong to comparison type such as "higher/lower than" or "significant difference", which means a relatively few bundle types, indicating, Chinese abstracts authors are active in adopting MOVE 'RESULT' for one thing, but favor some simple finding and quantity lexical types, and thus the lexical bundles in their abstracts lack a kind of diversity in form and meaning for another.

In Modality stance, Identification/focus and Topic elaboration / clarification, the type and token distributions in both CE and EE are similar, indicating the Chinese RA abstract writers and international RA abstract authors have much in common in these features.

Moreover, besides the three core functions of lexical bundles, there are many other clusters in CE abstracts which fail to belong to none of the classification categories of lexical bundles in that these clusters are not coherent enough, incomplete in form and meaning, and thus lacks a clear function.

5   Conclusion

Structurally, there is a shortage of 'Noun phrase + post nominal clause fragment' lexical bundles(eg., the ways in which, the extent to which) in Corpus CE, and these bundles are very beneficial to frame other parts of a whole sentence.

Functionally, compared with Corpus EE, the lexical bundles which are used to introduce the authors and then the topics and classified as topic introduction/focus, are underused, while those bundle types of 'Research findings/ focus' 'Quantity specification' are overused in CE abstracts, which are manifested in the bundle features of single form, meaning and function in spite of the larger bundle types and tokens.

Bundle research in RA abstracts facilitates an overall understanding of the structural and functional distribution of lexical bundles in abstracts, and is beneficial to develop the SLA learners' genre consciousness, to promote the fluency of abstract language and to enhance the richness and diversity of lexical bundles in RA abstracts.

Acknowledgements. This work was supported by the Humanities and Social Sciences Research Project of the Education Department of China (10YJA740074), the Natural Science Fund of China (No.60970083, No.61272221), the National Social Science Fund (No.14BYY096), 863 Projects of National High Technology Research and Development (No.2012AA011101), Science and Technology Key Project of Science and Technology Department of Henan Province (No.132102210407), Basic research project of Science and Technology Department of Henan Province (No. 142300410231, No.142300410308) and Key Technology Project of the Education Department of Henan Province (No.12B520055,No. 13B520381).

References

1. Altenberg, B., Tapper, M.: The Use of Adverbial Connectors in Advanced Swedish Learners' Written English. In: Learner English on Computer. Addition Wesley Publishing Company, London (1998)
2. Biber, D., Conrad, S.: Lexical Bundles in Conversation and Academic Prose. In: Hasselgard, H., Oksefjell, S. (eds.) Out of Corpora: Studies in Honor of Stig Johansson, pp. 181–189. Rodopi, Amsterdam (1999)
3. Biber, D., Conrad, S., Cortes, V.: Lexical bundles in speech and writing: an initial taxonomy. In: Wilson, A., Rayson, P., McEnery, T. (eds.) Corpus Linguistics by the Lune: A Festschrift for Geoffrey Leech, pp. 71–92. Peter Lang, Frankfurt (2003)
4. Biber, D., Conrad, S., Cortes, V.: If you look at … Lexical Bundles in University Teaching and Textbooks. Applied Linguistics 25(3), 371–405 (2004)
5. Biber, D., et al.: Lexical bundles in university spoken and written registers. English for Specific Purposes 26, 263–286 (2007)
6. Cortes, V.: Lexical bundles in published and student disciplinary writing: Examples from history and biology. English for Specific Purposes 23(3), 397–423 (2004)
7. Cortes, V.: Teaching lexical bundles in the disciplinary class: An example from history. Manuscript submitted for publication (2006)
8. Cortes, V.: The purpose of this study is to: Connecting lexical bundles and moves in research article introductions . Journal of English for Academic Purposes (2013)
9. De Cock, D.: A recurrent word combination approach to the study of formulae in the speech of native and non-native speakers of English. International Journal of Corpus Linguistics 3(1), 59–80 (1998)
10. Li, X., Wei, N.: Exploring lexical connotation and semantic prosody from the bilingual perspective. Modern Foreign Languages 35(1), 30–38 (2012). (in Chinese)
11. Liang, M., Li, W., Xu, J.: Using Corpora: A Practical Coursebook. Foreign Language Teaching and Research Press, Beijing (2010). (in Chinese)
12. Nattinger, J., DeCarrico, J.: Lexical Phrases and Language Teaching. CUP, Oxford (1992)

13. Niu, G.: A Corpus-based Study on Explicitation in English Translation of Chinese Research Paper Abstract. Journal of Xi'an International Studies University **21**(2), 112–116 (2013). (in Chinese)
14. Parley, A., Syder, F.: Two Puzzles for Linguistic Theory: Native-like Selection and Native-like Influence. In: Richards, J., Sehmit, R. (eds.) Language and Communication, pp. 191–225. Longman, London (1983)
15. Rayson, P.: From key words to key semantic domains. International Journal of Corpus Linguistics **13**(4), 519–549 (2008)
16. Pu, J.: Colligation, Collocation and Lexical Bundles in English Word Teaching. Foreign Teaching and Research **35**(6), 438–445+481 (2003). (in Chinese)
17. Scott, M.: Oxford WordSmith Tools 4.0 Manual. CUP, Oxford (2004)
18. Sinclair, J.: Corpus, Concordance, Collocation. CUP, Oxford (1991)
19. Stubbs, M.: Two quantitative methods of studying phraseology in English. International Journal of Corpus Linguistics **7**(2), 215–244 (2002)
20. Wei, N.: A Preliminary Study of the Characteristics of Chinese Learners' Spoken English. Modern Foreign Languages **27**(2), 140–149 (2004). (in Chinese)
21. Wei, N.: Phraseological characteristics of Chinese learners' spoken English: Evidence of lexical chunks from COLSEC. Modern Foreign Languages **30**(3), 280–291 (2007). (in Chinese)
22. Wray, A.: Formulaic sequences in second language teaching: Principle and practice. Applied Linguistics **21**(4), 463–489 (2000)
23. Wray, A.: Formulaic Language and the Lexicon. CUP, Cambridge (2002)
24. Zhang, X.A.: Corpus-based Study on the Characteristics of Lexical Chunks Used by Chinese Advanced EFL learners. Foreign Language World **140**(5), 48–57 (2010). (in Chinese)

Corpus Building for the Outcome-Based Education of the Ancient Chinese Courses

Bing Qiu[1](✉) and Qingzhi Zhu[2]

[1] College of Humanities and Social Sciences,
Beijing Language and Culture University, Beijing, China
bingqiu@gmail.com
[2] Department of Chinese Language Studies, Faculty of Humanities,
Hong Kong Institute of Education, New Territories, Hong Kong, China
qingzhi@ied.edu.hk

Abstract. Ancient Chinese is a core course of the Department of Chinese Language and Literature in most of related universities. However, the traditional teaching materials for Ancient Chinese are usually complied according to personal experience and preference, as a result of which, they cannot integrate with the modern teaching philosophy, especially the outcome-based education. To introduce a scientific, impersonal and quantitative foundation for the learning of Ancient Chinese, a corpus was constructed, which covers lexical and syntactic learning objectives based on the statistical inspection of selected typical literatures published in ancient times. The corpus will contribute to the transition from traditional experiential teaching to modern scientific teaching for the Ancient Chinese course.

Keywords: Ancient Chinese · Teaching materials · Corpus · Learning objectives

1   Background and Motivation

Due to the inheritance between Ancient Chinese and Modern Chinese, lots of Chinese language phenomena nowadays descend from ancient times. Therefore, the Ancient Chinese course is usually listed as fundamental compulsory courses in the Department of Chinese Language and Literature in most of related universities and colleges. Ever since 1950s, when the course was initiated, lots of academic attention have been drawn to the composition of its teaching materials. To the best of our knowledge, more than two hundred series of teaching materials have been officially published.

These teaching materials can be classified into two categories. The first group only focus on general theories, related to characters, phonology, grammar, vocabulary and so on. The representative instances include 古汉语纲要 (*Outline of Ancient Chinese*) by 周秉钧 (Bingjun Zhou) [1] and 古代汉语知识教程 (*Ancient Chinese Knowledge Tutorial*) by 张双棣(Shuangdi Zhang) etc [2]. The second group cover both general theories and a collection of literary pieces, such as 古代汉语 (*Ancient Chinese*) by 王力 (Li Wang) [3], 古代汉语 (*Ancient Chinese*) by 郭锡良 (Xiliang Guo) [4] and 古代汉语教程 (*Ancient Chinese Tutorial*) by 张世禄 (Shilu Zhang) etc [5].

© Springer International Publishing Switzerland 2014
X. Su and T. He (Eds.): CLSW 2014, LNAI 8922, pp. 358–368, 2014.
DOI: 10.1007/978-3-319-14331-6_36

The existing materials each have their own features and advantages, which have exerted a great influence on the development of the course of Ancient Chinese. However, in regards to their teaching philosophy and their composition of learning objectives, there are also some problems as follows.

Firstly, on the selection of the learning objectives, most teaching materials have not followed scientific standards. Instead, the authors usually evaluate the frequency and importance of the language phenomena subjectively and select and arrange the topics based on their personal experience and interest. As a result, the learning objectives in these teaching materials cannot meet the practical requirement for students to read ancient books.

Secondly, on the selection of the literary pieces, most editors have chosen them based on their own experience and preference, rather than the objective standards. Thus the articles selected by this way cannot effectively support the learning objectives, which may affect the educational outcome in some degree.

Thirdly, on the arrangement of the teaching units, the sequence of the learning objectives is usually determined according to some subjective judgment, rather than on a scientific, theoretical and progressive basis. Each unit is to be taught in fixed school hours, with no consideration of the current level or learning goals of the learners.

In brief, the classical teaching materials for Ancient Chinese are usually complied according to personal experience and preference, as a result of which, they cannot integrate with the modern teaching philosophy, especially the outcome-based education (OBE) [6-7]. In response to this issue, many scholars have appealed to rearrange the teaching materials for Ancient Chinese. Qingzhi Zhu [8] once pointed out, "It is a pressing matter to compile new teaching materials for the Ancient Chinese course, which are brand new, avoiding all limitations and disadvantages of the old and satisfying the need of contemporary college education; meanwhile, introducing the advantages of foreign teaching materials. They must not be the scraps or repetitions of the ones in use now."

This paper aims to partly solve the aforementioned problem. In particular, our contribution lies mainly in the following aspects. We will first analyze the lexical and syntactic learning objectives in the most representative literatures published in ancient times. Then we will preliminarily construct a new corpus, named Ancient Chinese Learning-oriented Corpus, abbreviated as ACLC. This corpus, which reflects the learning objectives in a scientific, impersonal, and quantitative manner, will contribute to the transition from traditional experiential teaching to modern scientific teaching for Ancient Chinese. Based on this corpus, the compiling of new teaching materials will also be discussed for tentative exploration.

2   Procedure to Build the Corpus

The selection of language materials is required prior to the construction of the corpus. In this paper, Ancient Chinese, or Classical Chinese, mainly refers to the written language during the classical period of Chinese literature, from the end of the Spring and Autumn Period (early 5th century BC) to the end of the Han Dynasty (220 AD). From the most influential texts during the Pre-Qin Period, we picked 16 works as the initial language materials for ACLC. These materials include 道德经 [Daodejing](Tao Te Ching),

论语[*Lunyu*](*The Analects of Confucius*) and孟子[*Mengzi*](*Mencius*). There are about 1.14 million Chinese characters in them, which cover the vast majority of the language phenomena. Other Pre-Qin texts and texts in future generations can be added into ACLC progressively later on.

There are several dimensions in teaching Ancient Chinese, such as vocabulary, grammar and pronunciation. To organize these teaching contents and build ACLC, we follow the steps below. The first step is to obtain and analyze the vocabulary in the selected ancient texts. The second is to determine the lexical learning objectives and the third is to recognize the syntactic learning objectives. The procedure is depicted in Fig. 1. Note that the phonic learning objectives are not taken into account at this stage.

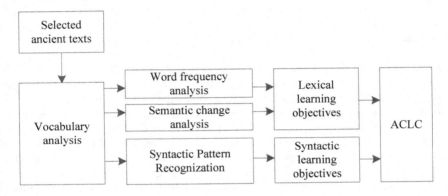

Fig. 1. The procedure to build the corpus from selected ancient texts

2.1   Analysis of Word Frequency

A Chinese word may consist of one, two or more Chinese characters. However, unlike the English text in which sentences are sequences of words delimited by spaces, the word boundary in Chinese is fuzzy. There is no immediate way of deciding which characters in the text should be grouped into words. In this paper, the word segmentation and the analysis of word frequency are on the basis of the Academia Sinica Ancient Chinese Corpus [9]. Words from the above 16 texts can be categorized by their number of syllables, as shown in the following table.

Table 1. The statistics of vocabulary in selected ancient texts

	Count
Monosyllablic words	20749
Disyllablic words	31962
Words of 3 or more syllables	2936
Total	55647

On the basis of above statistics, homographs with different parts of speech are counted separately; for example, pronoun "之[*zhi*]", auxiliary word "之[*zhi*]" and verb "之[*zhi*]" are taken as different words. Here the annotation of the parts of speech is also on the basis of the Academia Sinica Ancient Chinese Corpus. Among the vocabulary, the top-ten high-frequency words are listed as Table 2.

Table 2. The top-ten high-frequency words in selected ancient texts

Order	Word	Count	Part of speech	Remarks (very rough corresponding words in English)
1	之[*zhi*]	31492	Auxiliary	"of"
2	不[*bu*]	29620		"not"
3	也[*ye*]	28276		no corresponding words
4	而[*er*]	24599		"and"
5	之[*zhi*]	20094	Pronoun	"it"
6	以[*yi*]	18532		"by" or "with"
7	其[*qi*]	16680		"that" or "that person's"
8	曰[*yue*]	16591		"say" or "speak"
9	于[*yu*]	12416		"at", "in" or "on"
10	者[*zhe*]	10537	Pronoun	"person" or "this"

Let the vocabulary be ordered from largest to smallest by word frequency. The words in the latter part of the sorted sequence are accordingly in less use. The curve of the frequencies of words in terms of their ranks in the sorted word list is shown in Fig. 2, which obviously follows Zipf's Law [10].

As shown in Fig. 2, among about fifty thousand words in Ancient Chinese, about half of them appear only once in the corpus. About 6,600 words appear more than ten times, which account for less than 12% of the whole vocabulary. Among them, 1,100 words appear more than one hundred times, which only account for 2% of the whole vocabulary. Overall, the high frequency words occupy a very small proportion in the whole vocabulary.

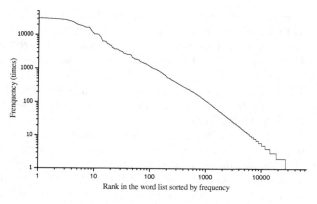

Fig. 2. The frequencies of words in terms of their ranks in the sorted vocabulary

Frequency is of critical importance to the learning of vocabulary. When we design the courses, we could prioritize the teaching of the high frequency words and delay or even ignore that of the rarely used ones. Obviously, the more high frequency words are presented, the higher coverage these words will have over the ancient texts. The curve of the text coverage in terms of the count of the learned high frequency words is illustrated in Fig. 3.

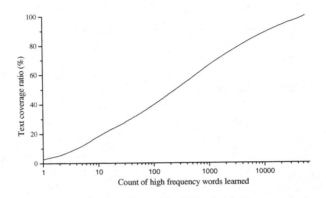

Fig. 3. The text coverage in terms the count of the learned high frequency words

As shown in Figure 3, when we know as few as the top 10 frequency words, we can still cover 4 percent of the whole selected ancient texts. If we know the top 100, we can cover as much as 66 percent. However, the curve adopts a slower smooth growth after that. We have to learn 3,795 high frequency words in order to cover 80 percent. For 90 percent, the number is 12,425. As expected, the statistics offer a scientific quantitative basis for the arrangement of teaching materials for different levels and different teaching units.

2.2   Lexical Learning Objectives

High frequency words are very important in the teaching of vocabulary. However, they cannot constitute the learning objectives directly, considering the prior knowledge base of the learners. They must be analyzed and categorized in order to fit the different levels of learners, according to what they have learned about the Modern and Ancient Chinese.

Suppose that the learners are familiar with Modern Chinese. A word can fall into any one of the following three categories, in terms of its meaning and usage in Modern Chinese and in Ancient Chinese.

Now, we consider the learners are familiar with Modern Chinese. Then a word can be divided into three categories according to the difference between its meaning and usage in Modern Chinese and those in Ancient Chinese.

First, the meaning and usage of the word are the same from ancient to modern times. That is to say, the ancient word is still used in modern times and its original meaning and usage remain the same. For example, "春[chun](spring)", "夏

[*xia*](summer)", "秋[*qiu*](autumn)" and "冬[*dong*](winter)", "贵[*gui*](expensive or noble)" and "贱[*jian*](cheap or humble)". These words can be ignored in the vocabulary teaching since they are already known by learners.

Second, the meaning and the usage of the word were some different in the ancient times than in the modern times. In other words, the ancient word is still used in modern times, but its meaning and usage are not exactly the same. For example, "金 [*jin*]" used to refer to "bronze" or "gold", but now means "gold" or "metal". For these words, we need to decide whether or when they should be taught, considering what the learners have known about Ancient Chinese.

Third, the meaning and the usage of the ancient word are vastly different in modern times, which means that the ancient word is almost extinct, or even though still in use, has totally changed. Two representative examples are "之[*zhi*]" and "去 [*qu*]". Whether or when these words should be taught depends on what the learners have known about Ancient Chinese, and they are usually among the most important learning objectives.

Now we also take the word frequency into account and then divide the lexical learning objectives into three levels as shown in Table 3. Generally speaking, if a word was frequently used in Ancient Chinese and is familiar to the learners in Modern Chinese, yet its meaning and usage have vastly changed over time, it should be regarded as an important lexical learning objective. In the last column of the table, the Level A means important lexical learning objectives, B means common ones and C means negligible ones.

It is difficult to determine the semantic difference between ancient words and modern words based on personal judgment. In order to get more accurate statistics, we must rely on the assistance of the authoritative reference books, such as 现代汉语 词典[*Xiandai Hanyu Cidian*](*Modern Chinese Dictionary*) and 古汉语常用字字典 [*Gu Hanyu Changyongzi Zidian*](*Dictionary of Ancient Commonly Used Words*), by which the meanings and usages of words in different times can be found and compared.

Table 3. The categories of lexical learning objectives

Word Frequency	Degree of Familiarity to Learners	Difference between Ancient Chinese and Modern Chinese	Level of lexical learning objectives
Frequently used	Familiar	Different	A
		Same	C
	Unfamiliar	Different	B
		Same	B
Not frequently used	Familiar	Different	C
		Same	
	Unfamiliar	Different	
		Same	

Since the proper nouns, such as toponyms, are not the targets of language teaching, we first filter the proper nouns out. For the rest in the high frequency word list, we follow the rules below to determine the difference between Ancient Chinese and Modern Chinese.

Firstly, for each word, we randomly select sample sentences from the selected ancient texts; the rule of thumb is that the sample sentences are scattered to as far as many literary pieces and words with higher frequency will be provided with more sample sentences. In this way, we try to have the samples cover a wider range of texts.

Secondly, we survey the sample sentences for each word, analyzing its meanings and usages in the ancient texts, comparing with its meanings and usages in Modern Chinese and labeling it according to Table 3. Take "之[zhi]" (auxiliary word) and "不[bu]" which were commonly used in Ancient Chinese as examples. The auxiliary word "之[zhi]" mainly has three usages: used between modifiers and central words to show a modifying and subordinative relationship, similar to "of" in English; used as a sign of preverbal objects; used between subjects and verbs to cancel the independent property of the sentence, not necessary to be translated. However, all the above three usages have vanished in Modern Chinese and might only be found in formal language use, which is not familiar to learners. Therefore, we label the word "之[zhi]" as B (common learning objective). "不[bu]" was and still is a negation word used in front of verbs, adjectives and adverbs; thus labeled as C (negligible learning objective).

We have investigated about 40,000 sample sentences for the top 3,800 high frequency words in the selected texts of Ancient Chinese. Among them, 748 words are tagged as A (important learning objectives), 896 are tagged as common learning objectives (C) and the remaining (about 2,000) words are tagged as C (negligible learning objectives). The lexical learning objectives in categories A and B, which should to be taught, are 1644 in total.

We have assumed that the learners in the Ancient Chinese course have obtained certain prior knowledge about the modern Chinese language. Due to the inheritance between Ancient Chinese and Modern Chinese, they should be able to understand ancient texts to a certain degree even before the course. However, no quantitative analysis is available in the existing studies and as a result, their learning outcome remains unknown.

Based on our statistic results, the learning outcome of the learners can be estimated. Prior to taking the course of Ancient Chinese, the learners have already mastered at least 2,000 lexical learning objectives in category C among the top 3,800 high frequency words, which cover about 33.5% of the ancient texts. That is to say, they can understand at least 33.5% of the texts. This is a conservative figure, since we have not taken into consideration what they might know about the non-frequency words. Given that the learners have acquired the top 100 lexical learning objectives in categories A and B, they can understand as much as 63.3% of ancient texts.

Generally speaking, the more lexical learning objectives the learners have acquired the more coverage ratio of the ancient texts they will reach. The data are listed in Table 4.

Table 4. The lexical coverage ratio in terms of learning objectives newly learned

Count of learning objectives newly learned	Coverage ratio (%)
0	33.5
100	63.3
300	68.7
500	71.2
800	72.9
1000	73.7
1644	75.4

As shown above, the teaching outcome can be evaluated in a quantitative manner. On this basis, we can set the teaching materials to meet the different requirements of elementary, intermediate and advanced courses of Ancient Chinese.

2.3   Syntactic Learning Objectives

Syntactic learning objectives constitute another important part when teaching Ancient Chinese. It is necessary to make clear of the differences between the syntax in ancient Chinese and that in modern Chinese, and then to organize the learning objectives into sequential teaching units from the learners' perspective. The differences lie in two aspects: parts of speech and sentence patterns.

In terms of the parts of speech, there are two substantial changes from Ancient Chinese to Modern Chinese. First is the shift of parts of speech. Ancient Chinese did not have a rich storage of content words and its syntactic rules were not strict. As a result, many of its vocabulary enjoyed great flexibility in parts of speech. For example, a noun can be used as a verb, causative verb, conative verb or adverbial modifier; a verb as a noun or causative verb; an adjective as a noun, verb or causative verb; a numeral as a verb. However, few examples of this phenomenon can be found in Modern Chinese.

Second is the difference in the use of numerals. In Ancient Chinese, there were very few measure words, especially for verbal actions. When counting, people put numerals right before the nouns or verbs, the same as in today's English. The definite numbers such as "三[san](three)", "五[wu](five)", "九[jiu](nine)" often represented indefinite numbers, similar to "some" or "many" in English. The words "将[jiang]", "几[ji]", "且[qie]" in front of the numerals indicated that these were approximate numbers. As for fractions, numerators and denominators were next to each other without any intervening elements. It is true that the above differences are very important syntactic learning objectives; however, since they can be taught along with the lexical learning objectives, they are not further discussed in our present study.

For the sentence types and the word order, there are also some obvious differences. In the declarative sentences of Ancient Chinese, the nouns and noun phrases are usually used as predicates, for example:

陈胜	者，	阳城	人	也。
Pinyin: Chensheng	zhe	Yangcheng	Ren	Ye
English: Chensheng	[is]	Yangcheng Town	Person.	

"Chensheng is a person of Yangcheng Town."

This is distinct from the Modern Chinese which used "是[shi](be)" as predicate. In Modern Chinese, the passive sentences are composed by the preposition "被[bei]", but they can be replaced by verbs or nothing in Ancient Chinese, which is called imaginary passive words. These words can be explained under specific context, for example, "拘[ju](arrest)" in:

文王	拘	而	演	《周易》
Pinyin: Wenwang	ju	er	yan	Zhouyi
English: Wenwang [is] arrested	and	deduce	Zhouyi	

"Wenwang was arrested and he deduced Zhouyi."

Here "拘[ju]" means "arrested". There are also some differences between Ancient Chinese and Modern Chinese in word order. The sentence structure in Modern Chinese is subject, adverbial, predicate and object. The sentence structure in Ancient Chinese is special: subject can be put in back of the predicate; object can be put in front of the predicate; adverbial can be put in back of the predicate and so on. The common used word orders include the following situations: preverbal object sentence, that is to say, object ahead of the predicate, such as:

沛公	安	在？
Pinyin: Peigong	an	zai
English: Peigong	which place	is in?

"Where is Peigong?"

Here prepositional phrase behind the central word, that is to say, move the prepositional phrase used to modify verb and adjective backward; modifier behind central word and subject-verb inversion.

Therefore, according to the main differences in Ancient Chinese syntax[11], we pick up four important parts: declarative sentence, passive sentence, preverbal object and prep-object phrases behind the predicate. The syntax patterns are then used to represent these four sentence types or word order based on a detailed investigation. Take the declarative sentence "夫[fu]..., ...也[ye]" for example. Its structure is "夫(NH) N, N 也(T)". Here "NH", "N" and "T" are the annotations in the Academia Sinica Ancient Chinese Corpus. We can retrieve, for example, "夫管子，天下之才也"[Fu guanzi, tianxia zhi cai ye](literally, Guanzi is a talent of the world.) according to the patterns. The implementation of the pattern queries are based on the regular expression and the related search engines.

Based on this method, we have sorted out the syntactic learning objectives of different ancient texts and has initially construct ACLC with these learning objectives. It is divided into 4 categories, 12 subcategories and 62 syntactic patterns, as shown in Table 5.

Table 5. The syntactic learning objectives

Categories	Subcategories	Patterns
declarative sentence	2	18
passive sentence	2	16
preverbal object	3	12
prep-object phrases behind the predicate	5	16

3   Conclusion

In traditional Ancient Chinese teaching, teaching materials are selected and sequenced based on personal experience and lack of scientific analysis and arrangement. To solve these existing problems in teaching materials, we have initiated a relatively systematic sortation and analysis of the vocabulary and syntax in the 16 influential ancient literary pieces, which were mainly a collection of proses, containing about one million characters. We adopt a perspective of corpus linguistics and evaluate the vocabulary and syntax in Ancient Chinese in terms of their frequency of use, familiarity to the learners and difference from those in Modern Chinese. We have taken an attempt to build a corpus for Ancient Chinese education.

The corpus is established with the intention of achieving a better teaching outcome with a more scientific curriculum design. After a quantitative analysis of the learning objectives in the ancient literary pieces, we are able to select teaching content and compile teaching materials in a systematic way, taking the difficulty and importance of the language points together with the capacities of the learners into consideration. In this way, the teaching of Ancient Chinese can be divided into stages while the learning can progress step by step. Besides, the clearly defined knowledge objectives also make it possible to evaluate the learning outcome of the students; at the same time, to set and realize learning objectives in respect of the outcome-based education becomes a feasible practice.

Building a corpus is a fundamental yet complicated task. As a tentative attempt to research on the corpus-based Ancient Chinese education, this study may have deficiencies and problems. We will improve our work in the coming studies and carry this research further forward.

Acknowledgments. The authors would like to thank the scholars who build the Academia Sinica Ancient Chinese Corpus. The authors also thank Ms. Junhui Qu and Ms. Lu Yang of Beijing Language and Culture University for their excellent technical assistance in the preparation of this paper.

This work was supported by Beijing Higher Education Young Elite Teacher Project (Grant No. YETP0869) and the funding of Hong Kong Institute of Education (Grant No. FLAN/TDG001/CHI/09-10), namely "A Corpus-based Study on the Content and Framework of the New Core Course Classical Chinese in Bachelor Degree (Language Studies) Program".

References

1. Zhou, B.: Outline of Ancient Chinese. Hunan Renmin Press, Changsha (1981). (周秉钧. 古汉语纲要. 长沙：湖南人民出版社) (in Chinese)
2. Zhang, S., et al.: Ancient Chinese Knowledge Tutorial. Beijing University Press, Beijing (2004). (张双棣等编. 古代汉语知识教程. 北京：北京大学出版社) (in Chinese)
3. Li, W.: Ancient Chinese (revised version). Zhonghua Book Company, Beijing (2010). (王力主编. 古代汉语(校订重排本). 北京：中华书局) (in Chinese)
4. Guo, X.: Ancient Chinese (revised version). The Commercial Press, Beijing (1999). (郭锡良主编. 古代汉语(修订本). 北京：商务印书馆) (in Chinese)
5. Zhang, S.: Ancient Chinese Tutorial. Fudan University Press, Shanghai (2008). (张世禄主编. 古代汉语教程. 上海：复旦大学出版社) (in Chinese)
6. Bonner, S.E.: Choosing teaching methods based on learning objectives: An integrative framework. Issues in Accounting Education 14(1), 11–15 (1999)
7. Pang, M., Ho, T.M., Man, R.: Learning Approaches and Outcome-Based Teaching and Learning: A Case Study in Hong Kong, China. Journal of Teaching in International Business 20(2), 106–122 (2009)
8. Zhu, Q.: The local vision: soft rib of current Chinese textbooks. Teaching Material Weekly 2009(4), 28. (朱庆之. 局部着眼，专家直指当前中文学科教材"软肋". 教材周刊) (in Chinese)
9. Academia Sinica Ancient Chinese Corpus. http://www.old_chinese.ling.sinica.edu.tw/
10. Newman, M.E.J.: Power laws, Pareto distributions and Zipf's law. Contemporary physics 46(5), 323–351 (2005)
11. Yang, B., He, L.: Ancient Chinese grammar and its development (revised version). Yuwen Press, Beijing (2001). (杨伯峻，何乐士. 古汉语语法及其发展(修订本). 北京：语文出版社) (in Chinese)

Building Chinese Semantic Treebank for Patent Text on the Basis of 3 Dimensional Dynamic Concept Model

Yateng Wang[1(✉)], Dongfeng Cai[1], Haoguo Feng[2], Qiaoli Zhou[1], and Mingru Wei[1]

[1] Knowledge Engineering Research Center, Shenyang Aerospace University,
Shenyang 110136, China
{wangyt_0823,wmrdllg}@126.com, zhou_qiao_li@hotmail.com,
caidf@vip.163.com
[2] Hebei Foreign Studies University, Shijiazhuang, China
fenghgnlp@163.com

Abstract. In this paper we proposed a method for building Chinese semantic treebank for patent text. On the basis of 3 Dimensional Dynamic Concept Model, we designed the semantic relations tagging sets with chunk as tagging object for patent translation. We proposed a top-down process for manually tagging and a standard for processing treebank, which is used for the level partition of a sentence and also can reflect core words. Building semantic treebank for patent text is very important for fully exploiting useful information of the patent text.

Keywords: Treebank · Chunk · Tagging set · Tagging process · Processing standard

1 Introduction

The patent is the world's largest source of information, which accounts for 90% to 95% of the world's scientific and technical information [2]. Compared with the general domain, the patent text has strong characteristics of the domain. There are many long sentences and complex sentences in the patent text, which brings a great difficulty in language processing. Most of the patent text is the description of some states of material objects or the relation between them, but less human consciousness or emotional content. Analysis and research on the characteristic of patent text will improve the accuracy of semantic analysis. Therefore, building semantic treebank based on patent text plays a very important role in fully exploiting the useful information of the patent text.

A number of semantic relations systems have been formed in related studies, such as HowNet [6], Verb Dictionary[4] and HNC theory[7]. But there are some drawbacks for

This paper was supported by the National Key Science & Technology Pillar Program No.2012BAH14F05.
This paper was supported by the National Basis Research Program under Project Number 2010CB530401-1.

© Springer International Publishing Switzerland 2014
X. Su and T. He (Eds.): CLSW 2014, LNAI 8922, pp. 369–379, 2014.
DOI: 10.1007/978-3-319-14331-6_37

patent text analysis. There exists deep semantic plane representing certain semantic structure in sentence. The deep semantic structure is mainly determined by the core verb of a sentence [3]. From the perspective of computer understanding and translating natural language, the predicate verb and adjectives acts as the center of syntax structure and interpretation of sentence [4]. In 3 Dimensional Dynamic Concept Model (3-DDCM) [5], the semantic combinational relations between the predicate verb and nominal phrases are concretely and exhaustively described and there are some intensive research on Chinese verbs and relative concepts in semantic or even deeper layer. The 3 Dimensional Dynamic Concept Model includes static axis, act axis and evolution axis. The static axis puts emphasis on relative equilibrium. The act axis puts emphasis on absolute motion, i.e. the cause of motion. The evolution axis is used to describe the general process everywhere apparent in Nature and Society. From the perspective of philosophy, the theory can be utilized as the basis for analyzing semantic relations in patent text.

In treebanks, dependency treebanks describe direct syntactic or semantic relations between words; phrase structure treebanks describe syntactic information of sentences, including syntactic units and part-of-speech of words and phrases as well as sentences, collocation and co-occurrence between words, internal structure and function classification of the phrase, etc [1]; there are also some treebanks reflecting semantic information with completed tagging of the predicate argument structure, which was built on the basis of above work. Due to the respective characteristic of each treebank, the syntactic structure, relations and semantic information cannot be shown simultaneously.

The previous study followed the bottom-up concept for building the Chinese Treebank[6]. The process includes word segmentation, POS tagging and follow-up work in order. Thus, the follow-up process will be limited by word segmentation and POS tagging. In Chinese, both word segmentation and POS tagging can cause ambiguous problems.

According to the above descriptions, we propose a top-down concept of building treebank based on chunk for patent translation, whose theoretical basis is 3 Dimensional Dynamic Concept Model, and determine the semantic relations tagging sets for patent text. Word segmentation and POS tagging will no longer interfere with the work of building treebank based on chunk. In this paper, the top-down concept of building treebank conforms to human thinking mode of firstly analyzing the largest chunk in linguistics. Thus, the process of building treebank will be more accurate and efficient. Our treebank shows not only information of chunk which is similar to the phrase structure treebank, but also semantic relations between chunks which are similar to the dependency treebank.

2   Tagging Sets

According to 3 Dimensional Dynamic Concept Model and semantic relations system of the Constructions Thought based on chunks and chunk sentences [9], we got the semantic relations tagging sets by improving the original semantic relations system for specific application. Our tagging sets are divided into chunks tagging sets and semantic relations tagging sets. Chunks tagging sets are used to describe category information of chunks, while semantic relations tagging sets are used to describe semantic relations between chunks as well as internal information. There are five chunk types in this paper, including dynamic chunk, scene chunk, role chunk, virtual chunk and sentence chunk. From the perspective of sentence structure and semantic understanding, dynamic chunk is the core of understanding the meaning of a sentence, such as verbs, adjectives, etc. Scene chunk is used to describe information about time, space or circumstance for an action which is driven by a dynamic chunk. Role chunk is involved in action which is also driven by a dynamic chunk. Virtual chunk has connection function in a sentence, such as punctuation, conjunctions, etc. In this paper, a simple sentence which is included in a complex sentence will be regarded as a sentence chunk, so that we can describe semantic relations between simple sentences through sentence chunk. In our semantic relation system, dynamic chunk is used as the core for describing semantic relations between all chunks. Further, semantic relations tagging sets are composed of five parts, including dynamic chunk tagging sets, scene chunk tagging sets, role chunk tagging sets, virtual chunk tagging sets and sentence chunk tagging sets. Among them, dynamic chunk tagging sets are used to describe semantic relations in the interior of dynamic chunks; scene chunk tagging sets are used to describe semantic relations between scene chunk and dynamic chunk; role chunk tagging sets are used to describe semantic relations between role chunk and dynamic chunk; virtual chunk is not involved in action which is driven by a dynamic chunk and it is used to describe relations between other chunks. In sentence chunk tagging sets, a simple sentence constituting a complex sentence is regarded as a sentence chunk to describe semantic relations between simple sentences. The following describes the detailed content of tagging sets.

2.1   Chunk Tagging Sets

In this paper, chunks are regarded as processing unit and we classify them as shown in Table 1.

Table 1. Chunk Tagging Sets

tag symbol	tag name	example
D	dynamic chunk	[D[不会]L] [D[提高]DC] (*do not increase*)
R	role chunk	[R[本发明]REE] (*this invention*)
S	scene chunk	[S[目前]TIM] (*currently*)
V	virtual chunk	[V[的]] (*of*)
SC	sentence chunk	[SC[两个冷凝器串联而成]] (*be made up of two condensers in series*)

2.2   Semantic Relations Tagging Sets

In this paper, we got semantic relations tagging sets by improving the original tagging sets. From the view of facilitating translation application, we transformed the relevant semantic information of static concept chunk, dynamic concept chunk, subjective concept chunk in original tagging sets through merging, adding, deleting or modifying into the semantic relations discussed in the paper. In the transformation process, we observed the following principles:

First, some semantic information can be replaced with other semantic information. Thus we will delete it. For example, "EXISTENT" is the expression of real things. There are some descriptions of state and relation about it. So we replace "EXISTENT" with "RELEVANT" or "STATUS" according to the context. To see an example, there is a sentence "镜体与镜体边框相连接(*Mirror body connects with mirror body frame.*)". In this sentence, "镜体(*mirror body*)" is "EXISTENT". The connection relation between "镜体(*mirror body*)" and "镜体边框(*mirror body frame*)" is described here, so we tag "镜体" as "RELEVANT". Second, several types of semantic information all express some commonality relation. For instance, "TIMEINI" and "TIMEFIN" express the relation about time, and their difference does not affect the result of translation. So we merge them and uniformly express their semantic relation with "TIME". For example, there are two phrases "剥离牺牲腔体层之前(*before stripping Sacrifice Cavity Layer*)" and "释放开口的覆盖层之后(*after releasing the opening cover layer*)". We only need to tag "之前(*before*)" and "之后(*after*)" to express the information of "TIME" relation. "之前" is translated into "before", and "之后" is translated into "after". Third, there are many words such as "是(*is*)" or "为 (*is*)" and they are used to express the *isa* relation. Therefore, we add two types of semantic relations, "ISS" and "ISB", to express *isa* relation between chunks. Fourth, for the rational expression of structure, we modify some original semantic information. For example, we modify "QUANTITY" expressing the relation in the interior of chunks in original system into "QUA" in our relation system. For example, there is a phrase "一种用于微光机电系统的制作方法(*a production method for micro elec-tromechanical system*)". Here a chunk "一种制作方法(*a production method*)" is separated into two parts by the chunk "用于微光机电系统(*for micro electromechan-ical system*)". We use symbol "QUA" to express their quantity relation between "一种 " and "制作方法". "QUA" is included in scene chunk tagging sets.

Following the above principles, we got our tagging sets. As follows:

a) Dynamic Chunk Tagging Sets

Dynamic chunk consists of five parts: left explanation, right explanation, up position, down position and dynamic concept. Among them, dynamic concept is the core of the five parts in dynamic chunk. In semantic understanding, other parts in dynamic chunk attach to dynamic concept and play a supporting role on the dynamic concept. In fact, every part of dynamic chunk is not necessarily to appear at the same time. One example for dynamic chunk: "[D[不会]L] [D[提高]DC]"(*do not increase*). There are no right explanation, up position and down position in this dynamic chunk. The detailed contents of dynamic chunk tagging sets are shown in Table 2.

Table 2. Dynamic Chunk Tagging Sets

tag symbol	tag name	example
L	left explanation	[D[不会]L] [D[提高]DC] (*do not increase*)
R	right explanation	[D[解决]DC] [D[了]R] (*solve*)
U	up position	[D[进行]U] [D[排列]DC] (*arrange*)
DP	down position	[D[转移]DC] [D[到]DP] (*transfer to*)
DC	dynamic concept	[D[涉及]DC] (*involve*)

b) Scene Chunk Tagging Sets

Scene chunk is the limiting description of the source or functional properties of role chunk, as well as of dynamic chunk, including range of activities, scenes, time or conditions. The detailed contents of scene chunk tagging sets are shown in Table 3.

Table 3. Scene Chunk Tagging Sets

tag symbol	tag name	example
TIM	time	[S[目前]TIM] [R[粉灰场粉灰]PAT] [D[输送]DC] (*Currently, the ash is transported from the ash field.*)
LOC	location	[R[谐振结构]STT] [D[位于]DC] [S[芯片中心]LOC] (*The structure of resonance is located in the center of the chip.*)
LOI	initial location	[V[从]] [S[存储器]LOI] [D[转移]DC] [D[到]RIG] [S[塑料瓶]LOF] (*The thing is transformed from the storage to the plastic bottle.*)
LOF	final location	[V[从]] [S[存储器]LOI] [D[转移]DC] [D[到]RIG] [S[塑料瓶]LOF] (*The thing is transformed from the storage to the plastic bottle.*)
DIR	direction	[R[所述PDMS衬底]PAT] [S[朝预设方向]DIR] [D[掀起]DC] (*The substrate is set off towards the default direction*)
QUA	quantity	[S[一种]QUA] [R[实施方式]PAT] (*an implementation way*)
SCO	condition	[S[在常温条件下]SCO] [R[气压]] [D[固定]DC] [S[在标准大气压]] (*Under normal temperature conditions, the barometric pressure is fixed at standard atmospheric pressure*)
FOL	following	[V[由]] [S[微机械的半导体材料]FOL] [D[制成]DC] (*be made of semiconductor material of micro-machining*)
LIM	limit	[R[调整机构]LIM] [V[的]] [R[主要部件]STT] (*the main part of the adjustment mechanism*)

c) Role Chunk Tagging Sets

In this paper, role chunk is the direct participant for action which is driven by a dynamic chunk, expressing state or relation. The detailed contents of role chunk tagging sets are shown in Table 4.

Table 4. Role Chunk Tagging Sets

tag symbol	tag name	example
AGE	agent	[R[本发明]AGE] [D[提出]DC] (*this invention proposes*)
PAT	patient	[D[设置]DC] [R[多个纳米结构]PAT] (*setting multiple nanometer structures*)
PRO	product	[D[形成]DC] [R[谐振梁图案]PRO] (*forming the resonant beam pattern*)
WHO	whole	[R[压力传感器元件]WHO] [D[包括]DC] [R[开口阵列]PAR] (*The pressure sensor element includes an array of opening.*)
PAR	part	[R[压力传感器元件]WHO] [D[包括]DC] [R[开口阵列]PAR] (*The pressure sensor element includes an array of opening.*)
POR	possessor	[R[所述电子设备]POR] [D[具有]DC] [R[较高的可靠性]PON] (*The electronic device has high reliability.*)
PON	possession	[R[所述电子设备]POR] [D[具有]DC] [R[较高的可靠性]PON] (*The electronic device has high reliability.*)
CAU	cause	[R[碰撞力]CAU] [D[导致]DC] [R[质量块发生振动]RES] (*The collision leads to the vibration of the mass.*)
RES	result	[R[碰撞力]CAU] [D[导致]DC] [R[质量块发生振动]RES] (*The collision leads to the vibration of the mass.*)
STT	status	[R[结构]STT] [D[简单]DC] (*The structure is simple*)
STE	state	[D[处于]DC] [R[静态状态]STE] (*in a static state*)
REE	relevant	[R[本发明]REE] [D[涉及]DC] [R[相关的芯片]REA] (*This invention relates to a relevant chip.*)
REA	relative	[R[本发明]REE] [D[涉及]DC] [R[相关的芯片]REA] (*This invention relates to a relevant chip.*)
ISS	isa-subject	[R[床垫的凹槽]ISS] [D[是]DC] [R[长体凹槽]ISB] (*The indentation of the mattress is a oblong shape indentation.*)
ISB	isa-body	[R[床垫的凹槽]ISS] [D[是]DC] [R[长体凹槽]ISB] (*The indentation of the mattress is a oblong shape indentation.*)

d) Virtual Chunk Tagging Sets

Virtual chunk plays the connection role in dynamic chunk, role chunk, and scene chunk. For instance, some conjunctions or some punctuation can be used as virtual chunk. For the information of virtual chunk, however, we only tag some virtual chunks that express parallel relation, such as "和(*and*)", "或(*or*)", etc. For other conjunctions and punctuation, we only identify them and do not tag semantic information. In addition, parallel relation between sentence chunks is not discussed here. The detailed contents of virtual chunk tagging sets are shown in Table 5.

Table 5. Virtual Chunk Tagging Sets

tag symbol	tag name	example
AND	and	[S[封帽]LOC] [V[和]AND] [S[底座]LOC] (*sealing cap and base*)

e) Sentence Chunk Tagging Sets

The sentence chunk tagging sets are used to describe semantic relation between simple sentences from a macro view. Those tagging sets in this part are proposed for processing complex sentences. A complex sentence is composed of several simple sentences. We consider a simple sentence as a sentence chunk, so the connection between simple sentences is converted into semantic relation between sentence chunks. The detailed contents of sentence chunk tagging sets are shown in Table 6.

Table 6. Sentence Chunk Tagging Sets

tag symbol	tag name	example
COO	coordinative	[SC[粘结剂具有高耐磨性]COO] [V[，]] [V[还]] [SC[具有高的度]] (*Binders have a high wear-resistance, and also have a high degree.*)
ATS	antecedent and succedent	[V[先]] [SC[刻蚀一定时间]ATS] [V[，]] [SC[获得硅纳米线阵列]] (*First, etching for a while and obtaining silicon nanowire arrays.*)
PRG	progressive	[SC[保证了成品率]PRG] [V[，]] [V[而且]] [SC[实现了批量生产]] (*Ensure the quality of finished products and achieve mass production.*)
ADV	adverse	[SC[本发明涉及话筒]ADV] [V[，]] [V[但是]] [SC[被封闭]] (*The invention relates to a microphone, but it is closed.*)
CTR	cause and effect	[V[由于]] [SC[本装置的安装]CTR] [V[，]][SC[美化了整体美观度]] (*The installation of this device beautifies the whole appearance.*)
COD	condition	[V[如果]] [SC[革新床是睡床时]COD] [[，]][SC[可用现有的产品]] (*If the bed is a bed of innovation, the existing products are available.*)
COC	concession	[V[即使]] [SC[在经受高的流速时]COC] [[，]] [SC[传感器是坚固的]] (*Even withstanding high flow rate, the sensor is strong.*)
PUR	purpose	[V[为了]] [SC[达到目的]PUR] [[，]] [SC[本实用新型采取如下技术方案]] (*In order to achieve the purpose, the following technical solution is taken in the utility model.*)
SUC	successive	[SC[系统设有管路系统]SUC] [[，]] [SC[管路系统设有并联管路]] (*The system is equipped with a pipeline system, and the pipeline system is equipped with parallel pipelines.*)

3   The Standard for Processing Treebank

The treebank in this paper can not only reflect the hierarchy of a patent sentence in a better way, but also express the semantic relations among different chunks, as well as distinguish between the main and the secondary. Furthermore, it is easier for people to understand the semantics, and the problem of complicated semantic relations of long sentences and complex sentences in patent text can also be solved. In the trees, the semantic structure of a sentence is presented by the relation between different nodes. Figure 1 shows a tree built on the basis of the processing standard of this paper. The original patent sentence is "于该探针下面形成一底切，用于将探针自基板分离。 (*Forming an undercut below the probe to separate the probe from the substrate.*)" The standard for processing treebank is as follows:

1) The Meaning of Node

The nodes of the tree represent different chunks. The node is tagged with its chunk type and the semantic relations between its child nodes (chunks), such as node "SC/LOC/PRO" in Figure 1, "SC" represents the chunk type "sentence chunk". The node has multiple child nodes (chunks), and dynamic chunk "D/DC" is the core. However, in the virtual chunk "V", no semantic relation will be tagged. Except the virtual chunk, the relations between other chunks and the dynamic chunk can be described from left to right. The "LOC" represents the semantic relation between child node "S" and node "D/DC"; "PRO" represents the semantic relation between child node "R" and node "D/DC". In addition, "D/DC" is a special node that "D" represents it is a dynamic chunk, and "DC" is a description of itself as a dynamic concept, not the semantic relation between different child nodes.

2) Processing of Virtual Chunk

The virtual chunk includes punctuation, words for connection, etc. Because the virtual chunk plays the connection role and has no special meaning, the semantic information can be derived from its own characteristics. Therefore, for most virtual chunks, we will not tag specific semantic relations. For example, the node "SC/COD" only expresses the semantic relation between child nodes "DC" and "SC", but does not tag the semantic relation of child node "V". "And" is a special virtual chunk that represents a coordination relation. It often appears in the patent text and has the special semantic information, so it is necessary to tag the "AND" relation.

3) Reflection of Core Word

In the tree, chunks of the same layer can be divided into the primary and the secondary, which is embodied by the structure and semantics. For multiple sentence chunks of the same layer, the right sentence chunk is the core of the left sentence chunk, e.g. in the second layer, the right "SC" is the core. If the scene chunk locate at left and the role chunk locate at right, the right is the core. When dynamic chunks exist in the same layer, the dynamic chunk with dynamic concept information is the core, e.g. in the third layer, "D/DC" is the core of "S" and "R".

4) Generation of Child Node with Dynamic Chunk as the Core

When a node includes a dynamic chunk, we need to generate a new child node; the leaf nodes at the bottom of the tree do not include dynamic chunk.

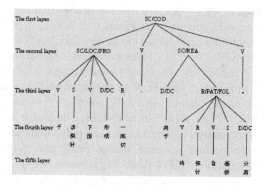

Fig. 1. A semantic structure tree

4   The Process for Tagging Corpus Manually

Currently, we have been tagging corpus manually. The core concept of the manual tagging process is top-down. For the building of treebank in the past, first step is Chinese word segmentation and second is part-of-speech tagging. On this basis, the treebank was built from bottom to top. But we think that the past concept does not match the thinking habit of human. Moreover, the largest chunk should be firstly analyzed as discussed in linguistics. That is to say, when we understand a sentence, we firstly understand the meaning as a whole and then understand every part of the sentence more deeply. So, from the view of matching the thinking habit of human, we proposed the top-down **tagging** process in which chunk is used as the processing unit. In addition, this process also avoids ambiguity caused by Chinese word segmentation and part-of-speech tagging. The manual tagging process includes: 1) identifying sentence chunks; 2) identifying dynamic chunks; 3) identifying other chunks; 4) tagging semantic relations.

Now we will show the manual tagging process by an example. An original Chinese sentence of patent is "于该探针下面形成一底切，用于将探针自基板分离。"(*Forming an undercut below the probe to separate the probe from the substrate.*) The first step is to identify sentence chunks. This complex sentence is composed of two simple sentences. According to the thinking habit of human, we analyze this sentence from the whole and identify two sentence chunks "于该探针下面形成一底切 (*Forming an undercut below the probe*)" and "用于将探针自基板分离(*to separate the probe from the substrate*)". We tag them by "SC". The second step is to identify dynamic chunks. Both of the two sentence chunks include dynamic chunks. There is only one verb "形成(*form*)" in the first chunk and it can express the core meaning of this sentence chunk. So "形成(*form*)" is the dynamic chunk of this sentence chunk. We tag it by "D". Similarly, "用于(*be used to*)" and "分离(*separate*)" also are both dynamic chunks in each sentence chunk. The third step is to identify other chunks. Based on the previous results, we continue to analyze them. "一底切(*an undercut*)" is a bearer of dynamic chunk "形成(*form*)", so "一底切(*an undercut*)" is a role chunk. We tag it by

"R". Similarly, "将探针自基板分离(*separate the probe from the substrate*)" and "探针(*probe*)" also are as role chunks. The chunk "于该探针下面(*below the probe*)" expresses place information where the action occurs. So, "该探针(*the probe*)" is as a scene chunk. We tag it by "S". For "于" (*There is no corresponding English translation for this word.*) and "下面(*below*)", they are virtual chunks with connection function. We tag them by "V". Similarly, "自基板(*from the substrate*)" is used to modify action which is driven by dynamic chunks, so "基板(*substrate*)" is as a scene chunk. "自 (*from*)", ", ", "。" and "将" are all as virtual chunks. The fourth step is to tag semantic relation. For the semantic analysis of chunks, we can judge that the first sentence chunk (SC) occurs before the second sentence chunk (SC), and they form an antecedent-succedent (ATS) relation. "于该探针下面(*below the probe*)" expresses the information of spatial location where the action occurs and the symbol of semantic relation is "LOC". "一底切(*an undercut*)" is the produce that is created by the action. So the semantic relation is "PRO". "探针(*probe*)" is the object of dynamic chunk "分离(*separate*)" and the tagging symbol is "PAT". "自基板(*from the substrate*)" is the accompaniment and the semantic relation is "FOL". "将探针自基板分离(*separate the probe from the substrate*)" expresses the relation of function semantics with "用于(*be used to*)", so the symbol is "REA". All the three dynamic chunks in this sentence are the core of semantic expression in each sentence chunk. So, the tagging symbol is "DC". The tagging results are as follows:

The first step: [SC[于该探针下面形成一底切]], [SC[用于将探针自基板分离]]。

The second step: [SC[于该探针下面 [D[形成]] 一底切]], [SC[[D[用于]] 将探针自基板 [D[分离]]]]。

The third step: [SC[[V[于]] [S[该探针]] [V[下面]] [D[形成]] [R[一底切]]]] [V[,]] [SC[[D[用于]] [R[[V[将]] [R[探针]] [V[自]] [S[基板]] [D[分离]]]]]] [V[。]]

The fourth step: [SC[[V[于]] [R[该探针]LOC] [V[下面]] [D[形成]DC] [R[一底切] PRO]]ATS] [V[,]] [SC[[D[用于]DC] [R[[V[将]] [R[探针]PAT] [V[自]] [S[基板] FOL] [D[分离]DC]]REA]]] [V[。]]

5   Conclusion

In this paper, we introduce some works on the building of Chinese semantic treebank for patent text. According to our tagging sets and processing standard, we have manually completed some tagging tasks. Those actual works prove the feasibility of building treebank with chunk as units and on the top-down concept. Thus the building process is no longer interfered by Chinese word segmentation and part-of-speech tagging. Meanwhile, it provides the foundation for exploring the automatic tagging methods in the future.

Currently, we only tag some sentences on small-scale patent corpus. On this basis, the language rules that have been found are inadequate and those semantic relations represented by tagging sets can not be utilized to fully describe all patent sentences. So, we need to further improve the tagging sets in future work, especially in terms of virtual chunk. Now our work mainly depends on manual method and the efficiency has been seriously restricted. Next, we need to explore the automatically tagging methods so that the tagging process can be automated and people just to assist. Thus we can improve the efficiency of building treebank and ensure the tagging accuracy with manual assistance.

References

1. Wang, Y., Ji, D.: The summary of Chinese Treebank. Contemporary Linguistics (2009). (王跃龙,姬东鸿.汉语树库综述.当代语言学 (2009)) (in Chinese)
2. Chen, Y., Huang, Y., Fang, J.: The collection and analysis for patent information. Tsinghua University Press, Beijing (2006). (陈燕,黄迎燕,方建国.专利信息采集与分析.北京:清华大学出版社 (2006)) (in Chinese)
3. Zhu, X.: Studies on Semantic Structure Patterns of Sentences in Modern Chinese. Peking University Press (2001). (朱晓亚.现代汉语句模研究.北京大学出版社 (2001)) (in Chinese)
4. Lin, X., Lu, C., Wang, L., Verb Dictionary. China Material Press (1994). (林杏光,鲁川,王玲玲.动词大词典.中国物资出版社 (1994)) (in Chinese)
5. Feng, H., Ye, N., Zhao, Q., Cai, D.: Chinese Verb Classification Based on 3 Dimensional Dynamic Concept Model. In: Liu, P., Su, Q. (eds.) CLSW 2013. LNCS (LNAI), vol. 8229, pp. 692–701. Springer, Heidelberg (2013)
6. Zhou, Q., Ren, H., Sun, M.: Build a large scale Chinese Tree Bank through Two-stages approach. In: The Second China-Japan Natural Language Processing Joint Research Promotion Conference (2002). (in Chinese)
7. Dong, Z., Zhou, Q.: HowNet. http://www.keenage.com (2013). (董振东,董强.知网. http://www.keenage.com) (in Chinese)
8. Huang, Z.: HNC (Hierarchical Network of Concept) Theory. Tsinghua University Press (1998). (黄曾阳. HNC (概念层次网络)理论.清华大学出版社 (1998)) (in Chinese)
9. Feng, H.: The building and application of patent verb frame base. Shenyang Aerospace University (2014). (in Chinese)

Statistics and Analysis of Coordination Structures in Patent Text

Mingru Wei[1(✉)], Guiping Zhang[1(✉)], Qiaoli Zhou[1(✉)], Yateng Wang[1(✉)], and Haihong Huang[2]

[1] Knowledge Engineering Research Center, Shenyang Aerospace University,
Shenyang 110136, China
{wmrdllg,wangyt_0823}@126.com, zgp@ge-soft.com,
zhou_qiao_li@hotmail.com
[2] Commercial Aircraft Corporation of China Ltd,
Shanghai Aircraft Design and Research Institute, Shanghai, China
Huanghaihong@comac.cc

Abstract. Based on the Chinese patent text, this paper thoroughly counts and analyzes part of speech and dependency relation distribution of coordination structures in the dependency treebank (wherein, the original corpus belongs to patent text.) from the perspective of morphology and internal and external linguistic features, and the dependency relations were compared in accordance with symmetry and asymmetry. For external linguistic features, we also investigate the modification relation of coordination structure. These investigations not only provide accurate analytical data for research on the structure, but also provide full knowledge of dependency parsing for difficulty in identifying the coordination structures in patent text.

Keywords: Chinese patent text · Coordination structure · Dependency relation

1 Introduction

Patent text records the details of technical invention, which is valuable technical information [1]. Due to dramatic increase in the number of patent text, the problems of traditional patent text analysis methods are increasingly evident [2]. Compared with general text, patent text has fixed format, standard expression, and a large number of coordination structure in addition to some high-frequency words and unknown words [3].

Coordination structure(CS) [4] is also named joint structure, consisting of two or more conjuncts. The immediate constituent in CS is usually called conjuncts which are connected always by conjunctions or commas or without any indicator.

From the characteristics of grammar and structure, CSs may be divided into simple CSs and complex CSs. A Simple CS presents several characteristics generally: it has no

This paper was supported by the Education Department of Liaoning Province, the general project under Grant No. L2012056.

This paper was supported by the National Basis Research Program under Project Number 2010CB530401-1.

X. Su and T. He (Eds.): CLSW 2014, LNAI 8922, pp. 380–389, 2014.
DOI: 10.1007/978-3-319-14331-6_38

more than five words; it includes only a single-layer CS which does not include other structures and is not included by other structures; for coordination with overt conjunctions(COC) , there is only one kind of conjunction; conjuncts of CS are consistent in syntactic and structural relationship. For complex CSs, due to their various forms, we defined those CSs other than simple CSs as complex CSs.

Example 1: BL【光源/n 和/c 图像/n (*Light source and pictures*)】

Example 2: BL【碳酸钠/n 、/wp 碳酸氢钠/n 、/wp 氢氧化钠/n 、/wp 磷酸钠 /n 和/c 乙酸钠/n (*Soda, baking soda, sodium hydrate, sal perlatum, and sodium acetate*)】

The sentence of Example 1 is a simple CS, which has one conjunction and three words.

The sentence of Example 2 is a complex CS ,which has two conjunctions of comma and "和(*and*)" and nine words.

Aiming at the statistic analysis and automatic identification of CS, researchers had investigated from many aspects.Dongbo Wang [5,6] detailedly counted and analyzed internal and external linguistic feature of COC before automatic identification of CS. Cui Shi [4] counted and analyzed internal and external feature of COC based on words and part of speech (POS) in Chinese patent text, but investigation on words and POS insufficiently shows the relationship between the syntactic constituents. Martin Popel [7] analyzed the problems of dependency in natural language processing by comparing the formats of encoding CS in dependency treebanks of 26 languages, which does not include Chinese due to bias in Chinese CS, demonstrating that analysis and identification of Chinese are more difficult compared to other languages. As in patent text, CS has intricate interior and exterior structures as well as various forms, it is also difficult to understand from either interior constituent or overall syntactic and semantic during automatic identification. Analysis only from phrase structure can easily result in ambiguous sentences, and the precision of phrase structure identification and dependency parsing would be improved if CSs were identified for syntactic analysis; on the other hand, dependency parsing can accurately and briefly show the dependence relationship between words, and then show the relationships of modifying and being modified in the interior or exterior of CSs, thus providing a great help to determine the left or right boundary of CS. In this paper, we focus on complex CSs in patent text and analyze their morphology and internal and external linguistic features, which provides full linguistic knowledge for automatic identification.

In the experiments, we adopt the patent text annotated by ourselves, in which dependency relation and POS are based on HIT label specification. After automatic word segmentation, POS annotation, automatic dependency parsing and manual proofreading, dependency treebank is formed, and "BL 【】" is utilized to mark the COCs in text. There are 6133 sentences and 190743 words, the average length of sentences is 31.06(word/sentence) [3]. 3731 sentences include 6253 CSs in total, and there are 5204 CSs when nested CS is considered as a single.

2   CS Morphology Statistics

In Chinese patent text, irregular CSs account for a large proportion, CSs with same number of words and same POS in conjuncts are symmetrical CSs, and the others are asymmetrical CSs, as shown in Table 1:

Table 1. Symmetrical statistics

	Number	Ratio
Symmetrical CS	2303	44.25%
Asymmetrical CS	2901	55.75%

Then we study the distribution of POS from different viewpoints according to the difference in symmetrical and asymmetrical CSs.

2.1   Symmetrical CS

For symmetrical CS, there are mainly two kinds of structures, one is CS with two conjuncts having one word each, and the other is CS with more conjuncts having more than two words, the more conjuncts, the less proportion in the corpus. Figure 1 gives the statistics of POS distribution on different kinds of symmetrical CSs (wherein, CJT indicates conjuncts; "&" indicates conjunction in the graph of the statistic result.)

Table 2. Symmetrical CS POS distribution

Number of CJT words	Number of CJT	POS distribution	Ratio(%)	Number of CJT words	Number of CJT	POS distribution	Ratio(%)
1	2	n&n	11.74	2	>=3	n n&n n&n n	0.10
		v&v	6.80			m q&m q&m q	0.06
		m&m	4.63			v n&v n&v n	0.04
		others	5.84			others	0.20
	3	n&n&n	1.36	3	2	n n m&n n m	0.27
		v&v&v	0.86			ws n n&ws n n	0.13
		ws&ws&ws	0.56			a n n&a n n	0.12
		others	0.65			others	1.40
	>=4	n&n&n&n	0.44		>=3	n n ws&n n ws&n n ws	0.06
		ws&ws&ws&ws	0.29			n ws n&n ws n&n ws n	0.04
		others	1.13			others	0.13
2	2	n m&n m	1.25	>=4	2	n n m ws&n n m ws	0.06
		n n&n n	0.98			m q b n&m q b n	0.04
		v n&v n	0.46			others	1.69
		others	2.92				

2.2   Asymmetrical CS

For asymmetrical CS, due to its irregular structure, we distinguish it with number of conjuncts to investigate whether the POS types corresponding to each number of conjuncts are the same, as shown in Table 3:

Table 3. Symmetrical POS distribution

Number of CJT	POS type	POS distribution	Ratio(%)	Number of CJT	POS type	POS distribution	Ratio(%)
2	same	n&n n	0.73	3	different	n&n&r n	0.21
		n n&n	0.71				
		v&v v	0.13			n n v ws ws u n&n ws m q n&b p n v u v u n	0.12
		others	0.46			others	9.20
	different	m&m q	1.15	>= 4	same	n&n n&n&n	0.06
		n n&b n n	0.69			n&n&n&n n	0.06
		v&d v	0.29			others	0.33
		others	34.51		different	p ws n n m v&p n m v&p n ws v ws v&p v v n n m	6.67
3	same	n&n&n n	0.17				
		n n&n&n	0.08			ws n&ws&ws&ws etc.	
		others	0.17				

From the Table 3, we can see that different POS types corresponding to each number of conjuncts account for a large proportion. Only from POS viewpoint, asymmetrical CS is difficult to identify by rules, and therefore, we perform deep statistic and analysis from dependency viewpoint.

2.3   Number of Conjunctions and Conjuncts

Conjunction is an important mark of CS, as well as an important tie to joint conjuncts. We count conjunction types of CS, in which one type accounts for 83.7%, but the number of conjunctions may be more than one, that is to say, this type also consists of complex CS, in which the types of conjunctions are the same; CS with more than one type of conjunctions accounts for 16.3%, which is typical complex CS, also difficult to identify, as shown in Table 4:

Table 4. Statistic of conjunction types in CSs

Conjunction kinds	Number	Ratio
2	958	15.32%
3	58	0.93%
4	3	0.05%

Example 3：BL【输入/v //wp 输出/v】 模块/n 1008/m 的/u 示例/n 包括/v BL
【键盘/n 、/wp 光标/n 控制/v 装置/n 、/wp 显示器/n 及/c 网络/n 接口/n】 。
/wp (*An example of the Input / output module 1008 includes keyboard, cursor control device, monitor, and network interface.*)

The sentence of Example 3 contains two CSs: the first is a simple CS, and the other is a complex CS that contains multiple conjunctions belonging to two types. In addition, systematic analysis is performed on the number of conjuncts contained in CS, and CS with two conjuncts accounts for a large proportion which is 75.94%; CS with more than two conjuncts accounts for 24.06%, which often has a large span and can be considered together with conjunction types during identification, as shown in Table 5:

Table 5. Statistic of conjuncts number

Number of CJT	Number relative to CJT number	Ratio
2	3952	75.94%
3	739	14.20%
More than 3	513	9.86%

2.4   Nested CS Styles

In patent text, nested CS accounts for a great proportion which is 13.08%. At the same time, nested CS consists of various styles, for example, two-layer CS includes 5 styles, wherein, two-layer CS with a one-layer CS accounts for 7.99%; two-layer CS with two one-layer CSs accounts for 3.54%; two-layer CS with five one-layer CS at most accounts for a small proportion which is only 0.04%, which is also the difficulty in the identification. There are 11 styles containing various layers of nested CS, which mostly contains one or more nested styles and also contains one-layer style, and its distribution is not focused, as shown in Table 6:

Table 6. Nested style statistics

Nested layers	Nested tags styles	Number of CSs	Ratio	Nested layers	Nested tags styles	Number of CSs	Ratio
2	BL【, BL【, 】, 】	416	7.99%	more than 2	BL【, BL【, BL【, 】, 】, 】	11	0.21%
	BL【, BL【, 】, BL【, 】, 】	184	3.54%		BL【, BL【, BL【, 】, 】, BL【, 】, 】	7	0.13%
	BL【, BL【, 】, BL【, 】, BL【, 】, 】	34	0.65%		BL【, BL【, 】, BL【, BL【, 】, 】, 】	3	0.06%
	others	12	0.23%		others	14	0.27%

3   Statistics of Internal Features

In the previous sections, we make the statistics for morphology of CS. In this section, we detailedly classify the relationship between conjuncts in CS from POS and dependency relation as follows.

3.1   One-Word Conjunct

When conjunct consists of one word, there is no dependency relation in the interior, therefore, we investigate its POS distribution, and the proportion is 36.6%, wherein, conjuncts with the same POS types account for 34.67%, and the frequency focuses on the case with two conjuncts, and the POS percentage decreases along with the increase of the number of conjuncts; conjuncts with different POS types account for 1.93%, demonstrating that this structures are mostly symmetrical CSs, and the methods based on rules may be used in identification, as shown in Table 7:

Table 7. POS types statistics of CSs with one-word conjunct

POS types	Number of CJT	POS distribution	Ratio(%)	POS types	Number of CJT	POS distribution	Ratio(%)
same	2	n&n	11.88	different	2	ws&n	0.29
		v&v	6.81			r&b	0.12
		m&m	4.62			a&d	0.06
		others	5.81			others	0.92
	3	n&n&n	1.44		3	b&n&b	0.06
		v&v&v	0.87			m&ws&ws	0.06
		m&m&m	0.58			others	0.22
		others	0.64		>=4	n&n&ws&n&n etc.	0.20
	>=4	n&n&n&n	0.48				
		ws&ws&ws&ws	0.29				
		m&m&m&m	0.15				
		others	1.10				

3.2   Multiple-Word Conjunct

When conjunct consists of multiple words, we cannot find its interior property only from the viewpoint of POS types. There is dependency relation in syntactic structure between words of conjuncts in case of multiple words. Therefore, we investigate the dependency relation distribution in conjuncts, and analyze and seek the core of identification respectively from the symmetry and asymmetry of dependency relation. Because analysis aims at interior dependency relation, exterior dependency relation is not included, and CS dependency relation between conjuncts is not included too, namely "COO". If the rest of dependencies relation of each conjunct are the same, then they are regarded as symmetrical dependency relations, accounting for 15.32%; otherwise, they are regarded as asymmetrical dependency relations, accounting for 84.68%. Table 8 and Table 9 show the main types:

Table 8. Symmetrical dependency relation

Dependency relation types	symmetrical
ATT	ATT& ATT
	ATT RAD &ATT RAD
	ATT ATT&ATT ATT
VOB	VOB &VOB

Table 9. Asymmetrical dependency relation

Dependency relation types	Asymmetrical
ATT	ATT
	ATT&null
	ATT &ATT ATT
ADV	ADV

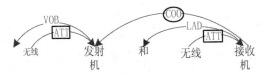

Fig. 1. (*Wireless transmitter and wireless receiver*) Symmetrical Interior dependency as "ATT" relation

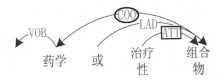

Fig. 2. (*Pharmacy or Therapeutic compositions*) Asymmetrical Right conjunct as "ATT" relation

Dongbo Wang[6] has counted the interior phrase distribution of COC. We count the interior dependency relation from symmetry, symmetrical dependency relation are parallel in structure, and if they are asymmetrical in POS, the boundary of CS can be determined according to dependency relation; while the CSs of asymmetrical dependency relation are identified in combination with statistic-based methods.

4   Statistics of Exterior Characters

4.1   Exterior Syntactic Structure

We count and analyze the external syntactic structure of CS from the viewpoint of dependency parsing based on the dependency treebank [8]. The results show that the CSs are located at the verb-object phrase(VOB), attribute center-word phrase(ATT), prepositional-object phrase(POB), the structure of "的(*de*)"(DE), etc. The frequency more than 100 accounts for 95.65%, and its distribution is shown in Table 10:

Table 10. Distribution of external dependency relation of CSs

Dependency relation	Frequency	Ratio	Dependency relaiton	Frequency	Ratio
VOB	1542	29.63%	RAD	263	5.05%
ATT	702	13.49%	APP	188	3.61%
POB	461	8.86%	VV	148	2.84%
HED	440	8.46%	QUN	147	2.82%
DE	436	8.38%	COO	147	2.82%
SBV	376	7.23%	ADV	128	2.46%

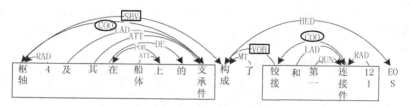

Fig. 3. (*The pivot 4 and its strut member on board constitute hinge joint and the first connecting piece 121*). CSs as SBV and VOB relation.

In Figure 3, subject is a complex CS which is shared modifier for the core word "构成 (*constitute*)", and forms SBV; predicate is a simple CS, which form VOB with core word. Cui Shi [3] simply counted and analyzed the dependency relation of COC. We deeply research the syntactic structure of patent text from the perspective of modification relation.

4.2 Modification Relation

In external information of CSs, whether or not the CSs are shared modifiers is important information of representing CSs. Martin Popel [7] illustrated that intricate problems exist in the precise representation of CSs in dependency treebanks, and one is whether the CSs are shared modifiers, and at the same time, CSs are also modified by other constituents or located at nested styles, the CSs included in nested CSs also have the relations of modifying and being modified, as shown in Table 11:

Table 11. CS commonly modify a constituent

Dependency relation types	VOB	ATT	POB	DE	RAD	APP	SBV	QUN
Number	1203	669	394	391	230	164	163	120

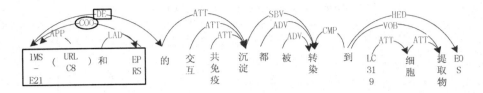

Fig. 4. (*Interactive coimmunoprecipitation of IMS-E21(URLC8) and EPRS are both transfected to LC319 cellular extract*). Shared modifiers relation of CS.

Shared modifiers account for 57.56%, in which the relation of VOB accounts for the largest proportion. The structure of "的(*de*)"(DE) of CS in Figure 4 is a shared modifier. This type of modification is easy to cause ambiguity, which is difficult to determine the right boundary, i.e. the shared modifiers may be mistaken as the private modifiers of the right conjuncts.

Table 12. CS is modified by the same constituent

Dependency relation types	ATT	ADV	SBV	LAD	CNJ	DE	QUN	VOB
Number	875	368	224	193	143	34	31	28

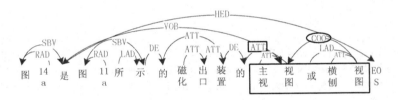

Fig. 5. (*Figure 14a is the main view or the transverse plane view of the magnetization exit device shown in Figure 11a*). The being modified relation of CS.

The percentage of being modified is 31.06%, in which the ATT relation accounts for the largest proportion. Figure 5 is contrary to Figure 4, the CS is modified by the structure of "的(*de*)"(DE), and its left boundary is easy to mistake, which may result in ambiguity, and this is a problem of identification.

5   Conclusions

In this paper, we investigate the patent text, and count and analyze morphology of CSs and internal and external linguistic features, in which we lay a lot of emphasis on the dependency relation distribution in internal feature when conjuncts consist of multiple words, and the features and types of modifying and being modified in external feature, which provide important rules information for automatically identifying CS. In future work, the rules information will be extracted by referring to the analysis results and adapting to the characteristics of patent text, and CSs are automatically identified based on statistics methods in combination with the machine learning strategy. Especially the particularity of CSs in patent text (such as the great percentage of asymmetrical CSs, etc.) is the critical problem to be solved. However, because of the limited text, the above statistics information is not enough, we will extend the text resource and the perspective of investigation to acquire more rules information. It is our goal to solve the problems of application in natural language processing.

References

1. Wang, Z.: Characteristics and Utilization of Patent Document. Modern Information (9), 151–156 (2008). (in Chinese)
2. Bao, H., Zhu, D., Li, J.: Knowledge Discovery in Patent Literatures. Forecasting **22**(4), 11–15 (2003). (in Chinese)
3. Shi, C., Zhou, Q., Zhang, G.: Analyzing the Linguistics Features of Coordination with Overt Conjunctions Based on Chinese Patent Literature. Journal of Chinese Information Processing **27**(5), 43–50 (2013). (in Chinese)
4. Feng, W.H., Ji, D.H.: The Dependency-based Analysis of Coordinate Structures and the Governor Status of Conjunctions. Linguistic Sciences **10**(2), 168–181 (2011). (in Chinese)
5. Wang, D.: The Automatic Identification of Coordination with Overt Conjunctions. Nanjing Normal University (2008). (in Chinese)
6. Wang, D.: Analyzing the Linguistic Features of Coordination with Overt Conjunctions Based on Tsinghua Chinese Treebank. New Technology of Library and Information Service (4), 12–17 (2010). (in Chinese)
7. Popel, M.: Coordination Structures in Dependency Treebanks. In: Proceedings of the 51st Annual Meeting of the Association for Computational Linguistics, pp. 517–527 (2013)
8. Lang, W.: Research and Application of Chinese Dependency Parsing Based on Rules and Statistics. Shenyang Aerospace University (2012). (in Chinese)

Syntactic Distribution, Semantic Framework, and Pragmatic Function of the Modal Adverb *Meizhun* (Maybe)

Hong Xiao[✉]

College of Chinese Language and Literature, Wuhan University,
Wuhan 430072, Hubei, China
xiaohong430072@163.com

Abstract. This paper divides the term *meizhun* into five homographs based on its morphemic structure and usage, and focuses on the modal adverb form that means *maybe* in English. *Meizhun* (maybe) generally appears in assertive sentences and can be used with auxiliary verbs, conjunctions, and other adverbs. Sentences with this term share the stylised frame of logical semantics. Its main textual functions are inference and definition, and the use of this term, which is derived from *meizhun* (uncertain/not sure), is now spreading rapidly among speakers of contemporary Chinese.

Keywords: Semantics · Modal adverb · *Meizhun* (maybe) · Homographs

1   Introduction

Although 没 准 (*meizhun*, or maybe) is widely used in contemporary Chinese, it has not yet become an established term. According to *The Contemporary Chinese Dictionary*, *meizhun* means "maybe" or "uncertain". For example,

(1)*Zhe shi meizhunr neng cheng.*

Maybe it can work out.

(2)*Qu bu qu hai mei ge zhunr.*

I am uncertain about whether to go.

The relationship between *meizhun* and *mei* + quantifier *ge*+ *zhun* is important and deserves further examination. In addition, *meizhun*'s syntactic forms, semantic meaning, and pragmatics also require additional attention.

2   Five Homomorphic Words for *Meizhun* in Contemporary Chinese

Based on an investigation of 532 examples in the Center for Chinese Linguistics (CCL) Corpus of Peking University, we identified two different categories of *mei* in *meizhun*:

© Springer International Publishing Switzerland 2014
X. Su and T. He (Eds.): CLSW 2014, LNAI 8922, pp. 390–402, 2014.
DOI: 10.1007/978-3-319-14331-6_39

mei_1 and mei_2. Mei_1 is a verb, whereas mei_2 is a negative adverb. In addition, *meizhun* is not a simple negation of the adverb *zhun*, which means "must". Instead, *zhun* carries four meanings: $zhun_1$, $zhun_2$, $zhun_3$ and $zhun_4$. $Zhun_1$ is a noun that represents certain ideas, methods, and rules and can serve as suffix for a non-syllabic "r". $Zhun_2$, a verb, means preparing or planning to do something or making advance arrangements. $Zhun_3$ is also a verb and indicates permission. $Zhun_4$ is an adjective, which means certainty or confirmation. In other words, contemporary Chinese contains five forms of *meizhun*.

2.1 *Mei zhunbei* (not ready)

According to the examples, "not ready" is generally embedded in four syntactic patterns:

(A) mei_1 $zhun_2bei$ + 0;

(B) mei_1 $zhun_2bei$ + verb phrase (VP);

(C) mei_1 $zhun_2bei$ + complement (好 (*hao*, or well);

(D) mei_1 $zhun_2bei$ + noun.

Mei + quantifier 个 (*ge*) + 准备 (*zhunbei*, or preparation) is sometimes used instead of mei_1 $zhun_2bei$ as the predicate in spoken Chinese.

2.2 *Meizhun* (not allowed)

According to example (3), mei_2zhun_3 is a usually used in a pivotal sentence, namely mei_2zhun_3 + telescopic form + verb. For instance,

(3) *Wo hai mei zhun ni zou, Gandaofu yanlide shuo: wo hai mei shuo wan.*

You are not allowed to go, Gandalf said sternly; I have not finished talking yet.

2.3 *Meizhun* (not exact/irregular)

The third usage is mei_1+$zhun_4$ + noun. As illustrated by the examples, this form can be collocated with time-related words such as 时 (*shi*, or hour), 点 (*dian*, or o'clock), and 日子 (*rizi*, or day). At times, it can also be collocated with other words, such as 主意 (*zhuyi*, or idea), 价 (*jia*, or price), and 姓 (*xing*, or surname).

Under these conditions, the quantifier 个 (*ge*) can be added between *mei* and *zhun*. Moreover, *meizhun* can be used to elaborate on time-related words, such as 点 (*dian*, or o'clock), as well as some other nominals, such as 名 (*ming*, or name) and 进项 (*jinxiang*, or income). In general, the nominal collocated with mei_1zhun_4 includes the quantity, namely [+ number]. When used with the quantifier *ge*, this inclusion of the quantity is more evident. For example,

(4) *Dangchu wa, wo taoyan ta dengche, yinwei dengche bu shi zhengjing hangdang, bu timian, mei ge zhun jinxiang.*

At first, I hated him being a rickshaw driver, because it is not a serious and decent profession with a regular income.

2.4   *Meizhun* (uncertain/not sure)

There are 18 examples of the use of mei_1zhun_1 as a predicate. These sentences take the form of subject(S) + *meizhun*.

First, the sentence is fragmented, with *meizhun* omitted. When *meizhun* is omitted, the sentences are unacceptable. The signified meaning of *meizhun* usually directs attention to the proximate subject. The subject is usually a noun or pronoun with metrological characteristics, and it often refers to time, distance, price, method, a particular rule, and so on. For example,

(5) *Yi wei xiu xie shifu shuo: Wo zai zheli gan hao ji nian le, mei ge huo shou duoshao qian meizhun.*

A shoe repairman said: I have worked here for several years, but I'm still not sure about how much a business should charge. (*Meizhun* refers to how much a business should charge.)

Used as a predicate, *meizhun* can include the quantifier *ge*, thus becoming *mei ge zhun*. We can also add *er* or *tou* after *zhun* as a suffix, forming *mei ge zhunr* or *mei ge zhuntou*. For example,

(6) *Xinli hai mei ge zhunr.*
I'm not sure whether I can make it.
(7) *Chizi liang dongxi, tanxing hao de shihou, liang de changxie; tanxing cha de shihou, liang de duanxie, mei ge zhuntou.*

The measurements made by a ruler are inconsistent: higher levels of elasticity produce longer measurements, whereas lower levels of elasticity produce shorter measurements.'

Second, *Meizhun* is used to modify 那 (*na*, **or that).** In the pattern of *na* + adverb or adjective + *meizhun*, if *meizhun* is removed, the sentence will be interrupted. The semantic orientation of *meizhun* is toward *na*, and *na* can substitute for methods or time. The words that are replaced will appear either in the preceding part of the text or be introduced in the text that follows. For example,

(8) *Zhuren shuo: Zhengce yao yunxu na ye meizhun. Shagua cai bu xiang yao nianqing guniang li.*

The chief said: "As long as the policy permits it, it is certain that everyone will want to date young girls".

(*Meizhun* corresponds to *na*, which refers to "no one wants to date young girls" in the following part of the sentence.)

Third, *meizhun* is used as an adverb, which directs attention to verbal phrases. For example,

(9) *Dagai bu hui jiang zhe shu tongdu le, huoxu hai hui dajiao shangdang er dang fei zhi mai le ta ye meizhunr.*

He will probably not read the book, or maybe he will sell it as a pile of waste paper, complaining that he was tricked into buying the book.

(*Meizhun* corresponds to "sell it as a pile of waste paper, complaining that he was tricked into buying the book". The adverbs *huoxu* and *dagai* share a meaning similar to that of *meizhun*.)

2.5 *Meizhun* (maybe/probably)

In this case, mei_2zhun_2 or mei_2zhun_2 + suffix r is the commentary adverb,[1] which means not predicted, possibly, or probably.

3 Syntactic Distribution, Semantic Framework, and Pragmatic Function of Commentary Adverbs: *Meizhun* (Maybe/Probably)

3.1 Syntactic Function of *Meizhun* (Maybe)

In most cases, *meizhun* is used in the adverbial form (i.e., *meizhun* + noun phrase (NP) + VP, or NP + *meizhun* + VP[2]).

(10) *Meizhun renjia lingmou- gaojiu le ne.*

Maybe he has found another, better job.

(11) *Zhe qian meizhunr neng pai shang yongchang.*

Maybe the money will turn out to be useful.

At times, *meizhun* is used independently as a parenthetic phrase that is separated from the main sentence with punctuation. For example,

(12) *Meizhunr, zhe ye keneng shi Xiaoxi gen ta de jiaohuan tiaojian ne.*

This is probably Xiaoxi's condition for doing business".

---

[1] A commentary adverb can function syntactically as a high-level predicate. They are used flexibly in sentences, expressing the speaker's assessment of and attitude toward an event. Zhang (2000, p. 18) and Shi (2003) proposed three standards for defining modal adverbs: its capacity to act as sentence constituents in combination with other constituents, its location when it co-occurs with the link-verb *shi* (be), and its location in the sentence.

[2] Duan (1995) noted that one characteristic of the modal adverb is that it can be used before the NP in subject–predicate sentences.

(13) *Meizhunr, shouhuoyuan lengbuding de paochu yi ju: Jiu wei zhe dian qian, zhide ma?*

The salesperson would probably suddenly throw the product and say, "It's worth more money than you are offering"?

3.2   Forms of Distribution of *Meizhun* (maybe)

First, like other commentary adverbs, *meizhun* is widely used in declarative sentences. However, it is seldom used in interrogative sentences (the word *meizhun* does not express doubt by itself, but it transmutes real interrogatives into pseudo-interrogatives),[3] and it is occasionally used in exclamatory sentences. *Meizhun* often appears in subject–predicate sentences, including ellipses and unmarked clauses. In addition, it appears in comparative sentences, passive sentences, the 把 (*ba*) structure, the verb-complement structure, 是 (*shi*) sentences, pivotal sentences, rhetorical questions, sentences with serial verbs, overlapping patterns, 连 (*lian*) sentences, negative sentences, assertive sentences, accusative subject sentences, quantity complements, parallelisms, elliptical sentences, and so on. There are two types of 是 (*shi*) sentence. The first is a judgment sentence in which 是 (*shi*, or be) is a copular verb. The second expresses emphasis, using 是 (*shi*) as a commentary adverb. For example,

(14) *Meizhun shang ci jiu shi ta jie de dianhua.*

Maybe it was she who answered the phone call last time.

(15) *Na nin chuli zhe gaozi ba, meizhun shi wo kan tai duo bian xian jinqu le.*

You should handle this paper. Maybe my problem is that I became obsessed after reading it too many times.

Second, the examples of *meizhun* demonstrate that it can collocate with many heterogeneous adverbs, auxiliary verbs, and conjunctions. The co-occurrence order is as follows:

(A) When meizhun is collocated with an auxiliary verb, such as 能 (neng, or can), 可以 (keyi, or can), 可能 (keneng, or maybe), 会 (hui, or will), 该 (gai, should), it should be located in front of the auxiliary verb.

(B) With conjunctions such as 而且 (erqie, or and), 可 (ke, or but), 但 (dan, or however) meizhun follows the conjunction.

(C) In terms of scope adverbs, such as 都 (dou, or all) and 只 (zhi, or only), meizhun precedes the adverb.

(D) With regard to adverbs indicating repetition, such as 又 (you, or again), 再 (zai, or again), 还 (hai, or still), and 也 (ye, or also), meizhun precedes the adverb.

---

[3] Duan (1995) summarised the pragmatic functions of the modal adverb, such as converting true questions into pseudo-questions, strengthening emotional coloring, and enhancing the colloquial characteristic of discourse.

(E) When used with time-related adverbs, such as 将 (jiang, or will), 要 (yao, or will), 已经 (yijing, or already), 正 (zheng, or just), and 刚 (gang, exactly), meizhun precedes the adverb.

(F) With regard to degree adverbs such as 更 (geng, or more) and 越 (yue, or more), meizhun often precedes the adverb.

(G) When used with correlative adverbs such as 就 (jiu, or and) and 也 (ye, or but), meizhun often precedes the adverb. However, if the referent of the adverb has already included meizhun as a commentary adverb, it should follow the correlative adverb.

(H) In terms of other types of commentary adverbs, meizhun often precedes the other adverb. If the other commentary adverb expresses emphasis, politeness, or un-expectedness, such as 就 (jiu [emphasis]), 也 (ye [politeness]), 到 (dao [mildness]), 却 (que [mildness]), 不过 (buguo [mildness]), meizhun often follows the adverb.

(16) *Ni zai na ji tiao yan, ji ping jiu shishi? Feidan bu gei ni ban shi, jiushi yijing ban hao de shiqing meizhunr ye gei ni za le.*

You'd better not bring more cigarettes and wine, as this will not help you solve the problem and may even make things worse"?

(17) *Yexu pingzhe congming, pingzhe piaoliang, jishi zhi jinguo chuzhong ketang, ye meizhunr zhen neng ba mou ge juese yan de liaorenermu.*

Although she received only a secondary school education, her intelligence and beauty may enable her to play certain characters perfectly.

(18) *Buguo dao ye meizhun ba hua shuo guotou le.*

But maybe it was overstated.

(I) When *meizhun* is collocated with a commentary adverb that expresses an ex-pectation, such as 或许 (*huoxu*, or maybe), 也许 (*yexu*, or probably), 或者 (*huozhe*, or or), 说不定 (*shuobuding*, or perhaps), 不一定 (*buyiding*, or uncertain), and 搞不好 (*gaobuhao*, maybe), *meizhun* can be used in the same sentence as the adverb or be used in the previous or the next sentence. When appearing in the same sentence, *meizhun* is always separated from these commentary adverbs, which differs from the situation discussed by Zhang (2001, p, 217). For instance,

(19) *Huozhe yexu buzhiyu gandao kunnan.*

It probably won't be difficult.

(20) *Zhen shuobuding yexu re si le.*

Seriously, we may be killed by the heat.

These situations are quite unusual for *meizhun*.[4] When appearing with other commentary adverbs, *meizhun* presents the commentary for the whole sentence, irrespective of whether it appears at the beginning or at the end of it. For example,

(21) *Meizhun na ge 'ta' yinggai huancheng 'ta' ye shuobuding.*

Probably, 'he' should be changed into 'she'.

(22) *Jiaru ni bu yuanyi jian wo de hua, wo keyi zhuan lai zhao ta; yexu yue ta*

chuqu zou yi zou, meizhun!

If you don't want to see me, I can come to see only her; I may ask her to take a walk!

(J) Modal particles at the end of the sentence can co-occur with *meizhun*, such as 了 (*le*, 23 cases), 呢 (*ne*, 31 cases), 的 (*de*, 5 cases[5]), 的呢 (*dene*, 2 cases), 吧 (*ba*, 2 cases), 哩 (*li*, 2 cases), 喽 (*lou*, 1 case), 啦 (*la*, (2 cases), and 哪 (*na*, 2 cases). Qi (2007) summarised the co-occurrence principles governing modal adverbs and modal particles at the ends of sentences. According to her statistics, the frequency with which subjective assessment modal adverbs (e.g., 大概 [*dagai*, or probably], 大约 [*dayue*, or possibly], and 也许 [*yexu*, or maybe]) co-occur with subjective assessment modal particles at the end of a sentence, and the frequency with which *dagai*, *dayue* and *yexu* co-occur with *de* or *le* is 60%; their co-occurrence with *ba* is 30%, and that with the interrogatives *ne* or *ma* is very low, possibly zero. *Meizhun* differs from *dagai*, especially when used with *ne*. They co-occur very frequently,[6] which may be involved in the affirmation problem related to the degree of suspicion associated with *ne*.

3.3   Semantic Framework of *Meizhun* (Maybe)

While analysing the examples in the CCL corpus, we found that sentences with *meizhun* share a stylised frame of logical semantics, namely the causal clauses, the hypothetical conditions, *meizhun* + the result clause or the causal clauses, *meizhun*, the

---

[4] *Meizhun* can be used with auxiliary verbs expressing possibility or assessment, such as 能 (*neng*, or can) and 可能(*keneng*, or may). For example, *Meizhun zhen you keneng ba Liang Daya zheng dao shan nabian qu* (They may really send Liang Daya to the other side of the mountain). However, we have not found a single example in the CCL corpus of Peking University in which *meizhun* is placed with adverbs that express possibility or assessment. In all the examples, the parentheses have been added.

[5] Three of the examples have the structure of *shi...de*, which expresses emphasis. In terms of the judgment structure of *shi...de*, *des*, which omits the object, is excluded from our statistics.

[6] Of the 3,560 examples of *shuobuding* taken from the CCL corpus of Peking University, 286 are examples of its co-occurrence with 了 (*le*) and 278 are examples of its co-occurrence with 呢 (*ne*). It co-occurs with the latter not infrequently. Moreover, there are also some examples with 吗 (*ma*). For example, *Shuobuding yexu zhende shi shigu ma?* Maybe it was a real accident?

hypothetical conditions, the result clause. Although an imperative sentence usually appears in this frame, the assumptions sentence may contain the imperative sentence. For example,

> (23) *Bie hui jia le, he laopo zai yiqi duo kuzao, ni jiu zhengxiu de he germen*
>
> *shenkan, meizhun hai neng kanyun geba yanjing shuiwangwang de nv xue*
>
> *sheng, jiuxiang dangchu kanyun wo yiyang.*

Don't go home. It's really boring to spend time with your wife. If you stay here with your brothers and spend the night talking freely, you may be able to trick some teary female student, just as you tricked me a long time ago.

The above includes the imperative sentence "don't go home" and uses "It's really boring to spend time with your wife" to explain the reason for this imperative. This text also contains a hypothetical conditional sentence, "stay here with your brothers and spend the night talking freely" as well as a result "you may be able to trick some teary female student".

> (24) *Wo zhen bu hui shou ciji, zhi hui wei ni gaoxing, ni jiu manzu yi xia wo de*
>
> *haoqixin ba, meizhun wo he ta hai neng chengwei hao pengyou ne—qiu ni le.*

I won't be hurt; I'll feel happy for you. Indulge my curiosity. Maybe I will become good friends with her—please.

These sentences first state, "I won't be hurt; I'll feel happy for you", a causal clause; this is followed by an imperative sentence, "Indulge my curiosity". The result clause, "Maybe I will become good friends with her", follows *meizhun*.

> (25) *Lao nin dajia qu bang Ding shifu chuli-chuli ba...Ruguo na liang ge ren*
>
> *chi de shi anmianyao, meizhun hai neng jiuguolai...*

Would you please help Mr. Ding deal with the situation ... The two people may be able to be saved if they only took hypnotics.

This sentence is an example of the semantic structure in which *meizhun* is typically embedded. It includes an imperative sentence ("help Mr. Ding deal with the situation"), a hypothetical conditional ("if they only took hypnotics"), and a result clause using *meizhun*, which forms a 还能 (*haineng*) + verb-complement structure.

> (26) *Chen Zai shuo ni de toufa you bu name houmi, jianduan le meizhunr hui*
>
> *xiande xixi-lala de.*

Chen Zai says that your hair is not very thick, so it will look thinner if it is cut short.

This sentence places "your hair is not very thick" at the beginning to provide a reason, and the hypothetical conditional, "if it is cut short", follows. The result clause, "*it will look thinner*", follows *meizhun*.

In addition, there are a few examples of *meizhun* in judgment sentences, and these differ from those in which it appears in the result clause. The semantic frame of *meizhun* in judgement sentences is a causal clause: *meizhun* + judgment sentence without the hypothesis. For example,

(27) *Yin Xiaotiao bu shuohua, Tang Fei jiu shuo, ta zhang de tai xiang wo jiujiu le, hng, meizhunr ta shi wo de biaomei.*

Yin Xiaotiao didn't speak. Then Tang Fei said: She really looks like my uncle. Hmm, maybe she is my cousin.

This sentence first explains "She really looks like my uncle". A judgment sentence, "she is my cousin", follows the word *meizhun*.

(28) *Zaishuo, haokan you you shenme liaobuqi, ta kuai liang sui le lian hua dou bu hui shuo, meizhunr ta shi ge yaba ne.*

What's more, it is no use to be beautiful. She can't speak although she is almost 2 years old. Maybe she is dumb.

This sentence, "She can't speak although she is almost 2 years old", presents the reason first. The judgment sentence, "she is dumb", follows *meizhun*.

3.4   Conjunctive Function of *Meizhun*

Some adverbs function as cohesive devices in texts. Zhang (2000, p. 298) found that the conjunctive functions of adverbs appearing in texts can generally be divided into six categories: sequence, addition, inference, explanation, disjunction, and condition.

3.4.1   Textual Functions of *Meizhun*

According to our analysis, the main textual functions of *meizhun* are inference and definition.

First, *meizhun* is always used to express an inference based on a logic judgment. That means that the conclusion can be derived from the conditions and information provided (Zhang 2000, p. 302). Inferences can be summative, comprehensive, and estimative. Most sentences with *meizhun* are estimative inferences. Given the context, it is reasonable to make the following estimate. In this kind of sentence, some verbal structures and discourse markers will be characterised by strong subjective qualifiers, such as "I believe", "I think", and "in my opinion". These structures emphasise the uncertain character of the result that follows *meizhun*. For example,

(29) *Wo juede, zhe ci zhongguo meizhunr neng na 5 kuai jin pai.*

I assume that China may be able to win five gold medals this time.

(30) *Wo kan meizhunr wo ye jie de dao.*

I guess I may also be able to borrow it.

Based on the facts and the situation described above, summative inferences can be used to draw conclusions and make judgments. *Meizhun* can also be used to represent a summative inference. For example,

> (31) *Kanjian Tianjian biaoqing, juede ta de xiaorong mianqiang, geng hen*
> *ziji shuohua maomei, na nv haizi meizhun shi ta de qingren.*

Judging from Tianjian's expression, I think his smile is quite forced. Thus, I hate myself for speaking rashly, because that girl may be his lover.

> (32) *Yilai wo zong shi shengguo da bing de ren, xianzai zhe bing shifou duan*
> *le gen ye nan shuo, cheng le jia meizhun you yao tuolei renjia.*

First, I used to be terribly ill. It's hard to say if I have been cured or not. I might be a burden if we got married.

When the format of *meizhun* + the result clause is used, the speaker is likely to have his expectation confirmed or proven. Therefore, in the double negation patterns that include *meizhun*, such as 没准没[*meizhun mei*] and 没准......不[*meizhun...bu*], the semantic meaning of *mei* is lost in *meizhun*, which renders the double negation semantically equivalent to a single negation, such as *zhunmei* (definitely not) or *zhunbu* (*definitely no*). For example,

> (33) *Wang Ming zai sixia shuo Xiaoyan yao pigu mei pigu yao xiong mei*
> *xiong, bie kan ta xianzai kuang, jianglai meizhun mei ren yao.*

Wang Ming said in private that Xiaoyan would definitely find it hard to find a boyfriend in the future because she had neither a big butt nor big breasts, although she was currently quite arrogant.

> (34) *Na ke bu xing, meizhun ni bu hui yong, nong cuo le jiu mafan le, wo jiao*
> *ni yi hui.*

That won't do. I'm sure you don't know how to use it. It's really troublesome if you get it wrong. Let me tell you how to use it this time.

In some assertive and negative sentences that contain *meizhun*, the intention conveyed by *meizhun* remains strong. In contrast, the negative connotation *mei* is weaker. Sometimes, *meizhun* can even be used to depict the climax of a sentence. For example,

> (35) *Dalama kending hui renwei wo hai le ta, meizhun hui sha le wo.*

Dalama must think that I should be blamed for his situation, so maybe he is going to kill me.

Second, *meizhun* can be used for interpretation, explaining the situation and content presented in the preceding part of the text via analysis and reasoning, including confirmatory and complementary commentary.

Confirmatory commentary extends the discussion and explanation related to the previous context, but from a different perspective, using affirmation and recognition (Zhang 2000, p. 304). For example,

> (36) *Zheme xiang shibushi youdian qiangjiayuren de weidao? Meizhun ta*
> *yagen ye bu chouchang shenme ye mei xiang jiushi chulai zhuanzhuan*
> *huozhe jiushi xiang yeshi xiang bieren.*

Isn't this idea a little compulsive? Maybe she is not worried about anything and is just going out for a walk, or maybe she is just thinking about somebody else.

Complementary commentary offers reasons that explain and validate the situation or that confirm the original expectation and fantasy based on facts and results. (Zhang 2000, P305) For example:

> (37) *Zhe hui haobu rongyi huai tai, huai le wu-liu ge yue, dou kanchu shi ge*
> *nanhai le, liuchan le. Zhe meizhun jiushi pingchang tai caoxin zhi gu.*

She was finally pregnant this time and, in the fifth or sixth month, it turned out to be a boy. But, unfortunately, she miscarried, which is usually the result of excessive concern.

This sentence refers to previous events and explains the reason for Sister Feng's miscarriage. It confirms and explains the previous phenomenon and situation by advancing causes and reasons as part of a complementary interpretation.

3.4.2   The Discourse Cohesion of *Meizhun*

Meizhun can be used at the beginning, the middle, or the end of a sentence.[7] For example,

> (38) *Ni qianwan bie guolai, meizhun women jiuyao chuqu, qianwan bie*
> *guolai.*

Don't come here, because we may be going out. Don't come here.

The location of *meizhun* in a sentence is flexible. According to an analysis of the semantic frame, *meizhun* is generally placed between the causal clause and the result clause. However, its location is not fixed when a hypothetical conditional clause or an imperative sentence is involved.

---

[7] Qi and Xu (2007) argued that the commentary ability of modal adverbs is represented by the continuum related to the order of the beginning, middle, and end of a sentence. Because of its location, the ability of a modal adverb to provide subjective commentary is weaker in static phrases (attributive clauses) than when it appears at the beginning of a sentence.

4   The Development of *Meizhun* in Contemporary Chinese

In contemporary Chinese, *meizhun* is usually used as a predicate, following the pattern of S + *meizhun*. In this pattern, S represents the interrogative pronoun, personal pronoun, demonstrative pronoun, and so on. The semantic orientation of *meizhun* consists of the phrases related to time, place, method, and regular pattern. In addition, its semantic features can be measured, and it generally appears in answers or in transitional complex sentences.

> (39) *Ruo wen ni shang na qu? Ni gaosu: Meizhun.*

If you are asked about where to go, you can answer: I'm not sure.

There are two examples that seem identical to mei_1zhun_4 and mei_2zhun_2, but they actually differ from them.

> (40) *Ya danchuan jiu shi yi san, ya shuangchuan jiu shi er si, dou shi liang menr du, bujiande zhundei shu, meizhun de shi.*

Betting on the odd numbers, i.e., 1 and 3, and betting on the even numbers, i.e., 2 and 4, are both just gambling, so you may not always lose. It's not a sure thing.

On the surface, this appears to be mei_1zhun_4. However, the frame is not 没 (*mei*, or not) + 准的事 (*zhun de shi* [permissible thing]) but is the 没准的 (*meizhunde*, or uncertain) + 事 (*shi*, or thing).

> (41) *Chulai bei ma gen zhongren daobie shuo:Wo zhe yi qu, buding si huo!*
> *Fanwang de piqi meizhun jiu xu ba wo sha le.*

He came out to prepare the horse and bid farewell to other people: I might die this time! Maybe I will be killed by the king, who has hot temper.

This sentence *Fanwang de pingqi, meizhun jiu xu ba wo sha le* (Depending on the mood of the king, maybe, maybe he will kill me) seems like mei_2zhun_2 (maybe). But it can also be considered *Fanwang de piqi meizhun, jiu xu ba wo sha le* (The king's mood is very labile; maybe he will kill me), which is still mei_1zhun_1 (uncertain).

The use of mei_2zhun_2 as an adverbial modifier and a parenthetic phrase has been increasing rapidly in contemporary Chinese. This usage conforms to the following pattern:

causal clause (S + mei_1zhun_1), hypothetical conditional, (adverb *jiu*) + result clause

↓   ↓

causal clause, hypothetical conditional, *meizhunr* + result clause or causal clause, *meizhunr*, hypothetical conditional, result clause

As we can see from the previous example (41), "The king's temper is very labile, and he might kill me", *meizhun* is used to emphasise the reason, *Fanwang de piqi meizhun* (The king's mood is very labile). In the result clause, *jiu xu ba wo sha le* (maybe he will kill me), *xu* means maybe or not sure, which has the same meaning as *meizhun*, which refers to maybe or not sure. In addition, the sentence omits the hypothetical conditional. Thus, it can be replaced by the sentence *Fanwang de piqi meizhun, yaoshi …, meizhun jiu ba wo sha le* (The king's mood is very labile, if…, maybe he will kill me).

5   Conclusion

Meizhun, which was used to highlight the uncertain character of reasons in modern Chinese, has been gradually transformed into a word that highlights the uncertain character of results. This is because *meizhun* always vacillates in a causal sentence and often follows the hypothetical conditional, appearing in front of the result clause. It can also be placed in front of the hypothetical conditional. In summary, it always appears between cause clauses and result clauses, and there is no significant relationship between its location and the hypothetical conditional. Additional research regarding the reasons for modifying the main point of sentences is needed.

References

[1] Duan, Y.H.: Distribution and Pragmatic Functions of Modal Adverbs. Journal of Chinese Learning (4), P18–P21 (1995); 段业辉《语气副词的分布及语用功能》,《汉语学习》1995 年4期 (in Chinese)
[2] Qi, C.H.: On the Cooccurrence Rules of Modal Adverbs and Sentence-ending Auxiliary Modal Words. Journal of Yunnan Normal University (3), P125–P130 (2007) (in Chinese)
[3] Qi, C.H., Xu, J.: A Study of the Pragmatic Functions of Modal Adverbs according to Their Syntactic Distribution. Journal of Yunnan Normal University (1), P118–P123 (2007) (in Chinese)
[4] Shi, J.S.: On the Scope, Types, and Order of Sequential Use of Modal Adverbs. Studies of the Chinese Language (1), P17–P31 (2003) (in Chinese)
[5] Zhang, Y.S.: Study on Modern Chinese Adverbs. Academia Press, Shanghai, P15, P298, P302–P304 (2000) 张谊生《现代汉语副词研究》,学林出版社 (2000) (in Chinese)

Preliminary Study on the Construction of Bilingual Phrase Structure Treebank

Kunli Zhang[✉], Hongying Zan, Yingjie Han, and Lingling Mu

School of Information Engineering, Zhengzhou University, Zhengzhou, Henan 450001, China
{ieklzhang,iehyzan,ieyjhan,iellmu}@zzu.edu.cn

Abstract. Treebank is an important resource for Natural Language Processing. Most existing treebanks are monolingual, but bilingual treebanks are the important basis of syntactical model in machine translation. In this paper, a bilingual phrase structure Treebank aimed for the application of machine translation was preliminarily constructed, which chose POS tagset and syntactic tagset of U-Penn English Treebank and Chinese Treebank as its tagging system. Chinese- English sentence pairs which were drawn from machine translation evaluation data in the treebank were pre-processed, with POS tagged, phrase structure annotated, and all processed data were proofread. Through the analysis of phrase structures which were modified in the proofreading process, it was found that Chinese functional words usages play an important role in Chinese phrase structure grammar.

Keywords: Bilingual Treebank · Phrase Structure Grammar · Chinese Functional Word Usages

1   Introduction

Treebank is a deep annotation language knowledge resource. It can be used to study various grammatical phenomena, the overall characteristics of language in corpus linguistics and quantitative linguistics, and to train and test syntactic analyzer in computational linguistics. Phrase structure grammar is the most popular syntax theory of Treebank construction. Most treebanks are constructed on its basis. Dependency parsing grammar which mainly describes the dependency relations between the words is another popular syntax theory [1].

Since Peter Brown, an IBM researcher, proposed the IBM machine translation models in the early 1990s, a variety of statistical machine translation models, such as phrase-based translation model, hierarchical phrase-based translation model, and syntax structure-based translation model have arisen and the quality of machine translation is also improving. But there are still limitations when the syntax structure-based model depending on treebank is adopted in machine translation. The main reason is that high quality parallel data is lack, though there are plenty of large-scale monolingual treebanks of source language and target language [2]. In this paper, we adopted Penn Treebank annotation scheme, extracted Chinese-English sentence pairs from evaluation data of

© Springer International Publishing Switzerland 2014
X. Su and T. He (Eds.): CLSW 2014, LNAI 8922, pp. 403–413, 2014.
DOI: 10.1007/978-3-319-14331-6_40

machine translation, and then artificially proofread the segment, POS and syntactic structure. These works were the preliminary attempt to construct the bilingual phrase structure grammar treebank.

The rest of the paper is organized as follows. In Section 2, we reviewed the works concerning treebanks. In section 3, we gave the construction process of bilingual phrase structure treebank. In section 4, we analyzed and summarized the syntactic structure which had been manually modified, and furthermore we discussed the impact of Chinese function words to syntactic structure. At last, we drew a conclusion and listed further works.

2   Related Works

At present, treebanks of various languages are being or have been established. The typical English treebanks are Lancaster-Leeds Treebank of England and Penn English Treebank (Penn-ETB) of University of Pennsylvania. The typical Chinese treebanks are Penn Chinese Treebank (Penn-CTB) of University of Pennsylvania, Sinica Chinese Treebank of the Academia Sinica in Taiwan, Chinese Treebank of Peking University, Tsinghua Chinese Treebank (TCT), Chinese Treebank of China National Language Commission, and Chinese Dependency Treebank of HIT-IR(HIT-IR-CDT), etc.

In terms of syntactic tagging level, on the basis of Chomsky's phrase structure grammar theory, clause level, function tags, grammatical role, and POS were annotated in Penn-CTB and Penn-ETB, in which the POS tagset adopted the Indo-European family tagset [3]. In Sinica Treebank, based on information-oriented case grammar, clause level, function tags, POS, and semantic role of noun phrases were all annotated[4]. Compared with Penn Treebank, in Sinica Treebank the POS is classified in more detail and the subclass of auxiliary words is simplified. Chinese Treebank of Peking University and the one of Tsinghua University, TCT, are both annotating sentence hierarchy based on Chinese traditional Analytic Hierarchy theory, and both adopting a relatively small POS tagset and annotating syntactic relations between direct components after POS tagging[5][6]. There are 19 syntactic relation tags in Chinese Treebank of Peking University, while there are 26 POS tags, 27 syntactic relation tags, and 16 component tags in TCT. And the Cotemporary Chinese Corpus of China National Language Commission adopted the construction idea similar to TCT[7]. On the basis of dependency grammar, HIT-IR-CDT adopted the POS tags of China National Language Commission which included 23 tags and developed a relation tagset which included 24 syntactic dependency relation tags [8]. These treebanks mentioned above have their own annotation schemes and characteristics respectively, and the annotation information included in treebanks determines the developed and potential application of treebanks.

3   Construction of the Bilingual Phrase Structure Treebank

The construction of Chinese-English bilingual Treebank involves four steps: choose annotation scheme, extract and preprocess Chinese-English sentence pairs, artificially proofread the result of automatic word segmentation, and artificially proofread the result of automatic POS tagging and parsing.

3.1 Annotation Scheme Choosing

The annotation scheme of both Chinese and English in Penn Treebank are consistent in POS tagging and syntactic tagging. So in this paper, the word segmentation, POS tagging and syntactic relations tagging of bilingual Treebank are all based on Penn Treebank standards.

The POS tagset of Penn-CTB has 33 tags [9]. In this tagset, verb and adjective are combined as one group, and the particle has a detailed division. The POS tagset of Penn-ETB has 36 tags [10]. In this tagset, according to the verb base form, past tense from, gerund or present participle, past participle, present tense other than 3rd person singular, and present tense 3rd person singular, verbs are divided into 6 categories , and "to" is a separate category, marked as "TO".

The syntactic relations tagset of Penn-CTB[11] has 2 clause level tags (IP, CP) and 15 phrase level tags (ADJP, ADVP, CLP, DP, DNP, DVP, FRAG, LCP, LST, NP, PP, PRN, QP, UCP, VP). The syntactic relations tagset of Penn-PTB[10] has 5 clause level tags (S, SBAR, SBARQ, SINV, SQ) and 21 phrase level tags (ADJP, ADVP, CONJP, FRAG, INTJ, LST, NAC, NP, NX, PP, PRN, PRT, QP, RRC, UCP, VP, WHADJP, WHADVP, WHNP, WHPP, X). There are 10 pairs of the same tags between Penn-CTB tagset and Penn-PTB tagset, which will provide a certain basis or rules for adjusting the syntactic parsing tree nodes of syntax structure-based translation model.

3.2 Corpus Extracting and Preprocessing

The Chinese-English sentence pairs in the bilingual Treebank were extracted from Chinese-English News training corpus of China Workshop on Machine Translation (CWMT). Giving consideration to sentence length and diversity of sentence structure in data extraction, 4000 sentence pairs were extracted, in which the longest length of Chinese sentences is 140 characters (96 words), and the corresponding English sentence 79 words, while the shortest length of Chinese sentences is 18 characters (10 words), and the corresponding English sentence 12 words. The following sentence (1) and (2) are examples of extracted Chinese-English sentence pair.

(1) 在博萨索·布尔奥和基斯马尤也有一些大的流离失所者集居点。 (*Other major areas of displaced settlements are in Bossaso ,Burao and Kismayo*)

(2) Other major areas of displaced settlements are in Bossaso,Burao and Kismayo.

In order to ensure the quality of the bilingual Treebank, the extracted Chinese-English sentence pairs were preprocessed and checked.

Firstly, some symbols in the corpus were replaced and deleted. There are mainly two kinds of situation. The first is to replace left bracket in corpus with "-LRB-" and right bracket with "-RRB-" in order to avoid confusing parentheses with syntactic marker symbol ("(",")"). The second is to remove symbols in digital form because the digital data with symbols, such as "," in digital "1,500", whether the digits are separated in segmentation, will be separated in parsing. The symbols that were replaced or removed in above situations will be restored at the end of artificial proofreading syntactic structure. Secondly, the sentence pairs that do not meet the requirements will be removed after proofreading, and then the pairs with similar length and pattern will be supplemented. Thirdly, the obvious local translation errors in the corpus will be revised. Because most Chinese sentences in sentence pairs were extracted from the translation of English sentences, there are some errors such as missing characters, redundant characters, or wrong characters in Chinese sentences. For example, the word in an English sentence is "subsequently", corresponding to word "后[*hou*](*after*)" in a Chinese sentence which should be revised to "随后[*suihou*](*subsequently*)".

3.3   Segmentation Proofreading

The Chinese-English sentence pairs in the corpus were automatically word-segmented, and then the result was artificially proofread. Proofreading of Chinese and English word segmentation is mainly based on the Penn Treebank segmentation scheme [9][12]. In this process, we found that the mistakes of Chinese word segmentation mainly lied in: names of persons or places and other proper nouns, adverbs, prepositions and time word segmentation. The mistakes of English word segmentation mostly existed in the sentences with symbol "/".

3.4   Syntactic Structure Annotation

Owing to adopting Penn Treebank annotation scheme as the bilingual Treebank annotation scheme, a syntactic parser is constructed by choosing Chinese and English annotated sentences in Penn Treebank as training data, which can automatically tag POS and parse Chinese and English sentences that have been word-segmented in the bilingual Treebank. The automatically annotated result of POS tagging and parsing is artificially proofread simultaneously.

The proofreading process of POS and syntactic structure is divided into two steps. The first step is to add constraints to the sentences that need to adjust the syntactic structure and automatically rebuild the syntactic structure by using syntactic parser, which can not only ensure the consistent with syntactic structure pattern of Penn Treebank, but also improve the proofreading efficiency. The second step is to manually modify POS tag and syntactic structure if the correct syntactic tree can't be generated according to the constraint file.

Each sentence format in the constraint file is as follows:

Segmented sentence @#@#@# {Syntactic tag}[span]

"@#@#@#"is the mark of division."Syntactic tag" includes phrase tags (such as NP, VP, etc.) and POS tags (such as NN, VV, etc.). It can be specified or not specified. "Span" consists of two span numbers. The left span number of the first word is "0", and the right one is "1", then encounter a word plus 1. "Span" specifies a syntactic node corresponding to span within the numbers.

If the parser mentioned above is unable to generate a syntax tree in all constraints, it will ignore some constraints to generate a syntax tree. Another problem is, after adding a new constraint the originally correct syntax structure gets wrong, and then some new constraints have to be added.

In order to improve work efficiency and reduce the error rate of proofreading, we developed a proofing tool which includes the automatic syntactic parser mentioned above. The interface of proofing tool is shown in Fig. 1. The Chinese sentence in the textbox at the bottom of Figure 1 is the proofreading one. The constraint including syntactic tags and span can be directly written after "@#@#@#" in the textbox. You can click on the button "重建[chongjian](rebuild)" to generate the syntactic tree and move mouse pointer to get the span number of nodes. If the correct syntactic tree can't be generated according to the constraint file you can directly edit POS tag and syntactic structure.

Take sentence (3) for example to describe the proofreading process. In sentences (3), the gray highlighted digit is the span number to indicate the position, not the real data.

(3) 0 在 1 整个 2 第二 3 季 4 , 5 再三 6 地 7 明确 8 要求 9 叛军 10 准许 11 向 12 粮食 13 严重 14 不 15 够 16 的 17 地区 18 -LRB- 19 包括 20 Gogrial 21 、 22 Yirol 23 、 24 Tonj 25 、 26 Pibor 27 -RRB- 28 空运 29 粮食 30 。 31 (*Specific and repeated requests were made to rebel factions throughout the second quarter for air deliveries of food to areas suffering severe food deficits , including Gogrial , Yirol , Tonj , and Pibor*)

Fig. 1 shows the partial generated syntactic tree without constraints. As can be seen from Fig. 1, the prepositional phrase structure"向粮食严重不够的地区(*to areas suffering severe food deficits*)" is not correct. After adding the syntactic tree constraint to the sentence, the correct syntactic tree is reconstructed, as is shown in Fig. 2.

Using the syntactic tree proofing tool, we can proofread Chinese-English sentence pairs at the same time, save the constraint file and proofread syntactic tree, and construct the preliminary bilingual Treebank.

4   Analysis of Syntactic Structure Adjustment

Up to now, we have finished 1000 Chinese-English sentence pairs proofreading according to the construction process mentioned above. There is a certain gap between the effects of Chinese syntactic parser and English because the great diversity of grammar features between Chinese (a typical analytical language) and English (a kind of Aryan language). By Comparing the automatic parsing result with the manual proofreading result, syntactic structures of 405 English sentences need to be modified and the modified structures focus on the parallel structure and prepositional phrase, such as the prepositional phrase in a sentence (4). A partial generated syntactic tree without constraints of sentence (4) is shown in Fig. 3, and the one with constraints is shown in Fig. 4.

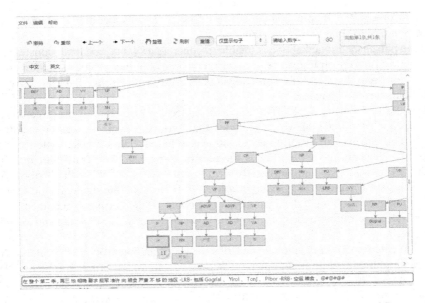

Fig. 1. Proofing Tool and Partial Generated Syntactic Tree without Constraints of Sentence (3)

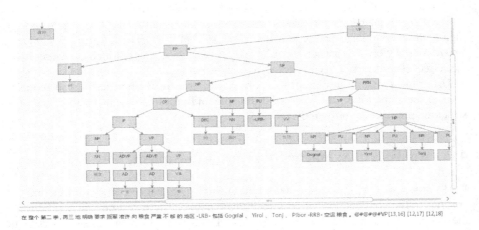

Fig. 2. Partial Generated Syntactic Tree with Constraints of Sentence (3)

(4) Those same countries have made headway in fostering macroeconomic stability through broad economic reform.

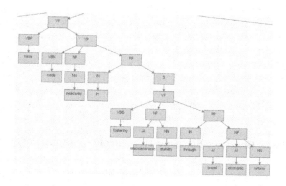

Fig. 3. Partial Generated Syntactic Tree without Constraints of Sentence (4)

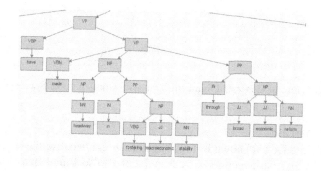

Fig. 4. Partial Generated Syntactic Tree with Constraints of Sentence (4)

There are 691 Chinese sentences needed to be modified in terms of syntactic structures, mainly on such three aspects as the parallel structure, prepositional phrase, and noun phrase including "的[de]()".

Parallel Structure

There are two conjunction "和[he](and)" in sentence (5), the first one connecting words "硫[liu](sulphur)" and "氮[dan](nitrogen)" as a parallel structure and the second one connecting phrase "电力厂的硫和氮气体洗涤器(sulphur and nitrogen scrubbers for power plants)" and "机动车辆的催化转换器(atalytic converters for motor vehicles)" as another parallel structure. As shown in Fig. 5, these two parallel structures in automatic parsing tree are not correct. The syntactic tree generated with constraints of sentence (5) is shown in Fig. 6. In the proofreading process, it is found that most modified parallel structures are connected by conjunctions or by punctuations.

(5) 其中包括电力厂的硫和氮气体洗涤器和机动车辆的催化转换器。（These include sulphur and nitrogen scrubbers for power plants and catalytic converters for motor vehicles）

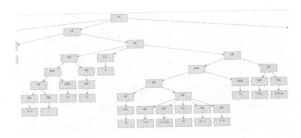

Fig. 5. Partial Generated Syntactic Tree without Constraints of Sentence (5)

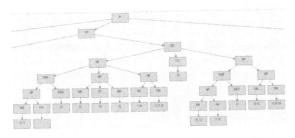

Fig. 6. Partial Generated Syntactic Tree with Constraints of Sentence (5)

Prepositional Phrase

The result of sentence (3) shown in Fig. 1 is not correct because the object of preposition "向[*xiang*](*to*)" isn't recognized correctly. It is also found that in the automatic parsing tree prepositional phrases including other prepositions such as "到[*dao*](*to*)" "在[*zai*](*in*)" have the similar mistakes for the same reason.

Noun Phrase including "的[de]()"

As shown in Fig. 7, the automatic parsing result of "重大的人力和物力牺牲(*great human and material sacrifices*)" in sentence (6) is a modifier-head structure noun and the head words are "人力和物力(human and material)". The right one should be "人力和物力牺牲(*human and material sacrifices*)", as shown in Fig. 8.

(6) *我国人民长期以来都为努力实现这个目标而作出了重大的人力和物力牺牲*

(*Our people has long striven for its achievement with great human and material sacrifices*)

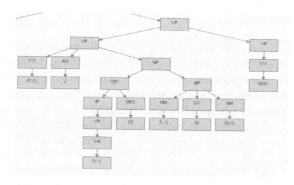

Fig. 7. Partial Generated Syntactic Tree without Constraints of Sentence (6)

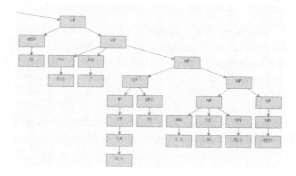

Fig. 8. Partial Generated Syntactic Tree with Constraints of Sentence (6)

From the Chinese syntactic structure adjustment, parallel structure, prepositional phrase and noun phrase including "的[de]()" all involve function words. In Chinese Function Knowledge Base (CFKB) the different usages of function words are described in detail and automatic identification of function words' usages with reference to the context is an important part of CFKB [13]. So in the following Treebank construction, we will try to utilize CFKB to improve the accuracy of automatic syntactic parsing result. As to parallel structure including conjunction words, we will use the method of literature [14]-[15] to identify conjunction phrases according to the conjunction usage, and then determine the parallel phrase, which contributes to automatically adjusting the parallel structure. As to proposition phrase, the automatic identification of proposition usages will be introduced to determine the right boundary of proposition phrase, which contributes to automatically adjusting the proposition structure [16]. The usage of auxiliary word "的[de]()" is more diverse and we will analyze its rules to the automatic adjustment.

5   Conclusions

Aiming at the requirements of machine translation, this paper adopted Penn-ETB and Penn-CTB annotation scheme as the tagging criteria, extracted Chinese-English sentence pairs from the training corpus of CWMT, and then made a preliminary attempt to construct a bilingual Treebank which included the work of preprocessing these sentence pairs and artificially proofreading the segmentation, POS tagging and syntactic structure parsing. Furthermore, the paper analyzed the sentence pairs whose proofreading had been completed, and summarized the syntactic structures which need to be manually modified.

Next we will continue to complete syntactic structure proofreading of remained sentence pairs, and complete the syntactic function tagging, Chinese-English bilingual word alignment and syntactic alignment. Besides, we will try to introduce the function word usage to automatic adjustment of syntactic structure, in order to construct a prefect bilingual Treebank.

Acknowledgments. This work was supported by the Natural Science Fund of China (No.60970083, No.61272221, No.61402419), the National Social Science Fund (No.14BYY096), 863 Projects of National High Technology Research and Development (No.2012AA011101), Science and Technology Key Project of Science and Technology Department of Henan Province(No.132102210407), the Humanities and Social Sciences Research Project of the Education Department of China (10YJA740074), Basic research project of Science and Technology Department of Henan Province(No. 142300410231,No.142300410308) and Key Technology Project of the Education Department of Henan Province (No.12B520055,No. 13B520381).

References

1. Du, J.H., Zhang, M., Zong, C.Q., Sun L.: Opportunities and Challenges for Machine Translation in China-Summary and Prospects for the Eighth Workshop on Machine Translation. Journal of Chinese Information Processing **27**(4) 1–8 (2013). (in Chinese)
2. Wang, Y.L., Ji, D.H.: A Review of Chinese Treebanks. Contemporary Linguistics **11**(1), 47–55 (2009). (in Chinese)
3. Xue,N., Xia, F., Chiou, F. D., et al.: The Penn Chinese Treebank: Phrase Structure Annotation of a Large Corpus. Natural Language Engineering **10**(4), 1–30 (2004)
4. Chen, F.Y., Jiang, B.F., Chen K.J., et al.: The Construction of Sinica Treebank. Computational Linguistics and Chinese Language Processing **4**(2), 87–104 (1999). (in Chinese)
5. Zhou, Q., Zhang, W., Yu, S.W.: Building a Chinese Treebank. Journal of Chinese Information Processing **11**(4) 42–51 (1997). (in Chinese)
6. Zhou, Q.: Annotation Scheme for Chinese Treebank. Journal of Chinese Information Processing **18**(4), 1–8 (2004). (in Chinese)
7. Jin, G.J., Xiao, H., Fu, L., et al.: Deep Processing and Construction of Modern Chinese Corpus Applied Linguistics **54**(2), 111–120 (2005). (in Chinese)

8. Liu, T., Ma, J.S., Li, S.: Building a dependency Treebank for improving Chinese Parser. Journal of Chinese Language and Computing. **16**(4), 207–224 (2006)
9. Xia, F.: The Part-of-speechTagging Guidelines forthe Penn Chinese Treebank(3.0). http://www.cis.upenn.edu/~chinese/
10. Ann, B., Mark, F., Karen K., et al.: Bracketing Guidelines for Treebank II Style Penn Treebank Project. http://www.cis.upenn.edu/~english/etb.html
11. Xue, N.W., Xia, F.: The Bracketing Guidelines for the Penn Chinese Treebank (3.0). http://www.cis.upenn.edu/~chinese/ctb.html
12. Xia, F., Mattha, P., Xue, N.W., et al.: Developing Guidelines and Ensuring Consistency for Chinese Text Annotation. In: Proceedings of the 2nd International Conference on Language Resources and Evaluation, Athens, Greece (2000)
13. Zan, H.Y., Zhang, K.L., Zhu, X.F., Yu, S.W.: Research on the Chinese Function Word Usage Knowledge Base. International Journal on Asian Language Processing **21**(4), 185–198 (2011)
14. Zan, H.Y., Zhou, L.J., Zhang, K.L.: Modern Chinese Conjunction Phrase Recognition Based on Usage. Journal of Chinese Information Processing **26**(6), 72–78 (2012). (in Chinese)
15. Zan, H.Y., Zhang, J.J., Lou, X.P.: Studies on the Application of Chinese Functional Words' Usages IN Dependency Parsing. Journal of Chinese Information Processing **27**(5), 35–42 (2013). (in Chinese)
16. Pang, Y.Y.: Studies on the Usage of Preposition and Conjunction in Phrase Structure Syntactic Parsing. Master Thesis. Zhengzhou University, Zhengzhou (2013). (in Chinese)

Quantitative Analysis of "ADV+N" via Cognitive Property Knowledgebase

Bin Li[1(✉)], Yan Ma[1], Xueyang Liu[1], and Xuri Tang[2]

[1] School of Chinese Language and Literature,
Nanjing Normal University, 210097 Nanjing, China
{libin.njnu,mayan.njnu}@gmail.com, liuxueyang1220@163.com
[2] Foreign Language School, Huazhong University of Science and Technology,
430074 Wuhan, China
xrtang@126.com

Abstract. The "ADV+N" construction is a special phenomenon in mandarin Chinese. The rule is widely accepted that the nouns having descriptive semantic features are more likely to be used in the construction. However, the descriptive semantic features are casually used in previous works. How many semantic features a noun has and how strong the relationship between the noun and feature are not well studied. In this paper, we consult the Chinese Cognitive Property Knowledgebase to get the semantic features of the nouns. We find that the salient features of a noun permit the noun to be used in the "ADV+N" construction. Then we put forward a metonymy model to explain the mechanism of the ADV+N construction. However, we also find that many nouns having salient features can not be used in the "ADV+N" construction.

Keywords: ADV+N · Cognitive Property · Language Knowledgebase · Cognitive Linguistics

1 Introduction

The "adverb + noun" construction is a special phenomenon in Mandarin Chinese, like "他很狐狸(*He is very fox*)", "她很小孩子(*She is very child*)". Usually, most of the nouns could not be used in the construction, as it is not acceptable to say "很桌子 (*very table*)"in Chinese. Many linguists in China try to explain why some nouns can be used in the "adverb + noun" construction while most not. [1] and [2] believe that it is the descriptive semantic features of the noun that provide the ability for the noun to behave like an adjective in the construction. For example, "狡猾(*cunning*)" is a salient descriptive feature of "狐狸(*fox*)". Thus "很狐狸(*very fox*)" means "很狡猾(*very cunning*)". On the contrary, "桌子(*table*)" doesn't have very salient features, so it is hard to say or understand "很桌子(*very table*)". It seems to be a solid explanation. However, how to define the semantic features of a noun is still a big problem. The types and number of the features of each noun vary from person to person. In this

© Springer International Publishing Switzerland 2014
X. Su and T. He (Eds.): CLSW 2014, LNAI 8922, pp. 414–424, 2014.
DOI: 10.1007/978-3-319-14331-6_41

paper, we want to testify the "semantic feature explanation" using the cognitive property knowledgebase CogBank[3], which is a large scale database containing the features of nouns in Chinese, such as "狐狸(*fox*)-狡猾(*cunning*)","狐狸(*fox*)-漂亮(*beautiful*)". 99 nouns from [4] are tested to find whether the explanation is solid.

2   Related Work

There have been many researches on the "ADV+N" construction. As early as 1960s, [5] regards it as an ill-formed structure for the noun playing as an adjective. In 1990s, most researchers take it as a rhetorical usage[6, 7]. Within the syntax level, [8] and [9] think the noun plays as predicate or adjective temporarily in the "ADV+N" construction. [10] argues that the verb 有(*have*) or 是(*be*) is omitted between the ADV and the noun. [1, 2, 11] consider the meaning of the noun as the key to explain the special construction. [2] believes it is the descriptive semantic features of a noun provide the possibility of the "ADV+N" construction. [4] follows this route and finds more real sentences as proofs to support the explanation. [12] conducts ERP experiments on Chinese "ADV+N" construction. The N400 effects support that the semantic operation exists in the comprehension of the construction. [12] also argues that the mechanism behind "ADV+N" construction is metonymy, which uses the noun to represent its semantic features.

Therefore, it is widely accepted that the noun's semantic features are the key to explain the "ADV+N" construction. We name it "Feature Assumption", which assumes that the strength and number of semantic features of the noun determine the ability for the noun to enter the "ADV+N" construction.

However, the semantic features are not fully examined in previous work. How many features a noun has and how strong the relation between the feature and the noun remain as unanswered problems. Different speakers have different judgments on the features of a noun. Thus, in this paper, we are going to use a new semantic knowledgebase CogBank to overcome the problem.

3   Data Recourses

The cognitive property knowledgebase CogBank is a database containing the "word-feature" pairs automatically collected from the web[3]. For example, "雪(*snow*)-白(*white*)" occurs 521 times in the database. The CogBank is automatically built as follows. Three simile templates "像(*as*)+NOUN+一样(*same*)", "像(*as*)+VERB+一样(*same*)", "像(*as*)+一样(*same*)+ADJ" are filled with the 51,020 nouns, 27,901 verbs and 12,252 adjectives from HowNet(ver. 2007) to query the search engine Baidu(www.baidu.com). Totally, 1,258,430 types (5,637,500 tokens) of "vehicle-adjective" items are gathered. Then, the items are automatic tagged with parts-of-speech and are filtered by nouns and adjectives in HowNet, leaving only 47,869 items. The items are available for search at http://nlp.nju.edu.cn/lib/cog/ccb_nju.php.

Table 1 shows the top 10 most frequent items with their frequencies and most frequent nouns.

Table 1. The Top10 noun-feature pairs and Top10 nouns

Top10 noun-feature pairs			Top10 nouns		
Noun	Feature	Freq	Noun	# of fes	Top 5 features
美玉 jade	美丽 beautiful	840	水 water	270	流畅 smooth, 稀 thin, 清淡 light, 纯净 pure, 温柔 gentle
纸 paper	薄 thin	660	孩子 child	164	好奇 curiosity, 天真 naive, 快乐 happy, 任性 willful, 无助 helpless
雨点 raindrop	密集 dense	557	花儿 flower	126	美丽 beautiful, 香 fragrant, 红 red, 灿烂 bright, 美 beautiful
雪 snow	白 white	521	猫 cat	116	贴心 sweet, 顽皮 playful, 慵懒 lazy, 敏捷 agile, 灵活 flexible
花儿 flower	美丽 beautiful	497	大海 sea	115	深 deep, 宽广 broad, 深邃 deep, 深广 deep broad, 蓝 blue
妖精 demon (female)	温柔 gentle	466	山 mountain	107	高 high, 沉重 heavy deep, 深重 deep heavy, 多 many, 重 heavy
细瓷 fine porcelain	完美 perfect	450	猪 pig	103	快乐 happy, 笨 stupid, 懒 lazy, 肥 fat, 幸福 happy
大海 sea	深 deep	402	花 flower	92	美丽 beautiful, 美 beautiful, 灿烂 bright, 漂亮 beautiful, 多 many
阳光 sunshine	灿烂 splendid	386	小孩子 kid	91	兴奋 excite, 好奇 curious, 任性 willful, 淘气 naughty, 天真 naïve
天神 deity	美丽 beautiful	341	狼 wolf	85	凶狠 rough, 狠 tough, 果敢 courageous and resolute, 凶残 savage, 机敏 smart

Most of the "word-feature" pairs are correct, while few of them are wrong due to the automatic collection procedure. But the automatic procedure avoids the different judgments of features of a word among people. The CogBank gives us a better proof to investigate whether the feature is crucial in enabling a noun to enter the "ADV+N" construction. It is rather hard to test all the nouns in CogBank to draw a full conclusion. And it is not easy to judge if an "ADV+N" construction is well formed and accepted by people. Instead, we use the 99 nouns observed in [4]. Among the nouns, 88 nouns(including location nouns, person nouns and common nouns) could form the "ADV+N" construction while the other 11 could not. Table 2 shows the nouns divided into 4 types.

Table 2. The 99 nouns from Wu(2006)

Type	Nouns
Location 16	东方*orient*,西方*occident*,大陆*mainland*,广东*Guangdong*,香港*Hong Kong*,东北*Northeast (of China)*,上海*Shanghai*,阿根廷*Argentina*,巴西*Brazil*,日本*Japan*,美国*America*,英国*Britain*,俄国*Russia*,法国*France*,韩国*Korea*,中国*China*
Person 26	高手*ace*,老手*old hand*,贵族*nobility*,贫民*pauper*,男人*man*,女人*woman*,知青*educated youths*,小人*villain*,个人*individual*,草包*idiot*,笨蛋*fool*,君*gentleman*,奴才*lackey*,书生*scholar*,笑面虎*smiling tiger(a friendly-looking villain)*,儿童*children*,淑女*lady*; 周杰伦*Jay Chou*,赵本山*Benshan Zhao*,唐僧*Tang's monk*,张曼玉*Maggie Cheung*,崔永元*Yongyuan Cui*,陈佩斯*Peisi Chen*,姚明*Ming Yao*,冯巩*Gong Feng*,林黛玉*Daiyu Lin*
Common Nouns 46	青春*youth*,集体*collectivity*,文化*culture*,技术*technology*,权略*tactics*,权术*power tactics*,兴致*interest*,理性*rationality*,感性*sensibility*,资本主义*capitalism*,风度*demeanour*,学问*learning*,缘分*predestined relationship*,个性*personality*,性子*temper*,经验*experience*,知识*knowledge*,潮流*trend*,境界*realm*,风采*mien*,气量*tolerance*,温情*warmth*,激情*passion*,雄心*ambition*,耐性*patience*,韧性*tenacity*,兽性*brutalization*,狭义*narrow sense*,广义*broad sense*,绝路*blind alley*,悲剧*tragedy*,喜剧*comedy*,狼*wolf*,狗熊*bear*,黄牛*yellow cattle*,海鸥*seagull*,乌鸦*crow*,古董*antique*,花瓶*vase*,蜡烛*candle*,权威*authority*,威望*prestige*,威信*prestige*,电子*electron*,民谣*ballad*,肌肉*muscle*
Unspoken 11	蚯蚓*earthworm*,海马*seahorse*,企鹅*penguin*,声望*reputation*,声名*reputation*,黑龙江*Amur River*,吉林*Jilin (Province)*,华中*Central China*,桌子*table*,窗户*window*,纸张*paper*

4   Data Analysis

4.1   Location

We test the 16 location names with the Chinese CogBank. Table 3 shows the features of each location. Only 4 locations are absent in the results. Most of the locations have many features. And the features can be profiled in different context. For example, "某地方很美国(*a place is very America*)" means the place is 强大(*strong*), 民主(*democratic*) and 富裕(*wealthy*). So, it seems the "Semantic Assumption" works. The features with high frequency tend to be the features profiled in a sentence. However, "某人很美国(*a man is very America*)" does not mean the man is 强大(*strong*) or 霸道(*overbearing*). It leads us to further investigation on the features of nouns. We find that the type of the subject noun should somewhat fit the type of the object noun in a sentence. In other words, "某人很美国" means "某人很美国人(*a man is very American*)".

Table 3. The features of locations

Noun	# of fes	Feature_ frequency
美国 America	27	强大 strong_58, 民主 democratic_18, 富裕 wealthy_9, 高 high_6, 霸道 overbearing _5, 有 have_5, 繁荣富强 prosperous_4, 畅销 best-selling_3, 富强 prosperous_3, 迟钝 dull_3, 大 big_3, 乱 disorderly_3, 伟大 great_3, 低价 cheap_2, 普及 widespread_2, 幸运 lucky_2, 像 like_2, 富有 rich_1, 富 rich_1, 多 many/much_1, etc.
中国 China	21	多 many/much_7, 有 have_6, 大 big_2, 大量 abundant_2, 地大物博 vast territory and abundant resources_2, 低级 low-grade_2, 如此 such_2, 快 quick_2, 听话 obedient_2, 古怪 weird _1, 独立 independent _1, 出色 outstanding _1, 复杂 complex _1, 革命 revolutionary _1, 共同 common _1, 很多 plenty _1, 软弱无力 weak _1, 真 distinctly _1, 穷 poor _1, etc.
上海 Shanghai	12	灯火辉煌 blazing_11, 普遍 widespread_11, 真正 true_4, 高不可攀 unattainable_2, 精彩 Wonderful_2, 低 low_1, 繁华 flourishing_1, 浮躁 blundering_1, 豪华 grand_1, 老年 elderly_1, 热 hot_1, 早 early_1
香港 Hong Kong	10	中西合璧 Chinese and Western_30, 繁华 flourishing_14, 多 many/much_9, 廉洁 clean-fingered_5, 疯狂 crazy_4, 是 is_3, 美丽 beautiful_2, 有 have_2, 好 good_1, 有序 well-organized_1
日本 Japan	9	富有 rich_12, 明亮 bright_4, 听话 obedient_4, 坚忍 persevering_2, 大 big_1, 好 good_1, 乌烟瘴气 foul atomsphere_1, 无耻 shameless_1, 合理 reasonable_1
法国 France	4	富强 prosperous_13, 惨 cruel_12, 浪漫 romantic_1, 安全 safe_1
英国 Britain	4	坦然 calm_10, 充分 sufficient _2, 有 have_1, 能 capable _1
东方 Orient	2	芬芳 fragrant _2, 白 white _1
西方 Occident	2	富强 prosperous_2, 民主 democratic_1
俄国 Russia	1	革命 revolutionary_1
广东 Guangdong	1	对 right_1
韩国 Korea	1	专业 professional_4
Unfound		大陆 Mainland, 东北 Northeast (of China), 阿根廷 Argentina, 巴西 Brazil

Table 4 lists the features of some location+人(man) phrases. Here, "某人很美国(a man is very America)" means the man is 富裕(wealthy) or 严格(strict) or 开朗 (optimistic). And 地道(authentic), 溜(fluent) and 流畅(fluent) are used in the context like "某人的英语很美国(somebody's English is very America)".

Table 4. The features of location+人(*man*)

Noun	# of fes	Features_ frequency
中国人 *Chinese*	21	懒*lazy*_11,有种*have guts*_8,苗条*slim*_7,勤劳*industrious*_7,热情好客 *hospitable*_6,常见*common*_3,一无所有*have nothing at all*_3,丑陋 *ugly*_2,微*tiny*_2,多*many/much*_2,矛盾*ambivalent*_1,拥挤*crowded*_1,坚 强*tough*_1,流利*fluent*_1,麻木不仁*apathetic*_1,聪明*intelligent*_1, etc.
美国人 *American*	14	地道*authentic*_19,富裕*wealthy*_7,严格*strict*_6,兴旺*prosperous*_4,开朗 *optimistic*_4,溜*fluent*_3,流畅*fluent*_2,懒*lazy*_2,如此*such*_1,活跃 *active*_1,富有*rich*_1,实事求是*realistic*_1,逍遥自在*easygoing*_1,好 *good*_1
日本人 *Japanese*	13	对*right*_10,无耻*shameless*_6,到家*excellent*_3,变态*psychopathic*_2,认 真*serious*_2,富裕*wealthy*_2,席地而坐*sit on the ground*_2,有礼貌 *polite*_1,婉转*mild*_1,精细*careful*_1,彬彬有礼*well-behaved*_1,精诚团 结*united*_1,可恨*hateful*_1
韩国人 *Korean*	6	地道*native*_35,团结*united*_1,丑陋*ugly*_1,漂亮*beautiful*_1,执着 *persistent*_1,狭隘*narrow-minded*_1
东北人 *northeasterner*	4	豪爽*great-hearted*_5,实诚*sincere*_2,实在*honest*_2,浑厚*simple and honest*_1
法国人*French*	3	好*good*_9,浪漫*romantic*_1,吊儿郎当*careless and casual*_1

Therefore, it comes to a new conclusion that the "ADV+N" construction may also demand the features of the subject noun phrase. The type or sub-part of the noun is also important in the comprehension of the "ADV+N" construction.

4.2   Person

Most nouns referring to person having salient features and thus can occur in the "ADV+N" construction. For example, "某女人很女人(*a woman is very woman*)" means the person is 美丽(*beautiful*), 细心(*careful*), etc. 姚明(*Ming Yao*) is famous in China. When people say "某人很姚明(*somebody is very Ming Yao*)", it means the person is 高(*tall*) and 优秀(*excelent*) etc.

4.3   Common Nouns

The common nouns referring the entities that are like the previous two types. For example, 狼(*wolf*) has salient features like 凶狠(*cruel*) and 狠(*ruthless*), which could easily be used in "ADV+N" construction. However, the abstract nouns referring to features are different. For example, 文化(*culture*), 技术(*technology*) are hard to find their features even by mankind. 17 abstract nouns cannot be found their features in the CogBank. Because these nouns are quite like features. [2] argues that these nouns become adjectives easily like the noun 科学(*science*) which developed the adjective usage in Chinese.

Table 5. The features of person nouns

Noun	# of fes	Feature_ frequency
女人 woman	85	美丽 beautiful_85,细心 careful_15,骚 coquettish_13,尖声尖气 in a shrill voice_8,复杂 complicated_8,妩媚 enchanting_8,紧 tight_7,溜滑 slippery_7,疯狂 crazy_7,感性 emotional_6,多愁善感 sentimental_6,婆婆妈妈 oldwomanish_6,啰唆 verbose_5,麻烦 bothersome_5, etc.
男人 man	84	战斗 fighting_666, 去 go_47, 剽悍 fierce_23, 顽强 tenacious_22, 果断 decisive_21,坚强 tough_20,豪爽 great-hearted_16,温柔 tender_16,膀大腰圆 heavy-set_14,勇敢 brave_14,坚挺 strong_13,自由 unconstraint_12,强悍 intrepid_9,花心 polygamous_8,强壮 strong_8, etc.
姚明 Ming Yao	12	高 tall_28,野 unrestrained_7,出名 famous_2,优秀 excellent_2,精准 precise_2,低调 undertone_2,辉煌 glorious_1,家喻户晓 well-known_1, etc.
儿童 children	8	矮小 runty_22,纯真 pure_17,天真 naive_8,高 tall_2,可爱 cute_2,活泼 lively_1,嗲声嗲气 childish_1,有趣 funny_1
唐僧 Tang's Monk	7	啰嗦 verbose_8,絮聒 chatter_6,好 good_4,俊秀 handsome_1,善良 kind_1,絮叨 garrulous_1,温柔 tender_1
个人 individual	5	骄傲 proud_2,半 half_2,对 right_1,别扭 awkward_1,有 have_1
奴才 lackey	5	百依百顺 submissive_2,贱 bitchy_2,伏贴 fit perfectly_1,卑微 humble_1,听话 obedient_1
林黛玉 Lin Daiyu	4	多愁善感 sentimental_67,娇弱 delicate_16,弱不禁风 be in delicate health_1,小心翼翼 cautious_1
淑女 lady	4	高雅 elegant_12,温柔 tender_11,优雅 graceful_1,文静 quiet_1
君子 gentleman	3	优雅 graceful_2,反 inverse_2,无私 selfless_1
周杰伦 Jay Chou	3	红 popular_38,幽默 humorous_9,酷 cool_5
贵族 nobility	3	骄傲 proud_93,优雅 graceful_9,饮用 drink_1
小人 villain	2	偷偷 catlike_3,像 like_1
笨蛋 fool	2	执着 persistent_3,浑 stupid_1
书生 scholar	1	文雅 gentle_2
崔永元 Yongyuan Cui	1	较真 take serious_4
张曼玉 Maggie Cheung	1	优雅 graceful_1
老手 old hand	1	老练 adept_3
赵本山 Benshan Zhao	1	有水平 have ability_1
Unfound		高手 ace, 贫民 pauper, 知青 educated youths, 草包 idiot

Table 6. The features of common nouns

Noun	# of fes	Feature_ frequency
狼wolf	79	凶狠cruel_114,战斗battle_106,狠ruthless _79,果敢resolute _44,凶残ferocious _22,机敏alert_18,强悍astute _11,自由unconstraint _9,坚忍persevering_8,忠诚faithful_8,团结united_8,坏bad_7,勇敢brave_6,狡猾sly_5,疯狂crazy_5,贪greedy_5,倨傲haughty_4,凶猛fierce_4, etc.
黄牛cattle	8	勤勤恳恳diligent_49,能capable_7,任劳任怨bear hardship without complaint_5,勤diligent_3,迟钝dull_3,憨厚honest_3,勤恳industrious_2,忠实dutiful _1
乌鸦crow	6	漆黑pitch-dark _21,坚韧不拔stick-at-itiveness_8,黑black_4,聒噪noisy _2,白white_1,难听harsh _1
花瓶vase	6	易碎fragile _33,脆弱fragile _10,美丽beautiful_2,弱不禁风as weak as water_2,空empty_1,徒其表specious_1
狗熊bear	4	笨拙clumsy_3,大big_2,摇摇晃晃groggy_1,粗壮hairchested_1
蜡烛candle	4	无私selfless_6,朴实无华unpretentious_3,朴实earthy_1,谦虚modest_1
古董antique	2	珍贵precious_16,稀有rare_2
海鸥seagull	2	坚强tough_12,尖锐shrill _1
喜剧comedy	2	简单simple_4,精彩纷呈wonderful _3
肌肉muscle	2	硬hard_3,通open_1
电子electron	1	自由free_1
青春youth	9	奔放unrestrained_4,美beautiful_4,壮健robust_3,繁茂luxuriant_2,摇摇晃晃groggy_2,渐渐gradual_1,短short_1,刺激exciting_1,自己own_1
理性rationality	1	疯狂crazy_4
缘分predestined relationship	1	有始有终have a beginning and an end_1
资本主义capitalism	1	悠久centuries-old_1
Unfound		集体collectivity, 文化culture, 技术technology, 权略tactics, 权术power tactics, 兴致interest, 感性sensibility, 风度demeanour, 学问learning, 性子temper, 经验experience, 知识knowledge, 潮流trend, 境界realm, 风采mien, 气量tolerance

4.4   Nouns Unspoken

There are 11 nouns that are regarded unable to be used in "ADV+N" construction listed in table 2. However, we find many features of the nouns 蚯蚓(*earthworm*), 企鹅(*penguin*) and 纸张(*paper*) as in table 7. And we can find some but very few sentences using these nouns in "ADV+N" construction by search engine Baidu. But it still remains the question why these nouns are not widely used in "ADV+N" construction.

Table 7. The features of unspoken nouns

Noun	# of fes	Feature_ frequency
蚯蚓 earthworm	14	弯弯曲曲bending_10,曲里拐弯bending_3,滑腻creamy_3,盘曲coiled_2,无声无息silent_2,突起protuberant _2, 灵活flexible_2, ,软soft _2,勇敢brave_1,细thin _1,突出protuberant _1,难看ugly_1,密密麻麻dense _1,没有声音without sound _1
纸张paper	7	柔软soft_11,苍白pale _4,薄thin_3,便宜cheap_2,轻light_2,薄弱weak_1,单薄thin_1
企鹅 penguin	4	小心careful_3,可爱cute_2,笨stupid_2,优美beautiful_1
桌子table	3	平flat_4,摇摇晃晃groggy_1,脚踏实地stand on solid ground_1

5   A Metonymy Model

In this section, we try to give a novel model to describe the conditions for a noun to be used in "ADV+N" construction. As [12] points out that the noun represents the features, so that metonymy is the basic mechanism of the "ADV+N" construction. We agree with the metonymy assumption and make a detailed description of the metonymy model. The typical sentence having "ADV+N" construction is "N1+ADV+N2". N1 plays as the subject noun. N2 plays as the object noun. Both N1 and N2 have many features, and the features of N1 and N2 may share. When a speaker uses "N1+ADV+N2", he/she has to choose a noun as N2 in mind. The key elements for his/her selection are the features he/she wants to profile in a context. So the features are pre-determined in the speaker's mind. The key procedure is to select a noun highly related with the features. The abstract nouns like 文化(culture) are already somewhat salient features, while other nouns need the metonymy to work.

The Chinese CogBank supplies the frequencies of the "noun-feature" pairs. We can see the higher the frequency is, the more salient the feature is. And the salient feature is more likely to play the adjective role in the "ADV+N" construction.

The problems left is to explain why words like 蚯蚓(earthworm) is hard to be found in "ADV+N", although the features of 蚯蚓 are of greater relation strength with other nouns. For example, 弯曲(bending) is more often expressed by弓(bow) and 蛇(snake) in Chinese.

However, we still could not explain a strange phenomenon that 山(mountain) and 猫(cat) have so many salient features (see Table 1) but they could hardly be used in the "ADV+N" construction. This is a new problem put forward by using the CogBank. Without a database like this, we cannot see the problem.

6   Conclusions and Future Work

In this paper, we investigate the factors that determine a noun's occurrence in the "ADV+N" construction. With the large quantity of "word-feature" pairs from the Chinese CogBank, we test the "Feature Assumption" that the descriptive semantic features of a noun permit the noun to be used in the "ADV+N" construction. We find that the nouns used in the "ADV+N" construction really have salient features, and that the nouns with only a few weak features are hardly found in the "ADV+N" construction. Then we build a detailed metonymy model to explain how the construction works. However, we also find that some nouns with salient features like 山(mountain) can not be used in the "ADV+N" construction. It is the data from CogBank which provides us a new sight of the "ADV+N" construction.

In the future, we plan to find new theories to explain why nouns like 山(*mountain*) can not be used in this construction. In addition, we want to investigate the history of the "ADV+N" through diachronic corpora and draw the timeline for the development of the construction. Third, we will try to build computational models for the automatic understanding and generation of the "ADV+N" construction.

Acknowledgments. We thank anonymous reviewers for their constructive suggestions. This work is the staged achievement of the projects supported by National Social Science Foundation of China(10CYY021, 11CYY030, 11AZD121) and National Science Foundation of China(61170181, 61272221).

References

1. Zhang, Y.S.: The Semantic Base and Function Variation of Nouns and ADV+N (名词的语义基础及功能转化与副词修饰名词). Language Teaching and Linguistic Studies, China **4** (1996). (in Chinese)
2. Shi, C.H.: The Descriptive Features of Noun and the Probility of the Construction of ADV+N (名词性的描述性语义特征与副名组合的可能性). Chinese Language, China **3** (2001). (in Chinese)
3. Li, B., Chen, J.J., Chen X.H.: Collection and Analysis on Chinese Cognitive Properties Based on Web Data. Applied Linguistics, China **3** (2012). (in Chinese)
4. Wu, L.H.: Studies on Chinese ADV+N (现代汉语程度副词组合研究). Dissertation of Jinan University, China (2006). (in Chinese)
5. Xing, F.Y.: On ADV+N (关于副词修饰名词). Chinese Language, China **5** (1962). (in Chinese)
6. Zou, S.H.: The Feature Emergence of Nouns (名词性状特征的外化问题). Chinese Construction, China **2** (1990). (in Chinese)
7. Yu, G.Y.: ADV+N (副+名). Chinese Construction, China **1** (1992). (in Chinese)
8. Hu, M.Y.: "Very Passion", "Very Yougth" ect. ("很激情""很青春"等). Chinese Construction, China **4** (1992). (in Chinese)

9. Peng, L.Z.: Very have NP (说很有NP). Chinese Studies, China **2** (1992). (in Chinese)
10. Zhang, G.A.: On ADV+N (关于副词修饰名词问题). Chinese Language Learning, China **6** (1995). (in Chinese)
11. Chu, Z.X., Liu, J.S.: Detail Emergence and ADV+N ("细节显现"与"副+名"). Chinese Construction, China **6** (1997). (in Chinese)
12. Cai, H., Sun, Y., Zhang, H.: The Emerging Idiomaticity: An ERP Case Study on the Degree Adverb+Noun Construction. Journal of PLA University of Foreign Languages, China **1** (2013). (in Chinese)

Annotating Principal Event Chain in Chinese Texts

Yu Chen[1,2], Han Ren[1,4(✉)], Jing Wan[1], Donghong Ji[1,3], and Guozheng Xiao[1,2]

[1] Hubei Research Base of Language and Intelligent Information Processing,
Wuhan University, Wuhan 430072, China
{wdchenyu,hanren,jingwan,dhji,gzxiao}@whu.edu.cn
[2] College of Chinese Language and Literature, Wuhan University,
Wuhan 430072, China
[3] Computer School, Wuhan University,
Wuhan 430072, China
[4] School of Foreign Languages and Literature, Wuhan University,
Wuhan 430072, China

Abstract. Cohesion in discourse represents not only lexical context, but also event subsequence, both of which have a close relationship in text understanding. This paper proposes a discourse annotation scheme based on principle event chain, which is derived from lexical and event chain. In this scheme, lexical chains are clues for searching principle events, while principle events in those sentences that includes words that are also in lexical chains are linked to build a principle event chain. Examples show that principle event chain represents cohesion relations in discourse and ensure consistent annotation as well.

Keywords: Cohesion · Discourse structure · Lexical chain · Principal event chain

1 Introduction

Cohesion, which is often achieved by referring to items common across sentences and paragraphs, is an important component in natural language discourse understanding and generation.

Cohesion in discourse involves semantic relations that exist within the text, and that define it as a text [2]. Halliday and Hasan [1] proposed a hierarchical taxonomy, in which cohesion forms are categorized as grammatical forms, including reference, substitution, ellipsis and conjunction, and lexical forms, including repetition, synonymy, antonymy, hyponymy, meronymy and collocation. This initial research of cohesion provides an option of estimation standard for discourse coherence.

Inspired by this idea, some discourse corpus are built, such as Penn Discourse Treebank (PDTB) and Rhetorical Structure Theory Treebank (RST), both of which are typical corpus annotating discourse structures and relations. Derived from Penn Treebank, PDTB represents text cohesion as connective-arguments structure by annotating connectives and the clauses (arguments) they connect, by classifying those connectives, and by generalizing some implicit logic relations[4]. Using rhetorical tree structure, RST divides each text into two main parts: nucleus and satellites, and then speculates the rhetoric methods that provide cohesion information[3].

© Springer International Publishing Switzerland 2014
X. Su and T. He (Eds.): CLSW 2014, LNAI 8922, pp. 425–433, 2014.
DOI: 10.1007/978-3-319-14331-6_42

However, it is difficult to annotate Chinese texts with PDTB or RST-style annotation scheme. The reasons are two folds: 1) it is difficult to annotate discourse phenomena of high-frequent paratactic cohesion, i.e., linking several text elements without any observable marker. Although those cohesion phenomena can be clarified by defining implicit connectives, it also brings more challenges on recognizing and coherently annotating implicit connectives. For example, the following sentence is well formed in Chinese without any explicit connective:

下雨了，地上湿了。
It rains, the ground is wet.
Three types of connective pairs are appropriate for the sentence:
（如果）下雨了，地上（就）湿了。
If it rains, the ground will be wet.
（因为）下雨了，（所以）地上湿了。
Because it rains, the ground is wet.
（之前）下雨了，（于是）地上湿了。
It rains, and then the ground is wet.

These connectives are mapped into different semantic relations such as 'conditional' 'causal' and 'temporal' for which the precise identification so far has not been sufficiently achieved.

2) PDTB and RST both focus on semantic relations between clauses. Besides clauses, sentences and sentences clusters can also be contributed to text cohesion. Moreover, with clear boundary, the sentence is better to define as text element.

This paper introduces an annotation scheme to find out PEC utilizing lexical chain (LC) that will be strictly defined in the next section. The LC would serve as in each sentence of a text a clue to seek for the PT that incorporates its direct argument into a function expression, namely PE, all of which would be put together to merge PEC that deliver the cohesion method and gist of the text. Moreover, PEC and LC are precious semantic resource from authentic corpora.

2   Principle Event Chain

Event is a structural text extracted from natural texts that provide some stylized information[7]. The Principal Event Chain (PEC) connects every Principal Event (PE) that consists of Principal Trigger (PT) and Principal Participants (PP) in each sentence of a text:

PEC=PE1+PE2+PE3+PE4+...+PEn
PE = PT + (PP1, PP2, PP3...)

The basic idea to construct PEC is to depict the events that help the text cohesion. Besides, PEC shows the principle narratives of a text, but this narrative is a structural text in which PT stands for the most important verb, and PP fills in the direct arguments for those verbs.

Compared with PDTB and RST, PEC boasts two advantages: (1) reducing annotation subjectivity while enhancing operability, since what PEC manifests is the physical sequence of a text that lineally expands a certain narrative without any generalization; (2) averting arbitrary assumption, owing to the fact that PEC follows the main points of a text, shunning additional information; (3) extracting structural information with much smaller granularity, so both the manual annotation and system recognition are more straightforward.

Principle event chains are recognized through clues of other cohesion relations. One typical relation is repetitive words, since they refer to limited topic the text exhibits. Furthermore, verbs in events are definitely associated with those words that usually play certain semantic roles for the verbs [5].

3   Lexical Chain Annotation

First and foremost, we need a rule not only with objective and unified feature but also with operability and legibility to define lexical chain: the units in a lexical chain have to appear in different sentences, semantically identical.

3.1   Identical Lexical Chain

We believe that the words with identical meaning are most likely to denote the same topic for which we extract lexical chains. The semantically identical lexical units can never shift to another narrative topic, so they can be perfectly merged into one lexical chain. Furthermore if we choose to link those identical words, we will come up with a very strict rule with much less subjectivity: only when the lexical units are replaced by each other without changing any meaning of the sentence can they be recognized as one lexical chain of which 3 types are specified: alias, reference, and substitution.

Alias is exactly the same referent with a different name.

Example 1: 波士顿【凯尔特人】和布鲁克林篮网完成大交易 。……早在今天选秀大会开始前，篮网和【绿衫军】的交易谈判就在进行中 。[1,2] (The Boston Celtics and the Brooklyn nets completed transaction.   Earlier in the day before the draft, the nets and the Green Jerseys trade talks in.)

Lexical chain: 凯尔特人 (Celtics)→绿衫军 (Green Jerseys)
Reference is the anaphora in a text that refers to the entity mentioned above.

Example 2: 美国航天局等机构研究人员27日在《科学》杂志上发表3篇论文指出，【"旅行者"1号】目前距太阳约180亿公里，依然处于太阳系中 。但从去年8

---

[1] Square brackets stand for Lexical Chain units. The subscript marks the identification for the chain.

[2] All the examples come from the Chinese prestigious web portals: Sina, Sohu, Neteasy. To save space, this paper leaves out some sentences that hardly affect our discussion. All the sentences chosen here are kept without any revise.

月底开始，【它】进入一处名为"磁场高速公路"的新区域，这里可能是太阳系最外围的疆域，也是进入星际空间的"大门"。(NASA and other researchers in "science" magazine published 3 papers pointed out, "the Voyager 1" now more than 18 billion km from the Sun, has been exploring an unexpected region of the heliosphere, the bubble of charged particles around our Sun, since late last August. NASA's Voyager 1 spacecraft has entered a "magnetic highway" that connects our solar system to interstellar space. This could be one of Voyager 1's last steps on its long journey to the stars.)

Lexical chain:旅行者1号 (Voyager 1)→它 (it)

Substitution is using synonym that repeats in different forms in a text for rhetorical reasons.

Example 3: 国民党第19次全代会下月10日将在台中市登场，"立委"颜宽恒还将作东【邀宴】"立委"及党政高层。当天中午【宴请】党籍"立委"餐叙，颜家也【邀请】江宜桦等党政高层。(The 19th National Congress of Kuomintang will be held on 10 next month in Taichung. Yan Kuanheng treats legislators and the party elite. At noon, Yan fetes legislators and invites Jiang Yihua and other senior party.)

Lexical chain:邀宴 (treat)→宴请 (fete)→邀请 (invite)

Treat, fete, and invite distinct from each other in many ways, but in this text, they can be correctly replaced by each other syntactically and pragmatically, so they can be regarded as one lexical chain.

How we handle with other lexical cohesion such as antonymy, hyponymy, meronymy, and et cetera remains to be a big problem. Our suggestion is to exclude them in the process of identifying lexical chain. The reason is that on one hand the sequence of a single topic does not necessarily require those lexical relations, and on another hand even if those lexical relations can be attributed to one topic, they stand for substitutions if with an intense semantic connection, or they represent a new but related topic if with a loose connection.

Example 4：据美国媒体报道，新闻集团已证实，该集团主席兼首席执行官【默多克LC1】向法院提出和妻子【邓文迪LC2】【离婚LC3】。【两人LC1/LC2】于美国当地时间6月13日向纽约州高等法院提出了【离婚LC3】申请。现年82岁的【默多克LC1】和现年44岁的【邓文迪LC2】1999年【结婚LC3】，育有两个女儿。(According to media reports, News Corp boss Rupert Murdoch has filed for divorce from Wendi Deng. The two filed in a New York City court on 13 June. The 82 year old Murdoch and 44 year old Wendi Deng got married in 1999, have two daughters.)

Lexical chain:

LC1默多克Murdoch→默多克Murdoch×→两人both

LC2邓文迪Wendi Deng→邓文迪Wendi Deng×→两人both

LC3离婚divorce→离婚divorce×→结婚marry

The word 'Both' is the holonym for Murdoch and Wendi Deng, but it is hard to decide which chain the lexical unit 'both' should follow. And if it links both chains, a topic would not be able to be mapped by a single lexical chain; consequently the indiscrete chains will puzzle the system making further decision. Our preliminary idea is to delete such relation in lexical chain granted it functions to some degree for text cohesion. This consideration also counts for Deleting antonym word 'marry'.

3.2   Lexical Chain Unit

The next question for lexical chain is how we define the lexical unit in Chinese text, as we know that no spaces or any other written interval between Chinese words. A simple solution is to make sure every unit is an inseparable semantic token with independent sense, with a mainstream Chinese dictionary determining.

But under some circumstances, some Chinese words can be separated like phrases. Some researchers call them spilt words. The way we annotate those words varies according to conditions: if the separated form appear in the text, we annotate two chains with corresponding parts in that word; if not, we just annotate the word itself:

Example 5：【俄罗斯LC1】不到1年损失10颗卫星 航天局长被【解LC2】【职LC3】（标题）(Russia had lost 10 satellites in seven failed launches in less than a year: space agency chief was dismissed.)

【俄罗斯LC1】总理梅德韦杰夫【解除LC2】了【俄罗斯LC1】联邦航天局局长弗拉基米尔·波波夫金的【职务LC3】。(Russian Prime Minister Dmitry Medvedev dismissed the country's space agency chief Vladimir Popovkin.)

Lexical chain:
LC1俄罗斯Russia→俄罗斯Russia→俄罗斯Russia
LC2解discharge→解除discharge
LC3职position→职务position

解职 dismiss is a spilt word, in this text the separated form 解除 discharge and 职务 position emerge below, hence we divide the word into 解 discharge and 职 position, linking different lexical chains.

Table 1. Some stop words

Light verbs	Link verbs	Functional words
发生(happen)+VP	是(be)	prepositions
进行(process)+VP	为(be)	conjunctions
加以(offer)+VP	系(be)	particles
作出(make)+VP	即(namely)	modal particles
让(let)+VP	属(belong to)	onomatopoetic words
要(be going to)+VP	属于(belong to)	interjections

Some other repetitive words only play grammatical roles and do not contain any entity or event sense but characterize the sense of quantization, modality, rhyme and consecution. Most of them are light verbs, link verbs and functional words. Those words are treated as stop words and, for annotators, are not taken for granted.

4   Principal Event Chain Annotation

Now we turn to extract PEC from the given lexical chains. As mentioned above, PE that scatters in each sentence in which PE narrates the lexical chain units with higher weight connects PEC. In a word, PE must talk about the most frequently repetitive topics, because what we need to get is the event that can be proven to be principal. Therefore, it is well-founded that our approach to find out PE begins with lexical chains. The calculation of the lexical weight for PE becomes the crux for which we design an annotation by introducing a new concept: cover.

Step1: in each sentence all verbs except those in stop list are PT candidates.

Step2: for each PT candidate, count the number of lexical chain units it covers. The positions the candidate is to cover are:

(1) The candidate itself
(2) The modifier of the candidate
(3) The head of direct argument for the candidate
(4) The modifier of direct argument for the candidate

Step3: the candidate with the maximum number from the counting is PT in this sentence, combining the head of its direct arguments (Argn) to get PE expression: PT, (Arg1, Arg2, Arg3...).

Step4: repeat the steps above in all sentences, and then connect all the expressions in the text sequence to get PEC. Here is an annotation practice below:

Example 6: 雁滩路甘肃行政学院门口路段地下埋设的【天然气LC1】主管道因施工不当造成断裂，发生【天然气LC1】【泄漏LC2】【事故LC3】。兰州公安消防支队迅速调集7个中队的17辆消防车和127名官兵赶赴现场应急抢险，同时紧急疏散了【泄漏LC2】点半径500米范围内的【群众LC4】2万余人。据了解，此次【事故LC3】导致周边3000余户【居民LC4】家中供【气LC1】中断，暂未造成人员伤亡。(The main natural gas pipeline buried under the road outside Gansu Institute of Public Administration ruptured due to improper construction. Lanzhou Fire Police detachment quickly assemble 7 squadrons, 17 fire engines and 127 staffs and soldiers rushed to the scene emergency. More than 20 thousand people, within 500 metres of the leak have been evacuated from its. Due to the accident, more than 3000 surrounding inhabitant gas supply cut off but that no americans were injured.)

Lexical chain:
LC1天然气 (natural gas)→天然气 (natural gas)→气 (gas)
LC2泄漏 (leak)→泄漏 (leak)
LC3事故 (accident)→事故 (accident)
LC4群众 (populace)→居民 (inhabitant)

In the first sentence, the candidates are埋设 （bury）, 断裂 （break）, and 泄漏 （leak）. The first two verbs both cover only one lexical chain unit 天然气 （natural gas）, while the verb泄漏 （leak） covers天然气 （natural gas） as well as itself 泄漏 （leak）, 2 chains in total. So the PT should be泄漏 （leak）, and PE is that: 泄漏 （leak）, （天然气 （natural gas））.

In the second sentence, the candidates are调集 （assemble）, 赶赴 （rush）, 疏散 （evacuate）. The first two verbs do not cover a single chain, while疏散 （evacuate） covers lexical chain units泄漏 （leak） and群众 （populace）. So the PT should be疏散 （evacuate）, and PE is that: 疏散 （leak）, （支队 （squad）, 群众 （populace））.

In the third sentence, the candidates are了解 （inform）, 伤亡 （injured and killed）, and中断 （cut off）. The first two do not cover a single chain either, while 中断 （cut off） covers two lexical chain units居民 （inhabitant） and气 （gas）. So the PT should be中断 (cut off), and PE is that: 中断 （cut off）, （供 （supply））[3]

PEC: 泄漏 (leak), （天然气 (natural gas))→ 泄漏 (leak), （支队 (squad), 群众 (populace))→中断(cut off), （供(supply))

Unlike tree structure from dependency analysis, this annotation would present a functional expression in which the benefit is to keep cardinal line from unnecessary detail, which guarantees that what we annotate is the core events in support of text cohesion.

Our annotation is aimed at Chinese text. But the complexity of the Chinese language is significantly reflected in texts that teem with special sentence patterns in particular. In this paper we will describe the annotation method for 3 sentence patterns that bother our annotation once for a while. They are named as verbal-object sentences, pivotal sentences and coordinate-predicate sentences. 3 of them have a complicated predicate system, resulting in the confusion for extracting PE.

1) Verbal-object sentences

The sentences can be codified as S+V1+V2+O, indicating an embedded event. The V2 event can be regarded as an argument of V1 event. So our approach is that the direct argument of V1 are S and V2, and that of V2 is only O, which means V1 can not cover O, while V2 can not cover S:

Example 7: 吉林：迎【今秋】【首场】【雪】 有利于过滤【雾霾】(JiLin: The first autumn snow helps to filter fog and haze.)

PE: 有利于(help), (雪(snow), 过滤(filter))

Example 8: 【欧盟】【批准】【建立】新【银行】【监管】【机制】(The European Union approved the establishment of the new bank supervision mechanism)

PE: 建立(establish), (机制(mechanism))

---

[3] In 供气中断(gas) supply cuts off, 供气(gas) supply is a noun narrated by the verb中断(cut off). For predicate-argument structure, it is generally accepted that the head is the predicate, so in this example the head is供supply.

2) Pivotal sentences

The sentences can be codified as S+V1+O1+V2+O2, also indicating an embedded event in which the patient of the V1 event is the agent of the second event. Therefore we decide that V1 and V2 share the argument O1; V1 can cover V2, but V1 never covers O2, and V2 never covers S.

Example 9: 【俄罗斯】外交部21日发表声明，【要求】【朝鲜】作出【解释】 。(Russian Foreign Ministry issued a statement on 21, asked North Korea to explain)

PE: 要求(ask), (俄罗斯(Russia), 朝鲜(North Korea), 解释(explain))[4]

3) Coordinate-predicate sentences

The sentences can be codified as S+V1+V2+O, seemingly the same with verbal-object sentences, but semantically different due to no embedded event; V1 and V2 are coordinate predicates with grammatical equality. Thus V1 and V2 cover S and O, and they both serve as PE in this sentence.

Example 10: 据悉，【其】家人及女友曾先后向【死者】家属、法院、检察院 道歉求情。(It is known that, his family and girlfriend beg and apologize to the families of the deceased, court and prosecutor.)

PE: 道歉(apologize), (家人(family), 女友(girlfriend))→求情(beg), (家人(family), 女友(girlfriend))

5   Conclusion

This paper introduces an annotation scheme to annotate cohesion in discourse by using Principal Event Chain (PEC). This chain with more event information and clear template is induced by Lexical Chain (LC) of which we build a very strict rule to identify the units: only the semantically identical words. Then, we find out the association between LC and PEC by virtue of cover. PEC, formed by PE from each sentence of the text, is a structural text displaying the most important narrative and cohesion pattern. The outcome of this annotation can be applied to text cohesion evaluation and automatic summarization.

Acknowledgements. This work is supported by Major Projects of National Social Science Foundation of China (11&ZD189), National Natural Science Foundation of China (61173095, 61402341), Fundamental Research Fund for the Central Universities (2012GSP017, 2014111010205), China Postdoctoral Science Foundation funded project (2014M552073).

---

[4] 作出(make) is a light verb, mentioned in given stop list.

References

1. Halliday, M.A.K., Hasan, R.: Cohesion in English. Longman Group UK Limited, London (1976)
2. Halliday, M.A.K.: The Linguistic Study of Literary Texts. In: Lunt, H. (ed.) Proceedings of the Ninth International Congress of Linguistics, pp. 302–307. The Hague, Mouton (1964)
3. Mann, W., Thompson, S.: Rhetorical Structure Theory: A Theory of Text Organization. ISI/RS-87-190. Information Sciences Institute, University of Southern California (1987)
4. Prasad, R., Miltsakaki, E., Dinesh, N., et al.: The Penn Discourse Treebank 2.0 Annotation Manual (2007)
5. Yuan, Y.: On the hierarchical relation and semantic features of the thematic roles in Chinese. Chinese Teaching in the World (3), 10–22 (2008)
6. Zhang, M.: A Study on Discourse Coherence Based on Event Chain. Doctoral dissertation, Wuhan University (2013)
7. Zhao, Y., et al.: Research on Chinese Event Extraction. Journal of Chinese Information Processing (1), 4–8 (2008)

A Study on Metaphors in Idioms
Based on Chinese Idiom Knowledge Base

Lei Wang[1]([✉]), Shiwen Yu[2], Zhimin Wang[3], Weiguang Qu[4], and Houfeng Wang[2]

[1] Key Lab of Computational Linguistics of Ministry of Education,
Peking University, Beijing 100871, China
wangleics@pku.edu.cn
[2] Institute of Computational Linguistics, Peking University, Beijing 100871, China
{yusw,wanghf}@pku.edu.cn
[3] College of Chinese Studies, Beijing Language and Culture University, Beijing 100083, China
wangzm000@gmail.com
[4] School of Computer Science, Nanjing Normal University, Nanjing 210000, China
wgqu@njnu.edu.cn

Abstract. In Chinese language, idioms are an essential part of its vocabulary and used in everyday expression. People like to use idioms for their power of expression, rhetoric skill and special effect, which are mainly created by the metaphors in most of the idioms. This paper introduces a tentative research on the idioms with metaphors based on the Chinese Idiom Knowledge Base(CIKB) by the Institute of Computational Linguistics at Peking University (ICL/PKU), in which the author expects to provide due help to research and applications on this topic. We believe that research as such will have benefit on NLP tasks like automatic metaphor recognition and processing, semantic role labeling etc. On the other hand, our work may also contribute to lexicography, Chinese linguistics study and teaching Chinese as a foreign language.

1   Introduction

As a language with a fairly long history, Chinese idioms are rich in cultural information and reflect the unique way of thinking of the ancient oriental nation. Being an essential part of Chinese, idioms serve as a typical representation for Chinese rhetoric and cultural sediment. By definition, an idiom is a fixed expression that is pragmatically habitual in usage and quite a number of them can be traced back to some ancient Chinese classics and historical legends. Semantically the meaning of an idiom cannot be deduced from its constituents, i.e. the words that it is composed of, but has a profound meaning and a vivid image holistically. This very compositionality makes most idioms only be understood metaphorically.

Metaphorical meaning refers to the new meaning produced by using the original meaning of a word to analogize another object. For this purpose, idiom users expect to boost his or her power of expression, produce a certain sense of humor or create other

X. Su and T. He (Eds.): CLSW 2014, LNAI 8922, pp. 434–440, 2014.
DOI: 10.1007/978-3-319-14331-6_43

special language effects. Hu[1981] in his *Modern Chinese* elaborates the metaphorical meaning of a word: "The extended meaning of a word can be obtained by its metaphorical use, thus it is called 'metaphorical meaning'. Different from other extended meanings, it is not directly deduced from the original meaning of a word but transferred from its metaphorical use." For instance, the word "玉[*yù*](*jade*)" in Chinese idioms has four metaphorical meanings: 1. smooth as in "珠圆玉润"[*zhū yuán yù rùn*[1]](Original[2]: be round as pearls and smooth as jade, Metaphorical: (of singing or words) be smooth and sweet). 2. perfect as in "金科玉律"[*jīn kē yù lǜ*](Original: the golden and jade-like rule, Metaphorical: an infallible law). 3. beautiful as in "如花似玉" [*rú huā sì yù*](Original: be as pretty as flowers and jade, Metaphorical: (of a woman) beautiful). 4. tasty as in "玉液琼浆" [*yù yè qióng jiāng*](Original: jade-like wine, Metaphorical: wonderful wine).

The metaphorical way of extending a word's meaning is based on the similarity to its original meaning. This similarity can be appearance, usage, characteristics, etc. For instance, the word "rat" is "a kind of rodent animal" as in "贼眉鼠眼" [*zéi méi shǔ yǎn*](Original: thief-like eyebrows and rat-like eyes, Metaphorical: mean expressions), but metaphorically it means evil as in "蛇鼠横行" [*shé shǔ héng xíng*](Original: Rats and snakes are on the rampage. Metaphorical: Wicked people are rampant.) Here wickedness is associated with the image of a rat and this similarity creates a new meaning for the word "鼠" as many other metaphorical meanings of a rat such as timidness as in "胆小如鼠" [*dǎn xiǎo rú shǔ*](Original: as timid as a mouse, Metaphorical: be timid), shortsightedness as in "鼠目寸光" [*shǔ mù cùn guāng*](Original: A rat cannot see beyond its nose. Metaphorical: be shortsighted). Besides, the metaphorical meaning can also be fossilized over the years of usage. For instance, the idiom "獐头鼠目" [*zhāng tóu shǔ mù*](Original: the head of a buck and the eyes of a rat, Metaphorical: ugly appearance and sly-looking) first appeared in the period of Five Dynasties (A. D. 907- A. D. 960) and has not changed ever since.

Metaphors in Chinese idioms play a crucial role in language usage and a thorough study on them is so necessary as to help us better understand and use idioms. They reflect the changes of not only the Chinese language, but also the values, morals, history of the Chinese nation in the past centuries. In the very process, they are like a living thing and in perfect accordance with the law of evolution: The better survives and the weaker becomes extinct. From them we know how ancient people use things around them or what they observe from nature to help express themselves and make their utterance as interesting and impressive as possible.

2   The Chinese Idioms with Metaphors in CIKB

The Philosophy of Rhetoric (1936) by I. A. Richards describes a metaphor as having two parts: the tenor and the vehicle. The tenor is the subject to which attributes are ascribed. The vehicle is the object whose attributes are borrowed. However, if we look

---

[1] This is Pinyin (拼音, literally "phonetics", or more literally, "spelling sound" or "spelled sound"), or more formally Hanyu Pinyin (汉语拼音, Chinese Pinyin) to mark the pronunciation of Chinese characters.

[2] Here "Original" and "Metaphorical" refer to the original meaning and metaphorical meaning of an idiom respectively.

at metaphor from a strict point of view, metaphor should be only one of the three typical figures of speech: simile, metaphor and metonymy. A simile is a figure of speech in which two quite different things are compared because they appear to be similar in at least one characteristic. Similes are as a rule introduced by "like" or "as". A simile is based on association and usually has four characteristics: 1) introduced by such comparative words as "like", "as", "as if", "as though", "as it were", "can be likened to", "be comparable to", "similar to", "akin to", "be analogous to", "be something of", etc. 2) involving two things, one of which being the primary term or tenor, the other secondary term or vehicle; 3) the two things involved should be completely different; and 4) the two things should be similar in at least one characteristic. And the criterion of effectiveness of similes varies from person to person.

Therefore from the above description we may conclude that simile is the most complete form of the three with all the elements: tenor, comparative word and vehicle. While by definition, a metaphor is a figure of speech that describes a subject by asserting that it is, on some point of comparison, the same as another otherwise unrelated object. In simpler terms, a metaphor compares two objects/things without using the words "like" or "as". A metonymy is a figure of speech in which a thing or concept is called not by its own name but rather by the name of something associated in meaning with that thing or concept. Table 1 makes a comparison among the three figures of speech taken by the idioms in CIKB.

Table 1. Formal comparison of simile, metaphor and metonymy

Type	Tenor	Comparative word	Vehicle	Example
simile	+[3]	like, as, as if, as though, as it were…	+	归心似箭[guī xīn sì jiàn] (When the mind is bent on returning, it is like a flying arrow.), 气壮如牛[qì zhuàng rú niú] (be as arrogant as an ox)
metaphor	+	is, become, grow, turn…/-	+	化干戈为玉帛[huà gān gē wéi yù bó] (Original: to turn hatchet into jade and silk, Metaphorical: to work for peace), 众志成城 [zhòng zhì chéng chéng] (When people are unified with a single will, they are as strong as city walls.)
metony-my	-		+	笼中之鸟[lóng zhōng zhī niǎo] (the bird in the cage) 万箭穿心[wàn jiàn chuān xīn] (Original: to drive tens of thousands of arrows through one's heart, Metaphorical: be greatly distressed)

---

[3] "+" indicates this field is required whereas "-" indicates this field is not necessary.

In addition to the three above-mentioned typical forms, the metaphors in Chinese idioms demonstrate another special form: comparative word plus vehicle without the tenor, as in "如花似玉" or "如虎添翼" [rú hǔ tiān yì] (Original: as tigers grow wings, Metaphorical: with might redoubled).

The vehicles of the metaphors in Chinese idioms can be served by the following: 1. natural objects. Many idioms contain metaphors that use natural objects or phenomena as its vehicles, for instance, human organs, animals, plants, etc. As in "情同手足" [qíng tóng shǒu zú] (Original: be as close as one's hands and feet, Metaphorical: brotherly love). Hands and feet are human parts, but here they are used to describe emotional intimacy. "冰" and "玉" in "冰清玉洁" [bīng qīng yù jié] (Original: be as pure as jade and clean as ice) are natural matters, but here they are used to describe the attributes of being pure-minded. 2. images or scences. Some metaphors are formed by the depiction of an image, an action, a scene, etc. As in the idiom "如坐针毡" [rú zuò zhēn zhān] (Original: like sitting on a mattress with pins and needles, Metaphorical: to feel ill at ease). One will naturally feel uneasy, even annoyed, when sitting on a mattress full of needles, thus the metaphor is formed by the description of the scene. For another idiom "一贫如洗" [yī pín rú xǐ] (Original: be as poor as having been washed away, Metaphorical: be very poor), the gerund "洗(washing)" illustrates the degree of being poor by creating an image of no possessions at all. 3. historical stories, legends, allusions, etc. Usually this type of idioms reflects the moral behind the story that it is derived (Lo, 1997). For example, the idiom "破釜沉舟" [pò fǔ chén zhōu] literally means "to smash the cauldrons and sink the boats." It was based on a historical story where General Xiang Yu in Qin Dynasty (221 B. C. – 207 B. C.) ordered his army to destroy all cooking utensils and boats after they crossed a river into the enemy's territory. He and his men won the battle for their "life-or-death" courage and "no-retreat" policy. Although there are similar phrases in English, such as "burning bridges" or "crossing the Rubicon", this particular idiom cannot be used in a losing scenario because the story behind it does not indicate a failure. Another typical example is the idiom "瓜田李下" [guā tián lǐ xià] which literally means "in the melon field or under the plum trees". Metaphorically it implies a suspicious situation. Derived from a verse called 《君子行》 [jūn zǐ xíng], meaning "A Gentleman's Journey") from Eastern Han Dynasty (A. D. 25 – A. D. 220), the idiom is originated from two lines of the poem "瓜田不纳履，李下不整冠" [guā tián bù nà lǚ, lǐ xià bù zhěng guān] which describe a code of conduct for a gentleman that says "Don't adjust your shoes in a melon field and don't tidy your hat under plum trees" in order to avoid suspicion of stealing (Wang & Yu, 2010) .

3   The Classification of Explanations of the Idioms that Contain Metaphors

For the importance of idioms in Chinese language and culture, an idiom bank with about 6,790 entries were included in the most influential Chinese language knowledge base – the Grammatical Knowledge Base of Contemporary Chinese (GKB) completed by the Institute of Computational Linguistics at Peking University, which has been working on language resources for over 20 years and building many knowledge bases on Chinese language. Based on that, the Chinese Idiom Knowledge Base had been constructed from the year 2004 to 2009 through the 973 National Basic Research Program of China (No. 2004CB318102) and collects more than 36, 000 idioms with more semantic and pragmatic properties added.

Basically the properties of each entry in CIKB can be classified into four categories: lexical, semantic, syntactic and pragmatic, each of which also includes several fields in its container -- the SQL database. Table 2 shows the details about the fields(Wang & Yu, 2010) of the entries in CIKB.

Table 2. Property categories of CIKB

Categories	Properties
Lexical	idiom, Pinyin, full Pinyin, bianti, explanation, origin
Semantic	synonym, antonym, literal translation, free translation, English equivalent
Syntactic	compositionality, syntactic function
Pragmatic	frequency, emotion, event (context), grade

The metaphorical meanings of the idioms in CIKB are mainly shown in the field of "explanation" which takes the following forms:

1. The metaphorical meaning as the sole explanation without its original meaning. This type can also be divided into two categories: A)with only one metaphorical meaning. "以卵击石"[yǐ luǎn jī shí] (Original: to knock the stone with an egg) means "to overrate one's abilities" metaphorically. "怜香惜玉" [lián xiāng xī yù] (Original: to be tender to fragrance and cherish jade) means "be tender towards pretty girls" metaphorically. B) with two metaphorical meanings. "捕风捉影" [bǔ fēng zhuō yǐng] (Original: to chase the wind and clutch at shadows, Metaphorical 1: to make groundless accusations, Metaphorical 2: to do something without a definite purpose)

2. The original meaning is given first and then its metaphorical meaning. This type can also be divided into three categories: A)Some key words in the idiom are explained first and then the metaphorical meaning is given, as in the idiom "朽木不雕" [xiǔ mù bù diāo] (朽木 : rotten wood ; 雕 : to carve. Original: Deadwood can't be carved. Metaphorical: people who do not make progress). B) Some key words in the idiom are explained first and then two metaphorical meanings are given. For example, "并蒂芙蓉" [bìng dì fú róng] (Original: twin lotus flowers on one stalk, Metaphorical 1: symbol of a loyal couple, Metaphorical 2: comparable in excellence or beauty), 蒂 : pedicel ; 芙蓉 : lotus) C)The origin of the allusion is given first and then the metaphorical meaning is given. For example, "愚公移山" [yú gōng yí shān] In *Liezi: Tang's Inquiries*, Father Yu tried to move two huge mountains Taihang and Wangwu in front of his village by human labor. Villagers laughed at him but he believed that by the efforts of his offspring this job could be done. Metaphorical: to do things with dogged perseverance and fear no difficulty.

3. The original meaning is given first and then its metaphorical meaning. But both meanings can be used. For example, "百发百中" [bǎi fā bǎi zhòng] (Original: Every shot hits the target. Metaphorical: to have 100 percent confidence to do something) and "馋涎欲滴" [chán xián yù dī] (Original: mouth drooling with greed, Metaphorical: to show one's greed).

4   The Tagging Method of Idioms with Metaphors

As for tagging the fields of those idioms with metaphors in CIKB, our principle is to add information as complete as possible with the purpose of practical application. The tagging of idioms may find application in two domains: 1. natural language processing; 2. Chinese language teaching/learning and linguistic research.

In natural language processing, the possible applications may be semantic tagging, automatic metaphor recognition and understanding, etc. For there are still disputes over a clear definition of idiom in the circle of Chinese linguistics, there are a number of idioms in CIKB that do not have metaphors in themselves even though some infulential Chinese idiom dictionaries include them. Here, we conclude that the criterion for distinguishing idioms and xiyus is whether they are metaphorical, i.e. whether we can get their meanings from looking at them literally (Wang et al, 2013).

The obvious mark to filter the idioms with metaphors is the word "比喻[bǐ yù]" used as a verb in the field of "explanation". Therefore we extract these idioms and get 8,3774 entries. In these entries, there are some idioms whose metaphorical meanings are the only meanings that are used at present and their original meanings have been neglected. There are some idioms that both their original meanings and metaphorical meanings are still in use. Thus we tag the former with the tag "M" and the latter "MO".

To improve the accuracy of the filtering, we also resort to the English translation fields of the entry. There are three fields of translation as we can see in Table 2 – Literal Translation, Free Translation and English Close. In spite of the fact that a literal translation of an idiom will not reflect its metaphorical meaning generally, it will still be of value to those who expect to get familiar with the constituent characters and may want to connect its literal meaning with its metaphorical meaning, especially for those learners of Chinese as a foreign language.

Those idioms with the field "Free Translation" definitely have metaphorical meanings. As to Chinese language teaching and research, we extract the vehicles of the idioms with metaphors. First we identify the comparative words in the entries, mostly "似", "若", and "如"[5] and assume the words following these comparative words are the vehicles we are looking for. The result is shown in Table 3.

---

[4] In the 8,377 entries, there are a number of idioms that are actually the variants of a popular idiom. For example, "狗续金貂", "狗续侯冠", "狗尾貂续" are the variants of "狗尾续貂"(gǒu wěi xù diāo, Original: to add a dog's tail to the sable coat, Metaphorical: a wretched sequel to a fine work).

[5] They all mean "like", "as", etc..

Table 3. The most common vehicles in idioms with metaphors

Compara-tive words	Formal Pattern	Vehicle	No. of Entries
如	A如B	水(water),　山(mountain),　玉(jade)...	654
	如A如B	醉(drunk),　痴(enchanted),　梦(dream)...	31
	A不如	猪狗(pig and dog),　禽兽(beast),　粪土 (dropping)...	37
似	A似B	火(fire),　海(sea),　箭(arrow)...	51
	如A似B	虎(tiger),　画(painting),　月(moon)...	11
若	A若B	狂(crazy),　惊(startled),　灰(ash)...	186

5   Future Study and Acknowledgement

At present, we are still working on theoretical research on metaphor in Chinese idioms. In the future, we are looking forward to find more applications for the metaphorical attributes of Chinese idioms, especially in the area of natural language processing. Our work is supported by National Natural Science Foundation(Grant No. 61170163 and No. 61272221) and Open Project foundation of National Key Laboratory of Computational Linguistics(No. 201302). This research was partly supported by National Natural Science Foundation of China (No.61370117, No.61333018) and Major National Social Science Fund of China(No.12&ZD227).

References

Hu, Y.: Modern Chinese (Enlarged Edition). Shanghai Education Press, Shanghai (1981). (胡裕树. 《现代汉语》(增订本), 上海:上海教育出版社 (1981)) (in Chinese)

http://en.wikipedia.org/wiki/Metaphor

Lo, W.H.: Best Chinese Idioms, vol. 3. Hai Feng Publishing Co., Hong Kong, China (1997)

Wang, L., Yu, S.: Construction of a Chinese Idiom Knowledge Base and Its Applications. In: Proceedings of the Workshop on Multiword Expressions: from Theory to Applications, pp. 11–18

Wang, L., Li, S., Qu, W., Yu, S.: Construction and Application of the Knowledge Base of Chinese Multi-word Expressions. In: Liu, P., Su, Q. (eds.) CLSW 2013. LNCS, vol. 8229, pp. 564–571. Springer, Heidelberg (2013)

Generalized Case Theory and the Argument-Omission Structure in Mandarin Chinese

Yong Yang[(✉)]

School of Foreign Languages, Fuyang Teachers College, Fuyang 236041, Anhui, China
40852094@qq.com

Abstract. Argument-omission structures in Mandarin Chinese, including omitting the subject, object and the head of "de" phrase, can be fully explained by Xu Jie's theory of Generalized Case Theory. Case assigner can be divided into two types: obligatory and optional, among which the nominative Case assigner in English is obligatory, while in Chinese, it is optional. Similarly, the accusative and genitive Case assigner in Mandarin Chinese is also optional. These facts directly lead to the argument-omission structures in Mandarin Chinese. The linguistic principles are surprisingly simple behind the unordered and rich linguistic phenomena, and the only difference among different languages is the values of the parameter in the language faculty.

Keywords: Generalized Case theory · Argument-omission · Optional Case assigner · Parameter

1   Generalized Case Theory

The hypothesis that every phonetically realized noun phrase (NP) must be assigned (abstract) Case is referred to the Case Filter in the literature of generative grammar (Rouveret and Vergnaud (1980), Chomsky (1981), among many others):

(1)   *NP,   if NP appears explicitly (phonetically realized) without Case.

The Case Filter has been kept and developed (Chomsky 1981, 1986, 1995, etc) since Chomsky(1980), which has played a very important role in the government and binding theory because the Case is the motivation of the movement and the quality inspection station of the factory of sentences.

That was called the standard Case theory by Xu (1993, 2001) who believed that the standard Case filter in this form is obviously a condition on Case assignees, i.e., the NPs, while saying nothing about the Case assigners, i.e., those grammatical categories that perform the assignment. But given that the theory of abstract Cases in its essence specifies a set of co-relationships between NPs and certain lexical or functional grammatical categories that are licensing the NPs in certain positions such as the relationship between a subject NP and Infl or between an object NP and a transitive verb, it is conceptually reasonable to assume that Case theory constrains the

© Springer International Publishing Switzerland 2014
X. Su and T. He (Eds.): CLSW 2014, LNAI 8922, pp. 441–447, 2014.
DOI: 10.1007/978-3-319-14331-6_44

Case assigners in addition to the Case assignees. Put differently, under a proper re-formulation of Case theory, not only does a Case assignee need a Case assigner, but also vice versa. A Case assigner, if obligatory, not only can assign a Case, but also must do so, requiring appropriate discharge. That was the Generalized Case Filter (GCF) proposed by Xu (1993) as in (2) below.

(2)   The Generalized Case Filter (GCF)

      i. *NP if lexical and no Case; and

     ii. *Obligatory Case assigner if un-discharged.

GCF not only includes the standard Case Filter, but also pushes it forward. The proposal in Xu (1993, 2001) takes the Case assigners and the Case assignees into consideration, which is the inheritance and development of the standard Case Filter. GCF is logical and feasible in theory and there are a lot of linguistic phenomena to support it in practice, possessing a marvelous power of explanation.

2   Argument-Omission Structures in Mandarin Chinese

Lv (1979) pointed out the two necessities for omission: firstly, the meaning of the sentence is vague without the context or the environment of the speaker, so some words must be added to transfer the clear information; secondly, the word(s) added is(are) possible and there is only one possibility. e.g.:

(3)   ta maile liangben huabao, wo ye maile yiben

    He bought two pictorials, I also bought one.

Without the first clause, we do not know what the "one" in the second clause refers to. With the aid of the first clause, we know we can only add "pictorial", so it is omission, while the following sentence is not the same case:

(4)   ni yiyan,   wo yiyu.

    You utterance, I utterance

      You say something, and I say something (Everybody joins in the conversation.)

Different words can be added before the "yiyan" and "yiyu", such as "say" or "utter" or "make", so it is not the omission, but the implication.

In a word, the omission refers to "the element which is indispensable structurally does not appear in certain grammatical condition" (Zhu 1982: 220). The construction of omission can be restored and there is the corresponding non-omission construction (that is the full form) in syntax. Wang (1985) divided the omission into three classes: semantic omission that is the omission in the thought; grammatical omission that is the omission in the structure and the pragmatic omission that is the omission in the communication, and these three ones belong to the semantic, syntactic and pragmatic categories accordingly. Here in this paper the omission in syntax is our only concern.

2.1   Subject-Omission Structures

More emphases are put on the meaning than the form in the Chinese language, so there exist lots of argument-omission structures in Mandarin Chinese. Firstly the subject can be omitted, which is reflected in the syntax as the zero-subject structures, or in the term of the traditional grammar "non-SVO sentence", whose opinion is that the subject is not necessary to restore or can not restore (Huang and Liao 2002, among others), Fang and Tan (2006) held that the null subjects do exist in the syntax, whose existence focus on the position in the sentence and it is an empty category in the linear chain of the syntactic level, for example:

(5)   a. mashang jiu   qu
         Immediately   go
         We will go immediately.
      b. yao   xiayu le
         will   rain le
         It will rain.

Xu (1993) divided the Case assigner into two kinds, obligatory Case assigner and optional Case assigner, which can be applied to explain the Extended Projection Principle (EPP) as follows:

(6)   Extended Projection Principle (EPP)
      There must be a subject even if one is not needed semantically.

According to the GCF, the nominative Case assigner in English is obligatory, so its assigning energy must be discharged, which does not allow the position of the subject is empty and an expletive ("there" or "it") is needed to satisfy its discharging demand even if it is nor necessary semantically. Accordingly, the nominative Case assigner in Chinese is optional so the null subject structure in which the position of the subject is empty is allowed in Chinese and it is OK for the nominative Case assigner not to discharge its assigning power[1]. This contrast can be clearly shown in the following examples:

---

[1] Of course, this phenomenon can be explained by the null subject parameter in the generative grammar, we can assume that there is a pro at the beginning of the two sentences, and the pro in these case dropped, so (5) can be reanalyzed as follows:
    （1） a. pro mashang jiuqu
          b. pro yao xiayu le
so Deng（2010）put the non-SVO sentence in Chinese into the category of SVO sentence, here we will not discuss it.

(7)   English: There arrived three doctors.

Chinese: laile   sange   yisheng.

Arrived   three   doctors

(8)   English: It is raining.

Chinese: xiayu le.

rained

2.2   Object-Omission Structures

The object can be also omitted in Chinese, which is projected into the transitive verb without complement in the syntax:

(9)   zai nvhaoli, Qing'e **buchi buhe**, dengzhuo yizhi yanjing tangzhuo, danqiu yisi.

*In the cell of the woman prison, Qing'e did not **eat and drink**, lying with the eye open, only waiting for the coming of the death.*

(10)   gongsi yigeyue zheng liangqian, yinian liangwan. Xianzai mai yitao liangjushi de fang yao sanshiwan, wo **buchi buhe** ye yao jin 15 nian caineng mai yitaofang.

*My salary in the company is 2000 Yuan RMB every month and 20,000 Yuan every year. Now it takes 300,000 Yuan to buy a two-roomed flat, even if I did not **eat and drink**, I can buy a flat in nearly 15 years.*

"Eat" and "drink" are transitive verb, which need two arguments, but in the previous two examples, the object was omitted.

In the daily conversation, the case of object-omission structures can be encountered here and there:

(11)   --ni daodi **jie**bujiehun?

Do you marry or not?

--bu**jie**!

No, I do not.

(12)   --chiguofan le ma? /jintian hejiu ma?

Do you have your meal? Do you drink (the wine)?

--**chi**le/**chi**guole; **he**le.

Yes, I do.

These kinds of phenomena posed a serious challenge to the Case theory of the generative grammar: how does the Case-assigning power of the transitive verb discharge? According to the GCF, Case assigner can be divided into two kinds, obligatory Case assigner and optional Case assigner. The Case-assigning power of the transitive verb in English must be discharged, or the construction is not grammatical, while in Chinese, the Case-assigning power of the transitive verb is optional, which means its power can be discharged or un-discharged, both of which are grammatical.

2.3 Argument-Omission Structures in the "de" Phrase

At last, argument-omission structures also reflected in the "de" phrase (He 2011: 119, 154-155, 171). The connotation of the "de" phrase focused here is rich, which not only includes the genitive structure, but also includes the PartP and CP composed by "de".

Noun, adjective, number-classifier phrase, and preposition phrase, with addition of "de", can constitute a PartP, whose head[2] can be omitted:

(13) **shengde** buhaochi, **shude** haochi.
    The uncooked is not delicious, while the cooked is delicious.

(14) shiwang haishi you **shaoxude**.
    There is still some disappointment.

(15) **mutoude** naiyong
    The wooden stand wear and tear.

(16) **zaixiaode** dou bixu shang wanzixi.
    Those who stay at the school must be attended the evening self-study.

Free relative is the relative composed by "de" but the head of the relative is omitted, and this kind of "de" phrase constitutes a CP, for example:

(17) wo buxihuan **xiaoli tiaode**.
    I do not like those xiaoli picked.

(18) haizimen dou xihuan chi **mama zuode.**
    Children all like the food mama cooked.

In this article, we only concern the head omission in the genitive structure:

(19) zheduishu shi **wode.**
    The pile of books are mine.

(20) zhangsande tiyi shoudaole dajiade renke, liside que meiyouren lihui.
    Zhangsan's proposal was accepted by all, while Lisi's was not cared about.

---

[2] Strictly speaking, in generative grammar, since Abney (1987) , because the head of "de" phrase is not the noun after "de", but "de"itself. In this sense, the head argument-omission structure in the traditional grammar is not the omission of the head.

Its tree diagram can be illustrated as follows:

(21)

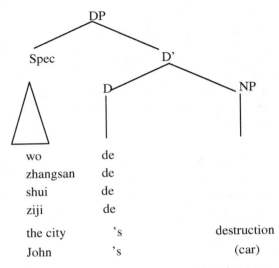

wo	de	
zhangsan	de	
shui	de	
ziji	de	
the city	's	destruction
John	's	(car)

According to Chomsky (1986), the Case is made up of the structural Case and the inherent Case. GCF is not only fit for the structural Case, but also for the inherent Case because the above mentioned genitive belongs to the inherent Case. The genitive in Mandarin Chinese is the obligatory Case assigner which means that its assigning power can be discharged or un-discharged. Actually, the similar linguistic phenomena also exist in English; the noun phrase after the genitive marker's can also be omitted, which is called independent genitive in literatures.

(22) My car is faster than John's (car).

(23) I saw him at my uncle's (house) last week.

(24) John lives near St. Paul's (Cathedral) in London.

(25) John bought the meat at the butcher's (shop).

3   Conclusions

There exist lots of argument-omission structures in Mandarin Chinese, including omitting the subject, object and the head of "de" phrase, which can be fully explained by Xu Jie's theory of Generalized Case Theory. Case assigner can be divided into two types: obligatory and optional, among which the nominative Case assigner in English is obligatory, while in Chinese, it is optional. Similarly, the accusative and genitive Case assigner in Mandarin Chinese is also optional. These reasons directly lead to the argument-omission structures in Mandarin Chinese. Through the unordered and rich linguistic phenomena, the linguistic principles are simple and the difference among different languages is only the different values of the parameter in the language faculty.

References

1. Abney, S.: The English Noun Phrase in its Sentential Aspect. Doctoral Dissertation, MIT, Cambridge, Mass (1987)
2. Chomsky, N.: Knowledge of Language: Its Nature, Origin and Use. Praeger, New York (1986)
3. Chomsky, N.: Lectures on Government and Binding. Foris, Dordrecht (1981)
4. Chomsky, N.: On Binding. Linguistic Inquiry **11**, 1–46 (1980)
5. Chomsky, N.: The Minimalism Program. MIT Press, Cambridge (1995)
6. Deng, S.: Formal Chinese Syntax. Shanghai Education Press, Shanghai (2010). (in Chinese)
7. Fang, H., Tan, X.: The Nature, Distribution of the Null Subject and the Related Problems. Foreign Languages Research **6**, 21–25 (2006). (in Chinese)
8. He, Y.: A Generative Grammar of Mandarin Chinese. Peking University Press, Beijing (2011). (in Chinese)
9. Huang, B., Liao, X.: Modern Chinese, 3rd edn. Higher Education Press, Beijing (2002). (in Chinese)
10. Huang, C.-T.J., Li, Y.-H.A., Li, Y.: The syntax of Chinese. Cambridge University Press, Cambridge (2009)
11. Lv, S.: Problems on the Analysis of Chinese Grammar. The Commercial Press, Beijing (2005). (in Chinese)
12. Rouveret, A., Vergnaud, J.-R.: Specifying Reference to the Subject: French Causatives and Conditions on Representations. Linguistic Inquiry **11**, 97–202 (1980)
13. Wang, W.: On Omission. Zhongguo Yuwen, 6 (1985). (in Chinese)
14. Wen, B.: An Introduction to Syntax. Foreign Language Teaching and Research Press, Beijing (2001). (in Chinese)
15. Xu, J.: An Infl Parameter and Its Consequences, Doctoral Dissertation, University of Maryland at College Park (1993)
16. Xu, J.: Grammatical Principles and Grammatical Phenomena. Peking University Press, Beijing (2001). (in Chinese)
17. Xu, J.: Sentence Head and Sentence Structure: A Study with Special Reference to Chinese. Pearson Education Asia, Singapore (2003)
18. Zhu, D.: Lecture Notes on Grammar. The Commercial Press, Beijing (1982). (in Chinese)

Author Index

Cai, Dongfeng   369
Cen, Ling   3
Chen, Bo   341
Chen, Yichen   286
Chen, Yu   425

Ding, Jing   12

Fan, Ming   251
Feng, Haoguo   369

Gao, Wei   231

Han, Yingjie   403
Hong, Jia-Fei   329
Hsieh, Shu-Kai   270
Hua, Min   278
Huang, Chu-Ren   12
Huang, Haihong   380

Ji, Donghong   286, 296, 341, 425
Jia, Yuxiang   251
Jiang, Yan   43
Jin, Peng   317

Kang, Shiyong   191
Kou, Xin   240

Li, Bin   112, 414
Li, Li   260
Li, Qiang   55
Li, Shoushan   231
Li, Xiangling   143
Li, Xiangnong   198
Li, Ying   99
Lin, Jingxia   181
Lin, Shanon Yi-Hsin   270
Liu, Dan   278
Liu, Hongyan   66
Liu, Liu   112
Liu, Pengyuan   317

Liu, Xueyang   112, 414
Liu, Yang   170
Liu, Youran   221
Liu, Zhenqian   143
Lo, Fengju   305
Long, Dan   221
Lu, Qin   305
Luo, Jianfei   3, 21
Lyu, Chen   341

Ma, Baopeng   66
Ma, Yan   414
Meng, Li   198
Mu, Lingling   403

Ni, Shengjian   286
Niu, Gui-ling   349

Qian, Maohua   278
Qiu, Bing   358
Qiu, Likun   317
Qiu, Qingshan   211
Qiu, Xiangyun   31
Qu, Weiguang   434

Ren, Fengmei   75
Ren, Han   425

Shen, Shaoshuai   143

Tang, Xuri   278, 414
Tian, Yuan   85
Tian, Zhen   191

Wan, Jing   425
Wang, Houfeng   170, 260, 434
Wang, Lei   434
Wang, Meng   231
Wang, Mengxiang   170, 260
Wang, Yateng   369, 380
Wang, Zhimin   251, 434

Wang Villaflor, Juan   99
Wei, Mingru   369, 380
Wei, Xiaomei   341

Xiao, Guozheng   296, 425
Xiao, Hong   390
Xiong, Dan   305
Xu, Jian   305
Xu, Jie   85
Xue, Yunxia   231

Yang, Daran   161
Yang, Haifeng   134
Yang, Hua   296
Yang, Yong   441

Yao, Yao   181
Yu, Shiwen   251, 434

Zan, Hongying   251, 403
Zhang, Guiping   380
Zhang, Kunli   403
Zhang, Longkai   260
Zhang, Mingyao   296
Zhang, Peicui   66
Zhang, Yichen   124, 143
Zhang, Ying   153
Zhang, Yingjie   112
Zhou, Guodong   231
Zhou, Qiaoli   369, 380
Zhu, Qingzhi   358
Zhu, Xuefeng   317
Zhuang, Huibin   143

Printed in the United States
By Bookmasters